2/28/19
$ 45.00
AS-14
3/19

Withdrawn

D0049291

WHITESHIFT

WHITESHIFT

Populism, Immigration, and the Future of White Majorities

ERIC KAUFMANN

Abrams Press, New York

Cataloging-in-Publication Data is available from the Library of Congress

Manufactured in the United States of America

ISBN 978-1-4683-1697-1
eISBN 978-1-4683-1698-8

1 3 5 7 9 10 8 6 4 2

Abrams books are available at special discounts when purchased in quantity
for premiums and promotions as well as fundraising or educational use.
Special editions can also be created to specification. For details, contact
specialsales@abramsbooks.com or the address below.

Abrams Press® is a registered trademark of Harry N. Abrams, Inc.

ABRAMS The Art of Books
195 Broadway, New York, NY 10007
abramsbooks.com

Contents

I

The Century of *Whiteshift*

We need to talk about white identity. Not as a fabrication designed to maintain power, but as a set of myths and symbols to which people are attached: an ethnic identity like any other. The big question of our time is less 'What does it mean to be American' than 'What does it mean to be *white* American' in an age of ethnic change. The progressive storyline for white majorities is a morality tale celebrating their demise, and, as I hope to show, much of today's populist reaction stems directly or indirectly from this trope.

Yet whites can no more hold back demography than Canute could command the tides. In the West, even without immigration, we're becoming mixed-race. This is not speculation, but is virtually guaranteed by the rates of intermarriage occurring in many Western countries. Projections reveal that faster immigration may slow the process by bringing in racially unmixed individuals, but in a century those of mixed-race will be the largest group in countries like Britain and America. In two centuries, few people living in urban areas of the West will have an unmixed racial background. Most who do will be immigrants or members of anti-modern religious groups like the ultra-Orthodox Jews. The reflex is to think of this futuristically, as bringing forth increased diversity, or the advent of a 'new man', much as Ralph Waldo Emerson, Israel Zangwill or *Time* magazine predicted for the United States.[1] But, if history is our guide, things are likely to turn out quite differently. Many people desire roots, value tradition and wish to maintain continuity with ancestors who have occupied a historic territory.

This means we're more likely to experience what I term *Whiteshift*, a process by which white majorities absorb an admixture of different peoples through intermarriage, but remain oriented around existing

I

myths of descent, symbols and traditions. Naturally there will be contestation, with cosmopolitans lauding exotic origins; but most people will probably airbrush their polyglot lineage out of the story to focus on their European provenance. This is rooted in Gestalt psychology, in which the brain simplifies sense-perceptions into a unified whole, screening out a great deal of information. We see this process of selective forgetting and remembering time and time again among ethnic groups in history. In Turkey, for example, many groups in the ethnic majority's DNA have been forgotten. Most Turks trace their origins to Central Asia, neglecting their Byzantine Christian ancestors and the large number of immigrants who arrived from far-flung parts of the Ottoman Empire.

Whiteshift has a second, more immediate, connotation: the declining white share of the population in Western countries. Whites are already a minority in most major cities of North America. Together with New Zealand, North America is projected to be 'majority minority' by 2050, with Western Europe and Australia following suit later in the century. This shift is replacing the self-confidence of white majorities with an existential insecurity channelled by the lightning rod of immigration. No one who has honestly analysed survey data on individuals – the gold standard for public opinion research – can deny that white majority concern over immigration is the main cause of the rise of the populist right in the West. This is primarily explained by concern over identity, not economic threat. I explore this data in considerable detail in the first part of the book. Not everyone seeks to maintain connections to ancestors, homeland and tradition, but many voters do.

The loss of white ethno-cultural confidence manifests itself in other ways. Among the most important is a growing unwillingness to indulge the anti-white ideology of the cultural left. When whites were an overwhelming majority, empirically unsupported generalizations about whites could be brushed off as amusing and mischievous but ultimately harmless. As whites decline, fewer are willing to abide such attacks. At the same time, white decline emboldens the cultural left, with its dream of radical social transformation. The last time this blend of ethnic change and cultural contestation occurred, in fin-de-siècle America, the anti-WASP adversary culture was confined to a small circle of bohemian intellectuals. Today, the anti-majority adversary culture operates on a much larger scale, permeates major institutions and is transmitted to conservatives through social and right-wing media. This produces a growing 'culture wars' polarization between increasingly insecure white conservatives and energized white liberals.

The Western tradition of opposing one's own culture begins with the so-called 'lyrical left' in the late nineteenth century, which lampooned bourgeois values. After the First World War, the cultural left turned against the nation, to the point that by 1930, according to the liberal George Orwell, essentially all English intellectuals were on the left and 'in left-wing circles it is always felt that there is something slightly disgraceful in being an Englishman'.[2] In the more diverse United States, the lyrical left's critique took the form of an attack on their own ethnic group, the Anglo-Protestant majority, whom they saw as oppressing European immigrants and enforcing puritanical laws like the prohibition on selling alcohol. In the 1960s, this countercultural movement, which I term left-modernism, developed a theory of white ethno-racial oppression. Its outlook superseded the logical, empirically grounded, left-liberal Civil Rights Movement after 1965 to become a millenarian project sustained by the image of a retrograde white 'other'. Today, left-modernism's most zealous exponents are those seeking to consecrate the university campus as a sacred space devoted to the mission of replacing 'whiteness' with diversity.

It's important to have people criticizing their own group: what Daniel Bell termed the 'adversary culture' spurs reform and creativity when it collides with the majority tradition. But what happens when the critics become dominant? In softer form, left-modernist ideology penetrated widely within the high culture and political institutions of Western society after the 1960s. This produced norms which prevented democratic discussion of questions of national identity and immigration. The deviantization of these issues in the name of anti-racism introduced a blockage in the democratic process, preventing the normal adjustment of political supply to political demand. Instead of reasonable tradeoffs between those who, for example, wanted higher or lower levels of immigration, the subject was forced underground, building up pressure from those whose grievances were ignored by the main parties. This created a market opportunity which populist right entrepreneurs rushed in to fill.

Ethno-cultural change is occurring at a rapid rate at precisely the time the dominant ideology celebrates a multicultural vision of ever-increasing diversity. To hanker after homogeneity and stability is perceived as narrow-minded and racist by liberals.

Yet diversity falls flat for many because we're not all wired the same way. Right-wing populism, which champions the cultural interests of group-oriented whites, has halted and reversed the multicultural consensus which held sway between the 1960s and late 1990s. This is leading to a polarization between those who accept, and those who reject, the ideology of diversity. What's needed is a new vision that gives conservative members of white majorities hope for their group's future while permitting cosmopolitans the freedom to celebrate diversity. Cosmopolitanism and what I term ethno-traditional nationalism are both valid worldviews, but each suits a different psychological type. Imposing either on the entire population is a recipe for discontent because value orientations stem from heredity and early life experiences. Attempts to re-educate conservative and order-seeking people into cosmopolitanism will, as the psychologist Karen Stenner notes, only generate resistance.[3] Differences need to be respected. *Whiteshift* is not just a prediction of how white identity will adapt to demographic change, but a positive vision which can draw the sting of right-wing populism and begin to bridge the 'nationalist–globalist' divide that is upending Western politics.

We are entering a period of cultural instability in the West attendant on our passage between two relatively stable equilibria. The first is based on white ethnic homogeneity, the second on what the prescient centrist writer Michael Lind calls 'beige' ethnicity, i.e. a racially mixed majority group.[4] In the middle lies a turbulent multicultural interregnum. We in the West are becoming less like homogeneous Iceland and more like homogeneous mixed-race Turkmenistan. But to get there we'll be passing through a phase where we'll move closer to multicultural Guyana or Mauritius. The challenge is to enable conservative whites to see a future for themselves in *Whiteshift* – the mixture of many non-whites into the white group through voluntary assimilation. Unmixed whiteness is not about to disappear and may return in the long run, but this is getting ahead of the story, so I hope you'll read on.

The Western media was shocked when the frontman of the Austrian Freedom Party (FPÖ), Jörg Haider, won 27 per cent of the vote in the late 1990s and the leader of the French Front National (FN), Jean-Marie Le

Pen, got 18 per cent in the second round of the 2002 French presidential election. When the centre-right Austrian People's Party (ÖVP) entered into coalition with the FPÖ, the EU was so outraged it moved to sanction Austria. Fifteen years later, the goalposts had shifted: both parties achieved nearly twice their previous vote share. The FPÖ under Norbert Hofer narrowly lost in the 2016 presidential election with 49.7 per cent of the vote while Marine Le Pen of the FN was defeated in the second round of the 2017 election on 34 per cent. This time the Western media breathed a collective sigh of relief, their outrage having long since ebbed away. Later in 2017, the FPÖ entered into coalition with the mainstream ÖVP, part of an established European pattern which aroused little controversy. Indeed, the news bookended an *annus horribilis* for Western liberals. On 23 June 2016, Britain voted to leave the European Union. Several months later, Donald J. Trump was elected President of the United States. Following the 2015 migration crisis, populist-right parties in much of Europe built on previous gains to post record numbers. The floodwaters were creeping up. It seemed the radical right was either in power or on the cusp of it.

These political earthquakes have their roots in a growing disquiet over ethnic change which began with a tripling of far-right support in Western Europe between 1987 and 2002 and the passing of California's anti-immigrant Proposition 187 in 1994 over elite Republican objections. Today's populist earthquake has little to do with economics. As white majorities in the West age and decline, their place is being taken by non-Europeans. This shift pervades the popular imagination across Europe, North America and Australasia. While cosmopolitans embrace the change, populist-right movements feed on anti-immigration sentiment. Elites stand helpless as immigration soars to the top of white voters' agenda. Mainstream politicians hector or dismiss populists, trying – and failing – to deflect white angst onto the familiar terrain of jobs and public services.

THE IMPORTANCE OF DATA

A chorus of analysts have attempted to divine the reasons behind Trump's victory, the Brexit vote and the post-2015 surge of right-wing populism. Most offer what social scientists dub 'overdetermined' arguments,

throwing a kitchen sink of explanations at the problem (economic stagnation, racism, distrust in politicians) without using data to distinguish
which ones matter and which don't. The manager of the Oakland A's
baseball team, Billy Beane, in Michael Lewis's *Moneyball* showed that
large-scale datasets could reveal truths that scouts acting on gut instinct
failed to see.[5] On-base percentage mattered more than how athletic a bat-
ter looked or how many big hits he had. The scouts, like all of us, think in
terms of vivid images, which lead us to make what Daniel Kahneman and
Amos Tversky term 'fast-thinking' decisions.[6] These can be misleading. In
approaching populism, many have been seduced by stories of 'left-behind'
working-class whites, the opioid crisis and rusting factories, so we've had
numerous media 'safaris' into Trumpland which tend to simply confirm
reporters' biases.[7] Journalists have been mesmerized by election maps.

Looking at fine-grained surveys of individual voters produces a
different picture, in which values count far more than economics or
geography. Maps often obscure what's going on. Why? Whites and
those without degrees are more likely to vote for Trump than non-
whites and university graduates. Since minorities and well-educated
whites cluster in cities, maps show cities as anti-Trump and the countryside as pro-Trump. Thus many commentators conclude, incorrectly,
that something about the culture and economy of rural areas makes
whites like him while the dynamic diversity of the metropolitan experience leads urban whites to reject him. The proper way to address the
problem is to look at whites of similar age, education and other characteristics living in cities and rural areas and compare their voting
behaviour. This reveals they back Trump at similar rates.

I take Beane's approach, trying to stick wherever possible to multi-
variate models based on representative surveys of individuals. Data
doesn't have to be quantitative to be valid – it might consist of large
numbers of interviews, or accounts based on historical documents –
but, in order to make causal claims, information needs to be as
representative as possible. Where I don't have large-scale representative
data I run small opt-in surveys on Amazon's Mechanical Turk (MTurk)
or Prolific Academic, which aren't too expensive, contain enough cases
to compare between groups and are widely used by academics. These
aren't as good as mass surveys but are better than anecdotes and
impressions. There isn't the space in these pages to present everything,
so I encourage you to visit this book's companion website.[8]

THE CENTURY OF *WHITESHIFT*

We hear a lot about populism, and some analysts encompass its left, right, Western, Eastern and non-European variants.[9] I'm less ambitious. While there are common threads, I think the Western situation has unique features. So I distinguish what's happening in Western Europe and the Anglosphere from developments in Eastern Europe. Right-wing populism in the West is different for two main reasons. First, it is not about recovering from national humiliation or pining for a better time before democracy arrived when a strong leader gave society a clear direction. These were important motivations for inter-war fascists like the Nazis, Mussolini, Franco or the Hungarian Arrow Cross, and remain important in Russia, Greece and a number of Eastern European states. Second, immigration is less important outside the West because migrants tend to avoid or pass through Eastern European states. It's a factor in some ex-Communist nations (if inside the EU), such as Hungary, which are not used to it, but the issue often ranks lower on voters' priority lists. Many of the forces which matter in the East count for less in the West, and vice-versa.

Anyone who wants to explain what's happening in the West needs to answer two simple questions. First, why are right-wing populists doing better than left-wing ones? Second, why did the migration crisis boost populist-right numbers sharply while the economic crisis had no overall effect? If we stick to data, the answer is crystal clear. Demography and culture, not economic and political developments, hold the key to understanding the populist moment. Immigration is central. Ethnic change – the size and nature of the immigrant inflow and its capacity to challenge ethnic boundaries – is the story. Indeed, if history is any guide, we shouldn't be asking why there is a rise in right-wing populism but why it hasn't materialized faster in places such as Sweden or the US. Politicians say diversity is a problem for the nation-state, but it's actually much more of an issue for the ethnic majority. The real question is not 'What does it mean to be Swedish in an age of migration?' but 'What does it mean to be *white* Swedish in an age of migration?' The Swedish state will adapt to any ethnic configuration, but this is much trickier for the Swedish ethnic majority. While Sweden can make citizens in an afternoon, immigrants can only become ethnic Swedes through a multi-generational process of intermarriage and secularization.

WHITE ETHNO-TRADITIONALISM

Whiteshift explores two interconnected topics: white ethnic majorities and the white tradition of national identity. Put simply, ethnic groups are communities that believe they are descended from the same ancestors and differentiate themselves from others through one or more cultural markers: language, racial appearance or religion. They are also typically attached to hazily defined 'homelands'. Nations are territorial-political communities with clear territorial boundaries and political aspirations, which ethnic groups need not have. Ethnic groups, like the Jews, unite around common ancestry, whereas nations – such as Switzerland – can be multi-ethnic.[10] White majorities in the West are every bit as ethnic as minorities are, but, for many, their sense of ethnicity and nationhood is blurred. If you're white, you may think, 'I don't identify as white, only as British.' This arises because being white in a predominantly white society, like being heterosexual, doesn't confer much distinctiveness. Even groups which are minorities, like WASP Americans, may have a weaker identity because their ethnicity forms the national archetype and thus is confused with it. Likewise, those at the cultural centre lose their identity: pronouncing words in a Thames Estuary accent, like most British TV anchors, similar to sporting a flat Midwestern accent in the US, means you won't think you have an accent, even though you do. On the other hand, Britain is very different from the world's other 195 countries, so when you're abroad, your British nationality is unmistakeable. Nations also promote themselves more vociferously than ethnic groups. The fact Britain is a political unit with a budget means the British nation has taken steps to inculcate identity in its citizens in a way the white British ethnic group has not. Finally, norms may discourage white identity: expressing white British identity is frowned upon due to the expansion of the meaning of anti-racism that has taken place since the 1950s. Taken together, this means majority ethnicity is backgrounded in everyday life.

If you're like most white Brits, your ethnicity is hidden at the centre of your national identity. It's present in the way you imagine your nation. You notice that non-white Britons are minorities. The racial image that comes to mind when people think of a typical Briton is a white one, which won't pose an identity issue for you because you fit it.

You'll tend to feel an uncomplicated connection to people from Britain who lived in the country prior to 1945, 1745 or even 1245. Minorities' sense of British national identity is less straightforward. As a thought experiment, imagine how your British identity might change if the country had been founded and inhabited by black people until the first major wave of whites arrived sixty-five years ago.

Because Western nations were generally formed by a dominant white ethnic group, whose myths and symbols – such as the proper name 'Norway' – became the nation's, the two concepts overlap in the minds of many. White majorities possess an 'ethnic' module, an extra string to their national identity which minorities lack. Ethnic majorities thereby express their ethnic identity as nationalism. In Hazleton, Pennsylvania, where the issue of illegal immigration divided whites and Hispanics in the 2000s, whites signalled their identity with the national flag, not a special white symbol. In England, conservative working-class whites use the English flag as a badge of ethnic identity, though it loses its racial connotations during the World Cup.

When it comes to 'seeing' our nation, we all wear a distinct pair of ethnic glasses.[11] Minorities' spectacles give them a clear sense of where their ethno-symbols end and national ones begin. White majorities don't, because many of the national symbols they think about, like Thanksgiving in the US or Joan of Arc in France, double as white ones. As the white share of nations declines, a thin, inclusive, values-based nationalism is promoted by governments which sidelines symbols many whites cherish, like Christopher Columbus or Robin Hood. In addition, some minorities challenge aspects of the national narrative like empire or Western settlement. This lifts the fog for many whites, making them aware of their exclusive ethnic symbols by separating these out from those that are inclusive, like the Statue of Liberty. Combined with falling white population share, this raises the visibility of white identity, drawing it out from beneath the shadow of the nation.[12]

Stepping back from the tide of history, we can see that ethnic majorities in the West are undergoing *Whiteshift*, a transition from an unmixed to a mixed state. This is a process that is in its early stages and will take a century to complete. Until the mixed group emerges as a viable majority which identifies, and comes to be identified, as white, Western societies will experience considerable cultural turbulence. American history offers a preview of what we're in for. We should expect a civilization-wide replay of the ethnic divisions that gripped the United States between the late 1880s and 1960s, during which time the Anglo-Protestant majority declined to less than half the total but gradually absorbed Catholic and Jewish immigrants and their children into a reconstituted white majority oriented around a WASP archetype. This was achieved as immigration slowed and intermarriage overcame ethnic boundaries, a process which still has some way to run.

Notice that identifying with the white majority is not the same as being attached to a white-Christian tradition of nationhood. Only those with at least some European ancestry can identify as members of the white majority. However, minorities may cherish the white majority as an important piece of their national identity: a tradition of nationhood. Rachid Kaci, a French centre-right secularist of Algerian-Berber origin, writes: 'The Gauls . . . are our collective ancestors, since they inaugurated . . . [French] history down to our days, via Clovis, Charles Martel . . . the Revolution, Napoleon . . . One who wants to be considered French adopts this history, or rather, lets himself be adopted by it . . .'[13] In the US, some 30 per cent of Latinos and Asians voted for Trump and many lament the decline of white America. In surveys taken soon after the August 2017 Charlottesville riots, 70 per cent of nearly 300 Latino and Asian Trump voters agreed that 'whites are under attack in this country' and 53 per cent endorsed the idea that the country needed to 'protect and preserve its white European heritage' – similar to white Trump voters.[14] Non-white Trump voters express a much higher level of sadness at the passing of a white majority than white Democrats.[15] A key question for the future of American politics is whether new generations of Hispanics and Asians will move closer to, or further from, the country's white-Christian traditions.

Is a common national 'we' not the solution to all this? I'm afraid not. Political scientists often differentiate 'civic nations', defined by loyalty to the state and its ideology, from 'ethnic nations', united by shared ancestry.[16] All Western countries have been trying to promote civic conceptions of nationhood to include immigrants, but the populist right shows that limiting nationhood to 'British values', the American Creed or the French Republican tradition doesn't address the anxieties of conservative voters. These universalist, creedal conceptions of nationhood are necessary for unity, but cannot provide deep identity in everyday life. Ethnic nationhood, which restricts citizenship to members of the majority, is clearly a non-starter. But things aren't so black and white. There is a third possibility, ethno-traditional nationhood, which values the ethnic majority as an important component of the nation alongside other groups. Ethno-traditional nationalists favour slower immigration in order to permit enough immigrants to voluntarily assimilate into the ethnic majority, maintaining the white ethno-tradition. The point is not to assimilate all diversity, but to strike a balance between vibrant minorities and an enduring white-Christian tradition. This is the view of many conservative white voters, though there is an important tranche of exclusionists on the far right who dream of repatriating minorities.

As we saw with minority Trump voters, it's important to recognize that a significant chunk of ethnic minorities are ethno-traditional nationalists because – like Welsh nationalists who don't speak Welsh – they are attached to cultural features that make their nation distinctive. Note the difference: they are not members of the *ethnic* majority, but are members of the *nation* with an attachment to its traditional ethnic composition. One often sees this among, say, outsiders who have moved to ethnically distinctive regions like Cajun country or Cornwall and oppose rapid erosion of the Cajun/Cornish share of the local population. At the national level, this means some ethnic minorities – especially Hispanics and Asians in America – have a vicarious attachment to the white majority and support majority ethnic aims like reducing immigration or resisting affirmative action. As minorities increase in size, an important question for electoral politics is whether they will incline towards ethno-traditional nationalism or multiculturalism.

MIGRATION AND ETHNIC GROUPS IN WORLD HISTORY

In order to understand today's populist upsurge we must stand back to take in a larger historical drama: the evolution of white-majority ethnic groups in the West. Ethnic groups such as the Persians, Jews or Chinese can be traced back over two millennia. Others, such as the Dutch or Russians, date from the medieval or early modern period, while WASP Americans, Taiwanese or Zulus emerged more recently. Some ethnic groups like the Jews have endured while many – Burgundians, Hyksos and Manx, to name a few – have gone extinct. By the end of our century, half the world's 7,000 languages – most of which define a tribal or ethnic group – will join them.[17] Excluding small island states, 80 per cent of the world's 156 major countries have an ethnic majority and half contain a majority of at least 70 per cent. Europe is one of three relatively homogeneous world regions, along with North Africa and East Asia. States in these zones often have ethnic majorities of 90 per cent or more, mainly because geoclimatic variation – topography and soil type – is lower. This reduced cultural diversity by facilitating historic assimilation. By contrast, mountainous places such as New Guinea or the Caucasus impeded these processes and thus are extremely diverse.[18] Australia takes after North-West Europe in homogeneity, with the United States, Canada and New Zealand closer to the world average.

We are told that migration is rapidly changing this picture – is it? As long as migrants assimilate, ethnic boundaries persist in the face of immigration. The Jews and Greeks have been around for millennia, but both contain a plethora of genetic inputs. Outsiders have been absorbed over time, but the key boundary markers – of religion in the Jewish case and language for the Greeks – have endured. Their proper names, myths of ancestry, aspects of memory and culture persisted in some form even as forgetting and revival also took place. Groups like the Greeks were thus able to absorb massive demographic incursions such as the Slavic settlements of the sixth to tenth centuries.[19]

Likewise, I contend that today's white majorities are likely to successfully absorb minority populations while their core myths and boundary symbols endure. This will involve a change in the physical appearance of the median Westerner, hence *Whiteshift*, though linguistic and religious markers are less likely to be affected. Getting from where we are now, where most Westerners share the racial and religious features of their ethnic archetype, to the situation in a century or two, when most will be what we now term 'mixed-race', is vital to understanding our present condition.

WHY NOW?

Why is all this happening now? Population change – demography – lies at the heart of the story. If you look at a line of human population growth, it's basically flat until the industrial revolution, then we see a takeoff, with most of the growth in human numbers occurring in the past fifty years. It took from the Dawn of Man until 1804 to reach 1 billion. We hit 3 billion in 1960. Now 7.5 billion of us share the planet. The West was the first to go through its demographic transition from high birth and death rates to low birth and death rates. East Asia soon followed, and now much of the rest of the world apart from a few spots in Central Africa and West Asia is following suit.

During a demographic transition, death rates fall first and there is a lag period when birth rates are temporarily higher than death rates, producing a population explosion. However, the historic demographic transition in Europe and its settler offshoots was different to that now taking place in the global South. Europe's transition began around 1750 and lasted until about 1950. It took a long time, but in 1750, 1850 or 1900 sanitation and medicine were not what they are today. The demographer Vegard Skirbekk shows that many of those who were part of Europe's population explosion died before reaching childbearing age, which is not true in the developing world. This means the European boom had a smaller impact on global population. Take one of Skirbekk's comparisons, Denmark and Guatemala. In 1775, prior to the onset of its transition, Denmark had a population of 1 million and a population density of about twenty people per square kilometre. In Guatemala in 1900, these numbers were about the same. Because Denmark's population boomed earlier, just two to three children per woman survived to adulthood during its transition. By the time Denmark's total fertility rate fell below 2.1 in the 1950s, its population had expanded to 5 million. By contrast, Guatemala's transition only began in 1900. By the 1990s, the average Guatemalan woman was giving birth to five children who survived to childbearing age. Today there are 15.5 million Guatemalans. When Guatemala's transition is complete, it is projected to have a population of about 24 million. Its transition will have produced a population expansion five times that of Denmark. Multiplied across many countries, this explains why the West's share of world population dropped so rapidly after 1950.[20]

The demographic transition is important for politics because it unfolds at different times between world regions, between nations and even between ethnic groups within nations. In Northern Ireland, for instance, Protestants entered the demographic transition sixty to eighty years before Catholics. That meant Catholic birth rates were higher than Protestant ones for decades, which is why the Catholic share of Northern Ireland increased from 35 per cent in 1965 to close to 50 per cent today. Since voting in Northern Ireland largely takes place on ethnic lines, this had serious political ramifications, which played a part in the violence which gripped the province between 1969 and 1994.[21] In other words, it is the unevenness of the demographic transition between groups which carries political implications.[22]

Now let's zoom out to the global level. The number of children a woman bears over her lifetime is called the total fertility rate (TFR). Countries in figure 1.1 are shaded by TFR. Ninety-seven per cent of global population growth takes place in a tropical belt from Central America through Africa and into West Asia, where TFR is well above the 2.1 level needed to replace the population. Some sixty-five countries are still early in their demographic transition with the average woman expected to bear between 3.5 and 7 children over her lifetime. The developed world – the West plus East Asia – has total fertility rates well below replacement. The population is ageing, producing societies such as Spain, in which over 40 per cent of the population will be over sixty in 2050.

In 1950 there were 3.5 Europeans and North Americans for every African. The UN's medium projection tells us that by 2050 there will be two Africans for every Westerner, and four Africans per Westerner in 2100. This is probably an underestimate, because the UN assumes Europe's TFR will magically return to replacement level even though this has not been the case since the 1950s. It's especially hard to see such a rebound taking place in Southern, Eastern or German-speaking Europe. So the actual numbers for Europe and its offshoots may stay much lower. Regardless, the West, especially its European-origin population, will be a demographic speck of a few percentage points by the end of the century. Meanwhile, economic power will continue to shift to other parts of the globe. All of which is likely to sharpen the awareness of European origins among tomorrow's mixed-race Western majorities.

Western Europe's fertility rate dropped below replacement almost fifty years ago. Demographic momentum takes about forty years, so Europe's ethnic majority population has been declining in absolute terms only since the 2000s. Fewer mothers mean fewer kids, which in turn means fewer mothers, and so on. Like reverse compound interest,

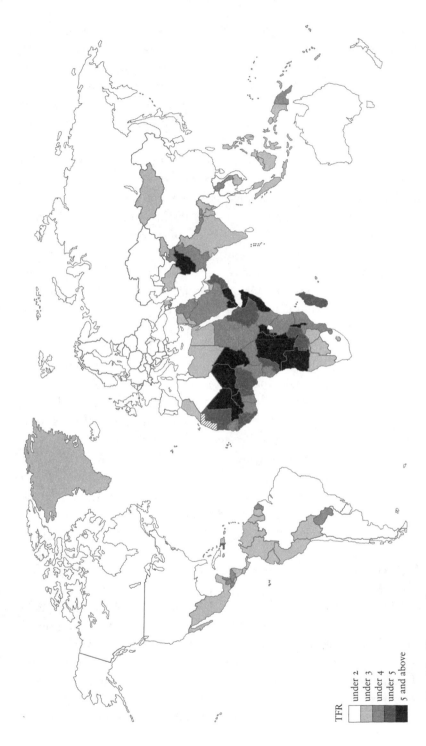

1.1. Total fertility rates by country

Source: CIA World Fact Book 2008

population decline accelerates logarithmically. If Italy's fertility rates continue at their present level for a century, its population will be only a third its present size. This is not speculation: demography is the most predictive of the social sciences because the fifty-somethings of fifty years from now have already been born. European fertility rates have risen slightly, but the continent's TFR is still only 1.5, enough to reproduce just three quarters of each generation of mothers. Demand for labour to staff hospitals and manual jobs and pay the taxes needed to meet growing pension bills will exert a powerful migratory pull. In the global South, a continuing population boom combined with low wages is generating a corresponding migratory push. While fertility is dropping quickly across most of the developing world, the population growth gradient between the global North and South will remain steep into the 2050s. In the decades to come, as young populations grow, we should expect significant migration pressure. The 2015 migration crisis showed the tragic lengths to which some in the developing world were prepared to go to reach Europe.

International migration has a long history: the share of the world's people living in a different country from the one they were born in has risen only modestly since 1960. But there has been a big rise in the number of people moving from the global South to Europe and North America. This figure more than doubled between 1990 and 2015 as 54 million people immigrated to Western countries. While nearly 40 per cent of those moving to European countries came from within Europe, 60 per cent arrived from beyond it.[23] Moreover, the vast majority of immigrants to North America came from Latin America, Asia, Africa and the Middle East – a big change from the period before 1980.

In East Asia, automation and guest worker programmes drawing on South-East Asian labour are ensuring that the region's demographic deficit will not produce multicultural nation-states. The same is true in Eastern Europe as rifts over accepting Syrian refugees showed in 2015. The Eastern rejection of cosmopolitan liberalism stands in stark contrast to the Western response, which emphasizes inclusion, multicultural citizenship and a celebration of diversity. This difference, I would argue, largely explains why right-wing populism has not reared, and will not rear, its head in Japan or Korea. These nations remain attached to what I call closed ethnic nationalism, in which proscriptions against intermarriage and tight ethnic boundaries coexist with

immigration policies designed to maintain majority ethnic predominance. Japan's foreign-born share is 1.5 per cent, Korea's 3.4, a fraction
of the 10–20 per cent we typically find in the West. In addition, many
who reside in Asia lack citizenship. This arguably leads to a class of
residents without the rights enjoyed by citizens.

The demographic revolution isn't the sole reason we're seeing conflict over immigration. The political winds are also favourable. The
decline of inter-state warfare since 1945, of organized religion since the
1960s and of communism since 1989 is opening more space for ethnic
politics to emerge. This is evident in the pattern of war. Over 90 per cent
of wars since 1945 have taken place within rather than between countries. Of these, most have been ethnic wars.[24] In developed countries
the same forces tend to produce contestation rather than violence, raising the importance of ethnicity in politics and society. In our more
peaceful, post-ideological, demographically turbulent world, migration-
led ethnic change is altering the basis of politics from class to ethnicity.
On one side is a conservative coalition of whites who are attached to
their heritage joined by minorities who value the white tradition; on the
other side a progressive alliance of minorities who identify with their ethnic identity combined with whites who are agnostic or hostile towards
theirs. Among whites, ethno-demographic change polarizes people
between 'tribal' ethnics who value their particularity and 'religious' post-
ethnics who prioritize universalist creeds such as John McWhorter's
'religion of anti-racism'.[25]

FIGHT, REPRESS, FLEE OR JOIN

In the following chapters, I chart the four main white responses to ethnic change: fight, repress, flee and join. Whites can *fight* ethnic change
by voting for right-wing populists or committing terrorist acts. They
may *repress* anxieties in the name of 'politically correct' anti-racism,
but cracks in this moral edifice are appearing. Many opt to *flee* by avoiding diverse neighbourhoods, schools and social networks. And other
whites may choose to *join* the newcomers, first in friendship, subsequently in marriage. Intermarriage promises to erode the rising diversity
which underlies our current malaise. I talk through these trends using
the latest data on immigration attitudes, populist-right voting, white

17

residential mobility, trust and intermarriage, beginning in the United States, then moving to Britain, continental Europe, and, finally, Canada and Australasia.

The focus throughout is on *Whiteshift*, the turbulent journey from a world of racially homogeneous white majorities to one of racially hybrid majorities. In the second half of the book, I explore racial population projections for Britain to the year 2300 to show that the mixed population, not ethnic minorities, will become the majority in the 2100s. The right to marry a foreign spouse, economic push-pull factors, legal barriers and international obligations make it difficult to reduce immigration below a certain level. At the same time, minorities' younger age profile will continue to power ethnic change. I work with a set of differing projection assumptions which affect the timing, but not the certainty, of a mixed-race future. This doesn't mean unmixed whites will disappear. Their fate preoccupies white nationalists and is also important for the future of Western societies, something I consider later in the book.

Fight

According to Karen Stenner, a social psychologist, rising diversity triggers two responses: conservatism and authoritarianism. Conservatism involves maintaining continuity with the past and resisting change.[26] If the West was diverse and became more homogeneous – as occurred in Poland or Vienna after 1939 – the conservative instinct would be to wax nostalgic about past diversity. Ethnic *change* is the irritant, not levels of diversity, which is why a meta-analysis of the academic literature I helped conduct shows ethnic change nearly always predicts increased anti-immigration sentiment and populist-right voting.[27] Psychological authoritarianism, by contrast, concerns the quest for order and security. Diversity, whether ethnic or ideological, however long its provenance, is problematic because it disrupts a sense of harmony and cohesion. Thus for authoritarians high *levels* of ethnic diversity are as much the problem as ethnic *change*. Even if the rate of change stays constant, high diversity levels increase discontent among those who value existential security and stability.

As Western cities have been overwhelmingly white within living memory, today's ethnic shifts are triggering both conservative and authoritarian responses. Many people have fond memories of youth, viewing this time as their halcyon days. Older conservatives look back on the way things were with profound nostalgia. Since Western populations are ageing, with the share over sixty projected to reach 30–45 per cent of various countries' populations by 2050, the average voter is getting older. The difference between nations' current ethnic composition and their makeup at the time today's median voter was twenty years old is widening. Given that old people vote at much higher rates than young adults, their nostalgia is an important ingredient in the rise of right-wing populism. On the other hand, today's young people are growing up with greater diversity, so begin with more polyglot memories. With some exceptions, such as Austria or France, they are less likely to support anti-immigration politics. If the rate of ethnic change slackens, the difference between the ethnic composition of 'golden age' memories and current reality will narrow, which could weaken support for right-wing populism.

A precedent can be found in the anti-immigration agitation of Protestant America in the mid-nineteenth century. The Irish famine and its aftermath saw over a million largely Catholic Irish immigrants move to America, a country which was over 95 per cent Protestant. By the 1850s, Catholics were a majority or large plurality in most northeastern cities. Horrific violence followed in which mobs torched Catholic churches, vandalized Irish neighbourhoods and attacked priests. Many white Protestants responded by forming anti-Catholic societies or voting for anti-immigration parties. The rise of the Native American ('Know-Nothing') Party of the 1850s was breathtaking. In the words of the historian Ray Allen Billington: 'The result was phenomenal. Whole tickets not even on the ballots were carried into office. Men who were unopposed for election and who had been conceded victory found themselves defeated by some unknown Know-Nothing.'[28] All but one of the 377 state representatives of Massachusetts were Know-Nothings. They won 22 per cent of the vote in 1856, the most successful third party in American history. Many thought a Know-Nothing President was inevitable until the North–South divide over slavery intervened.

Repress

A second white response is to repress ethnic instincts in the name of anti-racism. As humans we're always working with the grain of some of our evolutionary psychology and against other aspects of it. We may feel the urge to relieve ourselves at the dinner table, but ever since court manners evolved to frown on this in the late Middle Ages, we have opted to hold on until we find a bathroom. Tribalism is also something we can repress, and this repression of instincts may have made evolutionary sense. How? In the evolutionary race, people who cooperate with those who share more of their genes are more successful in passing on their genes. We are, as Jonathan Haidt remarks, part bee, hardwired to be tribal.[29] On the other hand, bigger tribes tend to beat smaller ones in battle. Tribes who trade do better than those too xenophobic to do so. So when it comes to social evolution, societies whose norms allowed them to transcend narrow tribalism may have aided individual survival. Evolution could also have selected for individuals who when conquered made the best of a bad situation and accepted amalgamation. Those who repressed their tribalism to adapt to these larger units may have been able to pass their genes on more effectively.

One study compared the Dinka and Nuer, two south Sudanese tribes, in the late nineteenth century. The Nuer tribes' more cooperative norms, buttressed by a religious belief system, permitted them to amalgamate their tribes into a larger political unit, whereas the Dinka tribes' worldview did not. This allowed the Nuer to expand in size, conquer many Dinka and assimilate them into their ethnic group.[30] Successful larger groups in turn spawn imitators, reinforcing the new cooperative norms. Religion evolved to permit cooperation in larger units.[31] Our predisposition towards religion, morality and reputation – all of which can transcend the tribe – reflects our adaptation to larger social units. Be that as it may, humans have lived in large groups only in the very recent past, so it is reasonable to assume tribalism is a more powerful aspect of our evolutionary psychology than our willingness to abide by a moral code. Today what we increasingly see in the West is a battle between the 'tribal' populist right and the 'religious' anti-racist left.

Even so, our evolutionary impulses can be harnessed in numerous ways. The fact our tribal makeup can be tricked to apply to sports teams or empires shows that evolution exerts only a distant force on behaviour. We favour genetic relatives, but this primordial tribalism is a weak tie-breaker that comes into play only when everything else is equal. A white American in a foreign airport usually feels closer to a black American than to a white Frenchman. Tribal instincts matter *within* social groups: a parent may favour a biological child over an adopted one if both are precisely the same in other respects, but the parent won't prefer her brother's child to her adopted one; the Arab Islamic fundamentalist will feel closer to an Arab fundamentalist than to a Pakistani fundamentalist but will feel a stronger bond to a Pakistani fundamentalist than to an Arab Christian. As long as political conflicts are centred on ideology or states, primordial tribalism remains latent. What matters most is economic and institutional heft, with nepotistic instincts deciding things only at the margin. A trans-ethnic social group like the left can harness our tribal instincts the same way white nationalism can. Only if the two institutional forces are equally resourced will evolutionary psychology hand victory to white nationalism because it resonates slightly better with our instincts.

Left-Modernism

Much of this book is concerned with the clash between a rising white tribalism and an ideology I term 'left-modernism'. A sociologist member of the 'New York Intellectuals' group of writers and literary critics, Daniel Bell, used the term *modernism* to describe the spirit of anti-traditionalism which emerged in Western high culture between 1880 and 1930. With the murderous excesses of communism and fascism, many Western intellectuals embraced a fusion of modernist anti-traditionalism and cultural egalitarianism, distinguishing the new ideology from both socialism and traditional liberalism. Cosmopolitanism was its guiding ethos. Unlike socialism or fascism, this left-wing modernism meshed nicely with capitalism and globalization. The left-modernist sensibility spread from a small elite to a much wider section of middle-class society in the 1960s with the rise of television and growth of universities, taking over as the dominant sensibility of the high culture.[32]

As it gained ground, it turned moralistic and imperialistic, seeking not merely to persuade but to institutionalize itself in law and policy, altering the basis of liberalism from tolerating to mandating diversity. This is a subtle but critical shift. Meanwhile the economic egalitarianism of socialism gave way to a trinity of sacred values around race, gender and sexual orientation. Upsurges of left-modernist fundamentalism became a feature of campus life in the mid-1960s and waxed in the late 1980s and early 1990s as well as in the period since 2013. While only a minority of academics – most of whom are centre-left rather than far-left – support campus radicalism, it has provided fodder for the right-wing media, raising the pitch of the so-called 'culture wars'. More importantly, left-modernism laid the basis for a new moral order – a redefinition of sacred and deviant – which pushed immigration restriction beyond the pale, keeping it off the political agenda. This permitted business and humanitarian considerations to override cultural concerns, facilitating the immigration-led ethnic changes which have powered right-wing populism.

The great liberal Isaiah Berlin makes an extremely important distinction between negative and positive liberty. Negative liberalism says we should allow people to pursue their goals as long as they don't infringe the rights of others. Positive liberalism consists of promoting particular goals, such as autonomy or diversity, as the proper aim of human individuals and societies.[33] Tolerating difference is critical for negative liberalism. Celebrating it is not. If someone doesn't have a taste for Marmite, asking them to celebrate it is a coercive form of positive liberalism with no roots in the Western legal tradition. This is why the attempt by the Law Society of Upper Canada in 2017 to force its members to promote diversity is being challenged in the courts.[34]

In the 1960s, resistance to left-modernism came from formerly socialist, primarily Jewish, intellectuals like Bell, Nathan Glazer and others. Glazer was an especially influential critic of the multicultural resurgence of the 1990s.[35] These criticisms shaped intellectual life on the centre-right and informed opposition to bilingualism and affirmative action in the United States. Even so, the multicultural narrative continued in the media while affirmative action was upheld by the courts and practised in elite universities. Events moved more quickly in Europe in the 1990s, where populist-right gains in countries such as France, Italy and Austria prompted mainstream politicians to abandon the rhetoric of multiculturalism. Where left-modernism was formerly able to portray national identity as dangerous, clearing the way for multiculturalism, political change desacralized multiculturalism, permitting it to be debated, whereupon it was swiftly replaced by civic nationalism.

Immigration was the next moral battleground. Liberal immigration had been facilitated by left-modernist norms of polite discourse that wrapped those who sought lower levels in a cloak of disrepute. By the 2000s, populist-right pressure on the European political centre led to an increasingly open debate over the volume of immigration, eroding the sway of anti-racist norms in this area and relocating the deviant–normal boundary. By the 2010s, the populist right was challenging proscriptions on anti-Muslim sentiment, endangering the religious liberty of conservative Muslims. This shift from contesting positive liberalism to attacking Muslims' negative liberty is, in my view, an overreach which needs to be reined in.

The tug of war between white ethno-traditionalism and anti-racist moralism is redefining Western politics. Among white liberals, moral considerations override nationalism so completely that the changing ethnic composition of Western cities and countries barely registers.[36] For white conservatives, the anti-racist taboo still restrains majority-ethnic impulses, but this is eroding. For instance, many French people who oppose immigration won't vote for the Front National because they see it as a racist party. Studies show that people reduce support for anti-immigration statements when they are told these come from far-right parties.[37] But the line of acceptability can shift. When populist-right parties make breakthroughs, they signal to other white conservatives that it's more acceptable to vote this way. This can generate a positive feedback loop in which higher votes facilitate even higher votes. The FPÖ's previous high of 27 per cent was vastly exceeded by its 49 per cent in 2016 partly because it had become more acceptable to vote for the populist right. The populist surge is not only about what's driving it, but what's no longer restraining it.

The same holds for immigration. The fact Trump openly talked about building a wall and banning Muslims and still won shifted the so-called 'Overton Window' of acceptable political ideas within the right-wing media. This weakened the anti-racist taboo among American conservatives and made it acceptable to openly campaign on a platform of reducing immigration. In Canada, by contrast, the taboo still holds on the right, so talk of reducing immigration lies beyond the bounds of the permissible. The only question is whether levels should remain the same or increase. Thus the Conservative government of Stephen Harper, which was strongly pro-Israel and willing to criticize conservative Muslims, didn't dare touch Canada's 'immigration consensus'. This has produced the highest immigration levels in the OECD and increased the non-European share of the Canadian population from around 2 per cent in 1970 to 22 per cent today. With this in mind, I pay close attention to the scope of the anti-racist taboo across different societies. Evolutionary psychology is not irrelevant, but the battle of ideas and political forces is what's decisive.

Flee or Join?

Right-wing populism dominates the news, but white majorities are also responding to ethnic change in quieter ways. The economist Albert Hirschman spoke of the difference between 'voice', fighting for change within one's social group, and 'exit', leaving it.[38] Likewise, if voting for the populist right is 'voice', a way of combating change, white 'exit' consists of withdrawal into white residential areas or social networks. White flight and avoidance of minorities is an important trend which often goes under the radar, especially outside the United States. Much of the work on integration has focused on whether minorities are self-segregating, ignoring what whites are doing. Lo and behold, white behaviour is turning out to be more important for the national segregation picture than minority behaviour. The polarization of American, and increasingly European, politics arises partly from the geographic consequences of whites' moving towards relatively white neighbourhoods and schools when they raise their children.

This is not the whole story, however. Many whites remain in diverse urban and suburban zones, and intermarriage is increasingly common. The 2011 British census found that the share of white Britons living in mixed-ethnicity households doubled from 6 to 12 per cent between 2001 and 2011. So while exurban and rural areas remain overwhelmingly white and are diverging from cities, whites in metro areas are increasingly exposed to difference. Intermarriage and inter-ethnic friendship are rising. In the Netherlands, Canada and Britain, around half the Afro-Caribbean population marries out. In the US, whites with children who remain in highly diverse neighbourhoods are often married to non-whites. Therefore, in addition to white 'voice' and 'exit', whites are joining the newcomers. These three responses – fight, flee and join – are not mutually exclusive. I explore how each is playing out in the US, Western Europe and the Anglosphere.

THE FUTURE OF WHITE MAJORITIES

What then is the future of today's white majorities? Talking about the future of race makes us uncomfortable; it's like discussing sex in Victorian Britain.[39] There is a great deal of conjecture as well, from the alt-right's white genocide and ethno-state to the radical left's multicultural cosmopolis. Being of white appearance, speaking the language without an accent and being Christian or Judaeo-Christian (or secular versions thereof) are the markers which differentiate white majorities from minorities. Of these markers, two are what Ernest Gellner terms 'counter-entropic', or resistant to assimilation.[40] Immigrant children typically speak the native language without an accent, but will tend to retain their religion and, if non-white, remain racially distinct. Non-Christian groups, apart from East Asians, generally remain religious over generations, though there is a slow process of secularization under way among Sikhs, Hindus and Muslims.[41] Physical differences likewise erode only over generations, through intermarriage.

Race does much of the work in demarcating whites from minorities today. Religion, despite the challenge of conservative Islam, is becoming less important as the West grows more secular. Current thinking on the role of racial appearance in nationalism divides primordialists, who think race matters because of our tribal instincts to cooperate with those who share more of our genes, and instrumentalists, who think it counts only because it serves people's material interests. I don't think evolutionary psychology on its own can tell us much about why group boundaries take the form they do. True, certain physical characteristics, such as white skin and blue eyes, co-occur together more often than black skin and blue eyes. But this clustering comes in the form of gradations from North to South, or East to West. Blood types and other genetic traits cut across these phenotypical traits, and there has been considerable gene flow since the Dawn of Man some 100,000 years ago. Cultural tradition, not genes, tells us which markers matter and which don't.

On the other hand, the view that groups like the antebellum Irish 'became white' when they served political purposes such as the interests of the southern Democrats is, in my opinion, overstated.[42] The Irish or Jews in America, though outside the Anglo-Protestant ethnic core, were distinguished from African-Americans or Chinese in daily social interactions. Some Latinos can pass as white: whether they do so is less dependent on census categories and laws than emergent, bottom-up social processes of social acceptance similar to those which eventually made gay marriage a non-issue in America. I'm a good example as someone who is a quarter Latino and a quarter Chinese but is considered white by most people, whereas some of my relatives with the same mixture are seen as Hispanic. Appearance plays a central part in this even if race isn't 'real': physicists tell us there are no actual colours in the electromagnetic spectrum, just a continuum. Yet we perceive colours and develop similar words for them across cultures. This is partly due to the way our brain processes electromagnetic stimuli and partly because of how cultures classify the primary colours.[43] A few small groups, such as the Namibian Himba, don't recognize the colour green, calling it a shade of blue.[44] Still, broadly speaking, there is cross-cultural consensus around colour and I don't believe this can be deconstructed. Is the same true for our established racial groups? Broadly speaking, I think so.

These racial archetypes matter for cultural-historical, rather than biological or economic, reasons. The paintings in the Uffizi, carvings on Mount Rushmore, statues in Pall Mall and faces in Hollywood classics preserve a white self-image which defines the ethnic majority. The hybridized whites of the future will need to forge connections back to these images, and tell a story which helps them navigate their ethnic past. One way visually 'unmixed' whiteness is likely to survive is through the unusually white features of pop icons, especially those who act in historical dramas. I explore this by looking at the endurance of Anglo-Saxon surnames among actors in contemporary Hollywood. Another mode of unmixed white survival may be through isolation, just as Irish-speaking communities endure in Ireland's Gaeltacht. With each passing census, the rural West is becoming a different planet from the cities. This raises difficult questions about whether countries are bifurcating ethnically, culturally and politically between 'metro' centres and 'retro' hinterlands, with little common ground.

In the final chapters I consider a number of ways 'unmixed' whiteness may persist, from the least to most likely. Might unmixed whites retreat into virtual reality? Could genetic engineering permit hybridized whites to 'whiten' themselves, much as Latin American elites have tended to do through selective marriage? I am sceptical. Much more likely is the survival of unmixed whiteness within fundamentalist religious sects I call 'time capsules' of whiteness. These groups, described in detail in my previous book, *Shall the Religious Inherit the Earth?*, have high birth rates and little interaction with the mainstream. They are religiously, not racially, motivated, but they rarely intermarry. The Amish, ultra-Orthodox Jews, Orthodox Dutch Calvinists, Hutterites, Finnish Laestadian Lutherans, Quiverfull Calvinists and Mormons will be a much bigger demographic force in a century than they are now. Already, the ultra-Orthodox are a third of Jewish-Israeli first-graders and by 2050 will form a majority of observant Jews in America and Britain. Since these groups are essentially all white, they push against the grain of the West's racial trajectory. Heavily Mormon Utah's population is increasingly diverging from the rest of the country, with a much whiter young population than neighbouring states. The main reason large sections of Brooklyn are becoming whiter is because of the rapid growth of the city's ultra-Orthodox Jewish community, where women bear an average of six to seven children.

Having surveyed the dynamics of *Whiteshift*, I set out a vision for a new centre, which entails accepting the legitimate cultural interests of reconstructed, open ethnic majorities. This can pave the way towards a more relaxed, rational political conversation. The West cannot simultaneously accept large inflows and maintain culturally neutral immigration policies. Yet I am not arguing that it should adopt the exclusive East Asian model. A better solution is to balance liberal and minority preferences for more immigration with the restrictionism of ethnic-majority conservatives. The key is that the majority be an open rather than closed ethnic group. An open majority group's conservative members will want slower immigration to help it maintain its share through voluntary assimilation – not exclusion and expulsion. Minorities should not be compelled to assimilate to a state-defined national identity, but, like white majorities, should be free to express their ethnically distinct versions of the common national identity – an arrangement I term multivocalism.

Immigration levels could be adjusted in response to concerns based in part on the best indicator of assimilation – intermarriage rates – to balance diversity increases with diversity abatement. Ethno-cultural, not economic, protection is what drives right-wing populism today, and policymakers need to become less squeamish about tracking cultural indicators to address majority concerns. It's better that these indicators be transparent and measurable than sublimated in favour of materialist rationales for restriction such as terrorism, crime or unemployment. The latter are rarely tied to data, target particular out-groups, and give rise to irrational panics. As my research shows, presenting evidence of intermarriage and assimilation to conservative audiences makes a significant difference in reducing support for right-wing populism.[45] Minorities should be free to maintain their ethnic boundaries, but when voluntary mixing occurs this positive story needs to be told to allay conservative fears about an excessive accumulation of diversity. When the majority sees itself as having a largely mixed-race future, it may become more open to immigration. Until that day arrives, proponents can make the economic and humanitarian case for immigration, but politicians should set levels that respect the cultural comfort zone of the median voter.

The liberal conceit that whites must be post-ethnic cosmopolitans has outlived its usefulness. Some warm to cosmopolitanism, others prefer to identify with their ethnic group. An unalloyed positive liberalism which insists on the value of diversity is unlikely to survive the populist moment. Even if conservative whites don't win elections, they are in a position to obstruct change, damage social cohesion and, perhaps, pose a security threat. Elites who use national and supranational institutions to advance a cosmopolitan vision are eroding conservatives' trust in liberal institutions. Conservative whites need to have a future and I believe most will accept an open form of white majority identity. Politicians should empathize with their anxieties so long as these are not – as is true of anti-Muslim politics – based on irrational fears of the other. In addition, we need to be more forthright about relaying good news about the pace of voluntary assimilation. Immigration will need to be slower than is economically optimal, but the result should be a more harmonious society. With these changes in place, the West can begin to refocus on priorities such as democratization, climate change, economic growth and inequality.

PART I

Fight

2

Prequel to *Whiteshift*: From WASP to White in American History

On 8 November 2016 a second populist explosion rocked the Anglo-sphere. Coming less than five months after Brexit, it unsettled elite opinion across the Western world and sent markets into a tizzy. As with Brexit, I doubted Trump could win and recall the same sensation of shock mixed with surprise when I heard the results the following morning. It's remarkable how two events could *feel* so similar. Both, it's fair to say, are an outgrowth of the first phase of *Whiteshift* – whereby rapid immigration of ethnic outsiders raises existential questions for the ethnic majority. In this case, around whether the white majority is losing predominance in 'its' perceived homeland.

In America, half of babies are Latino, Asian or black and the nation as a whole is slated to become 'majority minority' in the 2040s. Thirteen per cent of the population of the United States is foreign-born, no different to Britain. However, England is projected to be 73 per cent white in 2050, precisely where the US was in the year 2000. This puts America half a century ahead of Western Europe on the racial transformation curve. This has spread well beyond gateway cities: twenty-two of the top 100 metropolitan areas are currently 'majority minority', as are Texas, California, two smaller states and the District of Columbia. In Europe this is not the case. London, though just 45 per cent white British in 2011, is around 60 per cent white. If we include the additional 4 million in the commuter belt outside the M25 ring road, metropolitan London retains a white British ethnic majority as well as a white majority of some 70 per cent. The same is true of continental immigrant gateways such as greater Amsterdam or Paris. A ride on public transportation in New York, San Francisco or Chicago is generally a far more 'majority-minority' experience than taking the London tube or Paris metro.

The US was settled through waves of immigration. More importantly, it is the only Western country to experience large-scale ethnic transformation through immigration in the century prior to 1945. Canada, France, Switzerland and Australia received many non-core ethnic immigrants during this period as well, but ethnic majorities remained overwhelmingly dominant, both nationally and in major cities. In addition, much of our left-liberal lexicon on immigration – multiculturalism, cosmopolitanism, anti-whiteness, diversity – developed in America in the first two decades of the twentieth century. In order to get a sense of where Western societies may be heading in our age of ethnic transformation, we need to pay closer attention to the history of immigration politics in America than elsewhere.

A NATION OF IMMIGRANTS?

Europeans tend to view their immigration situation as unprecedented while downplaying American developments as somehow less consequential because the US is a 'nation of immigrants'. But is this convincing? British permanent settlement in the present-day US began in 1620. By the time of American independence in 1776, the free population of the United States was 98 per cent Protestant and almost entirely white apart from a small population of free blacks in the North. Eighty per cent of the colonists were of British descent, predominantly English, but with a significant Scotch-Irish component. The remaining 20 per cent were almost all of North-West European background – German, Dutch, Swedish, French or Irish. African-Americans and Amerindians comprised a fifth of the total, but were effectively disenfranchised and not considered part of the American nation. The Constitution in 1790 restricted citizenship to 'free white persons'. John Jay, despite his Huguenot ancestry, considered Americans 'essentially English' as did foreign visitors like Alexis de Tocqueville.[1]

Many of the American founders viewed Americans as descendants of the Anglo-Saxons who had fled the Norman yoke in England. This borrowed from British Whig historians who considered the British monarchy, which stemmed from the Norman Conquest, to be a tyrannical institution which quashed the primitive liberties enjoyed by the Anglo-Saxon tribes. The theory of republicanism held that societies based on independent farmers, or yeomen, were superior to those based on an aristocracy and tenantry. Whigs viewed the Anglo-Saxon Americans as returning to their yeoman roots, freed from British-Norman domination. This myth was not just a political lineage which viewed King Alfred's ninth-century Anglo-Saxons as kindred spirits. Rather, many of the Founders believed they were the actual descendants of the Anglo-Saxons. Ethnicity is a sentiment derived from a sense of common ancestry. Thomas Jefferson, a Founding Father who served as third president, wrote to John Adams after drafting the constitution that the Americans were 'the children of Israel in the wilderness, led by a cloud by day and a pillar of fire by night; and on the other side, Hengist and Horsa, the Saxon chiefs from whom we claim the honour of being *descended, and whose political principles* and form of government we have assumed'.[2] Notice the separate nod to Anglo-Saxon genealogical and ideological inheritances. In this sense, many Founders considered Americans a distinct ethnic group, especially as compared to the Norman-descended British elite.

The myth of Anglo-Saxon origins became the dominant interpretation of American history in the nineteenth century, though southern historians rejected it in favour of a Norman-Cavalier myth of descent prior to the Civil War.[3] In 1889, for example, in his sprawling history of America entitled *The Winning of the West*, the future President Theodore Roosevelt drew a direct line between the Anglo-Saxon conquest of Britain in the sixth century and the American Revolution, Indian wars, Mexican wars and Western settlement:

> The fathers followed Boon[e] or fought at King's Mountain; the sons marched south with Jackson to overcome the Creeks and beat back the British; the grandsons died at the Alamo or charged to victory at San Jacinto. They were doing their share of a work that began with the [sixth-century Anglo-Saxon] conquest of Britain, that entered on its second and wider period after the defeat of the Spanish Armada, that culminated in the marvellous growth of the United States. The winning of the West and Southwest is a stage in the conquest of a continent.[4]

In short, American political nationhood, as in much of Western Europe, was constructed around what the sociologist of nationalism Anthony Smith terms an 'ethnic core'.[5] We can think of two aspects to ethnic groups: a time dimension connecting them to ancestors, and a spatial dimension distinguishing them from neighbouring groups in the present. The spatial aspect is referred to in the literature as an *ethnic boundary* and its symbols typically include one or more of language, religion and physical appearance. At different times, and in different places, certain markers become more important. In Northern Ireland, the groups look and sound the same, but differ by religion. Hungarians and Slovaks look alike and don't differ much on religion, but language sets them apart. In Britain, Afro-Caribbeans have the same religion and language as white Britons but look physically distinct. Sometimes the boundary markers all matter and reinforce each other, as with white Afrikaner Protestants and black Zulu animists in nineteenth-century South Africa.

In the United States, the boundary markers for the ethnic majority were the 'W-AS-P' trinity of white appearance, unaccented English, British or Dutch surname, and Protestant religion. Having said this, Americans were an assimilationist ethnic group from the outset, so there was considerable fuzziness around the edges. Immigrants from foreign denominations like Lutheranism converted to Anglo-American denominations such as Methodism or Baptism rather than the other way round. Foreign accents faded, especially in the second generation, and many anglicized their surnames. Paul Revere's ancestors were Huguenots named Rivoire. Rittenhouse Square in Philadelphia is named after eighteenth-century inventor David Rittenhouse, whose German Rittinghuysen forebears settled in Pennsylvania. An American sociologist, Milton Gordon, referred to this process as 'Anglo-conformity', in which immigrants proceeded through seven steps from economic to marital to 'identificational' assimilation. His view was that immigrants assimilated to an Anglo-Saxon archetype. Here Gordon quoted Teddy Roosevelt.

> The representatives of many old-world races are being fused together into a new type, a type the main features of which are already determined, and were determined at the time of the Revolutionary War; for the crucible into which all the new types are melted into one was shaped from 1776 to 1789, and our nationality was definitely fixed in all its essentials by the men of Washington's day.[6]

This doesn't mean assimilation proceeded smoothly at all times. Benjamin Franklin worried about the 'white and red' skin tone of the English being overwhelmed by 'tawny' Swedes and Germans in colonial

Pennsylvania, but ultimately placed his faith in anglicization. More problematic were Catholics, who represented a seemingly indigestible element. Catholicism represented what the Czech-British sociologist of nationalism, Ernest Gellner, calls a 'counter-entropic' trait.[7] That is, retained through generations and resisting decomposition over time. Whereas language or accent tends to fade in the second generation, religion and phenotype are often inherited and therefore endure.

The share of foreign-born in the United States has fluctuated, but, apart from the earliest years of British and Scotch–Irish colonization in the seventeenth and early eighteenth centuries, never exceeded 15 per cent of the total. Immigration slowed during the early years of the American republic between 1776 and 1820, contributing just 3 per cent of population growth in 1810. However, as figure 2.1 shows, this changed from the 1830s. In addition to significant British immigration, German, Irish and Scandinavian inflows increased from the 1830s through the 1890s, with Southern and Eastern European immigration peaking between 1895 and 1924. Today, 13.1 per cent of Americans are foreign-born, a figure not seen since the 1920s, when anti-immigration sentiment was at its zenith. Inflows were actually somewhat higher

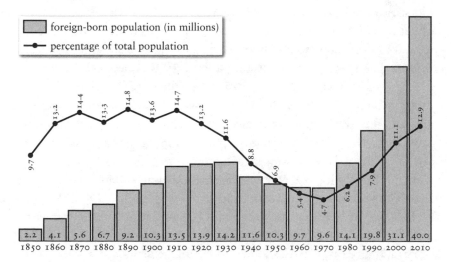

2.1. Foreign-born population and percentage of total population, for the United States: 1850–2010

Source: US Census Bureau, Census of Population, 1850 to 2000, and the American Community

35

in the nineteenth century than today, but the high native birth rate back then meant immigrants had less of a demographic impact than they do today.

ANGLO-AMERICAN 'NATIVISM'

In the 1820s, the Founders' lofty pronouncements about Anglo-Saxon origins found little echo in the population, most of whom remained attached to denominational, state and regional identities. This began to change with large-scale Catholic immigration from Ireland and southern Germany in the 1840s and 1850s. Immigration was concentrated in the northern states, especially in the cities of the eastern seaboard and the emerging Midwest. As today, immigrants concentrated in the larger cities. Boston, the heart of Puritan New England, was already a quarter Irish in 1844. By 1853 it was 40 per cent Irish and majority foreign-born. These sudden changes ignited ethno-nationalist sentiments in the Anglo-Americans who felt threatened by the increase in foreign, and especially Catholic, population. In the 1840s and 1850s, anti-Catholicism was a staple of the penny press which warned of papal plots. Anti-Catholic works such as Maria Monk's *Awful Disclosures* about sexual deviance in a nunnery sold hundreds of thousands of copies. Protestant mobs routinely burned Catholic churches and attacked priests. The spirit of anti-Catholic animosity was depicted in Martin Scorsese's film *Gangs of New York*, set in the 1850s, in which a Protestant gangleader played by Daniel Day-Lewis initiates a turf war against an Irish Catholic gang led by Liam Neeson. Anglo-Protestants saw themselves as the indigenous, 'native' population, descended from settlers who, as Day's character announced to Neeson's Irishmen, had won the Revolutionary War and built the country. This was distinct from Catholic immigrants who had arrived after the 1830s. As with perceptions of Islam in the West today, Catholicism was viewed as an alien faith with no place in American civilization.

From the 1840s, anti-Catholic political movements had begun organizing and contesting elections. By 1854, these came together as the Native American Party, known as the 'Know-Nothings' because of their oath of secrecy. The 'native' monicker resulted in a new American term, 'nativist', shorthand for Anglo-American ethnic nationalist. The party sought to reduce immigration and introduce a twenty-one-year residency requirement for citizenship. The Know-Nothing Party was the most successful third-party movement in American history. In the mid-term elections of 1854, the new party rampaged through the established order. In high-immigration Massachusetts, all but one of 377 representatives were Know-Nothings.[8] Commentators considered a Know-Nothing president inevitable in 1854, but by 1856, the issue of slavery split the northern and southern wings of the Know-Nothing convention. Though the Know-Nothings won 22 per cent of the vote in the 1856 election, war clouds were on the horizon. In 1860, the country entered the Civil War, the bloodiest episode in its history.

War can have many effects on a society. If a country loses, like Germany in the First World War, minorities like the Jews may be blamed and suffer. On the other hand, conflict can fuse different ethnic groups in mutual solidarity, and it appears the Civil War helped legitimate the German and Irish immigrant presence in the north. The conflict cost 618,222 lives out of a population of 31.4 million, an astounding casualty rate. The trauma of war and reconstruction hung over the nation for decades. Through the gloom, one outlet for national energies was the west. In the 1860s, settlers streamed west to settle the Great Plains, encouraged by Lincoln's 1862 Homestead Act granting settlers 150 acres of free land. There, ethnic configurations were different, historical roots shallower. Mexicans and Chinese were outsiders, but Irish and German Catholics were better accepted as part of the ethnic majority. The same was true in the south, where race could trump religion. For instance, Judah P. Benjamin, a Sephardic Jew, served as Secretary of War in Jefferson Davis's Confederate government during the Civil War. The colour line was a boundary condition for membership in the ethnic majority, even as anti-Catholic and anti-Semitic exclusions operated in some spheres to delineate 'true' Americans from arrivistes. Ethnic boundaries were also important as a litmus test for whether a territory could be incorporated as a state. New Mexico was admitted to the Union only in 1912, its entry delayed until Anglo settlers – a category which included white Catholics and Jews – predominated over Hispanics there.

THE LIBERAL IMMIGRATION
TRADITION

Chinese immigration was facilitated by the 1868 Burlingame Treaty with China. But this raises the question of who favoured immigration. Was it humanitarian liberals of the kind that champion open immigration today? Hardly. Liberal Progressivism would not emerge for another four decades. Instead, large businesses, pro-growth politicians and the Protestant clerical establishment comprised the main open-borders coalition. Intellectually, proponents of immigration could draw on an important set of symbolic resources which began with the Puritan concept of New England as a refuge from royalist tyranny. William Penn and the Quaker elite of Pennsylvania likewise established their colony as a refuge for oppressed sects.[9] With the establishment of the United States, American statesmen sometimes drew on this American tradition of asylum, as with Jefferson, who proclaimed in 1817 that he wished to keep the doors of America open, so as to 'consecrate a sanctuary for those whom the misrule of Europe may compel to seek happiness in other climes ... where their subjects will be received as brothers and secured against like oppression by a participation in the right of self-government'.[10]

The American asylum tradition was not an egalitarian project. Anti-racist egalitarianism played no part in liberal thinking at the time. Americans welcomed immigration to grow the country, and could wax lyrical about the US as a 'new' nation made up of various European peoples. At the same time, they considered themselves more Protestant and Anglo-Saxon than Britain. So Jefferson could affirm both the asylum and Anglo-Saxon traditions without cognitive dissonance. Here is the great American liberal philosopher and essayist Ralph Waldo Emerson, writing in 1846 about the US as 'The asylum of all nations ... the energy of Irish, Germans, Swedes, Poles and Cossacks, and all the European tribes, of the Africans and Polynesians, will construct a new race ... as vigorous as the new Europe which came out of the smelting pot of the Dark Ages.'[11] And around the same time he declared:

> It cannot be maintained by any candid person that the African race have ever occupied or do promise ever to occupy any very high place in the human family ... The Irish cannot; the American Indian cannot; the

FROM WASP TO WHITE IN AMERICAN HISTORY

Chinese cannot. Before the energy of the Caucasian race all other races have quailed and done obeisance.[12]

For Emerson, as for his contemporaries and writers throughout the nineteenth century, it was typical to rattle off a futuristic cosmopolitan pronouncement then affirm the country's Anglo-Protestant ethnic character, a mental feat Emerson called 'double consciousness'. Assimilation played a key part in squaring the circle. In his *English Traits* (1856), Emerson wrote that:

> forty of these millions [in the British Empire] are of British stock. Add the United States of America, which reckon (in the same year), exclusive of slaves, 20,000,000 people . . . and in which the foreign element, however considerable, *is rapidly assimilated*, and you have a population of English *descent* and language of 60,000,000, and governing a population of 245,000,000 souls.[13]

Emerson reflected the prevailing view among Anglo-American liberals that newcomers could be not only integrated but *ethnically* assimilated into the W-AS-P cultural markers and traditions. In the nineteenth century, the concept of ethnicity was relatively malleable – a stance I suggest white majorities must revisit. Many Anglo-American thinkers believed that the Anglo-Saxon tended to overwhelm other strains and would thereby prevail in the assimilation process. During the Mexican-American and Spanish-American Wars some even thought Latin America could be conquered and assimilated into an expanding Anglo-Saxon nation.[14] The most perceptive writer on American nativism, John Higham, observes that during the 'age of confidence', which lasted until 1890:

> the Anglo-Saxonists were pro rather than con . . . almost no race-thinker directly challenged a tolerant and eclectic attitude towards other European groups. Instead, Anglo-Saxon and cosmopolitan nationalisms merged in a happy belief that the Anglo-Saxon has a marvelous capacity for assimilating kindred races, absorbing their valuable qualities, yet remaining essentially unchanged.[15]

Political demographer Paul Morland suggests that the tremendous demographic expansion of Britain after the industrial revolution, when steady wages led to a lower age of marriage, facilitating higher birth rates, underlay this confidence. For instance, in 1700 France had three times Britain's population. By 1900, Britain had drawn level even while exporting 25 million people.[16]

ECONOMIC COMPETITION AND IMMIGRATION POLICY

Commercial interests drew on the asylum tradition in their call for more open immigration. In the 1850s, the 'elite developmentalist' wing of the Republican Party emerged as the chief vessel for commercial interests.[17] In 1864, the Republican Party enacted legislation permitting imported contract labour and 'reaffirmed the historic role of the United States as an asylum for the oppressed of all nations', endorsing a 'liberal and just immigration policy, which would encourage foreign immigration'.[18]

After 1849, thousands of Chinese – disproportionately male – entered California during the gold rush. By 1880, they made up over 10 per cent of the population of the golden state. Chinese contract labourers were first recruited in the 1860s, used by railway magnates to construct the transcontinental railroad because they could be paid a third less than white workers. 'All I want in my business is muscle,' declared a large employer in California in the 1870s. 'I don't care whether it be obtained from a Chinaman or a white man – from a mule or a horse!'[19] Southern elites, not least Ku Klux Klan founder Nathan Bedford Forest, called for Chinese immigration to quell black labour demands after the Civil War.[20] This neatly delineates the difference between the white nationalism of northern free-soil republicans and the white supremacy of southern slaveholders. Supremacists insisted only on white dominance, not on white ethno-territorial congruence.

Opposition to immigration was centred in the urban Protestant working class. An important part of the Republican base consisted of former Know-Nothings, many of whom were tradesmen. Pressure from this quarter led to repeal of the contract labour statute, but the battle would continue in California in the 1870s. Most Protestant Americans lived in the countryside and relatively few inhabited larger cities. Nevertheless, urban labour – especially mechanics and those in the craft unions – drew on the ethnic and racial traditions of American nationhood to call for restricted entry. Meanwhile, older waves of immigrants were progressively assimilated into the white working class. One index of assimilation was Irish-Catholic participation in the anti-Chinese Workingmen's Party in California whose agitation resulted in the 1882 Chinese Exclusion Act. Led by Irish-born Denis Kearney, it brought Protestant and Catholic together in what has been described as 'the most successful labour-based movement in American history'.[21]

Conflict between capital and labour was growing, with captains of industry squaring off against rising national unions such as the Knights of Labor and American Federation of Labor (AFL). For most of American history, notes Brian Gratton, capitalists were the main advocates of immigration while organized labour consistently opposed it.[22] But more than class conflict was at stake. At the elite level, the asylum tradition played an important part in legitimating immigration. John Hutchinson writes that national identities are not monolithic, but involve factions wedded to opposing interpretations of national identity.[23] The American asylum narrative was an idiom of nationhood that could be marshalled by pro-immigration forces to keep the country's doors open.

American Protestant clergy, meanwhile, cherished a laissez-faire theology in which God favoured America, with immigration a sign of divine providence. The more zealous maintained that the ingathering of the world's peoples was a prelude to the Second Coming. 'Why have we to make a better plan for the Almighty than He has made for Himself,' complained a minister, George Seward, in the midst of the debates over Chinese immigration in California. 'Can we not be just above things and leave consequences to take care of themselves?'[24] Preacher and writer Henry Ward Beecher agreed, and incurred the ire of the San Francisco press by insisting that the white residents of California should not impede God's will that the Chinese should come.[25] Laissez-faire theology dominated more strongly among the Protestant clerical elite of the eastern seaboard than in California, where local pastors generally opposed Chinese immigration. Nevertheless, until 1890, the liberal perspective prevailed at national conventions of the mainline Protestant denominations. Business-oriented Christian support for immigration is still recognizable at the upper level of both mainline and evangelical denominations, and in parts of the 'country-club' wing of the Republican Party.

THE RISE OF RESTRICTION

Chinese Exclusion didn't herald the dawn of a restrictionist era. Immigrants continued to pour in from Europe. By the 1880s, a rising share of the inflow stemmed from more culturally distant Italy, Russia and Poland. In Gratton's estimation, restriction in America is a function of both raw numbers and the distance of immigrants from the Anglo-Protestant cultural core. When numbers and cultural distance increase together, as they often do, pressure for restriction grows. Figure 2.1 showed that the share of foreign-born in the country remained high from the 1850s until the 1920s. Yet 1896 was the first year in which over half the country's immigrants came from Southern and Eastern Europe. This was a contributing factor in tipping the balance away from one of confidence in the majority group's capacity to assimilate to concern over immigration. More importantly, it helped draw a line between 'Old' North-Western European and 'New' Southern/Eastern European immigrant groups. This made it possible for anti-immigration voices to recruit the 'Old' immigrants to their cause.[26]

Even so, the shift in source countries cannot explain the explosive growth of anti-Catholic popular movements in the 1890s. The American Protective Association (APA) and second Ku Klux Klan – most of whose members were northerners who cared little about African-American questions – enrolled millions, united in their desire to reduce immigration, affirm their Anglo Protestant identity and defend America's Protestant character. At the elite level, ever more Protestant clergy grew sceptical of the pro-immigration theology of divine providence. As the country grew into an urban nation, the Social Gospel movement arose, uniting a concern for the working class and the ills of the industrial city with the belief that government should control immigration and enact social reform. Social Gospel cleric Josiah Strong's *Our Country* (1885) called for an end to unrestricted immigration and greater attention to workers' concerns. It proved a bestseller that defined the new era.

In the 1880s, rising concern for the social improvement of the working class in the burgeoning cities combined with a waning of the optimistic belief that Anglo-Protestants could assimilate Catholic immigrants to change elite attitudes. Prior to the Civil War, many Americans were unchurched, ministered to by itinerant preachers. However, after 1865, the Catholic Church became better organized and began expanding. It doubled in size between 1880 and 1900. The illusion that the new immigrants were going to become Protestants was fading. Catholics would begin converting to Protestantism in significant numbers, but not until almost a century later. In the meantime, Protestant anxiety grew, expressed in a growing populist movement for restriction. At the Baptists' annual convention, the mood changed from laissez-faire to restriction after 1887. 'An immense amount of twaddle has been uttered on this immigration question,' the Baptists' formerly pro-immigration paper the *Boston Watchman* editorialized in 1891. 'Speakers at our National Anniversaries have time and time again referred to the "Divine Providence" that has brought the scum of Europe to our shores. It would be well for these gentlemen to distinguish between "Divine Providence" and the cupidity of steamship and railroad companies.'[27]

Immigration restriction became a plank of the Progressive movement which advocated improved working conditions, women's suffrage and social reform. This combination of left-wing economics and ethnonationalism confounds modern notions of left and right but Progressive vs. free market liberal was how the world was divided in the late nineteenth century. A prominent plank in the Progressive platform was temperance, realized in the Volstead Act of 1920 prohibiting the sale of alcohol. The Prohibition vote pitted immigrant-origin Catholics and upper-class urban WASPs such as the anti-Prohibition leader and New York socialite Pauline Morton Sabin on the 'wet' side against 'dry' working-class, rural and religious Protestants. For Joseph Gusfield, Prohibition was principally a symbolic crusade targeted at urban Catholic immigrants who congregated in saloons and their 'smart set' upper-class allies.[28] This was a Protestant assertion of identity in an increasingly urban nation in which Catholics and Jews formed around a fifth of the population. Those of WASP background had declined to half the total from two thirds in the 1820s.

Nowhere was demographic change more evident than in northern cities like New York, Detroit or Chicago, where around a third of the population was foreign-born at the turn of the century, or in industrial towns like Lowell, Massachusetts where over 40 per cent were. Anglo-Protestants were often small minorities in these urban areas in contrast to the overwhelmingly Protestant rural and small-town districts where most Americans still resided. The south was relatively untouched by immigration, but in the north and Midwest urban ethnic change was rapid. This created a division outside the south between the immigrant-origin cities and mainly Protestant countryside, towns and provincial cities. Politically, the Republican Party spoke for northern Protestants while the Democrats emerged as the party of the immigrants and the south. 'It is not best for America that her councils be dominated by semicivilized foreign colonies in Boston, New York [and] Chicago,' declared Kansas Republican Edward C. Little to applause in the House.[29] In 1920, the rural-dominated House rejected the usual process of redistricting when it emerged that most of the country was now urban, claiming that wartime demobilization had produced an undercount of population in rural areas. If we exclude the south, the pattern echoes the divide between Democratic-dominated cities and Republican rural areas we see today. The difference is that in 1900 suburbs were much less important and the rural south was solidly Democratic. Today, the urban–rural divide structures political polarization in all regions of the country, with suburbs serving as a transition zone.

The parties were complex, with cross-cutting issue positions, but from 1896 anti-immigration sentiment was channelled primarily through the Republicans. Between 1896 and 1928, the Republicans won seven of nine presidential contests. Immigration restriction was an important part of their platform. The policy appealed not only to old-stock Protestants, but to German, Irish and Scandinavian 'Old Immigrants' and their descendants, who were well-represented in craft unions like the AFL. Most new immigrants from Southern and Eastern Europe backed open-door immigration but were less numerous and couldn't vote due to low naturalization rates.[30] Republican victories paved the way for increasingly restrictive immigration laws. In 1917, Congress enacted its first major anti-immigration measure, the Literacy Test. In 1921 the Republican president, Taft, passed the first restrictionist bill which created immigration quotas for European source countries based on the 1910 immigrant population. Since the 1910 immigrant population was much less Anglo-Protestant than the country, the basis for the quotas was progressively adjusted to match the composition of the American population. The much more encompassing Johnson–Reed Act of 1924 changed the quotas for source countries from the 1910 immigrant population to the more North-Western European 1890 immigrant population. The Act passed overwhelmingly, 323 to 71 in the House and 62 to 6 in the Senate. Johnson–Reed, popularly known as the National Origins Quota Act, represented a coalition between Anglo-Protestant and Old Immigrant voters. The framers of the original law proposed the 1890 immigrant population as the basis for quotas in order to win over German-, Irish- and Scandinavian-origin voters.

Once this had been achieved, however, Anglo-Protestant represent-atives sought to tilt the balance away from Ireland, Germany and Scandinavia towards Britain. Anglo ethnic interests were expressed through patriotic societies like the Grand Army of the Republic (GAR), American Legion and Daughters of the American Revolution (DAR). This was overlaid by support from Protestant organizations from the mainstream Freemasons to the more radical Klan, which enrolled a combined membership in the millions. In Congress, representatives from Anglo-Protestant districts sparred with Irish, German and Scan-dinavian societies over the fair basis for the quotas. By 1929, WASP interests had prevailed and the quotas came to be based on the WASP-ier 1920 population stock rather than 1890 immigrant population. Half the country's immigration quota was now allocated to Britain – the aim being to freeze the ethnic composition of the US population.[31] American national identity at this point is best described as racial, in the sense of excluding virtually all non-whites, and ethno-traditional, in seeking to maintain a population mix in which Anglo-Protestants remained a majority. This is distinct from ethnic nationalism, which would mean that only members of the WASP group could immigrate or be citizens – which was not the basis of the 1924 Act. Non-Protestant whites were included, even if they might be perceived as less American than 'old-stock' citizens. Ethnic barriers to Catholics and Jews were, however, present at the elite level to keep non-Protestants out of presti-gious institutions, occupations and clubs.

RACISM, ANTI-RACISM AND IMMIGRATION

A new feature of the discussions around immigration in the 1910s and 1920s was racism. American intellectuals considered anti-Catholic big-otry a backward sentiment, but hailed eugenics, the science of improving the inherited characteristics of individuals, to be modern and scientific.

Eugenics was connected with scientific racism, which ranked different ethnic groups as more or less advanced. This meant Catholic Irish and Germans were now 'Nordics', considered by some race scientists to be on par with Anglo-Protestants, an interpretation which many of the Old Immigrant representatives endorsed. Some race scientists demurred, ranking the Irish lower down the pecking order.

Eugenics, despite its scientific patina, was based on a slipshod methodology which confirmed pre-existing ethnic stereotypes. For instance, when it was discovered that African-Americans were under-represented in the prison population, eugenicists improvised an ad hoc argument that this was only because blacks worked on plantations so couldn't get into trouble. When Franz Boas measured skull sizes in a scientific manner and disproved eugenic arguments that immigrant groups had smaller brains, his work was ignored.

Scientific racism fed into the 1911 Dillingham Commission report which warned that the present American immigration policy would introduce a lower-quality population stock to the country, leading to criminality and endangering democracy.[32] It thereby concluded that the country must reduce immigration from Southern and Eastern Europe. What's interesting is that Anglo representatives did not make their case in ethno-communal terms, nor did they invoke the country's historic ethnic composition. Rather they couched their ethnic motives as state interests. Instead of coming clean about their lament over cultural loss, they felt obliged to fabricate economic and security rationales for restriction.

Much the same is true today in the penchant for talking about immigrants putting pressure on services, taking jobs, increasing crime, undermining the welfare state or increasing the risk of terrorism. In my view it would be far healthier to permit the airing of ethno-cultural concerns rather than suppressing these, which leads to often spurious claims about immigrants. Likewise, immigrants' normal desires to defend their interests are decried as 'identity politics'. So too in 1920s America. When minorities sought to defend their ethnic interests, this was attacked as disloyalty, as when President Wilson argued of Irish and Germans who opposed American entry into the First World War that 'any man who carries a hyphen . . . carries a dagger that he is ready to plunge into the vitals of this republic when he gets the chance'.

It is misleading to claim eugenics was the engine behind restriction, but it was a critical weapon in the bid to win elite backing. The mass of rural and working-class Protestants long opposed Catholic immigration, but Anglo-American thinkers were largely in favour until around 1890. Their change of heart is an important reason why restriction was able to prevail and points to the importance of elite discourse in shaping immigration and nationality. John Higham makes the point that the Anglo-Saxon ethnicity of nineteenth-century writers such as Emerson was more open and flexible than it became after 1890. Even Emerson's racism was more amenable to the notion of assimilation than the fixed, biological variant which prevailed after 1900. That increasingly biological, less fungible notion of ethnicity is one of the reasons why immigration restriction gained the upper hand over the laissez-faire tradition in *fin de siècle* America.

The foregoing doesn't mean the elite were unified around restriction. Indeed, the first glimmers of today's left-liberal, open-borders, anti-racism orientation were emerging and would gain power in progressive circles in the decades to come. Neither anti-racism nor religious toleration were important arguments for supporters of immigration until the twentieth century. Pro-immigration's intellectual foundations were classical liberalism, the American tradition of asylum and the theology of divine providence. Its handmaidens were growth-oriented politicians and commercial interests. Pro-immigration liberals like Emerson embodied the same unquestioned racist assumptions as immigration opponents. In the twentieth century, this changed, producing habits of mind and political constellations that remain influential to this day.

Anti-racism had a pedigree in the struggle against slavery and battle for the rights of African-Americans. Blacks were brought to the US against their will as slaves, then systematically disenfranchised in the post-1870s south where lynching remained a threat. In the north, urban blacks became increasingly segregated after 1900 and suffered from discrimination in the labour market as well as from race riots. Following an anti-black race riot in Springfield, Illinois in 1908, sixty individuals, predominantly white, but including W. E. B. DuBois and six other African-American intellectuals, formed the National Association for the Advancement of Colored People (NAACP). One of the NAACP's founders was William English Walling, whose intellectual trajectory tells us a lot about how anti-racist, anti-sectarian and pro-immigration views were beginning to coalesce into a coherent cosmopolitan outlook.

Walling was a member of the Socialist Party of America (SPA), a socialist organization dominated by WASP and Old Immigrant members. Most in the SPA considered immigration a threat to socialist revolution because immigrant workers held down wages and would delay the emergence of the working-class consciousness needed for socialism. Walling objected to both racist and Marxist theories, favouring the pragmatism of John Dewey, the relativism of Franz Boas and the liberal traditions of America and the Enlightenment.[33] These were denounced as bourgeois by the SPA, but indicated that a hybrid left-liberal tradition was emerging that blended concern for workers with classical American liberalism. Anti-racism, pro-immigration sentiment and left-wing politics were about to come together.

THE LIBERAL PROGRESSIVES

The Liberal Progressives were the first recognizably modern left-liberal open borders movement. They combined aspects of individualist-anarchism, ecumenism and Progressivism into a new synthesis. Two intellectual traditions nourished Liberal Progressivism: Anglo-American anarchism and secularized Reform Judaism. The former was represented in the persona of William James, the second by Felix Adler. James was an established New England writer who developed the philosophical stance known as Pluralism. Pluralism initially had little to say about ethnic diversity but rather called for people to combine aspects of multiple ethical systems in order to arrive at the truth. Adler was a German-Jewish writer and academic who took Reform Judaism's metaphorical storyline to its cosmopolitan conclusion. Where Reform Jewish theology called for Jews to work to unite the world's peoples under monotheism, Adler went further, suggesting Jews should dissolve themselves once the task was finished:

> The perpetuity of the Jewish race depends upon the perpetuity of the Jewish religion . . . So long as there shall be a reason of existence for Judaism, so long the individual Jews will keep apart and will do well to do so . . . when this process [of evangelization] is accomplished . . . the

48

individual members of the Jewish race [will] look about them and perceive that there is as great and perhaps greater liberty in religion beyond the pale of their race and will lose their peculiar idiosyncrasies, and their distinctiveness will fade. And eventually, the Jewish race will die.[34]

Adler's ideas naturally went down like a lead balloon among Jews, but James and other anarcho-pluralists applauded. By 1878 Adler had become president of the Free Religious Association, an Anglo-American freethinking outfit, and led the New York Ethical Culture Society from its inception in 1877.

Adler and James influenced each other and were formative influences on John Dewey, who would later gain fame as 'America's public philosopher'. Originally a Congregationalist minister, Dewey called for his New England denomination to 'universalise itself out of existence', much like Adler did for the Jews.[35] Between 1905 and 1910, Dewey developed the notion that all groups should give and receive cultural influence in cosmopolitan interchange. He was also the first to openly reject the Anglo-Protestant tradition of American nationhood. 'The dangerous thing', said Dewey, 'is for one factor to isolate itself, to try to live off its past and then to impose itself upon other elements, or at least to keep itself intact and thus refuse to accept what other cultures have to offer, so as thereby to be transmuted into authentic Americanism.' He further argued that 'neither Englandism nor New Englandism, neither Puritan nor Cavalier, any more than Teuton or Slav, can do anything but furnish one note in a vast symphony'.[36]

Where the Progressives saw the immigrant-dominated cities as open sores in need of social reform and assimilation, the Liberal Progressives viewed American diversity as an embryo of international cooperation and world peace. Instead of evangelizing and Americanizing, they called for the humane assimilation of immigrants into a universal civilization. An important figure here was Jane Addams, who bridged social work with immigrants with Dewey's cosmopolitan ideas. Addams, from a prominent Yankee family, led Hull House, a 'Settlement' in Chicago. The Settlement movement was a philanthropic one which began in Britain in 1884. It was based on a fusion of late Victorian social Anglicanism with the experimentalist romanticism of John Ruskin and William Morris. It sought to introduce idealistic upper-middle-class 'workers' to the urban poor in a programme of uplift and humanist education. In a period when few went to university, 80 per cent of American Settlement workers had degrees. Half had travelled abroad. The Settlements' non-denominational, pluralistic Christianity interacted with Addams's polyglot surroundings to incubate ethno-pluralist ideas.

For Addams, high-pressure assimilation, which culminated in the wartime '100 Per Cent Americanization' drive, was counterproductive. Instead, in a series of articles between 1904 and 1912, she called for immigrants to retain their culture in order to cushion the shock of adjusting to new surroundings. Hull House encouraged immigrant arts and crafts displays, an embryonic form of multiculturalism. Still, Hull House multiculturalism was envisioned as a transition phase towards assimilation. Thus Addams ultimately favoured the humane assimilation of immigrants over the course of three generations into a new cosmopolitan Americanism. They were to be guided by a 'better element', the upper-middle class of the spiritually advanced Anglo-American culture who would lead all towards a universalist endpoint. Notice the influence of Adler: Anglo-Americans now occupied the role originally reserved for Jews, and would lead the world's peoples towards a universal civilization. As part of the process, WASPs would terminate their own existence.[37]

The ideas of the Liberal Progressives influenced theologians within the mainline Protestant denominations. The *Boston Watchman*, which, as we saw, had turned against Chinese immigration by 1891, suddenly shifted its position back towards liberal immigration in 1905. Drawing on Addams's and Dewey's ideas, the paper urged that American children be taught foreign cultures in order to produce a 'cosmopolitan outlook' in which no ethnic group dominated America. Other denominations followed suit: Presbyterian spokesmen pivoted from anti-immigration to pro-immigration positions between 1904 and 1913, and now called for universal brotherhood. In 1908, Congregationalists first lauded the positive qualities of the new immigrants and, in the same year, a Methodist writer repudiated his previous position in favour of immigration restriction.[38] Notice how the rationale for clerical pro-immigration views changed from 'God's Will' prior to 1890 to secular cosmopolitanism and pacifism after 1910. In between, many had endorsed restriction because they believed this helped workers and would ameliorate the social problems of the cities.

Cosmopolitan tendencies were awakening among mainline Protestant theologians from other directions as well. The ecumenical movement in the nineteenth century aimed to overcome divisions within Protestantism. Its logic was initially anti-Catholic, to form a united front against the threat from Rome. After 1910, however, ecumenical clergymen yearned to reach across the larger doctrinal divides which separated Protestant, Catholic and Orthodox Christians. The ecumenical body for American Protestantism was known as the Federal Council of Churches (FCC, later NCC). Between 1905 and 1908, the FCC dropped its warnings about the dangers of Sabbath desecration, the saloon and foreign immigration. By 1910, it began reaching out to Catholic and Orthodox leaders. Leading figures in the FCC like Robert E. Speer and Albert R. Mott were well connected to the WASP governing establishment in Washington. During the First World War they welcomed Jewish and Catholic leaders as part of an inter-faith chaplaincy and successfully pushed for the cross to be removed from the chaplaincy's insignia. When the war was over, they took the lead in sponsoring the League of Nations.

After 1919, FCC leaders spearheaded the Goodwill movement, which encouraged inter-faith cooperation and denounced sectarianism and bigotry. During the revival of the second (anti-Catholic) Ku Klux Klan in the 1920s, the elite of mainline Protestantism in both northern *and southern* states editorialized tirelessly against them in their ecumenical and denominational papers. Denominations routinely fired pastors who backed the Klan. In churches where parishioners sympathized with the hooded order, liberal ministers often chose to be forced out by their flock rather than speak for the Klan. Locally, ministers joined civic leaders and journalists to denounce the organization. Even where a city was Klan-run, as in post-First World War Indianapolis, Protestant leaders, civic elites and local journalists showed their resistance to it by conducting war commemorations in which Catholic, Jewish and Protestant clergy gave joint addresses.[39]

Meanwhile, the mainline Protestant missionary effort, both overseas and among 'home' missions in the United States, lost its crusading zeal after the First World War and began to question its entire rationale. Beginning with a critique of Western imperialism, missionaries began doubting the wisdom of displacing non-Christian faiths. Eventually, they abandoned missionary activity altogether. John L. Childs of the YMCA revealed the transformation that had taken place in main-line Protestant thinking by the 1920s:

> In my opinion a third view which is now largely held by missionary workers will also have to be modified, namely the view which holds that in Christianity we have a final and complete revelation of moral and spiritual truth and that because of its inherent supremacy Christianity has the right to be the exclusive religion of the world. It is one thing to say that Christianity has its important contribution to make to the progress of the human race, and it is quite another thing to assert that the values which are found in Christianity are so unique, and completely satisfying, that it possesses the obvious and inherent right to displace all other religions.[40]

In 1924, mainline Protestant clergy were almost unanimous in their opposition to immigration restriction.[41] However, their liberal activism was out of step with the views of their parishioners. Soon after the First World War, the FCC became identified with the most liberal segment of public opinion and lost its former political influence while conservative churches left the organization to form a parallel evangelical body. During and after the Second World War, mainstream outlets like *Time* magazine would criticize the NCC as pacifists or 'pinkos'.

THE YOUNG INTELLECTUALS AND THE BIRTH OF MULTICULTURALISM

The Liberal Progressives are the progenitors of today's pro-immigration left, but they were not true multiculturalists. Addams's talk of humane assimilation of immigrants towards a cosmopolitan endpoint – not to mention the idea of Anglo-Saxons as spiritual leaders of such an enterprise – sounds distinctly off-key today. Of greater relevance for today's multiculturalist zeitgeist are the so-called Young Intellectuals of Greenwich Village, New York in the 1912–17 period. The Young Intellectuals were Anglo-American bohemian artists and writers rebelling against their own Protestant culture. Inspired by Nietzsche and Bergson's romantic individualism and modernism in art, they sought to overthrow what they perceived as a suffocating Puritan inheritance. The Young Intellectuals discovered the joys of Harlem's black jazz scene, experimented with drugs, exhibited modern art at Alfred Stieg-litz's '291' studio or read poetry aloud in Mabel Dodge Luhan's salon.

From a modern perspective, the most important figure to emerge from this milieu is Randolph Bourne. Viewed as a spokesman for the new youth culture in upper-middle-class New York, Bourne burst onto the intellectual scene with an influential essay in the respected *Atlantic Monthly* in July 1916 entitled 'Trans-National America'. Here Bourne was influenced by Jewish-American philosopher Horace Kallen. Kallen was both a Zionist and a multiculturalist. Yet he criticized the Liberal Progressive worldview whose cosmopolitan zeal sought to consign eth-nicity to the dustbin of history. Instead, Kallen argued that 'men cannot change their grandfathers'. Rather than all groups giving and receiving cultural influence, as in Dewey's vision, or fusing together, as mooted by fellow Zionist Israel Zangwill in his play *The Melting Pot* (1910), Kallen spoke of America as a 'federation for international colonies' in which each group, including the Anglo-Saxons, could maintain their corporate existence. There are many problems with Kallen's model, but there can be no doubt that he treated all groups consistently.[42]

Bourne, on the other hand, infused Kallen's structure with WASP self-loathing. As a rebel against his own group, Bourne combined the Liberal Progressives' desire to transcend 'New Englandism' and Protestantism with Kallen's call for minority groups to maintain their ethnic boundaries. The end product was what I term *asymmetrical multiculturalism*, whereby minorities identify with their groups while Anglo-Protestants morph into cosmopolites. Thus Bourne at once con-gratulates the Jew 'who sticks proudly to the faith of his fathers and boasts of that venerable culture of his', while encouraging his fellow Anglo-Saxons to:

> Breathe a larger air . . . [for] in his [young Anglo-Saxon's] new enthusiasms for continental literature, for unplumbed Russian depths, for French clar-ity of thought, for Teuton philosophies of power, he feels himself a citizen of a larger world. He may be absurdly superficial, his outward-reaching wonder may ignore all the stiller and homelier virtues of his Anglo-Saxon home, but he has at least found the clue to that international mind which will be essential to all men and women of good-will if they are ever to save this Western world of ours from suicide.[43]

Bourne, not Kallen, is the founding father of today's multiculturalist left because he combines rebellion against his own culture and Liberal Progressive cosmopolitanism with an endorsement – for minorities only – of Kallen's ethnic conservatism. In other words, ethnic minorities should preserve themselves while the majority should dissolve itself.

Cosmopolitanism must manage the contradiction between its ethos of transcending ethnicity and its need for cultural diversity, which requires ethnic attachment. Bourne resolved this by splitting the world into two moral planes, one for a 'parental' majority who would be asked to shed their ethnicity and oppose their own culture, and the other for childlike minorities, who would be urged to embrace their heritage in the strongest terms. This crystallized a dualistic habit of mind, entrenched in the anti-WASP ethos of 1920s authors like Sinclair Lewis and H. L. Mencken and the bohemian 'Lost Generation' of American intellectuals such as F. Scott Fitzgerald. All associated the Anglo-Protestant majority with Prohibition, deemed WASP culture to be of no value, and accused the ethnic majority of suppressing more interesting and expressive ethnic groups. The Lost Generation's anti-majority ethos pervaded the writing of 1950s 'Beat Generation' left-modernist writers like Norman Mailer and Jack Kerouac – who contrasted lively black jazz or Mexican culture with the 'square' puritanical whiteness of Middle America. As white ethnics assimilated, the despised majority shifted from WASPs to all whites. The multiculturalism of the 1960s fused the Liberal Progressive pluralist movement with the anti-white ethos of the Beat counterculture.

THE RESTRICTIONIST INTERREGNUM, 1924–1965

The Johnson–Reed Act and its alter ego, pluralism, are recognizably modern. Most would recognize this as the basis for the 'nationalist-globalist' polarization which increasingly divides Western societies. The situation by 1924 was a far cry from the pre-1890 dispensation, when a liberal-assimilationist Anglo-Americanism spanned both universalist and ethno-nationalist shades of opinion. Prior to 1890, most Anglo-Protestant thinkers held the view that their ethnic group could assimilate all comers. During moments of euphoria, they talked up the country as a universal cosmopolitan civilization; in their reflective moods, they remarked on its Anglo-Saxon Protestant character. By 1910, this Emersonian 'double-consciousness' was gone, each side of its contradiction a separate and consistent ideology. Most WASP intellectuals were, like New England patrician Senator Henry Cabot Lodge, ethno-nationalists who backed restriction, or, like Bourne and Dewey, cosmopolitans calling for diversity and open borders. Few ethno-nationalists favoured open immigration. No pluralists endorsed restriction. Herein lie the roots of our contemporary polarized condition.

After 1924, the proportion of Southern and Eastern Europeans entering the country dropped dramatically. The Great Depression reduced the demand for workers. By the 1930s, pluralism had become influential in liberal Democratic and Republican circles, but played little part in Franklin Roosevelt's New Deal. FDR did break new ground by employing an unprecedented number of Catholics and Jews in his 'brain trust' of advisers. Nevertheless, when push came to shove, he reflected the commonsense understanding of most Protestant Americans when he told Catholic adviser Leo Crowley in January 1942, 'Leo, you know this is a Protestant country, and the Catholics and Jews are here on sufferance.'[44] The Regionalist aesthetic of the New Deal, reflected in the public art and murals funded by the government, celebrated native-born, rural America and the country's settler past, not immigrant diversity or the modernism of the Young Intellectuals. As the prominent scholar of American ethnic relations Nathan Glazer put it: 'In the later '20's the Quota Act took its toll, then the depression began and nobody wanted to come, so for a long time American public opinion lived in the consciousness and expectation that America was completed . . . No one expected that America would again become an immigrant society.'[45]

In 1952, the McCarran–Walter Act was passed after President Truman's veto was overridden by a 2:1 margin in Congress. This reaffirmed the National Origins quotas of the 1924 Johnson–Reed Act. Beneath the surface, however, pluralism was making inroads into the national conversation. The Second World War helped bind Protestants, Catholics and Jews together in common cause. The Goodwill movement's spirit of trans-religious accommodation in the 1920s and 1930s was reflected in wartime novels such as Norman Mailer's *The Naked and the Dead* or James Jones's *From Here to Eternity*, which depicted the nation's inter-faith (though not racial) diversity.

Pluralists also managed to reposition the Statue of Liberty from its original basis as an emblem of renewed Franco-American cooperation into a symbol of immigration and pluralism. An 1883 poem, 'The New Colossus', by a Russian-Jewish émigré, Emma Lazarus, referenced the American asylum tradition in its lines, 'Give me your tired, your poor / Your huddled masses yearning to breathe free, / The wretched refuse of your teeming shore. / Send these, the homeless, tempest-tost to me, / I lift my lamp beside the golden door!' In 1903, a plaque of the poem was erected in an interior part of the Statue thanks to a private contribution by Georgina Schuyler, but only in the 1930s did the Statue acquire its contemporary significance as a symbol of open immigration.[46]

In the 1940s and 1950s, new school history textbooks began to appear which spoke of the country as a 'melting pot', talked of immigrant 'contributions' and used the Statue to illustrate the process. Irish-American Senator John F. Kennedy reflected the new pluralist sensibility in 1958 with his short book *A Nation of Immigrants* for the Jewish Anti-Defamation League's One Nation Library book series. The Statue and poem formed a cornerstone of Kennedy's interpretation of the national past, and he introduced the 'nation of immigrants' catchphrase that was new to the American lexicon and central to the progressive narrative of American nationhood.[47] The 'nation of immigrants' story tended to be linked with the 'All Men are Created Equal' phrase in the American Constitution, binding immigration and the American Creed into a new national narrative. This was a missionary nationalism with the liberal Creed at its centre, in which federal agencies and the country's battle against communism played a pre-eminent part.

Progressive educators of the National Education Association (NEA), itself inspired by John Dewey's ideas, battled to get the more pluralist, pro-immigration textbooks into the school system from the 1930s onward. Gradually, the new progressive texts displaced David Saville Muzzey's *American History* (1911), read by over half the nation's children between 1911 and 1961. Muzzey's text spoke from the perspective of an old-stock 'us' about the challenge of immigration. In the 1955 edition, readers learned that:

America has been called the 'melting pot' because of these millions of people of foreign speech and customs who have been thrown in with our native colonial stock to be fused into a new type of American. Some students of society (sociologists) think that the process has injured our country by introducing a base alloy. Others point to the benefits which the brains and the hands of the immigrants have brought. There is much to be said for each side of the question.[48]

The emergence of a more powerful American federal centre in the 1930s influenced the balance between more ethnic and more universalist interpretations of national identity. State bureaucrats during the Second World War and the Cold War sought to portray the US as a colour-blind universalist power. Immigration quotas didn't fit the narrative and could be used against the country by Japanese and Soviet propagandists. Inveighing against the restrictionist McCarran–Walter Act in 1952, the Democratic president, Harry S. Truman, warned:

> Our immigration policy is . . . important to the conduct of our foreign relations and to our responsibilities of moral leadership . . . The [McCarran–Walter] bill would continue, practically without change, the national origins quota system . . . The idea behind this discriminatory policy was, to put it baldly, that Americans with English or Irish names were better people and better citizens than Americans with Italian or Polish names . . . Such a concept is utterly unworthy of our ideals. It violates the great political doctrine of the Declaration of Independence that 'all men are created equal.' It denies the humanitarian creed inscribed beneath the Statue of Liberty proclaiming to all nations: 'Give me your tired, your poor, your huddled masses yearning to breathe free.' It repudiates our basic religious concepts, our belief in the brotherhood of man, and in the words of St. Paul that 'there is neither Jew nor Greek, there is neither bond nor free, for ye are all one in Christ Jesus.'[49]

Truman's speech bore the hallmarks of the older asylum tradition, the early-twentieth-century Liberal Progressive and ecumenical movements, and mid-century Statue of Liberty symbolism. Truman also highlighted the importance of the US as a 'moral leader', reflecting an enhanced missionary nationalism in the face of the communist threat. From the American state's viewpoint, the country was defined by its liberal-democratic ideology and political traditions. Its ethnic composition was immaterial.

Changes were also afoot on the right. In the early 1950s, Irish-American Senator Joseph McCarthy made his name by instigating an anti-communist witch-hunt of largely WASP federal bureaucrats. This meant anti-communism displaced WASPness as a litmus test of Americanism. Ironically, the WASP liberals who prised open the doors of opportunity to those of immigrant stock like McCarthy had become targets of a Catholic patriot. McCarthy's reconfiguration of right-wing nationalism indirectly benefited its first Catholic president, John F. Kennedy, who never once criticized the hawkish senator. During the 1960 election campaign when many Protestant Americans were wary of electing a Catholic, McCarthy's example of tough Catholic patriotism created space for Kennedy to convincingly rebut the charge that a Catholic was insufficiently American to hold the highest office.[50]

1965: AMERICA'S DOORS OPEN

During the 1950s, the McCarran–Walter Act reaffirmed the country's Anglo-Protestant ethnic tradition. However, liberal elements in both the Republican and Democratic parties were pressing for change. In the Republican Party, representatives of the East-Coast commercial wing such as Wendell Willkie, a lawyer and corporate executive, urged openness. Among Democrats, the liberal northern branch of the party was beginning to gain the upper hand over its powerful southern segregationist contingent. The Democrats' largely unbroken hold on power between 1932 and 1968 allowed it to shape the country's institutions in a progressive direction. In the early 1960s, for instance, the Democrats' more liberal Supreme Court ordered a reapportionment of seats in Congress where prior Courts had held this to be a state responsibility outside federal jurisdiction. This gave more power to the diverse cities because the state legislatures which are responsible for districting were dominated by rural interests. For example, one urban New York congressional district had a population of 800,000 while a rural one in the same state contained just 91,000 souls.[51]

Furthermore, social attitudes were beginning to shift. The average length of time in full-time education increased from under nine years to over twelve between 1940 and 1970; more importantly, the share of Americans attending college grew from 15 per cent in 1950 to a third in 1970. The country also came to be knitted together by a national electronic media centred in liberal Los Angeles and New York. Both helped spread progressive ideas which produced cultural value changes. In 1944, for example, 52 per cent of whites endorsed the idea that 'white people should have the first chance at any kind of job'; by 1972, just 3 per cent did.[52] The number of white Americans opposed to black–white intermarriage fell more slowly and steadily, from 94 per cent in 1958 to 56 per cent in 1983 to 13 per cent today. Similar liberalizing value shifts occurred in Europe after the 1960s, which Ronald Inglehart ascribes to rising material prosperity and security.[53] As attitudes change, they alter people's perceptions of what others think, leading to tipping points. Paul Krugman recalls that one summer, around 1965, large homes on Long Island suddenly repainted their little statues of coachmen from black to white in order not to typecast African-Americans in subservient roles.[54]

Attitudes to immigration were partially swept up in the current but also softened by the fact that the proportion of foreign-born in the American population had fallen from over 13 per cent in 1920 to less than 5 per cent by 1965. In 1953 and 1957, the percentage of Americans who favoured admitting East European refugees outside their national quota was about the same as those who opposed such a plan. Surveys also showed that the proportion of Americans calling for fewer immigrants had declined from 40 per cent in 1953 to 32 per cent in 1965. In that year, 51 per cent of the public approved of the shift to a 'colour-blind' policy based on job skills, while just 32 per cent wished to retain the National Origins quota system.[55] Institutional barriers and public opinion had budged enough to permit immigration reform. This came with the 1965 Hart–Celler Act, which passed overwhelmingly in Congress, with support from both parties.

However, during debates over the Act, sponsors of the bill deemed it necessary to reassure Congress that cultural change would be minimal. Since the bill was based on family reunification, they argued, it favoured existing groups. Thus its introduction would not lead to any major change in the ethnic composition of the population. In attorney-general Robert Kennedy's estimation, 'I would say for the Asia-Pacific Triangle it [immigration] would be approximately 5,000, Mr. Chairman, after which immigration from that source would virtually disappear.' Since immigrants were overwhelmingly European at this point and had been since the birth of the republic, few imagined that the legislation would lead the country to become increasingly non-European in origin in the ensuing decades.

THE AMERICAN MAJORITY: FROM WASP TO WHITE

Hart–Celler introduced a global immigration regime while the 1924 Act focused exclusively on Europe, with tiny quotas later added for Asia. Latin America, however, remained outside the quotas until the 1952 McCarran–Walter Act. This meant a steady stream of Mexican labour entered the country during the National Origins period, many under the Bracero temporary worker programme initiated during the war. However, as the number of Mexicans entering the country illegally began to rise, successive administrations began a heavy-handed programme of deportation, culminating in the mass eviction action known as Operation Wetback. During the Truman administration, the numbers of Mexicans deported each year rose from 200,000 to 726,000, peaking with Operation Wetback under Eisenhower in 1954 at over 1 million before dropping back to just 90,000 in 1956. By the time of the 1965 Act, the United States was 85 per cent white, 11 per cent African-American and only 3 per cent Hispanic. Asians comprised just 0.5 per cent.

Attitudes to marriage between Protestants, Catholics and Jews changed markedly from the 1960s. In the early part of that decade, three quarters of Protestants opposed marriage between Protestants and Catholics. By the early 1980s, over three quarters of Americans approved of both Protestant–Catholic and Jewish–Christian marriages.[56] Inter-ethnic marriage was increasingly common in mid-twentieth-century America but 90 per cent were intra-religious prior to 1970. After 1970, religious barriers fell to the point that half of Jews married outside their faith. Catholic and Jewish incomes also rose to WASP levels and they increasingly left ethnic enclaves for growing mixed-ethnicity white suburbs.

It's easy to forget how secure a WASP-dominated America seemed prior to 1970. In 1956, an American sociologist, C. Wright Mills, observed: 'Almost everywhere in America . . . the model of the upper social classes is still "pure" by race, by ethnic group, by national extraction. In each city, they tend to be Protestant; moreover Protestants of class-church denominations, Episcopalian mainly, or Unitarian, or Presbyterian.'[57] In his *Protestant Establishment* (1964), E. Digby Baltzell, an old-stock Philadelphian, urged the American elite to open up to other ethnic groups. Baltzell's and Mills's world has recently been brought to life by the television series *Mad Men* featuring a 'white shoe' (WASP) New York advertising agency from the early 1960s, Sterling Cooper, in which Anglo-Americans predominate.

Baltzell, it turns out, was pushing at an open door, for over the next few decades Catholics and Jews rapidly ascended the ladder of opportunity. 'For twenty years, the de-WASPing of the ruling elite in America has proceeded at a breathtaking pace,' observed Robert Christopher in 1989.[58] Meanwhile, ethnic social mobility and intermarriage to Protestants reconfigured the boundaries of the American majority, creating what a leading sociologist, Richard Alba, terms 'Euro-American' ethnicity. This early version of *Whiteshift*, from WASP to white, seemed to suddenly emerge, but was rooted in slow but steady mixing. For instance, in 1989, the share of Italian-Americans of mixed ancestry was less than 5 per cent among those over sixty-five but exceeded 80 per cent among the under-tens. Increasingly, white Americans were giving different answers to the ancestry question from survey to survey, or were simply calling themselves 'white' or 'American' on the census.[59]

Critical race theorists contend that white ethnics only 'became white' when they became useful to the WASP majority. Even Bill Clinton, a southern Protestant whose Irish heritage is undocumented, latched on to the idea that his Irish forebears 'became' white. Irish Catholics in the north, some claim, were important allies of southern whites in the struggle against Yankee republicanism, so southerners embraced the Irish.[60] I'm less convinced. The Irish, Jews and Italians may not have been part of a narrower WASP 'us', but they were perceived as racially white, thus part of a pan-ethnic 'us'. This entitled them to opportunities not available to African- or Asian Americans. Post-1960s intermarriage led to an extension of American majority ethnic boundaries from WASP to white but the foundations for expansion were already in place. From the 1960s on, the religious marker of dominant ethnicity came to be redefined from Protestant to 'Judaeo-Christian'.

Did the increasing assertiveness of African-Americans during and after the Civil Rights movement crystallize this unified white response? What about the increase in Latino and Asian immigration after 1965? This might explain why WASPs felt it was useful to enlist white Catholics and Jews to maintain their majority. Parts of this account ring true: we saw that Anglo-Saxon restrictionists appealed to North-Western Europeans' 'Nordic' identity to vote against the influx of Southern and Eastern Europeans. But it is far from clear this was motivated solely or even primarily by elites' desire for wealth and power. Moreover, similar processes of Catholic and Jewish inclusion took place in Canada and Britain in the absence of strong non-white challenges. In South Africa, Afrikaners who ran the apartheid regime had a clear incentive to make the Indians and Coloureds white but chose merely to accord them intermediate status. Large-scale social processes such as redefining ethnic boundaries emerge mainly as the result of millions of individual decisions which are only partly under the sway of political elites.

WHY WHITENESS IS MOSTLY ABOUT IDENTITY, NOT POWER

The struggle to defend the Anglo-Protestant tradition of American national identity gave way to an ecumenical whiteness. Critical race theorists view this through the prism of power: whites share a political, economic and status interest in keeping African-Americans and other non-whites in their place. Those on the far right would explain things differently: whites have common genes which exert a primordial pull for them to work together. Common material interests are clearly important, but the fact that American whites divided between inclusive liberals and exclusivist conservatives suggests interests are at best a partial guide to the location of ethnic boundaries. Genetic similarity likewise exerts only a distant pull on human action – think how unnatural it would be for a white American to support the white Serbian basketball team against the mainly black American 'Dream Team'! Instead, I favour a cultural explanation. Caucasian appearance, like Protestantism or the English language, has been a symbol of 'us', the American ethnic majority, since Independence. In addition, while the American nation has always contained racial diversity and illustrious minorities, the preponderance of its heroes and population have been white. The memes of whiteness and Americanness have come to be inextricably linked, though they are beginning to separate.

For many WASPs, their ethnicity and national identity seemed so closely related as to be coterminous. In *The Good Shepherd* (2006), set in the 1940s, an Italian-American mafioso played by Joe Pesci tells WASP CIA operative Matt Damon: 'We Italians, we got our families and we got the church. The Irish, they have their homeland. The Jews, their traditions. Even the Niggers, they got their music. What about you people, Mr Wilson, what do you have?' At this, Damon replies, 'The United States of America, the rest of you are just visiting.' In other words, American traditions are WASP traditions, and vice-versa.

From an ethno-traditional perspective, blacks and American Indians are also associated with the United States in a way less true of Latinos or Asians – whose ethno-symbols only dominate territorial identities in selected regions like the Rio Grande Valley of Texas or in urban pockets like San Francisco's Chinatown. In a fascinating psychological experiment, researchers Thierry Devos and Mahzarin Banaji asked a sample of Yale students: 'how "American" are people who belong to the following groups?' Students ranked African-, white and Asian Americans on a seven-point scale from 1, 'Not at all American' to 7, 'Absolutely American'. They were also asked about each group's association with American culture. Students consistently ranked Asians as less American than whites and African-Americans, with no statistically significant difference in the score assigned to whites and blacks. This provides empirical evidence for the strength of ethno-traditional nationalism in America.

The authors then repeated the exercise using an Implicit Association Test (IAT) in which students had to identify symbols flashed before them on a screen as 'American' or 'foreign'. Each symbol – the 'foreign' European Union headquarters or 'American' Mount Rushmore – had different faces pasted on part of them. When symbols like the American flag or Mount Rushmore were attached to an Asian or black face, students took a split-second longer to identify them as American than when they were overlaid by a white face. This time, the big difference was between whites and non-whites, not Asians versus the rest. More than this, whites were not the only subjects to make the 'white = American' connection on the IAT. African- and especially Asian-American subjects were also slower to label a US symbol American when it was paired with a non-white face. The one exception were African-Americans in a black–white comparison who were as quick to identify symbols as American when attached to black faces as white faces. Asians, by contrast, were faster to identify US symbols as American when overlaid with a white face, in both white–African and white–Asian comparisons.[61] Thus even though African-Americans are more closely associated with the nation than Asians, this seems a less automatic process than the 'white = American' equation. All of which may reflect the historic blending of white icons with national imagery symbolized in monuments like Mount Rushmore or on the American dollar.

Not only this, but even *within* white America, despite all the melting, the WASP remains the all-American archetype. In 1982, a survey asked Americans to rate the contributions of ethnic groups and discovered that the English were highest ranked, followed by the Irish, Jews and Germans, with non-European groups lower down.[62] In a convenience sample across three surveys on Amazon Mechanical Turk (MTurk) between 19 March and 1 April 2017, I asked 467 Americans, 'All surnames are equally American, but if someone from another country asked you what a characteristic American surname was, which of the following would you choose?' Answers were (rotated): Browning, Graziano, Hernandez, Schultz and Wong. Eighty-one per cent of those who gave a response chose Browning, the Anglo surname, including 86 per cent of Clinton voters, 78 per cent of Trump voters, 86 per cent of African-Americans, 85 per cent of Hispanics and 80 per cent of whites. In a similar question about religion, 72 per cent of 525 respondents – including 70 per cent of Catholics – chose Protestant rather than Catholic or Jewish as the characteristic American religion. Whether adopting the English language and Protestant-style congregational religious organization, or switching to Protestantism, the cultural slant of American society remains Anglo-conformist.[63]

Strong white identifiers tend, unsurprisingly, to be ethno-traditional nationalists that value the country's white and Christian symbols and traditions. Thus Ashley Jardina finds 57 per cent of high-identifying whites saying it is at least somewhat important to be white to be a 'true' American – with 23 per cent calling this very important. Fully 80 per cent say it is at least somewhat important to have 'American ancestry' and 62 per cent that it's somewhat important to be Christian in order to be a 'true American'.[64] As we'll see, conservative Hispanic and Asian Americans are also attached to the white-Christian tradition. In fact ideology is more closely associated with ethno-traditional nationalism than race.

This chapter underscores several aspects of American ethnic history that are relevant today. First, that the US, like most European nations, has had an ethnic majority since Independence. Second, that the Anglo-Protestant majority underwent a *Whiteshift* in the mid-twentieth century which permitted it to absorb Catholics and Jews, members of groups once viewed as outsiders. Finally, certain ethnic groups – notably Anglo-Protestants and African-Americans – have become symbolically intertwined with American nationhood. Two thirds of Americans are not members of these groups, yet many recognize them as ethno-traditional: part of what makes the nation distinct. On the right, an ethno-traditional nationalism focused on protecting the white Anglo heritage is emerging as an important force in American politics.

3

The Rise of Trump: Ethno-Traditional Nationalism in an Age of Immigration

The period after the passage of Hart–Celler turned a new page in American demographic history. Legal immigration to the United States in 1965 was about 300,000. This figure began to rise steeply, augmented by a growing flow of undocumented immigrants, largely from Mexico. In the 1970s, the country admitted 450,000 legal immigrants per year, rising to about 750,000 in the 1980s and over a million since the 1990s. The number of undocumented immigrants living in the country also increased, from around half a million in 1965 to over 12 million by 2008, despite a one-off amnesty for 1.8 million people as part of the Immigration Reform and Control Act (IRCA) of 1986.[1] A significant minority – up to half – of the legal inflow also consists of unauthorized immigrants being granted permanent residence.

Between 1960 and 2010, the non-Hispanic white share of the American population declined from 85 to 63 per cent. Hispanics, just 3 per cent of the US population in 1960, comprised 16.3 per cent by 2010, well ahead of the country's traditional black minority, at 12.3 per cent. The engine behind the change was a sharp increase in numbers combined with a major shift in the source of American immigration from over 80 per cent Canadian and European in 1965 to approximately 80 per cent Asian, Latin American and African by the 1990s.[2]

Fertility and immigration rates by ethnic group can certainly affect the future composition of the population, but much can be foretold by running today's age structure forward in time in projections software. In 1996, the US Census Bureau predicted that minorities would form a majority of the under-five population by 2020. They were too conservative: 2011 was the year minority births eclipsed those of whites. Subsequently they overcorrected, claiming the US would be 'majority minority' by 2042. The current forecast, based on lower Hispanic fertility and immigration, puts the date closer to 2055. In any event, by mid-century, a majority of the country will be Latino, black or Asian as it already is among the under-fives, in twenty-two metropolitan areas and in Hawaii, California, Texas and New Mexico.[3]

The surge of immigration after 1965 was largely Hispanic and initially concentrated in California, Chicago, New York and Miami. Miami was transformed most. It changed from a small city of half a million with a 4 per cent Hispanic population in 1950 to a 36 per cent Hispanic metropolis of 1.7 million in 1980. By 2015 its 2.8 million residents were two-thirds Hispanic. Over 70 per cent of residents of the city (as distinct from the metro area) spoke only Spanish at home.[4] Yet transformations at neighbourhood or even city level are arguably less momentous than those which encompass entire political jurisdictions.

California is often considered to be on the leading edge of American trends, from car culture and yoga to Flower Power and the personal computer. It's therefore fitting that it was the first major state to undergo what David Coleman terms the 'third demographic transition' from predominantly white to 'majority minority'. The state was 80 per cent non-Hispanic white as recently as 1970 and fell below the 50 per cent mark some time in the late 1990s. By 2050, California's department of finance projects that Hispanics will form 52 per cent of the population, with whites down to only a quarter. Hispanic growth was driven by immigration and higher fertility. In the year 2000, the number of children an average Hispanic woman was expected to bear over her lifetime (TFR) was 2.75 compared to around 2 for non-Hispanic whites and 2.1 for black Americans.[5] By the 2010s, however, Hispanic fertility had dropped to the replacement level of 2.1 and more Mexicans were leaving the country than entering it. Those from poorer countries in Central America, the Caribbean and the Andean cone of South America have replaced Mexicans in the illegal inflow.[6] Yet those countries are further away, their fertility is falling and they are developing, all of which intimate that future flows will abate. Figure 3.1 shows that during 2010–16, the number of illegal immigrants apprehended on the southwest border fell to early 1970s levels. Trump's enforcement policies halved this figure, reducing 2017 apprehensions to 1960s levels, though this rebounded in mid-2018 with a spike in Central American asylum claimants. Nevertheless, the demographic momentum of decades past

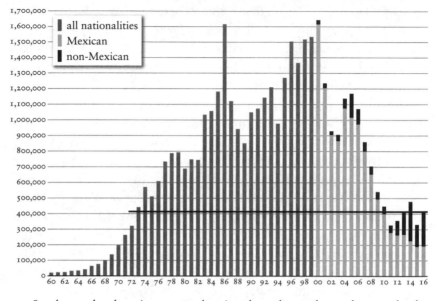

3.1. South-west border migrant apprehensions have dropped to early 1970s levels

Source: US Border Patrol

will continue to drive ethnic change for half a century even if Latino immigration slows to a trickle.

VALUES AND ANTI-IMMIGRATION POLITICS

Undocumented immigration was an important engine of ethnic change in California – as in the United States more broadly – in this period. Public opinion on immigration tends to sour when numbers increase and sources diverge from the ethnic core of the country. Why? There are three important value-driven segments of the electorate who generally oppose immigration.

Pat Dade from the market research firm Cultural Dynamics has been conducting values surveys for three decades based on the ideas of two social psychologists, Abraham Maslow and Shalom Schwarz. Dade fields surveys containing several hundred questions which enable him to map people's answers in two-dimensional space. These heat maps show how answers to a question such as voting populist correlate with a battery of other questions. From experience, Dade arrays the questions as dots on a map, with questions that tend to be answered similarly positioned close together. These surveys are often used to help companies or NGOs rather than political scientists, so it is all the more surprising how nicely they illuminate supporters and opponents of the populist right.

Dade identifies three zones in this value space: Settlers, Prospectors and Pioneers. Settlers prefer order, security and stability, eschewing change. Prospectors are hedonistic and status-conscious, focused on conspicuous consumption and success. Pioneers are interested in self-exploration, novelty and caring. The old left–right economic divide largely separated Pioneers from Prospectors, with Settlers somewhere in the middle. What's new is that today's identity divide pits Settlers against Pioneers, with the consumerist Prospectors looking on from the sidelines.[7] The maps are too detailed to reproduce here, but you can find several examples on this book's companion website.[8]

The base of support for anti-immigration politics in countries' populations is rooted in the Settlers. Most Settlers are psychologically *conservative*, seeking to secure their multi-generational group attachments and identity reference points for posterity. This is not the same as political conservatism. Many psychological conservatives will be on the right because right-wing parties often take conservative positions on cultural issues. But some cultural conservatives may have left-wing economic interests while others may be quiescent non-voters with little connection to politics. This is especially true in societies where anti-racist social norms or the dominance of economic issues prevents right-wing elites from appealing to the conservative instincts of these voters. Finally, psychological conservatives tend to be attached to established parties so are less likely to cut these cords to vote for insurgent right-wing parties.

Psychological conservatives benchmark their nation against the world they knew growing up. Ethnic changes are particularly jarring as they disrupt the sense of attachment to locale, ethnic group and nation. These ascribed identities provide a broader storyline which anchors their lives and lends meaning to their daily routines. In *ethnic* terms, rising diversity leads to a sense of white American demise and a fading connection between local referents and the white American presence.

Usually this takes the form of nostalgia for the loss of an unhyphenated 'white American' presence. In more specific 'white ethnic' neighbourhoods such as Italian-American Bensonhurst, Brooklyn or Irish-American South Boston, the narrative of white decline emerges as a higher-order property of Italian or Irish decline.

In *national* terms, ethnic change produces an erosion of the tradition of whites comprising a majority of the American nation. A fading of white cultural predominance further adds to the conservative malaise, but ethno-traditions will decline as a function of demographic change even if the content of mass culture remains oriented to white tastes and personalities. Culture is not ethnicity and the two have too often been conflated. Even if white culture remains the default mode, ethno-cultural decline may proceed apace. There are two separate ethno-cultural dynamics, white *ethnic* decline and the attenuation of the white tradition in American *national* identity. Only whites will be concerned with the former, but conservative-minded minorities may be attached to white ethno-traditions of nationhood. That is, they will wish to slow changes to the America 'they know'. The white tradition is of course only one of three strands of the broader W-AS-P tradition of nationhood which has declined substantially. Jewish-American Peter Schrag, inhabiting the very white but increasingly post-WASP America of the early 1970s, conveys a touch of this minority ethno-traditionalism in his *Decline of the WASP*: 'The old WASP character had been rooted in regions, each of them sufficiently distinct for "character," yet each also acceptably American ... Hester Prynne, Captain Ahab, Huck Finn, Horace Benbow, Temple Drake. Now much of that material is gone.'[9]

A second component of the anti-immigration Settler electorate are the order-seekers, known somewhat disparagingly in the psychology literature as 'authoritarians'.[10] Where conservatives seek to preserve the status quo, which might be multiracial, authoritarians always prefer less diversity and dissent. Conservatives are not the same as authoritarians. For instance, authoritarians dislike inequality – a form of economic diversity – thus may find themselves on the left. Conservatives prefer the status quo, however unequal. This means they will often be on the right unless society is becoming more unequal in which case they will hark back to a time of greater equality. But things can go the other way too. If blacks left the coastal south in large numbers, conservative whites might lament a decline in the historic black presence there whereas authoritarian whites would welcome it. However, immigrant-led ethnic change galvanizes both conservatives – who dislike change – and authoritarians, with their distaste for diversity.[11]

Importantly, this means conservatives will be most sensitive to increases in minority share but should become less worried as the rate of change subsides. This is clear in the data on neighbourhood change, where places that undergo ethnic shifts see higher white opposition to immigration but this effect disappears a decade after the change subsides.[12] Authoritarians, by comparison, are most sensitive to the stock of minorities. For instance, it is conceivable that the rate of ethnic change may taper but assimilation proceeds too slowly to prevent the stock of non-whites from continuing to rise. In this case, we should expect reduced conservative opposition to immigration in tandem with heightening authoritarian concern. In a meta-analysis of all academic articles published between 1995 and 2016 on the relationship between diversity and either opposition to immigration or support for populist-right parties in the West, Matthew Goodwin and I found that both ethnic change and raw minority levels counted at the national level – though minority *change* was a somewhat stronger predictor of white hostility than minority *share*.[13]

Needless to say, the survey and election data we have, much of which dates from the 1990s, makes it very difficult to disentangle the effect of levels from changes. It is clear that rapid changes such as the 2015 European migrant crisis increased concern over immigration and support for the populist right. As the flows subsided, concern began to retreat from its high-water mark. But what about minority levels? Is France, with its 10 per cent minority share, more at risk of populist-right support than Italy, with a lower minority share but a rapid rate of increase? Might countries with a high share be more susceptible to right-wing populism due to the greater insecurity of their ethnic majority authoritarians? Only by considering historical patterns can we arrive at a sense of whether the share of minorities may reach a tipping point, sparking a white political response.[14]

ETHNO-NATIONALIST INTELLECTUALS

Thus far we've discussed conservatives and authoritarians, who tend to be Settlers. But there is another, vital, part of any restrictionist coalition. Namely the small proportion of Dade's 'Pioneers' – open, self-directed and ideologically motivated – who are drawn to ethno-cultural preservation. These figures – such as Henry Cabot Lodge in the 1920s or Stephen Miller today – tend to form a small ethno-nationalist elite. In many historical periods, their psychological peers will be pro-immigration liberals. These intellectuals are not simply motivated by local and nostalgic considerations but often seek to return to a historic 'golden age' or imagined ethnic past before they were born. The Gaelic Revival in Ireland in the 1880s and Irish president Éamon de Valera's quest to make Ireland a Gaelic-speaking country once again is one example. Welsh nationalists' struggle to revive the Welsh language in recent decades is another.[15]

In certain periods, fashions may shift so that cultural conservatism becomes the ascendant elite worldview. The Romantic movement emerged as a counter-Enlightenment reaction in the early nineteenth century. In the Muslim world, Islamism became fashionable among formerly secular intellectuals after 1970 following the perceived failure of non-aligned socialism and secular nationalism. Often there is an inter-elite identity dynamic at work. Romanticism caught the imagination of German thinkers who resented the dominance of Parisian intellectual trends. Intellectuals in the Muslim world are attracted to the Islamic Revival as a riposte to the West, while nineteenth-century Russian intellectuals were drawn to Slavophilism because it elevated the worth of characteristics such as emotion and simplicity which were held in low regard by the Western Enlightenment.[16] In the 1930s US, provincial intellectuals and artists who resented the dominance of New York and the north-east gave voice to Regionalism. This rural-historical and working-class idiom challenged – though ultimately failed to overturn – the dominant modernist aesthetic in American arts and letters established by the Young Intellectuals.[17]

Might the intellectual mood turn from liberalism to conservatism in the West? It is difficult to imagine who the foreign liberal reference point could be for Western intellectuals to rally against. 'The West' might work as a foil for East European writers but fails for Western ones. Similarly, the integration of provincial intellectuals into national networks and identities militates against them spearheading a new anti-metropolitan cultural movement. Instead, a conservative intellectual climate is more likely to emerge as a response to changing 'facts on the ground' or to a popular new theory which plugs into one of modernity's holy trinity of liberty, equality and rationality. The rise of right-wing populism, for example, is a 'fact on the ground' which dragged centre-left intellectuals away from multiculturalism in Europe in the 1990s and 2000s.[18]

In a related vein, there is a new politics of the white working class. Their electoral assertiveness has challenged the prevailing intellectual climate as populist leaders brandish egalitarian arguments about peripheral whites being neglected and 'left behind' by metropolitan elites. 'Political correctness' about the white working class offers partial legitimacy to those resisting the subaltern identity groups favoured by left-modernists.[19] Finally, opponents of Islamic immigration in the West have keyed into liberal concerns over freedom of expression and rationalist worries about religious fundamentalism. For others, Islam is held to threaten the equal treatment of women, gays and Jews. Many of these writers also lean on security arguments to appeal to state elites and those concerned with crime and terrorism. These are modern arguments with little obvious connection to counter-Enlightenment themes such as Romanticism or the conservation of ethno-tradition.

In a modern differentiated society, purveyors of intellectual wares need to craft an appeal that resonates with many identities and interests. One of the reasons anti-immigration populists failed to achieve an outright majority in 1850s America or 1930s Scotland was because a chunk of the electorate, however sympathetic, was primarily concerned about issues other than immigration or anti-Catholicism.[20] This electoral logic means populist parties must broaden their appeal to capture voters for whom immigration is a second-order concern. This helps explain the populist right's embrace of Islamophobia. Focusing on Muslims appeals not only to ethno-nationalists but to an important minority of liberals, women, gays, Jews, Hindus and young hedonists.[21] The more issues that can be bundled onto the conservative anti-immigration core, the wider a party's potential appeal.

VALUE CHANGE AND IMMIGRATION
ATTITUDES AFTER 1965

The dramatic increase in American immigration, from 300,000 per year in 1965 to over a million by the 1990s, combined with the cultural distance of Latin American and Asian immigrants from the white Christian core, should, according to my 'voice' model of cultural anxiety, have led to rising anti-immigration sentiment. This is confirmed in Gallup's time series of opinion polls from 1965 to 1995. In 1965, 33 per cent of Americans wanted decreased immigration, 39 per cent favoured the current level, 7 per cent sought an increase and 20 per cent had no opinion. By 1977, the number favouring a decrease had risen to 42 per cent, reaching 49 per cent in 1986 and 65 per cent in 1993.

But what is striking, and runs counter to what we might expect from European patterns and much of American history, is the pronounced liberalization of attitudes since 1995. As figure 3.2 shows, the share of the population desiring a decrease in immigration went into reverse after 1995: dropping from 65 per cent in 1995 into the 35–50 per cent

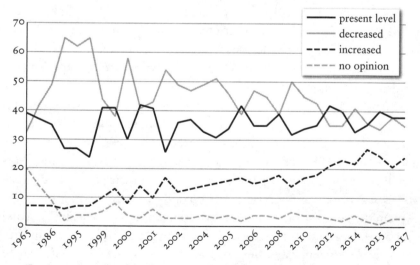

3.2. 'In your view, should immigration be kept at its present level, increased or decreased?', %

Source: Gallup 2017[22]

range after 1999. At the same time, the proportion of Americans favouring increased immigration rose substantially, from 6 per cent in 1995 to 27 per cent in 2016. How might this be explained?

The first point to bear in mind is that, unlike previous periods in American history, increased immigration from non-traditional sources took place against the backdrop of large-scale liberal attitude change within the American public. As noted, attitudes on race, religion, sexuality and women's roles shifted markedly between the 1950s and 1970s and continued as new liberal generations became a larger share of the electorate. Egalitarian and humanitarian attitudes have been shown to be especially strong predictors of the desire to *increase* US immigration levels, and this could underlie the steady post-1995 rise in pro-immigration sentiment from 6 to 27 per cent.[23] Cohort replacement – whereby older generations die off and new ones enter the electorate – led to steady liberalization in this period. The rising share of university-educated liberal Americans, spearheaded by the Baby Boomers, altered the profile of the median voter. The sexual revolution, anti-Vietnam War protests and Civil Rights movement of the 1960s recast the political culture by altering the values of the country's institutions. Not only were elite institutions 'de-WASPed', as Christopher puts it, but their ethos shifted from Anglo-conformity to universalist individualism. I would argue that the main reason attitude liberalization on this question only appears after 1995 is that the issue was barely present in many Americans' consciousness: it only gradually became politicized after California's Proposition 187 in 1994. Thus the steady rise in the share seeking increased immigration dates from this period.

Rising African-American political assertiveness led to a flowering of other forms of subaltern group politics that came to be labelled 'multi-culturalism' in the 1970s, including Latino, American Indian, feminist and gay movements. These were nourished by the cultural radicalism of the New Left, which reproduced many aspects of the 1910s Village adversary culture on a larger scale. The new minority social movements in turn energized the New Left and shifted the focus of left-wing activism from Marxism and industrial workers to disadvantaged cultural groups. Cultural politics had been a low priority on the American left during the Progressive and New Deal periods. While pluralist cosmopolitanism had become the dominant progressive outlook by the 1920s and was the guiding philosophy of the influential 'New York

Intellectuals' in the 1930s and 1940s, this did not translate into change within a Democratic Party that was still beholden to its southern segregationist wing. The expansion of education and a centralized electronic media, however, spread the anti-WASP outlook of the Young Intellectuals and Liberal Progressives to an educated stratum of society that was, by the 1960s, able to influence elite institutions such as the Democratic Party. In the words of well-known social critic and New York Intellectual Daniel Bell: 'the life-style once practiced by a small cénacle . . . is now copied by many . . . [and] this change of scale gave the culture of the 1960s its special surge, coupled with the fact that a bohemian life-style once limited to a tiny elite is now acted out on the giant screen of the mass media'.[24]

The sixties brought not only value change but individualism. Divorce rates doubled between 1965 and 1976, and the proportion of unmarried twentysomethings jumped two to three times between 1970 and 1987.[25] This was accompanied by the emergence of what Robert Bellah terms 'lifestyle enclaves'.[26] These are subcultural identities with their own identity narratives which displace those of ethnic group and nation. For instance, the hippies were a lifestyle group which came to encompass millions of young Americans in the late 1960s. Where the Young Intellectuals of the 1910s or New York Intellectuals of the 1930s and 1940s were small enough to form social circles, millions now participated in a countercultural identity. Other lifestyle enclaves formed around fashions and consumer tastes. The new subcultural identities were what Daniel Bell terms 'modernist' in sensibility, emphasizing novelty, immediacy and diversity of experience rather than tradition. They were necessarily disconnected from older multi-generational communities of ethnic group and nation.[27]

As the hippies grew up, they developed new group narratives around occupation and lifestyle. Often, members of countercultural lifestyle enclaves lived in identifiable sections of large cities such as Greenwich Village, the original home of the Young Intellectuals, or Haight-Ashbury in San Francisco. One index of rising bohemianism was the explosion in the number of artists in New York, from a few thousand in the 1960s to 100,000 by the early 1970s.[28] Meanwhile, the share of single households in Manhattan had surged to a third of the city's population by 1980. In the 1980s, upwardly mobile professionals, or 'yuppies', came to adopt aspects of bohemianism, combining economic self-interest with social liberalism. This is nicely explored by David Brooks's sardonic social commentary on the bohemian affectations of the American bourgeoisie, *Bobos in Paradise* (2013). One 'bobo' hotbed was the emerging tech hub of Silicon Valley, where countercultural values fused with venture capitalism and big science to form a new social ecosystem.

Techies, hippies, hipsters and yuppies represent different facets of the fragmentation of identity among young, well-educated modernist whites. Under the influence of the new social liberalism, mobile whites' meaning systems and attachments became increasingly divorced from ethno-histories anchored in locale, state and nation. This was accompanied by the breakup of white ethnic neighbourhoods in the 1960s which in many cases dated from the nineteenth century: places such as Philadelphia's WASP Main Line, Detroit's Polish Hamtramck and New York's Little Italy. Spatial assimilation into a new Euro-American melting pot was the main driver of declining local ethno-traditionalism. Nevertheless, expressive individualism accelerated the process by breaking down ethnic, religious and, ultimately, racial boundaries between neighbourhoods.

There is a parallel here with secularization, which Steve Bruce argues occurs in part because society becomes differentiated into many specialized occupations and leisure niches. Like the size of a slice in an increasingly crosscut pie, differentiation shrinks the niche occupied by religion even if a person remains a believer.[29] In a similar way, the proliferation of countercultural and consumerist lifestyle identities crowded out ethnic narratives. The only ethnic identities to resist differentiation were minority ones such as Latino or African-American, which worked with the grain of the new counterculture. Something similar took place for minority national identities like Québécois, Northern Irish Catholic or Scottish in the 1960s. These too came to be expressed in the new countercultural vernacular. The conservative white American narrative of revolutionaries, pioneers, settlers and industrial workers was much less fashionable, persisting most strongly among the less mobile: non-college, rural or older whites. A consequence of liberalism and its attendant individualist fragmentation was a hollowing out of ethno-traditional Americanism. This explains why, even during the period of rising opposition to immigration between 1965 and 1995, the issue fell well down Americans' list of electoral priorities. I suspect an American poll on immigration in 1855 or 1915 would look more like a West European one does today – with immigration ranking as a leading issue – than like an American survey from the 1990s.

A second reason for the low priority accorded to immigration in the 1965–95 period is elite agenda-setting. The economy, foreign wars and religious issues took precedence over immigration in the public mind. Social research tells us that cues from politicians and the media are often required to increase the importance of an issue for voters.[30] You can be in favour of reducing immigration, but if the issue is rarely raised in the media or by politicians, it tends to remain latent in your consciousness. Only if you are living in a rapidly changing neighbourhood will the issue strike you between the eyes. A more liberal post-1960s media elite, committed to calling out anti-immigration politics as racism, helped set the tone of political discussion in this area. The new mood music reoriented American political culture towards a cross-party consensus on immigration. This atmosphere discouraged both Democratic and Republican politicians from campaigning to reduce it. Debating measures to contain illegal immigration was legitimate because it concerned state security. Yet this had to be conducted with sensitivity given the ethnic differences between most Americans and the majority of undocumented migrants.

Finally, liberal social attitudes made a difference, especially as the Baby Boomers became the dominant segment in the population in the 1990s. This was symbolized by the election of Bill Clinton in 1992, the first member of the sixties generation to occupy the Oval Office. Despite the anti-immigration sentiment which rapid immigration usually produces, the rising liberalism of the Boomers was able to exert a countervailing influence on immigration attitudes. Later in the book, and in the online blog, I consider more rigorous evidence for this claim.

IMMIGRATION POLITICS IN
THE POST-1965 PERIOD

Legal and illegal immigration rose steadily from 300,000 per year in 1965 to 500,000 in the 1970s and 750,000 in the 1980s. This spurred anti-immigration organizing by the 1980s, but produced only a modest public response. In legislative terms, discussion focused only on illegal immigration. Some legislators pushed for employer sanctions to punish those who knowingly hired unauthorized workers. Liberals argued that regularizing the status of the undocumented was necessary for them to become productive citizens but this had not become a partisan issue. The 1986 Immigration Reform and Control Act (IRCA) ostensibly struck a compromise, but the amnesty provisions in IRCA – which led to legal status for 1.8 million undocumented people – far outweighed the bite of employer sanctions, which were only sporadically enforced. In 1990, recognizing reality, a new immigration act raised the official immigration cap from 270,000 to 675,000 per year while more than doubling employment-related visas and creating the H-1B programme for high-skilled immigrants.[31]

The IRCA amnesty may or may not have acted as an incentive for others to try their luck crossing the border. Alternatively, it may be that lofty legislation made little difference to the inflow, since apprehensions of illegal immigrants on the southern border continued at around 1 million per year.[32] Against the backdrop of rising illegal immigration and legal admissions, the Federation for American Immigration Reform (FAIR) was founded in 1978. The organization sought to 'end illegal immigration' and to 'set legal immigration at the lowest feasible levels consistent with the demographic, economic, and social realities of the present'. It eschewed ethnic quotas in favour of numerical limits, calling for a temporary moratorium on immigration to facilitate assimilation. However, FAIR also embodied important ethno-traditionalist concerns at leadership level reminiscent of those expressed by Theodore Roosevelt nearly a century earlier. 'One of my prime concerns', FAIR founder John Tanton admitted to a major donor, 'is about the decline of folks who look like you and me.' Elsewhere he told a friend: 'for European-American society and culture to persist requires a European-American majority, and a clear one at that'.[33]

Tanton, a small-town Michigan eye doctor, began his political career as an environmentalist who set up local chapters of Planned Parenthood, Zero Population Growth and the Sierra Club the 1970s. Family planning and environmentalism are strongly identified with the liberal end of the political spectrum in America, but Tanton attempted to convince his comrades that immigration control was important to advance the environmentalist cause. In 1998, the Sierra Club would have this debate, with members voting 3–2 against supporting the goal of 'a reduction in net immigration' after a noisy battle.[34] But at this point injecting concern about immigration into environmental discussions made Tanton's colleagues uneasy, jarring against deep emotional associations between left-wing environmentalism and left-modernism's open-borders inclination. 'I finally concluded', observed Tanton after being greeted with repeated awkward silences, 'that if anything was going to happen, I would have to do it myself.'[35]

Tanton set about creating an organization that would appeal to the centre-ground of public opinion. Racists and radicals were to be kept out of the new movement. FAIR went out of its way to reach out to anti-sprawl environmentalists, unions worried about job competition and African-Americans concerned Hispanic immigrants would compete for jobs, housing and schools. However, as Otis Graham Jr, a history professor and FAIR founding board member, recalls, liberal groups were unresponsive. Though a small number of Democratic representatives endorsed FAIR, liberal pressure groups viewed immigrants, legal or otherwise, exclusively through a protective lens. Unions, now under the sway of leaders sensitive to the ideological multiculturalism of the New Left and the pragmatic multiculturalism of the Democratic Party's 'rainbow coalition' of minorities, preferred to frame immigrants as potential members. This was virtually unprecedented in American labour history and a major change from the period from the 1830s to the 1960s when figures such as Samuel Gompers of the AFL railed against immigrants undercutting wages. Though the Democratic leadership was aware of the political opportunities offered by a large influx of low-income voters, the ideological shifts that had taken place in the party by the 1960s were arguably more important in moving it towards a pro-immigration stance. New Left ideas quite simply reframed the way the entire issue was perceived.

OFFICIAL ENGLISH

Tanton was increasingly active on other fronts, pursuing a cultural nationalist agenda focused on making English the official language of the United States. The impetus behind the move stemmed from the 1968 Bilingual Education Act, enacted by the Johnson administration to address poor performance among Hispanic children in Texas schools. The pragmatic law aimed to destigmatize Spanish, improve self-esteem and thereby enhance education outcomes. However, the Act would also encourage the bilingual and multicultural education movement of the 1970s and 1980s – an outgrowth of minority ethnic activism as well as lobbying from progressive groups such as the National Education Association (NEA). The NEA, inspired by Deweyite Liberal Progressivism, had played a key role in lobbying school boards to replace Anglo-conformist school textbooks like Muzzey's *American History* with more pluralist texts from the 1930s onward. It now sought to enhance the scope of bilingual Spanish-English education and develop a more multicultural, less Eurocentric curriculum.

The rapid increase in Spanish-speaking immigrants after 1968 and growing bilingual activism prompted a conservative response. In 1980, voters in ethnically transforming Dade County, Florida, approved an anti-bilingual ordinance. However, continued Hispanic growth in Miami and consequent redistricting demographically overwhelmed white restrictionism, resulting in the measure being repealed in 1993. Despite this, Miami voters had set the ball rolling, and in 1981 Virginia became the first state to make English an official language. Over the next ten years, ten Republican states adopted Official English statutes. These had little legislative bite, but served as symbolic statements about the country's linguistic identity. In order to advance the cause in more politically divided or liberal states, Tanton, together with Japanese-American Senator Hayakawa of California, founded US English in 1983. The aim was to use popular initiative mechanisms, where available, to compel reluctant legislators to enact Official English laws. The movement enjoyed rapid success, enrolling almost 2 million members by the early 2000s. More importantly, Official English ballots succeeded in Florida, Arizona, California and Colorado between 1986 and 1988.[36] To date, thirty-two states have some form of Official English statute. States which have not passed the measure tend to be those that are Democrat-dominated and lack popular initiative mechanisms. In addition, states with large historic non-Anglo communities, notably Alaska, Hawaii, New Mexico and Texas, have either not adopted a measure or have enshrined English as one of several official languages.

Official English took care, from its founding, to make a scrupulously civic-national rather than Anglo nationalist case. Its message remains popular across partisan and racial divides. Over 60 per cent of the public endorse making English the official language of the United States. Only among self-identified liberals and Hispanics is a majority opposed.[37] The scale of support was evident in Proposition 63, California's Official English vote, which passed 73–27 in 1986, the largest margin on a popular initiative recorded to date. This despite the fact the California political establishment – Republican Governor George Deukmejian, his Democratic opponent and Los Angeles mayor Tom Bradley and LA police chief Daryl Gates, stood united against it. Sixty-seven per cent of California blacks and 58 per cent of Asian voters backed the measure, though a majority of Hispanics and liberals demurred. Three years on, in 1989, support among Hispanics had risen to 63 per cent, possibly because they realized the measure would have few concrete implications in their daily lives.[38] Likewise, both the Republican vice-president, George H. W. Bush, and his Democratic adversary, Michael Dukakis, opposed the English Only position prior to the successful Florida, Arizona and Colorado English Only votes of 1988. Almost everywhere, opposition to Official English was bipartisan, uniting Republican and Democratic elites together with progressive organizations like the NEA and ACLU. Mainstream progressives rather than Hispanic advocacy organizations, who tended to be weak, organized the opposition. Yet virtually everywhere they were held, whether in conservative or liberal states, Official English initiatives succeeded.

NEOCONSERVATISM AND THE REPUBLICAN ELITE

Elite bipartisan opposition has repeatedly helped defeat attempts to enact a nationwide Official English law. Puerto Rico, a Spanish-speaking island, would make an Official English law an impossibility if it became a state. Yet more congressmen voted for Puerto Rican statehood (209–208) than for Official English (238–182) in 1998. The list of supporters of Puerto Rican statehood included Newt Gingrich and former religious-right figurehead Ralph Reed. Their backing coincided with the neoconservative ascendancy in the Republican Party, wherein fiscal, military and religious conservatives set the ideological tone. The leaders of these factions cleaved to the view of Republican strategist

Karl Rove that in order to win power for their ideas in an increasingly diverse country they needed to court the Hispanic vote. This would be achieved through an appeal to immigrants' religious and family values.[39] Needless to say, the Republican elite's ideological aims did not include white ethno-traditionalism.

Rove had cut his teeth in Texas gubernatorial and Senate campaigns working for both George H. W. Bush and his son George W. Bush. Texas Hispanics, who are predominantly of Mexican origin, have tended to vote Republican at a higher rate than Mexican-Americans elsewhere. For instance, they were key to George W. Bush's victory as governor of Texas in 1994. In 2000, Republican governor Kay Bailey Hutchinson won fully half the Hispanic vote. That year, Bush Jr became president, winning 35 per cent of the Latino vote nationwide, a figure that rose to 40 per cent in the 2004 election. His brother Jeb, meanwhile, was elected governor of Florida in 1998 on 61 per cent of the Hispanic vote and his Mexican-American wife was viewed as an asset with Latino voters that would one day help him become president. The Bushes' string of victories produced an optimistic mindset in which the Republican elite felt they could win Latino votes with a package emphasizing conservative social values and the work ethic.

Ideologically, the fall of the Berlin Wall gave rise to an optimistic 'End of History' spirit among American neoconservatives and interventionist liberals, symbolized by Francis Fukuyama's iconic book of 1992.[40] With communism defeated, liberalism, capitalism and democracy, under American tutelage, could finally become universal. A global framework based on the Pax Americana and the shared values of the 'Washington Consensus' would revolutionize humanity. Here was a classic form of liberal-democratic missionary nationalism in keeping with the country's 'City on a Hill' traditions. Some neoconservatives advocated the use of American military power to accelerate the regime changes needed to spread democracy. Then, on 11 September 2001, jihadi attacks destroyed the Twin Towers. This national shock energized neoconservatives in the Bush administration. First Bush intervened in Afghanistan to rid the country of Al Qaeda. He also placed the country on a domestic state of alert, replete with a powerful new Department of Homeland Security.

Some time later, the US government called for the ousting of secular-nationalist Iraqi dictator Saddam Hussein. This had been official US policy since 1998 under Clinton. Bush made this real by invading Iraq in 2003 on the grounds that Saddam possessed weapons of mass destruction. American involvement in Iraq only ended in 2011, and the last troops didn't leave Afghanistan until 2014. In addition to hundreds of thousands of civilian deaths, the former conflict claimed over 4,000 American soldiers' lives and the latter more than 2,300. Funerals for deceased servicemen became a routine aspect of the news during this period, helping to flag state nationalism to the population on a regular basis.

War abroad and readiness at home played to the more missionary, statist registers of American nationalism that had held sway since 1939. Ribbons in trees, military funerals and the obvious participation of Hispanic and immigrant soldiers kept state-led missionary nationalism to the fore. The enemy in this period were radical Islamists, an 'other' against which virtually all Americans – not least patriotic Hispanics – could unite. Authoritarian white voters could rally to the cause while embracing an inclusive civic nationalism and multi-ethnic military. Just as the Civil War dampened anti-Irish sentiment and the Second World War calmed anti-Semitism, it can be argued that the War on Terror muted white ethno-traditionalist opposition to the growing Hispanic and immigrant presence.

THE RELIGIOUS RIGHT

A second game-changer for ethno-traditional conservatism was the retreat of the religious right. In the late 1970s, the Republicans began to target white evangelicals, a group which increased dramatically over the course of the twentieth century due mainly to higher conservative Protestant birth rates – though defection from liberal denominations played a partial role.[41] Some of these voters went for Jimmy Carter in 1976, a fellow evangelical from Georgia, but had yet to throw their lot in with either party. This changed when two Catholic Republicans, Richard Viguerie and Paul Weyrich, joined Howard Phillips, a Jewish convert to evangelicalism. They forged links with the Southern Baptist preacher Jerry Falwell to create the Moral Majority, a Christian Right political coalition. Meanwhile, abortion, once a Catholic issue ignored by evangelicals, became a rallying cry for the movement following the landmark 1973 Roe v. Wade decision legalizing abortion.[42] In the

1980s, abortion figured prominently in the campaigns of Falwell's Moral Majority; in the 1990s, it was the top line for Pat Robertson's Christian Coalition and Charles Dobson's Focus on the Family.

The Christian Coalition alone boasted nearly 2 million members at its height in the mid-1990s. The New Christian Right formed a powerful grassroots network rooted in churches and para-church organizations. It soon went on the attack, winning control of state school boards and numerous local Republican Party branches. It sponsored candidates in the Republican primaries and became such a powerful faction that all Republican candidates were compelled to establish their religious bona fides. The movement's aims went beyond abortion to encompass the teaching of Creationism and opposition to same-sex marriage. In legislative terms, the religious right had its greatest success at state level, lobbying legislators to enact laws compelling minors to notify their parents when having an abortion and generally making life difficult for abortion providers. Religious conservatives also successfully sponsored state popular initiatives designed to repeal or block same-sex marriage. Under President George W. Bush, a declared evangelical, late-term 'partial-birth' abortions were banned. Bush created a new Office of Faith-Based Initiatives which channelled federal money to religious social service providers. In foreign policy terms, the political theology known as Christian Zionism, whereby Jewish conquest of biblical lands is deemed a sign of the Second Coming, crystallized evangelical support for Israel. It likewise won evangelical backing for Bush's hawkish foreign policy adventures in the Middle East.[43]

At the elite level, the religious right was universalist, not white nationalist. Its founding involved a collaboration between Catholics, a Jew and a southern WASP. Its cardinal issues – abortion, same-sex marriage, family values – drew Americans of many stripes together. The new 'culture war' of the 1980s, 1990s and 2000s pitted the faithful of all races and religions against seculars and moderates.[44] The inter-faith aspect of religious right politics is discernible in Bush's winning coalition, which knitted conservative Catholics, Protestants and Jews together. For instance, while 86 per cent of Catholics voted for Kennedy in 1960, 74 per cent of traditionalist Catholics chose Bush in 2004. Seventy per cent of Jews voted Democratic in 2004, yet two thirds of their Orthodox co-religionists voted for the former Texas governor.[45] Outside party structures, collaboration was even more successful. California's Proposition 8 (2008) banning same-sex marriage passed 52–48 as Latino votes overcame majority white opposition and black neutrality. Mexican television personality José Eduardo Verástegui was even enlisted to the cause in Spanish-language commercials, urging Latinos to support the measure. In organizational terms, conservative Mormons, evangelicals, and Latino and white Catholics joined forces to campaign for victory. Similar successes were notched up in Texas and Florida.

The religious right is willing to reach across religious and racial lines to advance its universalist agenda. At the leadership level, in the bible colleges and pages of *Christianity Today*, there is an awareness that nearly a quarter of evangelicals are non-white, a share that is rising while the proportion of evangelicals in America has been falling. White evangelical leaders interact closely with their black and Hispanic evangelical peers. The centre of world Christianity is in the global South, and many evangelical elites are excited by the opportunities for evangelizing Hispanic, Asian and African immigrants. In the pews, however, identities are far less universalist, reflecting the ethno-regional particularism of local congregations. Trump's victory in 2016 opened up a divide between evangelical elites and masses no less consequential than the one separating elite Republicans from Trumpists, or, for that matter, Republicans from Democrats.[46]

Internationally, conservative evangelicals have cooperated with Sunni Muslim imams, Shiite mullahs, Mormons and the Vatican to stifle UN family planning initiatives. Meanwhile the faith-friendly Bush administration defunded Planned Parenthood and forced successful family-planning programmes, such as Uganda's anti-HIV campaign, to terminate.[47] The universalist Americanism of the religious right is clear from the Christian Coalition's website of the late 1990s:

> The Christian Coalition is leading a growing new alliance of evangelicals, Roman Catholics, Greek Orthodox, Jews, African-Americans and Hispanics who are working hard for common-sense legislation that will strengthen families . . . It was the religious values of our people that made this nation a refuge for the poor, the outcast, and the downtrodden. America has lifted its lamp beside the golden door of entry to all immigrant groups, particularly Jews, and to victims of persecution the world over. We are part of that legacy. Let me be clear: the Christian Coalition believes in a nation that is not officially Christian, Jewish, or Muslim.[48]

EBB TIDE FOR THE RELIGIOUS RIGHT

The Christian Right surge of the 1990s ran out of steam, not least because the movement had impacted the lives of numerous Americans beyond its evangelical core – a core which comprised, at most, a quarter of the electorate. In September 2008, the country elected its first African-American president, Barack Obama, a devout Christian who invited evangelical pastor Rick Warren to deliver a prayer at his inauguration. However, he also won on the strength of the youth vote, which contained an unprecedented share of non-religious people. This was a chastening period for the religious right. At state level, Christian Right 'stealth' campaigns and ballot initiatives were being repealed or defeated in the courts. Even in the south, the Christian Right lost control of school boards and failed to institute school prayer, teach Creationism and restrict abortion. Newly mobilized anti-fundamentalist Democratic voters and Republican activists compelled religious conservatives to moderate their agenda. In 2008, 45 per cent of people agreed that religious leaders should not try to influence how people vote, up from 30 per cent in 1991.[49]

In fact the overreach of the religious right seemed to have accelerated a trend towards secularization among Millennial Americans. The proportion of Americans who never attend religious services increased from 15 per cent in 1995 to 22 per cent by 2008. The share with no religious affiliation reached 17 per cent of the total in 2008, and 23 per cent by 2014. In that year, 35 per cent of Americans born after 1981 had no religious affiliation, more than double the rate for the Baby Boomers.[50] The old wisdom that the United States was immune from European-style secularization was beginning to crack. Another index of creeping Europeanization was rising support for same-sex marriage, from 27 per cent in 1996 to 40 per cent in the 2000s to 53 per cent by 2012–13 and 64 per cent in 2017.[51]

The neoconservative trinity of military hawkishness, religious conservatism and free-market economics received a further blow with the 2007–8 financial crisis. Combined with stagnating real wages for American workers and rising inequality, the crisis shattered many thinkers and voters' formerly cocksure faith in the virtues of unfettered free markets. The neoconservative trinity remained powerful but had lost its primacy. The ebbing of its missionary nationalism created an opening on the political right which ethno-traditionalist Americanism stood ready to enter. During the Bush years, European observers saw American politics as profoundly alien. By 2016, it was to become thoroughly familiar.

PALEOCONS VERSUS NEOCONS

To understand the entry of ethno-traditional nationalism on the American right we need to revisit how it left the scene. This brings us back to debates between the so-called paleoconservatives and neoconservatives which resulted in neoconservatism's post-1960s victory. Neoconservatism's missionary nationalism fed off the country's struggle against communism. Recall that anti-communism, by shifting the litmus test of Americanism from Anglo-Protestant ethnicity to universalist ideology, permitted non-WASPs like Joseph McCarthy or semi-WASPs like Barry Goldwater to convincingly engage in the politics of patriotism. Neoconservatism's roots likewise lay in the immigrant, anti-communist, ex-leftist 'New York Intellectual' tradition. Stalin's Show Trials of the 1930s, and, later, the excesses of the 1960s campus revolts prompted many formerly left-wing, predominantly Jewish, intellectuals to move right. Figures such as Irving Kristol and Norman Podhoretz, writing in journals such as *Commentary* and the *Public Interest*, along with Catholic 'theocons' brought new vigour to American conservatism. As Edward Shapiro masterfully put it:

> Conservatives, they believed, belonged to country clubs, disliked blacks and immigrants, and came from the Protestant hinterland. They were not likely to be found on the Lower East Side, in the East Bronx, or on the West Side of Chicago . . . For the Jewish Neoconservatives . . . this was far too narrow a view of American culture. They emphasized the pluralism and openness of America and claimed that Americanism was less a matter of biological descent and European culture than of civic values and political ideology. Just as the neoconservatives stressed the ideological content of American diplomacy and asserted that American political ideology had well-nigh universal applicability, so they underscored the plastic character of American identity. Anyone was potentially

a good American just as long as he or she affirmed the fundamental American political precepts of the Declaration of Independence, the Bill of Rights, and the Gettysburg Address. The Neoconservatives, the traditionalists responded, exaggerated the appeal of American political principles to the rest of the world, and they underestimated the powerful hold which culture has, or should have, on its citizens.[52]

The Cold War struggle and the victory of the creedal 'nation of immigrants' version of American identity helped enshrine neoconservatism as the dominant force on the intellectual right. The older WASP ethno-traditionalism faded with the Civil Rights reforms of the 1960s, which delegitimized the racial and religious overtones of American conservatism. This was a contest between two versions of American nationalism: WASP ethno-traditionalism and American liberal exceptionalism. American exceptionalism is a missionary nationalism which perceives the US as the apostle leading the world on a universalist crusade for liberal-democratic-capitalism.[53]

Neoconservatism can also be viewed as a species of conservative thinking compatible with the new cultural liberalism of the sixties. Conservatism was adapting to the new racist taboos which set the parameters of political debate and were shaped by the once-radical ideas of the Liberal Progressives and Young Intellectuals. Yet this manoeuvre left the question of American ethno-traditionalism unresolved. No serious person could argue that discrimination against blacks was not a stain on the American past which persisted in some quarters. On immigration, all could agree that barring non-whites was racist. But was it also the case that limiting immigration to a level the ethnic majority could assimilate was racist? This assumption came to be smuggled into the cultural revolution of the period – a critical normative move. Curiously, this was never manifestly stated, nor did progressive politicians explicitly call for rapid increases in immigration levels as an antidote to racism. The representations of Bobby Kennedy and other supporters of the 1965 Hart–Celler Act in fact showed reverence for the country's ethno-traditions by envisioning minimal alteration to the ethnic composition of the country. In theory the question of American ethno-traditions would never need to be answered.

Yet by the 1980s this view had become untenable: diversity was rising and the 'browning of America' would enter the lexicon in the 1990s.

The new demographic realities increasingly laid bare the contradictions between universalist anti-racism and Kennedy's promise that cultural change would be minimal. With the emergence of 'majority minority' cities and states in the 1990s the question of what should happen to the country's white tradition, and to the ethnic majority, was re-emerging. Should whites 'die' by subsuming themselves in a futuristic cosmopolitan nation, as John Dewey argued? Should the country become a multicultural federation, with whites surviving as a tight-bounded minority, as Horace Kallen envisioned? Or should white Americans respond to ethnic change by embracing Randolph Bourne's injunction to reject their poisoned heritage and become cosmopolitans, celebrating the rich identities of immigrant groups?

Immigration and ethno-traditionalism are central to understanding the neocon–paleocon split. As the country became more diverse, a number of paleoconservative voices emerged warning that the country was on the verge of losing its ethnic traditions. In *The Path to National Suicide* (1987), Lawrence Auster, a Jewish-American who converted to Episcopalianism and subsequently to Catholicism wrote:

> The very manner in which the [immigration] issue is framed – as a matter of equal rights and the blessings of diversity on one side, versus 'racism' on the other – tends to cut off all rational discourse on the subject . . . Instead of saying: 'We believe in the equal and unlimited right of all people to immigrate to the U.S. and enrich our land with their diversity,' what if they said: 'We believe in an immigration policy which must result in a staggering increase in our population, a revolution in our culture and way of life, and the gradual submergence of our current population by Hispanic and Caribbean and Asian peoples.' Such frankness would open up an honest debate between those who favor a radical change in America's ethnic and cultural identity and those who think this nation should preserve its way of life and its predominant, European-American character.

Auster in turn influenced Peter Brimelow, an expatriate Briton and *National Review* editor whose *Alien Nation* (1995) became a widely discussed bestseller. Brimelow described the country as having a 'white' ethnic core. 'It is simply common sense that Americans have a legitimate interest in their country's racial balance,' he argued. 'They have a right to insist that their government stop shifting it. Indeed, it seems to me that they have a right to insist that it be shifted back.'[54] Brimelow argued against American exceptionalism, stating that the US was 'a nation like any other' with a historic white core. Brimelow formed part of a congeries of paleoconservative intellectuals including Chilton Williamson and *Washington Times* columnist Samuel Francis. To their right, the paleoconservatives had connections to white nationalist Jared Taylor. In 1990 Taylor founded *American Renaissance* magazine and in 1999 Brimelow established *VDare*, an anti-immigration website. Both are seminal influences on today's internet-based white nationalist movement which forms the core of today's alternative right, or 'alt right'.[55]

Neoconservatives preferred to endorse American exceptionalism, the idea that the US was a new type of post-ethnic nation. Most came to approve of Official English, opposed affirmative action and bilingual education and endorsed the need for immigrants to embrace a positive view of American history. They focused squarely on the creedal clements in the national repertoire. Francis Fukuyama, whom I interviewed soon after Brimelow's book came out, saw value in the country's ethno-traditions, thus deviating from the missionary nationalism of the neoconservatives. He argued that English was key for assimilation and traced the country's founding to its Anglo-Protestant forebears. Where Fukuyama was critical of paleoconservatism was over Brimelow's emphasis on a 'white' ethnic core rather than an Anglo-Protestant *cultural* inheritance which could be readily adopted by citizens of any background. Fukuyama was also of the view that immigration was not a growing issue in American politics, a position disputed by *National Review* editor John O'Sullivan, whom I also spoke to at the time.[56] Fukuyama was right: O' Sullivan was two decades early.

Michael Lind, former editor of the neoconservative *Public Interest* and Harvard professor Samuel Huntington operated between the neocon and paleocon positions. Lind's *Next American Nation* (1995) mounted a stinging critique of the American elite's universalist individualism. In the book, Lind offered a groundbreaking attack on 'mass immigration' as a policy which both right- and left-wing American elites favoured but which was opposed by working-class Americans of all races. John Judis endorsed this view, accusing the neoconservative right of fetishizing a free-market ideology which appealed to few ordinary Americans.[57] Huntington, in his final book, *Who Are We?: Challenges to American Identity* (2004), pushed back against the missionary creedal nationalism he had once endorsed, arguing that if America had been settled by French or Spanish Catholics instead of Anglo-Protestants it would have been a wholly different country. This put him in similar territory to Fukuyama on the question of the country's cultural antecedents. Rather than a nation of immigrants, Huntington identified the country as nation of native-born people who had assimilated immigrants into their Anglo-Protestant traditions over time. The volume and geographic concentration of Latinos, warned Huntington, was making them resistant to assimilation and could lead to the secession of the south-western United States.[58]

PAT BUCHANAN'S AMERICA FIRST

At the foot of Lookout Mountain in north-west Georgia in 2005, a former Nixon and Reagan adviser and presidential hopeful, Pat Buchanan, delivered the eulogy at the funeral of the prominent paleoconservative Samuel Francis, his friend and muse. Buchanan, a Donald Trump *avant la lettre*, ran for the Republican nomination in 1992 and 1996 on an anti-globalist, ethno-traditionalist, religious-right platform. In 1996, he wrote of the challenge to the country's ethno-traditions:

> Consider the change in our own country in four decades. In 1950, America was . . . 90 percent of European stock . . . By 2050, according to the Census Bureau, whites may be near a minority in an America of 81 million Hispanics, 62 million blacks and 41 million Asians. By the middle of the next century, the United States will have become a veritable Brazil of North America. If the future character of America is not to be decided by our own paralysis, Americans must stop being intimidated by charges of 'racist,' 'nativist,' and 'xenophobe' – and we must begin to address the hard issues of race, culture and national unity.[59]

In 1992, Buchanan attacked the Republican establishment for failing to stand up for American workers against Japan Inc. He assailed frontrunner George H. W. Bush on cultural issues: immigration, multiculturalism, gay marriage and feminism. Blending ethno-nationalist and religious conservatism with an appeal to the white working class, Buchanan came a close second to Bush in the pace-setting New Hampshire primary with 38 per cent of the vote. Nationwide, he finished with a respectable 23 per cent. At the Republican convention, Buchanan endorsed Bush and delivered a rousing 'culture war' speech. In it, he praised Bush's war record and foreign policy achievements, rallying the faithful behind religious issues. This was, however, a speech oriented to a mainstream audience: references to multiculturalism and immigration were conspicuously absent.

In 1996, the Republican establishment candidate was Bob Dole, a weaker, uncharismatic figure. In New Hampshire, an insurgent Buchanan stunned pundits by winning the state primary. Research shows that his campaign attracted a disproportionate share of votes from working-class and religious conservatives.[60] He won Alaska, Missouri and Louisiana as well, but finished with a similar national vote share to 1992, 21 per cent. At this point, however, opposition to immigration and multiculturalism was only a minor chord in Buchanan's symphony. Officially, even his immigration message centred mainly on border security rather than ethno-cultural threats. For the most part, Buchanan blended economic populism on NAFTA and Japan with an attack on out-of-touch Washington insiders. He praised the patriotic working man, God and guns – all fairly standard fare.

Buchanan's ethno-traditionalist radicalism increased after he had left the Republican Party in 1998. In 1999, he turned up the rhetoric on immigration. He called for a militarization of the border, repatriation of illegal immigrants and cutting legal immigration from a million back to its 'historic' level of 250,000 per year. In a May 2000 interview on National Public Radio, he said record immigration levels meant 'we're gonna lose our country'. That year, Buchanan won the nomination of the Reform Party but finished with a pitiful 0.4 per cent of the vote in the presidential election. Among his rivals for the Reform nomination was a political novice and property tycoon named Donald Trump. After losing to Buchanan, Trump lashed out at his rival for being politically incorrect on race and sex: 'Look, he's a Hitler lover . . . He doesn't like the blacks, he doesn't like the gays.' 'We must recognize bigotry and prejudice,' Trump added, 'and defeat it wherever it appears.'[61] Trump would apologize a decade later to Buchanan, but his remarks capture an ideological climate in which establishment conservatism, with its more 'politically correct' economic, military and religious chords, was firmly in the driver's seat.

PROPOSITION 187

At the mass level, Buchanan's run showed that immigration was not yet an issue that could mobilize the Republican membership. Buchanan suggests this is because ethnic change remained localized in hotspots like California and Miami and the Republican leadership had avoided politicizing the issue. Only with Hispanic dispersion did the pace of ethnic change become apparent to most white Americans, he argues. In his words, 'The numbers had reached critical mass, and native-born Americans saw immigration altering the recognizable character of the country they loved. The soil was more fertile for Trump because . . . by 2016, we no longer saw as through a glass darkly, but face to face.'[62]

Low immigration salience forms a clear contrast to Britain and several European countries where, by 2000, politicians were starting to convert anti-immigration sentiment into electoral hard currency. The one American jurisdiction where immigration was important was California. As the state most affected by undocumented immigration, it might be expected that its conservative white voters would be receptive. Nonetheless, immigration was an issue both major parties avoided. Since the 1960s, cultural liberals had become ascendant on the centre-left and the Democrats were now pro-immigration; on the right, business interests and neoconservatism kept restriction off the Republican agenda. Without elite cues, mass concern among authoritarian and conservative voters remained latent. Even where manifest, anti-immigration feeling found no ready political outlet.

This began to change by the early 1990s. In 1985, the Federation for American Immigration Reform (FAIR) established the Center for Immigration Studies (CIS), a think tank dedicated to, in founder John Tanton's words, making 'the restriction of immigration a legitimate position for thinking people'.[63] In the 1990s, FAIR began to function as a nerve centre for grassroots restrictionist groups and a bridge between local activists and Congress. It became increasingly active in issuing press releases and lobbying members of Congress, and its first success was Proposition 187 in California. California, on the frontline of undocumented immigration, is one of several states which permits citizens to raise popular initiatives (referendums) when a threshold of signatures is obtained. However, no ballot initiative had ever been held on immigration, which was deemed to be a federal matter. In 1994 FAIR helped coordinate grassroots organizations like Voice of Citizens Together (VCT) and Americans Against Illegal Immigration (AAII) to gather the necessary signatures to support the initiative they dubbed 'Save Our State' (SOS).

As a state ballot, Proposition 187 was not about border enforcement, a federal matter. Rather, its stated goal was to deny public services to illegal immigrants. In addition to acting as a deterrent, the measure would serve as a powerful symbol of local opposition to undocumented immigration. Despite its security and economic rationale, there was an important streak of white ethno-traditionalism among grassroots 187 activists. Nearly all contributors to the campaign were white and some 60 per cent were retirees, reflecting the fact California's seniors were considerably less diverse than its younger residents.[64] FAIR's leader, Tanton, as we saw, worried greatly about the loss of the country's Euro-American character.

The initial public reception to Prop 187 was enthusiastic, with 86 per cent of respondents to a Los Angeles *Times* poll approving of the measure. This was followed by a sustained counterattack by the media and sections of the political elite – largely but not wholly Democratic. Anti-187 activists organized street demonstrations, charging the initiative's supporters with racism and nativism. Supporters of the measure were placed on the defensive, repeatedly stressing its economic and security rationales. Despite the opposition of much of the media and large sections of the national political elites (including Ralph Reed of the Christian Coalition and Republicans like Jack Kemp), the measure passed with 59 per cent support. Sixty-four per cent of whites backed it, as did 57 per cent of Asians, 56 per cent of African-Americans and a third of Hispanics.[65]

Studies subsequently showed that citizens of southern California, where undocumented immigration had its largest impact, voted most strongly in favour of restriction. Democrats living closest to the border had a 64 per cent likelihood of backing it compared to 31 per cent for those situated furthest from Mexico.[66] However, whites in high-Hispanic counties weren't much more supportive, and whites in more Asian counties were less likely to back restriction. Anti-Latino stereotypes, conservative self-placement and republican partisanship were the most important predictors of support.[67] Among Latino citizens,

American-born and English-speaking Hispanics stood out as supporters of Prop 187 compared to immigrant and Spanish-speaking Latinos,
exposing a cleavage within the Hispanic community that would be laid
bare once again in the 2016 presidential election.[68]

Whereas the Republican Governor Deukmejian had opposed the
state's Official English bill in 1986, Governor Pete Wilson threw his
support behind 187. Wilson had trailed his Democratic opponent Kath-
leen Brown by 20 points prior to the election, but emerged victorious in
the 1994 gubernatorial election. Much of the credit was given to his
vocal support for Prop 187. Though the courts struck it down, the initiative helped shape the political agenda well beyond California. While
not quite Wilson's 'two-by-four [wood plank] we need to make them
take notice in Washington', it placed the question on Washington's
agenda. President Clinton, though an opponent, said he understood
Californians' desire to control illegal immigration and was working
on federal legislation. Prominent Republicans like Bob Dole, caught
between pro- and anti-immigration wings and mindful of Rove's
Hispanic strategy, were largely silent on immigration in 1994. But in
the 1996 election campaign Dole made immigration one of his issues,
and vowed to outdo Clinton on border security and deportation.

Meanwhile, in 1994, a bipartisan Commission on Immigration
Reform chaired by African-American Congresswoman and Democrat
Barbara Jordan tabled its long-awaited report. Its remit involved travelling the country to take soundings from 'Town Hall'-style meetings.
The commission recommended increasing money for the border patrol,
setting up a computerized registry, enacting employer sanctions and
reducing legal immigration to 550,000. The report's findings informed
President Clinton's Illegal Immigration Reform and Immigrant Responsibility Act (IIRIRA) of 1996. Though border enforcement was beefed
up, employer sanctions were never properly enforced, which reduced
the effectiveness of the measures. In addition, Jordan's recommenda-
tion to set a lower cap for legal immigration never saw the light of day.
Inflows remained at record levels.

In his analysis of why House and Senate bills sponsored by Congressman Lamar Smith and Senator Alan Simpson failed, citizenship and
migration scholar Christian Joppke shows that a coalition of special
interests from an unusually broad spectrum succeeded in quashing it:

Hardly had the ink dried, when the machine of client politics was set in motion. An unusually broad 'Left-Right Coalition on Immigration' included not just the usually odd immigration bedfellows of employers and ethnic and civil rights groups, but also the Home School Network, a Christian fundamentalist group rallying against the antifamily measures to curtail legal immigration . . . and the National Rifle Association, upset by the employment verification system (If you're going to register people, why not guns? they shouted). Richard Day, the chief counsel to the Senate Judiciary Subcommittee, characterized this unusual line-up as 'Washington groups' against 'the American people,' who had asked for 'some breathing space' from immigration.[69]

THE MEDIA AND IMMIGRATION SALIENCE

The flurry of legislative activity in 1994 and 1996 seems to have coincided with a bump in opposition to immigration. The ANES time series which began in 1992 shows that the share of non-Hispanic whites wanting reduced immigration levels jumped from 56 per cent in 1992 to 68 per cent in 1994 and 64 per cent in 1996 before slipping back to 52 per cent in 1998. In many countries, populist forces would have compelled politicians to take on the special interests. The fact this did not occur testifies to the fact that immigration was not a major issue on Americans' list of priorities. If it was, the collapse of immigration reform would have had political repercussions.

It's unclear whether Clinton's IIRIRA was responsible for lowering the temperature of the issue, but what can't be disputed is the relatively low salience of immigration throughout this period of record inflows and failed reforms. Figure 3.3 tracks the proportion of Americans naming immigration as the country's most important problem between 1994 and 2014. The measure remains below 5 per cent between 1994 and 2006. Thereafter, we see high volatility, with a baseline at generally higher levels than those recorded prior to 2006. Thus, even as the share of white Americans opposing immigration remained flat at 50 per cent, concern within the restrictionist half of the white population seems to have grown. A major reason is increasing post-2006 coverage

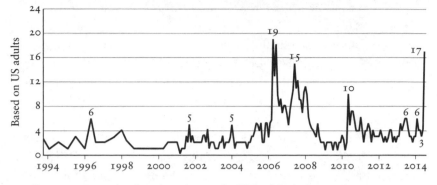

3.3. Percentage naming immigration as the United States' most important problem (based on US adults)

Source: http://www.dailymail.co.uk/news/article-2694508/Number-Americans-calling-illegal-immigration-important-problem-U-S-grows-SIX-FOLD-May-tops-issues.html

of immigration driven by immigration events. This coverage is generally negative: even in more liberal publications such as the *New York Times*, negative stories outnumbered positive ones by a 4:1 ratio.[70]

Periodic spikes in immigration salience correspond to high levels of media reporting about illegal immigration. In March 2006, for instance, Latino activists organized demonstrations over an eight-week period protesting against a bill that would criminalize those who assisted undocumented immigrants to enter or remain in the United States. Rallies took place in cities across America, with 100,000 marching in Chicago and 500,000 in Los Angeles. Many waved Mexican flags. The protests sparked a conservative backlash and helped increase support for volunteer border patrol groups like the 'Minutemen'. In a survey experiment conducted by Matthew Wright and Jack Citrin, 68 per cent of non-Hispanic Americans, and 86 per cent of conservatives, said they were 'bothered a lot' by an image of anti-immigration protesters waving Mexican flags. When people were shown pictures of protesters waving American flags, antipathy fell 10 points but still remained the majority view.[71] Congressional immigration debates during 2007–8 also kept the issue front and centre.

Likewise, in May 2010, protesters took to the streets to oppose Arizona's anti-illegal immigration law SB 1070. And in 2014 tens of thousands of Central American mothers and children fleeing drug-fuelled violence and poverty in El Salvador, Guatemala and Honduras crossed the southern border. This led to agonized debates and concern about impending waves of migrants. Once again, we see a spike in salience around this time in figure 3.3. From this point on, polls record a stable step-change increase in the share of Americans citing immigration as a top concern from under 5 per cent to a new steady-state of 5–10 per cent.

Among those identifying as Republican, the figures rose from 5 to 10 per cent and among the 'very conservative' figure 3.4 shows they jumped from around 5 per cent into the 10–15 per cent range. Terrorism surged even more: from under 5 per cent in 2012 to 20–30 per cent by 2017, while moral issues remained flat at 10 per cent. Those citing the economy as the top issue sagged from 40 per cent in 2012 to little more than 10 per cent by 2017 among both Democrats and Republicans reflecting both an improving economy and cultural polarization. On the right, non-economic questions had emerged as central, with security and identity issues overshadowing religious-moral themes.

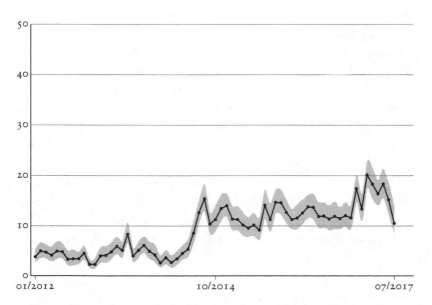

3.4. Share of 'very conservative' white Americans citing immigration as a leading issue, 2012–17, aggregated monthly figures, %

Source: Reuters Polling Explorer, accessed 31 July 2017

Researchers find that the salience of immigration rises and falls with the number of immigration-related news stories. Immigration is more salient for people living close to the Mexican border, partly because local newspapers carry more immigration coverage. A study using 2006 data shows that monthly coverage of immigration ranged from twelve to sixty articles during that year. All else being equal, 7 per cent of those polled during a 'slow' month (twelve articles) said immigration was the most important issue facing the country. In the busiest month, when sixty articles appeared, 43 per cent said it was the number-one issue.[72] In addition, whites in places with fast-growing immigrant populations are more likely to cite immigration as a serious problem, especially at moments when it features in the news.[73] Salience is critical because only then do political parties take notice and begin to campaign on an issue, shifting policy.

Another important change in public opinion is the strengthening association in the restrictionist mind between illegal immigrants and Latinos. ANES shows that whites' feelings towards blacks and Hispanics improved between 1988 and 2004 by 15–20 points, moving towards 70 out of 100 while their opinion of whites (their own group) declined from 86 in 1964 to 71 by 1996. This speaks to the generational liberalization on questions of race we visited earlier. After 2004, both sets of numbers went into reverse by 5 points, possibly hinting at a rising Anglo ethnocentrism captured in other work.[74] More importantly, Nicholas Valentino, Ted Brader and Ashley Jardina found that the difference between whites' 'thermometer' feeling towards their own group on a 0–100 scale and their warmth towards Hispanics came to be associated with their views of immigration. In 1992, opposition to immigration was linked with negative opinions of African-Americans but not of Hispanics. By 1994, during the debate over Prop 187, we see a big change, with negative views of Hispanics now closely tied to a desire to reduce numbers. From this point on, views of Latinos rather than blacks drive Anglo opinion.[75] Feelings towards Hispanics mattered more for immigration than feelings towards Muslims in 2012, but by 2016 anti-Muslim sentiment was slightly more important: a white person's chance of wanting less immigration jumps from 46 to 85 per cent when we compare a person who feels equally warm towards whites and Hispanics with someone who feels 50 points cooler towards Hispanics than whites. For Muslims the equivalent move is from 38 to 85 per cent support for restriction.

REVOLT OF THE GRASSROOTS: LOCAL AND STATE ANTI-IMMIGRATION POLITICS

In the 1990s and 2000s, Latinos increasingly left their initial settlement areas in Southern California and greater Miami for blue-collar jobs in whiter towns or states in the inland west, south-east or Midwest. Even recent Latino immigrants dispersed more widely. This brought a much broader range of white and black Americans into contact with significant numbers of Latino immigrants. North Carolina, for instance, saw its immigrant population increase fivefold between 1990 and 2000. Nashville (Tennessee), Atlanta, Charlotte (North Carolina), Fayetteville (Arkansas) and Boise (Idaho) were among the 145 places which experienced an average Hispanic growth rate of 61 per cent between 2000 and 2010.[76] Smaller towns generally felt less change, but there were many prominent exceptions: Latinos account for just 6 per cent of Wisconsin's population but in Republican governor Scott Walker's hometown of Delavan Hispanics now comprise a third of the total and nearly half the school-age population. The town was 7 per cent Latino in 1980, 11 per cent in 1990, 21 per cent in 2000 and 30 per cent in 2010. In Arcadia, Wisconsin, the increase was sandwiched into half the time as the share of Latinos rose from 3 per cent in 2000 to a third in 2015.[77] Dramatic shifts in local populations were especially common in towns with meat-packing plants such as Springdale, Arkansas, home to a large Tyson Foods facility.

Local opposition to immigration in all Western countries tends to increase in places which experience rapid ethnic change.[78] In the US, this is especially true of towns which have not had historically large immigrant populations. Whites in counties which were heavily white in 1990 and experienced rapid Latino growth in the subsequent decade were much more likely to say that immigration undermined American culture than whites in places with limited Hispanic increases.[79] In the 2000s, fast-changing locales and states began to take the lead on immigration policy, exasperated by what the Harvard demographer Michael Teitelbaum refers to as the bipartisan 'half-hearted and ineffectual enforcement of existing immigration laws' under the Clinton, Bush and Obama administrations.[80] By 2010, 370 jurisdictions had passed Illegal Immigration

Relief Ordinances (IIROs), often at the behest of grassroots citizens' groups. In Northern Virginia, for instance, police were required to check the immigrant status of those they picked up, business owners had to prove they were legal US residents and zoning laws clamped down on the number of people who could occupy a home. On the other hand, nearly 100 jurisdictions emerged as 'sanctuaries' which declared in support of unauthorized immigrants, declined to check documents or recognized Mexican identity documents. For instance, Takoma Park, Maryland laws stipulate that no official may help the Immigration and Customs Enforcement (ICE) – which is empowered by the federal government to cooperate with local law enforcement agencies – to carry out investigations into a person's status.[81]

Many locations at the forefront of the new local restrictionism were white middle-class suburban communities or small towns which experienced rapid ethnic change as part of the post-1990 Hispanic shift to 'new destinations'. Sometimes grassroots volunteer patrols like the right-wing Minuteman movement monitored unauthorized immigrants and informed law enforcement agencies. Their activities spilled over into local politics. Consider three places profiled by Thomas Vicino which adopted IIROs: Carpentersville, Illinois; Hazleton, Pennsylvania; and Farmer's Branch, Texas. In Carpentersville, the population grew from 26,000 in 1970 to 37,000 in 2009. The Latino share rose from 4 per cent in 1970 to 14 per cent in 1990 to 47 per cent in 2009; in Hazleton it increased from 5 per cent in 2000 to 24 per cent in 2009; and in Farmer's Branch, from 8 per cent in 1980 to 46 per cent by 2009.

In 2006, Judy Sigwalt and Paul Humpfer were elected to Carpentersville's board of trustees on an 'All American Team' ticket after nearly 2,000 residents received the following flyer:

> Are you tired of waiting to pay for your groceries while Illegal Aliens pay with food stamps . . . of paying taxes when Illegal Aliens pay NONE . . . of reading that another Illegal Alien was arrested for drug dealing . . . of having to punch 1 for English . . . of seeing multiple families in our homes . . . of not being able to use Carpenter Park on the weekend, because it is overrun by Illegal Aliens . . . of seeing the Mexican Flag flown above our Flag? If so, vote for the All American Team!

In addition to drafting measures to crack down on undocumented immigrants, these locales all voted to make English their official language.

Importantly, dissenters were present among whites in all locales, showing that struggling white communities are more complex than the stereotype. This highlights the importance of psychological and ideological differences which operate at the individual level within communities. As one Carpentersville liberal argued, 'This debate is about language, but everybody knows it's about . . . racism'. 'Why not rename the city Xenophobe's Branch,' complained pro-immigration Farmers Branch resident Glen Johnstone.[82]

Local legislation soon ran into legal challenges, mobilized by the American Civil Liberties Union (ACLU) in partnership with local law firms. The ACLUs challenge threatened to overwhelm Hazleton with legal expenses. However, Hazleton mayor Lou Barletta, who backed his town's ordinance, vowed to fight on, appealing against the local district court's finding that Hazleton had overstepped its jurisdictional powers. In order to meet the threat of being buried by legal costs, Hazleton set up an internet fundraising group, Small Town Defenders. The group ultimately managed to raise over $500,000 nationwide. 'If they stop Hazleton,' warned the site, 'they may stop your community next.' 'I'm confident the people of this country will back the city,' he declared.[83]

Barletta mounted a public relations effort that vaulted his local issue onto the national stage. In November 2006, Barletta appeared on CBS's 60 Minutes. He appeared regularly on Lou Dobbs Tonight, a CNN programme hosted by a prominent anti-immigration presenter who twice broadcast the show live from the Federation for American Immigration Reform (FAIR)'s national convention. Dobbs's support of FAIR, along with his perceived softness on supporters of the 'birther' conspiracy theory that Obama was born abroad, resulted in a campaign by the Southern Poverty Law Center and other liberal advocacy groups to force him to leave CNN. This he did in 2009. Dobbs resurfaced two years later at Fox News – a textbook case of how ideological pressures result in the sorting of journalists, contributing to a polarization of the country's media. In the end, mayor Barletta won the right to implement his IIRO, and the town's Hispanic population declined by over 5,000, even as many concrete aspects of the ordinance failed to be implemented.[84]

Expansion of California's border wall diverted more undocumented immigrants towards Arizona. Partly as a consequence, the state's Hispanic population tripled between 1990 and 2010, with much of the growth centred on Phoenix. Since the state's white population consisted of a disproportionate number of retirees, there were more Hispanics than whites in its school-age population by 2010. Indeed, by 2015, metropolitan Phoenix had the second-highest 'cultural generation gap' in the country: 85 per cent of seniors were white compared to 44 per cent of those under eighteen.[85] This set the scene for increased anti-immigration agitation in the state. In April 2010, Arizona governor Jan Brewer signed the state's SB 1070 into law, requiring citizens to carry documents and law enforcement officers to stop or arrest individuals if there is a 'reasonable suspicion' that they lack the right to be in the United States. State and local officials were compelled to cooperate with federal ICE agents. Those found aiding or sheltering illegal immigrants would be penalized. The measure was described as an 'attrition through enforcement' doctrine by its proponents. Polls showed Arizonans to be 64–30 in favour. National opinion surveys similarly found 50–60 per cent support for Arizona's law with fewer than 40 per cent opposed. SB 1070 caused Brewer's approval ratings to soar from 40 to 56 per cent, while those of her anti-1070 Democratic opponent Terry Goddard slumped.[86]

Importantly, the law split the Arizona legislature and national politicians along partisan lines with opponents worried that the bill's stop-and-search provisions would lead to the racial profiling of Latinos. Arizona's outgoing Democratic governor Janet Napolitano had vetoed all attempts at enacting similar legislation prior to leaving office in 2009. President Obama meanwhile, despite deporting a record number of unauthorized immigrants, expressed concern that SB 1070 would 'undermine basic notions of fairness that we cherish as Americans, as well as the trust between police and our communities that is so crucial to keeping us safe'. Democrat Linda Sanchez, from a mixed Anglo-Latino district of Los Angeles, warned: 'There's a concerted effort behind promoting these kinds of laws on a state-by-state basis by people who have ties to white supremacy groups. It's been documented. It's not mainstream politics.' This charge was angrily rebutted by Gary Miller, a Republican from a majority Anglo district in southern California who accused Sanchez of trying to reframe the debate around racism rather than law enforcement. While most Republican representatives were positive, Florida governor Jeb Bush and strategist Karl Rove, key architects of the GOP's Hispanic strategy, voiced their opposition.[87]

On 1 May, tens of thousands protested in Los Angeles, many waving

Mexican flags. Thousands also marched in Phoenix, Dallas and other cities. The Major League Baseball (MLB) association called for 1070 to be repealed or modified due to the adverse effects it may have on the quarter of MLB players of Latino background. The National Basketball Association (NBA) Phoenix Suns joined in, wearing special Spanish 'Los Suns' uniforms to protest against the bill. The gesture was lauded by Barack Obama but incensed some of the team's fans and conservative talk-show hosts like Rush Limbaugh. Meanwhile, Arizona Congressman Raúl Grijalva and others called for an economic boycott of the state. Liberal cities such as San Francisco, Seattle, Denver and Los Angeles responded by limiting their employees' travel to Arizona and severing business links with the state. New York Democrat José Serrano then called on MLB commissioner Bud Selig to move the 2011 All-Star Game from Chase Field in Phoenix, which he refused to do. At this, conservative supporters of SB 1070 – notably conservative radio hosts and the grassroots Tea Party movement – countered with a 'buycott' to support the state. In the end, the Arizona boycott was judged a failure.

SB 1070, like Hazleton's IIRO, was challenged in the courts. This time the federal Justice Department placed its weight behind a legal challenge, arguing that SB 1070 usurped federal authority. Supporters of Arizona responded that the state was only enforcing federal laws. Arizona senators John Kyl and John McCain released a joint statement to the same effect: 'The American people must wonder whether the Obama administration is really committed to securing the border when it sues a state that is simply trying to protect its people by enforcing immigration law.' Lower courts initially struck down most of SB 1070's provisions, which was appealed all the way to the Supreme Court. The Court rendered a 5–3 verdict in favour of modifying the law – the three dissenters being conservative justices Scalia, Alito and Thomas who favoured retaining it essentially intact. Yet overall the judgment was a victory for Arizona. State law enforcement officials would be able to check the residency status of suspects and could take action against 'sanctuary cities'. Soon afterwards, a range of other states passed or drafted similar measures. By 2015, only a handful of states, mainly in the liberal north-east, had failed to pass a measure on immigration enforcement.[88]

The conflict also launched the careers of three Italian-American Republicans, demonstrating how effectively the Euro-American melting pot had worked to create a sense of white identity among those whose ancestors were once viewed as not truly American. Hazleton's mayor Lou Barletta, who won the battle to keep his town's IIRO, became a Republican state representative in Pennsylvania. In Phoenix (Maricopa County), sheriff Joe Arpaio, who styled himself 'America's Toughest Sheriff', became a national figure. Arpaio only became attuned to the immigration issue in 2005 when Maricopa County Attorney Andrew Thomas was elected on a 'stop illegal immigration' platform. Arpaio soon initiated controversial police sweeps of Latino neighbourhoods and local businesses suspected of employing undocumented immigrants. In 2012, Arpaio and the Maricopa County Sheriff's Office (MCSO) were sued for racially profiling Latinos in their stop-and-search efforts. Arpaio and MCSO were found guilty, but Arpaio remained unrepentant, and frequently appeared on the national right-wing media scene. In 2016, President Trump officially pardoned him.

The third individual was Colorado Congressman Tom Tancredo, who ran in the 2008 Republican primary on a hardline anti-immigration ticket, winning 5 per cent support before pledging his support to Mitt Romney. Tancredo founded and led from 1999 to 2007 the Congressional Immigration Reform Caucus, which worked closely with FAIR to advance the anti-immigration agenda. In 2001, he sponsored a proposed moratorium on immigration entitled the Mass Immigration Reduction Act which called for immigration to be restricted for a period of five years to the spouses and children of American citizens. Though unsuccessful, it signalled a new assertiveness within the restrictionist movement.

FEDERAL IMMIGRATION BATTLES, 2005–2014

A chronically gridlocked Congress made it difficult for federal legislation on border enforcement or the fate of undocumented immigrants to pass – a vacuum increasingly filled by local and state IIROs. Democrats were largely united behind a liberal policy that granted a suite of rights and path to citizenship for the estimated 11 million undocumented immigrants. In general, they opposed Official English and supported bilingualism in service provision and education. They took pains to stress the law-abiding nature of most illegal immigrants and their contribution to the economy. This reflected their pluralistic, cosmopolitan conception of America which blended the Liberal Progressive and Young Intellectual traditions. The Republicans were divided between a missionary nationalist elite, motivated by free-market ideology, neoconservative foreign policy, family values and Rove's Hispanic strategy; and many ordinary congressmen and women from strongly Republican districts who – up for election every two years and vulnerable to challenges from the right – were alive to the concerns of their conservative constituents.

John McCain, despite backing SB 1070, stemmed from the party's establishment wing. In 2005, he co-sponsored a bill with Democratic senator Ted Kennedy which combined more funds for border enforcement with a temporary worker programme and a path to citizenship for unauthorized immigrants. The bill met strong resistance from both ends of the ideological spectrum: liberal Democrats and congressional Republicans. By 2007, the bill had gained the sponsorship of President George W. Bush, a senior Republican, Lindsey Graham, and the Democratic Senate Majority Leader, Harry Reid. It included the DREAM Act, designed to regularize the status of those who entered the country as minors and have met a number of conditions such as not having committed a crime and having graduated from high school. The bipartisan bill failed by fourteen votes, however, meeting resistance from conservative Republicans who claimed its provisions would act as a magnet for further illegal immigration. Senator Jeff Sessions of Alabama contended the bill would result in a further 8.7 million illegal immigrants arriving in the next two decades.[89]

During the debate in Congress, FAIR and a linked organization, Roy Beck's Numbers USA (which has since eclipsed FAIR), channelled popular anxiety directly to Congress, rallying popular opposition on conservative radio. At their behest, constituents besieged their representatives. They 'lit up the switchboard for weeks', said Senator Mitch McConnell of Kentucky. 'And to every one of them, I say today: "Your voice was heard." ' After the defeat, America's Voice, a pro-immigration lobby group for businesses and immigrants, went on a coordinated attack. The Southern Poverty Law Center called FAIR a 'hate group'. America's Voice placed ads warning Congress not to meet 'with extremist groups like FAIR'. Opponents focused on John Tanton, whose correspondence revealed an interest in eugenics and white nationalism.

FAIR's president, Dan Stein, and Beck disavowed Tanton's comments, and the organization weathered the storm.[90]

Barack Obama took office in 2008 promising, among other things, to reverse the defeat on immigration. In 2010, a combination of conservative Republicans and liberal Democrats, acting for diametrically opposing reasons, defeated immigration reform in the Senate. Meanwhile, Massachusetts governor Mitt Romney, in his bid for president in 2012, stood squarely on the side of the illegal immigration sceptics. He favoured a 2,800-mile fence and strict law enforcement, which would lead the undocumented to 'self-deport' and apply legally to enter the country. His stance on immigration was not, however, central to his nomination message in the Republican primaries, and was little discussed during the 2012 presidential election, which he lost to Barack Obama. Romney's defeat saw the Republicans win just 27 per cent of the Hispanic vote compared to Bush's 40 per cent and McCain's 31 per cent. In a report dubbed 'the autopsy', the Republican National Committee (RNC), chaired by Reince Priebus, reiterated the need for the party to appeal to Hispanics and young people by embracing immigration reform. The then reality-TV star Donald Trump echoed the RNC line: '[Romney] had a crazy policy of self-deportation,' he told the conservative website Newsmax. 'He lost all of the Latino vote. He lost the Asian vote. He lost everybody who is inspired to come into this country.'[91]

Bypassing Congress, Obama initiated the Deferred Action for Childhood Arrivals (DACA) programme in 2012 which allows undocumented immigrants who entered the country as minors to apply for a renewable two-year permit preventing them from being deported. DACA was widely criticized by the Republicans and in Arizona governor Jan Brewer refused to recognize those possessing DACA permits. In 2013, with a Democratic majority in the Senate, an immigration reform bill finally gained ground. It passed 68–32 on the back of all Democratic and fourteen of forty-six Republican votes. The legislation combined employer verification, border security and a path to citizenship for the undocumented. Tellingly, Republican supporters of the bill were establishment figures such as John McCain, Jeb Bush and Lindsey Graham. The RNC, Karl Rove, Grover Norquist, 100 conservative economists, the CATO Institute and the *Wall Street Journal* urged congressmen to pass the bill.[92] All Democrats were now onside, but when the bill came to the Republican-controlled House it suffered a crushing defeat.

Why did immigration reform fail? In a perceptive analysis, Christopher Parker of the University of Washington argues: 'House Republicans aren't motivated by true conservatism. Rather, they represent constituencies haunted by anxiety associated with the perception that they're "losing their country" to immigrants from south of the border.' Parker noted that over a quarter of Republican legislators won seats due to endorsement from the Tea Party. Parker identified a 70 per cent overlap between the Congressional Immigration Reform Caucus, which Tancredo had founded, and congressmen supported by the Tea Party. Formed after Obama's inauguration in 2009, the Tea Party reflected a wholly new right-wing ecosystem. Unlike the religious right, it didn't spring from a network of churches and para-church organizations but was nourished by activists linked via Fox News, talk radio and the right-wing internet. Religious and moral issues ranked lower on their priority list than secular concerns. Though composed of various strands, immigration was one of the movement's top priorities. Among Massachusetts Tea Partiers surveyed by Vanessa Williamson, Theda Skocpol and John Coggin in 2010, 78 per cent cited immigration as a leading issue, second only to 'deficits and spending'. Nationally, 80 per cent of Tea Party members considered immigration to be a serious problem.[23] Tea Partiers' oppositional, anti-politically correct orientation towards the Republican Party establishment distinguishes it from the religious right, which sought to win over and co-opt the party elite.

An estimated 10 per cent of Americans identify with the Tea Party, and Parker's survey shows they differ in important ways from other conservatives. Asked whether 'restrictive immigration policies are based in part on racism', only 18 per cent of Tea Party conservatives agreed, compared to 40 per cent of non-Tea Party conservatives. Racial-resentment measures (containing statements to the effect that blacks could succeed if they worked harder) correlated with Tea Party affiliation. There were also 20-point differences between Tea Party and non-Tea Party supporters on support for the idea that a child born in the United States should automatically get citizenship ('birthright citizenship') and support for the DREAM Act. Finally, 71 per cent of Tea

Parties agreed with the statement that Obama was 'destroying the country' compared to 6 per cent of non-Tea Partiers.[94]

Obama, who had been fairly tough on border security, took a much more liberal line towards those already in the country. Frustrated by the lack of legislative progress towards normalizing the status of the undocumented, he initiated both DACA and Deferred Action for Parents of Americans and Lawful Permanent Residents (DAPA), a programme to regularize the parents of lawful American residents (i.e. migrant parents of US-born children or the parents of illegals who subsequently acquired legal residency). 'Taken together,' Michael Tei-telbaum remarks, Obama's executive order 'would establish legal status for nearly one-half of the 10–11 million' illegal immigrants in the country. This led twenty-six of the nation's fifty states, all with Republican governors, to sue the government for failing to enforce US immigration law. The courts ruled in their favour, issuing an injunction preventing Obama from implementing DAPA, and the order was rescinded by Trump in 2017. Michael Teitelbaum notes that bipartisanship had almost completely collapsed compared to 2007–8, when an important minority of Republicans backed a path to citizenship. By 2014, Republican backing was confined to a handful of elite figures such as John McCain and Marco Rubio.[95]

In 2014, Tea Party candidate Dave Brat, an unknown figure, claimed the scalp of Eric Cantor of Virginia, the second-highest-ranking Republican in Congress, in a party primary. Cantor was convinced of the establishment position that the party needed to pass an immigration bill in order to reassure conservative Latino voters and safeguard its demographic future. Though generally quiet on immigration, he was on record as favouring the regularization of those who came to the country as children. During the campaign, Cantor tried to distance himself from Obama's 'amnesty', but faced a tough challenge from the upstart Brat, who declared: 'Eric Cantor is saying we should bring more folks into the country, increase the labor supply – and by doing so, lower wage rates for the working person.' The defeat of Cantor, who had been working quietly to salvage immigration reform, demonstrated the growing power of immigration on the Republican right.

IMMIGRATION AND
PARTISAN POLARIZATION

The patchwork of state and local ordinances broke on partisan lines between pro-enforcement and 'sanctuary' jurisdictions. This, and the public split among national politicians over SB 1070, sucked immigration into the ever-widening and more racialized partisan vortex of the 2000s. In the 1970s, American parties were weak and congressmen only slightly more likely to back their own party in roll-call votes. The median voter identified as conservative and Democratic, illustrating how ideology and partisanship were not neatly aligned. This began to change, especially in the 1980s, as Reagan ran on a more ideological conservatism. By 2000, polarization in Congress had exceeded its 1905 peak and shot past it. As the parties began to differentiate, the average American became better able to distinguish parties' stances on various issues. Previously, many voters, especially those without degrees, had difficulty pinning the tail of policies they supported on the donkey (or elephant) of party. Yet eventually even these Americans began correctly matching party to ideology. The era of mass polarization had begun.[96]

Party identities are linked to race as well as ideology. In the 1950s, the electorate was 95 per cent white, and there was only a modest difference between the parties' bases. As more southern blacks won the right to vote after the Voting Rights Act of 1965, they increasingly moved towards the Democrats while southern whites realigned to the Republicans. Then, in the 1990s, the growing Latino and Asian vote broke largely for the Democrats while northern white Catholics moved several points towards the Republicans each election. By the 2010s, figure 3.5 shows that minorities made up half the Democratic base but just 10 per cent of the Republican electorate. More than this, Republicans perceived Democratic voters to be 46 per cent black (rather than the actual 24) as well as 37 per cent LGBT (rather than the actual 6). Those with the greatest interest in political news had the most distorted picture of the other side's demographics and considered the opposing party's voters to be more ideologically extreme and socially distant.[97]

Race and attitudes to religious issues may have separated Republicans from Democrats, but immigration only emerged as a partisan issue in the late 2000s. As figure 3.6 shows, the gap on immigration

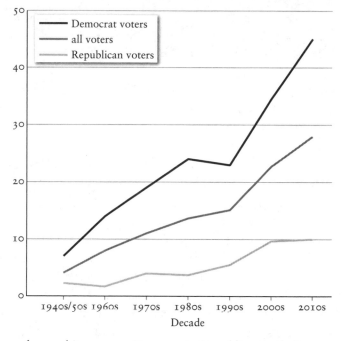

3.5. Share of non-whites among Democratic, Republican and all voters by decade, %

Source: Alan Abramowitz, 'How race and religion have polarized American voters', *Washington Post* (Monkey Cage), 20 January 2014

between white Republicans and Democrats in the ANES was no more than a few points between 1992 and 2008. This reflected wealthy suburban Republicans' predilection for low-cost, hard-working immigrants and white working-class Democrats' opposition to it. But between 2008 and 2012 Democratic voters became 3.5 points more liberal while Republicans grew 3.5 points more restrictive. By 2016, 69 per cent of white Republicans wanted less immigration compared to only 21 per cent of white Democrats, a yawning chasm. In high-immigration California, white partisans divided by a whopping 73–16. White Democrats had become 19 points less restrictionist nationally while white Republicans grew 15 points more so. The two effects cancelled each other out because the number of Democrats in the white population had declined while the number of Republicans among whites increased. The Republicans' outspoken stance on immigration had won them

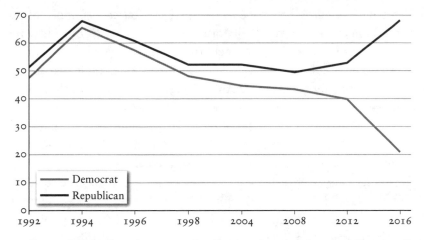

3.6. Share of white Americans wanting less immigration, by party identity, %

Source: American National Election Study (ANES) 1992–2016

white working-class Democrats, Independents and non-voters despite losing them sections of their wealthier suburban support base.

THE RISE OF A RIGHT-WING ELECTRONIC MEDIA

Political scientists emphasize that elite cues are important in shaping public opinion on issues and according them importance. American voters can be 'cued' by media as well as by political elites. When it comes to the rise of immigration politics, both are important. One of the liberalizing forces in American life after 1960 had been the expanding New York and Hollywood-based television media, with content produced by a media elite which leaned in a culturally liberal direction.[98] However, by the 1990s, cable television began to chip away at the primacy of ABC, NBC and CBS, the so-called 'big three' television networks. Market segmentation into speciality channels fragmented the media landscape.[99] In addition, in 1987, the Federal Communications Commission (FCC) stopped enforcing the 'fairness doctrine', which opened the door to conservative talk radio. In 1996, new laws enabled radio stations to become nationally syndicated.

So began the erosion of one of the institutional cornerstones of the country's post-1960s attitude liberalization. The growth of right-wing cable television, and, later, internet sites, induced a polarizing shift in American political culture. Between 1996 and 2000, cable was laid in 20 per cent of American towns. An influential study showed that towns which received cable – which came bundled with the right-wing Fox News channel – produced a small bump in Republican vote share and a major increase of as much as 28 per cent in turnout among registered Republicans.[100] The study design neatly ruled out the possibility that right-wing voters were selecting into Fox or lobbying for it because the cable was laid in an entirely random manner.

Conservatives selected away from the mainstream networks and radio stations towards conservative ones like Fox while liberals moved towards liberal outlets like MSNBC/CNN or National Public Radio. One study finds that Republicans who watch conservative cable news are more opposed to Mexican immigration than Republicans who don't.[101] My analyses of 2012 and 2016 ANES data show that, controlling for party identification, those who listen to conservative radio shows or watch conservative cable news are no more likely than others to want reduced immigration. However, people who watch or listen to liberal radio news shows – whether they be Republicans or Democrats, liberals or conservatives – are almost 20 points less likely to favour cutting immigration than other white Americans. Thirty-one per cent of white Democrats who listen to liberal radio stations favour restriction compared to 49 per cent of those who don't. Among Republicans who listen to liberal radio, the numbers jump from 41 to 60 per cent. Across a range of questions pertaining to the undocumented: whether to allow those under sixteen to acquire citizenship, whether police should be compelled to conduct background checks on suspects' immigration status, and whether to deport the unauthorized, liberal radio and news consumption is strongly correlated with attitudes. Support for deportation, for instance, is almost three times lower among white Republicans who listen to liberal radio programmes than among those who don't.

Conservative radio or news consumption makes a difference on the question of whether police should be required to conduct background checks on suspected non-citizens: support among white Republicans rises from 77 to 89 per cent and among non-Republicans from 50 to 69 per cent as we move from those who don't consume conservative news to those who do. On the key question of attitudes towards Hispanics, however, I could find no conservative media effect, though consumers of conservative TV news were a few points warmer towards whites than others in the population. All of which suggests the fragmentation of the news media is only part of the story of how the country began to polarize on immigration. Demographic change in white middle-class communities ignited the movement and led to copycat efforts in similarly affected areas. The tumultuous local battles to gain control over immigration enforcement began with grassroots activists, who shaped local and state legislation. The laws were popular – as much for symbolic as for practical reasons – and polarized national politicians and the media. Once signed up to the restrictionist cause, conservative media and politicians began providing the cues which shifted public opinion among the mass of people living in more demographically stable locations.

THE RISE OF TRUMP

American immigration politics since 1980 was driven by bottom-up dynamics which were ignored, to a greater or lesser extent, by the Republican establishment. Official English began as a grassroots endeavour that was initially resisted by conservative intellectuals and politicians, who soon realized, however, how popular these measures were and switched to endorsing them. Proposition 187 commenced as a socio-political movement which encountered opposition from Republican elites outside California. Similarly, local and state anti-illegal immigration laws in the 2000s reflect conservative white mobilization in ethnically shifting parts of the country. These efforts, channelled via the Tea Party, thwarted the Republican elite's strategy of yielding on immigration in order to win Hispanic support for an agenda based on economic liberalism, overseas regime change and social conservatism. The final nail in the establishment coffin was the election of Donald J. Trump as president in 2016.

Trump, a New York property tycoon and star of NBC's reality TV show *The Apprentice*, had a quixotic relationship with politics. Over the years he gave verbal or monetary support to George H. W. Bush, Hillary Clinton and Barack Obama. Though interested in American protectionism, his views on immigration were generally liberal or conventional. This changed in 2015 when he entered the race for the Republican leadership. On Tuesday, 16 June, he announced his intention to run. The speech contained a bombshell on immigration which walked all over the red lines in American public discourse: 'When Mexico sends its people, they're not sending their best ... They're sending people that have lots of problems, and they're bringing those problems with us. They're bringing drugs. They're bringing crime. They're rapists. And some, I assume, are good people.' He surpassed any previous candidate in the zeal of his immigration message, avowing: 'I will build a great wall ... I will build a great, great wall on our southern border and I will have Mexico pay for that wall.' In December he called for 'a total and complete shutdown of Muslims entering the United States'.

It's not entirely clear if Trump sincerely believes in immigration restriction or merely found it a useful tool to acquire the presidency. Some allege he was influenced by polling which showed that the immigration issue had immense potential within the active base of Republican Party members. Scott Walker, Rick Santorum and Ted Cruz all talked tough on illegal immigration though only Trump called for lower levels of legal immigration. Others argue Trump's anti-Mexican rhetoric reflected the views of conservative anti-immigration pundit Anne Coulter in her book *Adios America: The Left's Plan to Turn Our Country into a Third World Hellhole* (2015).[102] Trump continually surprised himself by how well he was doing.[103] He came second to Cruz in relatively evangelical Iowa, but won New Hampshire handily. On Super Tuesday in March 2016, Cruz won in Texas, Oklahoma and Alaska, but Trump secured seven states, many in the relatively religious southeast, which surprised pundits. By March, Trump was well ahead of Cruz, with establishment candidates Jeb Bush and John Kasich out of contention. Alarmed, fiscal conservative groups like the Club for Growth, as well as religious conservative pundits like Glenn Beck, got behind the 'Stop Trump Movement'. Bush and Kasich chose the lesser of two evils and endorsed Cruz, a populist in the religious-right mould who attacked Trump's 'New York values'. All to no avail. In April, Trump swept the north-eastern primaries, ending Cruz's challenge. The party establishment, used to weathering insurgent outsiders before getting its preferred candidate in place, was in shock. In July, at the

Republican National Convention, Trump officially became the Republican nominee.

Trump named Indiana governor Mike Pence, an evangelical, as his running mate and in August appointed Steve Bannon, head of the right-wing news website Breitbart, to run his campaign. Bannon, a former investment banker and media industry executive, moved in trans-national right-wing circles by the 2000s. In 2007, he wrote an eight-page treatment for a documentary entitled *Destroying the Great Satan: The Rise of Islamic Facism* [sic] *in America*. He has spoken approvingly of ethno-nationalist writers like Charles Maurras and Jean Raspail, author of the apocalyptic racist novel *Camp of Saints* based on a fictional account of a peaceful immigrant invasion of France. At Breitbart, his organization was routinely accused of publishing racist and anti-Muslim content and his appointment to Trump's Cabinet brought anti-racist protesters onto the streets. Breitbart has also been linked to the alt-right, a label which encompasses various forms of right-wing extremism but coalesces around the idea of white nationalism. Like Kellyanne Conway, whom Bannon was in conversation with by 2015, he believed the immigration issue could be used to win white working-class votes in critical swing states like Ohio, Wisconsin, Pennsylvania and Michigan.[104]

The strategy worked. On 9 November, I was floored by news that Trump had become US president, having won key Midwestern battlegrounds while taking Florida. Never had the country seemed so polarized. During the primaries and campaign, Trump's rallies attracted considerable protest from liberals, pro-immigration advocates, Muslim-Americans and others. On many occasions, protesters encountered hostility and were forcibly ejected by security, abused and even attacked by Trump's audience. Sometimes Trump appeared to condone the violence. In February 2016, he told an Iowa crowd, 'So if you see somebody getting ready to throw a tomato, knock the crap out of him, would you? Seriously, okay, just knock the hell. I promise you, I will pay for the legal fees; I promise, I promise.' After a protester at another Trump rally was punched, Trump answered, 'Maybe he deserved to get roughed up.'[105]

WHY TRUMP WON

In dissecting Trump's win, it's vital to separate his personal popularity from his election victory. I'll consider both in the pages that follow but let's begin with the election. Many loyal Republicans held their noses and voted for him in November. Most would have voted for any Republican candidate. On the other hand, the fact that Trump's outrageous statements about women and minorities were not a deal-breaker for many voters is an important indicator of the limited power that norms of 'political correctness' – not making remarks about minorities that are negative (or which might be construed as negative by left-modernists) – possess over much of the Republican electorate.

Attacks on political correctness were a signature of Trump's campaign and, as we'll see, one of the themes that resonated most strongly with many voters. The phrase repeatedly got the president out of tight spots during interviews and demonstrates how far he managed to stretch the 'Overton Window' of acceptable public discourse. Trump's repeated outrages and cavalier attitude to controversy seemed to blunt the force of the social sanctions which had, for instance, compelled FAIR to avoid any mention of cultural anxieties over immigration. Questioned by Fox host Megyn Kelly regarding his pejorative comments about women as 'animals', 'slobs' and sex objects, he replied, 'I think the big problem this country has is being politically correct.' Likewise, after NBC had severed links with him over his remarks about Mexicans, he retorted, 'NBC is weak, and like everybody else is trying to be politically correct.'[106]

As in Britain, right- and left-wing pundits endorse the 'left behind' explanation that white working-class voters voted for populism to protest against a selfish economic and political elite at a time of inequality and stagnant real wages. This permits them to shoehorn favoured policy solutions into the discussion, with the left calling for more public spending to reduce inequality and the right for less public spending to free up the economy. As with Brexit, the storyline also works for the right-wing populists themselves because it lends a 'we are defending the powerless' David-and-Goliath nobility to their cause. Countless observers point to work by Anne Case and Nobel Prize winner Angus Deaton to stake their claim. These researchers discovered a steady increase in non-Hispanic white suicide rates linked to an opioid epidemic among working-class white Americans.[107] Other authors favoured J. D. Vance's autobiographical and evocative Hillbilly Elegy, about growing up in backwoods poverty in Appalachia. Some tramped the byways of rust-belt Ohio or reported from struggling post-industrial towns to suggest that economic misery explained Trump's success. None performed any sophisticated individual-level data analysis.

Daniel Kahneman and Amos Tversky emphasize that our brains are wired to work with vivid images such as a coal miner in a down-at-the-heel West Virginia town.[108] Like Billy Beane in Michael Lewis's *Moneyball*, we are better off ignoring gut feel and looking at the individual-level data. It's much harder for us to digest the fact that the psychological differences between two Appalachian miners matter more for the Trump vote than the social distance between Youngstown, Ohio, and the northern Virginia suburbs. Electoral maps based on aggregate county results matched to census data offered the first snapshot of the social drivers of Trump, and it was apparent that education, not income, best predicted Trump success. Still, at first glance, maps reinforce stereotypes like the urban–rural divide.[109]

As with Brexit, income is correlated with education, but there are many wealthy people – think successful plumber – with few qualifications. Similarly, many resemble struggling artists, possessing degrees but little money. When you control for education, income has no effect on whether a white person voted for, or supports, Trump. Being less well-off produces an effect on Trump voting only when authoritarian and conservative values are held constant – and even then has a much smaller impact than values. Education is the best census indicator because it reflects people's subjective worldview, not just their material circumstances. Researchers find that teenagers with more open and exploratory psychological orientations self-select into university.[110] This, much more than what people learn at university, makes them more liberal. Median education level offers a window onto the cultural values of a voting district, which is why it correlates best with Trump's vote share. In American exit polls, Trump won whites without college degrees 67–28, compared to 49–45 for whites with degrees.[111]

VALUES VOTERS,
OF A DIFFERENT KIND

Values, the invisible social-psychological makeup of an individual, are much closer to explaining the vote than demographics of any kind, whether income, age, gender or even education. Most of the variation in values is within-group rather than between-group. For example, within the degree-holding population there is a great deal of social-psychological variation. Conservatives and authoritarians, who value stability and order, went strongly for Trump. These are the same people whom Dade classifies as Settlers and form the core of those Goodhart labels Somewheres.[112] Those preferring change and diversity voted instead for Saunders or Clinton. Plenty of university graduates in major metropolitan areas are conservative and authoritarian. Many high-school-educated rural whites are liberal. While whites without degrees broke 67–28 for Trump, don't forget white degree holders still favoured him 49–45. White women came out 52–44 for Trump over Clinton and whites under the age of thirty backed him 47–43.[113]

Indicators of psychological authoritarianism consistently predicted support for Trump. A subtle social-psychology question asks people whether it is more important for children to be considerate or well mannered. The two options sound alike but the first gets at empathy for others and the second adherence to rules. In a Policy Exchange (PX)–YouGov survey I ran in mid-August 2016 during the primaries, white Americans were asked to rate Trump on a 0–10 thermometer scale. The average warmth towards him was 4.34. Those who said it was more important for children to be considerate than well mannered rated Trump a 3.5 while people who answered that it was more import-ant for them to be well mannered gave him 5.5, a powerful statistical difference. White Americans who scored lowest on a measure of open-ness, one of the big five personality dimensions, scored Trump a 6.4 out of 10 while those who scored highest on openness gave him a 3.4.

I also asked one of Pat Dade's more outlandish authoritarianism questions which is one of the top predictors of populist-right support in Europe: 'How well does this describe the REAL you: I believe that sex crimes, such as rape and attacks on children, deserve more than mere imprisonment. I think that such criminals ought to be publicly whipped, or worse.' Those who most disagreed with this sentiment gave Trump a 2.2 out of 10 while those most in agreement scored him 5.7. Not only that, but the pattern of responses in the Trump questionnaire was a carbon copy of what I obtained in a survey of Brexit voting fielded in Britain on the same day: a big difference between those who strongly and 'somewhat' opposed whipping sex criminals, not much action in the middle of the distribution, and a big gap between those 'somewhat' and strongly in favour of whipping.

In the ANES, only 20 per cent of whites who most oppose the death penalty voted for Trump compared to 69 per cent of those most in favour of capital punishment. Trump did much better than Romney among these voters: in 2012 just 46 per cent of whites most in favour of the death penalty backed the Massachusetts governor. Among Latinos, Trump support likewise jumps from 12 to 35 per cent comparing the least and most pro-death penalty voters. But authoritarianism is less effective than conservatism in picking out Trump supporters. In the PX–YouGov data from August 2016, white Americans who strongly disagreed with the view that 'things in America were better in the past' rated Trump a 1.59. Whites who most agreed gave him a 6.85, a whopping 5.3-point differential. Recall that Karen Stenner distinguished authoritarianism – involving opposition to diversity – from status quo conservatism, a preference for continuity with the past. Both are important, but conservatism, as in the UK data, seems to correlate somewhat more strongly with right-wing populist support.

IT'S ABOUT IMMIGRATION

But even conservatism and authoritarianism are less important than immigration attitudes for Trump support because right-wing media and political elites have some sway in framing what their supporters should be conservative or authoritarian about. Should they be more worried about a threat to American military power or the loss of America's white Christian identity? The consensus from two decades of work on immigration attitudes in America is that cultural and psychological dispositions, i.e. conservatism and authoritarianism, drive attitudes. Economic factors are far less important.[114] Meanwhile the focus for conservatives and authoritarians has tilted away from foreign policy to domestic identity questions. Seventy per cent of white Trump voters want immigration reduced, rising to 75 per cent among strong Trump supporters. This compares to 20 per cent of white Clinton voters, a gap of more than 50 points.

Figure 3.7 reveals that when we control for age and education a person's probability of having voted for Trump *and* strongly preferring him over other primary candidates increases from 7 per cent among those who want immigration increased a lot to 45 per cent for those who want it reduced a lot. The tight and inconsistent lines for income, by contrast, reveal that a person's income had no real effect on Trump support.

Immigration and a cluster of attitudes labelled 'nativism' were likewise identified as the key drivers of Trump support in the primaries in an Ipsos study using sophisticated Bayesian modelling techniques. 'Simply put, it is all about nativism!' the author wrote.[115] Indeed, in the ANES data, a Romney vote in 2012 plus immigration attitudes on a five-point scale predict a striking 40.5 per cent of the variation in the probability of having voted for Trump. This compares with 3.6 per cent for a model combining age, income and education. It's not just that opposition to immigration is related to Trump support. The other side

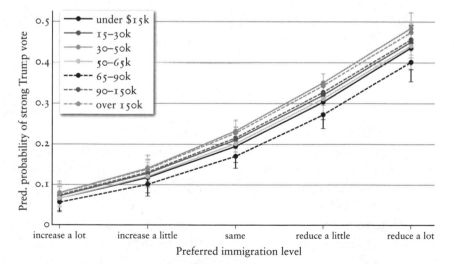

3.7. Strong Trump vote, by immigration view and income (US whites)

Source: ANES 2016. Controls: age, education, 2012 vote.

of the coin is that people who want liberal immigration, or think the past wasn't better than the present, are especially sour on Trump. My PX–YouGov 2016 data suggests liberal immigration opinion predicts 22 per cent of the variation in hard opposition to Trump while restrictive immigration attitudes predict 12 per cent of the variation in strong support for him. These numbers may not sound like much but are extremely powerful results for this kind of research. Immigration was also crucial for voters who shifted from voting for Obama or not voting in 2012 to voting Trump in 2016. Figure 3.8 shows that anti-immigration Obama voters were more inclined to switch to Trump than pro-immigration Romney voters were to switch to Clinton. Overall, the issue was a winner for the reality-TV mogul.

How much of a realignment was there? In the 2012 ANES, 47 per cent of whites who reported voting for Romney wanted immigration reduced. In the 2016 ANES, 63 per cent of people who said they voted for Romney in 2012 wanted immigration reduced. This suggests events and GOP cueing during 2012–16 moved Romney voters' opinion in the direction of restriction by 16 points. Opposition to immigration rises to 77 per cent across all 2016 Trump voters. Thus 14 points of the rise

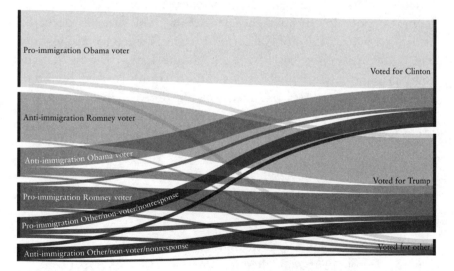

3.8. Shifts between 2012 and 2016 elections among those wanting immigration reduced or same/increase

Source: ANES 2016, using RAWGraphs.io.

(77 minus 63) is a result of switching. This tells us roughly half the increase in white Republican opposition to immigration between 2012 and 2016 was due to switching. The other half has to do with the changing content of conservatives' beliefs due to a combination of events such as the 2014 Central American child refugees, Trump's cues to Republican voters or the rising prominence of anti-immigration messaging on right-wing outlets like Fox. On the Democratic side, party and media cueing (including the response to Trump) rather than switching seem to account for the lion's share of attitude liberalization.

MINORITY TRUMP VOTERS

As in Britain, an important share of minorities in America want reduced immigration. In my PX–YouGov data, for instance, 39 per cent of African-Americans and 36 per cent of Latinos want less immigration. In the ANES, the figures are 33 and 31 per cent respectively. Trump surprised pollsters by taking 28 per cent of the Latino vote, without which he could not have won the election. This was a small improvement on Romney's performance with Hispanics and defied the conventional wisdom that Trump's remarks about Mexicans would lead to a crash in Latino support. It appears something similar took place as occurred as in 1994 when a third of California Hispanics voted for Proposition 187.[116] Immigration seems key to explaining Latino voting in both contests – anti-immigration Latinos enthusiastically backed Trump in a way restrictionist African-Americans did not. For instance, in the ANES, around half of Latinos who say immigration should be reduced voted for Trump, but this is true of only 10 per cent of restrictionist blacks. In the PX data, restrictionist Latinos score Trump a 5.1 out of 10 compared to 1.9 for Latinos who want current or higher immigration levels. Among blacks, the differences are not statistically significant in models: 2.1 out of 10 for restrictionists and 1.6 for others. This means restrictionist Latinos are marginally closer to Trump than the median white voter but less so than restrictionist whites, who rated Trump a 6.4 out of 10 and voted for him to the tune of 77 per cent.

While Latino restrictionists were undoubtedly motivated by economic considerations as well as intra-Latino social divides, I would argue that at least some were attached to the white ethno-tradition.

That is, they felt warmly about an America in which the majority of the population is non-Hispanic white. I asked a small opt-in sample of thirty minority Republicans on Prolific Academic how sad they felt on a 0–100 scale when they heard that the US would 'lose its white majority' by 2042. The average score was 47, with a score of 50 for Latinos. This was noticeably less than the 67 out of 100 among the fifty-five white Trump voters in the same sample and a bit lower than the 54/100 among the fifty white Trump voters in an MTurk sample where I asked the same question. But it was markedly higher than the 20/100 recorded for white Clinton voters or the 13/100 for the forty mainly Democrat minority voters in my MTurk sample.

This echoes the views of some 300 Hispanic and Asian Trump voters in a University of Virginia survey in which over half endorsed the idea that the US needed to 'protect and preserve its white European heritage'.[117] It chimes with work which finds that Hispanics are more likely than whites to say that being white and Christian are important to being 'truly' American.[118] It seems that minority Republicans are more attached to the white tradition of American nationhood than white Democrats. All of which underscores the difference between white ethno-traditional nationalism, which can be embraced by someone of any background, and white ethnicity, which is open only to those with at least some European ancestry. The decline of whites is experienced twice over by conservative white Americans: as ethnic loss and as national loss. Conservative minorities feel it only as national loss, hence their lower 'sadness' score.

IMMIGRATION SALIENCE, NOT IMMIGRATION ATTITUDES

Earlier I noted the importance of the *salience* of immigration for populist-right support, and not just attitudes about whether it should be increased or reduced. Immigration was the top issue for 10 per cent of white American voters in my mid-August 2016 PX–YouGov survey, high by post-1965 standards but low compared to Britain, where 20 per cent of white British voters said immigration was their most important issue. Importantly, immigration was the top issue for 25 per cent of those ranking Trump a perfect 10, a higher level than the white British average. Against this, only 2 per cent of the considerable number of white voters rating Trump a zero said immigration was the country's most important challenge, a 10 to 1 gap between strong Trump supporters and strong opponents.

Having said this, immigration is still not as prominent an issue in Trumpist America as it is in Brexit Britain. As in Britain, those taking the PX survey were asked to read a passage about the country becoming increasingly diverse, or managing to assimilate its immigrants. But the reassuring paragraph did not lead to a softening in American attitudes as it did in Britain. Instead, white anti-immigration voters who read *either* the 'alarming' or reassuring passage responded with significantly elevated immigration salience. That is, while 14 per cent of whites who want immigration reduced a lot but read no paragraph said it was their most important issue, this rose to 24 per cent among whites who read either the alarming or reassuring immigration message. Much of this increase seemed to come from those who would have named terrorism their top issue but when reading an immigration passage switched their priority to immigration.

The fact that reading a short immigration passage can significantly boost the ranking of immigration as a concern among anti-immigration whites suggests it has not reached the same saturation point in the American conservative consciousness that it has in Europe. Much will depend on how committed right-wing media and political elites are to the immigration-restriction narrative. If there is sustained momentum, spreading beyond anti-immigration pundits such as Tucker Carlson or Anne Coulter, then immigration has room to become even more important. If key anti-immigration figures in the administration such as Jeff Sessions and Stephen Miller are able to persuade Trump to keep anti-immigration rhetoric to the fore and downplay foreign policy threats like Russia and ISIS, this too could change the conversation on the right. A lot also depends on whether Trump's example shifts the message and priorities of future Republican primary candidates.

Next to immigration, 'left behind' issues are a busted flush. Just 4 per cent of whites who ranked Trump 10 out of 10 said inequality was the country's most important problem. Contrast this with the 40 per cent of those scoring him a zero who said inequality was the top issue, a tenfold difference. Compared to inequality and immigration, even the gap on terrorism, at around two to one, fades into insignificance.

The vote for Trump also doesn't seem to reflect a revolt against the rich and powerful. In Britain we saw that all measures of generalized anti-elitism failed to identify Brexit voters.

In March 2017, I asked 361 white American voters on MTurk, 'What annoys you most about the American elite?' Respondents could answer 'they don't annoy me', 'they are rich and powerful' or 'they are politically correct'. Clinton voters were actually marginally more annoyed by the American elite (64 to 60 per cent) than Trump voters, though this is not statistically significant. There is a current of resentment of the rich and powerful that runs through American society, but only 27 per cent of my sample of Trump voters said elites annoyed them because 'they are rich and powerful' whereas 55 per cent of Clinton voters did. On the other hand, 34 per cent of Trump voters but just 9 per cent of Clinton voters said it was the political correctness of elites that annoyed them. Thus Trump support, like Brexit, is distinctive in its opposition to *liberal* elites, not the elite in general, whom many voters from all parties dislike.

Ethnic change is central to explaining Trump's victory. We already noted how local anti-immigration ordinances tended to spring up in communities undergoing rapid ethnic change. Political scientist Dan Hopkins finds that, comparing two communities with identical characteristics, one which experienced an 8-point increase in immigrants in the 1990s had a .66 chance of adopting an anti-illegal immigration ordinance compared to .37 for one with no immigrant increase.[119] The political psychologists Eric Knowles and Linda Tropp suggest ethnic change tends to highlight people's sense of white identity. They asked 1,700 white Americans five questions about white identity including 'Being a white person is an important part of how I see myself' and 'I feel solidarity with other white people.' This was used to create an index with a range from 1, low white identity, to 5, high white identity. Whites in neighbourhoods with no Latinos scored a 3.1 out of 5 for white identity while those in neighbourhoods which were half Latino scored around 3.6, a significant difference. Moreover, during Trump's leadership bid, whites' propensity to support him rises from 20 per cent in a neighbourhood without Hispanics to 35 per cent in a half-Hispanic neighbourhood.[120]

Ethnic change also affects the politically vital *salience* of immigration in voters' minds. In my PX–YouGov data, ethnic change increases the importance of the immigration issue among voters who prefer less immigration. The threat effect is curvilinear: modest in areas changing a bit, but high in fast-changing locales. This accords with a large volume of work that shows that rapid ethnic change increases anti-immigration feeling.[121] For high-Latino areas that may not be changing so fast, there is a different effect. I find that whites in high-Latino neighbourhoods (ZIP codes) who are opposed to immigration are far more likely to say it is the most important issue facing the country when primed by reading an alarmist *or* reassuring paragraph on immigration. An anti-immigration white person in a neighbourhood with no Latinos who reads about immigration has a 12 per cent chance of calling it the nation's top issue; this soars threefold to 36 per cent among the same people in half-Latino neighbourhoods. This may explain why white attitudes to immigration polarized more between 2012 and 2016 in high-immigrant California than in the country as a whole.

More generally, many white Americans already think whites are a minority of the population.[122] Duke political scientist Ashley Jardina finds, across a range of surveys, that the share of whites who say white identity is 'very' or 'moderately' important to them almost doubled between the 1990s and 2010s – to the point that 45–65 per cent now say it matters. This is especially the case among authoritarian or low-openness whites, those who would be categorized as Settlers by Pat Dade. Older and southern whites also have stronger white identities, but, critically, identification as white is not related to antipathy to outgroups. This suggests that the common view that white identity leads to a dislike of minorities is misplaced.[123] Similarly, in the ANES, warmth towards whites is correlated with warmth towards both blacks and Latinos. A positive feeling towards whites, much more than negative feelings towards minorities, predicts whether a white person voted for Trump or wants less immigration. Only antipathy to Muslims has a similar (or slightly stronger) effect in predicting a Trump vote.

Many survey experiments which allocate one group of whites to read a news report or passage about whites' declining share of the population find that the group which reads about white decline experiences a higher sense of ethnic threat. In one study, whites who read about group demise expressed greater Republican identification and stronger support for conservative policies.[124] Other studies find that whites who read about their group's decline are significantly more likely to support the Tea Party. In addition, the effect is stronger for passages about white demographic decline than for fictional paragraphs which talk about whites losing their economic advantage, though both predict higher Tea Party support.[125] The effect is especially noticeable among high-identifying whites. Jardina finds a big jump in high-identifying whites' reported fear on a 0 to 1 scale, from .1 to almost .5, when they read about white demographic decline. These whites also reported higher anger and lower enthusiasm after reading the news story.[126]

THE MUSLIM FACTOR

Immigration is key for Trump support, but questions that combine opposition to immigration with an anti-Muslim security dimension are even more potent. In the January 2016 ANES pilot survey, 70 per cent of 301 whites who scored Trump above a 72 out of 100 said they greatly opposed Syrian refugees coming to live in America compared to a mere 10 per cent among the 302 whites scoring him less than 10 out of 100. The 2016 ANES shows that white Americans rate Muslims a 52 out of 100, considerably cooler than the 66 out of 100 accorded to Latinos. For the first time in the ANES series, coolness towards Muslims exceeded antipathy to Latinos as a predictor of the desire to reduce immigration. The new mood is reflected in Trump's 'total and complete shutdown of Muslims entering the United States' declaration in 2015 following a jihadi bombing at an Orlando gay nightclub. It also registered in his hastily implemented attempt in January 2017 to bar travellers from seven Muslim-majority countries from entering the United States.

Trump's legislation was not a Muslim ban but a seven-country travel order that quietly avoided targeting Saudi Arabia and other foreign policy allies with arguably more fundamentalist religious philosophies than the countries on the list. The first iteration of Trump's ban included an explicit preference for Christian over Muslim refugees and did not exempt green-card holders. It was struck down by the courts for discriminating among those already resident in the country (green-card holders). In late June, a suitably reformed version passed scrutiny and went into operation, affecting all travellers entering from Syria, Iran, Libya, Somalia, Sudan and Yemen apart from those with valid green cards.[127] The new legislation included a refugee cap of 50,000, a considerable decline from the previous ceiling of 110,000. Trump also attempted to enact a four-month freeze on all admissions through an Executive Order. Trump's freeze was stayed by federal judges and the case was appealed to the Supreme Court on the grounds that Trump's ban violates the right to equal treatment regardless of religion or race.

At stake is a key principle: whether the United States can select its immigrants on the basis of cultural criteria. This was clearly the case in the past with legislation such as National Origins or Chinese Exclusion. Trump even cited FDR's use of the Alien and Sedition Acts during the Second World War (in which German, Japanese and Italian-American citizens were incarcerated – though Trump criticized Japanese internment) as a precedent for his legislation. Many assume – because of the way anti-racism norms around Civil Rights came to be applied to the immigration issue – that the law prevents the country from selecting immigrants on the basis of cultural criteria. Trump's anti-Muslim tone was cited as evidence for the anti-religious motivation behind the ban. The Supreme Court, in contrast to more liberal lower courts, was not persuaded by this anti-discrimination line of reasoning. In a 5–4 decision that broke on ideological lines, it ruled that presidents have wide leeway to set immigration policy in the national interest.[128]

Trump's election has resulted in a tighter enforcement of immigration laws and a crackdown on 'sanctuary cities'. His Executive Order in January 2017 expanded the definition of those eligible for deportation to include minor felonies. As a result, ICE agents arrested 38 per cent more people in Trump's first 100 days than in the analogous period in 2016.[129] The number of illegal immigrants apprehended on the southern border in 2017 was half the level of 2016, which may indicate a deterrence effect.[130] Meanwhile, Trump appointee Stephen Miller is working on a bill with Senators Tom Cotton of Arkansas and David Perdue of Georgia to slash legal immigration from 1 million to 500,000 per year. If successful, this would represent a historic interruption of the post-1965 pro-immigration consensus: the first reduction in numbers since 1965 and a return to immigration levels not seen since the 1960s. In addition to its practical ramifications, the move is pregnant with symbolism because it politicizes legal immigration, a topic once considered outside the Overton Window of acceptable debate in American politics.

Between the Wall, cuts to legal immigration and the fate of the DREAMers – whose Obama-era protection from deportation was set to expire – immigration had become the central point of contention in American politics. In January 2018, the Democrats and Republicans failed to agree over the fate of the DREAMers, whom the Republicans promised to protect in exchange for concessions on the Wall and reductions in legal immigration. This produced a government shutdown. In effect, the Democrats were willing to see government – traditionally a Democratic bastion – go unfunded to force the Republicans to grant unconditional protection to the DREAMers. This tactic failed, and while an extension was passed, a further shutdown remains a possibility. Meanwhile the minority of pro-immigration Republicans in Congress joined with the Democrats to rebuff Trump's immigration proposals, preventing the Trump administration from getting the votes they needed despite the Republicans' congressional majority. As a result, the newly ascendant populist wing of the Republican Party is attempting to oust pro-immigration Republicans in local primaries to increase the likelihood of immigration restriction succeeding in the future.

Immigration remains a flashpoint for other reasons. In June 2018, facing a spike in Central American child and family refugees, the Trump administration began separating children from parents caught crossing illegally. According to a liberal court ruling, the Flores Agreement, children are not permitted to join parents in detention but must be released to accredited childcare or sponsors. This means children are divided from criminal parents as a matter of course. Thus when illegal immigration becomes a crime and parents are detained, more children wind up with extended family or carers. Trump's decision to alter first-time illegal crossing from a civil misdemeanour to a criminal felony did not invent the practice of separation but it did increase the number of family separations by over 2,000 in a six-week period, a much higher rate than under the Obama or Bush administrations.[131] A majority of Americans oppose the policy of separation, but a narrow majority also blame migrant parents more than Trump. In both instances, opinion splits sharply along partisan lines. For instance, 72 per cent of Trump voters deemed separations acceptable compared to only 4 per cent of Clinton voters; 83 per cent of Trump voters said parents of migrants were to blame for separations, compared to only 19 per cent of Clinton voters.[132] The separations also led to polarized reporting, which implied that separations were a new tactic designed to increase deterrence. Unfortunately, parts of the American mainstream media – which is reliable despite having a liberal tilt – allowed emotion to run away with the truth. In one case, *Time* magazine's cover showed a crying child looking up at President Trump. This was based on a picture which had gone viral, and which *Time* claimed, erroneously, involved the child being dragged from its parents. Even after publishing a correction, the magazine continued to defend the publication of the photo. Given Trump's oft-repeated and usually false charge of 'fake news', *Time*'s refusal to admit it made a mistake is disheartening.[133]

Trump's move is part of a series of reforms to end 'catch and release', an approach which permits illegal immigrants to enter society as their cases are processed, which often results in them disappearing into the US. Ideally, families would remain intact as asylum cases are adjudicated, but this can take years due to a backlogged system. Meanwhile, the 1997 Flores ruling and 2016 follow-up decision stipulate that children may be held for no more than twenty days, whether alone or as part of a family. It may even be interpreted as encouraging children to be separated and sent to relatives rather than remaining in custody with their parents. While Bush and Obama opted to allow the families of those caught crossing illegally the first time to remain intact until the twenty-day limit expired, then be released into the country, Trump initially chose the harsher alternative of separating the children, which expedites the processing of adult claims – most of which fail – to a month or two. Many argue the separations were designed to act as a deterrent, but it's also true the administration was compelled by liberal judicial decisions to separate families if it wished to speed up asylum processing and avoid releasing claimants into the US. A subsequent agreement between the government and ACLU lawyers enabled interned parents to waive the Flores mandatory-separation provision, allowing them to be reunited with their children beyond the twenty-day limit. The upshot is that Trump's administration moved the enforcement vs humanitarianism dial in the direction of the former.[134]

Some claim Trump's policy was spearheaded by Jeff Sessions and Stephen Miller. Regardless, it produced the tragic separation of thousands of children from parents, resulting in anguished scenes which were broadcast on television. The combination of Trump's enforcement policies, an underfunded asylum system and liberal judicial rulings caught the children in a vice. Democrats and some Republicans railed against the measure, while the administration was accused of using the kids as pawns in a struggle to secure backing for the Wall and deter future migrants. It's fair to say that the Trump administration should have anticipated the increase in scale and acted sooner to build more facilities for family detention to avoid having to separate families. Following adverse coverage, Trump responded with an executive order doing precisely this – though the action will most likely violate the judicial rulings mandating family (read: child) detention periods of under twenty days. The saga is not over.

A more humane solution that has a fairly high success rate in ensuring claimants turn up for their asylum hearings is ankle bracelets for those released pending their hearings, though it is not clear if Trump is willing to stomach the 20 per cent slippage rate. Is the problem similar to the ones which led to the EU–Turkey deal and Australia's 'Stop the Boats' policy? Namely, that if people can enter, make an asylum claim, and stay, this will incentivize others, overloading the system. Perhaps. Yet it is unclear whether Latin America is poor enough or demographically buoyant enough to generate a migrant crisis: the million refugees from chaotic post-Chavez Venezuela have opted for Colombia and Brazil, while Nicaraguans prefer Costa Rica. This leaves only Guatemala, Honduras and El Salvador, three relatively small entities, as source countries. Even here, Guatemalans sometimes choose Belize, rather than the US. Relatively prosperous Costa Rica and Panama are not far away.

More broadly, a sensible compromise on the fate of the country's 11 million undocumented is needed. The idea of an amnesty or 'path to citizenship' is anathema to most Republicans. But things need not be so binary. One possibility could be to offer a kind of second-tier citizenship to non-DREAMers who have been in the country for a period of, say, five or ten years. This official status would protect them from deportation (apart from major crimes) and allow them to access social services, jobs, banking and housing. However, in recognition of the fact they broke the law to enter, it would deny them membership in the nation and the right to vote. DREAMer citizens would be unable to sponsor undocumented relatives for citizenship. Alongside border-strengthening policies such as the Wall and employer measures like E-Verify, this would minister to Trump voters' symbolic desire to preserve a nation of laws while also addressing their concerns about the adverse electoral impact of the new residents. Needless to say, much depends on future illegal inflows. There is now a greater sensitivity to illegal immigration, but if flows return to the lower levels of 2016, this may make it easier to liberalize policy towards those already in the country.

THE NEW RESTRICTIONIST ELITE

For the first time in recent memory, conservative voters were more fired up about immigration than about religious questions. The secularization of American cultural conservatism was bringing it into line with the European right, for which immigration and Islam had long eclipsed questions of religion. Increasingly, on blogs and in politics, the populist right on both sides of the Atlantic riff off each other. Intellectually, right-wing talk radio, cable news and websites are giving increased oxygen to immigration and fears about the spectre of Islam in the West. A new online movement, the alt-right, sprang up around figures like Richard Spencer. Though the alt-right had only limited reach, a less radical but more influential restrictionist elite emerged online and in the right-wing media. Popular right-wing bloggers like Ann Coulter or Mike Cernovich, with followers numbering in the millions, routinely flag violent incidents involving illegal Hispanic immigrants and Muslims.

At the institutional level, Trump adviser Steve Bannon, though forced out of both Trump's White House and Breitbart News, helped lay the groundwork for the new cultural nationalism. Bannon was influenced by Jean Raspail's apocalyptic novel about a Third World immigrant invasion of France called *The Camp of the Saints* (1973) and was well versed in 'counter-jihadist' currents of European thought.[135] All successful nationalist movements require cultural elites, and while the new online right is less anchored in class and institutions than the patrician Immigration Restriction League of Henry Cabot Lodge's day it still constitutes a coherent network.

Bannon's anti-immigration approach was important for Trump's long-shot presidential bid which succeeded against all odds, bringing paleoconservative-cum-alt-right ideas into the heart of the Oval Office. Trump's outrageous comments about Muslims and Mexicans walked all over the taboos which had previously defined the limits of public discourse. Ethno-traditionalist and racist 'voice' had 'trumped' elite norms within the Republican Party and wider political arena which viewed the politicization of immigration as deviant. The fact that Trump was elected despite his comments sent a signal to many conservative voters that others shared their antipathy to political correctness and, for some, fear of minorities. This stretched the Overton Window still further, numbing the sting of anti-racism, emboldening other conservative voters and propelling a self-fulfilling dynamic. In chapter 8, I chart the erosion of the anti-racism norm around multiculturalism and immigration in the West. I also ask whether an expansive definition of racism, which depicts expressions of white group interest as racist, aggravates the white backlash.

Importantly, even Trump has not transgressed the anti-nativism taboo by directly invoking an ethnocultural rationale for restriction, citing materialist worries about terrorism, crime and welfare dependency instead. However, Europe can serve as a safe neutral screen upon which conservative white Americans may project their sense of ethno-cultural dispossession. These sublimated ethno-traditional concerns surfaced when Trump visited Britain in July 2018. 'Allowing the immigration to take place in Europe is a shame,' he told the *Sun*, a British tabloid newspaper. 'I think it changed the fabric of Europe and, unless you act very quickly, it's never going to be what it was ... I think you are losing your culture.'[136]

The changing racial demographics of America could permit the Democrats to consistently win first the presidential, then congressional, elections. Alternatively, the Republican establishment may be able to install a pro-immigration primary candidate. But is this a solution? With no federal outlet for white identity concerns or ethno-traditional nationalism, and with a return to policies of multiculturalism and high immigration which are viewed as a threat to these identities, it's possible the culturally conservative section of the US population could start viewing the government as an enemy. This is an old trope in American history and could pose a security problem. It is also how violent ethnic conflict sometimes ignites. For instance, the British-Protestant majority in Northern Ireland, where parties run on ethnic lines, meant Irish Catholics lost every election in the province between 1922 and the abolition of the Northern Ireland provincial government in 1972. This lack of political representation produced alienation which helped foment the civil war in 1969. What happens if rural and red-state America is permanently frozen out of power when it considers itself the repository of authentic Americanism?

The American hinterland is unlikely to support white terrorism, but Republican states or rural districts may become openly antagonistic towards the 'alien' federal government and the cities. As I'll argue, it would be far better if a transracial 'white' or 'American' majority could be forged which bridges rural and urban, as occurred when the largely rural Protestant population fused with predominantly urban Catholics and Jews to form a new white majority between the 1960s and 1980s.

4

Britain: The Erosion of English Reserve

On Thursday, 23 June 2016, Britain voted to leave the European Union (EU) by a 52–48 margin. It was a shock vote. Polling experts and those campaigning to Remain in the EU, including the Prime Minister, David Cameron, were confident the Remain side would win. In the 2014 referendum on Scottish independence, Scottish voters decisively rejected independence by a healthy 55 per cent to 45 per cent despite polls showing the two sides running neck and neck. Convinced that pragmatic British voters would err on the side of caution, Remain campaigners felt sure their warnings of the dire economic consequences of 'Brexit' would prove decisive. As in the Scottish referendum, polls had shown the two sides to be running a dead heat. But this time round British voters rejected the status quo and chose to leave the EU. Many in the white British ethnic majority had grown increasingly restive about the country's historically high immigration levels. They were persuaded that Brexit offered them control over immigration and a chance to reduce numbers and 'get their country back'. Referendum turnout was high – at 72 per cent – and the 4-point margin was sufficiently large to allay fears that the vote was too close to call. Anti-immigration populism had been viewed as a sporadic but manageable nuisance in Western politics. Now it punched into the real economy, damaging the interests elites really cared about.

I've lived in London since 1993, and have followed immigration and integration debates quite closely, so I've experienced much of what follows first hand. The idea that something as opaque as cultural nationalism could affect concrete economic relationships, such as the lucrative trade between Britain and the European Union, stunned London's financial and political elite. Finance is a pillar of Britain's economy, paying 11 per cent of the nation's tax bills. Forty-four per cent of Britain's exports (£222 billion) go to the EU, while the EU exports £290bn to Britain. London serves as the EU's financial capital, with many European and overseas firms locating there to leverage London's EU and global connections. Used to operating within an insulated world of economic policy, the city's bankers woke up to a revolt from the world outside. They immediately feared for the future of the City of London financial district, and worried that their banks would lose their right to offer financial services in other EU countries.

Outside of Scotland and Catholic areas of Northern Ireland, where separatist leaders urged a Remain vote, only London, major cities and college towns – with their young, diverse, highly educated populations – voted Remain.[1] According to Chris Hanretty, 421 of 574 constituencies in England and Wales voted to leave.[2] Few could pretend politics could still be 'managed' so that London's financial elite remained unscathed. Despite a chorus of elite voices from the Prime Minister, David Cameron, to the Bank of England's Mark Carney to most of the elite news media, Brexit forces prevailed. Cultural issues had rudely intruded into the economic sphere.

Britain had voted instrumentally to approve membership in the EEC, forerunner to the EU, in 1975. The country's economy was weak, hobbled by powerful unions, and many looked to the booming EEC as a lifeline. Britain's role in balancing European conflicts, its long history of democracy and its ties to the Anglosphere mean it has never felt as warmly about the European project as its continental partners. It has been an awkward, foot-dragging member of the EU, sceptical of the dreams of some Euro-federalists in the European Commission and European Parliament that the EU might one day supersede the nation-state.

While Britain's jaded view of the EU stands out, its immigration politics is fairly typical of many West European countries. Immigration has never been popular with most, especially among the white British ethnic majority. Economic, liberal and humanitarian motivations periodically opened the door to waves of immigration from the late nineteenth century onwards, but numbers were typically small. Only the internal migration of Irish Catholics to west-central Scotland between the mid-nineteenth century and the 1950s can compare to what is currently under way. Modest levels of Afro-Caribbean and South Asian immigration in the 1950s and 1960s proved a hot-button political issue. Thereafter, it was not until the late 1990s that the country began to receive large numbers. While the UK's 2016 net immigration figure of 248,000 per annum is considerably smaller in per capita terms than Canada's or Sweden's, it represents a major increase over the modest inflows of around 50,000 prevailing between the 1970s and the mid-1990s.

Today's historically high immigration is changing the composition of Britain's population, especially its cities, keeping the issue at the top of voters' priority lists. At the same time, the rising minority presence is reconfiguring patterns of internal migration and residential segregation. White Britons, especially families, are choosing relatively white schools and neighbourhoods, which is resulting in a growing number of superdiverse urban zones where whites are a shrinking minority. On the other hand, the encounter between majorities and minorities is also producing unprecedented levels of inter-ethnic mixing. One in eight households in England and Wales contain more than one ethnic group, rising to nearly one in five in London. Twelve per cent of couples are inter-ethnic among those under fifty, compared to 6 per cent among the over-fifties.[3] Those of mixed race, especially people of white and black Caribbean ancestry such as novelist Zadie Smith, are common, offering a foretaste of Britain's future majority population.

Meanwhile, continuing inflows have combined with pressure from the tabloid media and populist parties to change the conversation around immigration and multiculturalism. Britain, partly due to its competitive media tradition, never adopted as restrictive a set of norms around the discussion of immigration as some other Western countries. Since the 1960s, its politicians have generally sought to quietly limit immigration rather than pursue a strategy of 'moral leadership' to facilitate larger inflows. At the same time, British parties had been reluctant to explicitly campaign to reduce immigration. The accession of Tony Blair's Labour government to power in 1997 saw a departure from past practice, as Blair sought to win support for higher numbers on the back of a more open conception of Britishness. The backlash against this move opened the way for the right to openly court the anti-immigration vote, modifying Britain's political culture.

ANTI-IMMIGRATION POLITICS IN
HISTORICAL PERSPECTIVE

Immigrants had arrived in Britain since the 1600s, but numbers were not large as a proportion of the total population. Pogrom-era Jewish immigration, for instance, never numbered more than 10,000 per year to Britain around the turn of the twentieth century.[4] Current figures, even adjusting for Britain's smaller population at the time, are about twenty times larger. Despite this, the cultural distance and concentrated arrival of Jews in specific locales, such as East London, provoked some unrest. The British Brothers League, a restrictionist organization, was formed in 1902 with the support of important politicians, and their marches, agitation and media campaigns for restriction led to the 1905 Aliens Act, the first immigration control bill in the UK. Critically, the bill did not bar immigration from Eastern Europe and continued to permit those who could prove their ability to support themselves, as well as those fleeing persecution, to immigrate. Nevertheless, numbers remained small and some Jews moved on to America. The foreign-born share of the population remained under 2 per cent until after 1945, and stood at a mere 6 per cent as recently as 1991.

The one exception to the small-numbers rule were the Irish in Scotland. Ireland was part of Great Britain until 1922, but its population was mainly Catholic, a major cultural difference from largely Protestant England, Wales and Scotland. Scotland, as a small nation with a population similar in size to Ireland's in the nineteenth century, felt the impact of Irish immigration especially keenly. Even after Irish independence in 1922, the Irish retained the right to move to Britain and many crossed the Irish Sea to the industrial centre of Glasgow in west-central Scotland. Irish numbers grew consistently, drawn by the demand for labour in the country's industrial belt. As a result, between 1861 and 1961, the Catholic share of Scotland's population nearly doubled, from 9 to 17 per cent. In the greater Glasgow area, the proportion of Irish Catholics reached a third of the total.

This cultural demography was fertile soil for the growth of anti-Catholicism and a politics in which sectarianism cross-cut the left–right economic divide. In contrast to much of Britain, where economic divisions were paramount for politics, the strength of the Conservative

Party in central Scotland in the first half of the twentieth century lay in its cultural appeal to Protestant Scots. This included many Protestant workers, natural Labour voters who opposed the aspirations of Catholics and Irish nationalists. In the early 1930s, Alexander Ratcliffe's Scottish Protestant League in Glasgow, and John Cormack's Protestant Action in Edinburgh won as much as a third of the Protestant vote in municipal elections. Though these right-wing populists were opposed by the quasi-established Presbyterian Church of Scotland, known as the Kirk, it – along with establishment figures such as novelist John Buchan – actively petitioned the British Parliament to cut off immigration from Ireland. In 1923, the Church of Scotland issued a report entitled *On the Menace of the Irish Race to our Scottish Nationality*. Many in the Scots-Protestant majority feared that Irish Catholic immigration, in tandem with Scottish-Protestant emigration overseas, would for ever alter the ethnic and religious composition of their nation. World War II, secularization, slower immigration and growing intermarriage eased majority worries after the 1950s, though a ritualized form of ethnic conflict persists in the 'Old Firm' Glasgow football rivalry between Catholic-supported Celtic and Protestant-backed Rangers.[5]

Brian Gratton argues in the US case that, whenever the cultural distance or volume of immigration increases beyond a certain level, pressure tends to build for restriction.[6] The next wave of immigration to Britain to meet these criteria was the arrival, after 1948, of workers from British colonies in the Caribbean and Indian subcontinent. Around half a million came between 1955 and 1962, whereupon the Commonwealth Immigrants Act was passed, which ended the right of Commonwealth citizens to automatically enter Britain. From then on, about 75,000 entered per year, dropping to about 55,000 in the 1980s and early 1990s.[7] In 1992, just 27,000 of the 52,000 admitted came from the Asian, African and Caribbean New Commonwealth countries.[8]

The increase in the non-white population from a negligible amount before the war to around 2 per cent of the total in 1971 was enough to prompt considerable anti-immigrant hostility. The 1958 anti-black race riots in London's Notting Hill showed that tolerance was limited and racial prejudice widespread. In this climate, many politicians could see that it was important to enact anti-racism legislation. What is fascinating, however, is the extent of the rift between a small elite at Cabinet level in both the Conservative and Labour parties and the masses,

represented – in areas affected by immigration – by backbench populists. An older colonial-turned-Commonwealth sense of Britishness,
prevalent among the elite, made them sensitive to colonial opinion and
reluctant to restrict immigration between overseas possessions and
Britain. They were loath to restrict the rights of Canadians, Australians and New Zealanders to move to Britain, cherishing the idea that
these were components of an integrated unionist whole. Yet while privately few considered non-white colonies to be British in the same way,
they felt that open legislative discrimination in favour of the white
Commonwealth – as was the practice in these countries (and the US) –
would inflame opinion in 'New Commonwealth' countries like Jamaica.

While realism in international relations explains much of Britain's
openness in the 1950s and early 1960s, the liberal wing of the Labour
Party, together with left-liberal journals like the *New Statesman* and
immigrant advocacy groups, advocated free movement and tended to
attack restrictions as racist. Crucially, many did not draw a distinction
between equal treatment within Britain and non-discrimination in
immigration. Limiting the numbers of immigrants came to be associated with formal discrimination between white and non-white sources.
Yet many British politicians privately recognized that permitting colonial
subjects to migrate freely to Britain would cause a populist backlash.
In 1961, the Conservative government instigated the Commonwealth
Immigrants Act to control the migration of British colonial subjects to
Britain. This in practice meant those from the West Indies or other
non-white countries, with Ireland exempted. Without the legislation,
any resident of Jamaica, Hong Kong or other British colonies was free
to settle in Britain.

In late 1961 Labour's Hugh Gaitskell attacked the bill as 'a plain
anti-colour measure', promising to repeal it. His colleague Patrick
Gordon Walker called it 'open race discrimination'. The Tory elite was
sensitive to such charges and took steps to argue that it was also controlling Irish immigration, indicating their agreement with the view
that non-whites should not be excluded from Britain. Yet, despite its
rhetoric, Labour quietly dropped its opposition to the Act in 1962.[9] It
seems non-discrimination and free movement within the Empire could
be defended only when the numbers who took advantage of this freedom remained small. This recalls the words of Charles de Gaulle in
1959: 'It is very good that there are yellow French, black French, brown

French. They show that France is open to all races and has a universal vocation. But [it is good] on condition that they remain a small minority. Otherwise, France would no longer be France.'[10]

Continued immigration exposed the fiction that non-white immigration would soon come to an end. These concerns were galvanized by the radical pronouncements of the politician Enoch Powell in his infamous 'Rivers of Blood' speech of 1968. Here the Cambridge-educated Powell delivered a populist-right sermon *avant la lettre*. Most people voted for the two main parties, and the working class had secure employment. Elites were held in high regard. But Powell's message and the popular response to him is virtually indistinguishable from that of today's right-wing populists. This should make us wary of any theory which suggests that right-wing populism in Britain is driven by economic and political changes that have taken place since 1968.

At the core of Powell's message was a plea to protect the congruence between the English ethnic majority and the nation-state. He spoke of:

> areas that are already undergoing the total transformation to which there is no parallel in a thousand years of English history. We must be mad, literally mad, as a nation to be permitting the annual inflow of some 50,000 dependants, who are for the most part the material of the future growth of the immigrant-descended population. It is like watching a nation busily engaged in heaping up its own funeral pyre.

Powell urged the government to halt immigration and begin paying the Indian and Afro-Caribbean immigrants to return home, advocating a closed ethnic nationalism in which assimilation was unthinkable. Exclusion could be the only option.

Powell was also populist, drawing attention to the concerns of ordinary white working-class people. He spoke of his co-ethnics who were 'made strangers in their own country. They found their wives unable to obtain hospital beds in childbirth, their children unable to obtain school places, their homes and neighbourhoods changed beyond recognition, their plans and prospects for the future defeated ... more and more voices which told them that they were now the unwanted.' Here Powell intertwines people's sense of dispossession with commentary on the deleterious effects of immigration on the social services and economic condition of the white working class. This sounds strikingly similar to today's populist commentary on the 'left-behind' white working class.

In contrast, much of the Labour and Tory political elite accused Powell of racism. 'The flag of racialism which has been hoisted in Wolverhampton is beginning to look like the one that fluttered twenty-five years ago over Dachau and Belsen,' warned Labour MP Tony Benn. He suggested the Conservative leader, Ted Heath, was failing to take on Powell. 'If we do not speak up now against the filthy and obscene racialist propaganda ... the forces of hatred will mark up their first success and mobilize their first offensive.' The *Times* called it an 'evil speech'. Notice the emphasis on evoking emotions of disgust, signifying the violation of social taboos. The Holocaust was used as a warning of what could happen, with Britain's fight against fascism enlisted to legitimate opposition to Powell. In addition, the Civil Rights movement in the US – including the brutal southern white response – had begun to influence liberal left-wing politicians such as Roy Jenkins. Much of the Conservative Shadow Cabinet agreed, demanding Powell be fired from his post. Its right-wingers, however, dissented. Some, such as Gerald Nabarro, a Conservative MP of Sephardic Jewish origin who had converted to Christianity, used nakedly racist language, referring to the newcomers as 'buck nigger(s)'. Siding with most of his front bench, Heath removed Powell from his Shadow Cabinet position.

In centres of immigrant settlement such as London and Wolverhampton, the response to Powell's ousting was overwhelming. Tens of thousands wrote to him in support. Dock-workers in East London went on strike and over a thousand marched from East London to the Palace of Westminster where 300 entered the building and began verbally and physically abusing two East London MPs. A national survey found that 74 per cent agreed with Powell while just 15 per cent opposed him. In Powellism, we have all the ingredients in the right-wing populist cocktail. First, a liberal establishment, using the anti-racist taboo to defend an immigration policy which has not been sold to the people. Second, a populist leadership consisting of Powell and his defenders. Third, a popular base, representing the majority of public opinion.

Was Powell racist? Many didn't think so and some today continue to suggest he was right to raise the alarm. Powell's concerns have not gone away, and remain critical to explaining the populist ferment we witness today. In *The Trial of Enoch Powell*, a television programme aired on Channel 4 on the thirtieth anniversary of his speech, 64 per cent of the studio audience said he was not racist. This should make those of us who accuse him of racism think harder about what precisely it is that makes him guilty of the charge. Blanket condemnation and Nazi analogies, of the kind Benn proffered, are not – in my view – a productive way to make the case, especially in an anti-elitist era. Many have become jaded, and the racist charge is losing force. Benn's rhetoric may have helped sideline Powell, but it did not win hearts and minds. Benn and others should have acknowledged some of Powell's points while explaining clearly where and why his remarks were racist.

I define racism as an irrational fear or hatred of or prejudice against a member of another ethnic group, a violation of citizens' right to equal treatment without regard to race, or a desire for race purity. Violating this norm should disgust us. Powell called Black Britons 'wide-grinning pickaninnies', a derogatory term suggesting that blacks are inferior. He spoke of blacks gaining the 'whip hand' over whites, a fear-mongering proposition given the tiny numbers and benign intentions of the immigrants. He also called for minorities to be repatriated, clearly revealing that his conception of white British majority ethnicity was closed rather than open – based on a desire for race purity. Powell thus preferred exclusion to assimilation as his favoured mechanism of ethnic boundary maintenance. These facts make him racist.

Yet there are genuine majority grievances buried in Powell's message that are not racist. Powell's mention of neighbourhoods changing beyond recognition raises the valid point that the cultural impact of rapid immigration is perceived as negative by most whites in reception areas. The costs of immigration fall unevenly on the population and those affected feel they have no say in the matter – with injury augmented by the insult of being accused of racism. The government did try to direct more resources to the affected areas. However, it should have tried to win more hearts and minds to the idea of Commonwealth immigration. It might have used an assimilation story to reassure the majority population. Blacks had already been living in Liverpool and other British ports for generations and had readily intermarried into the local white population. The sense that the new waves of migration were small in national terms and could – as in the past – be absorbed through intermarriage is a message that, as we shall see, could have calmed nerves. At least this would have shown that the government empathized with those concerned about the ethno-cultural impact of immigration. Finally, the government might have planned for immigrant settlement rather than letting this occur in uncontrolled fashion. Ideally, migrants should have been housed in new developments with their own public facilities or in transient areas with prior experience of immigration.

At the height of Powellism, a mere 2 per cent of the population were non-white. My father-in-law, from Wigan in industrial north-west England, recalled that most people in the city around 1950 had never seen a black person and climbed poles to get a glimpse of black American soldiers. Even Powell recognized the localized impact of immigration in his speech. Despite the furore and public support for Powell, immigration was not a pressing issue for most. This highlights the crucial distinction between immigration attitudes and immigration *salience*. Most white Britons wanted little or no immigration, but aside from a few urban areas the issue was more distant from their everyday concerns than it is today. They had negative attitudes towards immigration, but the issue most likely ranked below other priorities like health care or wages. In the 1964 election, for instance, immigration played a role in just one constituency, Smethwick, near Birmingham. And among MPs only backbenchers from areas directly affected by immigration called for restriction, while those from the vast majority of the country where immigration was minimal followed the Cabinet's lead. Only in 1970, with Powell's intervention, did immigration emerge as an election issue, and even then its impact is disputed.[11] What has changed is not so much opposition to immigration – which is slightly lower than in the 1960s, reflecting broader liberal attitude changes attendant on growth in the university-educated liberal population – but the *salience* of the issue within the wider UK population. Once a social problem rises up people's list of priorities, it begins to affect election outcomes and structure ideological divisions.

THE RISING SALIENCE OF IMMIGRATION SINCE 1997

In 1970, two years after Powell, the British Election Study shows there was only a modest connection between party support and immigration attitudes. Fifty-one per cent of Labour and 55 per cent of Tory voters were 'very strongly' in favour of reducing immigration. Just 6 per cent of Tory voters and 10 per cent of Labour voters said there were 'not too many' immigrants. Only the supporters of the small Liberal Party, with 21 per cent saying 'not too many' and a mere 33 per cent strongly against, stood out. Through the 1970s, 1980s and 1990s, little changed. The share of people favouring lower immigration declined from around 90 per cent in 1970 to 70 per cent by 1990.[12] More importantly, few voters placed much importance on the issue. In 1975, when British voters cast their referendum ballots confirming membership in the European Economic Community (EEC), immigration opinion was completely disconnected from Euroscepticism. Even so, the leader of the Conservative Party, Margaret Thatcher, did not shy away from voicing her concerns over the issue. In a televised interview in 1978, just prior to the 1979 election, she opined that:

[If we go on] as we are then by the end of the century there would be four million people of the new Commonwealth or Pakistan here. Now, that is an awful lot and I think it means that people are really rather afraid that this country might be rather swamped by people with a different culture and, you know, the British character has done so much for democracy, for law and done so much throughout the world that if there is any fear that it might be swamped people are going to react and be rather hostile to those coming in . . . If you want good race relations, you have got to allay people's fears on numbers . . . We must hold out the clear prospect of an end to immigration because at the moment it is about between 45,000 and 50,000 people coming in a year . . . Every country can take some small minorities and in many ways they add to the richness and variety of this country. The moment the minority threatens to become a big one, people get frightened.

Thatcher's tough language was generally seen to have undercut the appeal of the far-right National Front. Despite a more measured tone than Powell, the underlying message here espouses a closed ethnonationalism. That is, that Britain is a white British ethnic nation which can accommodate small numbers of minorities for decoration but must maintain its ethno-national congruence through 'an end to immigration'. What is interesting is that Thatcher melded two arguments together, one about ethnicity, the other about British character and culture. In theory, culture could be acquired by ethnic outsiders and is thus a more inclusive rationale for reduction than simply saying white Britons must remain the overwhelming majority. Thatcher also mentioned population density as a further rationale for restriction.

While Thatcher's remarks were criticized on the left and were substantively the same as Powell's, they did not produce the kind of uproar that the latter's more emotive tone did. This indicates that the bandwidth of acceptable public opinion at the time was considerably broader in Britain than in North America or in much of Western Europe. The taboo against campaigning on immigration in most other Western countries was not breached until the 2000s, and then only by couching the argument in terms of threats to the poor or state interests. Yet, in Britain, Powell attacked immigration with vitriolic ethnocentric language, and was by no means the only British politician to do so. British exceptionalism may have to do with the wide range of opinion expressed by its freewheeling tabloid press. Yet it could also be due to the fact Britain's experience of immigration legislation was different from many others. It began the 1960s as the most liberal country on immigration due to free movement within its empire but was forced to confront the contradictions between this stance and the very real prospect of mass immigration. This arguably established the legitimacy of a politics of restrictionism for a new era. This was a very different institutional trajectory from North America's and Australasia's, where the politics of immigration started from a position of ethno-cultural preference and complete control and was pushed by the spirit of 1960s liberalism towards successively higher numbers and cultural neutrality, with the anti-racism taboo removing questions of cultural change from discussion. In Britain, a discourse of restrictionism was even established at the elite level, where quiet objections to immigration within Cabinet – referencing public opinion – were routinely voiced. This led the country to enact the most restrictive immigration policy of any major Western country between 1962 and 1997.[13]

Thatcher served as Prime Minister from 1979 to 1990. On the right of the party, the Monday Club, of which Powell was a strong supporter, launched an Immigration and Repatriation Policy Committee which seriously aired the idea of incentivizing non-whites to leave the country. Needless to say, repatriation was a mantra of the far-right National Front, in the late 1970s, and of its heir, the British National Party.

BRITAIN OPENS UP: THE BLAIR YEARS

In 1997, Tony Blair was elected Prime Minister on a modernizing plat-form. The economy had grown rapidly under Thatcher's premiership and London had developed into a lightly regulated centre of global finance. Blair sought to remake Labour as a social democratic party which could harness the fruits of global capitalism to ameliorate inequality rather than promote state intervention. He opted to ditch Clause IV of the Labour Party Constitution which emphasized state ownership. The youthful Blair, like his American contemporary Bill Clinton, appealed to the newly ascendant, presumably cosmopolitan, Baby Boomers. Blair's press secretary Alistair Campbell rebranded Labour as 'New Labour' and there was talk suggesting that Britain should be recast as 'Cool Britannia', a successful modern country, not a faded imperial power. Blair took the unorthodox step of inviting pop stars such as Noel Gallagher of the Britpop band Oasis to mingle with politicians at a reception in No. 10 Downing Street. A key component of Blair's approach was social liberalism, exemplified by a more open immigration policy and a rhetoric of multiculturalism.

The cultural liberalism of the 1960s was well represented in the upper echelons of Labour. In 2001, Blair's Foreign Secretary Robin Cook spoke of Britain as a global crossroads and a multicultural nation. 'The British are not a race, but a gathering of countless different races and communities, the vast majority of which were not indigenous to these islands.' He lauded Britain's 'diversity as expressed through . . . multiculturalism'. For Cook, chicken tikka masala was a symbol of modern Britain due to its fusion of Indian and British influences. In his somewhat London-centric speech, he referred to London's 300 languages and urged his countrymen to 'create an open and inclusive society that welcomes incomers for their contribution to our growth and prosperity'. He sought to deconstruct the notion of an ethnically homogeneous Anglo-Saxon England by pointing to Norman, Celtic and Norse waves of invaders. His remarks depicted a pluralistic, multi-ethnic Britain, increasingly diverse.

In doing so, he drew on a slender but influential liberal-cosmopolitan tradition. In 1700, Daniel Defoe spoke of the English as a mongrel race formed of waves of continental invaders: 'Thus from a mixture of all kinds began / That het'rogeneous thing, an Englishman.' By the 1960s, this melting-pot radicalism had morphed into an endorsement of multiculturalism as a permanent condition. Thus in 1966, as controversy swirled over New Commonwealth immigration, the Home Secretary, Roy Jenkins, a Welshman, replaced Defoe's melting pot with a multicultural vision:

> I do not regard [integration] as meaning the loss, by immigrants, of their own national characteristics and culture. I do not think that we need in this country a 'melting pot', which will turn everybody out in a common mould, as one of a series of carbon copies of someone's misplaced vision of the stereotyped Englishman . . . I define integration, therefore, not as a flattening process of assimilation but as equal opportunity, accompanied by cultural diversity, in an atmosphere of mutual tolerance.

It is unclear where Jenkins acquired his multicultural ideas, though the fact that he was addressing a British-Caribbean audience may have influenced his choice of words.

Immigration under Thatcher and Major's Conservatives during 1979–97 had been shaped by the aftershocks of Powellism as well as by Thatcher's own beliefs. The number of Commonwealth immigrants declined from approximately 75,000 per year in the 1970s to 55,000 through the 1980s and 1990s. This was about to change. Blair and his liberal Foreign Secretary Robin Cook presided over a new economic migration programme which plugged into booming Britain's demand for labour. Upon Labour's attaining office in 1997, immigration began to rise substantially. Some of the impetus behind this came from a brain trust of pro-immigration policy advisers such as Barbara Roche. According to former Blair speechwriter Andrew Neather, this group recommended from late 2000 that the government use mass immigration to make the country truly multicultural, to 'rub the Right's nose in diversity and render their arguments out of "date" '.[14] This cultural rationale was quietly excised in the final report in 2001 due to concerns over a white working-class backlash, with the case for immigration limited to economic arguments. This shows how swiftly the political winds had shifted against multiculturalism in just one year. The number of Commonwealth immigrants – mainly from former Asian, Caribbean and African colonies – increased from around 55,000 a year prior to 1997 to 82,000 in 1998 and 156,000 in 2004. Asylum claims, driven by wars in the former Yugoslavia, Iraq and Afghanistan, rose above the 100,000 mark by 2000, and routinely made headlines.

The increase in asylum numbers was roundly attacked by the new Conservative opposition leader, William Hague, demonstrating that the power of taboos over discussing immigration in Britain remained more limited than was true in Europe or North America. In April 2000 Hague spoke of the country being 'flooded' and 'swamped' by an uncontrolled flow of 'bogus' asylum seekers. In response, the Liberal Democrats' leader, Charles Kennedy, accused Hague of 'seizing upon the worst of prejudices' while the Labour Home Secretary, Jack Straw, charged Hague with pandering to the far right. Nevertheless, as with Thatcher, Hague stood his ground and repudiated the charge of racism.[15] Privately, Tony Blair expressed deep concern that the asylum issue was damaging Labour and resolved to take a firmer stance. He appointed David Blunkett, his tough, visually impaired, working-class Home Secretary, to address the problem. Under Blunkett, asylum numbers fell dramatically.

However, at the same time, several of Blair's policy advisers were bullish about economic immigration, arguing that the foreign-born had punched above their weight in contributing to Britain's economic ascent. Many rested their case on immigration's positive effect on Britain's free-wheeling economy. Immigrants were young and energetic, paying more into the Treasury than they took out. The booming economy and an increasingly diverse, vibrant London fed Blair's advisers sense of elite national pride. While many of them undoubtedly knew immigration wasn't popular, the Conservatives were in the political wilderness. Despite Hague campaigning on immigration in 2001 and his successor Michael Howard doing so again in 2005, the Tory vote barely budged, from 30.7 in 1997 to 31.7 in 2005. It seemed people really didn't care about the issue enough for it to shape their vote. That was about to change.

LIBERAL NATIONALISM IN BLAIR'S BRITAIN

The early Blair years represented the flowering of a liberal-egalitarian nationalism in Britain. Though some charge liberal elites with being post-national, it's more accurate to describe them as missionary nationalists. This is not a contradiction. When a country sees itself as blazing a trail for others to follow, or leading the world as the defender of a universal idea, it brings glory on itself. When the Soviet Union styles itself the vanguard of socialism, America the leader of the free world, France the 'Eldest Daughter' of the Catholic Church or Saudi Arabia the guiding light of Islam, these countries are engaging in what scholars term 'missionary nationalism'.[16] They may appear to be cosmopolitan, selflessly serving a transnational ideology, but they do so in part to court the approval of other nations and win glory for themselves. Indeed, studies show that national pride is not the preserve of the right. Those expressing pride in a country's artistic and scientific achievements, for instance, tend to be score more liberal than average.[17] Surveys I have run asking respondents to score the extent to which particular symbols make them feel nationalistic show that progressives tend to gravitate to different national symbols from conservatives. This was confirmed in a YouGov poll in early 2018 which found that 67 per cent of Conservative voters compared to 44 per cent of Liberal Democrats said Britain standing alone against Hitler made them feel proud to be British. When it came to the Suffragettes fighting for the vote for women, 58 per cent of Liberal Democrats but just 34 per cent of Tories said this made them feel proudly British.[18]

In Britain's case, New Labour was showing the world that its country, centred on the globalist capital, London, was at the forefront of liberal cosmopolitanism. This lent British elites international prestige. Not only did their pride swell when they met counterparts from other Western countries, but it was bolstered even when their audience was absent. As the social psychologist George Herbert Mead argues, our self-esteem reflects the opinions of our 'generalized other', those we hold in high regard and deem to be judging us even when not physically present.[19] In this sense, British liberals could bask in the glow of the imagined approval of their counterparts from around the world. New Labour advanced this form of nationalism prior to 2000.

There's a significant contrast in national identity between the New Labour elite and the mass of the white British population. Elite forms of national identity are strongly performance-based, tightly attuned to the opinions of elites elsewhere. Rather than identify with ascribed characteristics – history, physical appearance, religion, language – performance-based forms of nationalism focus on achieved status. In the World Values Survey (WVS) and European Social Survey (ESS), those with lower levels of education across the world – or who believe discipline is important for children – are significantly more likely than the well-educated or liberals to say that sharing the same religion as the majority or having ancestors from the country is important for citizenship. One's general liberalism, rather than the history of one's country, determines whether one endorses an exclusive 'ethnic' view of the nation or an inclusive 'civic' variant.[20]

Liberal missionary nationalism is qualitatively distinct from an ascribed 'ethnic' nationalism based on settled cultural traits, folk myths and memories. An ethnic sense of national identity is inflected by locale and region, rooted in characteristics handed down from generation to generation. There is no tension between being working class, a 'Geordie' (from the north-east) or a 'Scouser' (from Liverpool), English and British. The working-class Geordie views England as an extension of her own class and regional identity, and Britain as an extension of England. The national identity starts local and moves outwards to the nation-state. Local accents, customs and landscapes blend seamlessly into national reference points like the English flag and football squad. Their Englishness fills most of their imagined canvas of Britishness. They gain self-esteem from their collective identity by taking pride in their local particularity as 'truly English', an authentic expression of the nation. The audience for this expression of pride is national, not international. Those in other regions applaud the distinctive English type found in a city such as Liverpool. Region and class do not compete with national identity, but reinforce it. On the 2009–10 Citizenship Survey, 83 per cent of white skilled workers for whom class is a 'very important' identity also say their nation is 'very important' for who they are.

For most white British people, class, locale, ethnicity and religion are the identities which best complement national identity. This reflects a more particularist form of national identity that grows out from the local. The same is not true for those who say education and age are important to who they are. In the Understanding Society survey, only 36 per cent of university graduates who say their education matters a lot for their identity say their nation is very important for who they are. Thus the well-educated who identify with their credentials are less enthusiastic nationalists than others. They exemplify what writer David Goodhart terms the people from Anywhere, identifying more with achieved status than with ascribed characteristics.[21] Yet 'Anywheres' can also be nationalist. Binary questions about national and other identities such as those in the Citizenship Survey or Understanding Society may reflect popular notions of what 'pride in nation' entails – militarism, xenophobia and the like – but they miss the subtler progressive nationalism noted earlier which takes pride in artistic and scientific achievements, diversity, public services or alternative neighbourhoods. A large-scale BBC survey on Englishness discovered that 62 per cent of Remain voters said 'England's diverse cultural life' contributed strongly to their English identity, but this was true of only 38 per cent of Leave voters.[22] This shapes policy attitudes: when asked which should be a higher priority for government, 'promoting traditional British culture' or 'welcoming different cultures in Britain', Leavers favoured the former by a 76–14 margin compared to 22–50 for Remainers.[23]

On a progressive reading, when a country succumbs to cultural nationalism at the expense of the national mission, it loses face in the court of international public opinion. Brexit induces a sense of shame among many British missionary nationalists. In their minds, the country is now associated with anti-cosmopolitanism and a betrayal of liberal values so it contributes negatively to their self-esteem. As a result, some British liberals seek to distance themselves from a British national identity in favour of a London or metropolitan identity with the places which voted to Remain. Alternatively, they join the fight to get the country back on its former missionary-liberal track. When it comes to immigration, liberals are prepared to sacrifice elements of the cultural particularity of their nation on the altar of the liberal mission. This relegates ascribed nationalism in favour of achieved nationalism: local particularity and domestic approval is lost, but global applause is gained. Both are forms of nationalism, but one is based on international adulation for advancing an ideal, the other on intra-national recognition for exemplifying authentic cultural traits. Their intended audiences are different, as are their social bases.

THE DEMISE OF MULTICULTURALISM

The first indication that Blairite openness was beginning to falter arrived with the publication of the report of the Commission on the Future of Multi-Ethnic Britain, led by Bangladeshi-British peer Lord Parekh. The commission was launched by the Home Secretary, Jack Straw, at a time when multiculturalism was a cornerstone of New Labour's liberalizing project. Funded by the progressive Runnymede Trust, its remit was 'to analyse the current state of multi-ethnic Britain and propose ways of countering racial discrimination and disadvantage, making Britain a confident and vibrant multicultural society at ease with its rich diversity'. The much awaited report championed a multicultural, post-national vision of Britain deploying academic terms such as 'community of communities' and 'recognition', rooted in the work of multicultural political theorists like Charles Taylor and Will Kymlicka. Steeped in the language of critical race theory and multicultural political theory, it spoke of Britishness having 'racial connotations' and urged a root-and-branch reworking of Britain's national story. It urged the government to declare itself officially multicultural, as was true in Canada and, to a lesser extent, Australia.

Parekh himself is no radical, but rather a thoughtful mainstream political theorist. He has subsequently reconsidered the place of the white majority in more depth in his multicultural model and has influenced the important 'Bristol School' of multicultural political theory. The report's aim to give non-whites a stake in Britishness is laudable and many of its concrete anti-racism measures make sense. Nonetheless, reflecting the state of political theory at the time, there was little sensitivity to the cultural dilemmas faced by declining white majorities. It is difficult to see how members of the ethnic majority were supposed to fit into the notion of multiculturalism except as apologists for past misdeeds. One of those Parekh influenced, the British sociologist Tariq Modood, has subsequently taken this problem on board and is doing some of the leading work in analytic (as opposed to 'critical') political theory.[24]

Jack Straw initially planned to endorse some of the less controversial aspects of the report concerning anti-racism and policing. But he was blindsided by the negative response to its radical post-nationalism. The aftermath of the report was a case study in what happens when the progressive multiculturalist ideas holding sway in academia collide with the reality of public opinion. Politicians and the media, receptive to academic ideas but attuned to public sentiment, roundly condemned its more radical findings such as the claim that white exclusivity was built into the term 'British'. Straw dissociated himself from the report, reaffirming his commitment to British identity. However, Straw defined Britishness in terms of British values such as tolerance and diversity rather than by referring to a particular set of historical reference points.

A year later, the Mill Town Riots, pitting white against South Asian Muslim youths, broke out in several highly segregated northern post-industrial cities. Then came the 9/11 attack in New York, heightening security concerns. Ted Cantle, former chief executive of Nottingham City Council, was commissioned by the new Home Secretary David Blunkett to write the report on the Mill Town riots. The Cantle Report was as integrationist as the Parekh Report was multiculturalist. Cantle spoke of the 'parallel lives' lived by white and Pakistani-Muslim communities in the former mill towns. Rather than a multicultural celebration of difference, Cantle and New Labour championed British-ness and integration. Community cohesion, not the politics of difference, was to be the watchword. Suddenly, in mainstream and centre-left media outlets such as the BBC and the *Guardian*, there was talk of moving 'beyond multiculturalism'.[25] Even the government's Commission for Racial Equality – led by the high-profile Afro-Caribbean Briton Trevor Phillips who had formerly backed the Parekh Report – turned against it. On 3 April 2004, Phillips came out against multiculturalism and called for a 'core of Britishness' and integration.[26] He subsequently emerged as one of multiculturalism's most trenchant critics.

The discursive shift from multiculturalism to integration occurred earliest in continental Europe, spurred by the success of the far right. By the mid-1990s, Jean-Marie Le Pen's National Front (FN) was winning between 10 and 15 per cent of the first-round vote while Jörg Haider's Freedom Party reached 27 per cent of the poll in Austria in 1999. This prompted centrist parties, especially on the right, to denounce multi-culturalism and endorse an uncompromising civic nationalism. The hope was to undercut far-right support without adopting their exclusiv-ist ethno-nationalism. Islamist terror was also a force multiplier for change. In 2004, a series of Islamist attacks in Amsterdam and Madrid lent integration a new urgency. European critics dubbed London 'Lon-donistan', claiming its security services had tacitly agreed to permit Islamist extremists to congregate unmolested in exchange for peace.[27] For instance, jihadi radicals such as Abu Hamza, the imam at the important Finsbury Park Mosque, was largely left to his own devices until the mosque was raided and shut down in 2003. Two years later, on 7 July 2005, the London bombings ripped away the security blanket Britain had enjoyed through tolerating Islamist organizations. Fifty-six were killed and nearly 800 injured in a coordinated series of suicide attacks in the city. One of the bombs struck in the vicinity of my university, Birkbeck, claiming the life of one of our students, Benedetta Ciaccia.

This was the first suicide attack on British soil. Significantly, all the bombers were British-born, including three Pakistanis and one Jamaican convert, Germaine Lindsay. The three Pakistani Britons had associated through a youth centre in Beeston, an area of Leeds with a high Muslim concentration. Observers began to discern a connection between the concentration of Muslims in places like Beeston, radicalization and 'homegrown', or native-born, terrorism. Many now believed Muslim neighbourhoods such as Beeston or Brussels' Molenbeek helped incubate radicalism. In fact there is no evidence for this: Muslims are highly concentrated in a small number of places in Europe so there is a good chance an Islamist attacker hails from a Muslim concentration area. When one accounts for where European Muslims are clustered, those from Muslim-dominated zones are no more likely to have been terrorists than Muslims living in non-Muslim neighbourhoods. Data from the Home Office Citizenship Surveys shows that support for violence in defence of religion is actually lower among Muslims in high-Muslim wards than among Muslims in so-called 'superdiverse' areas where many ethnic groups live side by side. This chimes with evidence that those who participated in the 2011 London Riots lived disproportionately in superdiverse areas where ethnic communities are less able to monitor their youth.[28]

Events on the ground often change the intellectual conversation. Just as the Civil Rights era's black activism gave rise to multiculturalism, the rise of the far right and homegrown Islamist terrorism helped launch civic nationalism. Gone was talk of 'droit à la différence', to be replaced by an emphasis on integration and cohesion.[29] Britain followed suit in the early 2000s. Gordon Brown, who became Prime Minister in 2007, was one of the first prominent politicians to make British identity central to their thinking. I recall participating in an intimate *Prospect* magazine roundtable on Britishness in 2005 organized by editor David Goodhart in which Brown set forth his thoughts on the matter.[30] For Brown, British nationality largely revolved around so-called 'British values' such as tolerance, fairness and enterprise, rooted in British history.[31] Some version of Brown's shared values and institutions cropped up as the civic national identity in almost every Western country. Since the national identity was propagated by the state on a 'one-size-fits-all' model, it had to emphasize the thinnest, most inclusive, common denominators of society. Only the intolerant could be excluded. The end product was scarcely different from Jürgen Habermas's 'constitutional patriotism', which most civic nationalists assail. Given the need to thin out the identity to include everyone, these new civic nationalisms were, as writer Kenan Malik correctly observed, 'rather banal'.[32]

The turn away from multiculturalism became the established pan-European consensus soon after. Post-war Germany has generally been the most reluctant country to embrace right-wing trends so it was significant that, in a speech in October 2010, Germany's Chancellor, Angela Merkel, declared that 'multikulti' had 'failed, utterly failed'.[33] In fact multiculturalism had become so toxic by this time that during 2010–11 alone Merkel, David Cameron, France's Nicolas Sarkozy, the Australian ex-Prime Minister John Howard and José María Aznar, Prime Minister of Spain, all pronounced it a failure.[34] Multiculturalism had certainly suffered a setback, but one shouldn't overstate the change. For one thing, European governments had never embraced full-blown multiculturalism policy to the extent of allocating legislative seats, jobs or funding on the basis of ethnic quotas. Only in local governments controlled by the radical left did such policies occasionally emerge, and even then they were eventually forced to back down. All European countries eschewed US-style affirmative action in favour of softer minority-inclusion targets. Only in the symbolic sphere, when making official pronouncements about the nation, did rhetoric about multiculturalism and nation-as-diversity occasionally rear its head.

In that limited sense, the 2000s changed the discussion by reorienting the national storyline away from saying 'diversity makes us who we are' to 'values and institutions make us who we are'. But this was a rebalancing, and no more than that.[35] If the three legs of the national stool consist of the ethnic majority, minorities and common values, there was a transfer of weight from minorities to common values, but no concession to majority identity. Far from calling for assimilation to a majority identity, elites accepted that minorities would maintain their identities in private as society grew increasingly diverse. Implicit in this argument is that majorities should accept their ethnic decline and focus their identity on the common values which bind the civic nation. This is akin to asking the host country of a World's Fair to close its national booth and focus its sense of community exclusively on the fairgrounds.

Civic nationalism, it was hoped, would provide the ethnic majority with the reassurance it needed to stop fretting about immigration. But this logic only works if the majority's concern is of a piece with that of the state: namely political order, shared values and the smooth running of the economy. What happens if the conservative section of the majority is in fact exercised by the loss of its *ethnic* identity or of challenges to ethno-traditions of nationhood? Civic nationalism provides no answers to this deeper existential anxiety beyond its reflex to block such questions with charges of racism, xenophobia and pandering to the far right.

DIVERSITY OR SOLIDARITY?

The unprecedented level of immigration in Britain in the 2000s was posing questions which civic nationalism could not answer. The continued success of the radical right in Europe, and the ascent of the British National Party (BNP) and United Kingdom Independence Party (UKIP) in Britain, shows that the new civic nationalism had little effect on majority discontent. To wit, in my own analysis of Citizenship Survey and Understanding Society data attached to 2011 census figures at ward and district level, I found no consistent evidence that white Britons living in wards with minorities who are more 'integrated' – i.e. less segregated, UK born, English speaking, employed or well educated – are more tolerant of immigration or less supportive of UKIP. This indicates that political or economic integration, while laudable in its own right, ministers to the concerns of the state, not of the ethnic majority. In the main, this is because integrationist talk fails to address conservatives' cultural anxieties over immigration.

One of the first mainstream thinkers to question the diversity-in-civic nationalism consensus was David Goodhart. As editor of *Prospect* magazine, the country's leading centre-left current affairs monthly, and from a prominent family, Goodhart was an unlikely immigration sceptic. Yet in February 2004 he penned a controversial article entitled 'Too

Diverse?' published in both *Prospect* and the *Guardian*. He argued that Britain faced a choice: opt to be a high-solidarity, culturally homogeneous society such as Sweden; or move in the direction of diverse, low-solidarity America. He cited work from prominent American academics like Alberto Alesina and Robert Putnam showing that more diverse states and cities in America were less trusting and provided fewer public services to their citizens. In effect, when better-off older white taxpayers fail to identify with disproportionately minority welfare recipients or public, i.e. state, schoolchildren, they are reluctant to share their wealth. Diversity impedes the sense of common fate needed to facilitate redistribution.

In formulating his ideas, Goodhart drew on the thinking of David Willetts, a leading conservative intellectual and politician, who remarked in 1998 that there is a tradeoff between ethnic diversity and welfare provision, contrasting homogeneous, solidaristic Scandinavia with diverse, individualistic America.[36] Another important influence was centrist American writer Michael Lind, who argued that intellectuals and party elites in America were primarily motivated by expressive or economic individualism. Lind made the centre-left case for empowering the American federal state to redistribute wealth, but only as part of a new deal in which mass immigration is reduced and more attention is paid to national solidarity. Alongside critics of cultural individualism such as Daniel Bell and Christopher Lasch, Lind excoriated American elites for being postnational, universalist and out of touch.[37]

Goodhart, like Lind, came down clearly in favour of the high-solidarity model. Large-scale immigration, he cautioned, is undermining the social glue which convinces haves to share a large chunk of their income with have-nots rather than spending it on their children or on the needy overseas. Coming from a left-of-centre public figure, this shocked Britain's opinion formers, leading to a torrent of criticism. Robust challenges from multiculturalists such as Bhikhu Parekh were unsurprising. Even Trevor Phillips, who two months later angered progressives by attacking multiculturalism, accused Goodhart of 'liberal Powellism' and 'genteel xenophobia', urging the Labour government to open immigration even further. He implored it to ignore anti-immigration sentiments expressed in focus groups, emulate the pro-immigration politics of George W. Bush and stand firm in the face of a growing BNP challenge. Phillips has since moved closer to Goodhart's position, but at the time advocated a pro-immigration integrationism distinct from Lind and Goodhart's more immigration-sceptic brand of civic nationalism.[38]

EAST EUROPEAN IMMIGRATION

In 2004, ten new countries, mainly ex-communist states such as Poland, Lithuania and Slovakia, joined the European Union. Until that point, few immigrants had come to Britain from the EU. Only a trickle had arrived from poorer Southern EU countries such as Spain or Greece. This led a team of academic experts advising the government to predict that just 5,000–13,000 people would enter Britain each year from the new accession countries. Britain therefore opted not to impose transitional controls on migration from the new Eastern member states. The UK was one of only three countries, alongside Sweden and Ireland, to do so – and was the only large economy to throw open its doors. In the event, five to ten times the predicted number arrived, reaching 1.5 million newcomers by the 2010s. Early in the process, Southampton Labour MP John Denham worried that the New Labour leadership was growing increasingly out of touch with its working-class base. He related that in Southampton, East European immigrants had driven wages down among construction workers by 50 per cent and were placing enormous pressure on local services such as hospitals and further education colleges.[39]

Immigration to Britain has always been tricky to quantify because many Britons leave the country as well as enter it. Most analysts use net migration (immigration less emigration) as a rough guide to immigration levels. On this measure, numbers began rising in 1997 and never looked back. The rise in immigration led to growing concern about it. In effect, numbers matter. Bobby Duffy and his team at Ipsos MORI have done a sterling job tracking public opinion in Britain and show that, as net migration rose, three trends tracked it. First, the annual survey of Members of Parliament which asks them what their constituents are writing to them about began picking up growing mention of immigration. Second, the share of people saying immigration was the most important issue facing Britain began to rise. Finally, the number of news stories on immigration increased. The three trends rose together, so it is difficult to know whether the media shaped what people thought was most important or whether rising public concern created a demand for stories on immigration which the media capitalized on. Regardless, the result was dramatic. The proportion of survey respondents saying 'immigration/race relations' is the number-one issue facing Britain rose from 3 per cent in June 1997, prior to Blair's election, to 10 per cent by late 1999, and then moved into the 20s and 30s through the 2000s, occasionally approaching 50 per cent.

It's not that attitudes to immigration changed, but that immigration became a more central focus for voters who wanted less of it. Immigration consistently ranked as the first or second most important issue for Britons after 2001. Despite a change of government to David Cameron's Conservatives – in coalition with the Liberal Democrats – from 2010, net migration remained high, and the share of people calling immigration their most important issue hovered between 35 and 50 per cent after 2010. Figure 4.1 plots concern over immigration alongside net migration from the mid-1980s until 2014. The smoothed curves of the two series have a correlation of between 70 and 80 per cent. When it comes to explaining concern over immigration in Britain, numbers count. People tend to overestimate the share of immigrants in society

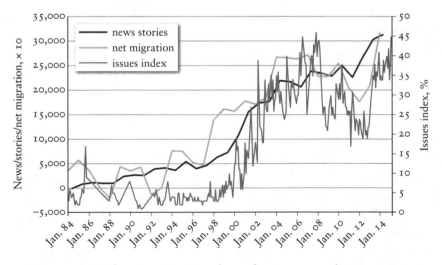

4.1. News stories about immigration, share of survey respondents mentioning immigration as top issue and net immigration over time

Source: Ipsos MORI 'Shifting Ground', 2015, p. 5

by a factor of two or more, but seem more accurate in their perceptions of change over time.

Numbers matter on many different levels. While immigration grabbed the headlines, quieter ethnic shifts helped prepare the soil of public opinion for the kinds of stories the media began to print. In 1991, about 90 per cent of the population of England and Wales hailed from the white British ethnic majority. In 2001, this declined modestly to 87.5 per cent, but by 2011 the majority share fell by nearly 8 points, to 80 per cent. The 2000s is remembered as a period in which several relatively poor East European countries joined the EU, hastening the flow of Poles, Romanians and others to Britain. Yet, away from the headlines, the population of non-European origin increased from 7 to 14 per cent of the total. In absolute terms, the non-European origin population more than doubled in size, from 3 to 8 million.[40]

This was partly due to higher rates of natural increase among the British minorities – South Asians more so than Afro-Caribbeans – but also because in the 2000s non-European immigration matched or exceeded European inflows. In 2016, for instance, net migration from the EU was running at 189,000 compared to 196,000 from outside Europe. Despite criticism of the EU's freedom-of-movement provisions, which gave East Europeans the right to live and work in Britain, the quieter increase in non-Europeans through immigration and natural increase arguably had a larger impact on majority perceptions. A 2017 YouGov–LSE (London School of Economics) survey of 3,600 people I was involved in showed that, despite Brexit, the average Briton was prepared to accept an annual inflow of 76,000 from the EU but just 61,000 from Asia, Africa and the Middle East.[41] Other surveys found a near-majority of Britons in favour of banning immigration from Muslim countries.[42]

THE RISE OF THE BNP

Politically, the first beneficiary of rising disquiet over immigration was the British National Party (BNP). Formed in 1982, the BNP had its roots in earlier neo-Nazi and neo-fascist formations such as the National Front (NF), which had been active since the 1970s. These movements were quite small, featuring both a street movement and a political wing.

Their street demonstrations often turned violent as the NF routinely clashed with left-wing anti-fascist radicals. The BNP languished electorally until the 2000s, when its fortunes began to pick up under its modernizing leader, Nick Griffin. On the back of the Mill Town Riots that took place in the summer of 2001 in the northern towns of Oldham, Burnley and Bradford, the BNP gained four local councillors in the 2002 local elections. Three were in Burnley. Downplaying crude racism and unpopular policies such as repatriating minorities, Griffin turned to anti-Muslim appeals to win over those who blanched at supporting the 'thuggish' BNP. This policy shift tells us that hostility to Muslims is seen as more legitimate than racism because it can be interpreted as stemming from a concern for liberal principles and not simply the defence of ethnic boundaries. Rather than appeal directly to racism, Griffin increasingly used multiculturalist language about the British government committing 'genocide' against the 'indigenous' British people through immigration. Under the radar, Irish Catholics, who had once been anathema to the far right, were included as an indigenous British people – especially after the guns fell silent in Northern Ireland in 1994.

At the 2004 elections to the European Parliament, the BNP won 800,000 votes, 4.9 per cent of the total. This despite the fact that the more moderate UK Independence Party (UKIP), also sceptical of immigration, secured 16.1 per cent. This was an early political bellwether of the rise in anti-immigration sentiment that had been building since 1997. Many scoffed that European elections were protest votes with low turnouts, hence poor indicators of what might happen in a high-participation, first-past-the-post national election. It's certainly true that supply factors – campaign resources and a local infrastructure of volunteers – are critical for winning national elections. While campaigning is also important in elections to the European Parliament, the electoral units aren't local while seats in the European Parliament are allocated on the basis of the popular vote. This neatly converts votes into seats, benefiting populist and single-issue parties whose support is spread relatively evenly across the country. Against this, UKIP's 13 per cent of the vote in British national (Westminster) elections in 2015 netted it just one seat while the Scottish nationalists, with only a third as many votes, gained fifty-five.

The BNP's ascent continued through the mid-2000s even at local level, where party organization matters a great deal. In the 2006 local elections, the inexperienced party focused its meagre resources on the one in ten seats it felt best able to win. In these, its average vote share was 18 per cent, resulting in an unprecedented forty-eight councillors, up from twenty-one the year before. The BNP's biggest impact was in the eastern outer-London borough of Barking and Dagenham. The district had largely been settled by working-class white Cockneys who maintained a distinctive culture based on accent and myths of place. Much of this was chronicled by the long-running *EastEnders* soap opera, whose largely white actors portray a lost Cockney landscape which now consists mainly of upwardly mobile white singletons and minority families. Many Barking families originated in the former Cockney heartlands of inner East London in the present borough of Newham which were ethnically transformed in the 1980s and 1990s. This was brought to life in 2016 by the controversial BBC documentary *Last Whites of the East End*. The fact that a programme with that title and content could be shown on the main public channel is a measure of how far the anti-racism taboo had lost ground in Britain. In Canada or Sweden, for instance, such a programme would be unthinkable due to moral constraints on the limits of acceptable debate.

The ethnic shifts of Newham were spreading further outward in the 2000s to Barking and Dagenham. The consensus of over 200 academic papers in the literature (an exhaustive sample up to 2016) is that increases in diversity almost always produce elevated anti-immigration and far-right support.[43] Only if change slows and a decade passes does local hostility to immigration return to its former level.[44] Accordingly, in 2006, in a shock result, the BNP won 20 per cent of the vote and twelve councillors on Barking's fifty-six-seat council. Barking nicely encapsulates the debate about the forces driving the rise of the populist right. On the one hand, the Ford auto plant was a major local employer which had been downsizing its workforce for decades. Did deindustrialization and the offshoring of jobs lead to working-class disaffection? A number of factors suggest otherwise. First, the ethnic composition of the shrinking Ford plant was 45 per cent non-white by 1999 – no longer representative of the wider borough.[45] Only a few thousand still worked there. Second, the car industry had declined in fits and starts over the course of several decades, yet far-right movements were not an important player in local elections until the 2000s. In 1997, for example, the BNP won just 2.7 per cent of the vote in local elections.

The more convincing explanation lies with the stunning ethnic transformation taking place in the district. In 2001, 81 per cent of Barking and Dagenham's people were from the white British ethnic majority. By 2011, this had fallen to 49 per cent. With its stock of roomy, low-rise, low-cost homes proximal to London's booming economy – initially built as public housing for workers – Barking attracted numerous African, Asian and East European-origin immigrants. Population turnover is a feature of urban areas and Barking relied on both natural increase and domestic in-migration to maintain its white population. Like a bathtub in which water is always draining away while more pours in, the balance between hot and cold inflows is crucial. A drop in white domestic migration and a rise in minority inflows was akin to turning up the hot tap and turning off the cold: the temperature in the bath soon increased. Notice this is a different process from 'white flight', in which local whites see minorities entering, fear the worst, sell up and leave, changing the composition of the area, which in turns prompts others to depart, fuelling a chain reaction.[46] There is virtually no evidence that this is happening anywhere in the West today.

Throughout the Western world, the dominant process is not white flight but white avoidance. This consists of white majorities moving towards areas that are heavily white, which involves a concomitant process of avoiding diverse places. In other words, when whites move, especially white families, they tend to bypass neighbourhoods with a significant minority population. American research suggests that whites greatly overestimate the share of minoritics in an area and wind up living in even whiter areas then they would actually prefer.[47] My analysis of Understanding Society data suggests that whites are sensitive not only to the share but to the ethnic *change* in an area. The whitest areas tend not to attract minorities, so these have both low minority shares and slow rates of ethnic change. The combination of low minority levels and high stability attracts and retains white residents, especially those with families searching for state schools to send their children to. The combined effect of a preference for both low minority levels and slow ethnic change is that whites gravitate to neighbourhoods that are over 85 per cent white. This pattern, as we'll see in chapter 7, holds in British, American and Canadian residential data, as well as in British school data.

Barking's rapid ethnic shifts were at the extreme end of a wider process of ethnic transformation centred in the cities of England and Wales. As minorities entered urban areas in larger numbers, white Britons departed or chose not to enter. For many established white residents, ethnic shifts were something inflicted on them by liberal elites based in London's Westminster political district. Though the BNP had an unsavoury reputation and a hooligan contingent among its activists, large numbers voted for them anyway. After 2006, local Labour MP Margaret Hodge led a campaign against the BNP, making a concerted effort to mobilize new voters, often from minority backgrounds. Turnout almost doubled, growing the electorate from just over 100,000 in 2006 to almost 200,000 by 2010. Though the BNP increased its vote from 14,800 to nearly 31,000, Labour's high-profile mobilization led the BNP to lose all twelve of its seats.

In the aftermath of the 2010 local contest, American political scientist Justin Gest conducted extensive fieldwork in the area and found strong resentment of elites among much of the local white population. Gest was present at one of Hodge's open forums with constituents, where Hodge met concerned constituents over tea. Approaching two local women, Eleanor Hodgkins and Poppy Moore, Hodge was challenged point blank about their number-one concern, immigration:

Eleanor: But where are [these foreigners] coming from, Margaret?

Hodge: Many are second and third generation immigrants. A lot of people have sold their houses and left Barking and Dagenham. Listen, you're never going to change it back again. All you can do is make it better for your children.

Poppy: But Margaret, they[immigrant renters]'re in and they're out. Why do we let them do it?

Hodge: With the buy-to-let people, no one is buying who has a commitment to the community. But you can't control it. It's no one's fault: the Government, the Council, no one's. But you can recreate the community spirit.

Poppy: The smells from the houses will make you heave! And on the Heathway, there's too many strange stores selling odd meats and vegetables.

Hodge: Well, some people like it.

Poppy: Margaret, would you please live here for two or three weeks and see what it's like?

Hodge: I'm here pretty often . . . Listen, times have changed and we have
    to move on with them.

Eleanor: I feel sorry for my grandkids.

Hodge: Look, we want good schools and jobs for them. What worries
    me is the 18-year-olds coming out of school or college with no work.
    That's the fault of the Tories and this Government with all their cuts.

Poppy: You would have made the same cuts.

Hodge: Not like this. Every young person would be employed, appren-
    ticed or in training. Now come on, don't mope. You don't have it
    that bad.

Poppy: [Brief pause] We're getting things taken away. I can't even get my
    eyes tested.

Hodge: Yes, you can.

Poppy: No, I can't.

Hodge: Yes, you can.

Poppy: No, I can't.

Hodge: Yes, you can.

Poppy: No, I can't.

Hodge: Yes, you can. Don't feel so cross.

Poppy: It makes me feel cross just to walk up the bleeding Heathway.

At this point Hodge excused herself. After Hodge had left, Gest spoke
with Poppy and discovered that she voted BNP and questioned Labour's
tactics in regaining the twelve BNP seats in 2010. She felt the BNP had
been ousted by a coup orchestrated by elites and their minority allies.
'They call them Nazis. But they're not. They're Britain for Britain. Labour
sent [immigrants] all down here and [Hodge] won't tell me where they
come from. I think they fiddled the votes, so that the BNP did not get one
candidate in . . . Why can't Margaret Hodge see the change in this place?'[48]

Two things jump out at me from Hodge's conversation with the
women. First, the women begin with a complaint about cultural change
in their area. Hodge does not consider this a valid argument: she tries to
get them to ignore ethnic change and forget about the past. One of the
women makes a racist remark about smells which Hodge rightly rebuts.
However, Hodge repeatedly seeks to deflect cultural concerns onto the
more comfortable terrain of housing and fiscal policy. There is not a
word of cultural reassurance from Hodge about, say, the likelihood
that many of the newcomers or their children will lose their cultural

differences and melt into the majority as in the past. Meanwhile, the women, who begin by expressing cultural unease, tacitly accept they must offer a material complaint about immigration in order to get a hearing from Hodge and not fall afoul of the anti-racism norm. Poppy therefore raises the highly dubious claim that she can't obtain an optometrist appointment. In the end, Poppy pivots from the optometrist angle to her true motivation, an emotionally laden ethnic grievance – at which point Hodge leaves the conversation.

I discussed ideas about how to navigate residents' cultural concerns with Hodge in her Westminster office, and I appreciate the difficulty she is in.[49] Hodge herself has no control over immigration or the number of people entering the borough, yet is held responsible for the change by many of her white constituents. She routinely encounters hostility from whites on the election doorstep. She expressed doubts about whether reassurance over long-term assimilation would be enough to satisfy disgruntled white working-class residents. She is probably right that the stunning pace of change in Barking means an assimilation message, or a plea to pan out to a larger geographic area in which white Britishness is more secure, is unlikely to minister fully to popular ethnic anxieties. Here Barking is truly an outlier and unrepresentative of the country, where most districts added only a few percentage points of diversity in the 2000s. Even so, validating and empathizing with cultural concerns and attempting to allay them – could have been more effective, especially as compared to the charge of racism brandished by left-wing activists campaigning for Labour who arrived from outside the borough.

Another powerful example of how the anti-prejudice norm sublimates ethnic concerns into faux-economic argumentation comes from a woman in a focus group I commissioned in 2014 in Croydon, south London, a suburb undergoing similarly rapid change. 'I might have been the only English person on that tram . . . I didn't like it . . . I could have been in a foreign country,' an older woman complained. Challenged by a liberal participant who asked, 'Why should that affect you that there's minorities on the train?', the woman swiftly changed her tune to a more acceptable, economic form of opposition to immigration: 'It doesn't affect me. It, um . . . I've got grandchildren and children . . . I don't think things are going to get any better or easier for them, to get work.' Once again, cultural arguments are recast in economic terms in order to comply with anti-racism norms which place boundaries on what can be expressed. These red lines shift over time, altering public opinion on immigration and support for populist-right parties.

Should we push for maximal or minimal anti-racism norms? When anti-racism norms retreat, opposition to immigration or backing for populist-right parties may rise because voting for such parties or holding anti-immigration sentiments is viewed as more acceptable. On the other hand, suppressing the expression of majority ethnic sentiment is a risky strategy: if the anti-racist consensus begins to fray, memories of past suppression of grievances turns into a force multiplier for the radical right. Meanwhile, those forced to sublimate ethnic concerns have to construct secondary arguments about pressure on public services which leads to policy distortions such as denying services to immigrants. This damages the lives of immigrants without addressing majority grievances. Permitting freer expression of the majority group's sense of cultural loss – as distinct from racist comments such as Poppy's comments on smells – is, in the long run, probably less dangerous than repressing them.

When anti-racism norms reach beyond the bounds of what people view as fair, this can produce a backlash. 'Racism is . . . a "mute button" pressed on someone while they are still crying out about a sense of loss – from a position of historic privilege, frequently in terms they have difficulty articulating,' Gest writes. 'Therefore, the preface "I'm not racist" is not a disclaimer, but an exhortation to listen and not dismiss the claims of a purportedly new minority.' Nancy Pemberton, one of Gest's working-class Barking respondents, goes further. 'I think the anti-racists have made it worse. They look for trouble. They construe everything as racist . . . These people are ruining our country. And we're the only ones who can be racist.'[50] Opposition to political correctness energized the BNP vote as it would later do with the Trump vote in America. The double standards inherent in today's anti-racist taboo (i.e. the proscription against expressing majority but not minority identities) provides cover for populist-right falsehoods pertaining to Muslim terrorism, immigrant crime or welfare abuse.

In the 2008 Greater London Authority elections, the BNP won just under 3 per cent of first-preference votes but over 6 per cent of second-preference votes, which gave the party a combined total of 5.3 per cent, enough to surmount the 5 per cent threshold and gain a seat in the London Assembly. Since its vote is almost exclusively white British, and white Britons formed just 45 per cent of London's population in 2011, this means one in ten ethnic majority voters backed the party. Thirty-eight per cent of London's white Britons have a degree compared to just 26 per cent in the rest of the country and just 45 per cent of white British Londoners lack secondary-school qualifications. In an important study of BNP voters by Rob Ford and Matt Goodwin during 2002–6 that sampled 150,000 people, just 6 per cent of BNP voters had a degree compared to 17 per cent of Labour voters.[51] Those without secondary-school qualifications outnumbered those with them in the BNP's base by a 4:1 margin. This suggests 20 per cent of white British Londoners without qualifications backed the BNP in 2008, a powerful statement of majority ethno-nationalism. In Barking, where the party won 20 per cent of the overall vote, the figure for those without degrees was undoubtedly somewhat higher.

As the map in figure 4.2 shows, the BNP's strength lay in white working-class Outer London boroughs such as Barking, Hillingdon,

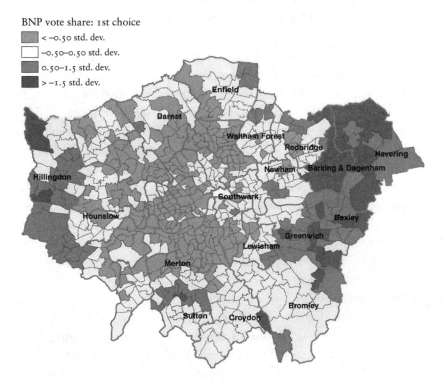

4.2. BNP vote share, 2008 London elections: first choice, standard deviation map

Source: Harris 2012.

Havering, Redbridge, Sutton and Croydon. Beyond London's boundaries, working-class exurban commuter-belt towns, such as those in the county of Essex east of the city, would prove even stronger redoubts of populist-right support. This reflects two ethno-geographic processes. First, ethnic transition in places such as Barking or Birmingham, which radicalizes conservative white voters. Second, the 'halo effect' whereby relatively homogeneous communities adjoining diverse ones fear they may be next to transition.[52, 53] Essex is in the eastern part of the halo surrounding diverse London, but similar patterns may be found in white working-class exurbs south of the city, or encircling diverse Birmingham or Bradford. Like a nuclear plant, people who live close enough to diversity to be comfortable with it, or too far away to think about it, are less radicalized than those just close enough to be fearful.

WHY THE LOCAL MATTERS LESS THAN THE NATIONAL

This said, I cannot stress enough that national perceptions are far more important in shaping people's views on immigration than local experiences. Differences between individuals matter far more than differences between places. Only in the most rapidly changing locations such as Boston in Lincolnshire or Barking in London do local ethnic factors strongly affect attitudes. The same is true for places with the longest history of high diversity, such as the borough of Lambeth in London, which are 10–20 percentage points less anti-immigration than the whitest boroughs when we account for age, education and ethnic change. This is because local whites are able to have more positive contact with minorities, getting to know them personally and taking the edge off misperceptions and prejudices. So at the extremes local diversity and change matter.

Still, only a fifth of white Britons live in wards that are less than 90 per cent white and the fraction in 'majority minority' wards is only 4 per cent. For the most part, attitudes are shaped by people's response to perceived changes to their imagined *national* community, not to their locale. Our security and identity is arguably more dependent on the nation than the neighbourhood. Nations inculcate an emotional attachment to myths and symbols much more than locales do. People may move neighbourhood but they are less likely to emigrate. They may risk their life for the nation, but rarely for their town. Consider the English village of Tyneham. Now a ghost town, it was requisitioned for a military range during the Second World War. The patriotic villagers duly agreed to vacate their village for the good of the nation. While a local change may be viewed as unsettling, threats to the nation may be perceived as existential. In addition, the political and economic decisions which most affect our lives are taken at the national level. The media focuses its coverage of political competition between groups on national institutions such as the British Parliament. This sharpens people's sense that changes to the national fabric count for more than local shifts.

National-level attitudes are often linked to views on the death penalty, trust, crime, political correctness and, more recently, the European Union. They tap into both authoritarianism – the desire for order and stability – and conservatism, a preference for continuity with the past. Perceptions of the nation are imagined through the media as well as by travelling around the country or hearing travel tales related by friends and relatives. Given people's tendency to 'fast think' through what Amos Tversky and Daniel Kahneman term 'system 1' cognition, vivid images and stories will tend to carry more weight than representative data and rational 'system 2' deliberation.[54] The media has an important role in reinforcing perceptions, but isn't the only influence on whether people imagine threats to the nation. Bottom-up, peer-to-peer transmission of emotional stories also matters. This can drive perceptions, creating fertile soil for the media. People are not dupes whose minds can be moulded like clay, yet their predilections are not completely fixed. This means the media has some leeway to shape attitudes. In particular, regular flagging and framing of issues can raise or lower the priority of issues like immigration in the public consciousness. As seen in figure 4.1, immigration rose up voters' agendas in the 2000s in tandem with more media coverage of it. This in turn began to influence the way people vote, with concerned individuals first opting for the Conservatives, then the upstart UK Independence Party (UKIP). The culmination of this was the Brexit vote.

THE EMERGENCE OF UKIP

Brexit, an unprecedented rebuke to the country's elite, could not have taken place without the rise of the UK Independence Party (UKIP). It originated as a middle-class party with a neo-liberal and sovereignty agenda, much like the early Swiss People's Party or the first incarnation of Germany's AfD. These parties were not originally motivated by immigration, only later entering this charged political space. As such, they tend to benefit from a 'reputational shield' against the charge of racism, an advantage not enjoyed by parties such as the Front National in France or BNP which stem from neo-fascist roots. Populist-right parties with a past that provides a reputational shield tend to do better than those which lack them.[55] The BNP's baggage made it harder to deflect brickbats from opponents seeking to attach the racist label to the party.

One study asked British respondents their opinion on Muslim schools. They read statements opposing Muslim schools which were attributed variously to the Conservatives and the BNP. When told that a message came from the BNP, people expressed less opposition to Muslim schools. This was especially true among those who scored highly on the Motivation to Control Prejudice (MCP) scale. Among those high in MCP, opposition to Muslim schools dropped from 76 to 67 per cent for the same message when people were told it came from the BNP rather than the Tories. UKIP had an intermediate effect, suggesting it was less toxic.[56] Even at the height of the BNP's popularity in 2009, 72 per cent of voters felt negatively towards the party, with 62 per cent 'very negative' in their assessment.[57]

This is critical because the policy agenda of the populist right is usually much more popular than the parties themselves. In Britain, as much as 60 per cent of white Britons want immigration reduced a lot but no more than 30 per cent have been willing to back a populist-right party. Even then, this high UKIP poll occurred only in the European elections, a relatively symbolic vote. Thus support for the populist right is the outcome of a tension between the attractiveness of the anti-immigration message and the disquiet people feel about transgressing the anti-racist taboo. Psychologists term this the 'dual-process' model, in which hostility to immigration collides with moral reticence.[58] This means that understanding what's going on with taboos is vital for predicting the populist-right vote.

Perceptions are vital in locating a party on one side or the other of the anti-racism line. The public has limited information on the actual opinions of populist-right party members when assessing whether they are beyond the pale. Hence they must rely on a party's brand, the biography and image of its leader and the portrayal of members' words and deeds. Perceptions are also based on what John Maynard Keynes termed a 'beauty contest': how people think others view a party. People must protect their reputations in front of others and manage guilt produced by their 'generalized other', the imaginary jury which George Herbert Mead argues we all carry around in our heads. Violating an anti-racist taboo, even covertly, induces guilt which affects self-esteem. But if others come out in support of a populist-right party, or a person perceives that others are happy to vote for it, this can detoxify its image, increasing support. A self-fulfilling dynamic kicks in whereby populist parties achieve a breakthrough level of support, signalling to fence-sitters that it's okay to vote for them. This in turn paves the way for the more reticent, who boost the party's numbers, which in turn convinces further waverers. The chain reaction only stalls when the party is compelled to reach beyond its core of conservatives and psychological 'authoritarians', or order-seekers.

In this sense, UKIP, much like the Swiss People's Party and German AfD, benefited from impeccably middle-class, non-racist roots. It was formed as an anti-EU party by Alan Sked, a libertarian London School of Economics professor, in 1993. Largely an offshoot of the Conservatives, it appealed primarily to middle-class Tories concerned about the EU's infringement of British sovereignty. This form of British nationalism was steeped in Thatcherite disdain for continental European – notably French – statism. As such, it pressed a traditional British sovereignist message. Though respectable, this held modest appeal beyond the Eurosceptic right of the Tory party. In the late 1990s, the Conservatives were in the political wilderness, rent by battles between Eurosceptics and Euro-pragmatists which hobbled the party.[59] By 2001 they had coalesced around a more Eurosceptic message, luring strongly anti-EU voters away from other parties, but surveys showed that the EU was simply not a high enough priority for most voters to persuade them to vote Tory.[60] In daily life, few could 'see' the EU, much less name any of its policies or politicians. At this point, UKIP were perceived as a quasi-pressure group of the Tory party, with many activists hoping to drag the Conservatives in a Eurosceptic direction until they could rejoin it.

In the early 2000s through to 2009, the BNP outpolled UKIP due to their single-minded focus on the immigration question, which most voters cared a lot more about than they cared about the EU. In addition, the BNP had a strong local-level network of committed activists. While the BNP targeted hard-pressed working-class voters in urban areas, UKIP's voting base was older, better off and centred in heavily white, provincial southern England. Only in 2011 did UKIP consistently begin to outpace the BNP in local elections.[61]

UKIP began opposing immigration in the early 2000s, and in 2004 scored an impressive 16.1 per cent vote in the 2004 European elections, a big increase over its 7 per cent share of 1999. It won 2.7 million votes, far more than the 1 million which the BNP recorded at its zenith in 2009. European elections, though largely symbolic contests, were a bellwether of growing discontent over consistently high rates of immigration and ethnic change. Once UKIP had politicized immigration, it began to encounter opponents attempting to tar it as racist in order to key into people's Motivation to Control Prejudice (MCP) and shut down the party's appeal. As early as 2004, the liberal *Observer* described them as 'the BNP in blazers':

> Under the headline 'Immigration soaring', a cartoon depicts 'overcrowded Britain', a shanty-town jumble of houses: across the sea, streams of eastern European immigrants pour into an entrance labelled 'Channel Funnel'. Inside, the leaflet adds: 'At last! A non-racist party that takes a firm line on immigration' . . . So is this little more than the BNP in blazers, as its critics suggest – a genteel, gin-and-Jag-belt version of the unsavoury messages peddled on council estates by the far right – or does it reflect a legitimate disenchantment with an over-mighty EU?[62]

This passage makes a clear distinction between the 'legitimate' cause of British political nationalism and the 'unsavoury' one of anti-immigration politics and cultural nationalism. Overlaid on this is the seeming respectability of Jaguar-driving suburban England compared to working-class public housing estates. For progressive papers in this period, politicizing immigration still carried the whiff of racism. In 2006, the new

Conservative leader, David Cameron, weighed in, dismissing UKIP as 'fruitcakes, loonies and closet racists'. In response, the new UKIP leader, Nigel Farage, defensively replied that his was a non-racist party which did not tolerate extremists or former BNP members. The presence of the BNP on the political scene, and UKIP's stated opposition to it, helped the party remain – for conservative voters at least – marginally within the bounds of non-racist respectability. But the party constantly had to police its boundaries and rhetoric in order to navigate the tension between campaigning to reduce immigration and avoiding the taint of racism which clings to anti-immigration parties. The shift in social norms to a more scaled-back definition of racism accounts, in part, for the party's rise in the early 2010s, a process I explore in chapter 8.

IMMIGRATION AND POLITICAL REALIGNMENT IN THE 2000S

As figure 4.1 shows, concern over immigration was rising sharply in the 2000s and was cited by over 30 per cent of voters as the most important issue facing Britain. In order to head off the challenge from the BNP and UKIP, the Conservative Party ramped up its rhetoric on the subject. Mindful of both the BNP and public attitudes, William Hague made headlines in 2000 with his plain-speaking critique of Labour's policy of permitting 'floods' of asylum seekers to enter the country. Michael Howard, who led the party from late 2003 until the 2005 election, likewise made immigration central to his campaign. Party billboards read 'It's not racist to impose limits on immigration', and 'Are you thinking what we're thinking?' Surveys showed that most people agreed with Tory immigration policy but felt uncomfortable embracing the party. Some analysts believed the party's hard-hearted reputation – a legacy of Thatcherite cuts combined with its position on questions like immigration – prevented many from voting for it.

The Tories' poor performance at the polls reinforced a sense that the party brand needed softening to reach voters in the centre. In 1997, Blair's Labour Party beat the Conservatives 43–31 in the popular vote. In 2001, the Tories barely improved, inching their way up to 32 per cent. At the 2002 Conservative Party conference, newly appointed chairman Theresa May, who would later become Prime Minister, urged the party to tone down its image. She first rebuked the party for its lack of female and minority candidates: 'Our base is too narrow and so, occasionally, are our sympathies, You know what some people call us: the nasty party.' In 2005, under Howard, the third in a string of opposition leaders chosen from the party's right wing, the Conservatives failed to improve on their 2001 performance, winning just 32 per cent of the vote. These failures prompted the party to select the youthful David Cameron as leader in late 2005. He broke with his predecessors, tacking to the centre on a modernizing, optimistic platform. Speaking warmly about green issues, he called for a compassionate conservatism that could appeal to younger, metropolitan voters.

In other words, while people might tell pollsters they wanted less immigration, when push came to shove, their sensitivity to Tory transgressions of anti-racist norms trumped their nationalist inclinations. As mentioned earlier, my point here is that the openness of a society to immigration is the outcome of a cross-pressuring between majority ethnic and nationalist 'voice' and anti-racist 'repression' of that voice. In the 2000s, it was assumed that campaigning to limit immigration transgressed anti-racist norms, damaging the Tory brand more than it helped it. The moral repression of majority ethnic 'voice' still predominated at this point. By the late 2000s, this was no longer evident. Longitudinal surveys such as the British Election Panel Study (BEPS) ask the same people questions year after year. These are more rigorous than snapshot surveys which can only compare individuals at one point in time. Geoff Evans and Jon Mellon at Oxford University used the BEPS to consider defection from Labour during the 2005–10 period. They found that half of 2005 Labour voters did not intend to vote for the party in 2010. Critically, the chance of someone defecting from Labour to the Conservatives rose from 10 per cent among those who thought Labour was handling immigration well to 20 per cent among those who thought the party was doing a poor job on immigration.[63]

Evans and Mellon found that immigration was the most important variable differentiating Labour defectors from Labour loyalists. Labour's perceived competence on the economy, for instance, had no impact on switching. In effect, concern over immigration rather than Labour's handling of the 2007–8 economic crisis is what tipped the vote in the Conservatives' favour. Many of these new Tory voters were white Britons who lacked educational qualifications. As in other Western countries, Labour, the main centre-left party, was losing much of its traditional white working-class base due, in part, to its cultural outlook. The New Left activist core of the party, increasingly motivated by cultural radicalism and liberal immigration, was a major driver of change. Between the mid-1990s and 2010, the share of the white working class who identified with Labour dropped from 55 to barely 30 per cent. Some gravitated to the Tories, their traditional rivals, but many entered the pool of disaffected, disconnected voters.[64] The latter would prove a particularly potent force during the Brexit referendum.

In peacetime, cultural changes are often the result of complex bottom-up dynamics in which individual changes create new social environments which reinforce change, in self-fulfilling fashion. This allows fledgling ideas to gain critical mass. The recent liberalization of attitudes to homosexuality in America is a case in point: liberalization made people aware that attitudes were changing, which convinced fence-sitters, who in turn shifted the cultural landscape, which helped change the minds of other waverers, and so on. Psychological authoritarians who resolutely oppose homosexuality will nonetheless accept its legitimacy if this is viewed as the 'normal' social consensus. Complexity theory tells us that large changes may make no difference while small changes, the proverbial straw that breaks the camel's back, do. Likewise, small shifts in cultural sensibilities at the margins can produce sudden swings in cultural mood. Consider the anti-racism norm as it pertains to immigration. The rise in immigration throughout the 2000s initially seemed to have little effect on the location of the anti-racism boundary in public life. Then, late in the decade, the ground suddenly began to shift.

One episode in the 2010 election campaign nicely captures the changing balance between two moral memes: the anti-racism norm and an emerging taboo against slights to the white working class. After being heckled in a televised debate by Gillian Duffy – a white working-class woman from hardscrabble Rochdale in northern England – the Labour Prime Minister, Gordon Brown, and his team arranged for him to speak with her. This would show Brown's common touch and responsiveness to the concerns of the ordinary person. Brown patiently listened to Duffy's worries about how some seemed to have access to income support while others did not. Then Duffy asked the Prime Minister point-blank: 'All these eastern Europeans that are coming in, where are they flocking from?' Brown managed to withdraw soon afterwards.

After the interview, Brown forgot to turn off his microphone. In private conversation with aides, he proceeded to describe the exchange with Duffy as a 'disaster', calling her a 'bigoted woman'. When the recording hit the air, the media, rather than brush off Brown's comments as an understandable reaction which served the cause of righteousness, turned on the Prime Minister. On BBC Radio 2's Jeremy Vine Show, the host asked Brown, 'Is she not allowed to express her views?' Brown, now on the defensive, swiftly replied, 'Of course she is.' Brown later apologized in person to Mrs Duffy, a signal that the relative power of competing social norms was shifting.

A TORY VICTORY

In the 2010 election, Cameron's Conservatives won 36 per cent of the vote to Labour's 29, ending thirteen years of Labour rule. This represented an increase of 4 points for the Tories over 2005 while Labour dropped by 6. Labour's result built on a pattern which began with Blair's election in 1997: the steady erosion of its white working-class base. Between 1945 and 1994, Labour won 50 to 60 per cent of working-class votes with its resolutely pro-union, socialist policies. After Blair's election in 1997 this dropped because Blair was viewed as representing the new liberal middle class. Whereas Labour had once received three quarters of its votes from the working class, this fell to a third.[65] From 1997, a second dynamic kicked in based on values, wherein culturally conservative working-class voters left the party. Some went to the Tories, but more became non-voters. Up until the 1990s around 75 per cent of working-class people turned up to vote. After 1997 half stayed away from the polls. Some joined working-class Tories by voting for UKIP and Brexit.[66]

Cameron and Nick Clegg of the Liberal Democrats governed in coalition from 2010 until the 2015 election. As Evans and Mellon show, the Conservatives had built up capital with anti-immigration voters in the wilderness years of the 2000s that finally paid off. This changed political thinking. From 1997 through 2005, the Conservative vote stalled despite the party's rhetoric on immigration. Many wondered aloud whether focusing on immigration was contributing to the 'nasty party' image at a time when a supposedly touchy-feely generation of voters craved optimism and an emotional connection to their leader. The perception was that the Conservatives damaged themselves more among former Blair voters by espousing a restrictive view on immigration than they gained from traditionalist folk voicing concern about immigration to focus groups and pollsters. By 2010, this reasoning was giving way to a realization that immigration really mattered for politics. It was clear that the balance between repression and voice on immigration had swung towards voice.

Thus, despite Cameron's empathetic image, he expressed scepticism of European integration and immigration. For the first time since Thatcher, a British politician set a clear target for reducing immigration. 'We would like to see net immigration in the tens of thousands rather than the hundreds of thousands,' he stated in January 2010. 'I don't think that's unrealistic. That's the sort of figure it was in the 1990s and I think we should see that again.'[67] Rhetoric aside, it soon became apparent during the coalition period that Cameron wasn't meeting the target. By 2015, net migration to Britain was exceeding 300,000 per year, a considerably higher figure than the 200,000–250,000 recorded during the late Blair years.

Continuing high numbers put the Conservative leader in a quandary. Half the flow was outside his control because Britain, as a member of the EU, had to accept as many European citizens as wished to enter. Britain's strong labour market stood in stark contrast to much of the continent, which hadn't weathered the 2007–8 recession well. The Eastern Europeans who had been arriving since their countries' accession in 2004 were joined by a growing influx from depressed Southern Europe. Even so, non-European immigration exceeded the European inflow through to 2016. In that year, 164,000 more non-Europeans arrived in Britain than departed. Family reunification, student overstayers, refugees and strong demand for low-cost labour kept numbers high. The Conservatives were fast losing the trust of the public on this key issue. Prior to the 2010 election, 75 per cent of voters disapproved of Labour on immigration while just 40 per cent said the same for the Conservatives. By 2013, disapproval of the Conservatives on the issue exceeded 70 per cent: higher than for Labour.[68]

Cameron's inability to reduce the influx spawned increasingly desperate gestures, such as the 'In the UK illegally? Go home or face arrest' vans which the Tories hired to drive around London. Criticized for using 'the language of the National Front' by Labour's Shadow Home Secretary, Yvette Cooper, even UKIP slighted Cameron's buses as ineffective. The ongoing influx prompted some Tory supporters to switch to UKIP to voice their concerns. One of Cameron's responses was to promise, in 2013, an 'In/Out' referendum on Britain's EU membership to placate his base and head off competition from UKIP. This was to be a momentous decision. Some contend that Cameron should never have pledged to reduce numbers to under 100,000, an unattainable target. But it can be argued this was as much a symbolic exercise as anything else. Polling in 2016 confirms that, while many voters don't believe the target can be met, they still want numbers below 100,000.[69] Setting a target and failing to meet it led to a decline in voters' trust in the Tories, but abandoning the target might have sent a potent ideological signal, causing even greater damage.

Despite high non-European immigration, politicians and the media constantly flagged the question of free movement and Eastern European migration. Why? The anti-racist norm played a curious role at this point, deflecting criticism away from Asians and Africans towards white immigrants from the EU. A naked appeal to reduce Asian and African immigration still carried racial connotations redolent of Powellism. As Labour MP Frank Field relates: 'The truth is, I wasn't brave enough to raise it [immigration] as an issue – though I thought it was an issue for yonks – until we were talking about white people coming in. And even then the anger that this was racist was something one had to face.'[70] Labour Cabinet minister Chris Mullin's diaries from 2004 revealed that, in relation to sham marriages within the South Asian community designed to facilitate immigration from South Asia, 'we are terrified of the cry of "racism" that would go up the moment anyone breathed a word on the subject'.[71] The post-2004 story of unchecked Polish, Romanian and Bulgarian immigration, whether voiced by politicians or the media, helped raise the importance of the issue in the minds of voters.

In this as in other ways, the anti-racist norm's proscription on expressions of majority ethnic anxiety was producing secondary fallout which damaged liberal causes. Work I have done with Simon Hix and Thomas Leeper of the London School of Economics based on a YouGov sample of 3,600 voters carried out in May 2017 shows that, despite the overwhelming focus of the media and politicians on EU immigration, the British public's desired level of EU migration, 76,000, remains significantly higher than its preferred 61,000 intake of non-EU immigrants.[72] At ward level (population around 6,500), my analysis of Understanding Society data likewise shows that the increase in non-European population share in a ward in the 2000s was a better predictor of a white British individual voting UKIP vote than the local rise in East European share.[73] By compelling the media, politicians and voters to express immigration concerns in an anti-EU idiom, the anti-racism norm inadvertently contributed to a climate in which the EU became a punching bag. This helped nudge the country towards Brexit.

VOICE, REPRESSION AND UKIP

In 1975, Britain opted in a referendum to remain in the European Economic Community, forerunner of the EU. Immigration played no role in the vote whatsoever. At the time, Britain's economy was moribund and Conservative voters, who tended to be more anti-immigration than Labour voters, favoured joining as a means of reviving the economy. Around 75 per cent of anti-immigration voters favoured joining the EEC in 1975 compared to barely 60 per cent of pro-immigration voters. By 2015, the reverse was true: the majority of anti-immigration voters were in the Leave camp while only 10 per cent of pro-immigration voters were. How did this reversal occur?

It's difficult to 'see' the EU in everyday life – many people in Britain can't name an EU politician and few understand how the EU works. EU flags are few and far between and its regulations, costs and benefits are largely hidden from view. Immigration, on the other hand, is much more present – both in everyday life and in the media. The trick for Eurosceptic politicians was to link something people cared about, immigration, with something they didn't, the EU. There is little doubt that this campaign was successful: recall that the share of people saying immigration was the most important issue facing Britain rose steadily through the 2000s. Evans and Mellon show that the difference in people's approval of the EU on a 0–1 scale between those who said immigration was the most important problem and those who said it wasn't widened from .5 in 2004 to .9 by 2015.[74] By 2016 the two questions had become two sides of the same coin.

What brought the two issues together? One answer lay with

anti-racism norms, which deflected rising anti-immigration sentiment and reportage almost exclusively against the EU and East Europeans. The second was UKIP, which worked tirelessly to yoke immigration and the EU in many voters' minds. UKIP billboards emphasized the slogan 'Take Back Control'. One famous poster featured an escalator rising up the white cliffs of Dover reading 'No Border. No Control. The EU has opened our borders to 4,000 people every week.' In the words of UKIP's leader, Nigel Farage, 'The goal was to get into people's heads that immigration and Europe are the same thing and that we are impotent.'[75] UKIP's share of anti-immigration voters in national surveys tripled between 2010 and 2013 as Cameron's Conservatives failed to bring numbers down.

UKIP's fortunes climbed steadily after 2009. In that year, UKIP won 16 per cent of the vote in the European elections, similar to its 2004 performance. After the 2010 election as immigration remained high, alienating anti-immigration voters who had switched to the Tories, UKIP began reaping the rewards. Its local election vote share increased from 4.4 per cent in 2012 to nearly 20 per cent in 2013 and remained in double digits thereafter.[76] Then, in the May 2014 elections to the European Parliament, UKIP won an astonishing 28.7 per cent of the vote, coming first overall. This was also the election in which the Danish People's Party won 26.6 per cent and the Front National 25 per cent, of their countries' respective votes. Though turnout is low for European elections and results often reflect expressive protest voting, these rumblings showed that ethno-nationalism was gaining power across the continent.

UKIP's rise prompted the question of who would benefit from their rise. Since Euroscepticism had a long history in the Tory party, it was generally assumed that UKIP was a Tory splinter-group whose departure would damage the Conservatives. However, Robert Ford and Matthew Goodwin's analysis remarked that UKIP was the most working-class party in the country. It was poised, therefore, to damage Labour as much as the Tories. A penetrating analysis by Geoff Evans and Jon Mellon using British Election Study (BES) data shows that, while most who voted for UKIP in the 2014 European elections voted Tory in 2010, many of these voters voted Labour, Lib Dem or did not vote in 2005 (figure 4.3). My own analysis of this data confirms that non-voters or voters for left parties who switched to the Tories in 2010 were significantly more likely to move on to UKIP than Conservatives who voted

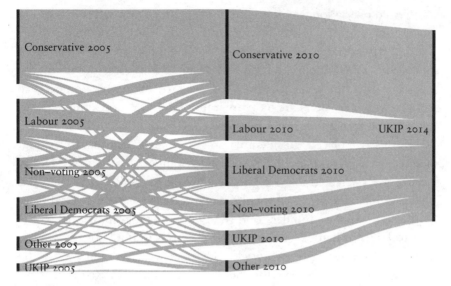

4.3. Sources of UKIP's 2014 European election vote

Source: G. Evans and J. Mellon, 'Working class votes and Conservative losses: Solving the UKIP puzzle', LSE British Politics and Policy Blog (30 April 2015).

Tory in both 2005 and 2010 – and were therefore party loyalists who could not shift to UKIP. Evans and Mellon suggest that many UKIP voters are ex-Tory voters living in strong Labour territory, though my own analysis indicates that UKIP captured roughly the same share of Tory votes across all types of constituency.

Using Britain's long-running British Household Panel Survey (BHPS), I established that most UKIP voters began life voting for Blair, but splintered to the Tories, Lib Dems and non-voting after 1997 before entering the Tory or UKIP folds by 2010. The doyen of British pollsters, Peter Kellner, identified the key differences between Labour loyalists and defectors in October 2012. Among 2010 Labour voters intending to vote Labour again, about half read left-wing papers such as the *Guardian* and *Mirror* and half consumed right-wing tabloids such as the *Daily Mail* and *Sun*. Yet among defectors *Sun* and *Mail* readers outnumbered *Guardian* and *Mirror* readers four to one. What really stood out were the immigration and Eurosceptic views of defectors: 78 per cent wanted 'net immigration reduced to zero' and 59 per cent wanted Britain out of the EU.[77]

Viewed over a longer time span, it is apparent immigration opinion among the ethnic majority became increasingly associated with partisanship after Blair's accession in 1997: Conservatives became more opposed while Labour and Liberal Democrat voters moved in the opposite direction (see figure 4.4). This is of increasing importance because younger voters are more tolerant of immigration and are flocking to Labour in even greater numbers than normal for those their age.

UKIP's rise placed considerable pressure on the Conservatives, and not just in the opinion polls. In August 2014, maverick Tory MP Douglas Carswell defected to UKIP. In September, Mark Reckless followed suit. Significantly, both held white working-class seats in coastal Kent in the south-east and understood these to be demographically favourable to UKIP. Their exit prompted by-elections in both constituencies. In Clacton-on-Sea, Carswell won in October with 59.7 per cent of the vote against 24.6 per cent for the Tory candidate. In Rochester and Strood in late November, Reckless held the seat with 42 per cent of the

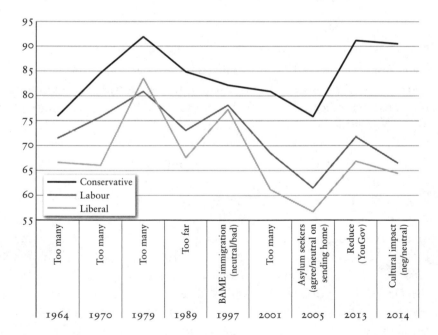

4.4. White opposition to immigration, by vote, 1964–2014, %

Source: BES 1964–2015; YouGov 2013.

vote against 35 per cent for his Tory challenger. All of which reinforced the perception of a rising, unstoppable UKIP tide.[78]

The tension between 'voice', ethnically motivated opposition to immigration, and 'repression' of racist concerns in the name of collective morality remained important as voters wrestled with their consciences. As the BNP's light faded after 2009, UKIP took over as the main anti-immigration force in politics. When UKIP's right flank disappeared, so did some of its moral insulation. As such, it had to work hard to include minorities in its ranks to protect its reputational shield. Those caught making racist comments, such as Andre Lampitt, who appeared in a UKIP election commercial, were expelled from the party. In May 2014 UKIP's leader, Nigel Farage, appeared at a rally with thirty or forty ethnic minority supporters, a stage-managed event designed to burnish the party's non-racist credentials. Calling it his party's 'Clause IV moment' in reference to Labour's modernization prior to the Blair years, he said, 'I don't care what you call us, but from this moment on, please do not call us a racist party.'[79] Minority UKIP activists such as Jamaican-born Winston McKenzie or the party's Pakistani-born small-business spokesman Amjad Bashir affirmed both their ethnicity and their party loyalty, challenging detractors to call them racist. Farage spoke of his minority supporters as 'wonderful men and women' from 'different backgrounds' who were united in wanting to reclaim Britain's sovereignty from the European Union. Scrupulously avoiding mention of non-European immigration, he urged Britain to renew ties to the Commonwealth (i.e. the Indian Subcontinent and the Caribbean), which it could not do with an 'open door' to East European immigration.

While keen to remain on the respectable side of the anti-racism line, Farage also used resentment of elite political correctness to his electoral advantage. He spoke of immigration as 'the biggest single issue facing the country . . . the establishment has been closing down the immigration debate for 20 years. UKIP has opened it up.'[80] Despite the rising volume of news stories and political rhetoric about the need to control immigration, most voters still felt not enough attention was being paid to the issue. Polling by Ipsos MORI in 2011 shows that 62 per cent of voters felt immigration was 'not discussed in Britain enough', 20 per cent said it was and 11 per cent said it was talked about too much. By 2014, the public were more satisfied: 43 per cent claimed it wasn't talked about enough, 28 per cent were satisfied and 26 per cent now said it was talked about too much.[81]

Tension between anti-racist repression of UKIP and anti-immigration 'voice' was acute. On the left, commentators urged voters not to permit Farage's party to be seen as respectable. For if it gained respectability as a non-racist party this would allow the Conservatives to use UKIP as their insulation against the charge of racism when politicizing immigration. To resist UKIP they sought to rely on the traditional method of shaming the party by activating the anti-racist taboo: 'If UKIP master using euphemism and politically correct language to couch their ideology and gain popularity, British political discourse will move even further to the right,' warned an opinion piece in the left-leaning *Independent*. 'We must beware the threat of UKIP's ideology in an acceptable garb . . . We must call it out when we see it . . . British political discourse needs voices prepared to speak out in favour of immigration and the EU, as well as the cosmopolitanism and multiculturalism that come with them.'[82] In the Rochester by-election the Greens made an overt play for the 'Anywhere' cosmopolitan vote, listing themselves as 'Green – Say No to Racism' on the ballot. This may account for their increase in vote share from 2.7 to 4.2 per cent.

Several UKIP activists such as Andre Lampitt and Godfrey Bloom made racist remarks, and Farage ensured they were quickly removed from the party. Yet for its critics this was mere window-dressing, concealing the racist fist within the party's velvet glove. Certainly there were racist sentiments and nastiness expressed by party members but what was lacking was a nuanced debate over the meaning of 'racism' and 'extremism' that might have sorted the racist wheat from the ethnotraditional chaff. Progressives cleaved to an expansive rather than forensic definition of these terms, effectively defining anti-immigration and anti-EU sentiment as racist and extreme. This was not only problematic in philosophical terms, but tactically questionable.

Consider the conclusion of a report into UKIP, *They're Thinking What We're Thinking*, published by Tory pollster Lord Ashcroft in December 2012. The Tory grandee conducted a massive survey of 20,000 people and fielded fourteen focus groups. In his words, the 'single biggest misconception' about UKIP's appeal was that it was based solely on the party's policies. Instead, offered Ashcroft, people voted for UKIP because it expressed their worldview and stood up to political correctness:

Certainly, those who are attracted to UKIP are more preoccupied than most with immigration . . . But these are often part of a greater dissatisfaction with the way they see things going in Britain: schools, they say, can't hold nativity plays or harvest festivals any more; you can't fly a flag of St George any more . . . you can't speak up about these things because you'll be called a racist . . . [These examples] were mentioned in focus groups by UKIP voters and led [UKIP] considerers to make the point that the mainstream political parties are so in thrall to the prevailing culture of political correctness that they have ceased to represent the silent majority.

The survey showed that, among respondents who might consider voting UKIP, 78 per cent agreed that 'UKIP seem to want to take Britain back to a time when things were done more sensibly', a sentiment nearly as powerful as the party's opposition to immigration and the EU.[83] In focus groups, Europe was rarely mentioned, but immigration and the way the anti-racist taboo constrained debate was a leading concern:

Many said they had noticed a significant change in the character of their local area over recent years. For them, the differences between this and previous waves of immigration were the sheer numbers involved . . . While a few thought the government was trying to control immigration, most felt that little was being done. They often thought this was because politicians seemed scared to speak out on the subject because of the constraints of political correctness and the fear that they would be accused of racism.

CLASS: A NEW FORM OF POLITICAL CORRECTNESS?

UKIP's rising fortunes, led by the charismatic, hard-drinking Nigel Farage, helped consolidate a new political culture in which political correctness about the patriotic white working class began to rival norms of political correctness around minorities. The first salvo had been the Gillian Duffy incident during the 2010 election. The scene would be repeated four years later when Emily Thornberry, an MP representing the 'champagne socialist' redoubt of Islington, North London, tweeted a picture entitled 'image from #Rochester' of a modest home in Rochester, Kent. The town is situated to the south-east of London and has a history of London East End working-class Cockney in-migration. Following close on the heels of Douglas Carswell's by-election win in Clacton-on-Sea and UKIP's stunning performance in the 2014 European elections, Mark Reckless's victory was viewed with considerable foreboding by 'Anywhere' liberals such as Thornberry.

Showing a house covered in English flags, with a white van parked out front, Thornberry's picture combined class snobbery with liberal anti-nationalism. The picture represented everything middle-class liberals derided about the patriotic white working class. The flying of the English flag, the Cross of St George, used to be associated almost exclusively with the far right and hooliganism. While this began to change when fans of England's national football team embraced the symbol in 1996, the flying of the flag outside periods of international football rivalry is still viewed by middle-class liberals as racist or distasteful.

As Angela, an older middle-class respondent and Labour councillor, told researchers Robin Mann and Steve Fenton: 'I always say I am British [not English] . . . Some of the pubs in the area celebrate St. George's Day in a very jingoistic way . . . and put up the red and white [George Cross] flag and they are ever so proudly English. But it's mixed up with the BNP and racism and a very anti-foreigner attitude.' For Linda, a lawyer in her fifties, 'When our people go on holiday they have a reputation for being lager louts and getting drunk. The English flag is something you are ashamed of.'[84]

By contrast, many white working-class people view the English flag as a statement of identity in a period of elevated political correctness. For Graham, one of the sociologist Michael Skey's Hastings-area respondents, 'the need to celebrate it [flag] comes from this feeling of that it's being actually suppressed'. 'It wasn't in your face,' claimed Janet, a south Londoner. 'But it's now in your face and you think "Hang on a sec, this is my country, so therefore I celebrate what my country is."' Many respondents evince a keen hostility to multiculturalism and political correctness. For Doreen, 'The silly nonsense about blackboards . . . everything that was black had to have the name changed, it's utterly ridiculous and it did cause of lot of resentment.' Derek, another of Skey's interviewees, claimed: 'there was hordes of them [English flags] on cars, buildings, the lot . . . I think that was the white community making a statement about immigration and about multiculturalism'.[85]

White vans, meanwhile, are the British version of the American

pickup truck, a symbol of white working-class masculinity often intertwined in the liberal middle-class mind with nationalism and racism.
When Thornberry tweeted her picture, the Conservative Prime Minister, David Cameron, made political hay out of the remark, castigating
the tweet as 'appalling . . . sneering at people who work hard, are patriotic, and love their country'. Internal criticism from within Labour,
a party struggling to retain its working-class base, compelled Thornberry to resign from her Cabinet post. Miliband, said to be 'furious'
over the tweet, swiftly responded that people should fly the England
flag 'with pride'.[86] In a period of right-wing populism, slights against
the nationalistic white working class had become as politically incorrect as talking about reducing immigration.

The contrast with Canada, where political correctness retains its
exclusive focus on minorities rather the white working class, is stark. In
2001, Hedy Fry, the Trinidad-born Minister of State for Multiculturalism in the Liberal government, said on the floor of the House of
Commons: 'Mr Speaker, we can just go to Prince George, in British
Columbia, where crosses are being burned on lawns as we speak.' The
comment, a figment of Fry's imagination, effectively smeared a British
Columbia pulp-and-paper town as a hotbed of racism. Having been to
the town on a number of occasions – once while planting trees, another
on a sawmill visit, I can attest to its frontier atmosphere and strong
First Nations influence. But there is no Klan or racist political activity
there, and never has been. The fact that Prince George is part of the
Conservatives' interior western heartland, and, like most rural Canadian communities, is predominantly white working-class, was enough
for Fry to brand it a racist backwater. Though compelled to apologize,
she didn't resign and received light treatment because in Canada's public discourse the white working class are considered fair game. Had this
happened in Britain in 2014 ('crosses burning in Sunderland'), her political career would have been over. Likewise, had Fry called for sharply
reduced immigration, her political life in Canada would have juddered
to a halt. This illustrates the different political norms prevailing in the
two countries. In Britain in the 2000s, immigration-scepticism and
white working-class identity politics had gained significant yardage
against norms seeking to repress majority ethnic sentiment. In Canada
by contrast, anything that could be construed as pro-white lay beyond
the racist pale.

BREXIT: BRITAIN LEAVES THE
EUROPEAN UNION

In 2015, the country went to the polls to elect their next government. David Cameron had governed with Nick Clegg's Liberal Democrats in a successful coalition. However, many of Clegg's youthful supporters felt let down by his U-turn on scrapping university tuition fees. Meanwhile Cameron's Labour opponent, Ed Miliband, was widely perceived as a weaker candidate than his brother David, having won the leadership only thanks to support from trade unions and the left wing of the party. The election was Cameron's to lose had it not been for UKIP, which threatened to eat into the Tories' right flank. In the event, UKIP won nearly 4 million votes, 12.6 per cent of the total. Curiously, one factor playing in Cameron's favour was the strength of the Scottish National Party (SNP). Scotland had only narrowly voted to remain in the United Kingdom in 2014. The thought of a Labour government in hock to its SNP coalition partner ruling the country helped push potential UKIP voters back to the Tories. On the doorstep, the Tories hammered home their 'vote UKIP, get Miliband' message. In strong UKIP constituencies, there was a noticeably greater swing to the Conservatives than predicted by the polls.[87]

The Conservatives emerged with a surprise majority: 331 seats on a popular vote of 36 per cent. One of the Tories' election promises was to hold an 'In/Out' referendum on leaving the European Union. There had been a strong Eurosceptic wing in the party since the 1990s and pressure from a rising UKIP and many Tory MPs led Cameron to promise in 2013 that a referendum would be held if the Conservatives won the next election.[88] On the night of the referendum to leave the European Union, I recall going to bed calmly believing that, as voters had done in the Scottish and Quebec referendums, British voters would opt for the status quo despite the tight polls. The following morning when my wife broke the news that the country had voted to Leave, I was stunned. A few months later I experienced the same set of emotions when waking up to Trump's victory. How did Britain's decision to Leave, 'Brexit', happen?

The increasing prominence of immigration and the rise of UKIP form the backstory to the Brexit vote. In fact constituency models which took UKIP's 2014 European election vote share and added 25 per cent strongly predicted the result.[89] The profile of immigration was raised by the 2015 migration crisis in Europe which began in earnest in February and crested in October. With over 100,000 people entering Europe each month, the issue gained prominence even as Cameron kept Britain's doors largely closed to refugees. But Cameron couldn't reduce the number of legal immigrants: in late 2015, the Office for National Statistics (ONS) announced net migration had reached a record 336,000.

One of the Prime Minister's manifesto promises was to renegotiate the terms of Britain's membership of the EU to gain better control of immigration. He hoped to persuade Brussels to offer Britain concessions on freedom of movement, one of the 'four freedoms' Brussels viewed as fundamental to EU membership. He didn't succeed. In February, Cameron returned from Brussels having secured a package of changes that included Britain gaining an opt-out of the symbolic 'ever closer union' clause and winning a qualified right to restrict benefits to new EU immigrants for a four-year period. Though Cameron tried to sell the deal as a success, most Eurosceptics viewed it as a failure. Despite telling focus groups that they worried most about immigrants putting pressure on public services, tightening benefits to immigrants was not the issue: most were privately far more concerned about numbers. For them, Brussels' refusal to accept British control over the inflow from the continent was the last straw.

Nevertheless, Britain's exit from Europe was far from certain. National politics is highly visible, EU politics is not. So when national politicians who back the EU are popular, EU popularity rides high. Cameron enjoyed much higher approval than Labour's new far-left leader, Jeremy Corbyn. Cameron's popularity should have buoyed the case for Remain. On the other hand, when the party that people support bashes the EU and says leaving Europe is an important issue, many voters tune in to that issue and follow suit.[90] UKIP played this role, raising anti-EU consciousness in the 2000s with its steady drumbeat of anti-EU soundbites and infomercials. Still, Harold Clarke, Matt Goodwin and Paul Whiteley show, using monthly survey data, that anti-EU sentiment was volatile after 2004: cresting at 54 per cent in 2011 before falling back to 37 per cent after Cameron's election in 2015, then beginning to rise again, until the EU referendum.[91]

In February 2016, upon returning from Brussels, Cameron announced that the referendum would be held on 23 June. The Remain camp featured David Cameron and prominent Remain Conservative frontbenchers such as George Osborne. Theresa May, the future Prime Minister, was in the Remain camp, but kept a low profile. On the Labour side, Jeremy Corbyn backed Remain. However, as an unpopular figure among centrist Labour voters who had himself voted against staying in Europe in 1975, Corbyn was of limited use to the cause. Each of the parties ran its own campaign, hoping to leverage party loyalty to convince its base to back Remain and turn out to the polls.

The Leave side, though structured as a cross-party effort, was equally divided. Vote Leave, the official Leave campaign, was chaired by Gisela Stuart, a Labour MP, but fronted by the Tory mayor of London Boris Johnson and Conservative MPs such as Chris Grayling, Andrea Leadsom and Michael Gove. Vote Leave's rhetoric focused on 'respectable' arguments around sovereignty and the freedom for Britain to make its own trade deals with growing economies. A second effort, Leave.eu, funded by UKIP donor Arron Banks and fronted by the party leader, Nigel Farage, was an insurgent campaign which concentrated on the immigration question. Farage's slogan, 'Take Back Control', resonated well with UKIP's base. While largely focusing on European immigration, Farage also made a high-profile pitch to those fearful of non-Europeans with his infamous 'Breaking Point' poster, shown in figure 4.5. The subtext being that large flows of Muslim immigrants who had washed ashore during the migration crisis would soon be arriving in Britain, courtesy of Britain's open door to Europe.

Reaction from all sides was immediate. Dave Prentis, of the Unison trade union, branded the UKIP poster 'an attempt to incite racial hatred' and reported it to the police. 'To pretend that migration to the UK is only about people who are not white is to peddle the racism that has no place in a modern, caring society. That's why Unison has complained about this blatant attempt to incite racial hatred and breach UK race laws.' At Vote Leave, Boris Johnson distanced himself from the poster, declaring, 'I am passionately pro-immigration and pro-immigrants.' The Archbishop of Canterbury accused the poster of 'pandering to people's worries and prejudices, that is, giving legitimization to racism'. Farage remained unmoved: 'This is a photograph – an accurate, undoctored photograph – taken on 15 October last year

4.5. UKIP's 'Breaking Point' poster.

Source: Reuters

following Angela Merkel's call in the summer ... most of the people coming are young males and, yes, they may be coming from countries that are not in a very happy state, they may be coming from places that are poorer than us, but the EU has made a fundamental error that risks the security of everybody.'[92] The racist charge is appropriate in my view because the poster encourages irrational fears of Muslim immigrants. What is less clear is how different the popular response would have been had the picture featured white East European Christians.

EXPLAINING THE BREXIT VOTE

Relations between Vote Leave and Leave.eu were acrimonious, but Clarke, Goodwin and Whiteley point out that the division had its upsides for Leave. Vote Leave could concentrate on waverers, often middle class, who didn't want to be associated with UKIP 'racism', while Leave.eu fired up the anti-immigration base.[93] This proved far more useful than the mixed messages delivered by the party leaders. Crunching survey data, the authors show that those with a positive view of Farage or Johnson inclined strongly towards Leave while those holding a positive view of Cameron and Corbyn were not swayed to vote Remain.[94]

A distinctive feature of the referendum was its 72.2 per cent turnout, considerably higher than the 66.1 per cent for the 2015 election. Since the vote was not structured on party lines, people were freed to vote for ideas rather than parties. This meant many white working-class voters who had disengaged from the Labour Party during and after the Blair years showed up to vote, pushing Leave over the line. Labour-leaning non-voters, mainly whites without degrees, made the difference. Figure 4.6, drawing on Understanding Society data, shows that a majority of Labour supporters who say they are 'not at all' interested in politics back Leave while barely 20 per cent of Labour supporters with a strong interest in politics do. Among Conservative supporters there is much less difference between the interested and apathetic, though even here those with no interest in politics incline more towards Leave.

No sooner had the referendum votes been counted than pundits began offering their take on why the country had voted Out. As with other populist-right votes, sources of information tended to be limited to vox pop interviews, impressions of the public mood 'on the street' or maps of the result. Maps plot the vote by district, which shows that populist-right support is larger in small towns and the countryside than in larger cities. Slicing districts by income typically results in poorer areas showing up as more strongly Brexit, Trump or a Le Pen. The take-home: those who

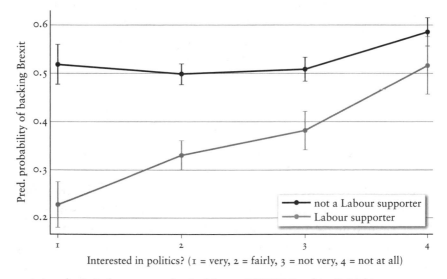

4.6. Apathetic Labour voters backed Leave (UKHLS, white British)

Source: Understanding Society, wave 8 (2015–16). Controls for major demographic and economic variables.

voted for the populist right are the 'left behind', who are angry about economic inequality and the political establishment.

This interpretation is largely wide of the mark. Why? First, impressions are often gleaned from members of the public who are outspoken. Interviews are then filtered to conform to a pre-cooked storyline which confirms the worldview of journalists who are typically well educated, liberal and from urban areas. A standard format is to contrast the older white working-class provincial with the young urban professional – our mind works with vivid images, not statistical means, and these profiles confirm our stereotypes. The voices of Remainers from the provinces or Leavers from London, who represent about 40–45 per cent of the vote in their respective districts, were seldom heard. Second, comparing aggregate results for districts from maps is very different from comparing actual individuals. Rural areas contain fewer ethnic minorities, people with degrees or twentysomethings than cities and college towns. When you strip out these demographic-compositional differences and compare apples to apples – a white working-class Londoner and white working-class resident of Middlesbrough – there is no rural–urban difference on Brexit.

Finally, many analysts bring a political lens to their analysis which inclines them to want to tell a story about wealth and power. Over half the country voted Leave and we can't condemn such a large group. So let's pretend populist voters are motivated by the same things we are: economic stagnation (for fiscal conservatives) or, for left-liberals, inequality and resentment of the establishment. Thus many analysts who peruse a map of the Brexit or Trump vote leap to the conclusion that rural and poorer districts voted for populists, confirming their view that resentment of urban wealth explains the vote. These quick explanations crumble when exposed to the harsh light of large-scale survey data. For instance, just 5 per cent of Brexit voters think inequality is the most important issue facing Britain while over 20 per cent of Remain voters do.[95] In addition, the BES asks a battery of five questions on anti-elitism such as 'the people, not politicians, should make our most important policy decisions' or 'politicians in the UK parliament need to follow the will of the people'. None of these items sorts Leavers from Remainers: socialist Corbyn supporters and Greens also tend to agree with them. As with the Trump phenomenon, opposition to a powerful, out-of-touch and wealthy elite does not explain the vote.

SOCIAL PSYCHOLOGY AND
THE BREXIT VOTE

More sophisticated data journalists such as John Burn-Murdoch of the *Financial Times* in Britain or Nate Silver in the US were astute enough to spot that average education, not income, is the best census predictor of Brexit or Trump support in a district.[96] Why education and not income? Education is a signal of worldview, not just material prosperity. Education and income are correlated, but it's possible to be a successful building contractor with no degree or a penniless graduate. In the BES, for instance, 16 per cent of whites without degrees earn above-average incomes and 29 per cent of whites with degrees are in the lowest income bracket. So there are plenty of well-educated poor people and less-educated wealthy people. The former tended to vote for Corbyn, the latter for UKIP. This reflects values not material position since education is the strongest demographic predictor of a person's views on immigration and the EU. University-educated people are far more socially liberal than those without degrees. Studies based on sampling schoolchildren's views at age thirteen show that this is because liberal-minded people select into university education more than because university makes them liberal.[97] If you know a person's income, your chance of guessing how they voted on Brexit is about 55 per cent, little better than chance. But if the only information you have on a person is whether they have a degree or not, this increases your accuracy to over 60 per cent.

Even better, though, is a direct window into people's deeply held values. As figure 4.7 shows, someone who strongly supports the death penalty (top right of chart) has about a 70 per cent chance of being a Brexiteer; a strong opponent, on the other hand, is at the bottom left of the chart on about 25 per cent. If we know someone's views on capital punishment we have a 7 in 10 chance of correctly guessing how they voted on referendum day, almost as good as knowing their opinion of the EU. By contrast, figure 4.7 tells us that the Leave vote rises only 10–15 points between the highest and lowest income lines. So, unlike the Trump vote, there is a 'left behind' income effect. Yet views on capital punishment are three to four times more important than income for understanding the Brexit vote.

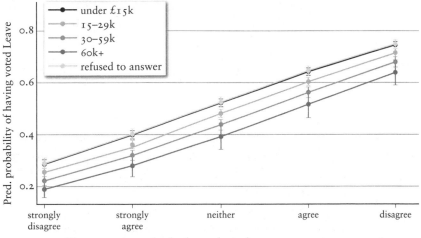

'For some crimes, the death penalty is the most appropriate sentence'

4.7. Income and support for death penalty and Brexit

Source: BES, waves 1–9 (2015–17).

This points to the importance of invisible differences in social-psychological outlook for explaining populist-right voting. These are considerably more important than social-demographic explanations. Nor is it the case that our values are the outcome of group memberships since the main social classifications such as age, class, ethnicity and education typically account for only about 10 per cent of the variation in conservative and authoritarian values. Hence social classifications based on metropolitan–provincial, winner–loser or even Goodhart's 'Somewhere–Anywhere'[98] divide only take us so far. A significant minority of people who lead highly mobile urban lives are what Stanley Feldman or Karen Stenner would call 'authoritarian' in outlook – preferring order and consensus to diversity and dissent. Others are conservative, favouring the status quo over change.[99] Meanwhile, an important tranche of people who have never moved from the town they were born in are liberal.

These differences may begin in the womb – twin studies suggest a third to a half of political behaviour is inherited – and continue with early childhood socialization related to strict or permissive parenting.[100] This induces a baseline receptivity to certain ideas which tends to be self-fulfilling. Someone with a mildly authoritarian predisposition is somewhat more likely to favour capital punishment. They internalize this value, which in turn opens them up to other conservative values on, say, child-rearing, immigration or Europe, as well as to a Conservative Party identity whose leaders cue their supporters to adopt certain positions across a wide range of issues. The connections are not only rational and logical, but emotional. Philosophically, it makes sense for a conservative to oppose immigration and support environmental protection; but if environmentalism and immigration restriction are cued by members of opposing parties, supporters will be emotionally repulsed from making logical connections.

Recall Pat Dade's division of the population into 'Settler', 'Pioneer' and 'Prospector' values groups. A good indication that psychology matters most for explaining differences between individuals on Brexit stems from the findings of household surveys, namely Understanding Society (UKHLS). Most households contain families or those in close relationships. Age, education, income and location tend to be the same among adult household members. In addition, there is considerable influence within the household and pressure among members to agree. This makes it all the more surprising how much difference there is within them on the question of Britain's membership of the EU. Kirby Swales of NatCen shows, using UKHLS data, that 29 per cent of two-person households were split on referendum day and over half of four-person households had a difference of opinion.[101] The fact that so many are divided testifies to how important psychological quirks are for explaining Brexit voting.

THE KEY ROLE OF IMMIGRATION

Within the Remain camp, strategists examined the polls and conducted focus groups. These convinced them that Leave owned the immigration issue. They concluded that 'there was no . . . argument that anyone could come up with on immigration that even slightly dented the Leave lead on the issue'.[102] The key narrative for Remain was 'Project Fear', a warning to voters of the grave economic risks of a Leave vote. Remain drew inspiration from the Scottish referendum, in which the anti-independence campaign focused on the threat to Scottish prosperity of leaving Britain. When confronted with questions on immigration,

Remain campaigners were told to change the subject to Project Fear rather than be drawn into debating questions they had no answer to. At the launch of Clarke, Goodwin and Whiteley's book in London, Trevor Phillips, who was on the board of the Remain camp, claimed this had been a mistake. By ducking immigration, he remarked, Remain had only increased the suspicions of swing voters.

Project Fear worked, claims Clarke and his co-authors. Independently of what voters thought about immigration and the EU, those who considered leaving the EU 'risky' did not vote to leave.[103] It's just that the fear effect was not quite enough to get Remain over the line. What this suggests is that many who plumped for Remain didn't do so out of love for the EU. A good rule of thumb is that about half of Remain voters were conflicted: torn between a desire to reduce immigration and the benefits of remaining in the EU: a PX–YouGov survey which I commissioned in August 2016, two months after the vote, shows that about half those who voted Remain wanted to reduce immigration, compared to 91 per cent of Leavers.

What really distinguishes Leave from Remain voters is their willingness to sacrifice economic benefits to cut immigration. Some economists estimate that leaving the EU could ultimately cost Britain up to 5 per cent of its GDP. Thus I asked people about their willingness to pay to reduce EU immigration, from paying nothing and having the numbers of EU immigrants remain at the current level to paying 5 per cent of their income to cut numbers to zero. Among Leavers, 70 per cent said they were willing to pay at least some of their income to reduce EU immigration whereas only 19 per cent of Remainers were. Furthermore, 35 per cent of Leavers gave the maximum answer: they were prepared to sacrifice 5 per cent of their income to cut EU numbers to zero.[104]

In a subsequent YouGov–LSE survey, Simon Hix, Thomas Leeper and I asked about people's tradeoffs on both EU and non-EU immigration. The 2016 EU inflow was 165,000. Remainers' preferred inflow was 74,000, but when presented with a sliding scale in which cutting numbers entailed a cost, the average Remainer settled on an influx of around 115,000. Leavers were more anti-immigration, preferring a European inflow of just 34,000, about 40,000 less than Remainers. But what jumps out is Leavers' willingness to sacrifice: when cutting numbers carried a cost, Remainers relented while Leavers were much more reluctant to do so. Even with costs attached, they were still only willing to admit 65,500

Europeans, 50,000 fewer than Remainers. The YouGov–Policy Exchange data also reveals that more than 40 per cent of Leave voters said immigration was the top issue facing the country, compared to just 5 per cent of Remainers – most of whom prioritized the economy or inequality. In short, many Remainers are anti-immigration but feel more cross-pressured by economic concerns than Leavers.

Could Remain have countered Leave's message on immigration? My work with the YouGov–Policy Exchange data suggests Trevor Phillips was right: had Remain been bold and imaginative enough to tackle immigration in the right manner, they could have persuaded enough Leavers to enable them to hurdle the 50 per cent bar. Recall that most Leave voters in my YouGov–Policy Exchange survey were willing to sacrifice part of their income to reduce EU migration. In the survey, I also divided respondents into three invisible groups to conduct an experiment. One group, the 'control' group, read nothing before answering questions on immigration. The second read what I consider to be the conventional civic nationalist narrative of immigration:

> Britain is changing, becoming increasingly diverse. The 2011 census shows that White British people are already a minority in four British cities, including London. Over a quarter of births in England and Wales are to foreign-born mothers. Young Britons are also much more diverse than older Britons. Just 4.5 per cent of those older than 65 are nonwhite but more than 20 per cent of those under 25 are. Minorities' younger average age, higher birth rate and continued immigration mean that late this century, according to Professor David Coleman of Oxford University, White British people will be in the minority. We should embrace our diversity, which gives Britain an advantage in the global economy.

Finally, a third group read what I term an open ethnic nationalist passage based on reassurance over assimilation:

> Immigration has risen and fallen over time, but, like the English language, Britain's culture is only superficially affected by foreign influence. According to Professor Eric Kaufmann of the University of London, a large share of the children of European immigrants have become white British. Historians tell us that French, Irish, Jewish and pre-war black immigrants largely melted into the white majority. Those of mixed race, who share common ancestors

with White British people, are growing faster than all minority groups and 8 in 10 of them marry whites. In the long run, today's minorities will be absorbed into the majority and foreign identities will fade, as they have for public figures with immigrant ancestors like Boris Johnson or Peter Mandelson. Britain shapes its migrants, migration doesn't shape Britain.

The share of Brexit voters wanting EU immigration cut to zero was 23 per cent among those who read the first or no passage, but opposition dropped to 15 per cent among those reading the second passage on assimilation. For 2015 UKIP voters, the proportion dropped dramatically: from 45 per cent favouring zero EU immigration for those reading the first or no passage to 15 per cent among the group which read the assimilation message. In other words, had Remain stopped ducking immigration and been brave enough to step away from civic nationalism and reassure majority conservatives using the facts of assimilation in Britain, they might have swung the vote in their favour. The conventional diversity-within-civic-nation message still has a role, but should be restricted to heavily minority or white-liberal audiences. Of course, this involves giving up on a one-size-fits-all civic nationalism and accepting that not all people share the same national identity: they connect to the nation in different ways.

A large chunk of the ethnic majority are what David Goodhart terms 'Somewheres'. A portion of these people have an exclusive sense of ethnic identity which views all immigration as a net loss, though most also accept you don't need to be white to be British.[105] Yet many others are what I term 'open' in their conception of white British ethnicity: content to maintain ethnic boundaries through assimilation under conditions of modest immigration. These open ethno-traditionalists will accept a reasonable inflow if convinced most newcomers are assimilating into their group over time.[106]

Some aver that in a post-Brexit era the country can select skilled immigrants like Canada or Australia and win public support for higher numbers. Liberal UK commentators like Open Europe or British Future make the case that a controlled, skilled inflow at current levels will win public support.[107] Leading academics report that, when European or American respondents are shown the characteristics of different immigrants and asked to indicate which they prefer, skill level is more

important than race or ethnicity.[108] The problem here is that many are
pro-immigrant but anti-immigration. A methodology asking people to
compare two individuals, one white and unskilled, the other non-white
and skilled, concentrates minds on a single person, ignoring the collective impact of numbers. There is also normative pressure not to give an
answer that could be deemed racist.

To get at what people think about immigration rather than immigrants, I fielded a PX–YouGov survey of 1,650 adults on 5–6 November
2017. I asked people:

> The government is considering its options for Britain's immigration policy
> after Brexit. Currently Britain has net migration of 275,000 per year of
> which about half is European. After Brexit, European migration is
> expected to decline. Two options are on the table, which do you prefer?:
> a) Increase skilled immigration from outside Europe, keeping net migra-
> tion at 275,000, raising the skilled share from 40% to 50%; b) Decrease
> skilled immigration from outside Europe, decreasing net migration from
> 275,000 to 125,000, lowering the skilled share from 40% to 20%.

The sample split evenly between the two options, with 52.7 per cent
favouring the status quo, though this was true of only 48.5 per cent of
white British respondents. This is much more positive than the current
75–25 split in favour of reduction, a finding which reflects the results of
the academic and policy literature mentioned above.

However, I then added the following riders to the questions: 'a) [cur-
rent levels of immigration] As a result, the white British share of the
UK's population will decline from 80% today to 58% in 2060'; and 'b)
[decreased immigration] As a result, the white British share of the UK's
population will decline from 80% today to 65% in 2060.' In other
formulations I added 'from Africa and Asia' after 'skilled immigration'. Once respondents saw that high numbers would bring faster
ethnic change, opposition swiftly returned to the present 75–25 split. In
other words, skill mix matters, but is overridden by concerns about
cultural change.[109] Given this climate of opinion, British parties are
unlikely to opt for a Canadian-style system based on skills and high
numbers.

THE AFTERMATH

Post-referendum shockwaves reverberated around Britain, shaking the country's political alignments. David Cameron stepped down as Conservative leader the day after, having gambled on winning the referendum and lost. In calling the vote, he had hoped to resolve, once and for all, the battle between Eurosceptics and Euro-pragmatists which had fractured his party since the early 1990s. His resignation set in motion a fast-moving piece of political theatre in which leading candidates Boris Johnson and Michael Gove eliminated each other in a plot reminiscent of *Julius Caesar*. This led to the emergence of Theresa May as Prime Minister.

May initially enjoyed an unprecedented advantage over Labour's Jeremy Corbyn. By 18 April 2017, when May called a general election, polling aggregators showed her leading 42–26 over her Labour rival, with UKIP on 11 per cent. But in the ensuing six weeks the mood of the country changed. Many saw May's gambit as an opportunistic attempt to increase the size of her majority. UKIP voters also began to defect to the parties from whence they came prior to 2015. By 17 May, UKIP had dropped to 5 per cent, with the Tories up 5 points to 47 and Labour up to 30. On 18 May, May released the Conservatives' new manifesto, which featured an extremely unpopular 'dementia tax' which sought to increase the amount that people would have to pay towards in-home residential care for the elderly out of their own assets. After heavy criticism, May climbed down, undermining her hard-won brand as a 'strong and stable' leader for the country in turbulent times. All of a sudden, the Tories began losing ground to Corbyn, who rose from 26 to 37 per cent in the polls just prior to election day.

When the votes were tallied, the Conservatives won with 42.3 per cent of the vote, an increase of 5.5 points over 2015. But the outcome was viewed as a setback for the Tories. First, they lost thirteen seats despite winning a larger share of the popular vote, and consequently had to make a deal with Northern Ireland's Democratic Unionists to regain the majority of seats needed to govern. Second, they benefited from a collapse in UKIP's vote from 13 to 2 per cent and from a dramatic drop in the popularity of the Scottish National Party. Without a surge of support for prominent Remainer Ruth Davidson's Scottish

Conservatives, May could not have formed a government. Soon after the election, Davidson made it clear she would be pushing May towards a 'soft' Brexit, meaning a deal which prioritized the economy at the expense of immigration control.

Labour, meanwhile, confounded the sceptics by winning 40 per cent of the vote. This despite being led by an 'unelectable' figure from the far left of the party with a history of sympathizing with the Irish Republican Army's struggle for a United Ireland. The result was a damning indictment of May's leadership, but also one which unearthed tectonic shifts in Britain's electoral landscape. Most importantly, the generation gap replaced class as the main dividing line in British politics. Two thirds of the country's 18- to 24-year-olds and 58 per cent of 25- to 34-year-olds voted for Corbyn, while a mere 23 per cent of those over 65 did. This recalled the age breakdown during the referendum when 18–24s broke 73–27 for Remain while 60 per cent of over-65s voted Leave. Never before or since have I witnessed young people talk politics as much as the day after the referendum. All I heard at my son's high school and from teenagers on my train was how the country had voted Leave and how this was bad news for them. In a mock poll, 94 per cent of pupils at my daughter's high school chose Remain, a fair barometer of sentiment among middle-class, academically minded London teens.

Behind the age gap lay a values gap. As in the referendum, Lord Ashcroft's polls revealed wide rifts on cultural issues – immigration, multiculturalism, social liberalism – between partisans.[110] As figure 4.8 shows, Millennials began diverging from older generations on the immigration question around 2004. In that year, Millennials were 5 points more tolerant of immigration than the pre-war generation. By 2013, the gap had grown to nearly 20 points.[111] Comparing under-25s and over-65s using the British Election Study (BES) shows that 80 per cent of over-65s and 69 per cent of under-25s in 2001 wanted less immigration. By 2014 the comparable figures were 76 per cent among over-65s versus just 40 per cent for under-25s. All told, young voters who had grown up in the more diverse, faster-changing Britain in the 2000s were more liberal than older voters whose formative memories were of a more culturally homogeneous Britain. Brexit may prove the Millennials' moment of political awakening, the issue which defines their politics. In 2005, BES data shows over-65s and under-25s both backed Labour to the tune of 40 per cent. In 2009, the young were

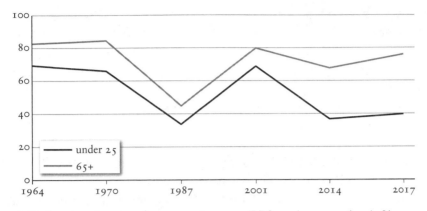

4.8. Reduce immigration, by age, 1964–2017 (BES, various questions), %

Source: BES 1964, 1970, 1987, 2001, 2014, 2017.

6 points more enthusiastic about Labour. By 2014, this had widened to 13 points, and by the 2017 election to a whopping 27 points.

Part of the explanation for Corbyn's polarizing effect by age is that young people didn't experience the terrorism of the Northern Irish troubles or Labour's battles over socialism, factors which make Corbyn anathema to many older voters. They are not especially attuned to his economic message: British Millennial attitudes towards economic redistribution are relatively right-wing.[112] May's inability to forge an emotional connection with younger voters, Labour's more advanced social media campaign and strong celebrity backing for Corbyn also played their part. Even so, the BES data indicate that at least half of Corbyn's advantage with young people predated the 2017 election campaign and stems from a generational divide over Brexit, which in turn reflects a generation gap over immigration. In the rest of Europe, as well as the US, there are also generational differences over immigration and populist-right support. Yet these are considerably smaller than in Britain.

None of this means Britain will favour open borders in a generation. First, the UK is an ageing society: a third of its population will be over sixty in 2050 so the grey vote will only become more important. Second, BHPS–UKHLS data, which has tracked voters for over twenty-five years, shows that Britons are more likely to vote Conservative as they age – typically when they move to Tory-dominated suburbs.[113] More importantly, events such as the post-1997 immigration surge in Britain tend to shift the attitudes of all generations, rapidly wiping out decades of cohort liberalization. Baby Boomers, for example, were 15 points more liberal on immigration than the pre-war generation in 1995, but by 2008 the inter-generational difference had narrowed to under 5 points.[114] An outspoken case in point is Roger Daltrey, lead singer of sixties Mod icons, the Who: 'I will never, ever forgive the Labour Party for allowing this mass immigration,' said Daltrey in 2013, a former Labour voter from a working-class London background. 'I will never forgive them for destroying the jobs of my mates.'[115]

Brexit has begun to reconfigure parties' support bases. Luntz Polling survey data from the day before the 2017 election shows that, among 2015 Tories, Remainers were 10 points more likely to switch to Labour than Leavers. Among 2015 Labour voters, Remainers were 13 points more likely to vote for Corbyn in 2017 than Leavers.[116] As Lord Ashcroft's exit polls showed, just a quarter of Remainers voted for May and a quarter of Leavers for Corbyn.[117] Corbyn made enough positive noises about Brexit and reducing the influx of cheap labour to convince some Labour Leavers, but the net effect of 2017 was a generational realignment reflecting a Brexit realignment reflecting an immigration realignment. Working-class whites continued to move to the Tories and the middle class to Labour to the point that class divisions no longer differentiated the parties. This was an unprecedented development in post-1900 British political history.

Stepping back from the flow of events reveals a wider panorama in which questions of immigration and the fate of England's ethno-traditions have been moving centre stage. Economic divisions based on class which structured British politics in the twentieth century are making room for a new identity cleavage in the twenty-first. Cosmopolitan–nationalist doesn't quite capture the division. Rather, it pits those wedded to an 'ascribed' multi-generational English ethnicity against people who define their nationhood on the basis of 'achieved' progress against moral and economic criteria. A 'soft Brexit' in which Britain agrees to a continued open flow of people from the EU could renew the British economy. But even a 'hard Brexit' in which Britain gains full control over immigration will not deflect pressure from business and the public sector for more immigrants – who are perceived as working more effectively, for lower wages, than native-born Britons.

As long as Britain's economy remains healthy – an aim shared by all parties and most voters – immigration will be difficult to reduce to 1990s levels. In such a world, the hopes of Leave voters for a return to the status quo ante-Blair will likely be dashed and cries of treason will fill the air. The YouGov–LSE survey data from May 2017 asked respondents who they would vote for if immigration remained unchanged after Brexit. This showed that 2015 UKIP votes which went to the Tories in 2017 would flow back to UKIP, returning the insurgent party to its former strength. If high immigration results from a 'soft Brexit' deal, this is even more likely. Brexit helped marginalize UKIP, but those who consider this a permanent blow to populism should think twice. The return to two-party dominance in 2017, far from a new normal, may represent an unstable prelude to populist-right renewal.[118]

5

The Rise and Rise of the Populist
Right in Europe

On 17 May 2016, liberal opinion held its breath for the results of the Austrian presidential election. When the votes were tallied, the press exhaled: in a two-man run-off, Alexander van der Bellen defeated Norbert Hofer of the Austrian Freedom Party (FPÖ) by a slender 50.3 to 49.7 margin.[1] The mood was one of relief rather than outrage. How things had changed. In 1999, the charismatic FPÖ leader, Jörg Haider, shocked Europe's political establishment by winning 27 per cent of the vote, little more than half Hofer's total. When the centre-right ÖVP and centre-left SVP failed to reach a deal to keep the FPÖ out of power, the ÖVP reluctantly entered into talks with the FPÖ, leading to a coalition government. Protests erupted in Vienna and across the international community. Israel recalled its ambassador. The EU imposed political sanctions.

The second explosion took place on 21 April 2002. In the first round of the French presidential elections, the Front National's leader, Jean-Marie Le Pen, stunned observers by coming second with 17 per cent of the vote, 1 point ahead of Socialist candidate Lionel Jospin. The front covers of the French papers said it all: 'The Le Pen Bomb' (*France Soir*), 'The Shock' (*Le Parisien*), 'The Earthquake' (conservative *Le Figaro*), 'France does not deserve this' (communist *L'Humanité*) and 'No' (left-wing *Libération*). Five days before the second round, on May Day, 1.3 million turned out to demonstrate. In the final vote, Le Pen managed only 18 per cent to Jacques Chirac's 82 per cent.[2] Looking back on these events, what comes across is how much the liberal response has faltered. The populist right in France and Austria surged past its previous milestones in the 2010s but the new high points failed to generate outrage. Instead, depending on the outcome, they were treated with resignation or relief.

Most European countries operate with a proportional representation (PR) electoral system in which votes translate into seats as long as a party meets a minimum threshold, typically 3–5 per cent. This makes it easier for the populist right to enter the legislature. In PR systems, governing coalitions are assembled from a range of parties, which presents an opening for populist-right outfits to influence policy. In order to forestall this possibility, national elites prior to the 2000s adhered to the norm that populist-right parties should not enter government. Mainstream parties repeatedly refused to accept the insurgent parties, erecting a cordon sanitaire around them which they hoped would consign them to the fringe.

We now know two things. First, the old wisdom that right-wing populists could not wield influence in the Anglo-American winner-take-all electoral system is false. UKIP may have gained only one seat for its 13 per cent vote share in 2015, but it forced other parties to bend to its anti-immigration, anti-EU agenda in order to limit losses to UKIP or woo its voters. In the US, populism emerged within rather than outside a major party, but the net policy result was the same. Second, attempts to bar the populist right from power failed. By the early 2000s, anti-immigration parties had entered coalition in Austria, Norway, the Netherlands, Denmark and Italy.[3] This removed some of the toxic sting which voters encountered when they first put the crosses in the far-right box. But the strongest detoxifiers were the vote totals themselves, which signalled to those worried about immigration and integration that they weren't alone and needn't feel guilty for backing anti-immigration populists.

Liberals fought against the 'normalization' of the far right, but with rising populist-right totals and coalition arithmetic pulling towards partnership it was only a question of time before the consensus gave way. The anti-racist norm against voting for the far right began to erode and centrist parties started adopting their policies. Elite obstruction may actually have contributed to an angrier anti-elite mood, recruiting yet more voters to the far-right banner. The anti-racist taboo against them has weakened but remains: more voters express strong anti-immigration views than are willing to vote far right.[4] Yet, as I explain in chapter 9, the higher the populist right's vote share, the more the taboo erodes. This eases their path to a higher total when conditions permit, setting in motion a self-fulfilling spiral.

POPULISM WEST AND EAST

There are many definitions of terms like 'far right', 'populist', 'fascist' and 'nativist'. I take the right–left axis to be about economics – whether to tax and spend more or less. Populist-right parties, as political scientist Cas Mudde notes, aren't principally concerned with economics.[5] Instead, their focus is cultural. In theory this could involve religious or social conservatism, but in today's West cultural concerns are ethno-nationalist. These parties are *populist* because they oppose the established elite in the major parties and cultural elite in the universities, arts institutions and traditional media. By contrast, nationalism in Quebec, Scotland or Putin's Russia is elite-led and therefore not populist.

Fascism is an ideology which calls for an authoritarian state commanded by a strong leader who represents the national will. It is nationalist, militarist and intolerant of dissent. In inter-war Europe, it had a powerful appeal. Today, far-right parties like Jobbik in Hungary and Golden Dawn in Greece carry forth its legacy, which is hostile to liberal institutions and democracy. Why? Liberal democracy in Greece, Spain, Portugal and Eastern Europe only dates from the 1975–90 period. The Southern and Eastern European far right is less patient with liberal democracy because pre-democratic memories, institutions and ideas are fresher than in North-West Europe. France is an intermediate case because liberal democracy was only stable there after an attempted coup against President Charles de Gaulle had been repulsed in 1961.

Historical traumas such as Hungary's loss of two thirds of its territory after the First World War, Spain's humiliation in the 1898 Spanish–American War, Germany's defeat in the First World War or France's withdrawal from Algeria in 1962 are important for explaining fascism. Anti-Semitism forms part of its belief system because Jews are a convenient scapegoat for societies suffering from the mental anguish of defeat. In France, neo-fascist themes like national humiliation, anti-Semitism and nostalgia for authoritarianism and empire informed Poujadism in the 1950s and Jean-Marie Le Pen's Front National in the 1980s. For instance, French settlers in Algeria who had returned to France after the war, known as *pieds noirs*, or 'black feet', were a key constituency for Le Pen.[6] Newer generations grew up who cared little for these old fights. Unless far-right movements or governments actively revive memories of pre-democratic glory and raise consciousness about the need to return to a glorious illiberal past, the embers of fascism tend to cool over time.

The mechanisms are different in the West. Immigration-led ethnic change, not national humiliation, is the main factor behind the rise of the populist right in Western Europe – just as it was in both the Trump and Brexit cases. In searching for a forerunner of today's West European populist right, we are better off examining the Native American ('Know-Nothing') Party of 1850s America than inter-war fascism. The Know-Nothings gave rise to the American word 'nativism', an imprecise term for majority ethnic nationalism. This is the idea that an indigenous or founding ethnic group should form the majority in society. Sometimes the indigenous are not the political founding group. In the US, WASPs are the founding group but Native Indians are indigenous. In Pakistan, the Mohajirs are the founders of the state while regional majorities like the Punjabis are indigenous. Elsewhere, indigenousness ('who came first') is contested, as in Israel–Palestine or in Sri Lanka, where the Sinhalese insist the Tamils are interlopers despite their having lived there for over a thousand years.[7] In Europe, indigenousness and political founding status generally overlap. Majority ethno-traditional nationalism comes closest to capturing the spirit of the modern populist right.

Immigrants bring ethnic difference, altering the composition of a country, region or city's population. The domestic migration of Irish Catholics to Scotland, northern Muslims to southern Christian Côte d'Ivoire, Han Chinese to Tibet or Castilian Spanish to Catalonia is not fundamentally different from the movement of Muslim Algerians to France. That is, both involve an immigrant challenge to majority ethnic groups' preponderance in 'their' homeland. If immigration slows, the majority can adjust to the presence of a minority, which becomes established over time. If, on the other hand, there is no end in sight, the majority must be confident of its ability to assimilate newcomers through intermarriage. Many in the ethnic majority will call for reduced immigration. Some may even seek to repatriate immigrant minorities. In Sri Lanka after 1964, over 300,000 Tamils were deported to India, many of whom had been in the country for generations.[8]

The foreign-born share of most western European countries was less than 1 per cent in 1900.[9] Domestic migration was more of an irritant than immigration. For instance, Swiss communes and German municipalities enacted restrictive citizenship laws against those from other localities. These later shaped national policies.[10] Catholic Germans from the south moving to jobs in the industrial Protestant north provoked discontent.[11] The Irish moved to Scotland and England, where they were considered an ethnic minority until the 1990s. In the twentieth century, poor Andalusians from the south moved to Catalonia and Sicilians migrated to northern Italy. Industrial capital cities in multiethnic empires were transformed by domestic migration after 1850. Vienna at the turn of the twentieth century, for instance, had a significant non-German minority of Hungarians, Czechs, Jews, Slovenians, Ruthenians, Serbians, Croatians, Bosnians and others. Berlin was only marginally less diverse by 1914.

Movements like the Scottish Protestant League of the 1930s prefigured the new anti-immigrant parties that would rise in the 1980s. In Italy, the Northern League initially aimed its ire at southern Italian migrants. Only in the 2000s did it shift to including them as part of the Italian 'us' resisting the Muslim immigrant 'them'.[12] Immigration was important earlier in France because the low French birth rate led to a policy of recruiting largely Catholic immigrants from Poland, Belgium, Italy and a number of other European countries. There was sporadic agitation against immigration in France, but the French state's military struggles with its British and German rivals acted as a force for integration.[13] This didn't mean things couldn't turn sour: between the 1880s and early 1900s anti-Semitism reached its height in France, as exemplified in the Dreyfus Affair. This was primarily driven not by immigration but by an elite discourse grounded in both the time-hallowed 'killer of Christ' brand of religious anti-Semitism and the new scientific racism.

Countries which are small and prosperous, notably Switzerland, are disproportionately affected by immigration. Between 1850 and 1910, Switzerland's foreign-born share rose from 3 to 15 per cent, making it an outlier in Europe. Switzerland is German-, Italian- and French-speaking and these immigrants came largely from these surrounding countries, but poor southern Italians were over-represented. Occasionally there were riots against them. Nevertheless, immigration was considered a local affair and a workingmen's problem. It became an issue only when the Swiss working class gained the vote and migration came to be centralized at the federal level.[14] The Swiss case reveals that local ethnic conflicts don't scale up to become a national problem until they are connected with the larger ideological frames which structure national politics. The same holds for immigration-driven ethnic tension in Vienna, Scotland or northern Italy, which failed to shape politics at the national level. While Jewish immigration to Berlin and Vienna had some effect on the support for Nazism, this acquired political significance only when combined with a resurgent intellectual anti-Semitism which sprang from eugenicist ideas and the country's humiliation in the First World War.

THE RISE OF THE POPULIST RIGHT

Populist-right parties in Western Europe emerged as a serious force in the 1980s and tripled their support in the following fifteen years. Figure 5.1

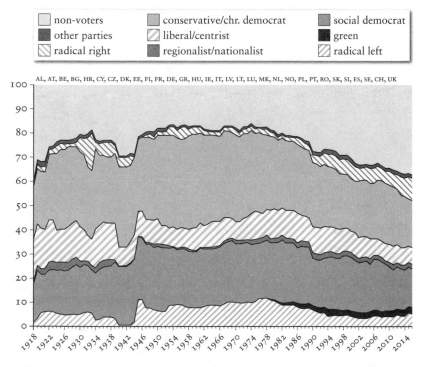

5.1. Percentage of votes in elections in thirty-one European countries, by political family

Source: Simon Hix, Twitter, 20 February 2017.

shows the vote by party family across thirty-one countries in Europe between 1918 and 2016. The populist-right vote share appears as the third-to-top layer in the graph. Notice the sudden rise in the late 1980s, a period of stability, and then another expansion beginning in 2013. By 2016, the 'radical right' share was similar to the fascist vote totals of the inter-war years. Notice as well that the proportion of non-voters, the top layer, began to fall in the late 1970s, reaching nearly 40 per cent by 2016.

Figure 5.2 focuses only on fourteen Western European countries for the period since 1949, removing non-voters. The two surge points from the late 1980s and 2013 are clearer, with the populist right notching up an unprecedented 15 per cent of the total.

How might we explain these changes? One argument holds that the end of the Cold War and the growing consensus of the parties on

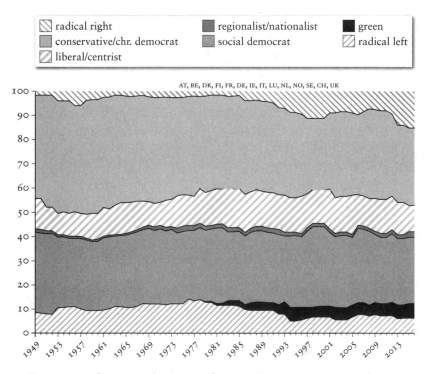

5.2. Percentage of votes in elections in fourteen European countries, by political family (excluding non-voters and others)

Source: Simon Hix, Twitter, 20 February 2017.

economic issues reduced the importance of the left–right dimension of politics. Another claim is that the increasingly secular and liberal social mores of younger, more educated generations led to a cultural backlash among older socially conservative voters.[15] Meanwhile, the rising proportion of non-voters we see in figure 5.1 may reflect the weakening ties between voters and their traditional institutions of church, union and party. In the Netherlands, for instance, the four separate 'pillars' or groups – Catholic, Protestant, Liberal, Socialist – which organized people's voting, recreation and news consumption, began to unravel in the 1960s. This is reflected in declining membership of the main parties. For Harvard political scientist Robert Putnam, this is connected to the weakening face-to-face connectedness of modern societies due to television and individualism. He discovered that Americans stopped having their neighbours over for dinner as often after 1960. They no longer bowled in leagues, but increasingly did so alone.[16]

Notice how the vote for the Green parties in figure 5.2 began rising in Western Europe in the 1980s, around the same time the populist right was growing and about ten years after voting turnout entered its slide. The increasingly unmoored, disconnected European electorate was beginning to depart from its traditional party loyalties and gravitate to parties along an 'open–closed' cultural axis which bisected the left–right economic one. The main parties, including the communists, who represented the old left–right order lost voters. The Greens and populist-right parties benefited. Yet these explanations can't fully explain what happened. From the 1980s onward, the share of ethnic minorities continued to climb in Western countries due to higher minority birth rates and immigration, albeit from a low base. This growth of the minority population raised questions about integration and the demographic position of the majority, creating the preconditions for the rise of the populist right. These parties viewed minorities as taking advantage of the welfare state or committing crimes at higher rates than natives, but material effects were not driving the trend. Rather, conservative opinion was hostile to immigration for identity reasons and viewed social problems through a pre-existing anti-immigration lens which pinned all problems on immigrants.

Economic rationales frequently disguise underlying psychological drivers. For instance, in small opt-in samples on Prolific Academic, one group of white Republican voters scored the problem of 'unchecked urban sprawl' a 51 out of 100, but another group of white Republicans who saw the question as 'unchecked urban sprawl *caused by immigration*' scored it 74/100 (italics added for emphasis). Likewise, among a sample of white British Brexit voters, the problem of 'pressure on council housing' scored a 47/100 but '*immigrants* putting pressure on council housing' was rated 68/100. In both cases, it logically cannot be the case that the immigration-driven portion of the problem of urban sprawl or pressure on council housing is more important than the problem itself. Thus what's driving opposition to immigration must be something prior to these material concerns. Likewise, the large-sample, representative British Election Study shows that concerns over the cultural and economic effects of immigration are tightly correlated. This suggests opposition to immigration comes first (Jonathan Haidt's unconscious 'elephant' moves us to act) and various rationalizations like pressure on public services follow (Haidt's conscious 'rider' telling us a story about why we acted as we did).[17] But rationales matter. If a morally acceptable rationale is not there, this inhibits a party's ability to articulate its underlying anti-immigration grievances. This is why restrictionists tend to don the cloak of economic rationalization.

In their rhetoric, Western European populist-right parties invariably focus on immigration. As Kai Arzheimer argues, 'it is difficult to overstate the importance of immigration for the modern (post-1980) Extreme Right'.[18] Marcel Lubbers and his colleagues show that for the 1990s the share of non-Europeans in a country is associated with a significantly higher populist-right vote share. In addition, the effect size of anti-immigration attitudes was twice that of dissatisfaction with democracy in predicting whether an individual in a European country voted for the populist right.[19]

The same was true in the early 2000s, with cultural threats many times stronger than economic threats in some models.[20] In a meta-analysis of the literature on the populist right between 1995 and 2016 that I conducted with Matthew Goodwin of the University of Kent, the effects of minority share on attitudes to immigration and on populist-right support were virtually identical, suggesting the two outcomes are closely linked. Populist-right support in a city, region or country was positively correlated with the share of minorities or immigrants in twenty-seven of thirty-five studies where a significant relationship was found. Nineteen of twenty-one studies which measured ethnic change over time found this to be associated with native white opposition to immigration or support for the populist right.[21]

A comprehensive review of the academic literature on immigration attitudes in the West by Jens Hainmueller and Dan Hopkins in 2014 found that personal income and economic circumstances explained little. Cultural attitudes emerged as the most consistent predictor of anti-immigration attitudes. Survey experiments can prove causation rather than mere correlation. One influential survey experiment asked a group of white Dutch respondents to read the following statement: 'People belong to different types of groups. One of the most important and essential of these groups is the nation which you belong to. In your case, you belong to the Dutch nationality. Each nation is different.' A second group read a statement that said, 'People differ in many ways and each human being is unique. One person likes music, another likes to go for a walk, still another likes to go out. Everyone is different.' The paper found that when relatively pro-immigrant Dutch people read the 'nation' passage, almost 70 per cent agreed that immigration should be reduced. This fell to just 45 per cent among those in the group reading the 'everyone is different' vignette. Reminding people of their national identity triggered an anti-immigration response showing that cultural-psychological factors like identity matter greatly for explaining immigration attitudes.[22]

Will attitudes to immigration grow more permissive as new generations of liberal young people enter the electorate and older conservatives die off? This happened with religion and social conservatism, so why not immigration? Figure 5.3 seems to support this interpretation. It shows that Austria, Switzerland and Ireland, which are more conservative on homosexuality, are less positive about the cultural effects of immigration than liberal Sweden, Denmark and the Netherlands.

We find a similar relationship worldwide between tolerance of homosexuality and ethnic nationalism – the belief it's important for someone to have ancestors from a country in order to be a citizen. It was once thought that some countries were born 'ethnic' nations and others 'civic' nations. Unlike secure-state nations like France which internally transformed from dynastic states to modern nation-states through revolutions or reforms, ethnic nations such as Germany or Norway had no state to begin with so had to unify or secede on the basis of ethnicity. This meant their understanding of nationhood was

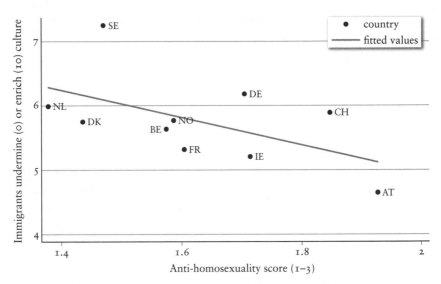

5.3. Attitudes to immigration and homosexuality, Western Europe, 2014

Source: European Social Survey (ESS) 2015.

kin-based rather than inclusive and territorial. Often formed in the nineteenth century, ethnic nations supposedly imbibed a more Romantic, counter-Enlightenment form of nationhood based on the idea of being an organic superfamily linked through mystical communion rather a set of individuals contractually attached to a state through a set of rights and duties.[23]

When we look at public opinion today, these historical legacies leave very faint traces. Compared to social liberalism, as measured by questions such as tolerance for homosexuality or believing children should obey, the circumstances of a country's birth count for little. Thus in figure 5.4 'civic' Sweden and 'ethnic' Norway both come out as highly civic nations whose members say ancestry is not an important criterion for citizenship. On the other hand, post-colonial 'civic' nations like Mali and South Africa rank as strongly 'ethnic' in their belief that people should have ancestors from the country to count as full citizens.

This data shows a relationship between social liberalism, inclusive nationalism and liberal immigration attitudes. This holds even more strongly between individuals within a country than between countries. In fact attitudes to homosexuality are a better predictor of views on

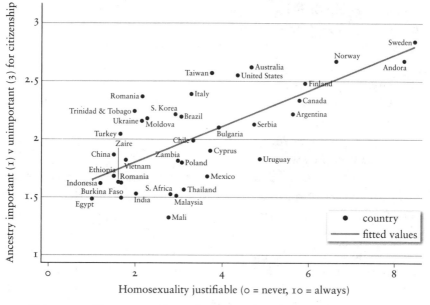

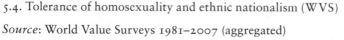

5.4. Tolerance of homosexuality and ethnic nationalism (WVS)

Source: World Value Surveys 1981–2007 (aggregated)

immigration than education level. Even so, only 3–6 per cent of the variation in immigration opinion among individuals in the 2014 European Social Survey (ESS) is accounted for by attitudes to homosexuality. This means we should not automatically expect attitudes to immigration to liberalize over time the way views on women's roles, religion, sexual mores, homosexuals or even racism have. As the work of Ron Inglehart – the doyen of value-change researchers – shows, social liberalism has been accepted, or is well on its way to becoming accepted, across the West.[24] Attitudes to immigration and the European Union, by contrast, have either remained static or gone in a more conservative direction since the 1960s. Thus questions pertaining to secular nationalism are following a different cohort trajectory from religion and social conservatism.

Does rising diversity lead to a backlash? Most surveys are taken at a single point in time, which makes it difficult to assess whether a higher share of immigrants is linked to more hostility to immigration. In 2010, Sweden, with its relatively large immigrant population, was more pro-immigrant than low-immigration Greece. We might conclude that higher immigration in Sweden has led to more tolerance of immigration, and that Greece would be more tolerant of immigration if it had more immigrants. But this would be erroneous if the reason Sweden has more immigrants and is more pro-immigrant than Greece is because its population is more socially liberal. What we need to do is compare Sweden in 1980 with Sweden in 2010. That way we screen out the confounding effects of social liberalism and other uniquely Swedish characteristics to see whether the rise in immigrants leads to greater opposition to immigration.

The most rigorous studies do this, using a panel design to measure change over time within European countries. These find that a higher immigrant share is a consistent predictor of higher opposition to immigration over time. Rising hostility to immigration is, over time, linked with voting for right-wing parties.[25] Work currently underway finds the same over-time relationship to populist-right voting. In a given year, on average, an increase in immigrant share correlates with an increase in populist-right voting.[26] It can be argued that after a short adjustment the new arrivals are less scary and produce mutual understanding and an easing of concern. We'll see there's some truth in this, but the weight of evidence is that a rising proportion of foreign-born people leads to more worries about immigration. This aligns with European studies that measure the rate of change in the share of immigrants in the recent past and almost always find that this predicts greater opposition to immigration.[27]

IMMIGRATION TO EUROPE

Immigrants from outside Europe began arriving in Western Europe in significant numbers in France as early as the 1930s. Yet for the most part non-European immigration was not a feature of the European experience until the 1950s. Colonial powers such as France, Britain and the Netherlands experienced a wave of settlement from former colonies in the 1950s and 1960s. In Germany, guestworkers from Turkey and Morocco arrived around the same time. Many Turks and Moroccans also settled in Belgium and the Netherlands. Immigration to Scandinavia took place somewhat later, with many arriving as refugees after the 1990s: Bosnians, Kurds, Iraqis, Afghans and

Somalis. Around half the non-European minorities in Western Europe are Muslim.

Roughly a million immigrants have reached Europe each year since the mid-1980s. The increase in non-European populations in Europe has been driven by both immigration and these minorities' younger age structure and higher birth rates. New generations of migrant background show considerably lower fertility, not much above native levels. This is because they are converging with local family-size norms and because fertility rates have declined sharply in their native countries. Turkey, for instance, has the same fertility rate as Sweden or France. Morocco's is 2.5 children per woman. In England and Wales, Pakistani and Bangladeshi immigrant TFR dropped from 9.3 to 4.9 between 1971 and 1996; in Belgium, Moroccan-born TFR fell from 5.72 to 3.91 between 1981 and 1996.[28] In Germany, the Turkish immigrant total fertility rate (TFR) declined from 4.4 children per woman in 1970 to 2.4 in 1996. Since then, these rates have moved even closer to host society norms. Nevertheless, the momentum of past high fertility will continue for around four decades, which will power minority natural increase – albeit at a slower rate than during the past fifty years

By 2002, cumulative immigration had produced an unprecedented foreign-born level in European countries, as shown in figure 5.5.

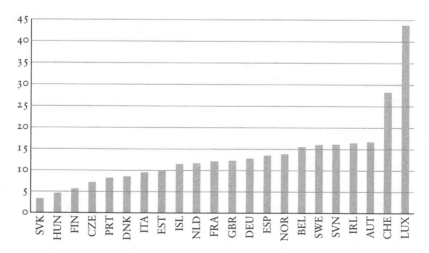

5.5. Percentage of foreign-born, by country, Europe, 2002

Source: Eurostat 2002.

Switzerland was nearly 30 per cent foreign-born, and the share reached almost 45 per cent in Luxembourg. Having said this, many of the foreign-born in these small countries were transient urban professionals from neighbouring European states.

Refugee inflows began to rise in the 1980s, first from the wars in the former Yugoslavia, then from conflict hotspots like Iraq, Afghanistan and Somalia. In 2004, the European Union expanded to include eight relatively poor Eastern European countries, mainly Central European and Baltic states. In 2007, two more, Romania and Bulgaria, joined. With freedom of movement inside the EU, this resulted in an increase in the number of residents from the ten accession countries residing in Western Europe: from 1 million in 1997 to nearly 5 million by 2009.[29] Residents were concentrated in the more prosperous countries, with over a million moving to Britain alone. The newcomers aroused fewer concerns than non-Europeans in most Western nations, but arguably contributed to a perception of majority decline and runaway diversity.

The economic consensus around mixed capitalism, in combination with falling social connectedness between citizens, led to a decline of centrist parties, an increase in non-voting and a rise in smaller parties on the ideological fringe. Rising immigration and minority levels provided the main source of latent conservative/authoritarian kindling which the new populist-right parties could light. It's important to recognize that the populist right grew dramatically before the Islam question took centre stage. Islamist terrorism and threats to liberalism added to populism's appeal, but the Islamic challenge is not the prime mover of these parties' success. If immigrants came from India or China instead of Muslim countries, I believe this would also stimulate these parties, though they wouldn't reach the level of support they currently enjoy.

ISLAM

In today's climate it's easy to forget that prior to the 1990s Western European publics cared little about Islam. During the Cold War, Islamists were heroes who resisted communism in Afghanistan and Saudi Arabia. This began to change after the fall of the Berlin Wall. The Iranian fatwa against Salman Rushdie and demonstrations in support of this by extremist British Muslims in 1989 shocked and angered Britain, but the effects faded. In 1995, the first Islamist terrorist attack on European soil took place in Paris in retaliation for that country's support of the Algerian government against the Islamists of the FIS. Again, the temperature of anti-Muslim politics did not surge in any lasting way. Then on 11 September 2001, Islamist terrorists destroyed the Twin Towers in New York. In 2004, Al Qaeda redefined Europe as a 'land of war', with 'defensive' jihad now obligatory for European Muslims.[30]

A spate of attacks followed, notably the Madrid train bombings of 2004 and the 7 July tube bombings in London in 2005. In the Netherlands in 2004, filmmaker Theo van Gogh was murdered in broad daylight by Mohammed Bouyeri. Bouyeri shot him several times, slit his throat with a machete and left his weapon planted in Van Gogh's chest where it pinned a note to Van Gogh's body. The message threatened outspoken Somali-Dutch critic of Islam Ayaan Hirsi Ali. Dutch society reacted with street protests. Forty-seven attacks on mosques and Muslim schools followed. In retaliation, Muslims attacked thirteen churches.

On 30 September 2005, the Danish newspaper *Jyllands-Posten* published twelve cartoons entitled 'The Face of Muhammad', one of which depicted the Prophet with a bomb in his turban. In January and February of 2006, protests erupted in the Muslim world and among European Muslims. The clash between Muslim religious sensibilities and freedom of speech suggested Muslims posed a danger to some of the most cherished Western values. Instances of Muslims protesting against plays and art exhibits critical of Islam made the news. For instance, when Sarah Maple, a Muslim artist, displayed her Islamic-themed work at the SaLon Gallery in London, the gallery's windows were smashed and she received death threats. Worse than this, Western politicians appeared to be caving in to the cultural sensitivities of conservative Muslims: the work of anti-Muslim polemicist Oriana Fallaci and fiction writer Michel Houllebecq were targeted for censorship.[31] In Britain in 2006, the Blair government's attempt to extend its hate-speech law to religion was defeated in the House of Lords after a campaign focused on the Islamic threat to free speech.[32] Honour-killings and female genital mutilation, though linked to ethnic traditions rather than Islamic texts, featured regularly in the tabloid press.

Anti-Islamic politics had yet to capture the far-right imagination. In 1999, when the Austrian Freedom Party was at its height, the main bugbear for its leader, Jörg Haider, was refugees from the former Yugo-slavia, whether Christian or Muslim. Even in 2004, the FPÖ didn't criticize the governing ÖVP when it announced that Muslim women had the right to wear the veil. It was not until 2007 that the FPÖ under its new leader, Heinz-Christian Strache, moved to an anti-Muslim stance, boosting FPÖ vote share. Whereas just 15 per cent of Austrians said they didn't want to live next to a Muslim in 1999, this reached 31 per cent by 2008.[33] Austria didn't suffer a terrorist attack, but its non-European population has a large Muslim component and Islam was the most visible source of cultural difference. The decline in Austro-German ethnic preponderance is the issue that links the Haider and Strache platforms. Islam should be viewed as an additional grievance rather than the FPÖ's engine, which is ethno-nationalism.

Further north, the Netherlands had been one of the first countries to break the elite consensus against criticizing multiculturalism. Frits Bolkestein of the centre-right VVD argued in the early 1990s that immigrants should integrate into the Dutch way of life.[34] So began a new era of anti-immigration politics. In 2001, Pim Fortuyn, a charis-matic, openly gay member of Bolkestein's VVD, left to form his own party. In a new departure, he criticized Islam from a liberal perspec-tive: as a threat to gays, freedom of expression and social liberalism. Dutch openness was contrasted with Muslim conservatism. When For-tuyn was gunned down by an animal-rights activist in 2002, he became a martyr and his party, the Pim Fortuyn List, won 17 per cent of the vote to become the second largest.[35] Fortuyn changed the conversation around multiculturalism and immigration, altering the direction of policy. In 2006, for instance, the Dutch government introduced a pack-age for prospective immigrants which included a film showing nude women sunbathing and gay men kissing. Though a perfectly legitimate expression of Dutch liberalism, the commercial also appeals to nation-alism in that liberalism serves as a marker of Dutchness against the Muslim 'other'.[36]

Fortuyn's 'homonationalism' created a template which Northern European populist-right parties like the Danish People's Party and Front National eagerly copied.[37] The support base for these parties, as with most on the populist right, was conservative and order-seeking. However, liberalism served to rationalize anti-immigration and anti-multicultural policies to a wider swathe of voters who may have felt uncomfortable voting for a 'racist' party. It also helped recruit a smaller but important contingent of younger, secular, liberal voters.

'I hear more and more testimonies about the fact that in certain districts, it is not good to be a woman, homosexual, Jewish, even French or white,' said Marine Le Pen in a speech in Lyon in 2010. Upon taking the FN's reins in 2011, Marine Le Pen opened her party to social liberals, including her gay chief lieutenant, Florian Philippot. In 2016, one poll found that nearly 40 per cent of married gay men backed the Front National.[38] Thirty-six per cent of Front National voters in 2013 supported gay marriage compared to 25 per cent of voters for the centre-right UMP.[39] The FN's share of the Jewish vote reached 13.5 per cent in the 2014 European elections, more than double its previous level.[40] Philo-Semitism was increasingly replacing anti-Semitism on the far right, something also evident in the pronouncements of the staunchly pro-Israel Geert Wilders in the Netherlands.

While taking care not to offend social conservatives within the FN, Marine Le Pen's opening to liberalism has helped the party detoxify its brand in a process known as 'dédiabolisation', making it more acceptable to voters uneasy about transgressing the anti-racist taboo against voting far right. Marine's next step is to rename the party in order to distance it even further from its fascist roots.[41]

This points to the importance of anti-racist norms (which govern the white response I term 'repression') in dampening populist-right parties' potential vote share.[42] While the identity motives driving FN support are significant, the moral legitimation which might smooth Le Pen's path to the presidency has proven a formidable obstacle. Some argue this problem is greatest for parties which spring from fascist roots, such as the BNP in Britain or the FN. Those that begin as middle-class libertarian parties, such as the Swiss People's Party, UKIP, Danish Progress Party or AfD in Germany, have generally been more successful. Political scientist Elisabeth Ivarsflaten looked at forty-one anti-immigration parties in Europe during 1980–2005 and found that only six had credible 'reputational shields' against charges of racism because they began as libertarian parties. All six achieved electoral success whereas only one with a fascist past, the FN, broke into double digits.[43] Women are more sensitive to violating perceived anti-racism norms, which is why they tend to vote for populist-right parties at lower rates despite being as opposed to immigration as men.[44]

Populist-right parties must surmount people's fears that they are thuggish extremists whose ultimate aim is to trample on the rights of minorities or threaten liberal democracy. They also struggle with how to ethically justify their opposition to immigration. Most conservative voters want less immigration but worry that this is viewed as a racist thing to do. Hence the recourse to policy arguments that focus on state priorities rather than ethnic majority grievances. Immigrants are accused of putting pressure on jobs and public services, threatening liberalism, gays, women and Jews. Crime and terrorism are state security issues, so are considered legitimate topics for debate. By contrast, white majority worries about losing the country they know, or their demographic preponderance in particular regions and neighbourhoods, is deemed out of bounds. The idea that the country has a traditional ethnic composition which people are attached to – what I term ethno-traditional nationalism – and which should not change too quickly, is viewed as beyond the limits of acceptable debate. This is a pity, because the 'legitimate' arguments stigmatize minorities and are often racist in a way the 'illegitimate' arguments about wanting to slow cultural loss are not. Only when the latter is taken to the extreme of wanting to bar certain groups or repatriate immigrants do they become racist.

IMMIGRATION RISES

After 2013, the rate of immigration began climbing in North-Western Europe. Figure 5.6 shows that net migration increased from about 1 million per year in 2013 to 1.4 million in 2014 and 2.2 million in the year ending 2015.

In contrast to the period before 2007, much of the new immigration was non-European. The middle line for the EU in figure 5.7 shows that the number of asylum seekers declined after the 1992–4 war in the former Yugoslavia, remaining low until 2012, when numbers jumped from 300,000 to nearly 600,000 due to conflicts in the Middle East, Afghanistan and Africa.

In 2014, populist-right parties posted record results in that year's elections to the European Parliament. European elections function as a protest vote because most people treat them lightly: the EU spends less than 1.5 per cent of Europe's GDP compared to the 40–50 per cent

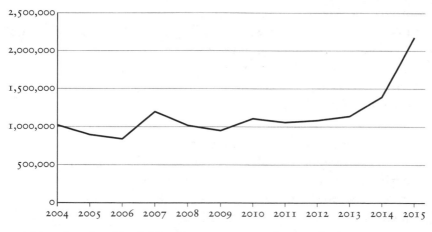

5.6. Net migration, North-West Europe, 2004–15 (year ending)

Source: Eurostat.

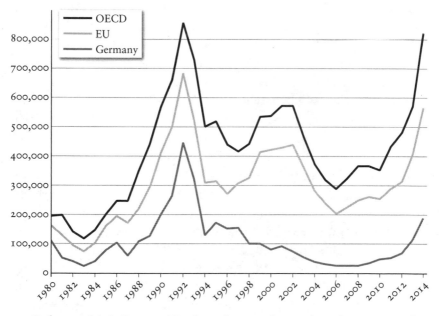

5.7. Refugee crisis in Europe. Number of new asylum seekers since 1980 in the OECD, EU and Germany

Source: UNHCR

disbursed by national governments. Nevertheless, in the 2014 elections, populist parties increased their vote in eight Western countries and declined in just three (Italy, Belgium, Finland). In the case of the True Finns, this was because they were in coalition in an unpopular government. Most impressive were the record gains posted by the UK Independence Party, up from 16 per cent in 2009 to 27 per cent in 2014; the Front National, from 6 per cent to 25 per cent; and the Danish People's Party, from 15 per cent to 27 per cent. The FPÖ also improved its vote substantially, from 12 per cent to 20 per cent.

Asylum applications to the EU had risen steadily in 2013–14, reaching 40,000 per month. With continued bloodshed in Syria, however, numbers swelled to 60,000 per month between mid-2014 and mid-2015. Many migrants took the convenient eastern Mediterranean route from Turkey to the Greek islands. On 25 August 2015, a German government agency posted a message on Twitter that 'We are . . . largely no longer enforcing Dublin procedures for Syrian citizens.' This meant Syrians didn't have to make asylum claims in their nearest third country but could proceed straight to Germany. At the end of August, the German Chancellor, Angela Merkel, made her country's stance clear and urged Europe to be true to its universalistic humanitarian mission: 'If Europe fails on the question of refugees, its close connection with universal civil rights will be destroyed. It won't be the Europe we imagine.' To her German audience she affirmed her commitment to the country's 'welcome culture' and said 'Wir schaffen das' ('We can do this'). This was an attempt to transform the narrative of German national identity from a 'qualitative' mode centred on history and culture to a 'quantitative' missionary nationalism based on being first among equals as the torchbearer for a universal humanitarian ideology.[45]

In response, a dramatically larger flow of refugees – Syrians, Afghans, Iraqis, Eritreans and others – began arriving from Turkey on the Greek island of Kos. Arrivals exceeded 100,000 in August and 200,000 in October, with daily headlines of flimsy and dangerous craft landing on Greek shores. Their route took them through Serbia, Hungary and Austria towards their final destinations in Germany and Sweden, and to a lesser degree the Netherlands and other points in Northern Europe.[46] What followed was an unfortunate, if predictable, rush of refugee claimants, most of whom were male, young and better off than many of their peers. If I were in their shoes and had the guts,

I would have done precisely the same thing, and it is hard not to be impressed by their perseverance and pluck. Watching it on television, many of us wanted them to succeed, and I am sure they are disproportionately endowed with entrepreneurship, intelligence and grit.

However, as policy, this free-for-all was a disaster. As Paul Collier observes, migration tends to be self-fulfilling, because established diasporas lower information and material costs for their slightly poorer or risk-averse compatriots, who in turn do the same for those further down the scale.[47] Those who may never consider migrating see others doing so and it becomes a possibility. There are 60 million refugees worldwide and estimates from the Gallup World Poll suggest 700 million people would migrate if they could – including 31 per cent of the population of sub-Saharan Africa.[48] If people saw their peers moving, the number could rise even further. What keeps most from moving is the knowledge that they cannot enter a host country, as well as the hardship, cost and uncertainty of migrating. The refugees that make it to the West are a relatively wealthy, male, risk-taking subsample of the total pool of potential claimants.

Money, not need, largely determines who comes to the West. Poor countries send few migrants because they can't afford to migrate. As they grow better off, more of them move. Middle-income countries send the most immigrants, but as countries pass an inflection point of $7,000–8,000 income per head, they send fewer immigrants.[49] Demographically expanding countries send more than those with a more mature age structure. Those in rich ageing countries move at low rates, which is why West European migration to North America declined sharply in the late twentieth century.

People are willing to take risks to pursue their dream. One study looked at five neighbourhoods in Dakar, Senegal. The proportion of those interviewed who would consider migrating was 92 per cent. Of these, 40 per cent indicated a willingness to migrate illegally – understandable given the difficulty of getting a visa. Most who said they would be willing to migrate illegally were men. Senegal is a peaceful African country well above the bottom of the income scale, yet the study found 77 per cent were willing to risk their life to get to Europe. Many thought they might perish and some said their chance of survival was only 50–50. Yet this didn't deter them. Half were willing to risk migrating even if the chance of dying was 25 per cent. Why? Because families receiving remittances from members living abroad have the highest status and wealth in the community. With high local unemployment, migration becomes the only route to high prestige for young men. Should they prevail, they bring honour on their family and themselves. Those with relatives abroad were substantially more likely to want to try their luck.[50]

The risk of dying is real for the migrants. The eastern Mediterranean route, where 3,771 people perished out of the million that attempted to cross in 2015, is much safer than the Libya–Italy (central) passage. Following the EU–Turkey deal which removed the incentive to use the eastern route, more opted for the longer, more dangerous central Mediterranean crossing. This is why 5,000 died in the Mediterranean in 2016 despite a much smaller flow than in 2015.[51] Libya itself is a failed state, with some migrants there being sold into slavery. The tragedy of signalling to migrants that they can acquire residence by getting close enough to Europe to be rescued is that it encourages others to try their luck.

Under specific conditions, as when migration comes from a middle-income country like Mexico, there is a limit to the numbers that will arrive. Even here, however, it took from the 1970s until 2014 for immigration from Mexico to the United States to subside, with hundreds of thousands arriving each year. In Europe, the exodus from Bulgaria and Romania began slowing in 2009 after around 2 million of their combined 28 million population had left, though more continue to arrive. These countries have incomes above $7,000 per capita, ageing populations and extremely low birth rates. Were this not the case, a much larger share would undoubtedly have emigrated.[52]

The economic and demographic gradient between the north and south shores of the Mediterranean is much wider than that separating Eastern and Western Europe. Those who argue that an open door will result in people moving seasonally in search of work without settling permanently rest their case on evidence from the US.[53] While it is true that many Mexican workers prior to the 1920s returned after working seasonally, this was largely because workers were mainly male. As more women began to accompany Mexican migrants after 1910, sex ratios fell, from 1.8 men per woman to 1.3:1 by 1930. More began to settle permanently, which facilitated others coming. Far from preventing illegal immigration, seasonal-worker programmes actually increased it.

The US response was large-scale deportation in the early 1930s and late 1940s/early 1950s ('Operation Wetback').[54] The only real difference between this period and the post-1965 era of undocumented immigration was a decrease in the political will to deport. It's also ironic that those who make the circulatory-migration argument are often the same people who prefer permanent settlement to guestworker schemes.

Following Merkel's signal that there would be no limits to Germany's generosity, liberal outlets like the *Economist* praised 'Merkel the bold' as 'brave, decisive and right'.[55] Many liberal critics attacked the Australian 'Stop the Boats' operation which ended uncontrolled flows of claimants to Australia, saving numerous lives. Between 2011 and 2013, the number of boats carrying migrants towards Australia rose from 4,500 to 20,000. Once facilities had been set up in Nauru and Papua New Guinea, the number of migrant boats dried up completely. Those who wish to claim asylum must do so from these locations. Despite its high-minded rhetoric, Germany has ended up in precisely the same place as Australia. In exchange for a large sum of money, the EU signed deals with Turkey and Libya which permit it to return claimants to these countries for offshore processing.

This is assailed by many, but the nub of the issue is that the world is an unequal place. The only reason there isn't large-scale migration to the rich world is that financial barriers and immigration controls prevent it. Once in a while, a crack appears in rich-country entry controls due to a refugee crisis, which permits better-off refugees in camps and those with an appetite for risk to have a chance at entering a wealthy country. This results in a gold rush of claimants – a perfectly reasonable response by migrants since windows of opportunity never last. So long as there is an incentive to enter European waters, the number of claimants will rise and more will die. The more that are accepted, and the fewer deported, the more that will arrive.

SAFETY IN EUROPE?

The tragedy is that there would be no need for offshore processing if claimants could be housed in secure, clean facilities in Europe without the prospect of permanent settlement. Building secure refugee facilities in the rich countries is the best way forward for the following reasons:

1. Where third countries are closed to refugees, those fleeing can be transported over them to safety in rich countries, so they won't die. This is the basic idea behind the term 'refuge'.
2. Western publics are more likely to accept the financial burden of housing refugees on a long-term basis than accepting them as permanent settlers because they care more about the cultural impact of refugee settlement than the economic costs.
3. This allows the world to absorb any number of refugees without discriminating on the basis of wealth, fitness to travel and risk appetite. Nobody dies in transit or gets attacked or enslaved en route.
4. The burden is taken off hard-pressed third countries, though refugees in Western camps would have the right to transfer back to camps closer to their home country at any time.
5. This will offer refuge, but not settlement, so only those genuinely fearing for their lives will remain. There would be no need to engage in the impossible task of sorting genuine refugees from economic migrants.
6. Refugees on Western soil will concentrate more minds on the problems in trouble spots, pressing for a solution. Western countries would have more of an incentive to bring camps in countries bordering conflict areas in line with Western standards in order to encourage refugees to return to those camps, or to prevent more people asking for a transfer to a Western facility. If the standard of facilities is high enough, refugees will prefer to be in places closer to their home countries.
7. Burden-sharing will become easier because countries will not be asked to alter their ethnic composition against their inhabitants' wishes – only to contribute funds and build facilities.

Long-term refugee camps are a reality in many countries, such as Kenya or Lebanon, bordering conflict areas. Why should this be unthinkable for us? Why is a secure camp in the West an affront to human rights while one in Turkey or Libya is not? If we are serious about the principle of offering a safe haven to those fleeing for their lives, we must accept this responsibility. Legal barriers could be surmounted if judges were willing to use their interpretive energies to do so. Hosting refugees in the

THE RISE AND RISE OF THE POPULIST RIGHT IN EUROPE

West would provide a good test of whether liberals are more interested in helping people take refuge or making the symbolic gesture of calling for more settlement – which is guaranteed to result in doors being closed. If the former, they will maintain support for secure refugee facilities. If the latter, they will label the facilities prisons, agitate to have camp residents resettled and call for facilities to be closed. If that happens, we'll revert to the status quo, in which many who flee war are sent back to die, unlucky migrants drown at sea or are preyed upon by criminals, the majority of refugees languish in underfunded camps and a small group of better-off risk-takers get lucky.

At time of writing, leaders of several European countries are groping towards these ideas. The first plan is to establish a facility in a less prosperous European non-EU country like Albania, a proposal tacitly endorsed by the EU's president, Jean-Claude Juncker.[56] After a populist Lega Nord–Five Star Movement government was elected in Italy, the Lega Nord interior minister, Matteo Salvini, made it clear that the Italians wanted a drastic reduction in the numbers arriving on their shores and greater dispersion of migrants to other EU states. Yet many EU states, notably the Visegrád countries, Austria and a German faction (the CSU) wanted frontline Mediterranean countries like Italy to prevent asylum seekers from moving north. Migration was emerging as the most important divide within the EU. During tense negotiations at an EU Summit in June 2018, Spain and France proposed the idea of secure migrant-processing centres within the EU alongside the earlier plan for centres in non-EU states like Albania or Tunisia. The agreement to develop secure processing centres, with a focus on deterring further flows, helped salvage a deal between the more liberal Merkel faction and more conservative Kurz–Salvini–Seehofer axis. This also helped prevent the collapse of the German government, a coalition between Merkel's CDU and Horst Seehofer's CSU, after Seehofer warned Merkel that a more liberal approach would lead him to terminate the seventy-year-old CDU–CSU alliance.[57]

In my view the plans are a positive move, but suffer from the fact that the onus is still on case officers to distinguish between true and false refugees, which could result in genuine refugees being sent back to their deaths or, if the system errs in favour of claimants, to a surfeit of people accepted for settlement, which will encourage others to migrate. I would prefer spacious permanent migrant centres across the full range of EU countries, alongside free transportation from conflict areas. This would cut deaths at sea, expand refuge, improve conditions in migrant facilities and increase the urgency of improving camps nearer the conflict zone.

My opinion is that the optimal scenario is one in which every refugee can flee a conflict zone and be protected, housed, clothed, educated and fed, receiving proper medical care. There should be recreational facilities and, ideally, an opportunity to work, as Paul Collier recommends.[58] This should be paid for by the international community, through either charities or contributions from wealthier countries. Much more needs to be done to bring the lives of refugees in camps up to an acceptable standard. This, for me, is where the attention of social justice campaigners should be focused. David Cameron's Conservative UK government gave a higher share of income to the camps than other European countries but admitted fewer – and then only on the basis of need – from the camps. This led to protest but was the correct decision.

WHY BLURRING THE LINE BETWEEN ASYLUM AND SETTLEMENT IS DANGEROUS

Paradoxically, pressure to widen the rights of asylum seekers inside Europe makes it harder to fulfil the mission of getting people to safety. Why? Because if countries believe admitting refugees is the first step to granting permanent settlement, they will be more reluctant to allow them in. Claimants in the West have their cases judged increasingly harshly due to domestic political pressure to limit the number accepted for settlement. Those whose cases fail and cannot escape lack the option to remain safely in a high-quality facility. It's estimated that thousands of genuine refugees are returned to countries where they risk being persecuted or killed.[59]

A consistent humanitarian position would be one that advocated transporting any refugee to safety in a camp, with overflow to Western facilities. Liberal activists and judges have strained to interpret international human rights law as generously as possible to the point where someone who arrives in Europe has a path to citizenship. The West doesn't have to practise what it preaches because money and geography prevent most of the world's 60 million refugees from arriving.

Paradoxically, tempering humanitarian idealism with realism so poor refugees could be evacuated would be far better for social justice than the current dispensation. Activist judiciaries have pushed for maximal interpretations of human rights conventions which prompts politicians to ensure that as few refugees as possible enter their countries.

The refugee system fails many where it should be welcoming. Turkey prevents refugees from Syria from crossing its border to safety and Lebanon periodically cracks down on those in the camps. In both countries, refugees cannot be contained in quality facilities so they enter the general population, stoking local resistance. Anti-immigration sentiment in Turkey is at record levels due to the refugee influx. It would be better if these people were in higher-quality facilities, locally or in Europe. The main reason Australia has to process refugee claims outside the country, where standards of care and protection fall short, is because if the claimants were processed in Australia, advocacy groups and judges would compel them to be settled. That is, they would urge authorities to grant asylum seekers access to appeals processes which would permit people to disappear into the underground economy. The same groups would then oppose deportation and support a path for the undocumented to obtain legal status. Again, tempering idealism with realism would lead to a better situation for claimants, but activists would prefer to agitate for maximalism even if this leaves refugees worse off.

The focus on settling refugees who can get to the West – who tend to be the fittest, brightest and richest – takes centre stage. Attention shifts away from pressuring governments and rich-world publics to improve the condition of the masses who are too frail or poor to move. Successful migrants may even worsen the mood of the unlucky folk stuck in the camps who can't pay a people smuggler. Finally, it's important to focus on those who are most needy. Someone who lives safely in government-controlled Syria or Afghanistan, or in a refugee camp in Turkey or Lebanon, is very unlucky. I thank God I'm not in their shoes. But they are in a better position than a South Sudanese peasant on the verge of starvation. War is the most grievous threat to human life, but ecological threats, especially lack of food, run a close second and affect many more people. Some 780 million people in the world are malnourished and 9 million people die of starvation every year. These ecological refugees would come to the West if they could. When I give my charity contribution each year, it always goes to those at the very bottom of the pile.

The current asylum regime urges the West to open its doors to those who can make it here. It only evaluates the moral claims of people who land on its shores, neglecting refugees languishing in camps from conflicts past and present. Conflicts in the news or nearby matter, while others are ignored. The selective worldview of the media puts pressure on Germany to fulfil its moral obligations towards Syrians but not Rohingyas. Both domestic and international law in this area has been subject to cosmopolitan interpretation, to the point where Western countries are essentially obliged to accept any refugee who arrives as a citizen – so long as they can make a subjective claim to being in danger. This stems from the expanding scope of human rights law since the 1960s, from its rightful focus on protecting people to a newer emphasis on the right to settle. 'The extension of rights to . . . foreigners in the decades following World War II', write three migration experts, 'is one of the most salient aspects of political development in the advanced industrial democracies.'[60] Christian Joppke observes that judiciaries took the lead in liberalizing settlement rules for temporary workers in Europe. In Germany they overturned a 'strong state' tradition in the 1970s to regularize the status of Turkish guestworkers and enable generous family reunification.[61] Activist judges and special interest groups, working with sympathetic bureaucrats, liberalized policy.

It's time to pull back from this cosmopolitan overreach. 'We need to restore refuge to its rightful place and understand what it is for,' argues Oxford Professor of Migration Alexander Betts. 'Refuge is not about migration . . . There is no absolute legal or ethical right to migrate.'[62] New forms of jurisprudence and internal institutional reforms are needed which interpret human rights conventions more reasonably to permit refugees to be housed in facilities in the West. State sovereignty should be respected as long as human rights are upheld. Failure to do this may lead mass publics to turn against institutions of liberalism such as the courts, endangering the rule of law and our hard-won freedoms.

The neediest in the camps should be prioritized and receive the lion's share of media attention and funding. I also believe in settling a quota of refugees in the West each year because the least lucky people on the planet deserve some hope. This should be done by lottery among those in camps or in areas threatened by drought and starvation. We should pay for them to fly safely here. When it comes to the lottery, those who have been in camps for more than a decade should gain access to a separate competition where the success rate is higher. This means those in the Kakuma camp in north-western Kenya, where nearly 200,000 people live and who in some cases have been there since 1992, should be considered ahead of Syrians in Turkish and Lebanese camps.

If Western countries are the nearest countries to a conflict, they should accept an unlimited number of refugees. A precedent is the 250,000 Belgians who sheltered in Britain during the First World War then returned home in 1918. The refugee burden should be redistributed to camps further afield, with financial contributions from all rich countries. It should be made clear that there is no chance of permanent settlement outside regular immigration channels or the refugee lottery. This preserves the meaning of national citizenship while offering a safety valve to those unlucky enough to be persecuted or driven from their homes through war.

Are Western liberals interested in ensuring that the locked doors the Jews encountered when trying to leave occupied Europe during the Second World War never slam shut again? Or is it more important to shame Western governments into accepting more refugees to settle, in order to burnish one's liberal credentials and hasten the multicultural millennium? The main reason Jews couldn't escape in 1938–9 is because the existing tradition of exile involved small numbers of political dissidents who received citizenship in the countries they fled to. The international system hadn't foreseen the need for a mass evacuation and countries weren't prepared to admit a large number of refugee-immigrants from a different culture.

If we are interested in the greatest good of the greatest number, we would focus on helping political and ecological refugees get to camps and make the lives of these vulnerable people better. Significant diplomatic pressure should be brought to bear on rich countries in East Asia and the Persian Gulf to contribute money and shelter refugees in facilities. Had this kind of system been in place during the Second World War, millions of Jews, including my great-grandparents, would have survived. The current approach is dangerous. Erasing the line between refuge and settlement makes it more likely countries will bar the door the way they did in 1939.

BACKLASH AND POLARIZATION

The increase in asylum claimants, crowned by the 2015 migration crisis, had far-reaching effects on European public opinion. The surge polarized European publics between a conservative majority and a liberal minority. The European Social Survey asks a sample of Europeans if they are willing to accept immigrants of a different race or religion to the majority in the country. Answers range from 'accept none' to 'accept many'. As figure 5.8 shows, the answers to this question have been stable since 2002, even registering a slight increase in tolerance between 2014, before the migration crisis, and 2016, after it. In most countries, the median response hovers between those who would accept 'few' and those who would accept 'some' non-Europeans. People's attitude to immigration is connected to their general social liberalism. This in turn relates to how psychologically conservative or authoritarian they are.

The form of question is very important, however. People tend to be

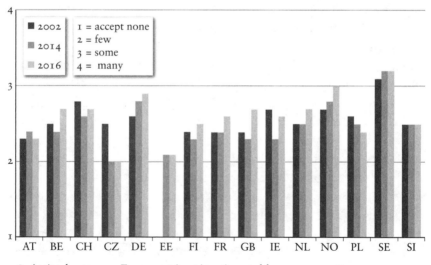

5.8. Attitudes to non-European immigration stable, 2002–2106

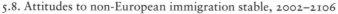

Source: James Dennison and Andrew Geddes, 'Op-ed: Are Europeans turning against asylum seekers and refugees?', www.ecre.org, 17 November 2017. Based on ESS 2002, 2014, 2016

more favourable when answering a question using the term 'immigrants' than the more impersonal 'immigration'. In February 2017, a Chatham House survey carried out before President Trump's first Executive Order restricting travel from Muslim countries discovered that a majority of Europeans agreed with the statement: 'all further migration from Muslim countries should be stopped'. This included respondents in traditionally liberal Germany. In most countries, as figure 5.9 shows, the share actively disagreeing was no higher than 25 per cent.

Though immigration attitudes are stable across Western Europe, a higher influx increased the ranking (salience) of the immigration issue among the majority of Europeans who desire lower levels. Populist-right parties tapped into this high salience, winning a higher share of the anti-immigration vote than had previously been the case.

Eurobarometer surveys show that concern over immigration ranked near the bottom of Europeans' priorities during the 2007–8 economic crisis. With the economy in free fall, voters cited economic problems

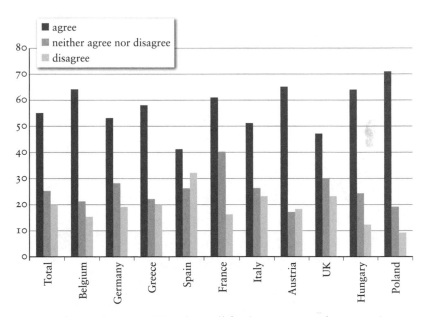

5.9. Attitudes on the proposition that 'All further migration from mainly Muslim countries should be stopped', %

Source: Matthew Goodwin and Thomas Raines, 'What do Europeans think about Muslim immigration?', Chatham House, 7 February 2017

like unemployment as the leading issues facing their countries. As the
Eurobarometer data in figure 5.10 shows, immigration scrapes along
the bottom as the least important concern for the public until 2013,
when it begins to rise, reaching a peak during the migration crisis of
2015. At this point it was named a top-two issue by 36 per cent of EU
voters. This data includes many Eastern and Southern European countries, but when we concentrate on North-Western Europe, the salience
is especially high. Of the six countries in the EU where immigration
ranked first in the autumn 2016 Eurobarometer, only Malta isn't in the
north. Terrorism also ranks highly in five countries, and again all lie in
North-Western Europe. Immigration was important in some Southern
and Eastern European countries, but unemployment and the economy
tended to rank higher.

In 2017, the Eurobarometer showed that EU citizens saw terrorism
and immigration as by far the most important issues facing the EU.

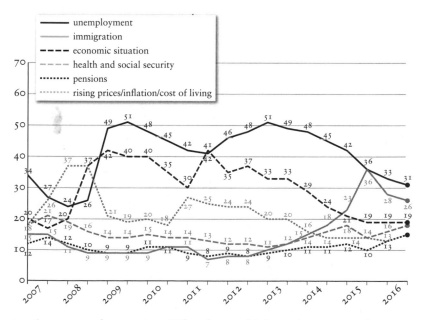

5.10. Answers to the question, 'What do you think are the two most important
issues facing [our country] at the moment?', %

Source: Eurobarometer, Autumn 2016

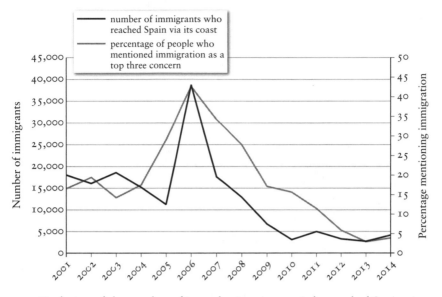

5.11. Evolution of the number of irregular immigrants (who reached Spain via the coast) matched against levels of concern over immigration

Source: Maria Mendes, Twitter, 25 November 2017.

Together, these began to rise in prominence in 2013 and were named top-two issues by 70–90 per cent of respondents compared to 50–55 per cent for the economic situation, unemployment and public finances combined. Salience tracks migration flows, especially asylum seekers. Figure 5.11 shows how tight the relationship between actual arrivals and immigration salience was in Spain between 2002 and 2014.[63]

The press is an important mediator. As immigration rises, the number of media stories increases and the prominence of immigration in the public mind rises. The studies that have been done on this – in Britain, Germany, the Netherlands and Spain – show that immigration, media coverage of immigration and salience rise together, as in figure 5.1.[64] This means numbers really do matter, even if people's perceptions of the actual inflows are inflated by a factor of two or three.[65]

SALIENCE AND
POPULIST-RIGHT VOTING

Figure 5.12, based on the work of James Dennison and Andrew Geddes, shows the relationship between immigration levels and support for Geert Wilders' PVV in the Netherlands. As immigration totals exceeded 150,000 per year after 2013, the PVV's projected seat total, based on opinion polls, rose dramatically. The authors find a significant correlation of .85 between annual immigration numbers and PVV support in the polls.[66]

Figure 5.12 shows there's a trend but also considerable volatility in the PVV vote. Prior to 2012, the PVV was part of an unpopular governing coalition, which damaged it. It subsequently joined a more popular one, which boosted its fortunes. Scandals and splits affect populist-right parties more than mainstream ones because insurgent parties lack an established brand like 'Christian Democrat' or 'Social Democrat'. The parties become heavily reliant on the charisma of their

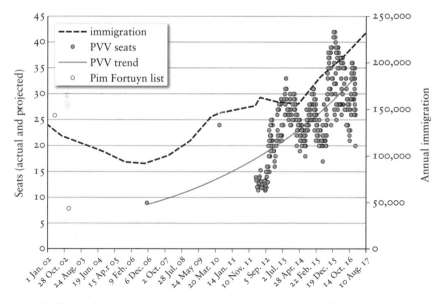

5.12. Relationship between immigration levels and support for Geert Wilders' PVV in the Netherlands

Source: Dennison et al., 'The Dutch aren't turning against immigration'

leader – Farage, Wilders, Haider – and may suffer succession problems. The template for populist-right success seems to involve a viable populist-right party with a capable leader which can serve as a vehicle for protest when immigration increases.

The relationship between the migration crisis and the rise of the AfD in Germany is a case in point. During the crisis, Frauke Petry replaced

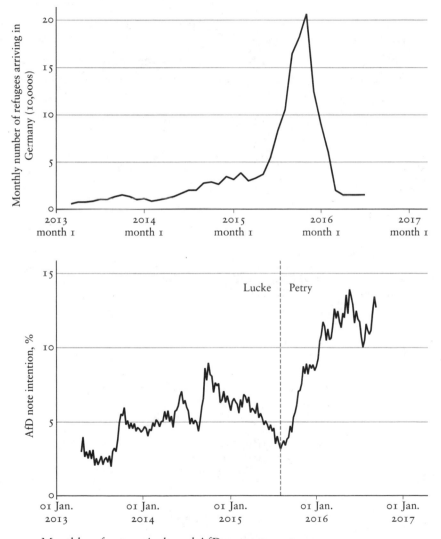

5.13. Monthly refugee arrivals and AfD support, 2013–17.

Source: Kappe, 'Media attention, party positioning and public support for right-wing populist parties'

Bernd Lucke, a founder of the party who was motivated by Eurosceptic economic concerns. In 2016, he left the party because he alleged it was becoming 'xenophobic'. As figure 5.13 shows, this unlocked an immediate surge in AfD poll numbers, reaching nearly 15 per cent by mid-2016. Political scientist Roland Kappe finds a significant statistical relationship between monthly arrivals and AfD support when accounting for change of leader. This is true not only of the trend but of monthly refugee fluctuations, which are correlated with the month-to-month change in AfD vote intention.

James Dennison and his colleagues find that between 2005 and 2016, immigration rates, immigration salience and support for the populist right were significantly correlated in nine of ten West European countries.[67] At a regional level, the 2016 Eurobarometer shows that concern over migration tracks the migrants' main route from Greece through Austria and Hungary into southern Germany, Sweden and the Netherlands. Across Europe, the migration crisis gave populist-right parties a shot in the arm while the 2007–8 financial crisis had no effect.

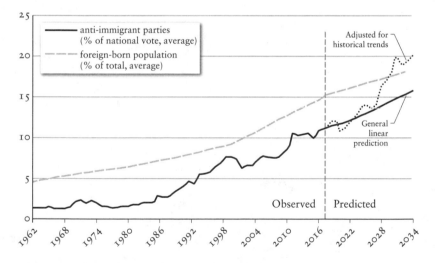

5.14. Foreign-born share and support for anti-immigration parties in Western Europe

Source: Nate Breznau, 'Europe's ageing societies require immigration to survive – and that means anti-immigration politics is here to stay', LSE British Politics and Policy blog, 21 December 2017

This demonstrates that immigration, not straitened economic circumstances, best explains the populist-right vote in Western Europe. Political scientist Nate Breznau finds that within seventeen West European countries, the increase in foreign-born share strongly predicts populist-right voting between 1962 and 2017 and forecasts continued growth because foreign share is expected to keep rising. Results are shown in figure 5.14.

It's also important to see that populist-right parties were capitalizing on a public mood, not manufacturing it. Had the latter been true, we would have expected more of a boost in right-wing populism during an economic crisis where such parties might have tried blaming elites and immigrants. To wit, in Europe, party messaging to supporters to get behind particular issues seems less important in shaping immigration opinion than in America. Public opinion and the populist right have led on this issue, with centre-right parties playing catch up.

THE MIGRANT CRISIS AND THE EUROPEAN UNION

The migration crisis swiftly sowed divisions within the EU. Germany's putting out the welcome mat clashed with the more restrictionist inclinations of politicians in most other member states. 'We will teach Brussels, the human traffickers and the migrants that Hungary is a sovereign country,' declared Hungary's Viktor Orbán, ordering the construction of a fence along the Serbian border which blocked the route to Austria and trapped migrants in Greece.[68] Since there is freedom of movement for EU citizens within the Schengen passport-free zone, migrants admitted to Germany could potentially enter other European states. This led to the reimposition of border controls in, among others, the Netherlands, Germany, Sweden and Slovakia, and weakened the legitimacy of an EU already battered by the financial crisis, and which would soon lose Britain as a member.[69]

The Visegrád countries in the East refused to accept their share of refugees, leading to an East–West standoff. 'Islam has no place in Slovakia,' argued Robert Fico, the country's Social Democratic Prime Minister.[70] This attitude, expressed by a centre-left rather than far-right figure, reflects a closed ethnic nationalism. While I support a safety-without-settlement policy for irregular migrants arriving in Europe, I also would argue that a quota of the most disadvantaged people should be admitted as immigrants to rich countries on humanitarian grounds. Slovakia as a sovereign state has the right to prioritize Christians from camps around the world, but should admit at least a symbolic quantity of Muslims – to see how they work out over a ten or twenty-year timespan. An identity based on ethnic or religious purity (as opposed to preponderance) is racist because it tends towards an unhealthy obsession with an imaginary racial essence. This typically produces an insular attitude towards outsiders and results in treating minorities as second-class citizens. Having said this, it would be considerably easier to get Visegrád ethnic nations to share the burden if this merely involved a financial commitment to maintaining secure facilities rather than opening up national citizenship, which is considered a sacred value.

Rogers Brubaker, a leading scholar of nationalism, explains that the Visegrád countries view immigration and refugees through the prism of resistance to foreign rule, be it Ottoman, Soviet or West European. Liberalism, with its defence of Roma, LGBT, Jewish and immigrant rights, is viewed as a foreign import like Soviet communism or Islam. In Brubaker's estimation, the anti-Islamic, anti-immigrant rhetoric in the East is more superficial and opportunistic than that in north-west Europe. Immigration is attacked because it represents an attempt at foreign interference over national sovereignty rather than due to its intrinsic threat to identity. Visegrád leaders also reference traditional mythic tropes about their countries serving as defenders of Christianity's frontiers against the Islamic threat.[71] Miloš Zeman's narrow victory in the 2018 Czech election focused on migration, Islam and the EU, and brought three of the four Visegrád countries into populist hands. Only Slovakia, where the mainstream parties have been vociferously anti-immigration, kept populists at bay, on 22 per cent of the vote. It should be noted that right-wing populism is strong only in ex-communist states with moderate income levels proximal to the Balkan migration route. It is weaker in the Baltic states, in poor Romania and Bulgaria, or in non-EU countries such as Serbia and Georgia.

Western European right-wing politicians admired Orbán's outspoken stance. In a pointed rebuke to Angela Merkel, Horst Seehofer of the conservative Christian Social Union (CSU) party, an ally of Merkel's Christian Democrats (CDU), invited Orbán to a CSU gathering in

Bavaria in September, at the height of the crisis, adding, 'We need Hungary to secure the outer borders of the EU.'[72] Two years later, the AfD won 13.3 per cent of the vote in the 2017 German election. Over a third of their vote came from those who hadn't previously voted, reflecting a dynamic common to Brexit, Trump and other populist-right phenomena.[73] This was a dramatic moment for a country whose fascist past led many to think it immune to the populist-right's charms. Despite her attempts to claim that what had happened in 2015 would never happen again, Merkel's CDU was badly damaged by the migration question, with the CDU/CSU losing 8.5 points. The left-leaning Social Democrats also lost out, slipping more than 5 points to just 20.5 per cent. By February 2018, they were being outpolled as the second largest party by the AfD.

Against the grain, the Free Democratic Party (FDP), a free-market party and usually reliable CDU partner, changed direction. Its young leader, Christian Lindner, accused Merkel of 'humanitarian narcissism' and promised a more controlled approach to immigration. This looks to have been a success, boosting the party's share from under 5 per cent pre-crisis to 8 per cent at the election.[74] In a sign of the times, Lindner failed to agree coalition terms with Merkel's CDU in part because of Merkel's liberal stance on the question of whether refugees should be able to bring their family members to Germany.[75] Meanwhile, the disgruntled CSU praised the example of Austria's successful centre-right leader, Sebastian Kurz, who adopted many of the FPÖ's hardline immigration policies.

IMMIGRATION AND POLITICAL TRUST

Growing concern over immigration is part of the explanation for a distrust of politicians, extending to reduced support for liberal democracy. Lauren McLaren finds that across Western Europe those concerned about immigration express lower trust in politicians, parliament and the legal system, even with a battery of control variables. Only dissatisfaction with the economy has a stronger effect.[76] In the 2016 European Social Survey (ESS), the same holds, with concern over immigration again strongly significant in lowering system trust, running second only to perceptions of the economy. What this tells us is not that immigration affects everyone's trust in elites and the system, but rather that it lowers the trust of the anti-immigration part of the public, notably the Settlers/Somewheres. As Karen Stenner observes, environmental triggers like immigration activate the latent anxieties of psychological authoritarians who prize stability and security.[77]

MUSLIMS IN THE SPOTLIGHT

The migration crisis placed Muslim immigration in the spotlight. Then, on New Year's Eve of 2015, hundreds of women were sexually assaulted in Cologne, Germany. Across German cities the total climbed to 1,200. Many of the perpetrators were reported to be immigrants. After an awkward silence from the authorities, the revelations caused a media storm.[78] Meanwhile a spate of terrorist incidents in France led to the intertwining of migration and terrorism in the minds of those predisposed to insecurity. In January 2015, two Islamist brothers, Saïd and Chérif Kouachi, burst into the Paris offices of the French magazine *Charlie Hebdo*. The publication had record of mocking religions, including Islam. The pair gunned down twelve and wounded eleven, four seriously, while yelling 'Allahu akbar.'[79] Then, in November 2015, at the height of the migration crisis, a series of deadly attacks rocked Paris, killing 130 and wounding a further 413, nearly 100 seriously. The worst carnage took place in the Bataclan theatre, where gunmen entered a packed Eagles of Death Metal concert, shooting indiscriminately. In the end, the death toll of young people stood at eighty-nine.[80]

Terrorist episodes seem to have a familiar effect on European publics. Immediately after the violence, progressives emphasize unity and the need to avoid racist attacks against Muslims. Conservatives mobilize, warning that Muslim immigration is a threat to the nation. The attack reverberates differently in different echo chambers. One paper based on ESS data pre- and post-Hebdo showed that liberals became more favourable to Muslims after the attack.[81] Concern rises among those in the middle of the ideological spectrum, but tends to fade gradually if time passes without incident.[82]

Earlier we observed how the populist right repositioned itself in the 2000s to foreground the Islamic threat. Work in political science, including the literature on anti-Catholic and anti-immigration politics, emphasizes that parties which campaign on a single issue – even one as important as immigration or nationalism – usually can't prevail. Some separatist parties like the Scottish National Party or Parti Québécois bundle nationalism together with a left-wing economic message. The populist-right strategy is to combine a traditional focus on protecting identity with an appeal to voters who value freedom of speech, gender and gay equality, material security and the welfare state. Populists make the 'welfare chauvinist' case that only they can protect the welfare state from abuse by undeserving immigrants who have not contributed to the system.[83] I maintain that these subsidiary issues act more as a legitimating device for a core message of ethnic defence and ethno-traditional nationalism. Yet many may rank immigration as their second or third concern after a more conventional liberal or material issue. By offering a distinctive take on such issues, the far right can secure the support of those for whom immigration is important, but not their highest priority.

The most successful populist-right parties in Western Europe, the Front National and FPÖ, have managed to combine an uncompromising immigration message with a liberal and material offer. This permits them to reach beyond their base to new categories of voter. Their age profile is thus much more even than that of newer right-wing populists like UKIP or the AfD, which rely more heavily on older voters.

Immigration and Islam together explain much of the appeal of the new parties. Figure 5.15 shows that in Western Europe there is a .63 correlation between projected 2030 Muslim share and the highest poll or vote share a populist-right party has achieved. Why is this relationship so strong? Data on the share of immigrants in Europe is not the best measure of the demographic shifts a country has experienced as many immigrants come from other, often neighbouring, European countries. Projected 2030 Muslim population provides a combined indicator of non-European population, Islamic presence and ethnic change, capturing both liberal anti-Islamic concerns and the ethno-national anxieties which motivate conservative and authoritarian voters.[84]

For instance, France has a higher Muslim share than Sweden, but Sweden's projected Muslim population in 2030 is almost as high due to its more rapid Muslim growth rate. Restricting the focus to Western Europe removes the distinctive historical forces which power the

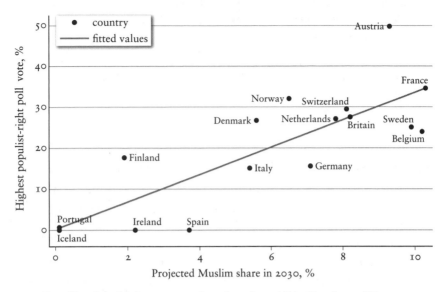

5.15. Populist right high-water mark and projected Muslim share, Western Europe

Source: Opinion polls, electoral results and Pew 2011 The Future of the European Muslim Population.

populist right in the East, where Muslim immigrants are rare. Finally, the high-water mark is important because these parties' vote shares are volatile. Splits, leadership succession problems and scandals cause their support to fluctuate over the short term. As vehicles for anti-immigration protest, many of their voters are recent converts from other parties or non-voting, with shallower brand loyalty. Maximum vote share, which occurs when leadership and opportunity is most favourable, provides a sense of how strongly the party's message resonates with voters.

The outliers in figure 5.15 are Spain at the low end, and Austria at the high end. Spain's painful experience with fascism, which lasted until 1975, and recent experience of domestic Basque terrorism may have acted as a prophylactic against the far right.[85] Immigration also peaked in 2008 and has been declining due to the country's weak economy. Yet Spain, like the German-speaking countries, has very low fertility and will therefore experience considerable economic pressure to increase migration. Only time will tell if it can continue to avoid the populist right.

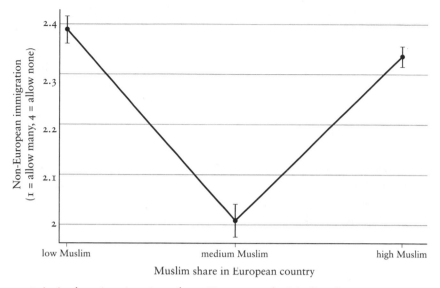

5.16. Attitude to immigration of non-Europeans, by Muslim share, Western Europe

Source: ESS 2016. N = 12, 274. Controls for age, education, income, trust in people, with country fixed effects. Ten West European countries.

The relationship with Muslim share is also not straightforward. When a country has little experience with Muslim immigration (i.e. Muslim share is below 2 per cent), fear and misunderstanding are high, so opposition is based on ignorance. After a country gets used to their presence, in the 2–4 per cent Muslim range, hostility declines. However, as numbers begin to rise beyond 4.5 per cent of the population, the relationship goes into reverse: figure 5.16 shows that increased Muslim share in a country beyond a medium level of 4.5 per cent is associated with greater opposition to non-European immigration among individuals. In models where I control for country income, the effect of a Muslim share above 4.5 per cent on anti-immigration sentiment greatly exceeds that of having a Muslim share under 2 per cent.

The foregoing suggests immigration stocks and flows have distinct effects. The share of minorities – regardless of growth rate – creates diversity, which is an issue for psychological authoritarians, who seek consensus and order. Change is the problem for conservatives, who benchmark the present against the golden age they knew growing up.

POLARIZATION

Opposition to immigration and a sense of being ethnically threatened tend to emerge among conservatives and order-seekers as societies grow more diverse. In the US, we noted how proximity to the Mexican border and living in a high-Latino area tended to polarize white American opinion on immigration between authoritarians and liberals, Republicans and Democrats.[86] The same relationship has been discovered in Europe. In more diverse or ethnically changing areas of Austria, Germany and Switzerland, a bigger gap on immigration attitudes is opening up between conservatives and liberals.[87]

We see something similar when comparing how homogeneous and diverse countries in Europe shape the voting preferences of security-oriented people. Figure 5.17 shows that the 25 per cent of European voters who say it's very important to be safe are sensitive to Muslim share. In more diverse countries such as France, the Netherlands and Sweden, they are twice as likely to vote for a populist-right party, but in homogeneous Finland they are actually less likely to back the

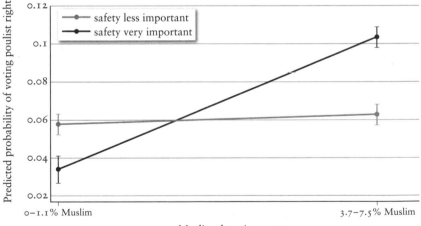

5.17. Muslim share, importance of safety and likelihood of populist-right vote

Source: ESS 2016 and Pew 2011 The Future of the European Muslim Population. N=16,815. Pseudo R2=.035. Controls for interpersonal trust, age, education, income, with robust standard errors. Ten west European countries.

populist True Finns. A similar pattern shows up for immigration attitudes: in relatively high-Muslim societies like France, those who worry
about their safety are much more restrictionist than those who don't.
Countries below 4.5 per cent Muslim have a smaller gap between the
more and less security-conscious. This backs Stenner's argument that
when consensus breaks down – in this case due to disagreements over
rising diversity – order-seeking voters are activated to vote for parties
that promise to limit change.

Rising diversity polarizes people by psychological outlook and re-
orients party platforms. As countries ethnically change, green parties
move to capture cosmopolitan liberals and the populist right targets
conservatives and authoritarians.[88] While attitude liberalization did
throw up cultural debates over religion, gay marriage and traditional
values, these are on their way to becoming marginal in Europe as liberal attitudes attain mass acceptance. The legalization of drugs and the
question of how best to address crime are live social issues, but neither
promises the same radical transformation of society as ethnic change.
Therefore it is ethno-demographic shifts which are rotating European
societies away from a dominant left–right economic orientation to a
globalist–nationalist cultural axis. The West is becoming less like
homogeneous South Korea, where foreign policy and economic divisions dominate, and more like South Africa, where ethnicity is the
main political division.[89]

The rise of anti-immigration parties in Western Europe presents challenges to the main centre-right and centre-left parties. After some
hesitation, the centre right in most European countries has attempted
to co-opt the populist right. This has paid off handsomely and placed
centre-left parties on the back foot.[90] From Norway to the Netherlands
to Austria, the centre right has either entered into coalition with the
populist right or tried to move onto its territory to win ownership of
immigration and integration issues.[91]

In Austria, the centre-right ÖVP entered into coalition with Haider's FPÖ after the latter's 27 per cent showing in the election. In France,
Nicolas Sarkozy gained a reputation as being tough on immigration
and Islam after the 2005 *banlieue* riots. In September 2009, he made
his views on the burqa crystal clear to a cheering crowd of lawmakers:
'In our country, we cannot accept that women be prisoners behind a

screen . . . The burqa is . . . a sign of debasement . . . It will not be welcome on the territory of the French Republic.'⁹² Only in Germany and
Sweden did the centre right, constrained by anti-racist norms, accede to
the bipartisan idea of isolating the far right and its agenda. This strategy collapsed under the weight of the migration crisis of 2015: the CDU
and Swedish Moderate Party have changed their tone on immigration,
though neither has yet entered into coalition with the far right.

In Britain, notwithstanding May's unpopularity, the Tories were seen
as the party of Brexit, permitting them to absorb UKIP support, reducing the populist right from its 12.7 per cent showing in 2015 to just 1.8
per cent. In the Netherlands, Mark Rutte's 'Act normal or leave' commercial burnished his anti-Muslim credentials, helping his centre-right
VVD best Geert Wilders' PVV in 2017. In Austria, 31-year-old Sebastian Kurz of the centre-right ÖVP positioned immigration and hostility
to 'parallel communities' – a thinly veiled reference to Islam – at the
centre of his message. This was a winning strategy. Kurz's 24 per cent,
combined with the FPÖ's 21 per cent, easily allowed the ÖVP-FPÖ
coalition to outdistance the Social Democrats' 26 per cent.

The rise of the populist right puts the social-democratic left in a
difficult position. Many white working-class voters are attracted to
anti-immigration politics and reject the 'cultural turn' of the left that
has influenced post-1960s cadres of party activists. Across Europe, no
social democratic party wins a majority of white working-class votes.
What should the centre-left do? Should it move to the right on immigration and multiculturalism, alienating many of its activists? Since the
left is less trusted on immigration, the best it can do is parry attacks
from the right accusing it of being soft on immigration and terrorism.
However, this carries risks. On its liberal flank, the centre-left stands
to lose cosmopolitan and ethnic minority voters to Green parties,
which have also gained ground.

Minorities are not yet a major voting bloc in most European countries.
Some centre-left parties have therefore decided that a pro-immigration,
multiculturalist platform is too risky. In Norway, the left has aligned
with the populist-right Progress Party's view that low-cost immigration
undercuts the wages of 'indigenous' workers. Something similar occurred
in Denmark. In Britain, Jeremy Corbyn qualified his initially open
immigration policy by criticizing firms which hire low-wage immigrant

workers instead of training British ones. This, combined with Corbyn's socialist Euroscepticism, helped him attract an important minority of Leave voters in 2017. My analysis of a survey conducted on the eve of the election suggests that while Leavers went Tory, many Leavers who voted for Labour before 2015 bucked the trend and went for Corbyn. In the Netherlands and Austria, however, the centre-left opted for a softer tone, hoping to redirect the political conversation towards its economic policies. This has been an electoral failure.[93]

The rising salience of immigration has arguably assisted the centre-right while weakening social democrats. Figure 5.18 shows how the moderate left vote share in seventeen Western European countries has declined to its lowest level since 1945. About half of this has been picked up by the far left, but parties to the right have captured the rest.

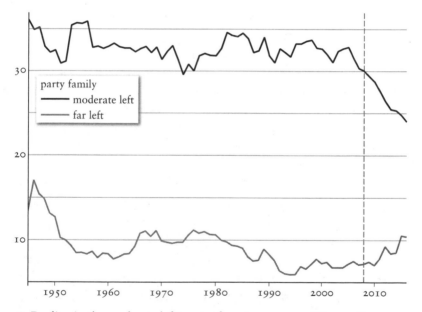

5.18. Decline in the moderate left's vote share in seventeen Western European countries, %

Source: Björn Bremer, 'Hope for Europe's Social Democrats? Why Martin Schulz might reinvigorate the SPD but struggle to become Chancellor', WZB Democracy Blog, 10 February 2017

Events and personalities buffet the political cycle, so no trend is absolute. In Germany, Martin Schulz of the SPD enjoyed a momentary run of popularity from January 2017, and looked to be catching Merkel's CDU before support ebbed and his party finished with a disappointing 21 per cent result. In France, the centrist Emmanuel Macron became social democracy's hero when he thumped Marine Le Pen 66–33 in the second round of the 2017 presidential election. Macron was a fresh face, heading a new party, in a country ripe for economic reform. These factors helped him cruise to an easy victory.

Macron's success underlines the importance of 'issue diversity' whereby parties must craft an appeal across a wide range of issues to win in a complex, pluralistic society. This is especially so when economic 'left-right' cleavages lose power.[94] Populist-right parties cannot win just by talking about immigration, but must satisfy a wider array of voters who may rank other issues first and migration second or third. Macron performed the obverse trick, mobilizing voters who value economic reform and optimism first, but also care about immigration. Accordingly, Macron spoke of France having to 'endure' migration. He resolved to open processing centres in Libya to stem the flow of asylum seekers and linked irregular migration with organized crime and terrorism.[95] Macron's populist style and conservative immigration policies reflected the influence of the populist right, not the turning of the populist-right tide heralded by some observers.[96]

In Northern Europe, unemployment and economic reform are not the pressing concerns they are in France and Southern Europe. This makes it harder for a Macron-style politics to emerge. Voters tire of the same old office-holders and centre-left coalitions can certainly win. The question is whether they can do so with the avowedly open immigration and multicultural approach that still holds sway in Canada and Australia. The evidence suggests they think otherwise. The centrist takeover of far right issues is not risk-free, however. If a centre-right party fails to control immigration, as in Britain during David Cameron's tenure, the populist right may come back even stronger. Should Rutte, Kurz, May and Macron prove unable to lower numbers, they will again be vulnerable to populist discontent on their right flank.

EUROSCEPTICISM

Macron vigorously defended the EU during his campaign, and with Merkel's star on the wane, is emerging as its saviour. But Macron has no plans to move Europe in a cosmopolitan direction. Instead, he is pushing to reform EU freedom of movement to compel firms employing workers from poorer Eastern countries to pay their social costs at Western, not Eastern, rates. Decrying 'social dumping', he also wants to reduce the job duration of detached employees to 12 months from the 24 months proposed by the European Commission.[97]

Opposition to immigration in Europe is not as closely associated with opposition to the EU as it is in Britain. While Northern European countries, who contribute more to the EU than they receive in transfers, are more Eurosceptic than poorer members, a clear majority in all countries support the EU. During the French election, Marine Le Pen's Euroscepticism was perceived as an electoral liability and the FN will likely jettison talk of 'Frexit'. While populist-right leaders and many supporters are reflexively opposed to the EU's liberal idealism, continental mass publics have a stronger European identity than in Britain. Each country has reasons for remaining attached. In the small Benelux countries, the EU offers a route to clout and prominence on the world stage. In Southern and Eastern Europe, the EU brings financial stability and subsidies.

History is extremely important. Most European countries have national myths of being defenders or leaders of Christian Europe. In other words, nationalism and Europeanism reinforce each other. France has a history of being the leader of Europe's counter-Reformation and the fount of its Enlightenment. The European 'republic of letters' spoke French. Macron relishes this imperial role. Austria and Germany occupy from the territories of the Holy Roman Empire, which sought to recreate the glory of Christian Rome on European soil. Poland's historic opposition to Russia pushes it culturally towards Europe while Spain, Portugal, Greece and Hungary possess nationalist myths of fighting against Moors and Turks to defend Christian Europe's honour. Scandinavian history is less invested in the mission of leading or defending Europe, which may explain its weaker enthusiasm for the EU.

All told, the intertwining of national and European histories helps bind the continent's people together even if many oppose particular EU policies. In the meantime, the EU has stepped back from supranational slogans like 'ever closer Europe', 'a Europe of the regions', or the 'bicycle' analogy which argues that integration has to keep deepening or the EU will fall apart. At an event I spoke at in the European Parliament in 2017, I was struck by the realism and moderation expressed in a speech by the Commission's vice-president, Jyrki Katainen. À la carte and 'multi-speed' integration have replaced the older idealism of the 'United States of Europe'. The Commission has upgraded elements of the 'Fortress Europe' tradition such as military and intelligence cooperation and increased support for Frontex, the EU's border control agency. This gives conservative voters assurances that the Union is not a vehicle for cosmopolitanism but also represents their civilizational identity. The rise of right-wing populism with its anti-immigration agenda doesn't threaten the integrity of the EU. Instead, the populist right is shifting the ideological compass in Brussels, just as it has altered immigration and integration policy in member states. Indeed, the EU's popularity rose after the Brexit vote, revealing its resilience in the face of repeated challenges.

THE BATTLE OF IDEAS

Europe's encounter with Islamist terrorism and large-scale immigration has also roiled the world of ideas though it is difficult to know how far-reaching these developments will turn out to be. In the 2000s, writers such as Bernard Lewis, George Weigel, Oriana Fallaci, Bruce Bawer and Niall Ferguson warned of the challenge that Europe's growing Muslim population posed to liberal values. A 'Eurabia' discourse emerged, declaring that Europe would be majority-Muslim as early as 2050 or 2100, something which I've argued is inaccurate given current demographic trends.[98] From this point on, concern over Islam became a talking point on the right, whether from a security, libertarian or nationalist perspective. Islam is also a major theme of the American libertarian right, encompassing online commentators such as Ben Shapiro, Gavin McInnes and Mike Cernovich.

Ethno-demographic change is becoming more openly discussed in mainstream right intellectual circles. Christopher Caldwell, a columnist for the *Weekly Standard* and *Financial Times*, argues that Europe would not be the same civilization without European people. Mass migration is altering its fundamental essence.[99] Thilo Sarrazin, a German Social Democratic politician and ex-central banker, penned his *Germany Does Away With Itself* (2010), which became a runaway bestseller, notching up sales of 1.5 million in its first year. He argues that low German birth rates coupled with non-European immigration is leading to the decline of the ethnic German population. Sarrazin is unsparing in its criticism of Islam, writing 'I do not have to acknowledge anyone who lives by welfare, denies the legitimacy of the very state that provides that welfare, refuses to care for the education of his children and constantly produces new little headscarf-girls. This holds true for 70 per cent of the Turkish and 90 per cent of the Arab population in Berlin'. In polls, half the German population agreed with Sarrazin's arguments and 18 per cent said they would vote for him.[100] These particular statements are exaggerations designed to instil anger against an outgroup, thus are racist. On the other hand, I would defend Sarrazin's right to express a sense of loss over ethnic German decline.

The French Nouvelle Droite (New Right) has influenced the intellectual evolution of the far right throughout Europe. This coterie of writers emerged in the late 1960s and initially published in mainstream right outlets such as *Le Figaro*. The New Right emphasizes ethno-national themes, opposing both racial integration and the Westernization of non-Western societies. Its identitarianism favours a halt to immigration, with groups remaining distinct and apart. Two newer stars on the French right are Renaud Camus, author of *Le Grand Remplacement* (The Great Replacement) and Éric Zemmour, an observant Jew of Algerian provenance who wrote for the centre-right *Le Figaro*. Zemmour's *The French Suicide* (2014) is the most successful, having sold 500,000 copies. Zemmour blames the free-market right and liberal left for France's plight, and he is especially scathing about the country's politically correct cultural and political elite. He goes further, arguing that Muslim minorities are paper citizens who do not belong to the 'real France'.[101]

From Sarrazin and Zemmour to the American alt-right, there can be no doubt that the overriding theme is the decline of the ethnic majority and erosion of ethno-traditions of nationhood. Economics and social mores barely get a look-in while civic nationalism is a busted flush.

Whereas the Eurabia discourse featured a strong libertarian and security streak, the newer French authors are more exercised by ethno-cultural
loss. With the end of ideology, decline of interstate war and ongoing
ethnic transformation, elements of the right on both sides of the Atlantic
right are coalescing around a common message of anti-elite ethno-
nationalism.

A milder version of these ideas has gained currency among centrist
intellectuals as well. A series of mainly Jewish, ex-leftist French writers
have emerged as spokespeople for the new concern over Europe's cultural demise. Figures such as Alain Finkielkraut and Pascal Bruckner
criticize the liberal-left for its preoccupation with white guilt and its
open-borders approach to immigration and refugees.[102]

Events on the ground have always affected the world of ideas. Immigration gave rise to ideas of multiculturalism, whether in 1910s America
or 1960s Europe. The rise of the populist right sparked multiculturalism's intellectual demise (outside academe) in the 1990s and 2000s and
is now affecting how society thinks about asylum and immigration. As
David Frum argues, Merkel's response to the 2015 refugee crisis, British
Labour's opening up to East European immigration and the American
Democrats' lax approach to illegal immigration produced populist
backlashes.[103] This ferment altered the boundaries of public debate and
restructured the intellectual right, empowering ethno-nationalist currents while downgrading previous conservative themes such as religion.
This matters because it affects the ideological orientation of centre-
right party activists. This in turn means the immigration issue will be
flagged more often to voters, raising its importance in voters' minds.

A NEW NORMAL?

The marked increase in immigrants and asylum seekers arriving in
Western Europe after 2013, culminating in the 2015 Migration Crisis,
shook European politics. The immigration issue shot to the top of conservative and authoritarian voters' priority lists. This fed a sharp rise in
populist-right vote share across the European Union to levels not seen
since the inter-war years. Support remains at an elevated level in many
countries even though the Migration Crisis has passed. The Crisis-
fuelled surge of populism also had the secondary effect of de-toxifying

the far right among a tranche of formerly wary voters, increasing its steady-state share and making it possible for right-wing populists to attain new heights in the future.

Centre-right parties either adopted the far right's ideas or went into coalition with them. Liberal Europeans counter-mobilized, insisting the new politics was driven by hate. The net result, as in America, is a polarization of opinion on psychological lines between change-oriented and order-seeking parts of the electorate. The difference in Europe is that polarization exists mainly within the left, between cultural progressives and old-left pragmatists who seek to retain the white working-class vote. By contrast, in the US, the right is now largely restrictionist while the left is overwhelmingly cosmopolitan.

Combined with Islamist terrorism, immigration has repositioned the main axis of politics in Europe from economics to culture. What comes next? Young Europeans are accustomed to a more diverse version of their countries and tend to be somewhat more tolerant of immigration. This could lead to attitude liberalization if these orientations endure through the life course. Europe's deals with Libya and Turkey may contain refugee flows, soothing anxieties and helping politics return to normal. France, a populist-right success story, may prove less hospitable to the Front National in the future due to its high native birth rate, robust Muslim outmarriage rate and relatively low immigration. On the other hand, Muslim populations continue to rise in France due to the demographic momentum from formerly high birth rates, which may offset this for some time. In the German-speaking world and Southern Europe, fertility rates are low and immigration pull factors will intensify as the aging crisis begins in earnest in the 2020s.[104] We should therefore expect the populist right to remain strong or improve its position in these countries. Scandinavia and the Low Countries are small, thus more affected by migrant flows, so should also prove fertile terrain for the radical right. Finally, should centre-right parties fail to control immigration, or if there is another influx of refugees, the populist right could surge yet again, perhaps winning outright majorities.

6

Canadian Exceptionalism: Right-Wing Populism in the Anglosphere

The rise of the populist right in America and Europe invites the question of why some Western countries remain unaffected. We've seen that Ireland, Portugal, Iceland and Spain lack viable populist-right parties, but all contain small Muslim populations and some have experienced declining immigration owing to weak post-2007 economies. Are there high-immigration countries that have not experienced a backlash? In this chapter I'll take a closer look at my own society, English Canada, to ask why it has not witnessed a populist-right movement. I suggest it may become increasingly distinct from other Western countries, including settler societies like Quebec, Australia, New Zealand and the United States.

Anglo settler societies have some of the highest rates of immigration in the West but most have right-wing populist movements which have influenced mainstream parties. For instance, New Zealand First, under the leadership of Winston Peters, achieved 8 per cent of the vote in 1993 on a platform which included opposition to immigration. Support crested at 13.4 per cent in 1996 and has hovered in the 4–9 per cent range since. The party entered governing coalitions with the right-wing National Party in 1996 and with Labour in 2005 and 2017. In 2017 the taboo-breaking promise by Labour's leader, Jacinda Aldern, to reduce immigration helped it win NZ First support. In Australia, Pauline Hanson's One Nation Party won 9 per cent of the vote in the 1998 Australian federal election, rising to 22.7 per cent in the Queensland state election. The party's success in rural Queensland was partly due to One Nation's approach to the aboriginal question, though opposition to immigration was a major aspect of its appeal.[1] After a decade in the wilderness, Hanson returned to politics and her party won over 4 per cent in the Australian senatorial elections of 2016. In its Queensland heartland in 2017, it reached 18–20 per cent in the polls.[2] While it didn't win seats, it rode a 13-point swing to garner 14 per cent of the vote in the Queensland election on 25 November of that year.

Australia and New Zealand have very high foreign-born populations but have traditionally drawn most of their immigrants from each other, the UK or Europe. In contrast to the US and Canada, where European immigration dropped to a minority of the flow by the 1970s, this didn't happen in New Zealand and Australia until the 2000s. As of 2006, a quarter of Australia's foreign-born population came from Britain, while in Canada the figure was below 10 per cent. Numbers for China, India and the Philippines increased rapidly only after 2006. The combined Chinese and Indian component of the foreign-born population rose to 16 per cent by 2016. By April 2017, UK immigrants made up only 4 per cent of the monthly inflow, while India and China comprised a third.[3] Figure 6.1 shows that the Asian portion of Australia's

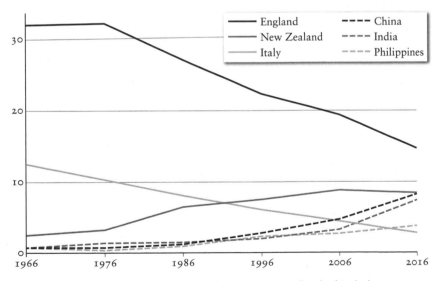

6.1. Percentage of overseas-born population in Australia, by birthplace, 1966–2016

Sources: Elle Hunt, 'Barely half of population born in Australia to Australian-born parents', *Guardian*, 27 June 2017; Australian Bureau of Statistics

substantial foreign-born population rose rapidly after 2006. There is also considerable growth from an array of smaller countries, many of which are non-Christian.

The 2016 Australian census found Australia to be 26 per cent foreign-born, with half the population having at least one immigrant parent; 2.6 per cent were Muslim and approximately 11 per cent were of non-European descent, with a heavy skew to younger age groups.[4] This means that, even if immigration ceases, the non-European share of the country is set to rise substantially.

The same holds, even more so, for New Zealand, which is only marginally less foreign-born than Australia, at 23 per cent. By 2001 China and India edged out the UK as the leading source of arrivals. As of 2016, about five times more were arriving from China and India than from Britain. Meanwhile, the number of immigrants soared as the country's economy pulled out of a slump. Net migration increased from 10,000 in 2013 to 41,000 in 2014 to 60,000 in 2015 and 69,000 in 2016 – this in a country of just 4.7 million people.[5] Against this backdrop, the Aldern-led Labour Party promised a reduction to 30,000–40,000 per year, while Winston Peters, her New Zealand First coalition partner, wanted numbers chopped to 10,000–20,000.

ETHNIC CHANGE: COMPARING ANGLO SETTLER SOCIETIES

Australia, New Zealand and Canada have approximately the same foreign-born share, around 20–25 per cent. This has risen since the 1960s, though each country has a long experience with immigration. In terms of ethnic composition, the US, with its historic black population, has a higher share of minorities, but its foreign-born total is lower, at 13.5 per cent. Figure 6.2 compares the approximate European-origin share of the main Anglo settler nations. In all cases, minority share is higher in these countries than in Europe, with ethnic transformation more advanced, even as Muslim share remains lower.[6]

The main reason the US had ethnic change at the same rate as other Anglo countries between 1965 and 2017 was the high fertility of its Hispanic population. However, this has recently dropped close to white-American levels. In the future, I would expect ethnic change to

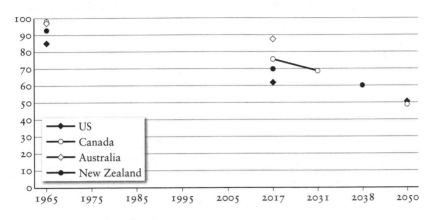

6.2. White share, Anglo settler countries, 1965–2050, %

Sources: Calculated from respective censuses based on race or ancestry questions. Projected figures from É. C. Malenfant et al., *Projections of the Diversity of the Canadian Population, 2006–2031*, Statistics Canada, Demography Division, 2010; P. Dion et al., 'Long-Term Contribution of Immigration to Population Renewal in Canada: A Simulation', *Population and Development Review* 41:1, 109–26, and National Ethnic Population Projections: 2013 (base)–2038 (update), *Stats NZ*, 18 May 2017. NB: New Zealand series assumes half of part-Maori offspring to be white.

be more rapid in Australia, New Zealand and Canada than in America. Canada and the US, for example, are both projected to pass the 'majority minority' mark around 2050 despite the relatively white character of contemporary Canada.[7] Cities will arrive at this point much sooner. The greater Toronto area (not just the city) surpassed the 'majority-minority' point in the 2016 census, with Vancouver close behind. In the US, twenty-two of the top 100 metropolitan areas were majority-minority in 2010.

ARE NEW NATIONS DIFFERENT?

One reason we might expect the New World to think differently about immigration is because people in settler nations may be accustomed to thinking of the nation in futuristic, frontier terms, with more of a sense that the nation is remade each generation. As Tocqueville described America in the 1830s:

Imagine, my dear friend, if you can, a society formed of all the nations of the world ... people having different languages, beliefs, opinions: in a word, a society without roots, without memories, without prejudices, without routines, without common ideas, without a national character, yet a hundred times happier than our own.[8]

Tocqueville exaggerates, but is there some truth to his observations? Do those in the New World have a more open attitude to immigration than those in Europe? A major review of cross-country research on immigration attitudes using data up to 2003 finds Canadians to be the most pro-immigration, followed by Australians and New Zealanders, Americans, West Europeans and East Europeans.[9] Against this, the World Values Surveys of 1995, 1999 and 2006 find Americans to be more restrictionist than either Europeans or those from other Anglo nations. Some studies find Americans to be no more open to immigration than West Europeans[10] The questions on large-scale surveys don't allow us to probe many aspects of cross-national differences, so I do this in a limited way by examining Britain and North America. In a combined Prolific/MTurk sample of 243 white Americans, Canadians and Britons from November 2017, I find that self-identified liberals from these countries tend to be equally pro-immigration. There is some cross-country difference among conservatives, but less so among those who are 'very conservative', most of whom favour reducing immigration, regardless of country. What really stands out is the extent to which moderates in North America are more open to immigration than moderates in Britain.[11]

About a third of the reason North Americans are more liberal on immigration than Britons is because more North Americans say that their country's tradition of immigration is important. North America obviously has a higher share of people whose ancestors arrived after 1800 than Britain does. However, it turns out that only those whose family arrived after 1945 or immigrated themselves are more liberal, in all countries, which doesn't explain transatlantic differences. Even when controlling for ideology, tradition of immigration and when a person's ancestors came to the country, figure 6.3 shows that Britons are more restrictionist than North Americans.

The idea that Britain is an older country than Canada or the US, or that people are more traditional in Britain, doesn't explain British

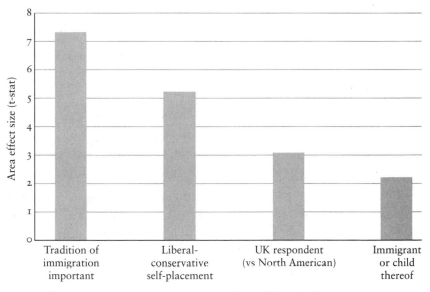

6.3. Predictors of immigration opinion in UK and North America

Source: MTurk/Prolific data November 2017. Limited to white respondents. N = 243 (152 USA, 72 Canada, 49 UK).

restrictionism. When asked how old their country is on a scale from 'very old' to 'very new', whether the country has old traditions that are important to preserve, or whether people think about the past or future more, none of the answers made any difference to explaining why Britons are more opposed to immigration than North Americans. The same is true of a question asking whether people saw their country as more of a team going through life together or as custodians carrying a torch passed down over generations. This suggests the antiquity of Britain is less important than the fact its tradition of immigration is less connected to the national epic than is true in Canada or the United States.

The MTurk/Prolific data is a small opt-in sample. My Policy Exchange–YouGov surveys are, by contrast, representative, and encompass 2,900 white Britons and Americans polled in August 2016. These show no significant variation in white opposition to immigration between the US and UK but a marked difference of priorities within the 40 per cent of white Britons and Americans who say immigration should be reduced a lot. Figure 6.4 shows that among those who want immigration reduced a lot (right side of chart), immigration is twice as likely to be the most important concern for white Britons (.42) as for white Americans (.21). Chapter 4 showed this to be a post-1997 development in Britain, accelerating in the 2000s, whereas salience (immigration as the most important concern) only began to rise in the US after 2014 and remains steady at around 10–15 per cent of conservative white voters.[12] For conservative Americans, the economy, terrorism and crime rank higher than in Britain. The materialistic, futuristic and individualistic orientation of North Americans noted by Wilbur Zelinsky may be important in explaining the lower salience of immigration compared to Europe.[13] This could explain why Americans seem more worried about the economic and security aspects of immigration than Europeans, and less about the cultural effects.[14]

Whether UK–North America differences are wholly to do with a history of immigration is difficult to discern. Argentina, another New World society with an immigration history, has immigration attitudes similar to Australia, Canada and New Zealand across three waves of the World Values Survey, with 40 per cent providing restrictive responses. However, in the past half-century, few have immigrated, so

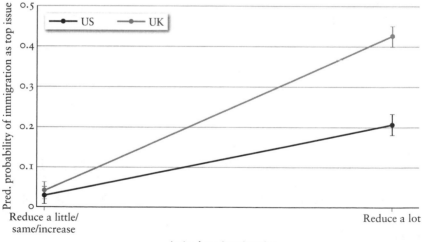

6.4. Immigration top issue, white anti-immigration British/Americans

Source: Policy Exchange-YouGov surveys, August 16–17, 2016

the country is just 4.5 per cent foreign-born. This may be changing, with a higher inflow from neighbouring South American countries like Bolivia and Paraguay. President Mauricio Macri has attempted to mobilize anti-immigration sentiment despite the small numbers: 'Nobody wants scum to come in from other countries,' he declared. 'Many foreigners come here because health services and education are free.' His opponents counter that the country has a long tradition of openness to immigrants.[15] On the 2017 Ipsos MORI survey, Argentinian opposition to immigration is closer to 60 per cent, well above that in America, possibly reflecting the new mood.

CANADIAN EXCEPTIONALISM?

The histories of Australia, New Zealand, the US and Canada have many similarities. All contain dominant ethnic groups based on British-origin cores which subsequently expanded to include other European groups. Canada is bi-national, with a French ethnic core in Quebec and Acadia and a British-turned-white core in the rest of the country. British cores have blended with other European groups, though 'white ethnics' were a much smaller share of the population in English Canada and Australasia compared to the US prior to the 1960s. English-speaking Canada, for example, was over 60 per cent British and Irish in 1971 while the equivalent figure in the US population was about 30 per cent.[16]

North America and Australia largely barred Asian immigration before the Second World War and favoured British immigrants over other Europeans. When Canada opened up to German and East European settlement under the Liberal Minister of the Interior, Clifford Sifton, during 1896–1904 in order to people the west and guard against American expansionism, this led to resistance from Canadian Britannic nationalists. These loyalist groups, including the Orange Order and Imperial Order Daughters of the Empire (IODE), joined other British-Canadians in successfully pushing for Sifton's resignation.[17]

The British share of Canadian immigration rebounded to 60 per cent by 1920, but subsequently slipped to a third of the intake by 1930. In response, Canada enacted an Imperial Preference immigration system in 1931 similar in intent to the US National Origins scheme of 1924. The categories, in order of preference were: 1. British subjects from Britain and the 'white' Dominions of Australia, New Zealand, South Africa, Ireland and Newfoundland; 2. US citizens; 3. Relatives of Canadian male residents; and 4. 'Agriculturalists with sufficient means to farm in Canada.' Oriental Exclusion acts were also enacted in 1923 and 1928. By 1941, the British share of immigrants was back up to 90 per cent.[18] Richard Bedford Bennett, the country's Prime Minister from 1930 to 1935, explained the country's immigration policy in the following terms in 1928:

> British civilization is the standard by which we must measure our own civilization . . . We desire to assimilate those whom we bring to this country to that civilization . . . That is what we desire, rather than by the introduction of vast and overwhelming numbers of people from other countries to assimilate the British immigrants and the few Canadians who are left to some other civilization. That is what we are endeavouring to do, and that is the reason so much stress is laid upon the British settler . . . [19]

After the Second World War, Canada had difficulty attracting the same number of British immigrants, and its desire to develop the country led it to slowly open up to other European groups. The British loyalism of English Canadians began to wane in favour of Canadian nationhood as the sun started to set on the British Empire. Sentiment in favour of retaining the Union Flag ('Union Jack') as the national flag, for example, declined from 42 per cent in 1943 to 25 per cent in 1963, and the new Maple Leaf flag was adopted in 1965.[20] In the 1950s, economic liberalism gained the upper hand over ethno-traditionalism in immigration policy, as it had in the Sifton period and during the 1920s.

British-Canadian conservatives kept ethnic considerations on the political agenda, however. The still-important Orange Order, for instance, which controlled the city of Toronto between the 1870s and 1950s the way the Irish Catholics controlled Boston, had an Immigration Committee which lobbied government officials to increase British immigration. In 1955 its Grand Master addressed the nearly 60,000 members across the country:

> Brethren, perhaps the most vital issue confronting our country . . . is that of immigration. The present policy of the Dominion government is so markedly against bringing people from the British Isles that if the present trend continues the whole racial picture of Canada could be drastically changed

in this generation . . . [Britons] who came equipped by language, traditions and law abiding instincts made them easily assimilable into the way of life prevailing in the country. We believe that Canada still needs an increasing flow of British immigration to see that the tremendous potentialities of this boundless country can be fully realized. But evidently the Ottawa government thinks differently, and I have no hesitation in stating that the reason they seem determined to keep immigration from the British Isles to around the 25 per cent level is that Quebec politicians, instigated by the hierarchy, have demanded it . . . Ottawa is complacently carrying out the avowed aims of the hierarchy of Quebec to reduce the proportion of British and Protestant stock in the country. The danger in this nefarious policy is evident and we, as an organization, should make it unmistakably clear that we still are determined to keep Canada British and Protestant.[21]

Notice how the immigration question was viewed through the prism of the historic Anglo-Protestant/French-Catholic political divide. Successive Orange leaders in the 1950s also warned of fascist and communist tendencies among Italian immigrants, who were arriving in large numbers in Toronto. Nevertheless, these accusations should be seen as secondary rationales to Britannic ethno-traditionalism, which was driving opposition.

The sentiments of the Grand Master were widely held among British-Canadian Protestants. Protestant-dominated Toronto and Ontario were loyalist and culturally conservative into the 1960s. However, French Canada formed around a third of the population rather than a quarter, as today. In addition, there was an important liberal bent among Irish Catholics and Scottish Presbyterians in English Canada.[22] This allowed the free-trading, growth-minded Liberal Party to win most of the time, facilitating occasional openings to immigration from beyond the British Isles. Given Britannic nationalist reassertion in the 1900s and 1930s, we might have expected a conservative pushback in the 1960s and 1970s, but two factors worked against this. First, the supply of British immigrants slowed as Britain's population growth declined. Second, the collapse of British-Tory loyalism and Orangeism destroyed the cultural tradition which had legitimated ethnically select-ive immigration.[23]

Anglo-Protestant Canadians were actual or spiritual descendants of American Tories who fled the country after the American Revolution.

Britishness was the bulwark of English-Canadian identity because in other respects – accent, lifestyle, folkways – Americans and Canadians were difficult to distinguish. As a Toronto poet, Dennis Lee, a descendant of American Tories, put it in the 1960s:

> The Dream of Tory origins
> Is full of lies and blanks
> Though what remains when it is gone
> To prove that we're not Yanks?[24]

The crisis of Canadian identity didn't mean Anglo-Canadians suddenly welcomed diversity – far from it. A majority of Canadians opposed immigration from outside Europe in a 1961 poll.[25] However, the collapse of the loyalist tradition created a vacuum which opened the way for left-modernism to emerge triumphant among Anglo-Canadian elites. In the guise of multiculturalism, it shaped the country's new national identity. In 1966, prior to the coining of the term, Frank Underhill wrote the foreword to a new liberal collection of essays on Canadian nationalism:

> Our authors . . . abandon the concept of British North America as defining the Canadian identity . . . Our new Maple Leaf flag will, one hopes, be taken by future generations as the epoch-making symbol marking the end of the era of the Wasp domination of Canadian society. At any rate, our authors are all post-Wasp in their outlook.[26]

Underhill began as a socialist, then became a liberal anti-imperialist in the 1940s who supported the merging of Canada with the United States. Later, he surfaced as a member of the Liberal Party. His ideas were informed by American pluralism – the term 'WASP' originated in American liberal circles – though it is difficult to draw a direct link to the ideas of Randolph Bourne we encountered in chapter 2. In any case, the Liberal government of Lester Pearson in the 1960s brought in non-discriminatory immigration, drawing on a generous interpretation of international human-rights law. During Pierre Trudeau's premiership in the 1970s, immigration policy shifted in a more left-modernist direction, from being primarily points-based to being predominantly focused on family reunification. The new provisions allowed my mother, who gained citizenship through marriage to a citizen, to sponsor her siblings and mother to enter the country from Hong Kong and Macau. This was a rational response by her and her extended family: I'd have done exactly the same thing.

In 1971, the Multiculturalism Act declared the country officially multicultural. The Act included commendable aspects of negative liberalism, such as respecting diversity and treating all people equally without regard to ethnicity, colour or creed. However, it also enshrined positive liberalism in the form of a duty to 'promote the understanding that multiculturalism is a fundamental characteristic of the Canadian heritage and identity and that it provides an invaluable resource in the shaping of Canada's future' and to 'advance multiculturalism throughout Canada'. Note the crucial slippage from 'respecting' to 'promoting' diversity. The new stand-in for a lost Britannic tradition left some wondering whether multiculturalism was simply an attempt to paper over the vacuum in Anglo-Canadian identity. Gad Horowitz, a political scientist at the University of Toronto, sardonically quipped that multiculturalism was 'the masochistic celebration of Canadian nothingness'. Richard Gwyn's *Nationalism Without Walls: The Unbearable Lightness of being Canadian* (1995) echoed a similar theme: namely, that a people without a cultural tradition trying to make up for this by plugging the hole with other cultures is engaged in a fruitless quest – there is no substitute for the cultural work required to reinterpret the history and folkways of the country.

The Act's provisions were subsequently enshrined in the 1982 Canadian Charter of Rights and Freedoms. It soon became apparent that even as English-Canadian elites flocked towards multiculturalism, French-Canadians – as one of the two founding political groups in the country – were not interested in being demoted to one of many 'cultures'. Multiculturalism has been an irritant in French–English relations ever since.[27] Quebec has repeatedly refused to sign the Charter and implements an integration policy known as interculturalism which repudiates multiculturalism.

Between 1975 and 1995, Canada became considerably more diverse, with non-Europeans increasing to over 10 per cent of the total. Yet support for immigration remained buoyant, with only 40 per cent calling for lower numbers. In 2005, opposition to immigration even dipped below 30 per cent, providing evidence of further attitude liberalization, though more-recent evidence based on online-anonymous polling techniques suggests the proportion in favour of reduction is around 40 per cent.

Indeed, an EKOS poll in 2015 discovered that 41 per cent of Canadians said there were too many 'visible minorities' among those immigrating to Canada.[28] As in other Western nations, there is an important constituency of conservative and authoritarian voters in English Canada who want fewer immigrants in the country. The difference is there are no political vehicles channelling this at the federal level.

CANADIAN ATTITUDES IN COMPARATIVE PERSPECTIVE

Immigration opinion across countries in the Anglosphere shows broadly similar patterns across multiple waves of the World Values Survey (WVS) and a survey run by Ipsos MORI in March 2017. As we see

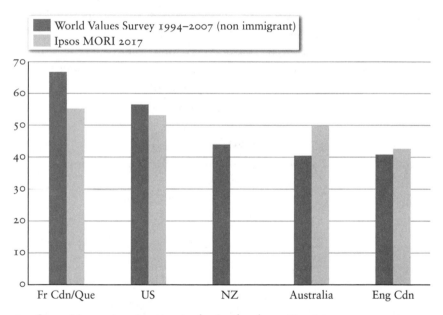

6.5. Opposition to immigration in the Anglosphere, %

Note: Options in WVS are 'let anyone come', 'as long as jobs available', 'strict limits' and 'prohibit people from coming'. The final two are counted as 'reduce'. In Ipsos MORI, the question is based on a five-point scale from 'increase a lot' to 'reduce a lot'. In the WVS, I use French language to identify French-Quebeckers, and in Ipsos MORI I use residence in Quebec as no French-language measure is available. NB: NZ not included in Ipsos MORI survey.

in figure 6.5, sentiment is most restrictionist among French-speaking Canadians, followed by Americans, New Zealanders and Australians, with Anglo-Canadians the most liberal.

This said, there isn't much difference between Anglo-Canadians and Australians. What differs is the issue's political salience. In the US, immigration is the top issue for roughly 7 per cent of voters, fluctuating between 4 and 13 per cent. In Australia, before the 2013 'Stop the Boats' operation, the figure reached 13.2 per cent but by 2017 had settled down to 7 per cent of voters naming immigration or asylum seekers as their most important issue. In New Zealand, the analogous figure hovered between 2 and 6 per cent between 2015 and 2017, averaging 4 per cent. In Canada, by contrast, immigration was mentioned as a top issue by fewer than 1 per cent of respondents in the 2011 Canadian Election Study.[29]

In view of Canada's rapid ethnic change and high foreign-born population, how has it managed to avoid right-wing populism? First of all, Anglo-Canadians share the relatively pro-immigration outlook common to all Anglo settler societies, whereas Britons are more restrictionist. Second, there is the linguistic cleavage in Canadian politics. Joshua Gordon, a political scientist at Simon Fraser University, remarks that the English–French divide splits the anti-immigration constituency between Anglo-Canadians who vote for the Conservative Party and French-Canadians who vote for the separatist Bloc Québécois. This means the federal Conservatives can't pool Anglo and French anti-immigration voters into a united voting bloc. They find it easier to bring right-wing whites and minorities together on a platform of social and fiscal conservatism.[30] The Tories have cultivated close links with representatives of the country's large Sikh and Chinese communities, for example.

While parties can raise the salience of an issue by cueing their members, I'm not convinced the French–English divide explains the low salience of immigration in Canada. First of all, the Tories' skirting of the issue should open space in the political marketplace for a populist conservative leadership candidate or third party similar to the Reform Party that broke through in the 1993 federal election. What's therefore more important are the boundaries of acceptable discourse in English Canada. American and European evidence suggests the media is a key intermediary. Where it unites behind a set of liberal norms, it can marginalize dissenting views. Canada, unlike Australia, lacks a conservative tabloid press. While there is a significant right-wing online site called Rebel, this is not a mainstream political force on par with Fox in the US or the Murdoch press in Australia. In addition, it reflects the Western libertarianism of the site's founder, Ezra Levant. It is therefore strongly opposed to Muslims and illegal immigration but has not, to my knowledge, called for lower levels of legal migration. In addition, a far from exhaustive search of its content suggests much of its immigration coverage is oriented to perceived problems in the US and Europe rather than Canada. Only a few scattered voices, writing occasional opinion pieces, call for reduced immigration – notably a former diplomat, Martin Collacott.[31]

Taboos which mark the boundaries of debate are very important in English Canada. The same holds to a somewhat lesser extent in Australia and used to be true in America. It arguably only became acceptable for a mainstream party to campaign on a platform of reducing immigration in the US in 2015 (and then only on the right) and in New Zealand in 2017. In chapters 7 and 8, we'll take a look at the question of 'political correctness' and its effect on immigration and multiculturalism in more detail. Suffice it to say that mainstream politics in Anglo settler nations diverged from much of Europe by placing these issues off-limits until the 2010s – at least until Trump's rise made legal immigration a legitimate issue for debate within the Republican Party.

While New Zealand First and One Nation in Australia campaigned to reduce immigration in the late 1990s and 2000s, they were viewed by the mainstream press and parties as beyond the bounds of moral propriety. Taboos relaxed somewhat in Australia after 2013, but only as regards illegal rather than legal immigration. In New Zealand, it took until 2017 for a major party to run on a platform of reducing immigration. Multiculturalism policies and rhetoric remain in place in both countries, despite suffering occasional attacks. Nothing of the kind has occurred in Canada. Though there is sporadic debate over border security and illegal immigration, support for high immigration and multiculturalism is currently unassailable due to anti-racist norms. When Kellie Leitch ran as a leadership candidate for the Conservative Party in 2017 on a platform that promised to screen immigrants for 'Canadian values' of liberalism and tolerance she was overtly or indirectly branded a racist by several politicians and commentators. Mike

Medeiros observes that in polls English-Canadian support for banning the burqa is identical to that in Quebec, but is not represented among politicians or the media. While Medeiros posits that 'the disconnect between elites and citizens in English Canada with regard to cultural sensitivity' could produce a populist backlash, it is equally possible that the system may withstand such challenges if it responds in unison, with overwhelming force.[32]

Tellingly, most of the high-profile critics of Canadian multiculturalism have been minority Canadians who can withstand the charge of racism. In 1994, Neil Bissoondath, a Canadian intellectual of Trinidadian-Indian origin, published *Selling Illusions: The Cult of Multiculturalism* in Canada, criticizing the way multiculturalism objectifies minority groups, castigating those on the left who brand any critic of multiculturalism a racist. In *Delectable Lie: A Liberal Repudiation of Multiculturalism* (2011), the academic and writer Salim Mansur adds a critique of the way multiculturalism's emphasis on cultural equality renders it blind to the threat posed by Islamic fundamentalism to liberal democracy.

Most minority critics have focused on multiculturalism but others have questioned the scale of Canadian immigration. In 2013, the Japanese-Canadian environmentalist and left-wing icon David Suzuki criticized Canada's immigration policy as 'criminal' for contributing to a developing world brain-drain and damaging the Canadian environment. Suzuki was attacked by the Canadian right, with the Conservative Immigration Minister, Jason Kenney, calling the remarks 'toxic' and the right-wing blogger Ezra Levant fulminating about Suzuki's 'xenophobic, crazy ideas that would put him to the right of the Ku Klux Klan on immigration'. Yet in an opt-in survey of over 9,000 respondents, 79 per cent said Suzuki 'had a point' while only 21 per cent called him 'out of line'.[33]

In Vancouver, foreign property investors, mainly from mainland China, were responsible for overheating the housing market, driving home prices beyond the reach of many Vancouverites in a city where the ratio of house prices to income is one of the highest in the world. When a Chinese-Canadian urban planner, Andy Yan, acting head of Simon Fraser University's City Program and a planner at Bing Thom Architects, noted that two thirds of upscale homes on Vancouver's West Side were being sold to those with Chinese first names (indicating mainland Chinese overseas buyers), Vancouver's pro-growth mayor, Gregor Robertson, quickly reached for the race card: 'I'm very concerned with the racist tones that are implied here,' he scolded. Bob Ransford, a real-estate industry public-relations figure, tweeted: 'of course it's racist', a charge echoed by a property developer, Anne McMullin, and endorsed by Pete McMartin, a liberal Vancouver columnist.

At this, Yan replied, 'My great-granddad paid the head tax. So to somehow use [concerns about] "racism" to protect your privilege? That's just absurd. This is an almost uniquely Vancouver reaction.' Albert Lo, the Chinese-Canadian head of the Canadian Race Relations Foundation, replied, 'In Canada, we are so used to the idea of tolerance that we sometimes find it odd to look at nationalities. That causes some people to jump up and start using the word "racism." I don't think it's helpful.'[34] In July 2016, with 90 per cent support among Vancouverites, encompassing all racial groups, the British Columbia (BC) government finally implemented a 15 per cent tax on non-resident property purchases in the city.[35]

In January 2016, Ujjal Dosanjh, a Sikh-Canadian former premier of British Columbia and ex-leader of that province's left-wing New Democratic Party (NDP), wrote a hard-hitting essay entitled 'The Silencing of the White Men of the West'. He began by noting how a commendable desire to reduce inequality had mutated into an ideological orthodoxy based on a neurotic desire to repudiate the sinful white man. As a result, integration was stalling and politicians were unable to address problems such as soaring housing costs in immigration gateways like Vancouver:

> What started as a legitimate change to bring about equality and transformation of how we viewed, treated and spoke about each other has now ossified into a rarely breached wall of silence; a silence reinforced by the onset of the West's indifference to its own – good, bad or ugly but – distinct societies, their values and norms; call it white man's burden or guilt; a guilt for the sins of the past now manifesting itself in the white man's fear . . . It seems some of us have so thoroughly shamed the white men into complete submission . . . [reflected in the Prime Minister, Justin Trudeau's] misplaced belief that Canada has no core identity or core values . . . On matters of race, religion, culture and [the] national identity of Canada the white men are reduced to either silence or non sequiturs. If the white men of Canada can't overcome the fear of rebuke from the enforcers of fear, Canadians can't ever have an honest debate about the

state of equality, race, culture and the place and space for religion . . .
The silencing of most good white men has provided an opportunity for
the Trumps of the world to rise. That is what happens when we suffocate
or silence rational debate.[36]

As we'll see in chapter 9, Dosanjh is correct that silence enables the
populist right to emerge, but this happens only once there is a crack
in society's consensus. Moral norms form a complex system in which
people act not only on their own beliefs, but from perceptions of what
others think is correct. So long as a critical mass of opinion formers
support – or fail to challenge – the rule that politicizing multiculturalism and immigration is racist, the system is stable. Only when there is
a breach of etiquette by a successful populist politician, which drags
the centre-right across a norm boundary, do memories of past suppression of these issues become a force multiplier for right-wing populism.

The Reform Party, a fiscally conservative western Canadian populist
party that emerged in the 1993 election, decimating the established
Progressive Conservatives, shows that populism is possible in Canada.
The success of the crack-smoking right-wing Toronto mayor, Rob Ford,
between 2010 and 2014, and his brother Doug, elected premier of
Ontario in 2018, is another case in point. Yet both scrupulously avoided
calling for immigration to be reduced. Reform's opportunity arose
mainly because the country did not have an economically right-wing
party. This because the Progressive Conservatives represented an older
elite 'One Nation'-style conservatism, shorn of the loyalist accoutre-
ments which once endowed it with a broader appeal.

Reform's leader, Preston Manning, concentrated on economic liberalism
and political institutions, avoiding immigration, yet was still routinely
accused of being racist. For Dalton Camp, a Progressive Conservative
commentator, 'The speechifying at the 1994 Reform Party convention
gives off acrid whiffs of xenophobia, homophobia, and paranoia – like
an exhaust – in which it seems clear both orator and audience have been
seized by some private terror: immigrants, lesbians . . . criminals.'[37]
Reform survived media attacks by avoiding immigration, but it isn't
clear that a party which campaigned to reduce it could do so, for it would
face the full force of the media and established political parties. Meanwhile, hate speech laws grounded in the provisions of the Multiculturalism
Act prioritize anti-discrimination. As Emma Ambrose and Cas Mudde

observe, 'it is the strict regulation of speech, and the very broad definition of hate speech, that could impact the ability of far-right parties to
develop, as opposition to immigration can easily be construed as hate
speech'.[38] Moreover, without an alternative conservative media to prime
conservative and order-seeking voters, the salience of immigration and
multiculturalism might not reach the level required to enable a populist-
right challenger to escape the margins. As long as there is no system
breach, English Canada may be able to repress criticism of multiculturalism and mass immigration indefinitely.

THE QUEBEC EXCEPTION

The one part of Canada where a politics of ethno-traditional nationalism
is on the rise is Quebec. In this predominantly French-speaking province,
attitudes to immigration and multiculturalism are similar to those in
Europe. Quebec and Canada have different angles on the question of
immigration and national identity. Quebec was founded by fewer than
10,000 French settlers who arrived in the early 1600s and resisted
attempts at anglicization in the 1840s. The French-Canadian majority
in Quebec descends from this small population of agrarian *habitants*
and makes up three quarters of the province. This gives Quebeckers a
deeper narrative of ethnic peoplehood than English-Canadians despite
attempts by the separatist Parti Québécois to define a civic identity
based solely on the French language and territory of Quebec.

When American settlers moved north to Canada to found English
Canada, they brought their individualistic, future-oriented culture with
them. The early-twentieth-century Canadian historian Arthur Lower
referred to Anglo-Canadians as 'four million economic animals' attuned
to personal advancement rather than the sense of common purpose
which he claimed, with approval, the French-Canadians possessed.[39]
This is somewhat misleading, as the history of Canadian loyalism
amply shows, though it may be more accurate today. Where Quebec
identity is territorial, historical and cultural, the contemporary Anglo-
defined Canadian identity is futuristic: a missionary nationalism centred
on the left-modernist ideology of multiculturalism. Charles Breton, a
political scientist, finds that when Quebeckers are reminded of their

Quebec identity, they become more opposed to immigration; when reminded of their Canadian identity the reverse is true.[40]

Quebec possesses a great deal of autonomy from Canada. It maintains a separate immigration programme which permits it to select who it accepts as a resident of Quebec. Criteria include whether an applicant can speak French, which allows the province to target French-speaking immigrants. Until recently, the aim of this programme was to ensure that Quebec received a higher share of Canada's immigrants than it otherwise would, and that it could attract French-speakers, regardless of ethnic background, to the province. This reflected the philosophy of the separatist Parti Québécois (PQ), which usually runs the province, that the new Quebec nationalism should focus on the French language rather than French-Canadian ethno-traditions. New laws, arguably draconian, were enacted which compelled new arrivals to send their children to school in French and prohibited signs in which English lettering was larger than French.

However, as enthusiasm for separatism fell from nearly 50 per cent in 1995 into the low 30s by the 2000s, ethno-traditional nationalism began to emerge. Immigration to Quebec has been lower than in English Canada, thus the rate of ethnic change has been more gradual. On the other hand, like other ex-Catholic European countries, the province has a relatively low birth rate. By 2016, those of non-European origin comprised around 15 per cent of the province's population, including a small but growing Muslim share of 3 per cent. Most immigrants congregate in Greater Montreal. The Montreal area is not changing as quickly as Toronto or Vancouver, and is predicted to remain nearly 70 per cent white in 2031 at a time when metropolitan Toronto and Vancouver will be only 30–40 per cent white.[41] Nevertheless, the ethnic shifts which are steadily changing Quebec are changing provincial politics.

In 1994, Mario Dumont formed a right-wing provincial party known as the Action Démocratique du Québec (ADQ) which was autonomist rather than separatist. Its platform was initially defined by economic liberalism, promoting measures such as a flat tax. But in the 2007 provincial election the ADQ rolled out a more anti-multicultural, anti-immigration message. This paid dividends as the ADQ won a plurality of the vote to form the official opposition to the PQ. In 2008, Dumont introduced a historic motion to reduce the province's immigration cap by 10,000. One of the justifications Dumont gave was to prevent Francophones from being outnumbered. While he did not explicitly mention 'pure laine' ethnic French decline, he did fret about the fall in the share of those of French mother tongue – which overlaps strongly with the French-Canadian population.[42] The statement runs directly counter to the joint Parti Québécois–Liberal Party commitment to increase immigration to the province by 10,000 per year. While Dumont's motion was rebuffed by these other two parties, it put immigration restriction on the Canadian political agenda for the first time since the 1950s.

The ADQ has been absorbed into a new party, the Coalition Avenir Québec (CAQ). In 2015, CAQ's leader, François Legault, proposed that immigrants be screened for compliance with Quebec's secular-liberal values and French language, and sent elsewhere if they fail after two attempts. In August 2016, he echoed Dumont by calling for Quebec to reduce its immigrant intake from 50,000 to 40,000 per year. The party also became more outspoken on Muslim issues. In both cases, the CAQ agenda was blocked by the PQ and attacked in some quarters as racist. Yet CAQ has not backed off, and may be taking inspiration from developments in France, which has long influenced the thinking of Quebec intellectuals and politicians. 'We have to open our eyes, we have a real problem [with conservative Islam],' Legault said. 'We have to ask questions, like the ones they're asking in Europe.'[43] When pressed on why he advocated lower numbers, Legault claimed this was to protect the French language, even though the existing selection mechanisms already achieve this. As elsewhere, it's still taboo to openly defend majority ethnicity or ethno-traditional nationalism. Instead, ethnic conservatism is sublimated into state-nationalist and liberal rationales such as protecting women's equality, secularism or defending the language.

Quebec also contains far-right street movements such as La Meute. These have emerged in force only since 2015, when attempts by local branches of the Europe-based PEGIDA were shut down by threats from counter-demonstrators. Far-right demonstrators focus on purported Islamization but also voice concern over 'La Grande Remplacement' of whites. This reference to Renaud Camus's recent book and the involvement of PEGIDA reveal how right-wing currents from Europe are affecting the lineaments of Quebec politics. In November 2017, 300–400 far-right protesters in Quebec City clashed with left-wing groups.

The white-nationalist protesters registered with police while anti-fascist groups did not, which meant the leftists were disproportionately arrested. Critics charge that these actions legitimize hate while others aver that Antifa's confrontational tactics tarnish the wider cause.[44]

The political mainstream in Quebec, as in Europe, is beginning to discuss ethno-nationalist issues. In October 2017, Quebec passed Bill C-62, banning the wearing of the burqa while receiving public services. Outside the province, there were numerous accusations of racism, but within Quebec 91 per cent of French-speakers approved. The split between the 75 per cent French-Canadian majority and Anglophone minority is revealing. While 68 per cent of Francophones 'strongly approved' of C-62, just 32 per cent of English-speakers in the province felt the same way – though 67 per cent approved somewhat or strongly. This could reflect the traditional antagonism between the Anglo minority and the French majority, however, since, in English Canada, opinion on the burqa aligns with that of Francophone Quebeckers.[45] This shows that ethno-cultural rather than country-wide factors, notably the distinct elite norms of English Canada, account for much of Canadian exceptionalism.

The French population has a 400-year-old ethno-history and well-defined traditions based on the myth of the *habitant*, or French agricultural settler, who settled the Lower St. Lawrence Valley in the early 1600s. Aside from Newfoundland, where British settlers put down roots in the late 1600s and which has a distinct identity, English Canadians only arrived in force after the American Revolution of 1776–83. These American loyalist settlers were joined by a larger wave of arrivals in the mid-nineteenth century, predominantly from Scotland and the northern half of Ireland.[46] While the American settlers established the accent and folkways to a large extent, no unified ancestry myth or set of native traditions developed akin to those of the French-Canadians. Cultural traditions such as Orangeism or the Union Flag were derivative of British models. The United Empire Loyalist founding myth did not lionize particular heroes, in part because the loyalists fled the victorious Americans. Even Canada and Britain's victory over the United States in the War of 1812, a potential touchstone, is not deeply embedded in the Canadian consciousness. Scottish and Irish settlement in the nineteenth century left only localized origin narratives. While Australia is no older and also has a Britannic-loyalist past, the myth of convict heritage, mateship and the exploits of folk figures like Ned Kelly form a more distinct majority ethnic tradition that is comparable to the American frontier/settler myth.[47]

Immigration is a federal matter, but provinces have some jurisdiction over border control. During the summer of 2017, 13,000 illegal immigrants crossed the Canadian border, most of whom entered through Quebec due to the ease of passing across the Vermont boundary. They were leaving the United States, fearful of being caught in President Trump's increasingly fine anti-illegal immigrant net. Many had family connections in Montreal. During the border crisis, Premier Couillard appealed for 'equality and compassion' but 60 per cent of Quebeckers disapproved of his handling of the issue, with 37 per cent 'strongly' disapproving. Among Anglophones, 57 per cent approved of the government's liberal approach compared to just 36 per cent of Francophones.

These issues were gaining salience: around 20 per cent of those polled said C-62 and immigration would rank as 'one of the most important factors' deciding their vote in the 2018 provincial election.[48] The poll also found that the CAQ's Legault had the strongest net approval rating (+14 per cent) while Couillard's, the Liberal premier, was −19 per cent and the Parti Québécois's leader, Jean-François Lisée, was rated −16 per cent. By late June of 2018, ahead of the autumn election, the CAQ led the polls with 39 per cent support, the highest ever for the party. Among the French-speaking majority, its lead over the second-place Liberals was 48–23.[49] With low birth rates working against the French-Canadians and a continued flow of immigrants arriving in the province, cultural questions of immigration and Islam are poised to become higher-profile issues in provincial politics.

CONTINENTAL DIVIDE: ENGLISH CANADA AND THE UNITED STATES

Immigration opinion is similar on both sides of the Canada–US border but where things differ is that immigration has been politicized by the American, but not the Canadian, right. White conservative Americans also possess a distinctive subculture which conservative Canadians largely lack. This stems from a working-class white American culture drawn from elements that are mainly upper southern in origin but spread nationwide after the Second World War, including country music and Nascar.[50] These draw on earlier white repertoires which link back to southern regional traditions and the motif of the frontier.[51] Republican politicians and conservative media key into these symbols while white identity has risen in salience as the country has grown more diverse.[52] In my Prolific/MTurk comparative data, white identity is stronger among white Americans than white Canadians or Britons. It predicts opposition to immigration and especially support for Trump.

By contrast, Anglo-Canadian conservative nationalism knows the culture it opposes, but not what it wishes to promote. The weakness of Canadian cultural conservatism in relation to its US counterpart reflects the collapse of the country's loyalist tradition in the 1960s. On the other hand, the Canadian left is arguably as rich in symbols as the American left. Consider this question, which I put to a separate sample of 251 American respondents in MTurk and 98 Canadian respondents on Prolific: 'A foreign tourist wrote up this list of things that struck him as typically American/Canadian. For each one, don't tell us whether you like it or not, but instead tell us how American/Canadian it makes you feel, from 0 (not at all) to 100 (very much).'

On 0–100 thermometer questions, answers below the midpoint signal coolness and those above it warmth. Figure 6.6 shows that white Trump and Clinton voters feel nationalistic about different symbols. Trump voters derive a sense of Americanism from a cluster of 'redneck' national symbols including country and western music, Nascar, cowboys and pickup trucks. These reference a rural symbol complex towards which white Clinton voters are significantly less receptive. On the other hand, white Clinton voters identify their Americanness more with the country's ethnic diversity and bohemian neighbourhoods like San Francisco's Haight-Ashbury. Partisans on both sides feel strongly American when contemplating icons like the Statue of Liberty and Mount Rushmore, but both also possess distinctly partisan-inflected national symbols.

A similar exercise in figure 6.7 shows Anglo-Canadians are also somewhat divided over their conception of the nation. But the symbols of white Canadian cultural conservatism are thinner. It may be that I didn't pick the correct symbols, though I think I have a fairly good feel for the ones that matter. Don Cherry, a hockey commentator and one of the few conservative Canadian television personalities, elicits the

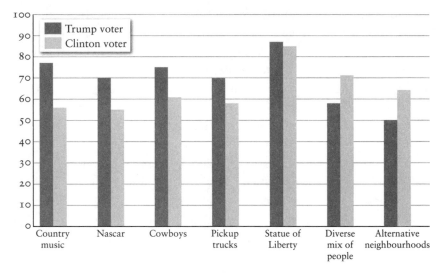

6.6. 'How American do these make you feel?' White Americans, by 2016 vote, %

Source: MTurk, 19 March 2017. N = 251 (95 Clinton, 156 Trump)

same enthusiastic patriotic response among left and liberal voters as Tory voters in this admittedly small sample. Hockey, potentially a symbol of white Canadian culture, produces no ideological disagreement. The biggest partisan differences are over symbols defined by left-liberal Canadians: the Canadian Broadcasting Corporation (CBC), ethnic diversity and the writer Margaret Atwood. Conservatives are cool towards these symbols, but the Canadian symbols they warm to haven't crystallized into an alternative vision of national identity.

Rural symbols such as pickup trucks, snowmobiles and resource towns matter more for Anglo-Canadian conservatives than liberals. Yet these tend to be low-profile and latent for politics compared to the US, where rural symbols are consistently referenced by the conservative media and politicians. The symbols the Tory party emphasizes, such as the Royal Canadian Mounted Police, Canadian history and the military, are supported by most Canadians. Whereas the 'redneck' cluster of American symbols strongly predicts a Trump vote even with liberal-conservative ideology and demographics held constant, this doesn't hold in Canada. Those who identify with rural symbols are no more likely to vote Tory once I account for ideology. On the other

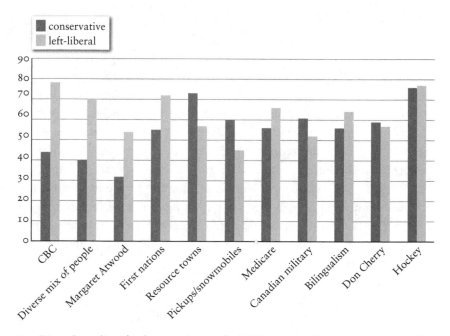

6.7. 'How Canadian do these make you feel? White Canadians, by 2015 vote, % N = 98 (86 left-liberal, 12 conservative).

hand, white Canadians who identify their Canadianism with the CBC, ethnic diversity and Margaret Atwood are much more likely to vote for the NDP, Greens or Liberals – even when controlling for ideology.

A DISTINCT SOCIETY?: ENGLISH CANADA AND THE WEST

Among high-immigration Western countries, only in Canada do all parties favour generous immigration and multiculturalism while facing no challenge from the populist right. On closer inspection, we see it is English Canada which is exceptional: Quebec, despite experiencing lower immigration levels than English Canada, has a populist-right party and a climate of opinion closer to Europe. No group invested quite as heavily in British loyalism as the Anglo-Canadians, and when the British empire broke up, this identity disappeared along with it. The collapse of loyalism removed the country's traditional counterweight to liberalism. The somewhat abstract notion of British Canada, fusing genealogical and political origins but not focused on any particular group of Canadian settlers (the United Empire Loyalist myth was entwined with Empire), meant that no ethnic founding myth or sense of peoplehood survived the fall of Britannic nationalism. There were potential historical resources for conservatives to construct an ethnic-majority narrative, but none actually in place. In the absence of the intellectual work required for ethnic revival, this means there are no important social forces protecting ethno-traditions as there are in Quebec. English Canada thus presents exceptionally fertile terrain for the cosmopolitan project with few analogues elsewhere. Liberals had an open path to cultural power and could fuse their traditional economic openness with left-modernism to entrench a missionary nationalism based on multiculturalism.

In Australia and New Zealand, a similar process took place but, if per capita membership in the Orange Order is anything to go by (ten times higher in English Canada than Australia), loyalism was arguably less central. Local myths and traditions remained for conservatives to work with to construct an alternative identity to multiculturalism. Immigration attitudes are nearly as positive in Australasia as in Canada while multiculturalism, though sustaining blows, remains part of its national rhetoric. The shift in immigration source countries since 2000 will, however, put pressure on Anglo-European traditions of nationhood in Australia and New Zealand in the decades to come. With populist right parties active in both countries, I expect European-style right populism to remain a consistent feature of Antipodean politics, shaping the agenda of centrist parties. Perhaps the 2017 New Zealand election, in which Labour and NZ First both campaigned to reduce immigration, is a harbinger of things to come.

The US is slightly more liberal on immigration than much of Europe but somewhat more conservative than Canada or Australia. Some of this stems from its white-Protestant settler traditions of nationhood but also from the fact that a great deal of immigration to the country has been unauthorized and low-skill. Had the US been able to select high-skilled immigrants, its immigration politics may be more similar to Canada's – as was true until 2015. America's populist turn is well in train, but a European-style mainstreaming of opposition to immigration and multiculturalism is evident only within the right-wing media and Republican Party. On the left, the media and the Democrats continue to champion multiculturalism and immigration in a more unvarnished way than any European centre-left party. Much of the American left implicitly welcomes illegal immigration, which makes it even more radical than leftist parties in Australia or Canada.

Traditions of immigration, along with Anglo settler societies' materialism and economic liberalism, help explain why New World countries are somewhat more open to immigration. However, all but English Canada are subject to increasing populist agitation, with growing pressure on the 'politically correct' consensus that multiculturalism and immigration should not be politicized. These societies will experience some of the fastest rates of white decline in the West over the coming decades. Right-wing populism is therefore likely to remain a force in Australasia.

In Canada, the linguistic divide makes it difficult for a mainstream party to broach the question of legal immigration levels or challenge left-modernist cultural dominance. Tory leadership candidates who wish to contest immigration or multiculturalism are likely be hemmed into the English language bloc, competing with libertarian pro-growth candidates and those who appeal to minority values voters. The strong economic performance of Canada's selected immigrants means minorities have a similar income and voting profile to whites.[53] Thus the immigration policy axis is unlikely to map on to the left–right economic divide which structures politics, as in America. The populist challenge will probably need to emerge from outside the Conservatives, in the face of near-unanimous media and main-party hostility. In order to shift the discourse, the new party would have to cost the Tories considerably more votes than the Conservatives' pro-immigration strategy delivers from minorities and libertarians. Probably the only way things could change is if there were a substantial non-white anti-immigration vote, or a minority anti-immigration candidate. This seems to have been decisive in the Vancouver non-resident tax debate. This is conceivable, but may require a decline of East Asian and Sikh immigration and its replacement by newcomers from other parts of the world in order to facilitate the recruitment of 'old' immigrants to the restrictionist cause, as in the US in the early 1900s.

Without a populist breakthrough which shifts centre-right discourse, Anglo-Canadian elite norms will continue to restrict the political entrepreneurs or media content which might prime opposition to immigration and multiculturalism. No populist spiral can start, therefore the system is stable. Anglo nationalist voters will have no choice but to stay at home or vote for their least worst option. Society won't work well for the conservative/order-seeking 30–40 per cent of white Anglos, just as Hungarian or Polish society is unkind to those of liberal-cosmopolitan bent. Quebec can regulate the character of its society and populist forces will probably lead the province to reduce immigration over time. This means Quebec's ethno-cultural divergence from an increasingly non-European Rest of Canada shouldn't create tensions which might otherwise challenge federal immigration and multiculturalism policy. This opens the door for English Canada to chart a different path from other Western democracies, becoming a truly multi-racial, multi-polar society such as Guyana or Belize in the second half of this century. This will produce a kind of Toronto-writ-large: a dynamic, low-cohesion, future-oriented society with an attenuated connection to its British and European past. So long as ethnic and income divides continue to crosscut, this configuration shouldn't challenge the welfare state or democracy, leaving society prosperous and stable.

PART II

Repress

7

Left-Modernism: From Nineteenth-Century Bohemia to the Campus Wars

Majorities may resist newcomers, but as the previous three chapters have shown, majority 'voice' is in tension with a second response: to repress anxieties in the name of anti-racism, the cornerstone of a liberal-egalitarian belief system that dominates Western high culture. All social systems work with the grain of some of our evolutionary psychology and against other parts of it. The repression of instincts occurs whenever we desire a gold watch or our neighbour's spouse. Controlling some evolutionary drives is a normal part of life, but the form this suppression takes varies from place to place. Historians and sociologists of emotion draw attention to how norms regulate which emotions can be expressed, by whom, in what social situations. Men are often discouraged from crying, for example, while women who don't cry at the death of a loved one may be sanctioned. Emotional norms may shift over time. The sociologist Norbert Elias writes of how the 'civilizing process' in Europe between the Middle Ages and eighteenth century increasingly restrained urges such as urinating at the table or settling arguments by duelling.[1] Norms work by triggering emotional rather than rational responses to violations. If someone relieves themselves at dinner, this is met with disgust, not a disquisition.

Norms can repress ideas as well as behaviours. Societies enshrine conceptions of the sacred and profane which derive from the dominant ideology of society. The anthropologist Mary Douglas surmises that all societies, not just religious ones, maintain conceptions of what is taboo. This is linked to notions of cleanliness and purity, helping to simplify a complex world and provide moral certainty in ethically ambiguous situations.[2] Ideas which run counter to sacred beliefs, like telling a Sioux tribal gathering that 'the Great Spirit is a social construction', violate these taboos. As with reactions to public urinating, taboos encourage an emotional response to transgression. They convey society's disapproval of norm-violating behaviour and shortcut the need to justify the norm each time it's invoked. Norms like patriotism or anti-racism are rarely explicitly codified. As an American sociologist, Kai Erikson, wrote in 1962, norms are the 'accumulation of decisions made by the community over a long period' which gradually gather moral force. 'Each time the community censures some act of deviance . . . it sharpens the authority of the violated norm and re-establishes the boundaries of the group.'[3]

No society can do without norms; the challenge is to ensure they rest on a sound ethical foundation, with the degree of emotional disapproval proportionate to the offence. We should express disapproval when someone suggests in casual conversation that mass murder is a good strategy for dealing with the poor. This said, the ethical foundations of taboos are often shaky. Expressing support for atheism in Pakistan today, homosexuality in Victorian England or communism in 1950s America activated taboos that lacked a sound ethical basis or a sense of proportion calibrated to the actual danger. What's more, there should be a space – the university – where arguments are not forbidden and can be aired and discussed rationally.

If conservative societies have dubious taboos, we shouldn't be surprised to find that liberal societies have unjustified norms. In the culturally liberal societies of the West after the mid-1960s, the emotional regime shifted from outrage at violations of traditional values to disgust at transgressions of liberal ones. Taboos now protect liberal ideas, especially those that can draw a connection to race or, to a slightly lesser degree, gender. Conservative taboos still exist in the West: the refusal of the NFL quarterback Colin Kaepernick to stand for the American national anthem was attacked as sacrilegious by outraged patriots. It's still impossible for an American president to be an avowed atheist. Yet within society's major cultural, economic and political institutions, norm violations increasingly consist of transgressions of liberal norms.

THE MORALISTIC STYLE OF POLITICS

Taboos are related to two concepts in the sociology of meaning: sacred/profane and deviant/normal. Ideologues truly believe that an idea, such as anti-racism or Catholicism, is sacred, to the extent that anything that can be construed as racist must be censured. Others instrumentally deploy norms to discredit political opponents. Often the two motives overlap.[4] Established powers like the Catholic hierarchy during the Spanish Inquisition, or challengers such as radical Islamists, with their heterodox ideas, understand what evolutionary psychologists have shown – that rational arguments alone rarely win the battle of ideas.[5] Therefore both use moralistic politics – which triggers our unconscious disgust mechanism – to gain the upper hand. Established groups accuse those with new ideas of being heretics, stooges of enemy powers, or even agents of the devil. Challengers accuse the establishment of betraying religious principle or selling out the uncorrupted people. Within their ranks, both establishments and upstarts enforce orthodoxy through shaming and excommunication.

Established and insurgent groups alike harness the power of herding, in which people fear to speak against orthodoxy lest this draw attention to themselves and make them a target. Pointing the finger at deviants signals virtue and loyalty to the group, endowing the accuser with a sense of moral superiority. At times, these emotional mechanisms set off a spiral in which fear of heretics or the desire to avoid being accused leads to further accusations, which increases fear, multiplying the number of accusations, which results in a witch-hunt. The frenzy also serves the function of providing an internal scapegoat to unify a group against.

The Inquisition, beginning in tenth-century Europe, is the most famous example of this dynamic, torturing suspected heretics and setting off a spate of moral panics. 'Crimes' committed by deviants are either evidence-free or grossly exaggerated.[6] The Terror following the French Revolution, the Stalinist Show Trials of the 1930s, McCarthyism in the 1950s and Mao's Cultural Revolution of the 1960s show how secular versions of the process operate. Splits within challenger movements such as the 1970s British left (satirized by Monty Python in the 'People's Front of Judea' skit in *Life of Brian*) or Irish republicanism (I once

297

visited an 'Official' IRA pub, commemorating some of those killed by the 'Provisional' IRA) may lead to similar purges or assassinations. There are moral struggles within groups and across society as a whole. A Danish anthropologist, Agner Fog, speaks of a battle between established social forces which use 'regalization' to enforce a moral order by censuring upstarts as deviants; the accused resist the charges in an attempt at 'kalyptization', to ascend the moral high ground.[7]

Scholarly attention has tended to focus on liberal challengers to social norms such as youth subcultures, cohabiting couples or homosexuals, who managed to eventually neutralize the stigmas against them. But the same process can work the other way, as conservatives challenge a liberal order. When a regalizing order fails to make a charge of deviance stick, the norm begins to unwind, leading to a period of intense cultural contestation. Competing groups police norm boundaries and marginalize deviants who are seen to have violated their community's sacred values. I maintain we are currently in such a period, in which hegemonic liberal norms known as 'political correctness' are being challenged by both populists and centrists, some of whom are trying to install new social norms, notably those defining Muslims and cosmopolitans as deviant.

Moralistic politics is deployed by both left and right. Some on the right are attempting to smear 'citizens of nowhere' and Muslims as beyond the pale, upbraiding cosmopolitans as unpatriotic and exaggerating the security risk Muslims pose. This is a tragedy as both cosmopolitanism and Muslim identity are perfectly respectable life choices. In the elite cultural institutions of society, by contrast, a left-liberal ideology dominates. This belief system polices norms by establishing what is sacred, namely subaltern racial and sexual minorities, and deviant – those who violate norms of racial and sexual equality or question liberal cosmopolitanism. These ideological disgust mechanisms staunch white majorities' response to ethnic change. When the dominant ideology considers whites' attachment to their majority ethnicity – or to a national identity in which whites form the largest part – to be racist, this represses and sublimates white opposition.

In order to grasp the wider moral context in which the populist backlash is taking place, we need to appreciate the historically unique fusion of egalitarian and liberal elements that constitutes the contemporary

Western intellectual climate: an atmosphere which, for example, makes us cringe when white identity is openly expressed. This reflects the ascent of what I term left-modernism ('equality-diversity') in Western high culture since the 1960s. Left-modernism triumphed despite the retreat of socialism. It originated in the 1910s, expanded in the 1960s and attained pre-eminence in high-cultural institutions in the 1980s. In universities, left-modernism continued to consolidate its hold into the 2000s and has become such a dominant force on campus that activist staff, administrators and students have begun restricting academic freedom – albeit in a less brutal manner than that carried out by McCarthyite anti-communists of the 1950s. Let's begin at the epicentre.

WHO IS RACIST?

On 16 September 2017, Bret Weinstein, a professor of biology at Evergreen State College in Washington state, resigned his post and settled out of court for $500,000 with the university for failing to protect him and his wife from verbal and physical abuse. The assailants were left-wing students who accused Weinstein of racism for failing to embrace the university's anti-racist equality and diversity initiative.

Weinstein's troubles stemmed from an email he wrote protesting about a change to his university's annual 'Day of Absence' in which white students, staff and faculty were told by the university to leave campus for the day. Some minority students and faculty members had observed a Day of Absence since the 1970s, meeting off-campus to discuss shared concerns. However, in late 2016, the new university president, George Bridges, decided on a more assertive strategy to tackle perceived racial inequality on campus. He convened a twenty-eight-member Equality and Diversity Council comprised of administrators and academics to take revolutionary new equity proposals forward. In November, his new Council presented its findings to the wider university community. The Strategic Equity Plan entailed sweeping changes to hiring practices and the structure of the curriculum, including an 'equity justification' for any new appointments. Offering no forum for debate, the meeting was designed to symbolically celebrate the new Plan. Building on the West Coast Salish Indian motif of a canoe, it urged staff to metaphorically climb aboard for a voyage towards equality and diversity. Two days prior to the meeting, on 14 November, an African-American Council member, the media professor Naima Lowe, posted on Facebook: ' "SERIOUSLY JUST BE QUIET. ONLY APPOINTED/APPROVED WHITES CAN SPEAK (AND ONLY WHEN SPOKEN TO).' Bridges, the president, who was aware of the post, remained silent.

After the Council meeting, Weinstein, whose views are best characterized as rational-progressive, raised questions about the process: 'this canoe metaphor felt like it was appropriated for the ironic purpose of cloaking an unstoppable train. You are either on board, or you are not. You can attempt to derail this proposal, or you can accept where the train is going.' In response, at two separate meetings, Lowe branded Weinstein a racist. Asking for an opportunity to defend himself against these charges, Weinstein was repeatedly told that a faculty meeting wasn't the appropriate venue. The president and provost failed to defend Weinstein, shrugging off responsibility for ensuring Lowe observed standards of common decency.

This reveals the tension between the two forms of liberalism that the Anglo-Jewish philosopher Isaiah Berlin termed negative and positive. Negative liberalism argues for procedures to ensure that people have the maximum freedom so long as they don't constrict the liberties of others. It argues we must *accept* a diversity of views and identities, whether we like it or not. Positive liberalism says we should *prefer* cultural diversity over homogeneity in order to be true to liberalism. Those who disagree may be deviantized as racists who have transgressed sacred values and therefore cannot be tolerated. This is a subtle but critical move. As such, Weinstein's negative conception of liberalism collided with the university's positive liberal mission to promote diversity.

The Equity Plan, claimed the university, was built on a statistical analysis of retention, achievement and graduation data. Yet when the crisis broke, an alumni and graduate student discovered that the discrimination data rested on an invalid statistical method. In response, Lowe, who had branded Weinstein a racist, claimed that to rely on data was to dismiss student concerns. The president and Council were determined that the Plan would go into action. One of its more ambitious outriders was a reconfigured Day of Absence. Rather than minorities voluntarily gathering together off campus, in keeping with tradition, a communication was sent by Rashida Love, director of Evergreen's First Peoples Multicultural Advising Services, urging whites to leave the campus. Weinstein replied with an email criticizing the policy as retrograde: 'On a college campus, one's right to speak – or to be – should never be based on skin colour.' An email exchange between Weinstein and Lowe was leaked, bringing social pressure to bear on him. In short order, Weinstein's attempt to question college policy was met with student intimidation as he was surrounded by fifty student protesters who berated him. The clip wound up on the internet and soon went viral. He was advised by the police not to come to campus the next day as students were searching vehicles for him.[8]

In a *Wall Street Journal* opinion piece, Weinstein wrote:

> The plan and the way it is being forced on the college are both deeply authoritarian, and the attempt to mandate equality of outcome is unwise in the extreme. Equality of outcome is a discredited concept, failing on both logical and historical grounds, as anyone knows who has studied the misery of the 20th century. It wouldn't have withstood 20 minutes of reasoned discussion. This presented traditional independent academic minds with a choice: Accept the plan and let the intellectual descendants of Critical Race Theory dictate the bounds of permissible thought to the sciences and the rest of the college, or insist on discussing the plan's shortcomings and be branded as racists. Most of my colleagues chose the former, and the protesters are in the process of articulating the terms. I dissented and ended up teaching in the park.[9]

The next day, around 180 students, some armed with baseball bats, protested against institutional racism on campus, taking over buildings, barricading themselves in a library and occupying the president's office for several hours. When the president, Bridges, asked to go to the bathroom he as told to just 'hold it'. Notwithstanding student actions, Bridges remained sympathetic to the equality and diversity project. Following the protests, he announced a suite of new measures, including mandatory diversity and cultural sensitivity training for all faculty members, a new equity/multicultural centre, a vice-president for equity and diversity issues, and a new policy mandating that every official event at the college start with an acknowledgment that Evergreen State stood on land stolen from Native Americans.[10] Norms are strengthened when the accused plead guilty to their 'crimes'.

The Evergreen disturbances reflected a growing assertiveness of left-modernists on campus, involving a synergy between a vocal minority of radical students and a group of activist administrators and faculty. Their actions were in turn enabled by the liberal inclination of the president and many staff and students, who disapproved of student extremism but felt their motives accorded with the progressive values they shared. Moreover, this silent majority was reluctant to challenge activists for fear of being branded racist, showing how regalizing forces harness group dynamics to repulse challenges to the normative order. The interaction between activist radicals and silent liberals on campus constituencies helps account for the rising demands for segregated 'safe spaces' for racial and sexual minorities at US universities, 'trigger warnings' for content which may offend progressive sensibilities and the 'no platforming' of controversial speakers. Sometimes there is a kernel of empirical truth to left grievances, but the danger is exaggerated, as was the threat posed by communist intellectuals in the US in the 1950s.[11] This justifies 'radical' remedies which infringe the liberty of deviants. Some, such as Antifa, even endorse violence.

Mentions of the terms 'safe spaces', 'trigger warning' and 'no-platforming' on Google Trends all show a pronounced jump beginning in mid-2015, documenting a new wave of left-wing campus activism. Likewise, the Foundation for Individual Rights in Education (FIRE) has compiled statistics on campus free-speech violations. These document a growing trend of largely left-inspired campus intolerance in America, including pressure leading to the disinvitation of speakers. In Britain, a 2017 survey found that twenty-one universities – around 20 per cent of the total – had no-platformed at least one speaker. Sixty per cent of UK universities 'severely restricted' free speech and 90 per cent maintained at least some restrictions. Activist student unions were typically in the lead, pressuring universities to ban the sale of right-wing newspapers such as the *Sun* or the wearing of costumes like sombreros. Prominent speakers to be no-platformed included UKIP politicians like Douglas Carswell or left-wing feminists with incorrect views on transgenderism like Germaine Greer. As a result, in October 2017 the universities minister, Jo Johnson, mooted the idea that a new Office for Students be empowered to fine universities engaging in no-platforming.[12]

Speakers have also been no-platformed from the right, albeit at a lower rate. Those who support abortion have been disinvited from universities with a Catholic ethos, like Boston College, and speakers critical of Israel's policies in Palestine, such as Robert Trivers, or who have blown the whistle on the military, like Chelsea Manning, have been barred from universities such as Harvard. Islamist speakers have also been targeted – and British academics have been told to report students expressing 'extreme' Islamist views. Academics have rightly pushed back against the latter, but should also be decrying the no-platforming of right-wing speakers. Indeed, the problem is primarily coming from the left: trends in figure 7.1 chart a rise in left-inspired disinvitations, mostly because a speaker contravenes perceived 'safe' views on race, gender and immigration.

Left-wing groups have participated in shouting down conservative or even liberal speakers. In some cases – as with the visit of the right-wing provocateur Milo Yiannopoulos to Berkeley in February 2017 – threats of violence from left-wing groups and the arrival of

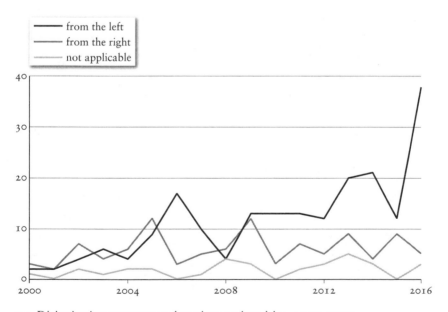

7.1. Disinvitation attempts at American universities, 2000–2017

Source: Sean Stevens, 'Campus Speaker Disinvitations: part 2', *Heterodox Academy*, 7 February 2017

thousands of protesters succeeded in forcing the university to pull the event on security grounds.[13]

American data from the General Social Survey (GSS) suggests younger generations are increasingly intolerant of speech they find offensive. April Kelly-Woessner, a political scientist, finds that twenty-somethings are 17 points less likely than those in their forties to say that 'Muslim clergymen who preach hatred against the United States' should be allowed to give a public speech. They are also less willing to permit communists to speak in public.[14] Prior waves of the GSS going back to the 1950s always found youth to be more tolerant than their parents, so liberalization appears to have gone into reverse. The big change has come from left-liberal students whose issue positions fit what Woessner calls a 'social justice orientation'. Whereas right-wing students were historically less tolerant, left-wing students have now pulled even.[15] Four surveys conducted during 2016–17 showed that nearly 20 per cent of students agreed it was acceptable to use violence to prevent a speaker who makes 'offensive or hurtful statements' from speaking. Eighty per cent agreed that 'speech can be a form of violence'. One survey found the share advocating violence to be as high as 30 per cent when the wording was 'using hate speech or making racially charged comments'.[16] A Cato Institute survey found 51 per cent of 'strong liberals' felt it was okay to 'punch a Nazi' compared to 21 per cent of strong conservatives.[17]

For Woessner, students' views reflect the new social-justice framework which permeates both secondary and university education and has displaced the primacy of free speech. She traces this to Herbert Marcuse, a paragon of New Left thinking, who coined the phrase 'repressive tolerance':

> Tolerance is extended to policies, conditions, and modes of behavior which should not be tolerated because they are impeding, if not destroying, the chances of creating an existence without fear and misery. This sort of tolerance strengthens the tyranny of the majority against which authentic liberals protested . . . Liberating tolerance, then, would mean intolerance against movements from the Right and toleration of movements from the Left.

An increase in ethnic diversity on campus may lie behind the new sensibility: Alison Harell uses Canadian data to show that students in more ethnically diverse social networks become less tolerant of racist speech but more tolerant of other dissidents. She uses the term 'multicultural tolerance' to describe this new orientation which ' "supports speech rights for objectionable groups" but not for "groups that promote hatred" '.[18]

Widening the definition of 'hate speech' has become a political project. The criteria for hate speech are not strictly delimited, but on modern US campuses are often set by the subjective sensibilities of the most affronted individual, or by what self-appointed defenders of subaltern groups imagine to be offensive. Expanding the definition of hate to include critics of transgenderism, like Germaine Greer, centre-right pundits, such as Ben Shapiro, or even defenders of individual liberties, like the American Civil Liberties Union, legitimates a silencing of those who challenge the 'sacred values'[19] of anti-racism and anti-sexism. These speakers may be wrong, but they should be free to make their case.

The game isn't only played by the left: the right deploys the charge of anti-Semitism to silence critics of Israeli security or settlement policy. Incidents of anti-Semitism in left-wing parties like Labour in the UK may be blown out of proportion. And in Canada in 2013, when the left-wing Japanese-Canadian environmentalist David Suzuki told a French reporter that Canada's OECD-leading rate of immigration put pressure on the country's environment, he was attacked as a racist by a right-wing pundit, Ezra Levant, and Jason Kenney, a minister in the ruling Conservative Party.[20] Bad arguments should be refuted by showing they have nefarious effects on people and society. Attempts to smear bad arguments as 'hate' without engaging with them gives them plausibility and narrows the sphere of reason and liberty.

LEFT-MODERNISM: THE HISTORY OF AN IDEOLOGY

The events at Evergreen State and other institutions represent the latest stage in the historical development of left-modernism. The evolution and progressive advance of modernist and egalitarian ideas culminated in the so-called 'cultural turn' of the left in the 1960s, of which Herbert Marcuse was one exponent. This marked a shift away from a story of the working class as the advance guard of socialism to a new narrative of cultural minorities as the vanguard of multiculturalism. On the moderate left, it resulted in a higher profile for identity politics and cultural grievances, resulting in less emphasis on the left's traditional economic message.

It's important to appreciate, as the philosopher John Gray does, that liberal societies are no different from socialist or fascist ones in holding to visions of societal perfection. Typically such dreams include a millenarian story of why history is inevitably moving towards an endpoint such as diversity or globalization.[21] The desire to actively bring forth the millennium often threatens negative liberty. This danger was evident even in nineteenth-century liberalism. John Stuart Mill, for example, believed enlightened individuals should pursue autonomy rather than collective tradition. More advanced social groups and countries should guide the less advanced towards these higher aims, which is why Mill felt Bretons shouldn't 'skulk on their rocks' in Brittany but should instead accept French culture and nationhood. Likewise, Mill supported the British Empire on the grounds that colonized peoples could learn from their British imperial tutors.

Both Mill and today's cultural left are, on Berlin's definition, positive liberals, because they not only specify that people have freedom, but elevate certain life goals and societal visions over others. It's fine to advocate these goals, but not to use society's liberal institutions to enforce orthodoxy. Once this happens, social sanctions are pressed into service to compel the recalcitrant to support ideas they don't believe in, reducing their negative liberty.

Much of the story of Western liberalism involves a struggle for negative rights and freedoms. The Whigs' battle for freedom from arbitrary arrest and the right to criticize the King in eighteenth-century England; anti-slavery and Catholic rights in the nineteenth century; women's rights in the early twentieth century; and black and gay rights in the later twentieth century are examples. But positive liberalism, often linked to radical beliefs about the transformation of society, shadowed the pragmatic victories of negative liberalism. The Jacobins' desire to destroy the old religious-aristocratic order during the French Revolution followed in the wake of the expansion of negative liberty set out in the Declaration of the Rights of Man. The Jacobins' zeal to achieve a purified liberal-egalitarian republic culminated in witch-hunts and the guillotine. Anarchism, especially the violent creed known as the

'Propaganda of the Deed', hewed to a similar millenarian belief: the avant-garde could, with an assassination or a bomb, bring about a revolution which would create the new heaven-on-earth. Socialism and fascism were fired by similar visions of radical action leading to a secular paradise. In each case, negative liberties were sacrificed on the altar of positive liberalism.

Fascism and socialism lost out after the Second World War, but what of the victor, liberalism? The Allies' victory did enlarge and protect the scope of negative liberty. But alongside this success a positive liberalism was smuggled in which advocated individuality and cosmopolitanism over community. Most, myself included, value individual autonomy, but one has to recognize that not all share this aim. Someone who prefers to wear a veil or dedicate their lives to religion is making a communitarian choice which negative liberalism respects but positive liberalism (whether of the modernist left or burqa-banning right) does not. This turns sour when those who fail to support a socially dominant positive liberal virtue like pursuing autonomy or preferring diversity are shamed, shunned or persecuted. This is acceptable in a voluntary organization such as Scientology where you know what you're signing up for, but not in a mainstream societal institution like a university, government bureau or large corporation. When mainstream institutions enforce positive liberal goals and punish deviation from sacred values, this shrinks the space for negative freedom in society.

Enlightenment individualism, which consisted largely of the rational, cognitive individualism of Descartes and Locke, gave way in the nineteenth century to a more romantic, expressive form of individualism. Expressive individualism advocates that we channel our authentic inner nature, or what H. G. Wells or Henri Bergson termed our life force, unconstrained by tradition or reason. Aesthetically, it tended towards what the influential American sociologist Daniel Bell terms modernism, rejecting Christian or national traditions while spurning established techniques and motifs.[22] Not only were traditions overturned but esteem was accorded to those whose innovations shocked sensibilities and subverted historic narratives and symbols the most. Clearly something happened between the nation-evoking historical and landscape painting of a Delacroix or Constable in the early nineteenth century and Marcel Duchamp's urinal of 1917. This 'something' was the rise, after 1880, of what Bell terms modernism and Anthony Giddens calls de-traditionalization.

For Bell, modernism is the antinomian rejection of all cultural authority. For Giddens, the shift is from a past- to a future-orientation and involves a decline in existential security.[23] A brief revival of nation-evoking art in 1930s America known as Regionalism, featuring the rural-historic realism of painters like Thomas Hart Benton and Grant Wood was superseded in the 1940s by the Abstract Expressionism of Jackson Pollock, Benton's student. In the 1940s, the Regionalists were accused by modernist art critics of being fascists. This regalization worked, marking Regionalism as a deviant in the art world. Never again would traditional themes ministering to mass sentiment be permitted to intrude into the high culture.[24]

The adversary culture of left-modernism was grounded in the lifestyle category of the bohemian, first romanticized in Henry Murger's 1845 novel *Scènes de la vie de Bohème*. Unlike dandies, who dated from an earlier period and focused only on fashion, bohemians were poets and artists who embodied a more radical expressive individualism. They tended towards left-wing politics, though the relationship became strained when socialists insisted on doctrinaire art forms such as the Soviet 'proletcult' of the 1930s. Importantly, the left-modernist form of positive liberalism has come through the major crises of the twentieth century with shining colours, meshing extremely well with global capitalism. The term 'work hard, play hard' encapsulates Bell's 'cultural contradictions of capitalism', combining a bourgeois puritanism at work with a bohemian consumerism at play. David Brooks's *Rise of the BoBos*, published in 2001, echoes Bell's bohemian-bourgeois synthesis, which underpins modern capitalism.[25] The rise of an adversary culture is one of the most distinctive aspects of the modern West. This self-critique is an asset which has unlocked cultural creativity and advanced the struggle for freedom and equality. But problems arise when there are no checks and balances to limit its domination of the high culture.

For Bell, modernism replaces contemplation of external reality and tradition with sensation and immediacy.[26] The desire to seek out new and different experiences elevates novelty and diversity into cardinal virtues of the new positive liberalism. To favour tradition over the new, homogeneity over diversity, is to be reactionary. Left-modernism continually throws up new movements such as Surrealism or Postmodernism in its quest for novelty and difference. The shock of the new is accompanied by a cosmopolitan pastiche of borrowings from non-Western cultures, as with the Primitivism of Paul Gauguin. Yet there is a tension between the expressive-individualist and egalitarian strands of left-modernism. Gauguin, for example, who considered himself a cosmopolite defending Tahitian sexual freedom against the buttoned-down West, stands accused by the New Left of cultural appropriation, colonialism, orientalism and patriarchy.

The rise of a discourse of cultural appropriation represents the elevation of left-modernism's moralistic egalitarian ego over its expressive-individualist alter, showing how the tension between these strands defines the adversary culture. Cosmopolitan modernism pushes the white-majority individual to construct the Self from a set of foreign influences, rejecting her own culture. Egalitarianism demands the opposite: respect for minority sensitivities, meaning she can't appropriate cultural forms from many places outside her own culture. David Johnston, the Governor-General of Canada, wandered into this difficult terrain. He signalled his modernist sensibility by claiming that Canada has no British-French founding culture and is defined by a de-traditionalizing repudiation of roots: 'We're a country based on immigration going right back to our, quote, indigenous people, unquote, who were immigrants as well, 10, 12, 14 thousand years ago.' After a storm of leftist criticism, Johnston swiftly paddled back: 'I want to clarify a miscommunication. Our Indigenous peoples are not immigrants. They are the original peoples of this land.'[27] New post-1960s egalitarian sensitivities trumped Johnston's attempt to strike a pose of cosmopolitan, self-abnegating WASP – a sensibility first cultivated by John Dewey and Randolph Bourne in the 1910s.

Hal Niedzviecki, editor of The Writers' Union of Canada (TWUC) magazine, stepped into the same trap when he sought to win cosmopolitan plaudits by proclaiming: 'I don't believe in cultural appropriation.' Saying most Canadian literature is written by those who are 'white and middle-class', he asked his writers 'to imagine other cultures', and learn from indigenous writers. He asked his writers to 'Win the Appropriation Prize.' The editorial led to an explosion of criticism on social media. This is classic moral politics, straight out of Kai Erikson's theory of deviance or Émile Durkheim's work on the policing of boundaries between sacred and profane. The union's Equity Task Force took Niedzviecki to task for writing an 'essay [that] contradicts and dismisses the

racist systemic barriers faced by Indigenous writers and other racialized writers'. Like Johnston, Niedzviecki duly apologized for 'fail[ing]
to recognize . . . how deeply painful acts of cultural appropriation have
been to indigenous peoples'.[28] Once again, an attempt to signal anti-
traditionalist virtue led a white liberal Canadian to violate the sacred
value of deferring to the (purported) feelings of members of totemic
social categories. The Canadian Prime Minister, Justin Trudeau, who
has sought to exemplify the left-modernist mission of Canadian identity, ran into the same contradiction on a trip to India, where his
repeated attempt to signal his cosmopolitanism by dressing in Indian
attire drew charges of cultural appropriation.[29] Transgressing one's
parochial outlook remains a core component of the left-modernist
belief system, but one must now be careful which culture one borrows
from in constructing one's cosmopolitan Self. Minorities, meanwhile,
are enjoined not to follow whites down the cosmopolitan path. Where
Randolph Bourne in 1916 lauded minorities who stuck proudly to their
culture because they were resisting a dessicated puritanical Americanism, today's left-modernism adds a moral imperative for minorities to
stick to their culture to resist white oppression.

Whether one violates liberal taboos is a decision which emerges from
among those who interpret the left-modernist canon. This diffuse secular priesthood may call forth an equally de-centred virtue police on
social media: typically minority activists or whites who interpret the collective mindstate of disadvantaged groups through a process of mutual
imagining. Indeed, there is little interest in positivist methods such as
conducting representative surveys of the opinion of disadvantaged groups.
There's also a hierarchy of protected categories. The distinct fates of
transgenderism and transracialism illustrate the pre-eminence of racial
over sexual minorities in the left-modernist hierarchy. Transgenderism
exemplifies the bohemian-modernist virtue of boundary-crossing, but
the trans community has also established a claim to disadvantage. Those
like Germaine Greer who seek to protect definitions of femininity against
transgression can thereby be criticized as reactionary.

On the other hand, when an untenured academic, Rebecca Tuvel,
argued in the feminist journal *Hypatia* that '[s]ince we . . . accept transgender individuals' decisions to change sexes, we should also accept
transracial individuals' decisions to change races', she was denounced.
Comparing the transgender odyssey of Caitlin (formerly Bruce) Jenner

with Rachel Dolezal, an activist whose claims to blackness were revealed to be fraudulent, Tuvel tried to argue the case for Dolezal's rights to have her claims accepted.[30] This chimes with the expressive individualist ethos of modernism, and Tuvel is right that it's logically inconsistent to support Jenner but not Dolezal. However, this misfired with black activists who mobilized a left-modernist backlash. This resulted in a social media uproar and the publication of an open letter signed by one of *Hypatia*'s associate editors apologizing for the article that garnered 830 signatures.

On questions of race, the 'left' side of the left-modernism juggernaut prevailed whereas for gender the opposite was true. Transgenderism seems to have won its right to boundary-cross because trans individuals are perceived as more disadvantaged than women. They thus have the green light from left-modernism's moral gatekeepers to transgress female boundaries. Transracials, by contrast, have not unseated people of colour in the disadvantage hierarchy so their attempt to surmount racial boundaries was construed as insensitive.

MODERNISM AND ANTI-NATIONALISM

The relationship between modernism and ethno-traditional nationalism is not as straightforward as it may seem. Modernism initially had an anti-religious rather than anti-nationalist thrust. Religion is often universalist and other-worldly where nationalism is particularist and this-worldly. This meant modernism was initially nationalist. Christianity celebrates a Middle Eastern religion and the classical world while ethnic nationalists in Europe romanticize pagan ancestors like the Gauls, Vikings and Anglo-Saxons.[31] In the French Revolution, the attack on traditional values opened space for French nationalism. So, for a time, modernism and nationalism could work together. Indeed, Italian Futurism became the basis for fascist art under Mussolini. Only after the First World War did the link between modernism and nationalism turn sour.

The same holds for the relationship between liberalism and nationalism. Liberals viewed the nation as a 'staging post in the ascent of humanity', a modernizing force helping to break down the parochialism of village life and open up new horizons.[32] In the United States, we saw how liberal cosmopolitanism and nationalism merged in Emerson's concept of 'double-consciousness'. Writers would simultaneously speak of the country's Anglo-Saxonism and its melting-pot cosmopolitanism. In Europe, where immigration was limited and the foreign-born made up under 2 per cent of the population in most countries in 1900, liberals blended political cosmopolitanism with nationalism. Mazzini, for instance, founded both Young Italy (in 1831) and Young Europe (in 1834) to advance what he thought were the linked causes of Italian nationalism and European unification. Equally, a German writer, Friedrich Meinecke, writing in 1909, declared that 'The best German national feeling also includes the cosmopolitan ideal of a humanity beyond nationality.'[33]

The left had a similarly ambiguous relationship with nationalism. In America prior to 1914, the Socialist Party of America along with unions such as the Knights of Labor or American Federation of Labor embraced the nation and opposed immigration. Socialism only adopted a consistently cosmopolitan approach after the First World War. In Europe, the chronology is similar: socialists of the First and Second Internationals (before 1917) endorsed colonialism, viewing non-European societies as too underdeveloped to bring forth socialist revolution. When war arrived in 1914, nationalism took precedence over universalism as the Second International broke up along national lines. Only with the advent of the Third (1919–43) International, backed by the Soviet Union, did European socialism opt for an anti-colonial, anti-nationalist outlook.[34]

The bloodletting of the Great War convinced liberals and the left in the West that nationalism was a retrograde, reactionary force. They had a point: German nationalism was a key driver of the conflict. On the other hand, two of the three Central Powers, Turkey and Austria-Hungary, were dynastic anti-nationalist empires, not nation-states. Even so, few could dispute that militarism and chauvinism were a negative force for mankind. The war ended any romance between progressivism and nationalism, prompting a swift decline in nationalistic history writing among Western academics. In the English-speaking world, the process was largely complete by 1919. Under the influence of the internationalist Union of Democratic Control, professional history replaced nationalistic narratives with limited conclusions strictly tied to documents and restricted to narrow slices of time.[35] Scientific 'history' vanquished national 'memory' at the elite level.[36]

In schools, nationalist narratives persisted but gradually shifted from ethnic to civic nationalism, as in the US, where a shift from an ethnically WASP-centred to 'nation of immigrants'-oriented national history was underway in the nation's schools by the late 1950s. From the 1960s, textbooks paid greater attention to the tribulations of African and Native Americans.[37] After 1980, American progressives promoted more critical school texts exposing whites' infringement of aboriginal, black or immigrant rights – whether as colonists, slaveholders, capitalists or the government. Despite facing conservative resistance, multicultural narratives made some headway in America, though this is less true in France.[38]

Popular internationalism also began to flower after the First World War. Between the wars, new social networks mobilized hundreds of thousands of idealistic Americans and Europeans into movements for Peace, the League of Nations and European unity. The scale of this activity was unprecedented. American Protestant ecumenists of the Federal Council of Churches (later World Council of Churches) who opposed immigration restriction in America in the 1920s played a leading part in spearheading the new international society. Meanwhile the Pan-European Union, the movement for European federalism, grew spectacularly under the leadership of the half-Japanese Austrian Count Coudenhove-Kalergi (who has a small street in Paris named after him). Kalergi successfully lobbied the French and Austrian governments on behalf of his Euro-federalist proposals, winning the backing of the French mainstream left. Prominent supporters included the foreign minister, Aristide Briand, who agreed to serve as secretary of the organization. In 1929 Briand presented his outline for a Federal Europe to the League of Nations. He then sent his Memorandum on a Federal Europe to European governments for consideration. Though these were rejected by other governments and criticized by the right at home, interwar pan-Europeanism set the scene for the emergence of what was to become the European Union after the Second World War.[39]

The excesses of Joseph Stalin in the 1930s undermined the popularity of state socialism among many Western intellectuals while Hitler's barbarism damaged the ethno-nationalist right. Left-modernist cosmopolitanism, which rejected both communism and fascism in favour of cultural radicalism and social democracy, emerged victorious from the war. The influential New York Intellectuals in the United States and anti-communist resistance movements in Europe helped advance its tenets. America's new federally directed state nationalism supported left-modernism by the early 1940s: the CIA even funded modernist art and the New York Intellectuals as a form of anti-Soviet propaganda. The US, which had rejected the League of Nations in 1918, now strongly endorsed the new United Nations. World Federalism became a popular movement for global governance in the 1940s, counting a future Republican president, Ronald Reagan, among its members.[40]

The Holocaust itself was not a force multiplier for left-modernism until it was pressed into service two decades later. The social penetration of left-modernist ideas would take a great leap forward only in the 1960s as television and university education soared. In America, the share of 18- to 24-year-olds in College increased from 15 per cent in 1950 to a third in 1970. Given the large postwar 'baby-boom' generation, this translated into a phenomenal expansion of universities. The growth of television was even more dramatic: from 9 per cent penetration in American homes in 1950 to 93 per cent by 1965.[41] The New York, Hollywood and campus-based nodes in this network allowed liberal sensibilities to spread from a small coterie of aficionados to a wider public. Rising affluence may also have played a part in creating a social atmosphere more conducive to liberalism. All told, these ingredients facilitated a marked liberal shift across a wide range of attitudes measured in social surveys from the mid-1960s: gender roles, racial equality, sexual mores and religion – with the effects most apparent in the postwar Baby Boom generation.[42] For the most part, these were attitudes which supported negative liberty and equality. However, a positive liberalism based on a preference for diversity and the sacralization of race and gender inequality above other forms of disadvantage advanced on the back of these attitude shifts.

Greater migration pressure in Europe and the United States after 1965 generated more opposition to immigration, offsetting what would have been a steady process of Baby Boomer-led liberalization. The proper question to ask, therefore, is what the Western response to non-European immigration would have been without the liberal attitude changes of the 1960s. Contrast the 'yellow peril' discourse on Chinese immigration in North America or Australia in the 1880s with the modest concern of the 1970s and you get your answer. All of which suggests attitude liberalization had an enormous impact in overturning national narratives and opening Western countries up to diverse new sources of immigration.

THE CIVIL RIGHTS MOVEMENT AND THE EMERGENCE OF IDENTITY POLITICS ON CAMPUS

The Civil Rights Movement was a social and political movement to ensure African-Americans' equal right to vote, access housing and otherwise realize the promise of negative liberty. Until the 1960s, the egregious violations of African-American civil rights in the south, and extra-legal segregation and discrimination against them in northern cities, weren't core issues for the Democratic Party. The party's southern wing was key to its electoral success, and its northern base of urban white Catholics wasn't especially sympathetic to African-Americans. When the Civil Rights movement prevailed in the 1960s, many whites realized they had taken too long to address the problem of racism. Racial attitudes swiftly changed: in 1944, 52 per cent of whites agreed that 'white people should have the first chance at any kind of job'. The next time the question was asked, in 1972, just 3 per cent did. The decline of opposition to interracial marriage was more gradual and generational, but just as enduring.[43] The Civil Rights Movement's effects rippled widely beyond America, inspiring campaigns for civil rights and nationalism in Quebec and Northern Ireland, as well as anti-racist movements in Europe. For the African-American professor John McWhorter, 'The Civil Rights Movement transformed the moral and intellectual fabric of this country.'[44]

As the dam broke and racial equality progressed, the American left responded by moving away from its pre-1960s emphasis on labour and welfare issues towards the concerns of subaltern identity groups. Some of this was necessary in order to realize the promise of negative liberalism: homosexuality was generally not accepted in society, racism persisted in many quarters and women found it difficult to access desirable jobs. But – perhaps due to the self-evident wrongs it had begun to right – left-wing intellectuals began to sacralize identity politics. Negative liberal goals such as equal rights gave way to the desire to realize a positive liberal ideal of diversity and invert a perceived cultural hierarchy. Cultural minorities replaced workers as the exploited category and agent of radical transformation. Left-modernist eschatology replaced the Marxist workers' paradise with the multiculturalist dream of equality-in-diversity. The New Left electrified the rising Baby Boom generation of intellectuals. Its tenets were less threatening to capitalism and thus, in softened form, more readily absorbed by large corporations, government and a rising cohort of knowledge workers.

This took time. The quickest strides were made in progressive circles, especially in universities. Baby Boomer scholar-activists began to occupy positions in the humanities and social sciences, instilling a more pronounced left-modernist ethos in these disciplines. For instance, leftist activists succeeded in using a ballot to install Alfred McClung Lee as president of the American Sociological Association (ASA), the discipline's professional organization, in 1976. The position had traditionally gone to individuals with a pedigree of academic achievements, which Lee lacked. Political mobilization was used to circumvent traditional esteem indicators and procedures. In this manner, the 'radical' academy, rooted in activism and anti-scientific epistemologies, was able to roll back the dominance of the scientific 'rational' academy in the social sciences. Here, then, was a successful example of what Agner Fog terms 'kalyptization', in which a new moral order emerges from a cadre of innovators, or what the neo-Marxist theorist Antonio Gramsci terms 'organic intellectuals'. The majority, which lacked a countervailing moral ethos beyond professionalism, acquiesced to the innovations of Lee and his confederates, resulting in a wider suite of views falling foul of the arbiters of propriety. A leading sociologist, James Coleman, for instance, had to endure protesters waving 'racist' placards on stage in 1975 as he outlined his research showing that the policy of busing was resulting in white flight.[45]

Activists also entered the university through direct action as part of a wave of rising protest activity on campus. In 1964, Berkeley students took part in a demonstration against the Sheraton Palace Hotel to protest at the hotel's discriminatory hiring practices, a stance consistent with negative liberalism. By 1966, the Black Panthers, a more radical African-American group based in nearby Oakland, began to influence the student movement. Then, in 1968, the amplitude of protests rose as students mobilized against the unpopular Vietnam War. Student protests spread nationally and internationally. In May 1968, French students protesting against capitalism and American imperialism sparked off civil unrest in Paris which led to strikes that involved 11 million workers and lasted two weeks.

One of the students' tactics was to demonstrate on university campuses and occupy the offices of the university president and administrators. On 5 November 1968, black students at San Francisco State College issued President Robert Smith with a list of ten demands. The first was the immediate creation of a department of Black Studies, with twenty positions. They also demanded a School of Ethnic Studies for 'Third World' ethnic groups, with fifty positions, called for Nathan Hare to be appointed chair of the Department of Sociology, and ordered the reinstatement of George Murray, a Black Panther student who had attacked the editor of the student newspaper. All non-white students were to be admitted, and 'any other faculty person chosen by non-white people' must be accepted. If the demands were not met, the students would strike. The Civil Rights Movement's success in furthering the negative liberty of African-Americans and the legitimacy of the anti-Vietnam War protests gave the movement a credibility which some now used to advance the left-modernist agenda.

President Smith agreed to the Black Studies and Ethnic Studies requests, but not to the appointment of Hare and Murray. When Smith failed to meet their demands, students instigated the Third World Strike from November 1968 to March 1969. The subsequent president sued for peace, reaching an agreement to end the conflict.[46] Direct action similarly forced the creation of an Ethnic Studies department at UC Berkeley in 1969. In the heat of the moment it isn't easy to realize when valid protests drawing attention to racial discrimination overstep the bounds of ethical consistency and begin to corrode the rational foundations of a university. But at some point in the second half of the 1960s protests replaced the early Civil Rights Movement's analytically consistent philosophy and negative liberty with an anti-intellectual, power-centred radical discourse. Arguments for Ethnic Studies based on gaps in the scholarly literature or unmet student demand would have been more consistent with Martin Luther King's exposure of liberal inconsistency than the students' hostage-taking approach. An oppression frame based on maximizing outcomes for one group, i.e. black Americans, could be balanced by a holistic overview which takes account of all group demands in an attempt to arrive at an optimal solution. This would still mean pursuing minority redress, but would also make it possible to appreciate competing demands and tradeoffs, leading to checks and balances. When institutions fall short, they should be held to account, but the students' strident demands based on unfalsifiable theories of oppression showed they were using white guilt and identity politics to infringe the spirit of reason which forms the basis of the university. And I say this as someone who works in ethnic studies and thinks it's one of the most important things we can study.

The student revolts had the side effect of producing a conservative intellectual awakening among former left-liberals, giving birth to early neoconservatism. Daniel Bell, like many of his fellow 'New York Intellectuals' group of mainly Jewish democratic socialists, shifted rightward in disgust at the anti-intellectualism of the student revolts. Bell, whom I met at his home in Cambridge, Massachusetts, in 2009, two years before his death, wrote of a 'radical egalitarianism' in the culture, superseding the 'older hierarchy of mind'. Claims to equal representation in the canon would now displace earlier conceptions based on merit or the mastery of an intellectual tradition.

For Bell, student radicals sought to erase the line between high culture and politics, democratizing standards in high culture while proclaiming that 'revolution is poetry'. This redounded, in his estimation, to the benefit of neither culture nor politics.[47] In the words of another New York Intellectual – who incidentally examined my doctoral thesis – Nathan Glazer, 'When I came to Berkeley in 1963, I still thought of myself as a man of the left, and for the first few months of the free speech issue, I was on the side of the free speech people … the key issue that labelled me a conservative, labelled a number of us as conservative, were [sic] the student unrest issues post-'64.' Bell recounts how he opposed the students' desire to set the curriculum at Columbia: 'I remember at one point a student saying to me, "Who the hell are you to tell me what to study?" I said because you don't know what you don't know. If you knew what you didn't know you could go out and study. That's what I'm here for, to show you what you don't know ... But they didn't even understand something as simple as that.'[48]

WHITE GUILT AND
THE RELIGION OF ANTIRACISM

After the 1960s, the riots subsided, but by the 1980s, the critical mass for the New Left's equality-in-diversity mission had been laid in the humanities and social sciences. In social psychology, for instance, the ratio of liberals to conservatives was about 2:1 in 1960. But, as figure 7.2 shows, this began to change rapidly in the 1980s, leading to a left-modernist monoculture. By 2014, the ratio of liberals to conservatives had reached 15:1.[49] In the same year, a survey of the 900-strong Society for Experimental Social Psychology, a professional organization of leading academics, showed that 89 per cent of the 335 academics who

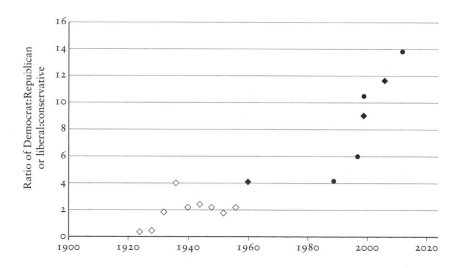

7.2. Ratio of Democrats/liberals to Republicans/conservatives among psychology academics in America, 1920–2014

Source: J. L. Duarte, et al., 'Political diversity will improve social psychological science', *Behavioral and Brain Sciences* 38 (2015).

answered placed themselves to the left and 3 per cent to the right, a 36:1 ratio. 94.7 per cent voted for Obama and just 1.2 per cent for Romney, a 76:1 balance. Answering a set of questions on policy preferences revealed psychology professors to be even further left-leaning than this: 96 per cent scored left of centre and just 0.3 right of centre, a 314:1 skew.[50]

Sam Abrams finds a similar pattern across the entire university, with the humanities and social sciences most left-wing, and New England the most left-leaning of all. His plot of faculty ideological position since 1989 is shown in figure 7.3.

An identical pattern is evident in Britain, where a 10-point Labour advantage over the Conservatives in the mid-1970s widened to a 25-point gap by the late 1980s. Since then, the trend has escalated, as in the US. Noah Carl, using an opt-in survey, found that in 2015 the left party skew in British academia had reached nearly 60 points. This was confirmed in representative Understanding Society data by the political scientist Chris Hanretty.[51] The lack of ideological diversity in the humanities and social sciences professoriate narrows the scope of

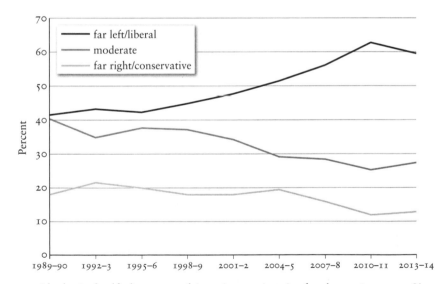

7.3. Ideological self-placement of American university faculty, 1989–2014, %

Source: Abrams, S. 'Professors moved left since 1990s, rest of country did not', *Heterodox Academy*, 9 January 2016

intellectual enquiry and generates orthodoxy, rendering it socially and professionally costly to criticize dominant theories such as the majority-minority paradigm in ethnic studies. This means the scientific process, whereby theories gain robustness by withstanding repeated attempts at falsification, is impeded. Entire lines of enquiry go unexplored for fear the final product will not be published or could expose the author as a conservative, potentially affecting their chance of employment or tenure and making college life difficult.[52] It's my sense that many social science academics are on the centre-left, eschewing the far left as well as the right. For instance, few UK political scientists supported the far-left Jeremy Corbyn before he became more moderate, during the 2017 election. Even so, the partisan imbalance is undeniable, and this state of affairs led the prominent social psychologists Jonathan Haidt and Chris Martin to co-found Heterodox Academy in 2015 to fight for academic freedom and increased viewpoint diversity on campus. I'm pleased to be an early UK-based member.

LEFT-MODERNISM OFF CAMPUS

In the culture more broadly, beginning in the late 1980s, the trinity of left-modernist sacred values – race, gender and sexuality – greatly expanded their reach, prompting the phrase 'politically correct' to come into common parlance. Political correctness refers to speech violations of left-modernist taboos. Such taboos, if well calibrated to harms, have a place – transgressions of well-justified norms should be verbally condemned. But what is a reasonable tradeoff between sensitivity and freedom of expression? Or consider the struggle between reason, which depends on mutually agreed, measurable concepts such as oppression and racism, and the progressive desire to spiritualize these categories into sacred values which cannot be traded off against other social goals, ranked in proportion to other sources of inequality, or empirically scrutinized.

Whatever one's view, it's clear that the period beginning in the late 1980s featured a logarithmic increase in the use of the terms 'racist', 'sexist' and 'political correctness' as the 1960s radicals began to set the cultural tone. This is a classic example of regalization, in which adherents of an ideology use moralistic politics to entrench new social norms and punish deviance. The trend in the use of 'racist' and 'sexist' – new ways of calling out deviants – in the English-language corpus of Google Books is presented in figure 7.4. 'Racist' began to be used with some regularity after 1960, rising between 1965 and 1970 before hitting a plateau, then ascending swiftly again after 1985 to peak in the late 1990s. 'Sexist' emerges in the 1970s, rising sharply in the late 1980s to peak in the late 1990s. 'Homophobia' and 'politically correct' follow the same trend of a swift ascent in the late 1980s to reach a late 1990s apogee. Use of 'anti-Semitism', by contrast, jumps up from the 1930s to 1946 but remains fairly stable thereafter. The pattern of increase tracks the shift towards ideological uniformity in the professoriate apart from the fact that in the wider culture these terms reach their zenith in the late 1990s, while in academia they are able to rise unabated in the 2000s, reaching near-saturation in the humanities and soft social sciences by the 2010s.

Similar processes occurred in other Western countries. In German, 'rassistisch' follows a straight-line trajectory from 1960 to the mid-1980s before tracking the English trend of reaching an apogee in the late 1990s. In French, 'racisme' has a straight-line ascent after 1950 but shows the same upward growth. Between 1960 and 2008, the use of 'racist' increased fivefold in Spanish, Italian and French, tenfold in

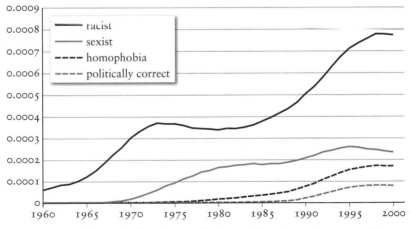

7.4. Frequency of use of selected terms in Google Books, 1960–2000, %

Source: Google Books Ngram Viewer

German and fifteenfold in English. What is fascinating, however, is that in Russian, the only East European country tracked on Google Books, mentions of 'racist' emerge in the 1940s and 1950s but remain stable thereafter at levels similar to those recorded for English in 1960. Whatever cultural change led to the rise in the word's usage in Western Europe doesn't seem to have affected Russia. I suspect the trend in Eastern Europe is closer to Russian than English, reflecting an increasingly important East–West values divide within Europe's elite culture and institutions.

Google Books Ngram Viewer doesn't continue into the present, so figure 7.5 presents results from Google Trends, which does. It covers a much wider range of sources then Google Books but only runs from 2004. The vertical axis measures the frequency of searches for a given set of terms relative to their maximum search level of 100, which in figure 7.5 is searches for 'racist' in April 2014. This source shows that use of 'racist' and 'sexist' enjoyed another growth spurt after 2009 while 'homophobia' and 'politically correct' (not shown) remained stable. This suggests racism is a more salient feature of Western debate than sexism though both of these core components of left-modernism have been rising in importance in recent years.

The trends can also be viewed geographically, illustrating how the

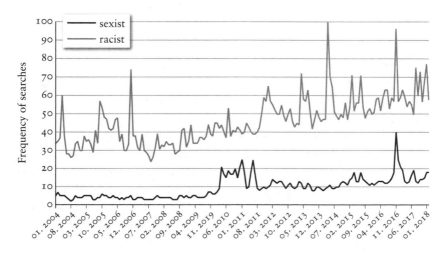

7.5 Frequency of use of selected terms in Google Trends, 2004–17

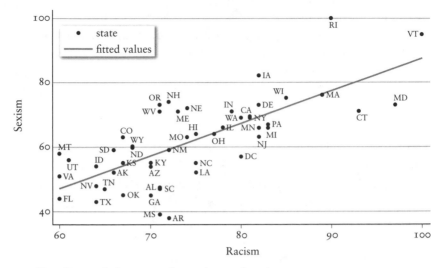

7.6. Google search frequency for racism and sexism, 2004–17

Source: Google Trends.

left-modernist belief system is especially pronounced in liberal US states. Figure 7.6 plots Google search scores for 'racism' and 'sexism' in American states during 2004–17. This reveals a .52 correlation between the state-level frequency of searches for the two terms, rising to .70 when I control for percentage African-American in a state (assuming black search patterns may differ and that racism is a more prominent concern in states with a higher black share). This again indicates that a concern with racism and sexism forms part of an integrated worldview. It also reveals that states with liberal white populations such as Vermont have a considerably higher per capita volume of searching for these left-modernist terms than states with more conservative white populations.

Discussion of racism is much more prevalent in Western than in Eastern Europe. Figure 7.7 compares the frequency of the term racist in Hungarian, Swedish and Polish. This contrasts two small countries, Sweden and Hungary, with the much larger Poland to reveal that 'racist' is used far more in Sweden than in the Eastern European countries, despite Poland's larger population size.

Even within countries there are important differences. In Canada, as noted in chapter 6, left-modernism is more powerful in the Anglophone

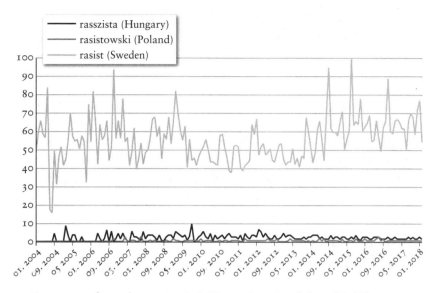

7.7. Frequency of search term 'racist', Hungarian, Swedish and Polish, 2004–17

provinces than among Francophone Quebeckers. Hence the English term 'racist' is searched for twenty-eight times more often than the French 'raciste' in Canada, even though English speakers outnumber French speakers only 3:1. In Quebec, where the French outnumber the English 4:1, there are still more searches for 'racist' than 'raciste'!

THE 'RELIGION OF ANTIRACISM' AND WHITE PRIVILEGE

Anti-racism stands as the highest value within left-modernism, resulting in what John McWhorter terms the 'religion of antiracism'. This elevates the laudable goal of formulating policies to reduce racial inequality into what Scott Atran, an anthropologist, terms a 'sacred value.'[53] Within a community of believers, sacred beliefs such as 'Jesus died for our sins on the cross' or 'Western society is racist' are not open to question. They are deemed to lie beyond what may be legitimately exposed to the scientific method or empirical falsification. McWhorter writes that this religion comes complete with a high priesthood, in the form of revered authors such as Ta-Nehisi Coates, to which genuflection rather than criticism is due. Coates's analysis is not really up for dissection and discussion, but is a call whose appropriate response is 'Amen'. For McWhorter:

> The call for people to soberly 'acknowledge' their White Privilege as a self-standing, totemic act is based on the same justification as acknowledging one's fundamental sinfulness is as a Christian. One is born marked by original sin; to be white is to be born with the stain of unearned privilege . . . Coates is telling [liberal white] people that they are sinners . . . and they are eagerly drinking in the charge, 'revering' him for it. This, ladies and gentlemen, is worship, pure and simple.

McWhorter believes the 'religion of antiracism' hampers the progress of American blacks by shielding aspects of black male honour culture from critique and reform. Shelby Steele, an African-American conservative scholar, adds that there are political and fiscal incentives for African-American leaders to focus on white discrimination rather than on more pressing problems in the black community.[54] For Coleman Hughes, progressives have responded to the undeniable reduction in actual racism with a concomitant expansion of its definition: it becomes 'a conserved quantity akin to mass or energy: transformable but irreducible'.

I recall similar dynamics at work in a political theory seminar at the American Political Science Association where a Native Indian speaker from Canada berated a co-panellist, the cosmopolitan theorist Jeremy Waldron, about '400 years of oppression' without engaging with his arguments. During the aboriginal speaker's presentation, the heads of the predominantly white audience nodded in religious unison. The only member of the audience willing to challenge the Native presenter's logic was an African-American woman who prefaced her statements by talking about her slave ancestors in order to gain the moral platform to debate with the speaker. McWhorter and Steele observe that rather than being motivated by a desire to enact policies most likely to pragmatically reduce racial inequality, the religion of anti-racism ministers to white progressives' symbolic need for the absolution of sin. I would add that this ideology runs alongside a wider Western millenarian belief in radical social transformation, from oppressive monoculturalism to egalitarian multiculturalism. Ritualistic aspects include shaming those who violate taboos around immigration or multiculturalism while applauding people who perform 'virtue-signalling' affirmations of sacred anti-racist values. This signalling-approval dynamic is identical to the 'Amen' which a fundamentalist preacher's flock chants after the pastor divines signs of Satan's or God's presence in innocuous events. Left unopposed, the ecstasy can spiral out of control, leading to moral panics of the kind seen at Evergreen State.

CONFLICT OVER THE MEANING OF RACISM

While positive liberals seek to expand the scope of the anti-racism taboo, negative liberals defend it only for a narrower range of infractions. For instance, restricting the right of a Muslim woman to wear a burqa runs counter to procedural liberalism. While proponents of a ban argue that patriarchal Muslim culture compels women to wear the burqa, a negative liberal cannot second-guess a person's motivations. Negative liberalism can criticize Salafi norms and intervene to prevent people forcing adult women to go uncovered, but it can't push the positive liberal ideal of autonomy on Muslim women who make a religious decision. Negative liberalism would likewise resist a ban on minarets as a limit on free association and expression. This said, it's inconsistent to decry the positive liberalism of the burqa removers while approving of the positive liberalism of the multiculturalism movement, which considers a diverse environment to be an inherently virtuous goal rather than one preference among others. While France bans the burqa, left-modernists censure ideas such as immigration restriction, which are deemed to violate the sacred values of anti-racism and diversity. The right smears non-violent Islamist ideas as 'extremism' while the left tries to prohibit ethno-traditional nationalism as 'hate speech'. Both reflexes are illiberal.

Since so much of the debate around the boundaries of the permissible revolves around racism, we need a rigorous – rather than political – definition of the concept. It's very important to specify clearly, using analytic political theory and precise terminology, why certain utterances or actions are racist. Only in this manner can we defend a racist taboo. I define racism as (a) antipathy to racial or pan-ethnic outgroups, defined as communities of birth; (b) the quest for race purity; or

(c) racial discrimination which results in a violation of citizens' right to equal treatment before the law. Let's deal with each aspect of racism in turn.

First, antipathy to outgroups: even if one is at liberty to call immigrants 'poison' or Muslims a threat, doing so impugns a minority group and perpetuates irrational feelings of hatred or fear towards them. Since most Muslims acquire their faith at birth through being members of particular ethnic groups, attacking Muslims represents an injury to these groups and ignores the fact there is a diversity of viewpoints among them. When Geert Wilders talks of having fewer Moroccans or Donald Trump speaks of a 'total and complete shutdown' of Muslims, this targets one or more ethnic groups, generating hostility towards them, which threatens their safety, equality and liberty. Criticizing Islam is, however, fair comment so long as one takes care to contextualize. That is, to criticize Islamic texts for opposing homosexuality is fine, but one should mention that several religious traditions also do so; or to focus on Salafi jihadism rather than Islam as the source of terrorism.

Second, racial puritanism: attachment to one's own ethnic group or race is not, in my view, racist. However, if this translates into a zeal for purity, it results in outgroups being viewed as 'pollutants', which leads to ill-treatment of minorities and carries an enhanced risk of genocide. Calling one's country white or Christian explicitly excludes minorities. It makes them second-class citizens, opening the door to maltreatment. Following this logic, it's racist to ban all immigration and want a hermetically sealed gene pool, but not to argue for a slower inflow in order to limit cultural disorientation and allow more time for voluntary assimilation.

Third, racial discrimination. This is often motivated by a positive attachment to one's own group rather than a hatred of outgroups. Like helping a relative, someone who is attached to their ethnic group may wish to favour them for a job. Since this doesn't involve irrational fear or hatred, I see it as qualitatively different to the forms of racism outlined previously. Nevertheless, it's still harmful to people and can generate immense frustration, leading to conflict. In terms of intent, there is no difference between a white British lawyer hiring a white Briton in a law firm and a British Pakistani taxi operator hiring a Pakistani because they are attached to their own group and its interests. The difference lies in the effects, since being a lawyer is a more lucrative position than being a taxi driver. In both cases applicants should be assessed without regard to ethnicity, because only in that way can people be treated equally before the law. This doesn't mean there aren't grey areas. In a fascinating *Freakonomics* episode, Stephen Dubner and Steven Levitt explore situations, such as hiring French waiters in a French restaurant or Indian cooks in an Indian one, where an argument in favour of ethnic discrimination can be sustained. This is a similar justification to Rihanna replacing a Hispanic musician with an African-American to create an all-black 'look' on stage – which may be defended on artistic grounds.[55]

Being white in Europe or North America confers some advantage, depending on the sector or social situation. The same is also true of being Japanese in Japan or Tswana in Botswana. All social groups maintain a view of what's typical: those who are different – such as redheads, 'weird' personalities or unattractive people – draw attention and could be disadvantaged if we aren't careful. It's commendable that the left has brought attention to this, for a good society should seek to minimize sources of bias while recognizing that until 'normal' is abolished (which is impossible because of bell-curve distributions of height, looks and other traits) society will always need to work against biases towards those in the tails of the distributions. The problem is that left-modernism has established racial inequality as an outrage rather than one dimension – and not generally the most important – of the problem of inequality. If racial inequality is one facet of inequality, it should be considered alongside other aspects such as income, health, weight or age. To focus the lion's share of attention on race and gender disparities entrenches 'inequality privilege', wherein those who suffer from low-visibility disadvantages are treated less fairly than those who fit totemic left-modernist categories. A white male who is short, disabled, poor and unattractive will understandably resent the fact his disadvantage is downplayed while he is pilloried for his privilege.

Reducing cultural inequality is an important goal but not an absolute one. Sometimes inequality is egregious and simple to resolve, like ending slavery or racial discrimination in law. But we have picked this low-hanging fruit. Today's cultural disadvantages rarely consist of a simple injustice requiring immediate restitution by whatever means necessary. Like measures to reduce income inequality, there is a downside to redistribution. One cost is efficiency: Somerville College at

Oxford University moved to unisex bathrooms in January 2018, which is fairer as it doesn't discriminate against non-binary individuals. But it means fewer people are processed, so queues are longer for all. Similarly, strict racial or gender quotas may result in lower-quality candidates in fields such as computer science where the minority or female applicant pool is small.

There are other costs to cultural egalitarianism. The drive to purify language of putatively offensive speech reduces expressive liberty. If it closes off avenues of enquiry – such as research prioritizing culture over power and economics; or work challenging the 'blank slate' approach to human nature – it reduces human rationality. Finally, when majority ethnic groups, men or other advantaged categories are prevented from developing their culture and identity, there is a cost to community. If this leads to resentments which drive populism, this polarizes the nation. Therefore, as with the equity–efficiency tradeoff in economics, the drive towards cultural equality carries costs in terms of liberty, rationality, equality and community. These must be weighed against gains to ensure the greatest good of the greatest number, while leaving nobody below a minimum level.

The appropriate policy response is similar to the way we currently approach the economy: a compromise between equity and efficiency, between those who seek more redistribution of wealth to ameliorate inequality and those who argue that government spending crowds out investment. Discussion is guided by a rational evaluation of costs and benefits. If ending any trace of racial discrimination requires racial employment quotas in all sectors and strict racial income equality, alongside restrictions on any speech which the most sensitive member of a minority group might construe as racist, the price is too high and we have to settle for an imperfect outcome in the short run. Unobtrusive measures such as anonymizing CVs or abolishing interviews are less costly than imposing quotas – though I would not rule the latter out if equity gains from these measures were repeatedly demonstrated to be large. We cannot expect racial equality to occur overnight, but it can remain an important social goal, much like reducing income inequality.

By contrast, if racial inequality is a sacred value, anything less than perfect equality is a profane, deviant outrage – not subject to policy tradeoffs and rational discussion. This is especially problematic when those making the case for inequality eschew a scientific method based on measurement and variable-centred logic in favour of ethereal concepts such as structural oppression or 'systemic' racism. Historic structures are real. As Arthur Stinchcombe, a sociologist, explains, historicist causation occurs when the outputs of a system become its inputs, reproducing the system through time. Power holders in the Catholic church in France in the 1600s devoted resources to disseminating their values and selecting people who believed in those values into powerful positions. Catholic institutions ensured it was in the interest of ambitious French people to be devout Catholics.[56] These causes and effects can be measured and evaluated over time. White structures of oppression in the Deep South in the 1950s left measurable fingerprints everywhere: segregated water fountains, underfunded black schools, laws against intermarriage and racist attitudes in surveys.

Indicators of structures of white oppression have largely disappeared, so left-modernists argue that racism is now 'hidden', offering racial income disparities or anecdotal evidence to back up their claims. The meaning of racism has also expanded. Nick Haslam, a psychologist, uses the term 'concept creep' to refer to the widening remit of psychological concepts such as abuse, bullying, mental disorder and prejudice. The last is especially germane in that cognate terms such as white supremacy, racism, violence and refugee have been applied more broadly in order to make moral claims to marginalize competing arguments. Some even include patriotism and capitalism under the 'racist' rubric. There are two issues at work here. First, whether it makes empirical sense to engage in what Giovanni Sartori, a political scientist, calls 'conceptual stretching'. Second, whether it makes ethical sense to apply a morally charged label such as racism to new sets of phenomena, expanding the scope of a taboo and collapsing the distance between serious and minimal harm. Matters have clearly gone too far when opposing affirmative action and questioning the continued pervasiveness of racism is operationalized by social psychologists as 'symbolic racism'.[57] Social scientists have also developed measures like 'racial resentment', which recently have been shown simply to tap resentment of laziness among those of all races.[58]

Arguments based on critical race theory, history or income differences do not constitute rigorous evidence of a structure of white privilege. Too often proponents make unfalsifiable claims which intimate that white privilege is engraved into the soul of society. Without contemporary evidence, such arguments cannot be distinguished from, for example, the view that Protestant discrimination against Catholics, which runs through most of American history, is an ineradicable feature of American life. Historic structures may persist, they may have led to countervailing structures working in the opposite direction, or may simply have ceased to operate. These are competing hypotheses which need to be tested. Claims that language is power can also be evaluated empirically. Those who wish to make this case should conduct replicable experiments in which a sample of white respondents is split into those who are exposed to politically correct and un-PC language to see if this significantly affects their attitudes, biases or behaviour.

A scientific way to assess discrimination is to run field experiments. This means sending two identical applications to a job, with only the name or picture changed, to look for a difference in callback rates. An important field study in Boston and Chicago found that an applicant with a white-sounding name needed to apply to ten jobs to get a callback compared to applicants with African-American-sounding first names such as Lakisha and Jamal who had to apply to fifteen to get a callback. This represents a 50 per cent discrimination gap.[59] However, this could be because stereotypical African-American first names carry lower-class connotations, similar to a lower-class white name like Jimmy Bob. A replication which removes class-inflected first names finds no evidence of anti-black discrimination, but one can legitimately question the study's claim that there are recognizable black surnames.[60] On the other hand, there is no disputing the fact that those with Muslim names applying to jobs in European countries are discriminated against – all studies show a callback penalty.[61] These results provide powerful evidence that discrimination exists, though it would be useful to run experiments which can better separate the distinct effects of name and appearance since many African-Americans have white-sounding names. One study found, for instance, that French employers favour black Senegalese with French-Christian names over black Senegalese with Muslim names.[62]

Broadly speaking, the studies show that employment discrimination against Muslims and the over-fifties is the most serious problem, followed by discrimination against the obese and then blacks.[63] Rectification should involve foregrounding the results of rigorous experiments such as these in bias training, as well as using CV anonymization and other nudge techniques wherever possible. I wouldn't rule out targets, but these shouldn't move ahead of evidence on effect size from replicated experiments or multiple regression analyses that have survived attempts at refutation. After all, there are many reasons for racial disparities, whether we are speaking of the over-representation of Jews in nationalism studies (three others in my subdiscipline share my surname!) or the under-representation of Somali Britons in the boardroom. To enact quotas for some groups may lead to discrimination against others, such as Asian Americans at Ivy League universities.

Those with immigrant or black names are discriminated against, as the experiments show. This is an important problem. But is immigrant or black underprivilege the same as white privilege? Proving the case requires a study which shows John Wong or Mike Hernandez receive fewer callbacks than John Smith. My guess is that work hasn't been done because researchers suspect nothing will turn up. More importantly, field studies haven't found that whites discriminate more than other groups do. If Asian and Hispanic taxi drivers or recruiters discriminate against blacks as much as whites do (i.e. anti-black discrimination among the almost entirely non-white pool of Los Angeles taxi drivers), or if blacks and whites discriminate equally against Muslims, then it's problematic to attach a white-male label to the problem. [64] When the available studies show that black officers are just as likely to shoot black suspects and more likely to arrest them than white officers, we need to question simplistic majority–minority interpretations. [65] If those of all races share an equal responsibility for dismantling stereotypes and questioning biases, then the white-male shaming conducted by Equality and Diversity officers at Google or Evergreen State College represents a left-modernist animus rooted in sacred values, not evidence. A collaborative approach which acknowledged the complexity and mutuality of the problem would win wider support.

Overzealous liberal norm-policing is contributing to a toxic, polarizing atmosphere. It's time to bring our norms under control. Surely humanity has reached the point in its development where it requires a moral jurisprudence to accompany the rational deliberation which refines the application of our law. Law and norms are related, but perform different functions. Norms lack legal teeth but can enforce crippling social sanctions. Yet the way our norms function today is pretty much unchanged from hunter-gatherer days: taboos are established in a Hobbesian manner in which the powerful and ideologically committed set the tone. Conservative and liberal elites have, over the years, manipulated society's red lines to protect their cherished values from rational debate. I'd love to see a politically balanced online task force use rigorous studies of harm, principles of political philosophy and analytic logic to judge high-profile accusations of norm violation. They could decide which statements and actions contravene social norms, and comment on how severe the social sanctions should be based on logical consistency and evidence. Such judgements wouldn't have force of law, but could serve as a reference point for the wrongly accused to contest their excommunication or for norm violators to be properly shamed. As an impartial voice, the task force might be able to change the conversation and win backing on both left and right, reducing polarization. Such a process could tame our anarchic moral universe that has, since the dawn of man, exacted an enormous cost in human life and happiness.

THE MULTICULTURAL MIRAGE

One of the cornerstones of contemporary left-modernism is the belief that ethno-demographic change will produce a new millennium of racial equality. Ta-Nehisi Coates makes the argument that African-Americans will never be fairly treated by American society. After Coates discussed his pessimistic book *Between the World and Me* on Jon Stewart's *The Daily Show*, Stewart asked Coates whether America's changing demographics might rectify things. Coates said little would change, whereupon Stewart replied, 'I hope you're wrong.' This episode provides a useful glimpse into the left-modernist belief system. For adherents like Stewart, the decline of white America and its replacement by a Guyana-style mixture of minorities portends a bright future of racial equality. The underlying premise is that whites are incurable oppressors whereas new groups unencumbered by racism will treat blacks fairly. But is there any evidence that African-Americans will do better in a multicultural America than the current one?

Left-modernism's power-centric worldview posits that a higher minority share will lead to a more equitable form of politics, support for progressivism and less racial inequality. Yet a larger share of minorities and smaller white population means the whites that remain will become scarcer, increasing the value of their cultural capital as a historic founding group to increase white privilege. Asians and Hispanics may feel fewer obligations to blacks than whites. Casual observation would suggest that being black in diverse San Francisco is not necessarily better than being black in white-majority Fargo. I speculate, so let's look at some evidence. Figure 7.8 examines the relationship between white share and black–white income inequality in American states and Puerto Rico. Diverse Washington, DC, Louisiana and Puerto Rico have high racial inequality, as do non-diverse Minnesota and Wisconsin. On the other hand, white–black inequality is low in both diverse Hawaii and non-diverse Vermont. The change in racial inequality over 2000–2015 is similarly uncorrelated with the decline in white share over that period. There is nothing here to suggest that a more diverse America will offer blacks a better deal. It looks like Coates's account is more realistic than Stewart's.

Perhaps white share needs to fall nationwide in order to enable

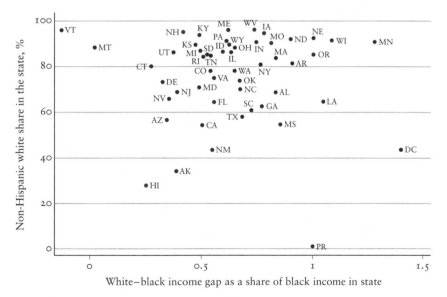

7.8. White share and white–black inequality

Source: US Census 2010. American Community Survey 2015.

minorities to take power and redistribute wealth away from the white oppressor? Yet the story is the same across nations. The Americas-barometer measures respondent's skin colour alongside income, allowing us to gauge racial income inequality across Latin American countries. Are whiter Latin American countries more unequal? Figure 7.9 again shows no relationship. Racial inequality is at rock-bottom in the mostly non-white Dominican Republic, but is also bad in pale-skinned Uruguay. Diverse Panama and whiter Chile or Costa Rica both score well. All of which casts doubt on the millenarian belief that we will attain racial equality when whites are no longer in the majority.

I've performed a similar exercise for the world, looking at whether majority–minority income differences are lower in countries with smaller majorities. Nothing much comes out, though trading minorities of Chinese, South Asians and whites tend to be small and wealthy, which may affect the results. In short, racial inequality is a higher-order property of society maintained by all groups in complex interaction with each other.

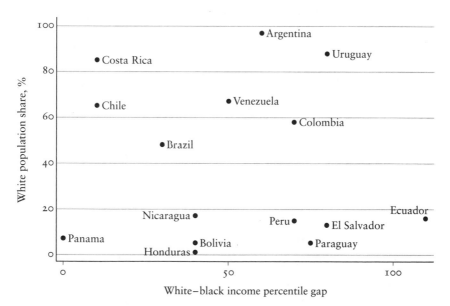

7.9. White income advantage over blacks, Latin America
Adapted from Bailey, S., et al. (2014). "Race, color, and income inequality across the Americas." Demographic Research 31, p. 739. Racial composition by country provided by data from Vanhanen, T. (1999). Ethnic Conflicts Explained by Ethnic Nepotism. Stamford, CT, Jai Press.

Whites' economic advantage – to the extent this exists – is unrelated to their share of the population, thus immigration is no panacea. Inequality must be tackled in its own terms by monitoring everyone's bias and improving policy. Whether whites express and maintain their ethnic identity is tangential to white privilege. Indeed, by antagonizing those who are attached to their white identity, high immigration justified in the name of anti-racism may make it harder to build the progressive coalition that can reduce inequality of all kinds, including race.

LEFT-MODERNISM BEYOND ACADEMIA

The expanded anti-white norm radiates outwards from its nucleus among the minority of scholars in academia who adhere to radical epistemologies. The more this belief system collides with the real world – selling news content, winning votes, competing with other businesses – the more it's forced to moderate. Hence anti-white radicalism fades into what I term 'soft radicalism', an often-restrained Equality and Diversity agenda in centre-left parties, government and corporations. Off-campus, purveyors of New Left ideas are usually less utopian than on it, even if they continue to prioritize race and sex over other aspects of disadvantage. Anti-white radicalism typically only thrives off campus in pockets where countervailing pressures are weak or the political culture strongly favours left-modernism, as in English Canada, the metropolitan US or Sweden.

The extent to which companies will permit left-modernist activism in their human resources departments depends on how much it affects their bottom line. At Google, for instance, the uncompromising Equality and Diversity culture which led the firm to fire James Damore for advancing a carefully reasoned argument about the gender gap in programming – whether one agrees with it or not – carries few costs for this quasi-monopolist. Yet the company is not about to implement quotas. Its activism cannot conceal the fact its workforce is only 4 per cent Hispanic and 2 per cent African-American. Whites, at 56 per cent, are not over-represented, despite the 'mostly white' headlines that tend to follow the release of its human resources reports.[66] Asians make up 35 per cent of Google staff and have been steadily eroding white share despite forming just 5 per cent of the US population. Yet their sevenfold over-representation is not a news item. As with debates over affirmative action, Asian over-representation doesn't easily fit the narrative of white privilege.[67]

THE 'RELIGION OF ANTIRACISM' AND NATIONAL IDENTITY

The 1960s witnessed, understandably, a romantic mythologization of the anti-racist project. The Civil Rights Movement's achievements are a great success and deserve to be lionized. But this legitimate avant-garde identity mutated into a more proactive creed focused on the irretrievably fallen white, male 'other'. Anti-racism morphed from an evidence-based policy resting on violations of negative 'do unto others' liberalism into a sacred value promoting positive liberalism. This represents a shift from a liberalism which accepts a variety of competing life plans – ethnic, religious, cosmopolitan – to one which enjoins minorities to be ethnic and whites to be cosmopolitan. Whites must not just tolerate diversity, a hallmark of negative liberalism, but celebrate it.

This subtle shift from negative to positive liberalism occurred suddenly in the mid-1960s. Indirectly shaped by Randolph Bourne's ideas of a half-century earlier, sixties multiculturalism was a more strident, ambitious and large-scale application of Bourne's double-standard of applauding the Jew who 'sticks to his faith' while urging the WASP to leave his culture behind and become a cosmopolitan.[68] The New Left took Bourne's rebellious experimental progressivism and electrified it with a moralistic charge. His cosmopolitan modernism was married to an expanded definition of racism in which whites' attachment to their identity would be treated not as regrettable parochialism but as an outrageous violation of sacred values. In Canada, for instance, Native peoples and minorities are encouraged to adopt an uncritical romantic ethno-traditionalism while whites are urged to reject a white identity and celebrate diversity. Only in this way can we understand the ethical U-turns of Anglo-Canadian liberals like Governor-General David Johnston or Hal Niedzviecki.

The post-1960s cultural earthquake went on to shape the official version of national identity in several Western countries. The left-modernist dream of multiculturalism emerged as the state religion, ushering in competition between multicultural 'missionary nations' such as English-speaking Canada, Sweden, Australia and Germany. Moral imperatives reconfigured national identity. Each country had a distinct reason for embracing multiculturalism. The decline of empire loyalism in Canada, Australia and New Zealand in the 1950s and 1960s created a vacuum at the heart of national identity which multiculturalism was well placed to fill.

British loyalism had been especially important in English-speaking Canada due to a long-standing identity crisis caused by the Americans, who are culturally similar but ideologically distinct. An index of the relative power of British Unionism in Canada is the key role played by the loyalist Orange Order, a Protestant-Unionist fraternity brought to Canada by Irish immigrants. The Orange association furnished four Prime Ministers and numerous provincial premiers as well as many city mayors until the 1950s. It was up to ten times as powerful – on a per capita basis – in Canada than in Australasia. Membership began to fall after the First World War, but rebounded after 1945 and began its steady decline only from the 1950s. The collapse of the country's 200-year tradition of empire loyalism left a hole in the English-Canadian identity, offering fertile soil for multiculturalism.[69]

In Europe, Germany's desire to bury its history of twentieth-century militarism and racism rendered its elites, especially the '68er generation, more receptive to multiculturalism and European unity. Sweden's predominantly social-democratic elite had influenced the character of official national identity in a progressive direction by the 1960s so was more open to new currents of progressive thought like multiculturalism. The extent to which multiculturalism shaped national identity and public policy in a given country is a matter of degree: France partly resisted it due to the republican tradition, but, even there, aspects of New Left discourse – such as guilt over white colonialism and racism – were important for progressives, informing proclamations such as 'Droit à la différence'.[70]

Regardless of national history, the rise of left-modernism in the high culture prompted an attack on majority ethnicity. For settler societies, this meant a dual focus on aboriginals as dispossessed natives and non-white immigrants as a welcome source of diversity who experience discrimination. In Australia, it's common for progressives to preface their talks by thanking the local aboriginal tribe as the 'rightful owners of the land', and this was also a demand of the Evergreen State protesters. In 1998, Australia formalized white repentance in the form of a 'National

Sorry Day'.[71] Genocide against aboriginal peoples is important to expose, but this needs to be contextualized. As Jared Diamond outlines in *Guns, Germs and Steel*, agriculturalists have replaced hunter-gatherers – mainly due to differences in immunity to animal-borne diseases – throughout human history. This is as true of the Bantu cattle-herding ancestors of African-Americans, who largely wiped out the indigenous pygmy and San peoples of Central and Southern Africa, as it is of Europeans in the New World. We also know that the chance of being violently killed is ten times higher in hunter-gatherer societies than in agricultural civilizations.[72] On the Great Plains, the Comanche were able to master the Western technology of horsemanship before white settlement and used this to brutally conquer other Amerindian groups, nearly wiping out the Apache. None of which means today's Comanches should feel ashamed of their identity and dwell on the foibles of their ancestors. A balanced perspective which acknowledges positives and negatives of Western settlement rather than a 'social-justice' lens narrowly focused on white original sin would be considerably truer to the facts.

It may also be the case that, as McWhorter writes for African-Americans, the focus on white guilt removes a sense of agency from aboriginal groups, worsening their plight. Victim status may bring lower resilience and worse social outcomes. As Greg Lukianoff and Jonathan Haidt point out, the ideology of victimhood elevates precisely those habits of mind – such as viewing others' innocent statements as malign or relying on emotional reasoning ('I feel it, it must be true') – which produce depression and anxiety. Cognitive behavioural therapy (CBT) is explicitly designed to correct such neuroses through building resilience, yet left-modernist ideology seems intent on doing the opposite.[73] It's certainly the case that the severe problems of suicide and substance abuse among Canadian and Australian aboriginal peoples haven't improved since the 1960s. Anti-Western tropes can also be used by developing-world politicians like Robert Mugabe who leaned on postcolonial leftist arguments to deflect attention from his misdeeds.

The French philosopher Pascal Bruckner views white guilt as a trope that appeals to whites' narcissistic desire to keep Europeans at the centre of world affairs, even as demographic, economic and political power flows elsewhere. Everything bad that happens in the world is a result of white actions, past or present. Bruckner ridicules the left-modernist emphasis on victimhood as the fount of moral authority, asking the reader to imagine a schoolyard in which the sins of the fathers are visited on the children. The kids introduce themselves as descendants of slaves or slave traders, colonized peoples or colonizers, bandits or crime victims. They compete to unearth the title-deeds of victimhood from their family histories. Bruckner, despite being Jewish, sees the Holocaust as the West's second Golgotha, 'as if Christ died a second time there'. The new 'penitent state' rewrites history as a series of shameful episodes, with the categories of victim and victimizer producing absolute moral clarity.[74]

The double standard inherent in Bournian multiculturalism lauds subaltern ethnicity while decrying majority ethnicity. *Völkish* native authenticity is championed for aboriginal groups against European migrants to the New World but downplayed for aboriginal Europeans in countries receiving non-European immigrants. There is a logical tension between being a 'nation of immigrants' and supporting aboriginal nativism, which the Canadian Governor-General, David Johnston, stumbled upon. In Europe, no such tension exists because all indigenousness falls foul of left-modernism. This gives a free hand to the 'nation of immigrants' interpretation. Historic waves of invasion are drawn upon as evidence that European countries are immigration nations despite very limited annual inflows through most of their history. Population geneticists find that invasions left only a trace genetic footprint in most European countries compared to the base populations formed from Cro-Magnon aborigines speaking Basque-related dialects and the descendants of agriculturalists from the Middle East who arrived some 9,000 years ago.[75] Middle Easterners settled Europe not long after Asian settlers arrived in the Americas, but the first are deemed immigrants while the second are natives with a spiritual connection to the soil.

Eastern Europe was insulated from left-modernism because it lay behind the Iron Curtain until 1989. Left-modernist ideas had little impact on Eastern Europe's elite culture and institutions, even as the USSR's Cold War propagandists attacked Western countries as racist and imperialist. As a negative liberal and moderate egalitarian, I criticize the lack of support for the rights of minorities like the Roma in these countries while at the same time respecting the way Eastern Europe has avoided the excesses of left-modernism. In ploughing ahead with positive liberalism – in the form of multiculturalism and political correctness – the West is handing the enemies of liberty and equality in the East the ammunition they need to reject reform.

8

Left-Modernism versus
the Populist Right

On 11 August 2017, a group of far-right demonstrators gathered in Charlottesville, Virginia, to protest at the removal of a statue of the Confederate general Robert E. Lee from a city park. The statue was viewed by the city council as an insult to the African-American community because Lee was a champion of the pro-slavery cause during the Civil War. The park itself had been renamed from Lee Park to Emancipation Park two months earlier, not long after a white supremacist gunned down worshippers at a black church in Charleston, South Carolina. Many Confederate statues were erected by white-supremacist southerners in the 1920s during the segregationist Jim Crow era, well after the war. The Confederate cause was unambiguously wrong, so I support removal and would argue that statues should be preserved in museums or private collections for historical purposes. But the group who gathered at the park had other ideas. Their insignia included Klan and Nazi symbols, anti-Semitic signs, as well as Trump's signature 'Make America Great Again' caps. One of their slogans was 'You will not replace us', a reference to the increasingly influential idea that the left, Jewish and liberal elite is pursuing a programme of 'white genocide'.

Leftist counter-protesters arrived in force and clashed with far-right supporters, leaving fourteen people injured. The next day, a far-right sympathizer drove into a crowd of counter-demonstrators, killing one protester, Heather Heyer, and injuring nineteen others. President Trump issued a statement two hours later saying: 'We condemn in the strongest possible terms this egregious display of hatred, bigotry and violence on many sides, on many sides.' He also described some of the pro-Confederate groups as containing 'fine people'. Only later was this qualified by a condemnation of 'violence, bigotry, and hatred. Of course that includes white supremacists, KKK, Neo-Nazi and all extremist groups.' Trump argued that his comments reflected the fact that the far-right demonstration was legal while the counter-demonstration was not. Much of the media and many politicians struck back, claiming the counter-protesters' cause was ethical while the far-right's wasn't, and this was an important difference. Moreover, the fatality was on the counter-demonstrators' side. Trump's strategist Steve Bannon was accused of being behind the strategy of drawing a moral equivalence between the rival groups.[1] In polling conducted after the event, whites, by a 59–18 margin, blamed the far right for the violence; however those who backed Trump said by a 35–27 margin that the counter-demonstrators were at fault.[2] A non-binary question discovered a more even picture: 31 per cent said both sides were responsible, 28 per cent said white supremacists were, and 10 per cent blamed the anti-fascist left.[3]

In this chapter we'll observe what happens when left-modernism and a rising ethno-traditional nationalism collide. The events at Charlottesville are important because they brought increasingly assertive left-modernist and white-nationalist activists into direct conflict. These are actors in a larger drama involving, on the one hand, surging left-modernist protests on campus and in cities; and, on the other, growing white consciousness and anti-immigration politics. The institutionalization of left-modernism led to a successful attempt to expand the meaning of racism to encompass new policy areas, permitting social norms to curtail discussion of particular issues.[4]

Left-modernist ideas which enjoyed a fairly steady march through elite institutions between the 1960s and the 1990s have begun to encounter significant nationalist resistance. This initially took the form of populist-right agitation and attacks from right-wing provocateurs like Milo Yiannopoulus, but is now also coming from mainstream parties, liberal scholars and the media. Institutional norms of anti-racism rested in part on the economist Timur Kuran's notion of preference falsification, in which people believe others observe a norm, so follow suit.[5] When a moral narrative starts to be challenged, sceptics realize others share their doubts. This has initiated a self-fulfilling process of norm unravelling which has produced a rollback of anti-racist taboos, first over multiculturalism, then over immigration and Islam. It's unclear where the process will stop: I'd argue it has gone too far with respect to Muslims. The rollback in turn stimulates left-modernist attempts to assert normative control in the institutions where they hold sway. Meanwhile the overreach of the left on campus becomes a red flag for the right in the culture wars, leading to growing conservative animus against universities. This is new terrain.

At Charlottesville, the tactics of leftist counter-demonstrators can be criticized; I'd argue their cause was right because slavery is unambiguously evil. However, subsequent attacks on more complex figures like Christopher Columbus show the radical left doesn't make reasonable distinctions between whites who pursued singularly bad causes and those whose legacy combines positive and negative deeds. Soon after Charlottesville, activists branding themselves 'Popular Resistance' damaged the oldest American memorial to Christopher Columbus, over two centuries old, in Baltimore. Filming the event and posting it on YouTube, one of the activists held a sign reading: 'Racism, tear it down'. The scenes recalled ISIS vandalism at Palmyra.

They also reflected an increasing symbolic radicalism. Many cities across the US are in Democratic hands due to their large minority, young and university-educated populations. In recent years, Albuquerque, Portland and St Paul changed their long-standing Columbus Day holidays to 'Indigenous Peoples' Day'. The state of Vermont followed suit in 2017 and New York's mayor, Bill de Blasio, ordered a review of the city's statues and monuments, including the statue at Columbus Circle. Often, radical students are at the centre of these efforts, as in Baltimore itself, where a similar campaign failed.[6]

In response, President Trump defiantly stood up for the Euro-American heritage, speaking to both white identifiers and Americans of all races who value the European tradition: 'Five hundred and twenty-five years ago, Christopher Columbus completed an ambitious and daring voyage across the Atlantic Ocean to the Americas . . . The permanent arrival of Europeans to the Americas was a transformative event that . . . changed the course of human history and set the stage for the development of our great Nation.' The speech did not mention Native Americans, incurring the ire of liberal outlets like CNN, who retorted: 'Never mind the disease and slavery wrought by Christopher Columbus' voyage.' At this, Pat Buchanan enthused about the president's 'In-your-face defiance of the dictates of political correctness [which] has solidified Trump's base behind him.'[7]

Trump also lauded Columbus's Italian heritage, and some Italian-Americans defended Columbus as an ethnic hero. This carried some weight, illustrating the power of subaltern 'ethnic' narratives to leverage the multiculturalism which prevails in American high culture. This was in tune with the mood of many across the country, for whom the attacks on Columbus statues were extremely unpopular. Even when it comes to Confederate monuments, just 27 per cent of Americans call for their removal compared to 54 per cent who want them to stay.[8] President Trump echoed this view, arguing against removal just because these figures were slaveholders. 'Robert E. Lee, Stonewall Jackson – who's next, Washington and Jefferson?' he tweeted on 17 August 2017. The spate of progressive local initiatives and the president's tweet reveal an intense political clash between conservative and progressive interpretations of the American past that is rising to the surface of politics. The important distinction between the legacies of Lee and Washington is obscured on both sides.

The positive feedback loop between left-wing and right-wing radicals seems to have begun with left-modernist success in institutionalizing political correctness. This built up a fund of conservative grievances, with surveys showing PC to be unpopular among a majority of Americans. The vanguard of the politically correct movement on college campuses dates from the late 1980s, but has been amplified by social media and online forums since the early 2010s.

Google searches for 'racist' and 'sexist' begin rising in late 2009, while searches for 'white privilege', 'whitesplaining', 'homophobic', 'transphobic' and 'microaggression' begin to rise in 2012–13 and take off during 2014–15, prior to Trump's arrival on the scene. Bradley Campbell and Jason Manning document the efflorescence of the new progressive crusade against microaggressions in their 2014 paper and subsequent book.[9] Meanwhile, Zach Goldberg's work shows that consumption of social media and online websites soared, and appeared to be exerting a radicalizing effect on liberal whites' opinions on race, sex and gender. In 2008, about 30 per cent of white liberals and conservatives got their news online, but by 2016 liberals were skewing online, with some 60 per cent acquiring their news content this way compared to only 40 per cent for conservatives and moderates. Meanwhile, the share of white liberals who visited the left-wing sites *Buzzfeed* or

Huffington Post in ANES data jumped from 15 to 34 per cent between 2012 and 2016. White liberals who regularly visited these sites were 60 per cent more likely to view sex and race discrimination as a problem than white liberals who didn't.

Social media use was also rising quickly, from about 45 per cent of respondents to 75 per cent between 2010 and 2016. White liberals who sent Facebook or Twitter posts on any political topic were over twice as likely to perceive racial or sexual discrimination as a problem in America than white liberals who didn't. The combined radicalizing effect of online news and social media is noteworthy. Between 2009 and 2016, the perception that blacks, Hispanics and women were being discriminated against jumped among white liberals during a period when minorities and women were reporting record low (and falling) levels of harassment, discrimination and hate crime. In 2009, just 20 per cent of white liberals thought there was 'a lot' of or 'a little' discrimination against African-Americans, rising to 40 per cent in 2012 and nearly 80 per cent in 2016. For discrimination against Hispanics the increase in the same period was from 30 to 42 to 50 per cent, and for discrimination against women it rocketed up from 20 per cent in 2011 to 25 per cent in 2012 and 45 per cent in 2016. Meanwhile surveys picked up a 50 per cent increase in white liberal support for affirmative action, warmer feelings towards minorities and illegal immigrants, and a cooler attitude towards whites.[10]

In effect, the 2010s represent a renewed period of left-modernist innovation, incubated by near-universal left–liberal hegemony among non-STEM faculty and administrators. Most academics are moderate liberals rather than radical leftists, but in the absence of conservative or libertarian voices willing to stand against left-modernist excess, liberal saturation reduced resistance to the japes of extremist students and professors. Social media and progressive online news acted as a vector, carrying the new left-modernist awakening off-campus much more effectively than was true during the first wave of political correctness of the late 1980s and 1990s.

High-volume real-time interaction between fervent, often anti-intellectual, partisans of right and left increased substantially. First, Trump's emergence in 2015 seems to have functioned as a force multiplier for left-modernism. Second, the expansion of social media and online sites allows contending forces to invade others' echo chambers, increasing direct conflict in comment threads and ramping up the temperature of the culture war. Angela Nagle finds that leftist radicalism emerged first, attracting a far-right response. One of the first to trace the emergence of this polarizing dynamic, she shows how, in left-modernist online chat groups, those who stake outlandish claims about white male oppression win moral and social plaudits. These in turn are lampooned by the alt-right, who leverage left-modernist excesses to legitimate blatant racism and sexism. This begins a cycle of polarizing rhetorical confrontation. Alt-right message boards adopt a playful countercultural style, emphasizing their rebellion against a stifling, puritanical-left establishment.[11] Whereas bohemians like the Young Intellectuals of the 1910s and 1920s lauded African-American jazz and immigrant conviviality as a riposte to an uptight Prohibitionist Anglo-Protestant culture, the alt-right champions white maleness as a liberation from the strictures of the puritanical left.

The anti-racism taboo represents the successful institutionalization of liberal and left-modernist ideas, but the scope of the taboo is eroding or under challenge in most Western societies. 'We have erected a whole series of taboos that we cannot debate without being immediately described as incendiary,' announced Laurent Wauquiez, aspiring leader of the French centre-right Les Républicains in October 2017. 'The nation, massive immigration, identity, the transmission of values, Islamism.'[12] Wauquiez's attempt to steal the populist right's clothing was a promising technique whose worth has been proven by the success of other centre-right leaders in capturing these voters, including Mark Rutte in the Netherlands, Sebastian Kurz in Austria and Theresa May in Britain. For our purposes, what jumps out is Wauquiez's politicization of the term 'taboo', a frequent refrain of conservative politicians going back to Pim Fortuyn in the Netherlands and William Hague in Britain in the early 2000s. This is true even on the left, where some, like David Blunkett in Britain and Bernie Sanders in America, have criticized political correctness.

Taboos are underpinned by both negative and positive liberalism. While negative liberalism delimits a narrower scope for the anti-racism taboo focusing on verbal attacks on minorities, positive liberalism seeks to expand the definition of racism to protect symbolic policies such as multiculturalism and large-scale immigration. When politicians decide what to campaign on and voters think about how they'll vote, they may suppress their desire for greater ethnic homogeneity to adhere to the anti-racism norm. In terms of evolutionary psychology, this pits whites' tribal drive to protect the group, i.e. the white majority, against their religious instinct to adhere to a sacred anti-racist moral code. The result is what social psychologists term the 'dual-process' model, in which decisions are the product of a tension between tribal and moral motivations.[13]

Figure 8.1 maps the retreating sway of anti-racism taboos since the 1990s. It depicts the front lines in the battle between voicing and repressing various forms of nationalist anxiety. The outer ring of the circle, multiculturalism, was the first liberal taboo to fall. Multiculturalist rhetoric about celebrating diversity was in retreat in continental Europe and on the American right by the 1990s, and in the UK after 2000. Moving inward one ring to immigration, we see that in Europe mainstream politicians and media commentators began to openly call for lower migration levels in the late 1990s and early 2000s. This took much longer in the United States: Trump was the first American post-war politician to call for less *legal* immigration, seeking to halve the numbers from 1 million per year to 500,000. Prior to Trump, there had been a strong presumption in favour of immigration – especially legal – even in the right-wing media. The norm against voicing a desire for lower immigration remains in the so-called 'mainstream' American media, but no longer in right-wing outlets like Fox News.

In Sweden and Germany, the sheer scale of migration during the 2015 Migration Crisis forced governments and the media to discuss limits. As late as 2013, Tobias Billström, immigration minister in the centre-right Moderate Party of Fredrik Reinfeldt, was attacked in the media for suggesting Sweden needed to debate the volume of immigration to the country. Then in 2014 the anti-immigration Sweden Democrats shocked the establishment by winning 13 per cent of the vote. Mainstream politicians had their parliamentary seats unscrewed and moved to avoid sitting next to the upstarts. Politicians vowed never to go into coalition with them. Then came the 2015 Migration Crisis. With the Sweden Democrats polling as high as 20–25 per cent, the centre-left government began scaling back its refugee intake and closed the border with Denmark.

In 2017, the flagging centre-right raised the possibility of going into coalition with the Sweden Democrats. Ahead of the 2018 election, both

left and right now speak openly of numerical reduction. For the political scientist Stig-Björn Ljunggren, 'The big parties are talking about it
[immigration control] more now, trying to reach the electorate and tell
them "we notice your concerns, the Sweden Democrats are not the only
ones trying to handle this or address it".'[14] Meanwhile, in Germany, the
AfD have altered the mood music of mainstream politics. In the wake
of the AfD's rise, the Free Democratic Party, a small pro-business party,
ran on a platform critical of Merkel's refugee policies. Its young leader,
Christian Lindner, was expected to join Merkel's CDU and the Greens
in a coalition that pointedly excluded the AfD. However, in a blow to
tradition, the FDP refused because they were unwilling to back Merkel's
call to permit refugees to settle their families in Germany.[15]

So too on the other side of the world. Following several years of
rapid immigration to New Zealand, the young Labour Party leader,
Jacinda Ardern, announced – despite activists' accusations of racism –
that the party would cut immigration levels from 72,000 to around
40,000. It was an unprecedented move which boosted the party's fortunes and led to a coalition agreement with Winston Peters' anti-
immigration New Zealand First party. This enabled Labour to form
the government in 2017.[16] There are always challengers to taboos on

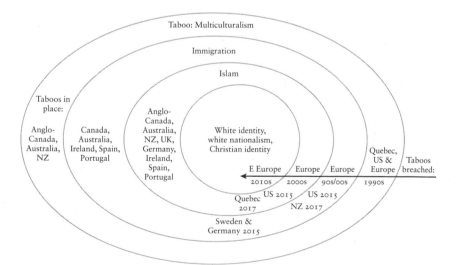

8.1. The erosion of anti-racism taboos in the West, 1990–2017

the fringes of public debate, but in figure 8.1 I try to locate the centre of gravity of acceptable public discourse, or the 'Overton Window'.[17]

Calls to curtail Muslim liberties – banning burqas, restricting the wearing of hijabs in state schools, outlawing the construction of minarets or new mosques – entered the political lexicon in Western Europe in the 2000s. Pim Fortuyn and Geert Wilders in the Netherlands and Marine Le Pen in France were at the front end of the new anti-Islamic politics. In 2004, France clamped down on the wearing of hijabs in state schools. From 2011, France and Belgium banned the burqa, followed by partial bans in the Netherlands in 2015, Switzerland in 2016 and the Canadian province of Quebec in 2017.

The inner sanctum in figure 8.1 consists of anti-racist taboos against expressions of white identity and white or Christian nationalism. This too has been breached, though only in Eastern Europe, where discursive restrictions arguably never existed but failed to surface because of the paucity of immigrants. The stand against accepting Muslim refugees taken by the Visegrád countries – Hungary, the Czech Republic, Slovakia and Poland – during the 2015 Migration Crisis, drew a clear line in the sand. 'Islam has no place in Slovakia,' said the country's leftist Prime Minister, Robert Fico. 'Migrants change the character of our country. We do not want the character of this country to change.'[18] In March 2017, the Hungarian Prime Minister, Victor Orbán, called migration a 'poison', extolled the benefits of 'ethnic homogeneity' and urged his audience to 'keep Europe Christian'.[19] Anti-racist taboos pertaining to immigration had never taken root in these societies, but open ethnic nationalism of this kind from political leaders in the European public sphere had been rare.

MULTICULTURALISM IS NOT DEAD

Despite the breaches of the 1990s and 2000s some countries remain at the outer edge, possessing the full menu of left-modernist taboos. Left-modernist activists had once sought to portray opposition to multiculturalism as morally deviant. This was achieved by defining multiculturalism, a slippery term, in a misleading manner. Multiculturalism can refer to the demographic fact of many groups living in one place or a public policy of recognizing ethnic diversity as the identity of society and a basis for redistribution. Critics from the right and centre contest multiculturalism in its second guise, stressing they do not oppose multi-ethnicity. Left-modernists, by contrast, occlude the definitions in order to paint critics of multiculturalism as monocultural racists.

This discursive strategy has successfully rebuffed challenges to multiculturalism policy in English Canada and, to a lesser extent, in Australia and New Zealand. In 2006, the Australian Treasurer, Peter Costello, decried 'mushy, misguided multiculturalism', adding that sharia law had no place in Australia and urging newcomers to adopt Australian values. This led to considerable criticism from the left. The Prime Minister, John Howard, did not heed the left's calls to censure Costello, but he didn't scrap the country's multiculturalism policy. Only after he left office in 2007 did he mount a direct attack on multiculturalism. In Canada, the Conservative leadership candidate Kellie Leitch's call for immigrants to be screened for 'Canadian values' and her proposal for an anonymous hotline to report forced or underage marriages led critics to brand her a racist in March 2017. One of her challengers claimed she was using the test to keep Muslims out of Canada and that this would brand the Conservatives an 'anti-immigrant party'. The chill effect seems to have worked, since Leitch picked up only 9 per cent of delegates and no other Tory candidates took on multiculturalism.[20]

The immigration taboo also remains in place in both countries: neither Stephen Harper's Conservative government nor mavericks like Leitch or the Ford brothers in Ontario dared breach the Canadian immigration 'consensus' by calling for fewer to be admitted. When the Liberal Prime Minister, Justin Trudeau, increased immigration targets from 260,000 to 340,000 per year in 2017 – equivalent to three times American or West European levels – the Conservatives were only willing to criticize the skill mix, not the numbers. When a commission appointed by Trudeau mooted the idea of accepting a staggering 450,000 immigrants per year – equivalent to a US annual intake of 4–5 million – it only pulled back due, it claimed, to opinion polling. The Conservatives were unwilling to be portrayed as anti-mass immigration despite the preferences of many of their voters.[21] Trudeau isn't the only high-profile Canadian to engage in anti-racist virtue-signalling: a welter of prominent opinion leaders are openly calling for a Canadian population of 100 million by the end of the century.[22]

In Australia, the Prime Minister, Tony Abbott, oversaw the country's tough 'Stop the boats' policy towards refugees in 2013, but – despite pressure from Pauline Hanson on the populist right – did not campaign to reduce legal immigration until he was out of office in February 2018. In Ireland, which has a high foreign-born share but a low Muslim population, anti-immigration politics is in its infancy. Protests from anti-racist groups have greeted attempts to form populist-right parties in the country. Identity Ireland, formed in mid-2015, was accused of being racist and has had its press conferences and meetings disrupted by protesters. In November 2016, the Merrion Hotel in Dublin was forced to cancel a meeting by the fledgling National Party in November 2016. Shane O'Curry of the European Network Against Racism Ireland, which asked followers to lobby the Merrion, hailed this as 'a great day for common sense and humanity'.[23]

Left-modernists in each country promote a missionary form of national identity based on exemplifying multiculturalism. 'The most multicultural country in the world,' is the proudest boast of liberal-left parties in these societies. In the words of the Prime Minister, Justin Trudeau, Canada is a completely new society with 'no core identity [and] no mainstream'. The country is a 'post-national state', he told *The New York Times*.[24] Trudeau's attempt to elevate Canada as the leading exemplar of left-modernism is similar to Iran or Saudi Arabia's competing attempts to style themselves the leading proponent of Islam. In the seventeenth century, France styled itself the 'Eldest Daughter of the Church', defining France's identity as the leading missionary for Catholicism. After 1917 the USSR took its identity not from its history but from a futuristic ideology, as the foremost champion of international socialism. In all cases, exemplifying a millenarian belief system brings glory to the nation and serves as the foundation of its official national identity. This 'quantitative' nationalism emphasizes universalist moral achievements, as opposed to a 'qualitative' nationalism celebrating ethnic uniqueness and historic particularity.

What's difficult to envisage in the current climate is the reintroduction of a taboo after it has been repeatedly transgressed to the point this becomes routine. Might it once again become *verboten* to criticize multiculturalism in Britain or call for fewer immigrants to France? It's difficult to imagine. Like sealskins on skis that run flat downhill but grip going backwards, it's hard to rebuild the climate of preference falsification that sustains a normative order once cracks in its legitimacy have appeared. In the American case, the country's polarized culture means taboos persist on the Democratic side of the political aisle and in much of the mainstream media, but not on the right. It's a stretch to imagine a return to a norm frowning on criticism of current levels of legal immigration on Fox News given the mainstreaming of anti-immigration narratives within it and the GOP.

In other instances, taboos hang on, resisting attacks from the margins. When Pauline Hanson wore a burqa in the Australian Parliament and called for banning it in August 2017 she challenged a taboo, but the media and most politicians remained united, so were able to turn back her insurgent challenge and deter others from following suit. The norm against politicizing immigration may be on the verge of tipping, however. In February 2018, mindful of pressure from One Nation and polls showing a majority of Australians favouring reduced immigration, the ex-Prime Minister Tony Abbott called for the country to reduce its legal intake from 190,000 to 110,000 per year and alleged that the conservative (Liberal Party) Home Affairs minister, Peter Dutton, had raised the subject of a modest reduction with his Prime Minister, Malcolm Turnbull – an allegation Dutton and Turnbull subsequently denied. Abbott went on to accuse the 'talking classes' of betraying the 'working classes' and referenced the rising populist mood in Western countries.[25]

The rise of the populist right has usually been the engine of norm shift. Populist pressure from below has driven political realism and intellectual shifts on multiculturalism and immigration. This is a distinct process from the elite-led institutionalization of negative liberalism from the 1960s which did a lot of good before overreaching in the direction of positive liberalism. Consider the outer ring of the circle consisting of support for multiculturalism – the idea of recognizing ethnic diversity and defining the nation on the basis of difference. This was the first left-modernist redoubt to give way and has since faded across Europe. The rise of the populist right in Western Europe after 1987 led centre-right politicians to move away from officially celebrating diversity. This dragged centre-left parties and intellectuals in the same direction, such that many began to prioritize integration over difference by the late 1990s. Indeed, a counter-mood emerged across Europe in the 2000s making it nearly impossible for national leaders to advocate multiculturalism and be taken seriously.[26] The comment by the German Chancellor, Angela Merkel, that multiculturalism had 'failed, utterly failed' in 2010 marked its death knell.[27] Only among mayors of diverse cities like London does it remain a mantra.[28]

Something similar took place for immigration. The populist right's coalitions with the centre-right in Austria, Norway, the Netherlands, Denmark and Italy in the late 1990s and early 2000s placed immigration squarely on the political agenda, defying previous attempts to erect a cordon sanitaire around populist-right parties and the immigration question.[29] The populist right's continued success and the rise of Islamist terrorism in the 2000s consolidated a new norm permitting the overt politicization of immigration. A Dutch journalist, Kustaw Bessems, persuasively argues that the taboo against criticizing immigration in the Netherlands has now altered its charge to frown on those favouring immigration.[30] Later in the 2000s it became permissible to target Muslims, campaign to ban conservative Islamic dress and prohibit minarets or mosques. While I endorse the dismantling of left-modernist taboos against criticizing immigration and multiculturalism, many of the proposals regarding Muslims cross a negative-liberal red line, which should be resisted.

Moral norms may shift gradually or suddenly give way. With multiculturalism, politicians like David Blunkett of Britain's Labour Party recall having to fend off radical activists as early as the mid-1980s: 'As leader of Sheffield council 30 years ago, I had to slap down well-meaning equality officers who wanted the local authority and the schools (which were much closer to the local authority then) to avoid using words such as "blackboard": this was so patently ridiculous that a stand needed to be taken, to make the opposite point that we did not help race relations by irritating the populace as a whole and by creating absurdities.'[31] Nevertheless, Labour paid lip service to multiculturalism with Tony Blair's victory in 1997. Robin Cook's invocation of chicken tikka as an archetypal British dish and the party's commissioning of the Parekh Report in 2000 signalled this new direction. Labour's backpedalling after media reaction to the Parekh Report led it to swing sharply against left-modernism, suddenly removing the stigma of racism that had surrounded elite expressions of British nationalism.

THE RETURN OF THE REPRESSED

The erosion of left-modernist control of the bounds of acceptable debate over immigration can set off the spiral of populist-right mobilization illustrated in figure 8.2. First, opposing immigration and voting for right-wing populists becomes less toxic, permitting more people to vote for these parties without incurring a guilt or shame penalty. This further erodes the anti-racist norm, reducing guilt even more, increasing support for such parties once again, in a self-fulfilling spiral. The rise of the populist right and unravelling of political correctness proceed hand in hand until the supply of psychological conservatives and authoritarians – which is finite – is exhausted. In some cases, like the United States, attempts to defend taboos may even backfire, further fuelling the populist right.

The Trump vote proved a demonstration of the model in figure 8.2. Prior to the vote, a significant portion of white Americans were reluctant to admit they wanted fewer immigrants to enter the country. This is illustrated by list experiments which permit respondents to remain anonymous. List experiments involve a survey which is split in two groups of respondents. People filling out the survey in each group indicate how many statements on the list they agree with. In one case the immigration question is included in the list, and on the other it is asked as a separate question from the list. When you indicate the number of

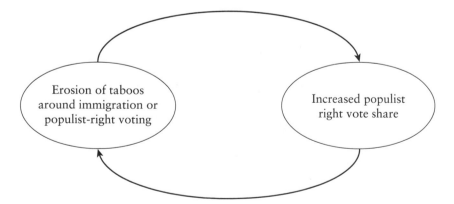

8.2. The spiral of populist-right mobilization

statements you agree with, you aren't revealing which statements you support, so your answers to the immigration question are concealed. The average of the first list can be compared with answers to the average of the second list plus the free-standing immigration question. Using this technique, the sociologist Alexander Janus discovered that 60 per cent of white Americans supported cutting immigration to zero when their identities were concealed by the list. The comparable figure for the open question of wanting immigration cut to zero was just 39 per cent. University graduates were far more likely to conceal than those without degrees.[32] Anonymity releases individuals from the shame of taboo violation, increasing their stated opposition to immigration and support for the populist right. Joshua Gordon, a political scientist at Simon Fraser University, shows that the share of Canadians willing to say there are too many immigrants and visible minorities doubled to over 40 per cent when the polling firm EKOS altered its methodology from face-to-face to anonymous online surveys.[33]

Populist success can similarly draw shy supporters out of the woodwork. An experiment by Leonardo Bursztyn and his colleagues found that 54 per cent of Americans were prepared to donate to an anti-immigration organization associated with maintaining a white majority if their anonymity was assured. This dropped to 34 per cent among those told that researchers might contact them in a follow-up. Soon after Trump's victory, however, the difference between the open and anonymous conditions fell away, suggesting Trump's win had altered social norms, making it more respectable to express anti-immigration attitudes.[34]

If this is the case, the left's quest to widen the definition of racism and harness guilt and shame to repress criticism of immigration can be said to have worked well between the mid-1960s and 1990s. Is the left's best strategy to fight any norm erosion, conceding no ground? Should its aim be to continue to push the boundaries of anti-racism as far as possible within its strongholds – academia, schools, Hollywood – and pressure centrist institutions like social democratic parties and the mainstream media? Possibly. In studies of ethnic civil war, state repression does limit violent secession.[35] Xinjiang, for example, is unlikely to mount a successful secession from China because of overwhelming Chinese military dominance over the Uighurs.

The danger zone, however, lies in the middle, when repression falters, perhaps due to external factors like the American invasion of Iraq, which opened the door to secessionist groups like the Kurds. During periods of repression, rebels consolidate their networks and identity, and coalesce into organizations. When the opportunity arises, they are poised to act.[36] When repression lifts and full democratization ensues, society is more likely to become peaceful, but in the transition period things may get rocky. This is also why authoritarian states like North Korea are more internally calm than semi-democracies like Côte d'Ivoire.[37]

Repression can also contain secessionist movements, but its apparent success may prove short-lived. Which is more effective, Britain's strategy of permitting the Scots to hold a referendum on independence or Spain's technique of suppressing a Catalan independence vote? There is a risk Scotland will leave, but permitting a vote allows people to have their say and can begin the process of reducing separatist sentiment. In Quebec, after a very close independence vote in 1995, support for it has sagged into the low 30s and not recovered. Support for Scottish independence is also on the back foot after the vote. There are no guarantees, but a repression strategy is more likely to manufacture grievance, driving more Catalans to the independence banner and leading to a greater long-run risk of secession.

With this paradigm in mind, I argue that a moral-repression strategy for containing white conservative discontent, if perceived as an illegitimate overreach, could result in blowback at a later date. How might this happen? Figure 8.3 shows that expanding anti-racism norms allows high immigration and multiculturalism policies. Few conservative and authoritarian voters directly experience campus political correctness, but its outriders reach them through the liberal policies that an expansive anti-racist norm enables. Political correctness initially inhibits white conservative grievances, populist-right voting and centre-right mobilization against immigration and multiculturalism. However, once the populist right breaks across a threshold, the system shifts. Populist-right success leads the centre-right to adopt anti-immigration policies, which in turn weakens the hold of taboos. Once this occurs, political correctness, instead of acting as a brake on white conservative grievance and populist-right voting, is exposed and can propel populism to greater heights. At the very least, anti-racist repression becomes a mixed blessing. The risk here is that the illegitimate expansion of the anti-racist norm is rolled back to the point that legitimate anti-racist

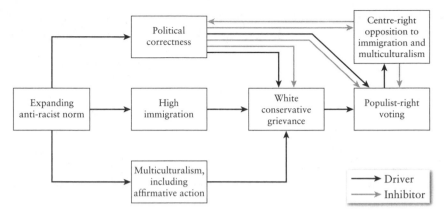

8.3. Expanding anti-racism norms allows high-immigration and multiculturalism policies

norms come under attack. We see this already in the new anti-Muslim laws and political rhetoric.

Nowhere has political correctness become as important a recruiting sergeant for the populist right as in the United States. Left-modernist excesses on campus now routinely make headlines, exposing the fundamentalist core of a belief system which many Americans only experience in watered-down form, such as the multilingual Coca-Cola commercial during the 2014 Super Bowl or requests to press '2' for Spanish. Second, the emerging right-wing media is focusing on political correctness as a key front in the 'culture wars' against their left-liberal antagonists. At Evergreen, the clip of students verbally assaulting Bret Weinstein spread like wildfire across conservative and alt-right social media. Weinstein was interviewed on Tucker Carlson's 'Campus Craziness' segment on Fox News and on the right-leaning Dave Rubin show on YouTube, incurring the ire of Weinstein's liberal colleagues. Far-right social media trolls stormed the Facebook accounts of identifiable left-wing students and racially abused Evergreen Equality and Diversity administrators, engaging in the practice known as doxxing, by which individuals' personal details are exposed on far-right websites. A right-wing group, Patriot Prayer, came to the university, clashing with anarchists on campus.[38] The conservative response to political correctness, more than the ideas themselves, is what's new about the late 2010s. Nothing of this kind occurred in the 1980s and 1990s.

An irreverent Mexican-American blogger and Sanders supporter, Greg Scorzo, describes a new online free-speech counter-culture which has arisen in response to left-modernist excess:

> The new counter-culture is about social media, memes, and music which is distributed through Facebook, soundcloud, itunes, and Spotify . . .This new counter-culture isn't really a youth culture, even though it contains many young figures. In fact, it mostly lampoons angry young left-wing activists, portraying them as entitled, pampered, and censorious bigots. What is perhaps most shocking about this counter-culture is its lampooning is largely justified.[39]

The storm of activity by left-modernists on campus also seems to be accompanied by activity on the alt-right. Figure 8.4 shows trends in the frequency of the use of the leftist slogan 'white privilege' and alt-right meme 'white genocide' on Google since 2011. 'White privilege' is searched for much more often (as the un-normalized data would show), but the growth pattern for the two terms is similar. A plausible hypothesis is that the perceived erosion of the anti-racist norm prompted a reaction from the fundamentalist left while Trump's emergence emboldened the alt-right.

Political correctness is now a staple of right-wing media discourse in

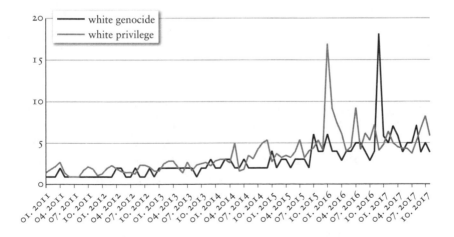

8.4. Mention of terms in Google Trends (US), 2011–17, as ratio of 2010 mentions

both the US and Britain. Campus Reform, a conservative US website, reports on incidents of intolerance perpetrated by left-modernist students, faculty and administrators. These infractions have provided oxygen to right-wing online stars like Milo Yiannopoulus, Ben Shapiro, Mike Cernovich, Anne Coulter and others. Campus Republican groups regularly invite these controversial speakers, knowing they will fuel protests, exposing radical-left intolerance. As a small minority, right-wing students possess a keen sense of ideological identity. The first generation of culture wars in US politics in the 1990s pitted religion against 'secular humanism', operating within the ambit of political correctness. Even the most doctrinaire fundamentalist Christians such as the Quiverfull movement were careful to reject whiteness and embrace immigration.[40] The Christian Coalition and Republican elite, like the evangelical elite today, were pro-immigration and opposed the restrictionist views of their rank-and-file.[41]

The campus political correctness of the 1980s and 1990s produced conservative books and editorials against Afrocentrism, speech codes and attacks on the Western canon, but was largely ignored by politicians.[42] As portrayed in figure 8.3, conservatives aimed their fire at the outriders of political correctness rather than the campus itself. This meant campaigning against affirmative action and bilingualism, but not political correctness *per se*. This time around, things are different.

'I will assess the facts plainly and honestly,' promised Trump in his acceptance speech: 'We cannot afford to be so politically correct any more.' Whenever opponents questioned his outrageous remarks on gender or race, Trump was able to deflect these as examples of political correctness. The Democratic contender Bernie Sanders agreed that Trump won in part because of this. '[Trump] said he will not be politically correct,' said Sanders. 'I think he said some outrageous and painful things, but I think people are tired of the same old politically correct rhetoric. I think some people believe he was speaking from his heart and willing to take on everybody.'[43] Sanders was subsequently criticized for these remarks by many in the media and his own party and forced to recant.

Public opinion seemed more receptive to the anti-PC message than ever before. In December 2015, 7 in 10 Republicans agreed that Trump 'tells it like it is'. When Trump made racist statements about Mexican and Muslim immigrants, many conservative Americans disagreed, but quietly approved of the principle of challenging anti-racist taboos. In late June 2017, seven months after the election, Americans were asked about political correctness in American life. Figure 8.5 shows the country split fairly evenly between those who felt he should be more politically correct and those who said he was about right or should be less PC. Aside from the question about Trump, more Americans thought political correctness was too powerful than too weak in society. These sentiments are strongest among Republicans but are also held by many Democrats – even in the Trump era.

In Canada, a national survey conducted in late August 2016 during the Trump campaign showed remarkable agreement about the extent of political correctness. Fully 76 per cent of Canadians said political correctness had gone too far. In the US, the equivalent figure was 68 per cent. While only 37 per cent of Democrats felt PC had gone too far, in Canada this sentiment cut across the political spectrum, with 60 per cent of Liberals and 62 per cent of left-wing New Democratic Party voters agreeing. On the right, almost 80 per cent of Canadian Conservative and American Republican voters agreed.[44] Though Canadian Conservative politicians have begun to occasionally attack their opponents as

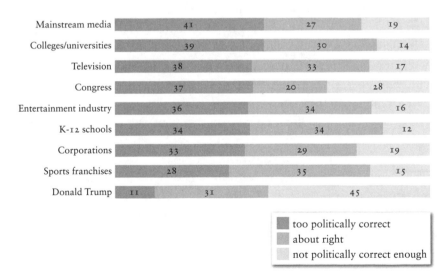

8.5. People don't consider Trump 'PC', %

Source: 'Poll: Majority of Trump voters say his political correctness is "about right"', *Morning Consult*, June 29, 2017

politically correct, these figures show the issue doesn't structure Canadian politics the way it does south of the border. This speaks to the Canadian Conservatives' reluctance to politicize cultural questions. The same is true in Britain, where surveys show that opposition to political correctness is 10 points higher than in the US but partisan gaps are, as in Canada, narrower. While Leavers are 20 points more likely than Remainers to say that 'people are too easily offended', the corresponding distance between Republicans and Democrats is over twice as wide.[45]

The campus is the centre of left-modernism, but only recently have Republican voters begun to focus their fire on universities. Figure 8.6 reveals that partisan divisions over universities have increased sharply since 2015. In 2010, 58 per cent of Republicans said colleges had a positive impact on the country compared to 32 per cent who replied in the negative. Among Democrats the margin was 65–22. Thus, despite the rise of political correctness in the 1980s, 1990s and 2000s, there was only a modest 7–10 point premium in favour of universities among Democrats in 2015. In the next two years, this changed dramatically: by 2017, 58 per cent of Republicans said colleges had a negative impact, a stunning 26-point shift. Democrats grew slightly warmer towards colleges, giving them a 72–19 endorsement. Once viewed as apolitical – possibly due to their sports teams, which are an important cultural reference point for many provincial Americans – colleges are increasingly being perceived as Democratic bastions. This is accurate for faculty, so, to the extent perceptions are catching up with reality, this could put universities in conservatives' crosshairs.

In a September 2017 survey, 43 per cent of Republicans gave professors a 'cold' rating, compared to 7 per cent of Democrats. This was especially pronounced among Republicans over sixty-five, of whom 63 per cent gave professors a cold rating compared to just 4 per cent of older Democrats.[46] Politics is beginning to respond: Republican state legislatures, most recently in Wisconsin, have begun censuring universities which do not uphold free speech on campus and are beginning to agitate for more conservative faculty and content.[47] A similar initiative was floated by several Conservative politicians in Britain in October 2017 but has not materialized.

Does the importance of the new anti-PC culture war vary by country? In a Prolific opt-in sample on 17 July 2017, I asked fifty-five white Republican identifiers – not necessarily Trump voters – and fifty-three

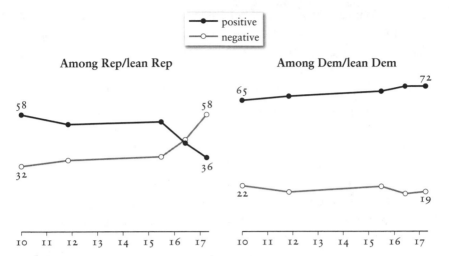

8.6. Since 2015, Republicans' views of the impact of colleges have turned much more negative (percentage who say colleges and universities have an effect on the way things are going in the country)

Source: Pew, 10 July 2017

white British Brexit voters how strongly they agreed with the following statement, on a scale from 0 (disagree most) to 100 (agree most):

> White liberal elites in this country are pushing 'political correctness'. Taking their cue from 'Social Justice Warriors' and anarchists, they call ordinary White Americans [British] who are proud of their identity racist while encouraging the opposite among minority groups. They should feel proud, we should feel guilty. They get an identity, we get multicultural-ism. Immigration benefits them and causes us to decline but we are prevented from expressing our feelings about the change.

The average score in both countries was exactly the same, 66, indicating strong agreement in both countries. I then asked the Americans, 'Which do you think was a stronger motivation for Trump's rise in the primaries and victory in the election?' Options, rotated, were 'Opposition to immigration for putting pressure on jobs and services', 'Opposition to elite political correctness (i.e. the previous statement)' or 'Other'. Sixty per cent answered political correctness, 20 per cent immigration and 20 per cent 'other'. In Britain, however, with respect to the Brexit vote, 64 per cent chose economic effects of immigration, while only 36 per cent selected political correctness. Had I included an 'other' option on the British sample, the political correctness score may well have dropped further. This again indicates political correctness is a more pressing concern among American than British populist voters.

It would be misleading to conclude that political correctness is more important than immigration in accounting for the Trump vote because the priming effect of the above statements affects the answers. A better barometer comes from a representative sample of 874 white Americans in the ANES 2016 pilot survey conducted during the primaries, in which opposition to political correctness scores only slightly below immigration attitudes in predicting how a white American rates Trump on a 0–100 thermometer. Results are graphed in figure 8.7. Note that any score below 2 is not statistically significant.

Another way of approaching the problem, which is more indirect, is to ask whether white Americans feel whites are being discriminated against compared to blacks. Figure 8.8 displays results for reported Trump vote based on the ANES post-election survey in late 2016. The

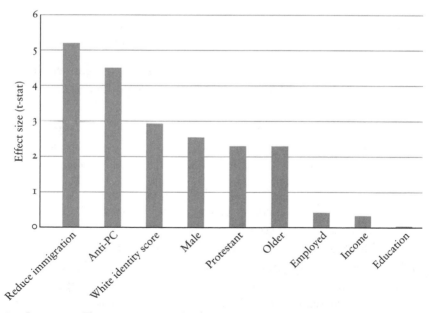

8.7. Impact on Trump support (US whites)

Source: ANES 2016 pilot survey. N = 874; R^2 = .419. Controls for party identity, with state fixed effects and design weights.

belief that whites were discriminated against in relation to blacks was more strongly associated with an actual Trump vote than views on immigration – even though immigration mattered slightly more in predicting a person's warmth towards Trump.[48]

A more rigorous test of the direction of causation was conducted by Ashley Jardina of Duke University. In August 2016, before the election, she fielded a survey experiment which illustrates how the racist charge is turning into an own-goal for the left. She split a sample of white-American respondents into groups. Group 1 was either asked (a) whether they support or oppose removing the Confederate flag from state buildings or other government property; or (b) whether they would vote for Trump in the November 2016 presidential election. This group were told that (a) some support and some oppose the flag on buildings; or (b) some support and some oppose Trump for political reasons. For a second group, the preamble to the questions was subtly modified to read that some people opposed the Confederate flag on buildings 'because it is racist'. The Trump question was also touched up to read that some oppose him 'because he supports racism'.

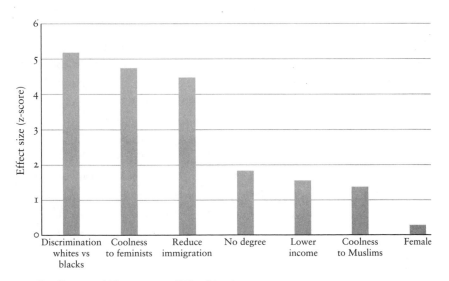

8.8. Predictors of Trump vote (US whites)

Source: ANES 2016 main survey. N = 1329; Pseudo R^2 = .579. Controls for party identity, with state fixed effects and design weights.

The results showed that white Americans high in 'racial resentment' – i.e. who agreed with statements such as 'group x can get ahead if they tried harder' – became 30 per cent more likely to support the flying of Confederate flags or vote for Trump when the word 'racist' was included in the question. For those low in racial resentment there was no effect – though recall that the racial-resentment measure actually taps attitudes to laziness, not race. In another exercise, people read about a white student who tried to start a student group for whites on campus, with one group reading that this 'was denounced as racist'. Whites high in 'racial resentment' who read the 'denounced as racist' version reacted by becoming 20 per cent more hardline in their opinions on welfare spending.[49]

There is powerful evidence that the power of anti-racism norms has faded in the US between the early and late 2000s, even with respect to anti-black sentiment. In Tali Mendelberg's famous work from the 1990s, whites who scored high in implicit prejudice on an IAT test responded with tough-on-crime attitudes to 'dog whistle' racial codes such as 'inner-city crime' with a picture of a black man next to it. But when the words 'black crime' were explicitly used, people's conscience kicked in and the appeals failed. By the mid-2000s, and especially the 2010s, the difference between 'dog whistle' and explicit appeals had disappeared, suggesting the power of the taboo to induce guilt and shame had gone. Whereas George H. W. Bush's use of the Willie Horton commercial portraying an African-American criminal in the 1988 election turned negative for Bush when it was accused of being racist and Trent Lott was forced to resign his Senate leadership post in 2002 after praising the segregationist Strom Thurmond, Trump shows this may no longer hold. 'Our core conclusion,' write the political scientists Nicholas Valentino and Fabian Neuner, 'is that the substantial power of racial attitudes in mainstream American politics no longer varies according to the ways in which race is discussed.'[50]

Frank Bruni chronicles the fading power of the anti-racist norm in his *New York Times* column: 'Conservative commentators and die-hard Republicans often brush off denunciations of Donald Trump as an unprincipled hatemonger by saying: Yeah, yeah, that's what Democrats wail about every Republican they're trying to take down.' When Romney was running against Obama in 2012, he was called a 'race-mongering pyromaniac' by *The Daily Beast*. On MSNBC, an

African-American commentator charged him with the 'niggerization' of Obama into 'the scary black man who we've been trained to fear'. Trump's campaign awakened a sense of nostalgia in the Democratic camp for Romney, McCain and the Bushes. As Harold Wolfson, Hillary Clinton's 2008 communications director who also worked on the 2004 and 2012 campaigns, admitted, 'I'm quite confident I employed language that, in retrospect, was hyperbolic and inaccurate, language that cheapened my ability – our ability – to talk about this moment with accuracy and credibility.' The 'cry wolf' effect seems to have dulled or even reversed the polarity of the racism charge on American voters and conservative politicians.[51]

This still doesn't mean opposition to political correctness ranks above immigration in motivating the Trump vote. When I asked around forty white Republicans on Prolific on 22 October 2017 what the first, second and third most important issues facing the country were, immigration was mentioned as a top-three issue by 36 per cent, compared to 17 per cent for 'political correctness against whites'. Among those who voted Trump the numbers were 46–18 in favour of immigration. So opposition to political correctness on race probably remains a second-tier concern for most Trump voters, even if rising in prominence. This indicates that left-modernism is generating a backlash, but this is still operating indirectly through concrete policy issues like immigration more than via direct anti-PC sentiment as per the model in figure 8.3.

RACIAL SELF-INTEREST

We've tracked the ebbing of anti-racist norms as they pertain to immigration and multiculturalism. In what follows, we'll see this rollback is contentious. In fact its effects are a mirror image of those we're picking up for rising diversity. As such, they polarize the electorate along the open–closed psychological dimension which is restructuring Western politics. At the crux of this debate is the question of whether whites can legitimately defend their group interests through restricting immigration. Liberals insist this is racist, while conservatives see it as a normal expression of group partiality.

In an insightful piece penned soon after Trump's election, the Brookings Institution, Arab-American scholar Shadi Hamid argues that, were he white, he could imagine voting for Trump as an expression of racial self-interest:

> For me, the more useful question isn't why Trump voters voted for him, but, rather, why they wouldn't. It seems self-evident that minorities would generally vote for the party that goes out of its way to consider – and protect – the rights of minorities . . . Why would whites, or at least a large percentage of them, act any differently? . . . [If I were white] I can't be sure I wouldn't have voted for Trump. This may make me a flawed person or even, as some would have it, a 'racist.' But it would also make me rational, voting if not in my economic self-interest then at least in my emotional self-interest.[52]

Hamid adds that ethnic group interest is a near-universal theme in human history and the demographic struggle for power between ethnic groups is a persistent feature of the modern world.[53]

Hamid argues that being attached to an ethnic group and looking out for its interests is qualitatively different from hating or fearing out-groups. This is a distinction social psychologists recognize, between love for one's group and hatred of the other. As Marilyn Brewer writes in one of the most highly cited articles on prejudice:

> The prevailing approach to the study of ethnocentrism, ingroup bias, and prejudice presumes that ingroup love and outgroup hate are reciprocally related. Findings from both cross-cultural research and laboratory experiments support the alternative view that ingroup identification is independent of negative attitudes toward outgroups.[54]

To illustrate, glance at figure 8.9, which plots how warmly white Americans in the 2016 ANES feel towards whites and blacks on a 0–100 thermometer scale, where 0 represents coldest and 100 warmest. Overall, the pattern is a strongly positive, upward-sloping relationship: white people who feel warm towards whites also feel warm towards blacks. There are some people in the top-left corner who are warm towards blacks and cold towards whites, and somewhat more people in the bottom-right corner who are warm towards whites but cold towards blacks. Yet most have similar feelings towards both.

This is not to say in-group favouritism is completely unproblematic. When groups perceive themselves to be locked in a zero-sum conflict, in-group love can beget outgroup distrust, fear or hate. But in most

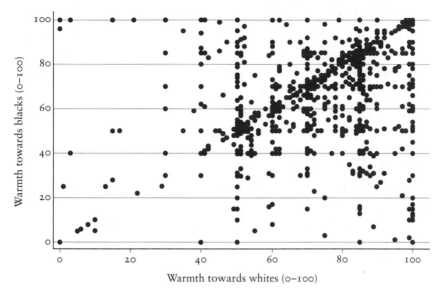

8.9 White Americans' warmth towards whites and blacks

Source: ANES 2016. $R^2 = .229$, N = 2683.

societies the two aren't related.[55] Therefore, like Hamid, my view is that expressing a white identity or group self-interest, or an ethno-traditional national identity which includes a white-majority component, isn't racist. The same holds for black, Muslim or other minority identities. Only if exclusive or directed against other groups do these become ethically dubious. The exception, as noted above, is when in-group attachment leads a person to favour their own group for a valued economic or political good like a high-status job. This automatically discriminates against outgroups, violating citizens' right to equal treatment.

Some aver there cannot be a legitimate white self-interest in Western countries because whites are the dominant group. I think this is erroneous for two reasons. While whites have no legitimate power interests in majority-white societies, they may have reasonable economic and demographic interests. How so? First, when we speak about the black or Muslim interest, we refer not just to the fact individuals in these groups experience discrimination and use identity politics to stand up for their individual rights. There is also a question of collective dignity: if my group is not treated fairly and experiences poverty, even if I am rich and experience no discrimination, the group's subaltern condition affects me. I share its pain. Whites generally are not discriminated against, but there are exceptions, such as affirmative action, which could be a source of legitimate white grievance. Here it's noteworthy that Asian opposition to affirmative action in California is considered legitimate whereas white opposition is not. This is inconsistent. Whites may also lack community structures akin to those for minority groups when they experience failure, depression or loneliness. This is partly the legacy of their individualism and partly because they have not had to develop group institutions in the past to protect themselves.

A more important form of legitimate white self-interest in most countries is demographic. We can understand this once again by starting with minorities, as their group interests are easier to grasp. If blacks are becoming a minority in Harlem due to a white and Asian influx and this changes the historically black character of Harlem, or if Afro-Caribbeans are dwindling in Britain due to intermarriage, this decline affects the well-being of members who identify with the group. No individual rights are affected, but people have collective identities which matter to them. It's psychologically much harder to decline than to grow. Many whites may also experience a sense of loss in contemplating the idea of Harlem losing its black character. As a consequence, black residents, as well as white Harlem residents with an ethno-traditional neighbourhood identity, will wish to advocate policies to slow the rate of change. In Harlem this might involve zoning to prevent gentrification of low-cost housing or a sons-and-daughters policy in public housing to retain black residents. In Britain, prospective immigrants from the Caribbean could receive extra consideration because they are an established group in decline.

Adjusting our scale to the level of regions such as Cornwall in England, where there has been an influx of people from around Greater London, illustrates once again why groups may have demographic interests. It's not just about house prices: the Cornish may have a distinct identity that is affected by excessive English in-migration. In Xinjiang, Han Chinese have recently displaced the native Uighurs as the majority. There is an economic and power imbalance in favour of the Han, but even if this were not the case, the Uighurs would still have a legitimate ethnic self-interest in slowing their rate of decline in their home region.

The same holds for countries of immigration, which includes

black-majority South Africa as well as most Western countries. The established population will tend to resist their relative decline. One could argue that no group should have a self-interest unless it is a minority. Yet this would exclude most of the human race: only 31 of 156 major countries lacked an ethnic majority in 1999, and even where there is no majority, minorities typically dominate their home regions.[56] It's not clear in ethical terms why there is something rights-conferring about the figure of 49 compared to 50 per cent of a country or region, and I have never seen this logic defended from a political-theory perspective. So long as the preferences of minority groups and post-ethnics are accommodated, it's hard to see a problem with whites placing their group self-interest on the table as one factor to consider in a rounded immigration policy debate.

If politics in the West is ever to return to normal rather than becoming even more polarized, white interests will need to be discussed. I realize this is very controversial for left-modernists. Yet not only is white group self-interest legitimate, but I maintain that in an era of unprecedented white demographic decline it is absolutely vital for it to have a democratic outlet. Marginalizing race puritanism is important, but muzzling relaxed versions of white identity sublimates it in a host of negative ways. For example, when whites are concerned about their decline but can't express it, they may mask their concern as worry about the nation-state.

Paradoxically, it becomes more acceptable to complain about immigrant crime, welfare dependency, terrorism or wage competition than to voice a sense of loss and anxiety about the decline of one's group or a white-Christian tradition of nationhood. It's more politically correct to worry about Islam's challenge to liberalism and East European 'cheap labour' in Britain than it is to say you are attached to being a white Brit and fear cultural loss. This means left-modernism has placed us in a situation where expressing racism is more acceptable than articulating racial self-interest. This is perverse and twists political reasoning to produce counterproductive outcomes like denying welfare to immigrants, preventing them from working, and, in America, prompting the electorate to vote to cut spending on schools, roads and hospitals.[57] I'd argue that sublimated white-majority cultural expression also underlies rising Islamophobia, Euroscepticism, populism, polarization and declining trust in liberal democratic institutions.

IMMIGRATION AND RACISM

The main faultline between left-modernism and populist conservatism revolves around immigration: whether it's racist to want fewer immigrants, especially for cultural reasons. When talk of reducing numbers became more acceptable in the 2000s in many European countries, it was typically dressed up as concern over pressure on wages and public services. In Western high culture, there is still a 'cultural cringe', a sense of unease in addressing immigration. This sustains a growing fragmentation of the media into left- and right-wing echo chambers with each bubble processing events differently and reinforcing prevailing worldviews. Terrorist attacks cause the left-wing press to tell the story of innocent Muslims and fret about Islamophobia, while the right steps up calls for security and protection from a rising Muslim threat.[58]

It's well-known that the American public is polarized by partisanship, with each side responding to how parties cue their voters to think on issues like building a border wall. What is less visible are the deeper divides within the white populations of Western countries over the scope of race taboos. On the 2016 ANES pilot study, 5–10 per cent of American whites say they have a lot of white guilt, depending on how the question is asked. A wider category is the roughly one third of white Americans who respect the left-modernist line that white group partiality on immigration is racist and who say they have at least 'a little' white guilt. Another third of white Americans have a strong identification with white racial identity or a white-inflected national identity, say whites experience a medium to high level of discrimination, and want immigration reduced a lot. This is the core Trump base. The final third have a moderate identification with whiteness, want immigration reduced a little, don't consider white group interests racist and report no white guilt.[59]

A critical demarcation across all Western countries is between the 63–80 per cent of whites who believe there is such a thing as a legitimate white self-interest on immigration and the 20–36 per cent of whites who think this is racist. The outcome of this conflict over the definition of racism determines whether it's legitimate to deploy social norms to repress opposition to immigration. To get at this, I undertook a small opt-in pilot survey of around 200 Americans using MTurk.

MTurk skews towards secular white liberals, but it's the comparison that is of interest here rather than perfect representativeness. For a set of statements, I asked people to indicate whether a statement is (a) racist, (b) not racist, or (c) don't know. Excluding don't knows produces the results in figure 8.10. The table shows that whites and minorities in America largely agree on what is and isn't racist. The only significant difference is over whether racial quotas in university admissions are

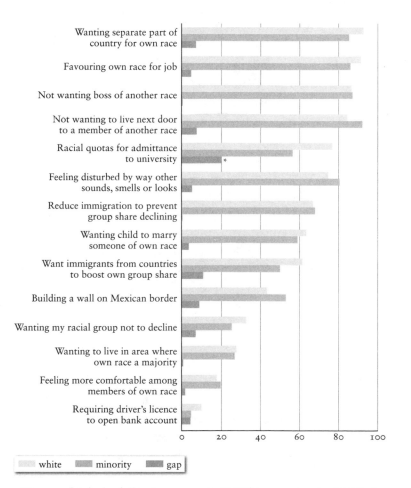

8.10. 'Do you think the following are racist?' (White vs minority.) MTurk (relatively Democratic) sample, %

Source: M Turk survey. N = 155–192. *Statistically significant difference between whites and minorities at the p<0.5 level.

racist, and, even here, a majority of both non-whites (57 per cent) and whites (77 per cent) say they are.

Figure 8.10 shows that even among this relatively liberal sample, most don't think it's racist to feel more comfortable among members of their own 'race' (defined by US census categories) or to want to live in an area where their group is in the majority. Trump's proposal to build a wall on the border with Mexico divides opinion, though a slim majority – even in this Democrat-leaning sample – say this isn't racist. Importantly, there is no statistically significant gap between whites and minorities on whether the wall is racist.

Figure 8.10 showed that whites and minorities place the racism/non-racism boundary in a similar place across a wide range of questions, but when we compare white Trump and Clinton voters, big partisan divides open up. In seven of twelve measures the difference is significant at the 1 per cent level, which is not true of any of the white-minority differences in figure 8.10. Figure 8.10 was sorted by the share who think a statement is racist, but in figure 8.11 I sort by the size of gap between Clinton and Trump supporters to give a clearer picture of where the divides are.

Large divides characterize two types of statement. First, questions identified with party positions, such as building a wall or affirmative action: 72 per cent of those who voted for Hillary Clinton in the sample view Trump's proposal to build a wall on the Mexican border to be racist compared to 4 per cent of Trump voters. On racial quotas, the tables are turned: 52 per cent of Clinton voters – but fully 96 per cent of Trump voters – think this is racist. The second set of differences revolves around questions of group partiality. As Haidt suggests, liberals have a difficult time understanding the moral psychology of majority group loyalty. Thus 79 per cent of Clinton voters think it's racist to wish your child to marry someone of the same race, compared to 33 per cent of Trump voters. 47 per cent of Clinton voters also think it's racist to even want one's racial group not to decline. Just 12 per cent of Trump voters concur.

It's important not to forget that there is common ground as well. Whites from both parties consider a white ethno-state à la Richard Spencer to be racist. On the classic racism items like not wanting a boss or neighbour of a different race or favouring one's own race for a job there is widespread agreement. So while there's a gulf over whether defending white demographic interests is racist, the overwhelming majority of Trump voters agree that certain thoughts and behaviours are racist.

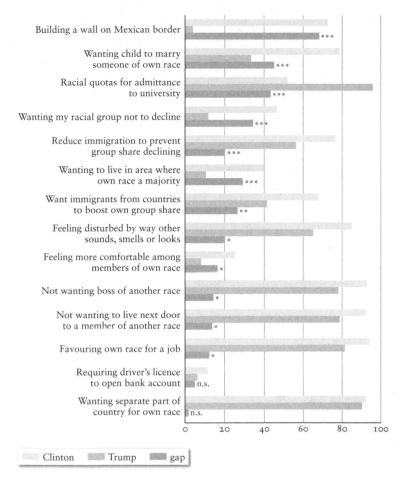

Building a wall on Mexican border
Wanting child to marry someone of own race
Racial quotas for admittance to university
Wanting my racial group not to decline
Reduce immigration to prevent group share declining
Wanting to live in area where own race a majority
Want immigrants from countries to boost own group share
Feeling disturbed by way other sounds, smells or looks
Feeling more comfortable among members of own race
Not wanting boss of another race
Not wanting to live next door to a member of another race
Favouring own race for a job
Requiring driver's licence to open bank account
Wanting separate part of country for own race

Clinton   Trump   gap

8.11. 'Do you think the following are racist?', % (by 2016 vote)

Source: MTurk survey, 29 November. N = 117–144. *Statistically significant at the p<0.5 level; **p<0.1; ***p<0.001. n.s. – not significant.

The MTurk samples are small and skew young and left, but this data is borne out in larger representative samples. In order to explore the findings in figure 8.11 on a larger scale, I commissioned, as part of a project with the think tank Policy Exchange, two YouGov surveys of over 1,500 individuals. These were fielded on 7–8 December 2016, one in the US and one in Britain. I was interested in whether respondents considered individuals racist for supporting immigration policies that favour their group. Consider this question, noting what is underlined: 'A <u>White</u> American who identifies with her group and its history supports a proposal to <u>reduce</u> immigration. Her motivation is to <u>maintain</u> her group's share of America's population.'[60] Is this person: 1) just acting in her racial self-interest, which is not racist; 2) being racist; 3) don't know.' Removing those who answered 'don't know' yields 61.4 per cent of Americans who say the person is not being racist versus 38.6 per cent who say she is. This is a more conservative average than the MTurk data in figures 8.10 and 8.11 because the YouGov sample is weighted by vote, education and other variables to be representative.

My strategy on the survey was not simply to ask a question, but to employ an experimental technique whereby different people see an alternative version of the question. So I swap Asian, black or Latino for white to see whether the answers change as well as altering 'decrease' to 'increase' immigration, and 'maintain' to 'increase' group share. For example, compare this question with the previous one: 'An <u>Asian</u> American who identifies with her group and its history supports a proposal to <u>increase</u> immigration from Asia. Her motivation is to <u>increase</u> her group's share of America's population.' Altering the three underlined fields across the four main US racial groups allows us to see how people's answers change as the group in question shifts and the direction of policy changes from a reduction to a selective increase. I can also watch how the results differ between whites and minorities as distinct from liberals and conservatives.

The bottom line is that white liberals overwhelmingly consider white attempts to reduce immigration to be racist. Their view changes considerably when minorities adopt the same strategy or if whites seek European immigration to boost their numbers. Conservatives and minorities are also biased, but the degree of inconsistency is lower. Consider these results:

- 73 per cent of white Clinton voters say a white American who wants to reduce immigration to maintain her group's share of the population is being racist.
- 57 per cent of white Clinton voters say a Japanese or black American who wants to reduce immigration to maintain her group's share of the population is being racist.

- 34 per cent of white Clinton voters say a white American who wants to increase immigration from Europe to boost her group's share of the population is being racist.
- 18 per cent of white Clinton voters say a Latino or Asian American who wants to increase immigration from Latin America or Asia to boost her group's share of the population is being racist.

And on the other side:

- 11 per cent of white Trump voters say a white American who wants to reduce immigration to maintain her group's share of the population is being racist.
- 18 per cent of white Trump voters say a Japanese or black American who wants to reduce immigration to maintain her group's share of the population is being racist.
- 29 per cent of white Trump voters say a white American who wants to increase immigration from Europe to boost her group's share of the population is being racist.
- 39 per cent of white Trump voters say a Latino or Asian American who wants to increase immigration from Latin America or Asia to boost her group's share of the population is being racist.

So both sides are biased, but the skew is heavier among white Democrats. When we control for demographic variables like age and education, what emerges is a strong preference among white Democrats for labelling someone of any racial group racist if they favour reducing immigration. In fact they are more likely to think a Japanese-American who wants less immigration to protect Japanese share is racist than a white American who wants more Europeans to immigrate to boost white share. This means the definition of racism is elastic: for white Democrats it turns on whether the proponent wants less immigration. Finally, all else being equal, white Democrats are 16 points more likely to consider someone racist if they are backing white interests. Something similar shows up in ethical experiments which find that liberals are significantly less willing to sacrifice a person with a black-sounding name to save white lives than to sacrifice an individual with a white name to save black lives. Conservatives, by contrast, are colour-blind.[61]

All told, the partisan difference on whether immigration restriction to maintain white share is racist is vast, at over 60 points. Figure 8.12 shows that among white, Clinton-voting university graduates – the group that largely comprises the cultural elite – this sentiment is near universal, at 91 per cent. But among non-white Clinton voters just 58 per cent agree: many see whites who want less immigration for group-interested reasons as racially self-interested rather than racist. A similar finding turned up in a 2017 Pew survey which asked whether 'discrimination is the main reason blacks can't get ahead'. Ninety-one per cent of the largely white 'solid liberals' agreed, but only 40 per cent of the mainly non-white 'devout and diverse' group did.[62] At the other end of the scale, just 11 per cent of white Trump voters see the white woman in my question as racist but 73 per cent of white Clinton voters do. In line with their left-modernist beliefs, white educated Clinton voters have an expansive definition of racism which perceives white racial

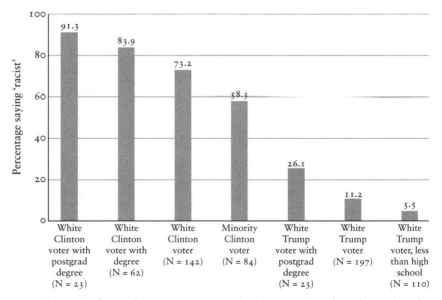

8.12. Is it racist for a white person to want less immigration for ethnocultural reasons?, % (USA)
Birkbeck–Policy Exchange–Yougov survey, 7–8 December, 2016.

self-interest to be racist. White Trump voters generally view this as non-racist while minority voters lie somewhere in the middle.

In the United States, morality, in Jonathan Haidt's phrase, 'binds and blinds', serving as a partisan boundary marker and producing logical blind spots.[63] Outside the US, partisan differences are smaller, and fewer people think it's racist for a member of a white majority in their country to want less immigration to maintain white group share. In Britain, for instance, the YouGov survey found that just 24 per cent of white Britons said the statement was racist compared to 37 per cent in the US. What predicts the difference in most countries is opinions on immigration: those who want current or higher levels tend to feel that restricting numbers for ethno-cultural reasons is racist, and vice-versa. In Britain there is an enormous divide between the 80 per cent of university-educated pro-immigration white British Remain voters and the majority of the white British population who want lower immigration. Educated, pro-immigration Remainers – for instance, most of those working in academia or higher levels of the culture industry – say the sentiments were racist. This falls to 45 per cent among white British Remainers overall and plummets to just 6 per cent among white British Leavers. Among white British Leavers without qualifications, the share calling the statement racist is precisely zero.

Ipsos MORI ran the same question on an eighteen-country representative survey.[64] Here we changed the majority ethnic group in line with each country, so 'white Hungarian' in Hungary or 'Hindu' in India. Aggregated to country level, excluding 'don't know' responses, it's again clear that a majority *do not* think it's racist to want less immigration for ethno-cultural reasons. The proportion considering this motivation racist varies, however, from a high of 36 per cent in the US to a low of 13 per cent in South Africa (where Xhosa are the reference group). Divides within countries also matter. In Canada, 37 per cent of English-Canadians say the sentiment is racist – similar to the US – while just 15 per cent of Quebeckers do. In Belgium, 32 per cent of Brussels residents but only 19 per cent of those in Flanders agree.

Those who want current or higher levels of immigration tend to believe it's racist to restrict it. At first glance, this seems unsurprising. It could be argued that asking whether immigration restriction is racist or racially self-interested amounts to the same thing. But if the theory that the politics of immigration is about economic interests were true, it should be possible for someone to support immigration as a boost to economic growth or a country's working-age population without thinking group-motivated restrictionists are racist. Across all countries, the majority say tribally motivated restrictions are not racist, but among pro-immigration respondents views are more evenly split: 51 per cent of pro-immigration people say the statement is racist. Education also counts. In many countries, the university-educated are 10–25 points more likely than those without high school to think that a person who wants less immigration for ethno-cultural reasons is racist. The biggest education gap on this issue, at 26 points, is in Germany.

Alternatively, someone may want less immigration to reduce pressure on public services while agreeing that someone who wants less for ethnic reasons is racist. Yet we find that a mere 12 per cent of those who want less immigration say a person who wants fewer immigrants for ethnic reasons is racist. This makes for a bad fit with the mainstream narrative that people want less immigration because they're hard up. This said, the racism/racial self-interest divide strongly predicts variation in support for immigration. Most notable is that the

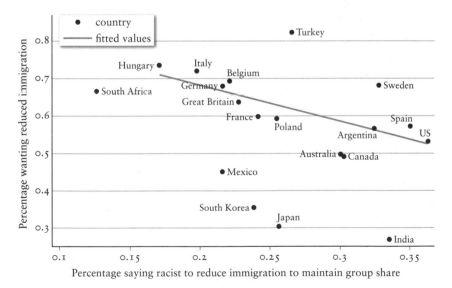

8.13. Perceived relationship between opposition to immigration and racism

Source: Ipsos MORI Global @dvisor Survey, 18 countries, 15 March 2017. N = 14,014. Aggregated data. Includes minority respondents.

anti-racism-pro immigration relationship holds more strongly in white-majority societies than elsewhere. The line of best fit for Western countries is shown in grey in figure 8.13. Notice that India, South Korea, Japan, Mexico and Turkey fall well outside the line. This underscores the sharper association between one's view of what racism is and one's immigration opinion in the West as compared to the rest of the world. As migration and ethnic change proceed, conflict over the proper scope of the racism taboo is becoming a growing political issue.

This is confirmed in the individual-level data presented in figure 8.14, where the grey line for the white-majority countries is steeper than the black one for non-Western countries. In the West, a person of average age, income and education who thinks it's racist for a white person to want less immigration to maintain her group share has a 30 per cent likelihood of wanting immigration reduced. Restrictionist sentiment jumps to 72 points among those saying that the sentiment is racial self-interest, not racism. Outside the West, the difference in probabilities is only half as large, at 55–34. In essence, immigration is much more of a

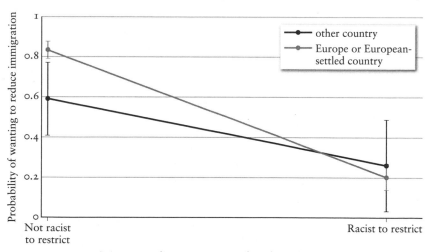

Is it racist to limit immigration for ethnocultural reasons?

8.14. Is it racist to restrict immigration for ethnocultural reasons?, % (West vs non-West)

Source: Ipsos MORI Global @dvisor Survey, 18 countries, 15 March 2017. N = 14,014. Non-European countries: India, South Korea, Japan, Mexico, Turkey, South Africa. Controls for individual's education, income, gender and age.

moral issue in the West than elsewhere: divergence on the remit of anti-racist social norms distinguishes pro- from anti-immigration opinion in the West more sharply than outside it. What this suggests is that when it comes to understanding the politics of immigration, it's just as important to grasp people's views on the morality of restriction as it is to explain what's motivating them to seek reduced immigration.

CHALLENGING DOUBLE-STANDARDS MODERATES OPINION

We saw that white Clinton and Trump voters altered their views of what's racist depending on whether a person wanted to reduce or increase immigration and whether the reference group was white, Hispanic or Asian. Is it possible for people to be less partisan and inconsistent? In a subset of my YouGov sample, I had people answer two versions of the same question. For instance, whether it's racist for a white person to want fewer immigrants to maintain group share and whether it's racist for a Hispanic person to want more to boost group share. When people were made to answer in sequence, their answers became slightly more consistent. What really made the difference, however, was asking people to answer four versions in sequence and justify their answers in a textbox, something I did on a smaller follow-up sample of 200 in MTurk.

The results were quite dramatic. Just 48 per cent of white Clinton voters now said it was racist for whites to want reduced immigration to maintain their group. This compares to 73 per cent of white Clinton voters in the YouGov sample, a dramatic difference. Meanwhile 29 per cent of white Clinton voters now said it was racist for Latinos to want more Latin American immigration to increase their group share, considerably more than the 18 per cent in the YouGov sample. Trump voters also adjusted their views: 22 per cent of white Trump voters now said it was racist for whites to want less immigration to maintain group share compared to just 11 per cent in the YouGov sample. Whereas 39 per cent called Latinos racist on the YouGov survey for wanting more Latin American immigration to boost group share, the level in the MTurk sample – where people are asked to justify their responses – was just 25 per cent. So we see a much higher level of consistency when people are asked to answer four sequential questions and explain the pattern of their answers. This is unlikely to be an artefact of the differing survey samples because MTurk's liberal bias should move all responses in that direction rather than narrowing partisan gaps.[65] What is revealing is that with greater consistency came a shift away from seeing the desire for reduction as racism to accepting racial self-interest: when people think about it, fewer are willing to level the racism charge at restrictionists.

Respondents in my MTurk follow-up sample showed more consistency, but big partisan divides still remained. Nearly half the Clinton voters still felt that a white desire to restrict immigration to maintain white share was racist, but that a Hispanic who wants to increase group share through immigration was simply acting in her racial self-interest. How was this justified? Consider the following answers, which were quite typical:

'I think the difference is whether the person is acting in a way that will benefit others or acting in a way that will restrict the freedoms of others.'

'The idea of allowing others to have the same chances that you've had are not particularly racist, but the idea of limiting others from coming to America because you've already had the chance and established yourself can be.'

Both statements reflect a perception that preventing people from entering the country is racist. Facilitating immigration widens freedom while restriction narrows it and is therefore racist. The sentiments reflect an open-borders liberalism rather than a left-modernist desire to radically transform society, but they are radical in that they entail accepting the expansive definition of racism institutionalized by left-modernism.

Another common justification was more directly influenced by left-modernism: that minorities sought opportunities while whites were after domination, as in the past:

'The white person's support for bringing in more Europeans is to maintain power over other racial groups, while the Hispanic person wants her group to gain power to bring them on an equal foothold with whites.'

'Racism refers to an imbalance in structural power, which racial minorities do not have, and probably still won't have even if white people stop being the majority by number. I assume the people in [questions] #27 and #29 want to increase the number of their racial group because they want to stop being marginalized so hard. White people on the other hand have only white supremacy as a possible reason to increase white numbers.'

'Of course it is worse when white people do it because at least in the case of the others they have been historically oppressed.'

Here respondents are interpreting the question through a politico-economic rather than cultural lens, despite the fact the question specified that the white person identified with a group and its history.

Conservative inconsistency was motivated by either straightforward white nationalism or a fear of minority retribution, as with:

'America should be a white nation but others are trying to commit white genocide.'

Or:

'As a white person it makes me nervous more than sad to not be the majority any more. I do not consider myself a racist and I strive to not consider the color of a person in my daily dealings, but I know most people do. I don't want it to turn into a situation of groups feeling like they need to pay back whites and make us suffer for years of perceived injustice.'

Two groups of consistent respondents emerged. One is a liberal group who defined illiberalism as racism. This cleaves to the expansive definition of racism propounded by left-modernism, but applies the standard consistently across all groups. Among ethno-communitarians, who made up a large share of consistent respondents, most said it was natural for people to want the best for their group, whether this meant increasing selective immigration to boost share or decreasing numbers to maintain group share. These offer clear examples of Hamid's concept of racial self-interest:

'I didn't find anything about those questions racist, it didn't say anything about those people hating on another race, just they wanted more people like themselves around.'

'Racism is the being prejudicial towards other races. Trying to increase immigration populations isn't being prejudicial to another race.'

'The motives weren't based on any sort of perception that other races were inferior or less worthy. They were instead cold calculations based on social blocks and relative voting power.'

Needless to say, I share the views of this final group of respondents, who represent the views of the overwhelming majority of people in the West and beyond. I also think these sentiments are supported by the social-psychology literature. This isn't to say policy should bow to group interests. Only that they be freely expressed and traded off against other aims when making policy.

PART III

Flee

PART III

9
Hunkering Down: The Geographic and Social Retreat of White Majorities

So far I've discussed white resistance to ethnic change, in tension with an opposing response: repressing anxieties to abide by liberal norms. But there are other options available to white majorities. 'Fight or flight' is our way of characterizing how an animal reacts to a threat, and humans are no different: we often flee or bypass difficulties. The next reaction I want to consider is flight – whether to white-dominated neighbourhoods or into predominantly white social networks.

People are inclined to flock together on the basis of social characteristics, so the more choice they have, the more segregation. A UK study finds that when public-housing tenants are permitted to choose where to live, ethnic segregation tends to increase.[1] In Singapore, by contrast, most housing is publicly owned and allocated. The government ensures ethnic groups can't cluster, so segregation is engineered out of the system. Some might think that's a good thing, but, quite apart from the loss of freedom to choose, minorities often have better health and well-being when they are able to rely on co-ethnic support networks in areas where they are densely settled.[2] Economic factors are also important in structuring where people live inasmuch as many minority groups tend to be poorer than whites – so minority areas are often more deprived. When ethnicity and income overlap a lot, as in much of continental Europe and the USA, mixed-income development can promote integration. Continental European countries such as Germany, which maintain a good standard of public housing with mixed development, can mitigate segregation to some extent.[3]

On the other hand, there are plenty of poor whites in Western cities, especially in Europe. Poor whites and minorities may be in the same economic boat, but they still have some choice over which deprived area to reside in. At the other end of the social scale, wealthy minorities are no longer compelled to choose lily-white areas if they want to move up, but can select a more diverse middle-class area in which to live. In urban Canada, and increasingly in the US and Britain, there is a large minority middle class. In addition, there are a growing number of prosperous 'ethnoburbs' such as Richmond in Vancouver, Harrow in London, or Cupertino, California, where upwardly mobile minorities move – and which white middle-class families increasingly avoid.[4] This means minority upward mobility doesn't automatically translate into integration. Mixing housing sizes in a development may just result in a blend of wealthy and poor people from the same ethnic background living in the area.

Most work on segregation focuses on where minorities choose to live. Segregation is typically measured using either the Index of Dissimilarity (ID) or Index of Isolation (II). The ID is about how evenly a group is spread, the II about how isolated it is from contact with other groups. Both measures are needed to arrive at an accurate picture. The ID runs from 0, meaning no segregation, to 1, total segregation. If you took a group and randomly distributed it across neighbourhoods, the ID would be zero. If you took the group and clustered it entirely in one place, the ID would be 1 because the share of the group would be so much higher in that place than elsewhere. But a small group like Jews in Tartu, Finland, can be completely concentrated in one neighbourhood and still be a small minority there. Their ID could be at the maximum of 1, but they won't be isolated from contact with Finns, so their isolation from others (II) will still be low. On the other hand, a large group like the ethnic Finns might be evenly distributed across Finland but still have very little contact with minorities, on average. Their ID is low, but their II is high.

Whites have been the overwhelming majority in the West, and most social scientists are still white, so they tend to be interested in minorities, who seem different. Moreover, ethnic discrimination in housing has historically been a problem, so it's unsurprising that scholars have focused most on minority segregation. In the US, African-Americans were kept out of white neighbourhoods by discriminatory practices such as 'steering', in which real-estate agents directed African-American customers towards black neighbourhoods. This is now against the law, but is difficult to police. Landlords can also discriminate against tenants. Field experiments which send in two identical enquiries and only alter the names or photos, or have a black and a white person show up with identical economic backgrounds, find that ethnic discrimination persists. In the US, there is modest evidence of discrimination against lower-income African-Americans in recent studies (blacks received 2–6 per cent fewer callbacks than whites for sales and rental enquiries), but not against Hispanics or upper-income blacks. In Spain, housing discrimination against immigrants is closer to 15 percentage points. In Sweden, the gap between Middle Eastern and white Swedish enquiries reaches 25 points; and in Greece the disparity with Albanians soars up to 46 points.[5]

WHITE FLIGHT

Despite the persistence of discrimination, this is unlikely to account for today's segregation picture. For instance, studies find discrimination is often worse in the rental than in the sales market, but segregation isn't noticeably lower in areas with more homeowners. There is also plenty of evidence of minorities entering heavily white areas. In 2001, the whitest fifth of wards in Britain was 98 per cent white. In 2011 it was 94 per cent white. In the US in 2010, the census tract (population around 7,500) of the average white American from a tract that was 90 per cent white back in 2000 had fallen to 83 per cent white, a 7-point decline.[6] This mirrored overall shifts in the top 100 metropolitan areas, where the average white person saw their tract change from 79 to 72 per cent white between 2000 and 2015.[7] Minorities are clearly entering heavily white areas, suggesting discrimination is not the barrier it once was. However, whites are generally not moving to high-minority areas.

Whites are also declining in the new 'superdiverse' zones, often suburbs, which are growing rapidly and absorbing the rising minority population. In an important paper focusing on small-scale movements within output areas (which average 300 people in Britain), Ron Johnston and his colleagues at the University of Bristol in the UK found that the share of minorities living in their own-group areas had declined, but so had the proportion living in heavily white areas. Minorities were increasing in lily-white areas but this was not keeping pace with the overall numerical growth of minorities. Instead, minorities were growing fastest in superdiverse places such as Wembley in London, where minorities are a majority but no single minority group dominates.[8] The same is true for Afro-Caribbeans, who have been leaving Brixton, an initial London settlement area, for suburbs like Croydon. This pushes segregation indices down when comparing single groups like Afro-Caribbeans with whites or the general population. However, at the same time, white British have been leaving or avoiding places like Croydon. In fact the only ethnic group to become more segregated in London in the 2000s are the white British.[9] As others move towards ethnic strangers, the white British seem to be moving towards themselves.

For instance, the map in figure 9.1 shows where Bangladeshi Britons in London lived in 2001, and the areas where they grew fastest in the 2000s. This shows that Bangladeshis were static in their heartland in inner east London but expanded out of it during this decade. Look at similar maps for the white British and it is clear the white Brits retained population best in white outer London boroughs like Bexley, where they were already concentrated in 2001. The ID for white-minority segregation in England didn't fall during 1991–2011 the way the ID for, say, Bangladeshi segregation did. Furthermore, some of the fastest segregation declines were for intra-minority measures, such as Bangladeshi–Pakistani or Hindu–Muslim, as these groups met each other in superdiverse neighbourhoods. British Muslims, for example, are largely unsegregated from other religious minorities in superdiverse wards, but are strongly segregated from whites in whiter wards, where they concentrate in specific blocks.

A similar pattern appears in the US, with whites avoiding not only ethnic 'ghettoes' but also superdiverse 'global' neighbourhoods where whites are the minority.[10] And so we see Asians living near Hispanics and African-Americans, but whites – especially white families – declining rapidly in diverse areas. This is producing a growing number of all-minority neighbourhoods in America's most diverse metropolitan areas, where whites are the only major group electing not to enter.[11] In the future, I would expect the Index of Isolation of minorities from whites in superdiverse places like Brent in London, Scarborough (except for the Lakeshore) in Toronto, or the Bronx, New York, to continue to rise – even as individual minority groups deconcentrate. This will be especially apparent in schools, which are even more segregated than neighbourhoods. The segregation problem is likely to shift from concerns about

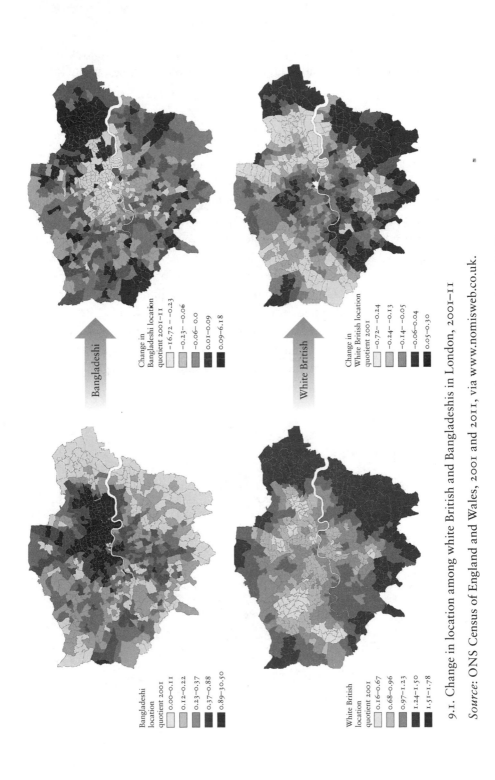

Bangladeshi
location
quotient 2001

- [ ] 0.00–0.11
- [ ] 0.12–0.22
- [ ] 0.23–0.37
- [ ] 0.37–0.88
- [ ] 0.89–30.50

Bangladeshi →

Change in
Bangladeshi location
quotient 2001–11

- [ ] -16.72 – -0.23
- [ ] -0.23 – -0.06
- [ ] -0.06 – 0.0
- [ ] 0.01–0.09
- [ ] 0.09–6.18

White British
location
quotient 2001

- [ ] 0.16–0.67
- [ ] 0.68–0.96
- [ ] 0.97–1.23
- [ ] 1.24–1.50
- [ ] 1.51–1.78

White British →

Change in
White British location
quotient 2001

- [ ] -0.72 – -0.24
- [ ] -0.24 – -0.13
- [ ] -0.14 – -0.05
- [ ] -0.06–0.04
- [ ] 0.05–0.30

9.1. Change in location among white British and Bangladeshis in London, 2001–11

Source: ONS Census of England and Wales, 2001 and 2011, via www.nomisweb.co.uk.

Pakistanis or Somalis segregating themselves to worries about minority schoolchildren in global neighbourhoods never meeting a white kid.

ARE WHITES FLEEING?

The results of the 2011 census of England and Wales, released in late 2012, made the headlines. London's population had grown by over a million, yet the white British had declined by 620,000. Their share of the city dropped from 58 to 45 per cent in a decade. The BBC's Home Affairs editor, Mark Easton, netted over 2,000 comments for his 'Why Have the White British left London?' article in early February 2013 before comments – mostly negative – were cut off. But change was not confined to London. In cities up and down England, minority growth at ward level in the 2000s was inversely correlated with white growth. The picture in London is shown in figure 9.2. Notice how city-wide trends are amplified at this fine geographic scale: London neighbourhoods where East European or non-European minorities grew quickest

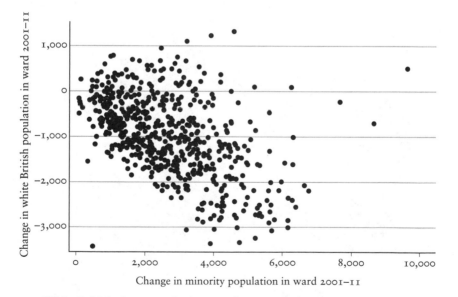

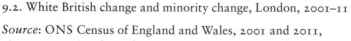

9.2. White British change and minority change, London, 2001–11

Source: ONS Census of England and Wales, 2001 and 2011, via www.nomisweb.co.uk.

experienced the largest white British losses. This is not just because there is a fixed supply of housing, though this is part of the story. Approximately a quarter of a million new homes were constructed in the city in this decade.[12] More importantly, Ian Gordon of the London School of Economics shows that 40 per cent of London's immigrant influx in this period was accommodated through crowding.[13] Ben Judah, a journalist who used his language skills to go undercover as an East European labourer, describes how many of the new immigrant proletariat subsist: 'Undercover, the worst doss house I ever lived in was 15 shoved into three rooms. They shared beds, and one night worker time-shared a bunk in the day.'[14]

White British decline in London, and urban England, is less a story of white flight than one of white British families avoiding dense and diverse neighbourhoods. In many parts of large English cities, 10 per cent of the population moves in or out each year, so over five years an important part of the population churns.[15] In short, inflow really matters. Imagine a bathtub with a hot and cold tap, with water draining out at a steady clip. If you turn off the cold water and twist open the hot, the tub heats up pretty quickly.

White avoidance is also important in Northern Europe. Åsa Bråmå demonstrates that ethnic Swedes are bypassing diverse high-rise public-housing developments such as Husby, on the periphery of Stockholm. It's not that ethnic Swedes flee Husby, though more native Swedes left than immigrants. Rather, the bathtub effect resulted in few white Swedes moving in. This left room for new minority entrants and natural increase, which steadily changed the area's ethnic composition.[16] Swedish residential segregation, according to one of its leading segregation researchers, 'is a result of decisions taken by the Swedish majority, who tend to cluster in Swedish-dense neighbourhoods and avoid immigrant-dense housing estates'.[17] In the Netherlands, minorities are concentrated in four cities – Utrecht, Amsterdam, Rotterdam and The Hague – where they make up a third of the population. Here again, studies find that the white Dutch are avoiding areas with large shares of minorities.[18] Yet the significant share of housing that is public in the Netherlands allows for some insulation against the general pattern.[19]

In order to get at what's driving segregation, it's important to move down from aggregate patterns to the level of individuals. The ONS Longitudinal Survey (ONS LS) is a 1 per cent sample of the population of England and Wales which is followed at every census.[20] This makes it a goldmine for tracking mobility. In the ONS LS, a white British and minority person aged thirty-five, each with two kids, with a degree and from the same occupational class, who leave a neighbourhood that averages two-thirds non-white and move the same distance will, on balance, choose ethnically different places to move to. And this is with controls for the urban density and deprivation of origin and destination wards. The white Briton has a 15-point greater likelihood of moving to a whiter area than the minority person. In *Understanding Society*, white Brits from diverse areas move to a ward that is 10 points whiter than that chosen by an otherwise identical minority mover, all else being equal.

In the US, native-born American movers tend to select destinations that contain just a third to a half as many immigrants as the neighbourhoods they left.[21] In Sweden, white Swedish out-migration and limited white in-migration contributed to ethnic change in diversifying neighbourhoods, but in-migration was around twice as important. All told, whites choose whiter places to move to than minorities who originate in the same neighbourhoods and share the same social characteristics, such as age and income. Multiply that across the population and the effect, at least in Britain, is that white-minority segregation (ID) has remained frozen for two decades. In fact, 44 per cent of non-whites in England and Wales live in just 502 of 8,571 wards (population 6,500 on average) – places where the white British are a minority. Meanwhile, barely 4 per cent of white Brits live in these 'majority minority' wards. Eighty per cent of England and Wales remains more than 90 per cent white.

In the 2000s, two thirds of white British movers chose whiter wards, 12 per cent went to more diverse places and the rest selected wards of similar diversity. For minority movers, only 25 per cent opted for whiter wards, while 40 per cent chose more diverse wards to move to. It may be that white-minority segregation is being reproduced by minorities, but this is belied by the fact that different minorities are increasingly meeting each other in superdiverse neighbourhoods.[22] Minorities are clearly not sticking to their own, so who is? As the urban West gets more diverse, the finger increasingly points to the white majority as the engine of segregation. White majorities are retreating towards places where they are relatively concentrated. This throws light on larger patterns like the white British departure from London. The ONS LS shows that white British left the city at three times the rate of UK-born minorities in the 2000s. Controlling for all the usual socioeconomic factors – education, class, age, marital status, children, housing tenure, distance moved, neighbourhood deprivation and population density – white Britons were still 13 points more likely than other ethnic groups to leave the city. They were also significantly less likely to enter it. In an increasingly expensive city, working-class whites were also much less likely to move to London than their middle-class counterparts.

Another unusual twist is the relationship white Brits now have with the city over their life cycle. In the 1970s, London was still depressed and somewhat run-down, and wouldn't become a centre of global finance until the roaring 1980s. More white twenty-somethings left it for other parts of England and Wales than entered it. As the capital became a more attractive destination for young professionals, this changed. In the 1990s and 2000s, about 25 per cent more white British twenty-somethings moved to London than departed. But London's growing attractiveness made little difference to white families. In the 2000s, 20 per cent more white Britons with children – a much larger group than twenty-somethings when you count their kids – left the city than moved in.[23] The cyclical pattern of moving to London in your twenties then then leaving the city to start a family is much less apparent for minorities. In the 2000s, the number of British-born twenty-something minorities coming to London was almost exactly offset by minorities leaving. For non-white families with children, there was a net outflow, but at only a third the white British rate, so ethnic factors again played a key role.

In the future, these patterns may shift somewhat – minorities are an important element of the urban core of many towns around London and are growing rapidly in satellite cities such as Slough or Milton Keynes. East Europeans have fanned out more widely than non-Europeans, changing the character of towns such as Boston, Lincolnshire, or Peter-borough. In the United States, Hispanics left their initial settlement areas in southern California and greater Miami in the 1990s and 2000s for the less Hispanic states of the inland west, north-west and south-east. I experienced this first hand when crossing into Washington State from the Canadian side, a trip I have made on many occasions over the years. A number of roadside towns now have significant Hispanic populations, and Hispanics are a majority in some agricultural communities east of the Cascade mountains. William Frey identifies 145 Hispanic 'new destinations' where Hispanics form just 7 per cent of the population but increased 119 per cent in the 2000s – places like Fayetteville, Arkansas, Boise, Idaho, or Oklahoma City.[24] Hispanics who moved to these new destinations tended to be lower-income folks taking up opportunities at the bottom end of the labour market, suggesting hard economic realities drew them away from places which may have offered them more by way of cultural support networks. Generally speaking, the affluent are more likely to be able to select the social characteristics of the places they live.

However, it isn't clear the unusual Hispanic growth in new destinations will continue. If a city has one Hispanic family and another moves in, that's a 100 per cent Hispanic growth rate so the numbers required to continue posting fast growth go up exponentially. With slower Hispanic immigration, lower fertility and upward mobility, Hispanics may choose to remain closer to their co-ethnics. Also, there are only a limited number of unskilled jobs. After the financial crisis in 2007–8, Hispanic dispersion to new destinations was cut in half and hasn't recovered.[25] In Britain, minorities living in heavily white wards tend to leave for more diverse places at a much faster clip than whites, suggesting that when they have a choice, many minorities would rather not inhabit a lily-white area. In Canada, many immigrants who are initially compelled by the government to settle in the relatively homogeneous Maritime provinces subsequently move to diverse metro areas. Today, successful minorities who leave inner-city neighbourhoods must often choose a whiter one if they want better amenities. As diversity rises, successful minorities may be able to opt instead for one of many emerging ethnoburbs – places like Johns Creek in Atlanta – which offer both cultural comfort and material amenities.

WHITE RETREAT?

It's easy to focus on eye-catching exceptions to rules, but more important to step back and appreciate the broader tableau: namely, that most Western countries, including Canada and the United States, are overwhelmingly white across most of their geographic expanse. This is abundantly clear from the new dot-per-person ethnic maps of Canada and the US you can find on the book's website.[26] Immigration is transforming large metropolitan areas while leaving most of these countries relatively untouched. Most whites are experiencing more diversity, but not as much as they might in the absence of segregation. For instance, the average white person in America lives in a tract that is 8 points whiter than average.

Nevertheless, the insulation effect is much greater for rural and small-city whites. Major American metro areas dropped from 70 per cent white in 1990 to 56 per cent white in 2010. The 14-point fall compares to a 10-point decline for whites in smaller metros and a 6-point drop in rural areas.[27] Even here, rural minority growth tends to be concentrated in a small number of districts near industrial facilities or metro areas. For many isolated places, minority increase is glacially slow, with Hispanics forming less than 5 per cent of the population. Twenty-two of the top 100 American metropolitan areas were 'majority minority' in 2010 and metro areas are 7 points less white in 2015 than they were in 2000. Yet outside the top 100 metros the average white person's neighbourhood became only 4 points more diverse, from 84 to 80 per cent white. In rural areas, things were even more stable, with the average slipping just 3 points, from 88 to 85 per cent white, in these years.

Some of this is because minorities are attracted to where they are concentrated, but consider figure 9.3. The graph shows a fairly clear positive relationship between the white share of a state's metropolitan population in 2000 and the rate of change in the raw number of white people living in urban areas of the state during 2000–10.[28] Thus urban Idaho, which was 91 per cent white in 2000, experienced a 10 per cent increase in its white urban population in the ensuing decade. Metropolitan California, which was only 47 per cent white in 2000, lost almost 15 per cent of its white urban population in the 2000s. No state with less than a two-thirds white urban majority in 2000 experienced absolute growth in its white urban population the following decade. And if a state's urban population was over 85 per cent white in 2000, it was guaranteed to retain at least 94 per cent of its white urbanites. In effect, the more diverse a state's metro population in 2000, the greater the loss of its white metro population in the ensuing decade. Frey and Liaw consider a large sample of inter-state movers from the 1995–2000 period and find that the difference between the ethnic composition of the origin and destination state is second only to geographic distance in predicting which state an individual will move to.[29, 30]

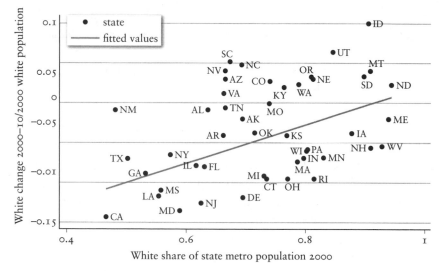

9.3. Metro US white population growth, by state, 2000–2010

Source: computed from Longitudinal Tract Database 2016

Of course, most moves are short distance and people have a lot of choice within states. And this is where the patterns begin to look uncannily similar across time, scale and country. Figure 9.4 compares trends in British wards with those in American tracts, a comparable unit. I focus only on tracts or wards that experienced population growth because many peripheral white places lose population and this distorts the results somewhat. Patterns in both countries tell a similar story: metropolitan neighbourhoods with a higher initial white share experience slower white decline or faster white growth than those which are initially more diverse. Think of how unusual this is: if people moved randomly, we should see the balls gravitate to the mean. Whiter places should lose the most white people while diverse areas should gain them. Instead, we find the opposite pattern. In addition, a curve based on the square of initial white share, not a straight line, best fits the data in both cases. As the curve reaches 85–90 per cent white in 2000–2001, it appears to kink upwards.

Naturally there are exceptions like Brixton in London or Brooklyn, New York, where gentrification has taken place. This shows up as the line of dots on the left side of the American graph where there is a spike of places that were less than 10 per cent white in 2000 but had

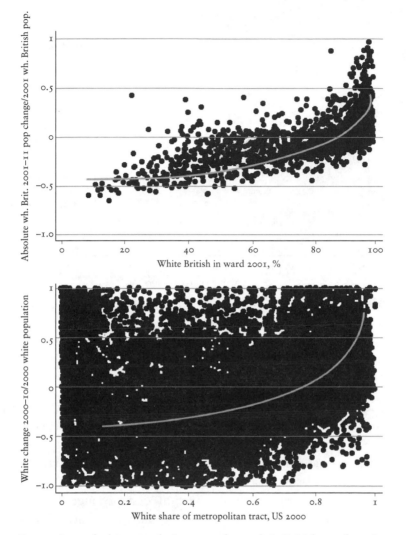

9.4. Comparison of white population growth trends in British wards and American metropolitan tracts

Source: Census of England and Wales 2001, 2011. US Longitudinal Tract Database.

rapid white growth in the 2000s. Still, the overwhelming story, which the statistical models tell, is one in which whites are moving towards the most heavily white neighbourhoods. An identical pattern can be found in Stockholm neighbourhoods in the 1990s, and appears to hold within many American cities.[31] We see it as well in urban British Columbia and

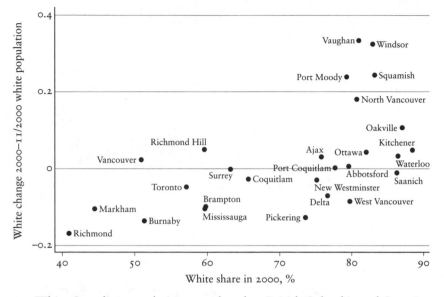

9.5. White Canadian population growth, urban British Columbia and Ontario communities, 2001–11

Source: calculated from Census of Canada 2001, 2011.

Ontario, Canada, in figure 9.5. Once again, white growth is greater in initially white communities, and the non-linear curve rears its head.

A sceptic might argue that the pattern above arises because whites are better off and white areas are more expensive so only whites can afford them. Yet controls for socioeconomic factors like unemployment, population density or deprivation don't change the results. Running the exercise for minority groups fails to replicate the same pattern: in Britain, Afro-Caribbeans or Bangladeshis are moving out of concentration areas, and African-Americans and Hispanics are doing the same in the US. This tells us we are staring at a white dynamic.

What is that dynamic? A number of researchers have, in my view, drawn the wrong conclusions from population patterns. They argue that when minority share exceeds 10 or 15 per cent, there is a tipping point beyond which whites flee an area. This draws on the work of Thomas Schelling, a game-theory genius. He demonstrated that if you imagine black and white pieces evenly spaced on a chessboard, with each piece a person, and each white person has a different tolerance threshold for the share of black pieces in the surrounding squares, a single move would increase the number of black pieces surrounding a white piece enough to make the person move to a less black environment. This would leave the former environment with fewer white pieces, which would breach another white person's tolerance threshold, making them move, and so on, setting off a cascade which ends in complete segregation. As applied to the US, the thinking is that if a small number of African-Americans enter a white neighbourhood, they alter its composition enough to prompt intolerant whites to flee, which increases black share enough to cause the next most intolerant whites to flee, and so on.

Today, however, few whites are this skittish and there aren't many lily-white areas. More than one white-to-minority household shift is needed to meaningfully change a neighbourhood. More importantly, research with individual-level data finds only limited support for the argument that, all else being equal, whites are more likely to leave diverse or changing neighbourhoods than white ones. They have a slightly higher preference to move, but don't actually do so. Those who argue for white flight ground their claim in white tolerance thresholds, but data which tracks people over time, notably Understanding Society (UKHLS) in Britain, tells us that Brexit- and Remain-voting whites, UKIP- or Labour-voting whites, or white liberals and conservatives, move to similar places once we account for demographic and economic factors.[32] In Britain, conservative whites are actually *less* likely to leave diverse wards than liberal whites because movers tend to be more liberal and better educated than stayers. Finally, it is a bit odd to argue that whites are fearful of change at a threshold of around 85 or 90 per cent white, but are relaxed about minorities when an area drops below 85 per cent white. Intuitively, if flight was the mechanism, we should see a gentle slope on the right side of the charts, then a tipping point at, say, 50 per cent white, below which the white population crashes.

Rather than account for the pattern in figures 9.3 through 9.5 through white flight and tipping, we can better grasp it as stemming from white attraction to whiter, ethnically stable neighbourhoods. Heavily white neighbourhoods are unattractive to minorities: UK data show that non-whites tend to avoid wards which are over 85 per cent white. This means the heavily white wards are *both* very white and ethnically stable. White residents are sensitive to both white levels and ethnic change when selecting a neighbourhood. In addition, they often overestimate minority share, so may opt to move to an area that is whiter than they would actually prefer.[33] The net result is a steady white flow towards the whitest neighbourhoods, districts, communities and even states.

DO INTOLERANT WHITES LEAVE DIVERSE AREAS?

Thanks to an innovative set of survey experiments asking people to indicate their preferred neighbourhood racial composition, we know that whites have the most exclusive ethnic neighbourhood preferences. When shown a card with twelve houses on it, some white and some shaded to represent minority groups, whites prefer a majority of houses to be from their own group – an average of around 70 per cent. This holds equally in the US, Netherlands and UK, where these studies have been done. In the US, African-Americans are most integration-minded, while Hispanics and Asians fall in between – though they are generally opposed to having many black neighbours.[34] What's remarkable is that whites emerge as the most exclusive group, even though you would expect them to be most swayed by pressure to prove to an interviewer they are not racist. We should therefore consider 70 per cent white to be a lower bound on actual white preferences. Why this white exclusivity? It could be because whites are accustomed to being a majority and setting the cultural tone in Western countries, whereas minorities are used to being what their name suggests: in the minority. Others foreground a status dimension, in which many – including minorities – deem white-majority neighbourhoods to be more prestigious than super-diverse ones even when the former are no richer and have similar amenities.[35] Yet even when told that minority residents in a hypothetical neighbourhood would be highly educated, half of white Dutch respondents said they would be uncomfortable living in a majority-minority area.[36]

A further possibility is that whites are less tolerant of difference than minorities. The showcard studies in the US and Netherlands find, for example, that whites who view minorities as a cultural or economic threat, or perceive them as prone to crime, prefer a much higher share of whites in their neighbourhoods. Others find that the tipping point beyond which whites no longer increase in US urban neighbourhoods is connected to how racially liberal the local whites are.[37] This would explain why whites in diverse neighbourhoods are generally less anti-immigration and anti-minority than whites in whiter areas.[38] In England and Wales, for example, even when we account for the fact whites in diverse places are more likely to be single, university-educated twenty-somethings, those in the most diverse neighbourhoods are 10 points more open to current immigration levels than those in the least diverse places. This is commonly ascribed to the fact that whites in diverse areas experience more positive contact with actual immigrants or minorities, reducing fears and misperceptions. But could it instead be due to selection: liberal whites moving to more diverse areas while conservative whites depart?

The showcard studies imply that intolerant whites select out of diverse neighbourhoods, leaving liberal whites behind. It's a story which makes sense on the surface and emerges strongly in qualitative research, captured well by the controversial BBC documentary *The Last Whites of the East End*, which aired in May 2016. Paul Watt's ethnographic work similarly relates how whites with conservative attitudes such as Jane, a working-class 'Cockney' retiree who moved from increasingly immigrant east London to exurban Essex, speak about diversity. Here she describes the diverse east London neighbourhood she left:

> My dentist is there, that's it, that's the only reasons [*sic*] to go back there. We don't go back there for anything else. Even to the market, it's changed. It's not the old English market that it was. It's like all the Indian stuff and things, and you know, you're just not interested in that sort of thing, and they're taking over the fruit stall and things like this, and it's not the same. [. . .][39]

Another respondent, Sonia, bemoaned the fact that even in parts of Essex things were changing: 'Some of the market stalls have changed, half of it's Asians now. It's a different atmosphere, it's not the same, not as friendly. Everyone used to say "hello" to you . . . We go in the café and it's run by Bozzos [Bosnians] now.'[40] These sentiments are real, but the problem is that a large majority of all white working-class Londoners, whether they have 'fled' to whiter areas or not, share them. Do whites who remain behind in diverse spots like east London hold more tolerant attitudes than those who leave for whiter zones such as Essex? Here I turn to longitudinal surveys, notably Understanding Society, which asks 40,000 British people each year which party they support and where they live. In 2016, it asked people whether they preferred Britain to leave or remain in the European Union. We know the Leave vote was weaker in diverse areas compared to whiter places: does this mean Brexit whites, most of whom strongly oppose immigration, tend to flee diversity?

Actually, no. What people say and do seem almost totally disconnected. Brexit-voting, UKIP-voting or Conservative-voting whites who live in diverse wards (less than 60 per cent white) are more like to *say* they want to move than Remain, Liberal Democrat, Green or Labour voters, but are less likely to *actually* do so. With sociodemographics controlled, 35 per cent of white British Leave voters want to leave diverse neighbourhoods compared to 28 per cent of Remainers. But while 9 per cent of white British Remainers move from diverse wards in a given year, just 5.5 per cent of white British Leavers do. And this takes income, education, age, area deprivation and other socioeconomic factors which affect both moving and Brexit voting into account.

In Stockholm, Lina Hedman shows that ethnic Swedes leaving the most diverse parts of the city are if anything slightly more tolerant of diversity than whites remaining behind, even when controlling for demographics and income. Those who stay in diverse places differ from movers mainly in having more social connections in their neighbourhood.[41] It's not that white liberals are hypocrites who flee diversity, but that liberals – those David Goodhart dubs 'Anywheres' – are more likely to be mobile. Conservatives may be more attached to their routines and hence more likely to stay than liberals, regardless of whether a neighbourhood is diverse or not.

There's little evidence white conservative movers choose whiter areas than liberals when they move. Whites select whiter places to move to than minorities, but it's hard to fit a paper clip between liberals and conservatives. Controlling for all the usual confounders, white British Leavers, UKIP/BNP voters or right-wing voters move to places a few points whiter than white British Remainers and left-wing voters, but the difference is small. In the US, there is no equivalent data, so I turned to geocoded pro- and anti-Trump tweets. This work, with a data scientist, Andrius Mudinas, finds a similar pattern to Britain. Namely, white Americans move to significantly whiter places than minorities, but whites who are pro- and anti-Trump move to equally white areas.

This echoes a growing number of US studies using voter registration files which find that the partisan composition of areas is not what attracts white Republicans or Democrats there. This isn't the same question as whether white Democrats move to more diverse places than white Republicans, but it reflects a similar process in which ideology is a weak driver of ethnic mobility. Bill Bishop and Robert Cushing rightly note that the share of Americans living in landslide Republican or Democratic counties rose from a quarter in 1976 to about half by 2004.[42] But the reason for their 'Big Sort' of Democrats into Democratic areas and vice-versa for the Republicans has more to do with the fact that whites, African-Americans, the poor or those with degrees move towards their own. That is, they choose, or can only afford, areas where their social group lives – and these groups have distinctive voting profiles. As the authors note, degree-holders were relatively evenly distributed around the country in 1970. But, as the tertiary sector grew over the next few decades, they began to cluster in Silicon Valley, New York and other centres of the knowledge economy. This enhanced the Democratic character of large metro areas.

People generally don't move to neighbourhoods for explicitly political reasons, but the partisan character of an area can shape the vote choices of people – especially those without strong prior ideological leanings. In the UK, a study using BHPS data tracking people over an eighteen-year period found that those in Conservative-dominated constituencies trended more Conservative in their voting over time, though the same was not true of Labour areas.[43] Amenities also matter, and account for why partisans wind up moving to where they are already dominant. Those who value walkability and public transport, for instance, are more likely to be Democrats: 77 per cent of 'consistent liberals' prefer to live in communities where houses are closer together and schools, stores and restaurants are within walking distance. Seventy-five per cent of 'consistent conservatives' prefer a place where houses are larger and farther apart, and amenities are several miles away.[44] These values collide with reality: jobs tend to be in metro areas and good schools in the suburbs. This draws Republicans and Democrats into areas they would prefer to avoid. As the political geographers James Gimpel and Iris Hui remark, 'If it were not for the economic influences pulling people towards larger cities, the nation would surely exhibit far greater partisan segmentation across small geographic units than it does.'[45] Finally, the character of areas shapes the way people vote due to peer pressure, norms and influence, which accentuates partisan skewing.

Thus far I've made the case that whites who dislike diversity don't retreat from it any more than pro-diversity whites do. But this isn't completely true. At the extremes, we do find an effect. A YouGov survey I fielded with the think tank Demos in August 2013 asked people if they had moved from a more or less diverse ward over the past ten years. It also enquired about voting, immigration attitudes and minority tolerance thresholds. White British movers who said they would feel uncomfortable if their neighbourhood dropped below 90 per cent white were more likely to have moved towards a whiter ward than white British movers who had higher minority tolerance thresholds. But this low-tolerance group formed a mere 3 per cent of the total survey sample. Those who wanted immigration reduced a lot – a much larger portion of the sample – didn't have a history of moving to less diverse neighbourhoods than pro-immigration whites. Attitude differences between white liberals and conservatives *do* affect moving behaviour, but only for a tiny 3 per cent subgroup. The discrepancy between the showcard studies – where attitudes to diversity matter – and actual moving behaviour, where attitudes don't, could arise from the fact that white social networks tend to steer whites towards white neighbourhoods, regardless of attitudes to diversity. Alternatively, it may be that liberals and conservatives both have ethnic preferences but liberals are less willing to own up to them.

Attitudes also influence moving behaviour for a somewhat larger slice of people: anti-immigration whites who already live in heavily white areas. White British Leave voters who moved from heavily (over 95 per cent) white neighbourhoods make up around 12 per cent of white British movers. They have a .64 probability of choosing another lily-white neighbourhood when they move, compared to .51 for white British who originate in the whitest areas but voted to Remain in the EU. And this controls for many individual and area characteristics which affect destination choice.[46] The same pattern holds for UKIP and non-UKIP voters, and, to a slightly lesser degree, for voters for parties to the right of centre compared to those on the left. What's interesting is that among white voters originating in even moderately diverse wards (over 5 per cent minorities) there is no significant difference between conservatives and liberals in where they move. So it seems white conservatives used to a lily-white status quo prefer to move to other homogeneous areas, while white conservatives, once they experience some diversity, don't differ from white liberals. I haven't found the same pattern among white pro- and anti-Trump voters, but data quality is lower for the US because it's based on Twitter profiles.

It seems whites move to white areas more than non-whites, but white liberals and conservatives barely differ. How then can we explain the dramatic pattern of whites moving towards whites? One possibility is that white preference is operating at a subconscious level among white liberals, drawing them towards whiter places. Another is that whites have a stronger sense of community in lily-white areas, which attracts white liberals. Figure 9.6 is based on the Citizenship Surveys in Britain

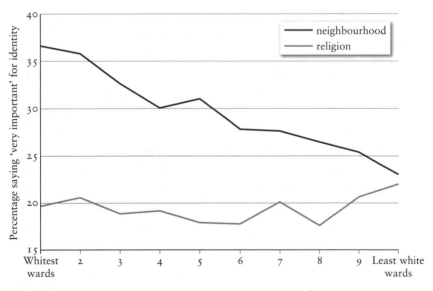

9.6. Neighbourhood is 'very important' for self-identity, for white British, by ward diversity, 2007–11

Source: Citizenship Surveys 2009–11. N = 33,055.

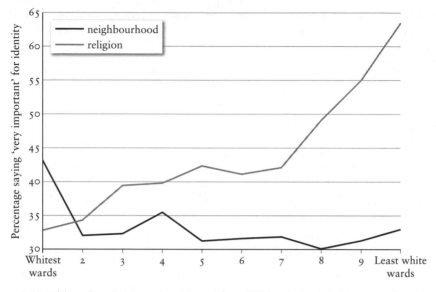

9.7. Neighbourhood is 'very important' for self-identity, minority respondents, by ward minority share or religion, 2007–11

Source: Citizenship Surveys 2009–11. N = 33,055.

that ask people how important neighbourhood is to a person's sense of 'who they are'.[47] The share of white British who say neighbourhood is 'very important' for their identity declines from 36 per cent in the whitest wards to 22 per cent in the most diverse. Among minorities, however, there is no difference in their propensity to say the place they live is very or quite important to them as the share of minorities in their neighbourhood rises. On the other hand, figure 9.7 shows religion is much more important to minorities living in high-minority areas than among minorities in white areas, reflecting the fact minority-specific places of worship are located in ethnic enclaves and attract co-ethnics. The same holds with controls for ward population density and deprivation as well as individual characteristics. All of which suggests whites may be gravitating to whiter areas to find social cohesion or a sense of community – motives which cut across the liberal–conservative divide.

An Indian-American writer, Anjali Enjeti, nicely captures the new phenomenon of liberal whites leaving and avoiding superdiverse suburbs. Johns Creek, her neighbourhood in suburban Atlanta, is a paragon of diversity: 'Persian and Indian markets bookend strip malls. Japanese,

Vietnamese, Thai, Indonesian, Korean, and Chinese restaurants perch on the corners of major intersections.' Though still 60 per cent white as of the 2010 census, it is changing rapidly. At the local high school, the number of whites fell from 397 to 195 in a decade, from 55 to 23 per cent. Enjeti describes herself as having a front-row seat on the suburb's white flight. 'The majority of these white families ... move across a newly expanded four-lane road to the adjacent northern county, Forsyth, a stone's throw from their former domiciles.' She quotes a sociologist, Samuel Kye, an expert on ethnoburbs, who told her that a significant presence of minorities in a prosperous suburb is 'a near perfect predictor' of 'white exodus'.

Though the Asian presence is what Jonathan Haidt terms the 'elephant' – the unconscious motive – for white flight or avoidance, Enjeti picks up on what Haidt calls the 'rider', our conscious rationalization for our subconscious decisions: namely, the liberal rationale that white children will be adversely affected by competitive Asian students and will perform better in a more holistic scholastic environment. As she puts it: 'The white parents in Johns Creek, who in the same breath decry the police killings of unarmed African-Americans, do not hesitate to tell me they do not want their children measured against Asians.'[48] Enjeti's reportage seems consistent with what the large-scale data is telling us: white liberals, like white conservatives, are generally avoiding superdiversity – especially when they settle down and have kids.

Work on school segregation confirms that segregation is greater among schoolchildren than in the general population – i.e. schools are more segregated than areas. San Francisco, for example, is 42 per cent white. Its school-age population is 28 per cent white. Yet its public, i.e. state, schools are only 13 per cent white, with a majority of white kids attending private schools.[49] Likewise, school segregation in England and Wales tends to be more pervasive than residential segregation in part because whites opt out of the state sector for private or religious schools.[50] It turns out the pattern of white growth in the whitest schools resembles what we saw for the whitest neighbourhoods: namely, that above a threshold of about 85 per cent white, absolute white pupil growth is highest. Figure 9.8 presents official data for growing schools in the south-east of England for 2010–15, showing our now-familiar kink at the right of the chart. The same graph, only with denser dots, could be shown for all of England.

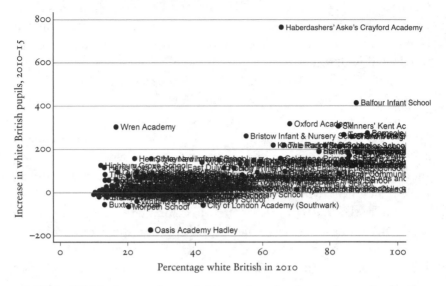

9.8. White British share and growth in growing schools, south-east England, 2010–15

Source: England School Census 2010–15. Department of Education.

Notice that a majority of the schools which gained over 200 white British pupils in these five years were in schools that were over 80 per cent white British in 2010. Among these growing schools, those in places where pupils were over 80 per cent white British all gained white British students. Below 70 per cent initial white British share, schools grew just as fast, but many lost white British pupils while gaining minority and European pupils. Much of this reflects residential choice, but not all: when I control for the 2010 white British share in the ward in which a school is located, this only accounts for half the impact on white British pupil growth in the ensuing five years. The other half is explained by variation in the 2010 white British share in schools *within* wards. This again speaks against the view that fearful whites flee schools with a high share of minorities. Instead, the pattern suggests they are attracted to schools with a high share of their own group. An unacknowledged desire for community and cohesion could be the motivating factor.

TWO NATIONS?

The relative shift of white populations towards whiter neighbourhoods, often in exurbs, rural areas or small cities, combined with minority growth in large metro areas, is producing higher-order geographic divisions. Moreover, knowledge work is concentrated in metropolitan areas, luring university-educated rather than unskilled whites. The result is a polarizing tendency towards the emergence of 'two nations' within Western countries. One 'nation' consists of large diverse metros like New York, Paris or London, where a largely minority proletariat lives alongside a wealthy knowledge class which is primarily native-born. Beyond these diverse metro areas lies a second 'nation': rural districts, small towns, provincial cities and the exurban fringes of major cities. This part of the country is overwhelmingly white, with a lower share of university-educated professionals and a higher average age. The American writer Michael Lind argues that the two represent different models of society, with considerable inequality in the cities and a more even distribution of income in the communities outside them:

> The social liberalism of these high-end service meccas cannot disguise caste systems reminiscent of Central American republics, with extreme wealth and income stratification and a largely immigrant impoverished menial-service class whose complexions differ from those of the free-spending oligarchs. The gap between richest and poorest in New York City is comparable to that of Swaziland; Los Angeles and Chicago are slightly more egalitarian, comparable to the Dominican Republic and El Salvador[51]

The ethnic composition of the urban elite is not as white as Lind suggests if we count all white-collar professionals as members and should become less white over time: in the second half of the twentieth century, the American urban elite 'de-WASPed' at a rapid rate, absorbing upwardly mobile white ethnics.[52] However, given current trends, whites are likely to become a vestigial element of the American urban panorama late this century, much like WASPs in New York, who make up 3–5 per cent of the city's population. In Europe, the process is at an earlier stage, but is following a similar trajectory.

In the US, the terms 'metro America' and 'retro America' have been used to denote the two nations mentioned above. Politically, the metropolitan nation is liberal and progressive, reflecting the dominance of young, mobile, credentialled or minority residents. In many metropolitan areas, the foreign-born make up a large chunk of the population. Toronto is 46 per cent foreign-born, mainly citizens or permanent residents. Add in those of immigrant parentage, and this means a majority have new-immigrant roots. New York, London, Los Angeles and Sydney trail closely behind, at 37–9 per cent foreign-born.

Owing to ethnic residential preferences and economic forces, hinterlands are much whiter and more ethnically stable than larger cities. They are more likely to vote for nationalist parties, usually conservative or right-wing populist. I don't wish to make the same mistake as the pundits: political-geographic differences are shades of grey, not black and white. Many in large cities identify with the nationalist hinterland and plenty of those in the exurbs consider themselves cosmopolitan. However, when votes are tallied on a district-by-district basis, even small differences swiftly produce a map of sharp contrasts. The new political cleavage in the West turns on a value axis between open/globalism and closed/nationalism. Globalism finds its expression in the hub-and-spoke network of large cities with their international migration flows, while nationalism predominates in the more settled areas outside major nodes. The maps of the vote for Brexit, Trump or the Austrian Freedom Party on the book website reveal how most of these countries' geographic expanse tilts towards right-wing populism, while cities and university towns favour globalism.

We've seen that most of the voting differences between cities and rural areas arise because different types of people live in them: young or old, white or minority, unskilled or university-educated. But there are also modest contextual effects arising from peer pressure and cultural atmosphere at the local level. A feedback loop of mutual enmity can arise, with those from homogeneous hinterlands feeling alienated from the diverse cities and vice-versa. Peer pressure from the kinds of people found in retro or metro social contexts has some effect on voting behaviour, tilting the politics of the two nations towards polarization. Most commentators exaggerate the impact of the liberal atmosphere of cosmopolitan cities like London on public opinion, but at neighbourhood level, strongly globalist or nationalist environments do shape attitudes. For example, living in a ward that voted strongly Remain exposes you to social influence from Remainers as well as Remain messaging. This contextual effect is a larger influence on a person's Brexit vote than their education or age.[53] The effect of being in a Remain Local Authority (Local Authorities are a unit ten to thirty times larger in population than wards) is considerably weaker because the influence is less intimate. At the city or region level the contextual effect disappears.

As cities grow and become increasingly powerful engines of globalist politics, the metro/retro political divide may widen. In the US, the principal political divide in the northern states between the 1890s and 1960s pitted largely immigrant-descended urban areas of the northeast and upper Midwest against the mainly Protestant countryside and towns. This standoff marked the nation's politics for decades. However, the fact that rural southern whites voted for the same Democratic party as northern Catholics and Jews moderated rural–urban alienation and resulted in moments of unity such as FDR's New Deal. Today no conservative section of the country votes Democratic, so there is no moderating force. The county-level voting map is mostly Republican red with Democratic blue patches in the cities, and, since Bill Clinton left office, the contrast has been growing more extreme every election. This also shapes interpersonal networks, with three quarters of Americans only discussing politics with those of their own political persuasion.[54] As cities become more ethnically diverse and progressive, and the populist right gains force or is co-opted by a nationalistic centre-right, the urban–rural split is likely to widen.

'HUNKERING DOWN': WHITE SOCIAL NETWORKS

We've seen that whites tend to move towards schools, neighbourhoods and communities where they're concentrated. Among growing communities there is a marked tendency for white population growth to take place in the heavily white areas. Of course, most people don't make long-distance moves. Many are compelled by circumstances to live in more diverse locations than they would prefer. Thus most whites are experiencing steadily rising diversity in their neighbourhoods and schools. But this doesn't necessarily translate into a great deal more mixing. Indeed, as diversity rises, white social networks are becoming less representative of the places they inhabit.

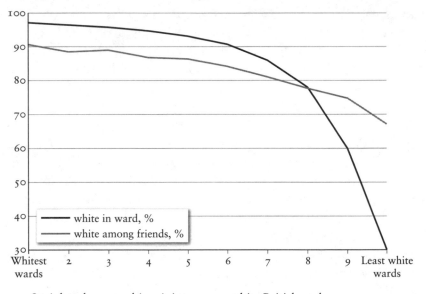

9.9. Social and geographic mixing among white British under-25s, 2009–11

Source: Citizenship Surveys 2009–11. Note: friendship share approximated from a 4-category response. N=1,282.

Figure 9.9 is drawn from Britain's Citizenship Surveys for the years 2009–11, capturing 16,000 white British individuals. What it shows is that native-born whites aged sixteen to twenty-five living in the most diverse wards, which average only 30 per cent white, have friends who average 68 per cent white. Thus the white skew in their friendship network is 38 points. Whites in wards in decile 8, which averages 78 per cent white, have friends who are roughly a fifth non-white. That is, their social ties perfectly reflect their neighbourhood. As wards exceed 90 per cent white, native whites' friendship networks become more diverse than their areas, which makes sense insofar as people make friends at work and in other more diverse situations beyond their neighbourhood. But, again, what really jumps out is the way white social networks begin to diverge from their surroundings as neighbourhoods become highly diverse. This is true even among the young people portrayed in figure 7.

In 2014, Britain's Social Integration Commission, chaired by Matthew Taylor, Chief Executive of the Royal Society of Arts and former head of Blair's Policy Unit when he was Prime Minister, commissioned a large survey of over 4,500 people. Respondents were asked about their most recent social gathering of five people or fewer, and to state the social characteristics of each guest. It turns out that in London, the supposedly cosmopolitan capital and most ethnically diverse part of the country, whites' social networks were the most skewed of all.[55] This reflects the pattern shown in figure 9.9 in which a white person's social networks become increasingly unrepresentative of their surroundings as their area grows more diverse.

Some of this is certainly because people make friends outside their neighbourhood so the mismatch would be expected to be larger where whites inhabit a diverse area. However, in keeping with findings from a study of how American students make friends at university, much of the effect seems to turn on 'like with like' ethnic homophily.[56] At work, with less choice, there is more interaction: 65 per cent of white Britons in the 2009–11 Citizenship Surveys who lived in a ward averaging 30 per cent white interacted with other ethnic and religious groups on a daily basis at work, but only 14.5 per cent did so in their (or others') home. That's a 50-point gap. In the whitest neighbourhoods the corresponding numbers were 23 and 2 per cent, a 21-point gap, which is much smaller. People connect less with people at home than at work, but the home vs work pattern indicates something more: that when whites in diverse areas have the choice, i.e. of whom to invite or visit, they interact much less with diverse groups than at work, where there is less choice. Here again, network segregation is higher for whites in diverse places because if people interacted randomly we would expect whites to have much more contact with minorities in their homes.

The pattern seems even more pronounced in the US. Using a convenience sample of 730 individuals – including 612 whites – from MTurk, I found that 50 per cent of whites living in ZIP codes that averaged just 30 per cent white said their most recent gathering of five people or fewer was all-white. Only a quarter said their most recent gathering wasn't majority white. Roughly speaking, the pro-white skew in this US white sample for those in the most diverse neighbourhoods is 50–60 points, arguably even higher than the 35–40 points in the UK recorded for the friendship measure, though the questions are not strictly comparable. It seems that even where whites are exposed to high levels of diversity in their neighbourhood, social contacts remain largely white.

We've seen that political attitudes and social behaviour are only modestly connected. In our British Citizenship Survey sample, 65 per cent of native-born whites who want immigration reduced 'a lot' have all-white friends compared to 42 per cent of native-born whites who want immigration to stay the same or increase. In Understanding Society, the gap between Leavers and Remainers on the 'all white friends' measure is 61–51. About half the difference can be accounted for by the younger age and higher education of whites in diverse cities, since the young and educated say they have more minority friends. Still, even controlling for these factors, when it comes to having all-white friendship networks, there is a 14-point gap between pro- and anti-immigration voters and a 6-point gap between Leavers and Remainers.

Likewise, 62 per cent of Americans in the MTurk sample who want less immigration had an all-white intimate social gathering, whereas only 49 per cent of those backing higher immigration did. White Trump voters in the MTurk sample were modestly more likely to have an all-white network than white Clinton voters, but this disappeared with controls for age and education. We shouldn't conclude from this that liberals have more minority friends than conservatives. As we saw for white flight and avoidance of diverse areas, these selection effects are small. Instead, the gaps are best explained by positive contact – i.e. having minority friends makes whites slightly more tolerant of immigration or less likely to back right-wing populists. Once again, when it comes to the ethnic composition of whites' social networks, being white matters a lot more than being liberal or conservative. Whites and minorities differ a lot in which ethnic groups they invite to dinner, but white liberals and conservatives don't – they both inhabit predominantly white worlds, even when they reside in diverse neighbourhoods.

DIVERSITY AND SOLIDARITY

Whites' unrepresentative social networks in diverse communities suggest society may be more fragmented in superdiverse locales. Does this reduce social solidarity? In a seminal article, the influential political scientist Robert Putnam argues that ethnic diversity and communal solidarity are in tension. Diverse places are less cohesive, with people expressing less trust in their neighbours than in relatively white areas.

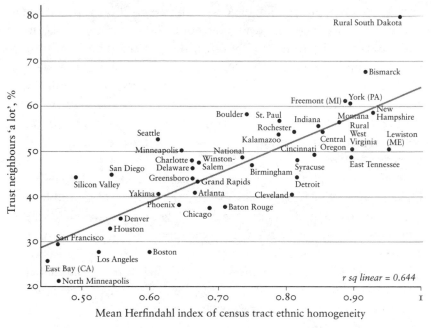

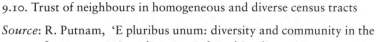

9.10. Trust of neighbours in homogeneous and diverse census tracts

Source: R. Putnam, 'E pluribus unum: diversity and community in the twenty-first century'. *Scandinavian Political Studies* 30(2): 148

Not only do people trust neighbours and members of outgroups less in places with a high share of minorities, but they also trust members of their *own group* less. Figure 9.10, reproduced from Putnam's essay, shows that the proportion saying they trust their neighbours 'a lot' is much higher in homogeneous census tracts than in diverse ones. At one end of the scale is high-trust, non-diverse South Dakota; at the other low-trust, highly diverse San Francisco.

Probing this in more depth for North America, Dietlind Stolle, Stuart Soroka and Richard Johnston asked North American survey respondents the following: 'If you lost a wallet or purse with two hundred dollars, how likely is it to be returned with the money in it if it was found by (1) strangers, (2) neighbours, (3) police.' Respondents could answer from 0, not likely, to 3, the most likely. Combining the responses yields a single trust index for an individual from 0 to 3.[57] They discovered that even when they controlled for education, age, religion, being an immigrant or minority, language and the deprivation level of neigh-bourhoods, more diverse neighbourhoods were strongly associated with lower trust in strangers. The effect was present in both the US and Canada, but was stronger in Canada, where there is a higher general level of interpersonal trust. There, whites in tracts with no minorities were almost a full scale point more trusting than whites in tracts with the highest minority share. Minorities were also less trusting in tracts with a higher share of minorities, but the effect was much stronger for white Canadians.[58]

Reviewing some ninety studies of diversity and social cohesion in Europe, North America and Australasia, Tom van der Meer and Jochem Tolsma found that diversity was linked with lower neighbourhood trust in the majority of studies, even with controls for area deprivation. The effects were especially consistent for whites in diverse areas, whereas for minorities some tests showed their trust to be higher in diverse neighbourhoods.[59] Many things can affect trust in neighbours, and unmeasured factors such as traffic may be related to ethnic diversity. Any snapshot of variation in diversity and trust across places at one point in time can't rule out unmeasured factors.

However, a number of longitudinal studies have now examined what happens when places become more diverse. This offers a rigorous test of the diversity–solidarity hypothesis. By focusing on what happens to people over time, the researcher can screen out the many confounding influences that could be associated with both differences of local diversity and individual trust at any one time point. In Denmark, one longitudinal study found that a shift from 0 to 30 per cent minority in an area between 1980 and 2009, the maximum recorded, corresponds to a .23 loss of trust on a scale running from 1 – 'people can be trusted' – to 0 – 'you can't be too careful'.[60] In Britain, two social researchers, James Laurence and Lee Bentley, using the BHPS, the precursor to Understanding Society, tracked over 4,000 individuals over an eighteen-year period from 1991 to 2009. They found that among people who stayed in their neighbourhoods levels of community attachment declined significantly as their communities became more diverse.[61]

ARE DIVERSE SOCIETIES
LESS COHESIVE?

The evidence from a generation of studies since Putnam's provocative article confirms that he is clearly right in one respect: local diversity reduces local trust and attachment among whites. But Putnam and others make a more contentious claim, that diversity reduces national levels of trust in politics, making it harder for societies to share wealth and provide effective public services. David Goodhart dubs this the 'Progressive Dilemma' in that those on the left are compelled to choose between two cherished policy aims, diversity and solidarity. He quotes David Willetts, Minister of Education in David Cameron's Conservative government:

> The basis on which you can extract large sums of money in tax and pay it out in benefits is that most people think the recipients are people like themselves, facing difficulties which they themselves could face. If values become more diverse, if lifestyles become more differentiated, then it becomes more difficult to sustain the legitimacy of a universal risk-pooling welfare state. People ask, 'Why should I pay for them when they are doing things I wouldn't do?' This is America versus Sweden. You can have a Swedish welfare state provided that you are a homogeneous society with intensely shared values. In the US you have a very diverse, individualistic society where people feel fewer obligations to fellow citizens. Progressives want diversity but they thereby undermine part of the moral consensus on which a large welfare state rests.[62]

The inverse relationship between diversity and solidarity draws on a substantial body of work showing that diverse countries are poorer and more conflict-ridden than homogeneous societies. Sub-Saharan Africa, for instance, is the most ethnically diverse part of the world. Earlier we noted that ethnic diversity within African countries is high mainly because the typical African country has more geoclimatic diversity than countries in other parts of the world. Jungles, mountains or other barriers allow linguistic differences to develop in small pockets, increasing ethnic variety, whereas flat plains or deserts facilitate assimilation. Diverse countries tend to have a higher incidence of civil war than homogeneous ones, but the relationship is 'u'-shaped, with conflict risk highest in polarized places such as Rwanda or Northern Ireland, which have two large groups, and lower in countries with hundreds of small groups like Tanzania.[63] With many groups, coalitions shift over time so they are less likely to become locked in a zero-sum struggle.[64]

What is less contested is diversity's impact on the economy. In a famous article, the economists William Easterly and Ross Levine show that between 25 and 40 per cent of the difference in economic growth between 1960 and 1990 between East Asia and Africa can be explained by the fact that East Asian nations are among the most ethnically homogeneous while Africa is the most diverse.[65] And, within Africa, homogeneous Botswana is considerably more prosperous than diverse Liberia. Part of this relationship runs the other way: as societies develop and cities grow, ethnic diversity declines.[66] Yet East Asia began at a similarly low level of development. Even with modernization, the legacy of geoclimatic diversity remains in the form of higher African ethnic diversity.

Diversity reduces solidarity in developing countries by making it more difficult for governments to agree on where to build a road or hospital, which goods to tax, or how to distribute wealth and government posts. This is because these decisions alter the distribution of benefits between competing ethnic groups. In one natural experiment, researchers looked at what happened in two slums in Kampala, Uganda, when budget problems forced the government to cut back on policing. In ethnically homogeneous Kitale, residents organized their own policing, keeping crime low. In diverse Kifimbura, they couldn't organize, which permitted crime to rise.[67]

Turning to the developed world, Alberto Alesina and his colleagues find that ethnic diversity has a negative impact on public provision in the United States. Controlling for education, income and the proportion of elderly in a community, the authors find that the level of racial diversity is by far the strongest predictor of whether useful public services (garbage collection, public education, infrastructure) are provided in a US county or metro area.[68] They find that, even with a range of control variables, states with larger Hispanic and black populations have more conservative and Republican-leaning whites. Wealthier, often older, whites tend not to wish to pay for public services used most by poorer, often younger, minorities. In fact, getting people in Europe and the US to answer questions about their views on immigration

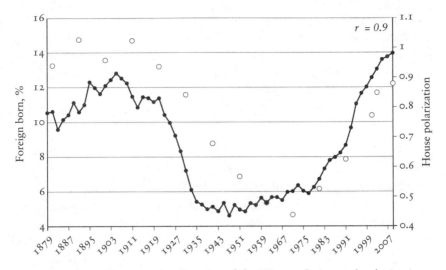

9.11. Correlation between the diversity of the US population and polarization in the House of Representatives

Source: N. M. McCarty, et al., *Polarized America: The Dance of Ideology and Unequal Riches*. Cambridge, MA, MIT Press, 2016

before answering questions on redistributing wealth produces less support for redistribution than when the questions are asked the other way round, illustrating the negative priming effect of immigration on support for the welfare state.[69] Given this evidence, and the clear relationship between local diversity and low neighbourhood trust we encountered earlier, it seems logical that the dynamic is the same – more diversity equals less solidarity. As the West becomes more diverse, support for the welfare state and trust in government will erode. This seems true of the US, where figure 9.11 shows a 90 per cent correlation between the diversity of the American population as measured by foreign-born share (the line of squares), and polarization in the House of Representatives as represented by the dots.

But things aren't so simple. First of all, in many countries, such as South Africa, Malaysia or Fiji, minorities are richer than the majority. In these cases, the incentive for a majority of voters in diverse societies is to strengthen the welfare state, increase tax and implement a kind of affirmative action for majority groups. Sometimes there is violence against rich trading minorities like the Chinese of Indonesia.[70] In the US and Europe, by contrast, minorities tend to be poorer than average, so diversity inclines some white voters away from redistribution. But there are Western exceptions. In Australia or Canada, where predominantly Asian minorities earn a similar amount to whites, we wouldn't expect rising diversity to erode support for the welfare state. Work on Canada shows precisely this – that while diversity leads to reduced local trust, it has no effect on support for redistribution.[71] In America, a higher share of Asians – who earn more than whites – in a state is associated with greater white support for social programmes.[72]

It's also the case that local mistrust doesn't automatically scale up to the national level. Diversity consistently reduces local trust, but has no clear effect on national trust. James Laurence shows that whites in more diverse wards are less trusting of their neighbours; but because they encounter more minorities in their daily lives they are more trusting of ethnic minorities than whites in homogeneous areas.[73] Thus diversity may simultaneously lower 'bonding' within communities while increasing 'bridging' connections across ethnic groups. While diversity reduces local connectedness, this may displace cohesion: people connect socially outside the neighbourhood.[74]

The mechanisms seem to be the same as with immigration opinion, and reflect general patterns in the politics of population change: namely, that local conflicts don't scale up to national conflicts unless national media and politicians become interested in local demographic shifts. Local diversity and ethnic change provide tinder which national politicians can light. However, without elite framing, these embers remain localized and dormant. In order to activate local grievances, national politicians need to make the connection between higher local diversity and welfare abuse, calling for cuts in response. If they do this, low local trust in diverse places helps the message sell. If they don't, the welfare state remains unaffected.

In the West, there appears to be a modest relationship between increasing diversity and falling support for welfare states.[75] But many other factors matter, such as national traditions and economic trends. At the national level, ideological polarization of the population has an even stronger effect than ethnic diversity in reducing trust. Where people are furthest apart in their political ideologies, such as America, they report the lowest levels of interpersonal trust.[76] Often ethnic diversity results in protectionist 'voice' rather than wholesale abandonment of the welfare state. In Europe, for instance, the populist right rarely calls for a smaller state. Instead they demand that those who have 'paid in' should have exclusive access to benefits, not recent immigrants. This 'welfare chauvinism' is especially important for populist parties trying to attract white working-class supporters who benefit from redistribution but oppose immigration.[77] America is somewhat distinct because worries about diversity are exclusively taken up by the Republicans. Within the GOP, opposition to diversity fuses with the party's anti-tax tradition to bolster the case for welfare cuts. Even so, Trump's victory showed that many conservative whites support welfare programmes that favour older white recipients, such as social security, and are concerned about public infrastructure.

As in the case of support for deporting illegal immigrants or voting for the populist right, local diversity doesn't have a singular effect on white attitudes. Figure 9.12 illustrates how the likelihood of someone belonging to their neighbourhood changes when they live in a diverse neighbourhood. The Citizenship Survey data shows – after controlling for age, ward deprivation, population density and several other factors – that

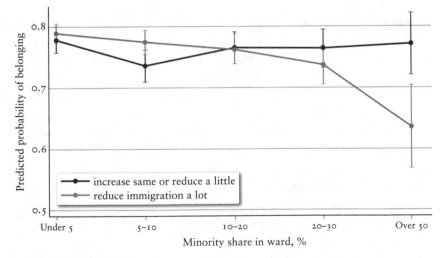

9.12. White British belonging to neighbourhood, by ward minority share and immigration opinion

Source: Citizenship Surveys, 2009–11. N = 12,319. Controls for major demographic and economic variables.

local diversity affects neighbourhood attachment only among the 60 per cent of white Britons who are strongly opposed to immigration. For the 40 per cent who accept current levels or want only a small decrease, local ethnic composition has no effect. In wards where at least half the population is non-white, whites who want immigration reduced a lot are about 15 points less likely to be attached to their neighbourhood than either pro-immigration whites or anti-immigration whites residing in white wards. In other words, diversity lowers trust only among conservative whites.

Specifically, local diversity reduces the local trust and belonging of anti-immigration whites or those who report negative experiences with minorities.[78] Whites who are satisfied with immigration levels or report positive dealings with minorities are unaffected. As we saw in chapter 5 with immigration attitudes, diversity appears to interact with values to produce a polarized white response. Liberal whites are barely affected, but a chunk of conservatives lose trust and psychologically 'exit' from their communities.

TRIBALISM, EXIT AND VOICE

Attitudes to immigration and voting don't have much effect on where people choose to live. By the same token, it's striking how little attitudes – to immigration or the EU, for instance – are affected by actual neighbourhood diversity. In the UK, the share of people saying immigration is a problem in their nation is 50 points higher than the share who say it's a problem locally. Most of the variation in attitudes to national-level immigration is psychological – linked to personality and values rather than the local environment; or it's connected to the general political discussion, i.e. the social power of competing ideas in a country. As a nation experiences ethnic change, mainly in cities, people encounter it in visits to the city. They hear about it through the media, and this appears to distort perceptions to the point where most people – white or non-white – think the share of immigrants is two or three times larger than it is, and the share of Muslims three to five times greater.

In the US in 2016, people guessed the country was 17 per cent Muslim, even though the correct number is 1 per cent. In France, the average estimate for Muslim share was 31 per cent instead of the actual 7.5. French respondents also thought this proportion would rise to 40 per cent by 2020 rather than the officially predicted 8.3 per cent.[79] Minorities' perceptions are even more skewed than those of whites, in part because minorities tend to live in diverse areas.[80] This doesn't mean numbers don't matter. While people get the levels wrong, they have a better feel for trends over time such as the pace of ethnic change or rate of immigration, as we saw with the link between immigration rates and the salience of immigration across Europe. They also can compare the ethnic composition at present with what they experienced growing up – an important source of cognitive dissonance that leads many to report that they don't recognize their country any more (61 per cent of whites said this in a 2011 UK sample).[81]

Those who study the politics of population change in developing countries find that local population dynamics, such as high birth rates leading to pressure on scarce cropland or migrations of outsider tribes into an ethnic group's perceived homeland, can result in low-level conflicts. Population shifts significantly affect the chance of small-scale (under 1,000 killed) violence. But local population change doesn't usually lead to civil wars where more than 1,000 are killed because larger conflicts require national-level mobilization. This means local actors must forge links to ideological players headquartered in the capital.[82] In Ivory Coast, local tension between southern Christians and Muslim immigrants recruited from Burkina Faso to work on southern cocoa plantations didn't flare into violent national conflict until competitive elections were introduced. The southern-based FPI mobilized voters around the issue of illegal Muslim immigration, questioning northerners' citizenship and voting rights – in part to disenfranchise voters for the northern-based RPR.[83]

We find the same pattern with local ethnic shifts and political conflict in the West. Local actors like anti-illegal immigration forces in Hazleton, Pennsylvania, had to catch the eye of the national Republican Party in order for ground-level ethnic shifts to become a national issue. If an ideology like multiculturalism, Islamism or neoliberalism is ascendant, local grievances about ethnic change are ignored, failing to shape national discussion. We see this in 1930s Britain, where Scottish pleas to curb Irish immigration fell on deaf ears at the national Parliament in Westminster; and in Washington after Prop 187 passed.

National politicians' ideological concerns lay elsewhere. Likewise, our evolved nepotistic instinct to cooperate with our genetic relatives has more of an effect on small-scale behaviour – who we choose to befriend, marry or live near – than on our views on national issues.[84] Our attitudes to bigger political questions are influenced more by the national media, politicians, cultural traditions and institutions. While white conservatives scale up their ethnic attachments from the intimate community to the national 'imagined community', liberals' sense of ethnic primordialism extends no further than their intimate network. Beyond it, they endorse pluralism. The institutional power of liberal ideas in countries such as Sweden or Canada accounts for the powerful disjuncture between whites' relatively tribal local behaviour and their more cosmopolitan orientation towards immigration and national identity.

Will whites in Western cities become a highly self-conscious, segregated minority with strong proscriptions against intermarriage, as in South Africa, Mauritius or the Caribbean? Or will they, like WASP Americans, intermarry to the point where they become virtually indistinguishable from other whites? This is the question I turn to next.

PART IV

Join

10

Mixing or Moulding? Interracial Marriage in the West

White majorities may resist the ethnic changes that come with immigration or repress that anxiety to align with an anti-racist moral code. Some may flee change. But, as the saying goes, 'If you can't beat 'em, join 'em.' White majorities may respond to change through adapting to the minority presence or mixing with newcomers residentially, socially or in marriage. In this chapter I consider evidence which shows that white majorities are adapting to change and increasingly blending with minorities. But what is emerging is less a futuristic new compound than a reproduction of established racial categories, albeit with fuzzier boundaries. This suggests the mixed population may ultimately accrete around existing white ethnic cores to form a new 'white' majority containing significant non-white admixture.

Before exploring intermarriage, it's worth mentioning an intermediate form of accommodation based on majorities becoming more accepting of previous waves of immigrants. Previous chapters have concentrated on white fight or flight, but acceptance is also important. There's a paradox in studies of local ethnic change and populist-right support. When the share of minorities in a white person's local area increases, this produces higher opposition to immigration and greater support for the populist right. Yet the higher the share of local immigrant-origin minorities, the lower are white opposition to immigration and support for the far right. The effect is not enormous: only in the fastest-changing places, like Barking, England, or Arcadia, Wisconsin, does opinion shift by over 5 points. And the difference in attitudes to immigration between the whitest and most diverse areas, once you account for other characteristics, is typically no more than 10 points.[1] Ethnic changes lead to hostility, higher minority levels to toleration, but in order to have a high level of minorities, ethnic change had to happen at some point. How does threat morph into toleration?

I investigated this using British data and found that, provided the rate of ethnic change slows, the radicalizing effects of changes fade after ten years. Moreover, the longer a place contains a large and stable minority population, the lower the local white opposition to immigration and the weaker its support for the populist right. These local effects are not large, but they do tell us that whites get used to a minority presence. The more time that passes, the more the local minority comes to be viewed as established. In addition, local whites have a higher degree of contact with minorities than in white neighbourhoods, which reduces anxiety among whites who opposed immigration out of fear.[2]

These results are not produced because intolerant whites have left. White residential sorting is too modest and gradual to account for these effects. Having said this, we must bear in mind that whites in whiter areas bordering diversity (the 'halo') will tend to have heightened opposition to immigration, fearing their areas will change next.[3] An example of the halo effect is the increase in Republican vote share between

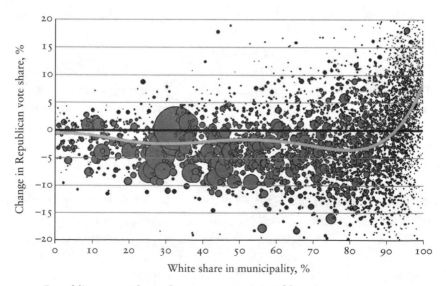

10.1. Republican vote share change, 2012–16: top fifty metros

Source: Myron Orfield, cited in Thomas Edsall, 'White-on-white voting', New York Times, 16 November 2017

Romney's candidacy in 2012 and Trump's in 2016 in the small white municipalities which tend to be located in the 'halo' of exurbs around US cities, as shown in the right-hand side of the chart in figure 10.1.

The halo effect offsets the habituation effect in metro areas, but what's happening nationwide? Here we also find a relaxation effect during periods of slower immigration. In Britain, anti-immigration sentiment declined 20 points between 1970 and 1990 as immigration slowed and fell off the political agenda.[4] In the US, opinion softened during the immigration restrictionist period of 1924–65. If immigration remains low in Europe, we should see immigration come down the political agenda while the anxieties produced by the Migration Crisis should begin to fade. James Dennison and colleagues already find some cooling of European attitudes after the 2015 Migrant Crisis.[5] But this is not certain. What works against relaxation is the continuing demographic growth of minorities due to their younger age structure and slightly higher fertility rate. The level of minorities may affect opinion nationally in a different way to how it operates locally. Instead of creating calm after a decade, habituation may take longer to set in. This seems to be what my meta-analysis of the literature on the contextual effects of diversity on attitudes shows, with minority levels reducing hostility at local but not national levels.[6] If this is the case, then even gradually rising minority population levels – perhaps above a threshold of 5 or 10 per cent of the population – may be sufficient to maintain elevated support for the populist right.

A second form of habituation is generational turnover. Younger cohorts like the Millennials grow up with a different idea of what Austria, America or Britain looks like, so they don't feel like 'strangers in their own country' the way many older whites do. Cohort liberalism is the centrepiece of Ron Inglehart's and Pippa Norris's argument that what we are experiencing is turbulence on the road to a more liberal-cosmopolitan West that is comfortable with higher diversity.[7] I think there's something in this approach, but these authors can't disentangle life-cycle and generational-turnover effects because findings are based on snapshot surveys rather than longitudinal surveys that ask people the same questions over time. UK longitudinal data shows people become more conservative as they age.[8] In Britain this seems to point to a shift of around 20 points over a lifetime.[9]

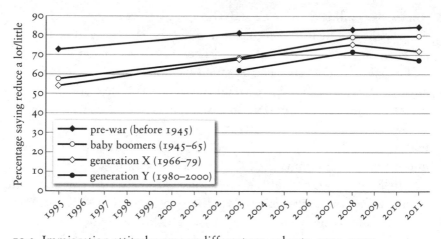

10.2. Immigration attitudes among different age cohorts, 1995–2011

Source: B. Duffy and T. Frere-Smith, *Perception and Reality: Public Attitudes to Immigration*. London, Ipsos MORI, 2014, p. 18

In most European countries and the United States, the age gap on immigration attitudes between the oldest and youngest whites falls inside 20 points, so is in my view unlikely to lead to liberalizing attitude change. In the 2016 ANES, for instance, 38 per cent of white Americans under thirty want less immigration compared to 55 per cent of whites seventy-five and above. Only in Britain, where the immigration attitude gap reached 38 points in 2017, might we expect generational turnover to reduce opposition as society ages. Even this needs to be qualified, however, because when rising immigration numbers shift attitudes, they can rapidly erase decades of gradual cohort liberalization. Figure 10.2 shows that immigration attitudes among the Baby Boomers in Britain converged with those of the pre-war generation between 1995 and 2009. Decades of potential cohort liberalization were wiped out in under ten years.

This process also explains why attitudes to religion, racial prejudice, premarital sex and women's rights in Europe can all liberalize with cohort change, while feelings towards the European Union can move in the opposite direction, as shown in figure 10.3.[10]

Despite the caveats, I can't help but feel that the changing baseline against which new generations judge the country's ethnic composition

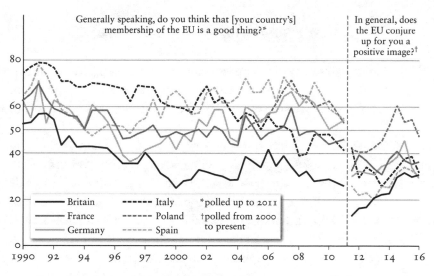

10.3. Love lost: favourable opinions of the EU, percentage polled

Source: 'The future of the European Union,' *Economist*, 25 March 2017

will, all else being equal, have some liberalizing effect on attitudes to immigration. Yet all things rarely are equal. Matters could change if – as in Austria and France, where the populist right has done well among young people – immigration is construed as a threat to personal freedom. Perhaps more importantly, if new intellectual currents on the right revive memories of a whiter 'golden age' past, this can generate a majority ethnic grievance of having had their birthright 'sold out' by liberal elites. An analogy can be drawn to work on the study of memory. The last British survivor of the First World War, Harry Patch, died in 2009. At some point, the last Holocaust survivor will also pass on. Our memory of these events is not personal, but mediated.[11] If the memory of an ethnically homogeneous nation is transmitted by political forces in society, this could generate anti-immigration hostility and populist-right voting even when people's lived reality is of a country that has always been diverse.

INTERRACIAL MARRIAGE

White rates of intermarriage are almost certain to rise. Much of this is mathematical: as minorities increase their share of the population, there is a greater share of minorities in a white person's social orbit. This increases the likelihood they will find a friend or mate of a different racial background. Imagine a country, perhaps Jamaica, that is 99 per cent non-white and 1 per cent white. If partnering were random, the white person would marry out 99 per cent of the time. The flipside of this is that blacks would marry out only 1 per cent of the time since they are so dominant. Small groups face a dilemma: have strict rules against marrying out or accept dissolution. Parsees are not supposed to intermarry, but there are so few of them they often have no choice.[12]

All other things being equal, whites will have higher intermarriage rates and a greater chance of having a minority neighbour or friend in a less white environment. But things aren't always equal because intermarriage is taboo in some contexts. Religion may be a barrier to intermarriage, as may caste or race. In India, there is virtually no intermarriage between Hindus and Muslims, and cross-caste marriage is limited. In Northern Ireland, Protestants face strong community disapproval if they marry a Catholic. Despite whites' tiny share of the population in the Caribbean, Mauritius or South Africa, these are tightly knit minorities which rarely marry outside their racial group. Elsewhere in the world, such as Latin America or sub-Saharan Africa, inter-ethnic marriage and assimilation are more common, with looser ethnic boundaries. Descent rules play a part in determining the strictness of group boundaries.[13]

Whites in the United States, especially the south-east, where blacks make up 25 per cent of the population, used to disapprove of interracial marriage. Indeed, interracial marriage was illegal in many southern states until the Supreme Court's landmark Loving v. Virginia decision of 1967. In the pre-Civil Rights south, those with more than 1/32nd 'black blood' were classified as non-white under the 'one drop' rule even if they looked white and were socially considered as such. Attitudes to intermarriage were equally uncompromising: 94 per cent of white Americans disapproved of black–white intermarriage in 1958. As recently as 1990 the figure stood at 63 per cent. Today it has plummeted to 15 per cent.[14]

Minorities likewise differ in their propensity to marry outside the group. In 2001, there were only around 2,500 Bangladeshis and Pakistanis living in a Bangladeshi–Pakistani couple out of the groups' combined population of more than 1 million. This despite the fact that both are Muslim South Asian ethnic groups living in urban areas of Britain. Antagonism, group location and customs limited intermarriage. These groups were more likely to marry white British than each other, though South Asian–white intermarriage was still unusual: just 4 per cent of Pakistanis, 7 per cent of Indians, and 3 per cent of Bangladeshis were married or cohabiting with a white British partner according to the 2001 ONS LS. Shares were much higher among Afro-Caribbeans, East Asians and Black Africans. Afro-Caribbeans are a small group like Pakistanis and Hindus; Chinese are similar in size to Bangladeshis and Sikhs. Thus these differences pertain to ethnic and religious norms governing partnering. Religion is an important part of this, but Muslim South Asians were no less likely to marry out than Sikhs.

The mixed-race component of unions is 17 per cent in the United States, approximately 4 per cent in Britain and 5 per cent in Canada. Part of this stems from how races are defined in the US, with Hispanics counted as a separate category even though half of them state their race as white. The higher rate of mixing in America also follows from the larger share of non-whites there (37 per cent) compared to Canada (22 per cent) and Britain (12 per cent). But there is more to the American story. In the US, a relaxation of attitudes to black–white intermarriage facilitated a rise in the share of black newlyweds marrying outside their race, from 5 per cent in 1980 to 18 per cent in 2015. So much so that in 2013 an American Cheerios cereal commercial featured a black–white interracial couple and their mixed-race daughter. This was considered controversial by some Americans and drew negative commentary from racist groups on social media.[15]

The number of American blacks who outmarry is still well below that of blacks in Canada or Britain, reflecting the small size of black populations in those countries. Offspring of mixed black–white unions in Canada and Britain are likely to marry whites due to the paucity of own-group partners: in Britain, 78 per cent of those of mixed Caribbean–white heritage were partnered with a white person according to the 2001 ONS LS. This points to a trajectory of assimilation into the white British majority.

Among white Americans, the increase in intermarriage has been steady if not quite as dramatic as for black Americans: from 4 to 11 per cent in the same period. Tellingly, the large Hispanic population of 16 per cent has maintained a high intermarriage rate of 27 per cent despite its increasing size. This gives a clue about the main type of intermarriage in America, which involves a white person partnered with a Hispanic. White–Hispanic unions comprise nearly half of American mixed-marriages, with white–Asian the next most common pairing at just over 10 per cent. Hispanics seem especially likely to intermarry as they achieve upward mobility. Among Latinos without high school qualifications, just 16 per cent are intermarried. Among those with degrees, the share is 46 per cent.[16]

As Mexican inflows fall, assimilation may accelerate. In 2014, more Mexicans left the US than entered it. While some of the slack has been taken up by immigrants from Central and South America, these countries are further away and have alternative migration options such as Costa Rica, Spain, Chile and Argentina. As immigrants become a smaller share of the Hispanic population, Hispanic intermarriage should rise.

Asians have a similar intermarriage rate, but this is partly to do with the group's smaller size – at less than a third of Hispanic share. Asians are now the largest immigrant group in America. As they grow, they will likely become less prone to marrying outside the group. Between 1980 and 2015, the share of Asians who outmarried (nearly all to whites) dropped from 33 to 29 per cent. Among Asians without degrees, the numbers slipped from 36 to 26 per cent.[17] One study compared Canada and the United States and found the intermarriage rates to be identical when controlling for which ethnic groups are in each country and their relative size. Chinese are a large group in Canada, for instance, so have less need to marry out than in the United States, where they are smaller. Blacks are a small group in Canada, with a high intermarriage rate, but in the US they are much larger so have a lower propensity to marry outside their group.[18] Whites in the two societies differed little in their intermarriage propensities despite the stereotype of a more liberal Canada. Indeed, even in Toronto, where nearly half the population was non-white in 2011, just 8 per cent of marriages crossed racial lines. In Vancouver, whose minority share is close to Toronto's, the share of whites marrying out was barely higher, at 10 per cent.[19]

In continental Europe there is no census data on ethnicity, but surveys show that Christian or secular minorities intermarry at higher rates than non-Christian minorities. One study found European-born Muslims marry out more than their immigrant parents, but the level is modest: 10.5 per cent compared to 6 per cent for the parental/immigrant generation. Algerian French men are the outlier driving the increase: half married out in 1992. Afro-Caribbeans on the European continent tend, as in Britain, to intermarry at high rates: in the Netherlands, 26 per cent of the immigrant generation of Caribbeans married native-born whites, rising to 53 per cent in the second. Another study found the rate to be 50–70 per cent.[20]

A German study of some 3,000 adult Muslim migrants found intermarriage rates to be lowest among Turks (1.1 per cent), Bosnians and South Asians (4 per cent), intermediate among Arabs and Iranians (13 per cent), and highest among North Africans (22 per cent) and sub-Saharan Africans (20 per cent). A majority of single Muslim migrants said they would consider marrying someone who wasn't Muslim; 63 per cent of those with daughters said it would be all right for their daughters to do the same.[21] A more comprehensive survey of patterns in the Netherlands, the UK, Germany and France found that around half of French Muslim men married white French women, and some 40 per cent of French Muslim women married white French men. Figures were lowest among Turkish women, of whom only 7–13 per cent married white Europeans while a majority married men from Turkey. So there is considerable variation by ethnic group.

One barrier to realizing a higher level of mixing is communal pressure to take a spouse from the homeland – in part to surmount tight immigration controls. In Holland, 71 per cent of second-generation Turks and 59 per cent of second-generation Moroccans between 1988 and 2002 chose a spouse from the homeland. The pattern is similar in Belgium. A majority of British Bangladeshis and Pakistanis, French and Dutch Turks, and Dutch Moroccans also select marriage partners from abroad, with many taking the form of arranged marriages – especially for women.[22]

Do tough immigration laws increase the share of Muslims taking foreign brides or grooms? Possibly. On the other hand, Dutch, German and Danish laws which set a minimum age for foreign spouses, demand language proficiency and stipulate waiting periods have reduced marriage migration. Denmark's is the most demanding: those under twenty-four who take partners from outside the EU cannot reside in the country. This disproportionately affects Danish Muslims. Indeed, the share of Danes of non-European background who marry someone from abroad declined from 63 to 38 per cent between 2002 and 2005.[23]

In Europe, religion is the clearest example of what the leading British sociologist Ernest Gellner termed a 'counter-entropic' trait that allows a group to resist assimilation. Gellner was writing about Jews in nineteenth- and early-twentieth-century Europe but the concept seems also to apply in the present era.[24] While some Muslims groups, notably Franco-Algerians and Franco-Moroccans, look to be embarking on a journey of assimilation, the pattern is slower among Muslim groups elsewhere, as well as among Hindus and Sikhs. Seculars from these groups tend to be the most intermarried because religious loss tends to promote intermarriage and vice-versa.

Christian minorities are therefore most likely to experience secularization, with rates of religious decline highest among Afro-Caribbean Christians. Figure 10.4 shows the change in the share of British people from various ethnic backgrounds who declared themselves to have no religion in 2001 and 2011. The share of religiously unaffiliated white British people shot up from 15.4 per cent in 2001 to 28 per cent in 2011 as Christian identity dropped due to secularization. The share of white European seculars reached nearly 19 per cent and the share of non-religious Afro-Caribbeans approached 13 per cent. But among predominantly non-Christian groups, few ticked the 'no religion' box: a mere 3.1 per cent of Indians (who are Sikh, Hindu or Muslim) and less than 1.5 per cent of the almost entirely Muslim Pakistanis and Bangladeshis. Theories of secularization claim that where there is a religious difference with the mainstream of society, religion serves as an identity marker, with religion and ethnicity reinforcing each other to the advantage of both.[25] It should be noted, however, that there was a small upward shift in non-religion across all groups in the 2000s. British Muslims who moved to less Muslim areas during 2001–11, were in a mixed-ethnicity household in 2001 or were of mixed white–South Asian background were several times more likely to shift to non-religion than other Muslims. Entering university predicted a doubling in the rate of Muslim disaffiliation. The census also records that some three to four times more people moved away from Islam during 2001–11 than towards it. In other words, mixing and secular modernity do lead

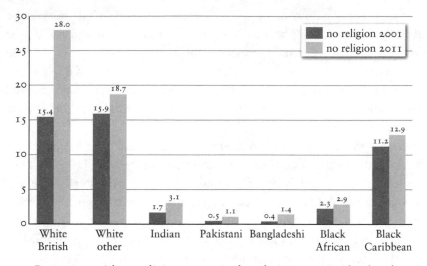

10.4. Percentage with no religion, 2001–11, by ethnic group, England and Wales

Source: ONS Census of England and Wales 2001, 2011

to Muslim assimilation in Britain, albeit at a much slower rate than in France.[26]

Again, there are the usual exceptions among non-Christian faiths. Sixty per cent of second-generation French people with at least one Algerian parent report no religion. One reason stems from the homeland. In the 1999–2000 World Values Survey, Algeria had the lowest share claiming to be religious (55 per cent) of any Muslim country. French football star Zinedine Zidane, like many Algerian French Muslims, is of Berber descent from the Kabylie region. Kabyles tend to identify with Francophone traditions and a less public form of Islam in contrast to the Arab majority of Algeria.[27]

A NEW MAN?

'The New Face of America,' proclaimed the cover of *Time* magazine in November 1993, which featured a computer-generated image of a woman's face created from fusing various racial images. *National Geographic* performed a similar exercise for its 125th anniversary edition in

October 2014, publishing a series of faces based on what the average American of 2050 might look like. Could immigration and mixing be leading to the futuristic American 'New Man' Hector St John de Crèvecoeur prophesied in 1782? Some are enthusiastic: 'We live in an increasingly diverse and increasingly mongrel society, a nation of blurred boundaries and bizarre extremes,' proclaims Scott London. 'Never before in history has a society been as diverse as the US is today. And never before have so many different traditions, beliefs and values been integrated in a single culture.'[28] Though inaccurate – the US is of moderate diversity worldwide – the quote tells us a great deal about the modernist sensibility of some commentators. I'm more sceptical. Rather than a radical transformation, I think it's more likely those of multiracial background will tend to identify, and be identified, with an established racial category based on their appearance and cultural cues.

Part of this stems from how we perceive colour. Richard Dawkins remarks: 'While we happily interbreed with each other, producing a continuous spectrum of inter-races, we are reluctant to give up' racial categories. Yet, for Dawkins, races are not simply arbitrary social categories:

> Physicists tell us that the rainbow is a simple continuum of wavelength . . .
> It is biology and/or psychology, not physics, that singles out particular
> landmark wavelengths along the physical spectrum for naming. Blue has
> a name. Green has a name. Blue-green does not . . . there is substantial
> agreement over such namings across different cultures. We seem to have
> the same kind of agreement over judgements of race. It may prove to be
> even stronger and clearer than for the rainbow.[29]

Not all cultures have the exact same colour words; only modern societies do. The Himba, for example, isolated semi-nomadic herders in Namibia, don't have a word for green in their language. This seems to be a feature of a number of several other isolated communities.[30] But as societies grow complex they all seem to move towards the same set of colours.[31]

If this is correct, trying to reconstruct our racial categories from above through politics may be as difficult as trying to get people to unlearn the primary colours. This doesn't mean categories can't evolve, but it suggests the process is complex, evolutionary and bottom-up. As the median racial type changes, the boundaries of whiteness may expand because people judge categories based on the average type they encounter. One study blurred Japanese and Caucasian facial features in different proportions and found that most Japanese exchange students in America considered the Japanese face to become Caucasian when it acquired 30–35 per cent Caucasian features. Whites had a more expansive definition of their group which included whites with up to 40–45 per cent Japanese features. Intriguingly, the Japanese students who had been in the country longest shifted part way towards the white perceptions over time, reflecting their experience of race in America. There was also wide variation among individuals in their judgements of where the racial boundary line lay.[32]

A good example of how existing categories frame those of mixed ancestry are the professional golfers Tiger Woods and Rickie Fowler. Woods is half African-American (itself probably a mixture of black, white or Native Indian), a quarter Thai, an eighth Dutch and an eighth Chinese. Fowler is a quarter Japanese and a quarter Navajo Indian.[33] Woods in particular claims to be multiracial, calling himself a 'Cablinasian'. Yet for most Americans their colour perception and society's established ways of categorizing lead them to view Woods as African-American and Fowler as white. Part of this arises because of the 'other-race effect', whereby people tend to see distinctions within their own race but not within others, who tend to 'all look the same'.[34] This develops early in childhood, though as the racial configuration in a society changes, the median type will change and people will probably adjust their category boundaries accordingly.

In 2008, the US elected its first 'black' president, Barack Obama. Why was Obama black rather than just another in an unbroken line – bar Kennedy – of presidents of WASP ancestry? Mainly because the US is a white-majority society. The country's predominant cultural gaze tends to perceive those with some African features as black. The same is true in Canada and Britain, despite their very different histories, but in black-majority Jamaica Obama would be considered part of the 7 per cent light-skinned minority.

Societies have established racial categories which tend to sort those of mixed background into one box or the other, even as people understand that some people lie close to a racial boundary. Like Rickie Fowler or the British politician Iain Duncan Smith, who are both part East Asian, I'm generally perceived as white. Yet when I mention my Chinese and Latino ancestry, people are suddenly able to see it. The same mix in my cousins shows up differently, so some of them look more Latino. In other cases siblings may be classified as racially different. There are also numerous whites who may not be aware of their polygenetic origins. In provincial England, Cedric Barber discovered he was the descendant of Samuel Johnson's freed slave Francis Barber from over two centuries ago.[35] The blonde American actress Heather Locklear has a Lumbee Indian surname. Even Craig Cobb, a white nationalist, discovered he was 14 per cent black.[36]

In Brazil, where the European component makes up half or less of the country's origins and considerable mixing has occurred over centuries, the black–white–brown colour categories, while fuzzy at the edges, are reproduced each generation. I would argue this is an emergent, bottom-up process, shaped by the same forces Dawkins mentioned for colour perception. The precise nature of the boundary between groups will vary, however, with socioeconomic status and dress 'whitening' how an individual is perceived. Nevertheless, one shouldn't overstate the role of status, as this is less important for categorization than physical appearance and family background.[37] Events can also affect self-perceived race: negative events such as incarceration increase the tendency to identify as non-white while positive events incline an individual towards white identity.[38] We can go further, pointing out that racial classification may change with information: an initial judgement may be based on physical appearance, complemented by cultural and status cues. A subsequent appraisal takes into account a fuller set of information on self-identity and family background.

SHIFTS IN MAJORITY ETHNIC BOUNDARIES

Majority ethnicity is similar – someone's surname may be Cruz and he may look Hispanic, but we then discover his first name is Ted, he is half Anglo in heritage, identifies as an unhyphenated American, is married to a white woman, and is a committed Republican and patriot. This may lead us to re-categorize Ted Cruz as white. The 'beiging' of America due to white–Hispanic intermarriage means that the share of Americans with European ancestry is not in decline. A leading sociologist of ethnicity, Richard Alba, notes that the US census bureau defines anyone with 'one drop' of minority identity to be non-white. This over-states the decline of whiteness. In 2013, half the country's newborns were categorized as non-white in census terms, yet 60 per cent had at least one white parent. At mid-century, three quarters of Americans will have some white non-Hispanic ancestry.[39] In addition, a significant number of Hispanics – half of whom identify their race as white on the census – tend to 'disappear' into the white category over time.[40] Indeed, 80 per cent of third-generation Americans with Mexican ancestry are the product of intermarriage.

These 'mixed-race' Hispanics have a higher socioeconomic profile than other Hispanic Americans and a significant portion tend to 'drop out' of the Hispanic category on the census to identify as white – which makes Hispanics seem less upwardly mobile than they actually are. Even among those who identify as Hispanic, very few identify as racially non-white.[41] The process may well be partial: Reihan Salam points out that lower-status Hispanics often live in largely Latino worlds and may not assimilate as quickly.[42]

Ethnicity is about subjective myths of descent, thus how people choose to identify is a critical question. The other is whether their identity claims are 'objectively' true enough to be accepted. Rachel Dolezal, who has no African-American heritage but claimed to be black, and the Englishman Archibald Belaney, known as 'Grey Owl', who claimed to be half Apache, are considered frauds. Had they had some black or Native Indian ancestry like the one-eighth Indian Metis leader, Louis Riel, they could have sustained their claims. This suggests those with some European background should be able to claim a white identity in the future.

Hispanics, like the Italians before them, may become part of the ethnic majority in the not-too-distant future. Many white Americans currently view those with Spanish surnames or Hispanic features as outsiders. A majority of Hispanics see themselves as white, but only 6 per cent of Hispanics who identify as white say they are accepted as such by American society. Even among those with just one Latino grandparent, 58 per cent identify as Hispanic.[43] Yet this may change with increased intermarriage, cultural assimilation and the arrival of more culturally distant groups. Already, lighter-skinned Hispanics are more likely to vote Republican or live in the same neighbourhoods as whites.[44] As group lines are blurred by intermarriage, ethnic boundaries may shift:

Ramirez may be considered an Anglo-American on a par with De Niro. Hispanic surnames are unlikely to be 'counter-entropic' barriers to assimilation. This assimilation process is a major reason why the centre-left writer John Judis revised his thesis that America's changing demographics will automatically produce Democratic victories in the future.[45]

As the left-wing writer Jamelle Bouie argues, 'If the pattern of the past holds, the future won't be majority–minority; it will be a white majority, where Spanish last names are common.'[46] In Louisiana, for instance, some French-origin Cajuns have Spanish surnames. We see something similar in other contexts: in the South Tyrol, a region of northern Italy that is predominantly ethnic German, Germans can have Italian surnames and vice-versa. In Northern Ireland, the Irish-Catholic politicians Gerry Adams and John Hume carry British surnames, while the Unionist-Protestant leader, Terence O'Neill, has an Irish surname. Surnames are not markers of an ethnic boundary, even though they are one clue to group membership and form part of the ethnic arche-type, something we'll come to in the next chapter.

Sometimes there's a wholesale shift in ethnic boundaries whereby characteristics that were once viewed as irredeemably 'other' become part of 'us'. In the US and Britain, Catholics and Jews are now con-sidered part of the ethnic majority. Notice this is a different process from whether to categorize those of mixed background like the half-WASP, half-Jewish 1964 presidential candidate Barry Goldwater as part of the dominant group. When the criteria for defining who is in or out of the majority change, whole chunks of the population who are not of mixed origin – like the fully Irish John F. Kennedy – suddenly become part of the ethnic majority. The analogy would be if fully Hispanic or Asian Americans came to be viewed as white. I deem this unlikely, given the proximity to Mexico and the established nature of the racial categories noted by Richard Dawkins. What seems more likely is that the high rate of intermarriage between Latinos and whites, as well as the rising share of native English-speakers, Protestants or seculars among them, may expand the boundaries of whiteness to include those of mixed parentage. That is, those with some European background who are culturally assimilated and have Anglo first names – but who have Spanish surnames or a Hispanic appearance – may be accepted as white.[47]

African and Asian migration now exceeds the Hispanic inflow to America and this is likely to become even more pronounced as Latino inflows subside. A foretaste of the future came in 2008, when an Immigration and Customs Enforcement raid led to the arrest of 200 illegal Hispanic immigrants working in a meat-packing plant in Grand Island, a town in southern Nebraska. The loss of workers prompted management to advertise in immigrant networks, leading to the arrival of Somali refugees, who are legal residents. At the plant, the Somali workers asked for shifts to be scheduled to accommodate Muslim prayer breaks. Management agreed to their demand for an earlier end to the workday to accommodate their need to take a dinner break close to sundown. This concession led to protests from over 1,000 largely Hispanic workers and unease among the town's residents. 'The Latino is very humble,' argued Raul Garcia, a 73-year-old worker at the plant. 'But they [Somalis] are arrogant . . . They act like the United States owes them.' Mayor Margaret Hornady admitted that the sight of hijabs in the town made people think of Osama bin Laden and terrorism.[48] If scenes like this grow more frequent and Latinos become anglicized, the majority-minority boundary could shift to include Latinos.

The line between whites and Asians, especially East Asians, is also blurry. American Asians are generally viewed as high status. They make up around 20 per cent of the student body in the nation's elite universities despite having to achieve higher SAT test scores than other racial groups. Their average income exceeds that of whites and they are increasingly occupying elite positions in the occupational structure. Since 2000, whites' share of new recruits in prestigious occupations has declined considerably, from 85–90 per cent in the 1980s and 1990s to below 70 per cent in the 2010s. As the large (35 per cent) and growing share of Asians at Google demonstrates, Asians are increasingly being hired for these positions. White–Asian marriage is common and those of mixed white–Asian background have higher income than either Asians or whites. They tend to incline towards their white heritage, occupy white social worlds and overwhelmingly marry whites. One study found that 36 per cent of white-Asians ticked the 'white box' on the census, 22 per cent ticked the 'Asian' box and the rest chose a mixed category. 'When their children grow up . . . many of them may view themselves as whites,' writes the sociologist Richard Alba.[49]

A decline in Latino immigration combined with their rising mobility would indicate that the absorption of Hispanics into the white group is likely to take place. However, the process may become slower for Asians – especially those of non-Christian religion – if their share of the population continues to rise quickly. This seems to be true of Vancouver and Toronto, Canada, with their large Asian populations, where Asian outmarriage occurs at a considerably lower rate than in America.[50]

In Europe, Caribbean-Christian and East Asian groups are following an assimilation path which points to the eventual absorption of many into the majority over generations. This includes European royalty: Prince Harry's nuptials in May 2018 to an American actress, Meghan Markle, who is half African-American, may one day be viewed as a sign of things to come. Assimilation is also evident on the populist right, where the quarter African-American Steven Woolfe served as UKIP's immigration spokesman. The assimilation of non-Christians who are religiously observant into the ethnic majority is much less likely due to religion's function as an ethnic boundary marker. Islam is not unique here – the same holds for Hinduism and Sikhism.

Mixture is therefore more likely to occur among secularized members of non-Christian groups. The French elite is more racially exclusive than that of the Anglosphere, but given French North Africans' high rate of intermarriage and secularization, their mixed offspring may become accepted as white. The same seems true of Britons of mixed Indian–white heritage, some of whom pass as white and many of whom are of middle-class background. In 2011, there were 342,000 Britons of white–Asian background, only slightly smaller than the 427,000 of white and black Caribbean origin, and increasing at the same rate. Many Britons of white and South Asian background resided in the affluent suburbs north-west of London.[51]

Outside France, Muslims are less likely to intermarry. Even those who do not take spouses from the home country will have a larger pool of potential Muslim partners, which, all else being equal, will counter the effects of assimilation, reducing intermarriage. Muslims are projected to more than double to between 10 and 20 per cent of the population of West European countries by 2050. Even 30 per cent is not beyond the bounds of the possible for Sweden.[52] This means a continual increase in Muslim intermarriage due to cultural assimilation – the pattern so far – is not a foregone conclusion. Economic stratification caused in part by discrimination could lead Muslims to continue to occupy the lowest rung of the occupational ladder, limiting assimilation.[53] Yet in some countries ethnic differences among Muslims reduce the pool of eligible Muslim partners, which should lead to higher rates of outmarriage. Thus the polyethnic Muslim population of Sweden or Norway – Kurdish, Syrian, Somali, Iraqi, Bosnian – should marry non-Muslims at higher rates than the more Turkish- or Moroccan-dominated Muslim populations of Belgium or the Netherlands.

THE GEOGRAPHY OF ETHNIC MIXING

Unsurprisingly, mixed-race individuals are more likely to live in diverse cities and, within them, in racially integrated areas. Whites in mixed-race relationships also tend to remain in diverse or 'majority-minority' neighbourhoods far more than whites in single-race relationships.[54] White British people who were intermarried or living in mixed-ethnicity households in 2001 are far less likely than other white Britons to have left diverse wards and more likely to have moved into them during 2001–11. According to the 2011 ONS LS, 17 per cent of white British people in London and 12 per cent of whites in 'majority-minority' wards across the rest of England and Wales lived in a mixed-ethnicity household. Most were partnered across ethnic lines (includes with European groups).

Critically, white Britons in mixed-ethnicity households who moved between 2001 and 2011 were far less likely to choose a more white British area to move to than white Brits in mono-ethnic households. The effect, with a wide variety of area and individual controls, was between a third and a half as strong as the countervailing effect of being white British (which pulled individuals towards whiter neighbourhoods). This suggests mixed-race households exert a powerful integrating force, preventing whites from leaving or avoiding superdiverse neighbourhoods.

Looking ahead, as metropolitan areas become more diverse, a substantial share of the whites who remain in superdiverse neighbourhoods will be in mixed-race relationships. In highly diverse neighbourhoods of American cities, as much as half the white population live in interracial households.[55] Whites gravitate to whiter neighbourhoods, but many need to live in urban areas for work, and the pace of ethnic change increases the proportion of minorities in a white person's environment considerably faster than white residential sorting reduces it. In the US, whites in urban areas are much more exposed to minorities than was the case even a decade ago.[56] This means interracial friendship and marriage grow more likely. Of course, the more diverse the neighbourhood, the more white friendship networks depart from what we would expect on the basis of random friendship. The same holds for partnering: even in the most diverse British wards, where just a third of residents are white British, the 2011 ONS LS tells us 88 per cent of white British people live in mono-ethnic households. This makes their choice of mate hugely unrepresentative of their neighbourhoods compared to whites living in mainly white areas. Still, diverse environments shape the partnering possibilities for white residents to some degree, leading us to expect that the rate of whites intermarrying with minorities will be highest in immigration gateways like Los Angeles, London, Paris or Amsterdam.

The increase in mixed marriage is producing a rise in the proportion of Western populations that are of mixed-race descent. The share of Americans with more than one race (white, black, Hispanic, Asian) in their background has reached 7 per cent. The proportion of American infants with a multiracial background increased from 5 per cent in 1980 to 10 per cent in 2000 to 14 per cent in 2015. However, this is measured by who the kids' parents are, not how they identify or are socially identified. Many – perhaps most – will tick one of the established racial boxes in the census when they grow up. In addition, it may be the case that outsiders are even more likely to classify these multiracials as being from an established racial category. As noted earlier, the sum of millions of perceptions and decisions assigns individuals to established social categories. Institutions like the census, with its racial categories, have some effect on how people categorize, but this is often overstated by social scientists. Colour perception, which is unconscious, plays a powerful role. Even if there were a concerted effort to deconstruct the primary colours and get us to centre our categories on the shades in between, I'm pretty sure this would fail. In the next two chapters, we'll consider some plausible scenarios for the future of white majorities in the West.

11

The Future of White Majorities

When Samuel Huntington asked 'Who are We?' in 2004, he spoke of the American nation-state in the context of large-scale immigration from Latin America. He raised questions about American security, unity and prosperity – an established idiom in security studies and a well-trodden topic of conversation. Yet the American state can work with almost any ethnic or religious configuration, adopt any official language, and still function pretty well. Divided loyalties are unlikely to matter for the state in our era of limited interstate war. Huntington touched on questions of majority ethnicity and ethno-traditional nationhood, warning of the alienation of white Americans, but didn't venture to ask what should, or would, happen to the white majority.[1] I'd argue that these, and not the security questions, are primary. That is, 'Who are we?' and 'Where are we going?' are not so much questions for the American state as they are issues for those attached to their white ethnic identity or to the idea that Euro-Americans have traditionally been the largest ethnic component of American nationhood.

It's therefore time to think about the ethnic future of Western nations, and, within this, of the white majorities that comprise between 62 and 95 per cent of the population of Western countries. There are three major possibilities:

1. Ethnic unmixing, in which minorities leave or are forced to leave, resulting in a return to 1950s levels of homogeneity.
2. A melting pot, in which the white group melts with others, forming a larger or smaller component of the total depending on the openness of its ethnic boundaries; or a new hybrid majority emerges.

3. A salad bowl, in which whites remain a tight-bounded group but become an ever-diminishing share of a multicultural society of discrete groups.

Option 1 is extremely unlikely for a host of reasons. Given what's going on in today's most racially diverse societies and has historically taken place, my view is that we will move closer to situation 3 but ultimately evolve towards option 2. Time to consider each in turn.

ETHNIC UNMIXING

In the summer of 2017, I visited the town of Motovun, a beautiful hilltop village in Istria, Croatia. If you go there, you can enjoy a meal of truffle pasta, the local specialty, admiring the magnificent views from your table. Wandering the town, you'll come across a museum dedicated to the Formula 1 driver Mario Andretti, who was born there before the Second World War when it, like many towns in the region, had an Italian majority. The Adriatic coast, part of the Austro-Hungarian Empire, was given to Yugoslavia after the First World War but had once been part of the Venetian Empire, so was coveted by Italian nationalists. With Italy's defeat in the Second World War, life became difficult for the Motovun Italians and they left for Italy or, like Andretti's family, emigrated to America. Across Europe, ethnic Germans met a similar fate, evicted to Germany from countries like Estonia, Poland or Czechoslovakia where they had lived for centuries and influenced urban life.

Almost all 'unmixing' migrations are involuntary and occur due to war or conquest. As the Ottoman Empire retreated from the Balkans or the Caucasus, many Muslims emigrated or were forced out. Crimean Tatars or Circassians, for instance, were compelled by the invading Russians to emigrate to Turkey. The collapse of the Austro-Hungarian Empire after the First World War resulted in numerous ethnic Hungarians and Germans migrating from lands where they had lived for many generations.[2] Sometimes migrations are part of a diplomatic arrangement, as in 1923, when a Greek–Turkish population exchange saw hundreds of thousands of Greeks from present-day Turkey and Muslims from present-day Greece move to their assigned countries. In most cases the minorities had lived as religious diasporas for centuries and had no familiarity with their new homelands. The partition of India in 1947 was both a diplomatic event and a violent conflict, which produced slaughter and involuntary migration among Hindus and Muslims caught in the 'wrong' country.

War between countries virtually ceased after 1945. Nearly all wars since have taken place within rather than between countries. Yet even civil wars have been on the decline since 1991. This is because, as Andreas Wimmer notes, civil wars tend to take place in waves during periods when empires, including the Soviet Union, break up.[3] Now that most of the world's empires have been consigned to the dustbin of history, we should see fewer systemic bouts of civil war. Steven Pinker argues this is part of a pattern of declining violence in human history. It's more profitable to trade with countries than to invade them, and state sovereignty removes the insecurity that leads to private violence.[4] This doesn't mean we've seen the end of war: religious and ethnic divisions are the basis for most civil wars such as those in Syria and Afghanistan. Yet the regional mayhem that created the conditions for unmixing are increasingly rare. Where there has been genocide or civil war within a single state, as in Bosnia, Rwanda, Syria or Northern Ireland, unmixing has been partial rather than total. In these cases unmixing involves populations moving to homogeneous enclaves within countries rather than leaving them.

In the West, the far right calls for 'voluntary' repatriation of minorities to create white ethno-states. Placing the obvious ethical problems to one side, there are two reasons why this is a near-impossibility. First, minorities tend to identify primarily with the host countries, apart from very recent arrivals: 75 per cent of British Muslims, for instance, identify as British first rather than with an ancestral nation-state. Among those born in Britain, the British-identifying share is higher still.[5] A British Bangladeshi who visits Bangladesh is considered British. British Bangladeshis tend to see their Bangladeshi-ness through a British lens. This means symbolic reference points such as chicken tikka masala, a dish created in Britain by Bangladeshi chefs, or Tower Hamlets, an area of London with a large Bangladeshi concentration, become part of their identity. These symbols have no resonance among Bangladeshis back home, all of which means the British-Bangladeshis are rooted in British soil and extremely reluctant to leave. Only force could make them do so.

Attempts to ethnically cleanse minorities like the Bangladeshis would have virtually no public support. Even voluntary repatriation – paying people to leave – which was seriously mooted on the right of the British Conservative Party until the late 1970s, is a vote-loser. The British National Party removed repatriation from its platform in order to have a hope of winning even the small slice of votes it garnered during its 2006–9 peak. Most conservative and order-seeking white voters in Western countries want to slow ethnic change, but would be horrified at the thought that innocent families could be ethnically cleansed because of the colour of their skin or religion. Opening the door to racial purification would also mean hunting down those of mixed-race background, who are very numerous, and scrutinizing family histories for impurities, as occurred under the Nazis or in the Jim Crow south. The chance of this happening is not zero, but pretty close to it.

There is another option, which Paul Morland terms 'soft demographic engineering', in which political lines are redrawn in order to reduce heterogeneity.[6] The partition of Northern Ireland from the Republic in 1922 was designed to create a Protestant majority in the North. In the same year, Lebanon was carved out of Syria as a Christian-majority state. After the First World War, the principle of self-determination of peoples was designed to grant sovereignty to ethnic groups, with borders determined by referenda. The location of the Israel–Palestine boundary has also been influenced by the ethnic geography of the region. Ethnic partition is sometimes the best option for a divided society, especially if well-designed.[7] A case can be made that a partition of Syria, guaranteed by the Great Powers, might have averted much of the bloodshed that occurred. Few can argue that holding the Czechs and Slovaks together against their will would have been a better idea than permitting divorce, and if Catalonia or Scotland vote to leave, they should be permitted to do so.

However, I think the chance of whites in North America or Europe creating ethno-states is remote. Almost every secessionist movement takes place in a historic territory where the inhabitants have mythosymbolic ties to what the sociologist of nationalism Anthony Smith terms 'poetic spaces'.[8] The Promised Land of Israel from 'Dan to Beersheba', England's 'Green and Pleasant Land', the French-Canadian attachment to the lower St Lawrence Valley, and other cultural-territorial connections develop over long periods. Artificial ethno-states lack these roots. This deprives them of the symbolic power that comes from the association between a territory, political tradition and the inhabitants' myth of ancestry. Most people are attached to their national territories and myths, not artificial new tracts. In addition, the chance of states ceding sovereignty to such entities is virtually nil, as in South Africa, where the Afrikaner *volkstaat* of Orania in the Northern Cape is unlikely to ever gain independence.

Finally, a handful of far-right extremists wish to commit genocide against minorities and a similarly tiny band of far-left zealots would liquidate all whites. Neither of these infinitesimal possibilities is worth wasting time on.

THE DYNAMICS OF MELTING

This leaves us with options 2 and 3, the melting pot and salad bowl. Let's consider option 2 first, the melting pot. The share of Americans with more than one race (white, black, Hispanic, Asian) in their background has reached 7 per cent. The proportion of American infants with a multiracial background increased from 5 per cent in 1980 to 10 per cent in 2000 to 14 per cent in 2015.[9] Will most Westerners be mixed-race? This depends on both intermarriage and immigration. The rate of non-white immigration bears a different relationship to this process from what you might think. For instance, beyond an initial share of minorities, the faster the rate of immigration, the longer it takes the mixed group to become the majority. Why? Imagine the minority populations of the West all married whites and had children who in turn married other whites, and so on. Over several generations, even with no further minority outmarriage, non-white ancestry would spread within the white population to the point whites become mostly mixed, even if the non-white admixture is too small to affect people's physical appearance. This explains how most African-Americans have European heritage and why the share of those identifying as Hawaiian has been rising even though there are only a few thousand 'pure' Native Hawaiians.

PROJECTIONS

Most ethnic projections undercount the mixed population because it's more difficult to model. One that does so uses 2006 Canadian census data and immigration levels to project ahead to 2106. In that year, if there were no mixing between the descendants of post-2006 immigrants and the pre-2006 population, approximately 62–71 per cent of Canadians would descend from post-2006 immigrants.[10] About 20 per cent of Canadians in 2006 were non-white and immigrants to Canada are about 80 per cent non-white. So we can use the share descended from post-2006 immigrants as an approximation of the non-white population.

In reality, the white share of immigrants to Canada will almost certainly decline as Europe becomes more diverse, but, to be cautious, let's say it doesn't. With no interracial marriage, 29–38 per cent of Canadians in 2106 will be white and 62–71 per cent non-white. Of course, post-2006 immigrants and their descendants are likely to intermarry with the existing population. This leads to exponential growth in the mixed population because the product of any marriage between a mixed person and a white or non-white person is also counted as mixed. This increases the supply of mixed mothers and decreases the number of unmixed mothers. The result is that in 2106, if intermarriage were random, the share of unmixed whites in Canada would be between 9.5 and 13.5 per cent. We know that marriage in Canada is far from racially random. Even in 'majority-minority' Toronto and Vancouver only 8–10 per cent of whites marry those of other races. However, models show that even a modest amount of mixing quickly produces a rapidly rising mixed-race population. This means unmixed whites will probably comprise just 20 per cent of Canada's population in 2106.

In Europe, Giampaolo Lanzieri of Eurostat has projected the size of foreign-born populations in Europe. Using those of foreign birth as a proxy for those of non-majority ethnicity, and based on current rates of immigration and fertility, the minority share will grow to between 22 per cent in France and 75 per cent in Luxembourg in 2061. Among those under fifteen, the share runs from a low of 24 per cent in France to a high of 82 per cent in Luxembourg. The projected foreign share is lowest in France due to its high native birth rate of around 2.1 children per woman, and highest in Southern Europe and German-speaking countries, where birth rates are low – especially ones like Switzerland or Luxembourg with small populations.

A majority of the foreign-born in European countries are other Europeans, who will probably assimilate into ethnic cores over time. An alternative measure of non-European share is projected Muslim population. For 2050, Pew estimates a medium scenario in which most West European countries are between 10 per cent (Switzerland) and 21 per cent (Sweden) Muslim, with Portugal on the low end at 2.5 per cent. A high projection, which I deem unlikely, puts the share at between 13 per cent (Switzerland) and 31 per cent (Sweden), with France, Britain and Germany in the 15–20 per cent range. All countries have some East Asian, black Christian, Latino and Hindu share, so a reasonable estimate is that most Western European countries will be 15–40 per cent non-white in 2061.[11] David Coleman of the University of Oxford comes up with a broadly similar figure of 15–35 per cent by 2050.[12]

Yet these projections assume no mixing. One which does is Coleman's and Scherbov's model, which shows a white British minority by the 2060s. However, since Europeans intermarry with white British at a high rate and their children tend to identify as white British, I think it's more realistic to assume non-British whites will ethnically assimilate. This leaves us with three main British groups: white, non-white and mixed. Much of the mixed share will disperse to the white or non-white categories, but let's bracket this for the moment. Coleman and Scherbov's median assumptions produce a British population of 2100 that is 40 per cent white, 30 per cent mixed and 30 per cent non-white.[13]

Let's perform a thought experiment in which 80 per cent of immigrants to a Western country are from outside Europe and 20 per cent from Eastern Europe. As Eastern Europe develops economically and loses population, it's unlikely to send many immigrants, so this is the most likely scenario. Imagine a large cup of milk with a leaky bottom. This represents a Western country today, with a predominantly white population and below-replacement fertility. Coffee and milk are entering the cup in a 4:1 ratio, with coffee representing non-European immigration and milk the East European inflow. As these ingredients enter the cup they begin to mix, and the longer they remain in the cup, the more the initial ingredients become unrecognizable due to blending. In the long run, the cup will contain a perfectly blended mix that is 4/5 coffee and 1/5 milk. The level of 'immigration' of coffee and milk – the speed at which it enters the cup – doesn't affect the composition of the latte in the cup. 'Immigration' affects only two things: (a) the speed with which the initial milk gives way to a mix; and (b) the time it takes for the coffee and milk to blend into a latte.

Let's consider a live example, Britain. The first point to bear in mind is that Western populations have higher death rates than birth rates. Without immigration, they would decline substantially. A UN projection based on existing fertility rates for Northern and Western Europe suggests this region's population will fall from about 270 million in 2000 to 185 million in 2100 even with immigration.[14] Population decline means that if immigration is used to keep population stable, most of Europe's population after 2100, as in Canada, will be the descendants of post-2000 immigrants. Thus the character of immigration will have a major impact on population composition. In order to explore mixing under various scenarios into the distant future, I asked Edward Morgan, a demographic researcher at the London School of Hygiene and Tropical Medicine, to run some projections using the most recent census inputs from England and Wales, and a cohort-component projection methodology. This gives us a glimpse into the West's long-term racial future.

I begin with what I consider to be the most likely scenario for the future composition of England and Wales based on three groups, white, non-white and mixed. Anyone with some blend of white and non-white is considered mixed even if they are socially white or non-white. The larger a group gets, the lower its intermarriage rate because there are more potential own-group partners. Immigration at 250,000 per year, with current birth and death rates, and an immigrant inflow that transitions from 50 per cent white in 2011 to 10 per cent white in 2120, produces the racial scenario in figure 11.1. The minority share rises from 12 per cent in 2011 to 21 per cent in 2050, then plateaus through 2120. White share falls from 86 per cent in 2011 to 71 per cent in 2050 to 32 per cent in 2120.

More importantly for our purposes, the mixed-race group takes decades to get moving, but once it does, it grows exponentially. Whites and non-whites produce mixed kids, who grow up to become mixed-race mothers and fathers. They in turn intermarry with the unmixed groups at rapid rates, eroding them further. So the mixed share has two

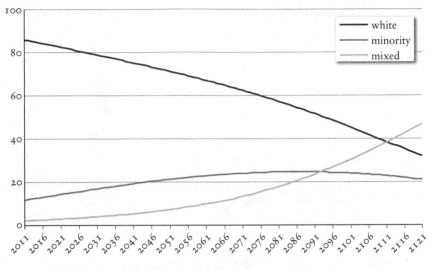

11.1. Racial composition of England and Wales to 2121, %

Note: Assumes 250,000 annual net migration, with flow 50 per cent European, declining to 10 per cent European in 2120.

engines of natural growth which simultaneously subtract from the future population of unmixed folk: intermarriage between white and non-white, and intermarriage between unmixed and mixed. My mother and I are both examples of the latter process.

Against this, the unmixed can only expand through immigration. The upshot of this is that the mixed group really starts to takes off after 2060. According to projections in figure 11.2, mixed overtake non-whites by 2095 and exceed whites after 2110. By 2125, the mixed are an outright majority of the population of England and Wales, breaking 90 per cent by 2167. The initial milk and subsequent coffee have produced a latte. There are reasons to believe that the unmixed – especially whites – will make a comeback by then, something I explore in the next chapter. But the big picture is that we are moving towards a mixed-race majority after 2100, with *Whiteshift* largely complete by the late 2100s. The multicultural millennium never arrives and the 'majority-minority' dream evaporates as diversity declines from the 2080s. This of course depends on how the mixed group identifies, and is identified, something I'll address later.

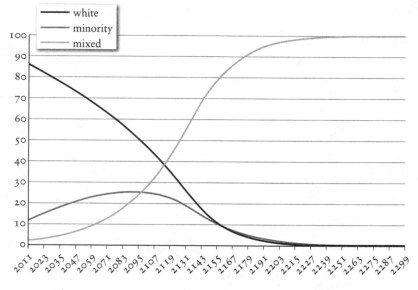

11.2. Racial composition of England and Wales to 2299, %

Note: Assumptions as in figure 11.1.

It doesn't make much difference whether immigration is zero, 50,000 or 350,000 per year (or even higher), the end result is the same: a mixed majority after 2100 and pretty much everyone mixed by the early 2200s. What the rate of immigration *does* affect is the amount of white admixture within the eventual mixed population. A 350,000 per year intake produces a mix in 2200 that is about a third white and two thirds minority, perhaps similar to the mestizos of Nicaragua. A 50,000 annual inflow produces one that is about 60 per cent European and 40 per cent minority, like the mestizos of northern Mexico or Costa Rica. In 2300, when global economic and demographic convergence is more likely, the 350,000 immigration scenario means a 10:90 white–non-white mix (Bolivia?) compared to around 50:50 (Brazil?) for a 50,000 annual influx. But in the *very* long term, if the British population continues to have below-replacement fertility, it will have a 10:90 admixture regardless of immigration level.

Immigration level is also important because it accelerates the speed of initial white decline, which could prove culturally disorienting, igniting the populist politics we see today. Figure 11.3 illustrates, using

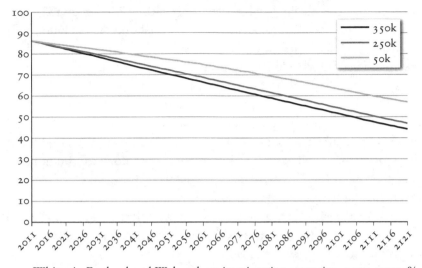

11.3. Whites in England and Wales: three immigration scenarios, 2011–2121, %

Note: Projection assumes somewhat slower growth in mixed population than figure 11.2.

a method which assumes a slower rate of mixed growth than figure 11.3 in order to recognize the fact that many of the mixed in this period will be whites with a modest share of minority admixture. The point here is that immigration can still unsettle the cultural security of whites in the medium term, even though the share of unmixed whites will be pretty similar in the 2100s regardless of immigration level. The pace of immigration will matter a lot because whites will feel they are in rapid decline until they begin to see themselves and the mixed population as part of the same group.

HOW WILL THE MIXED IDENTIFY?

The projections in figures 11.1 and 11.2 measure the mixed share as a function of who the kids' parents are, not how they identify, or are identified by others. Many of these individuals are likely to identify with an established racial group and be treated as such. The census or government equal-opportunities monitoring forms, which establish the ethnic categories through which the population is enumerated, have some effect on people's perception of group boundaries, but this is often overstated. As noted earlier, the sum of millions of perceptions and decisions, informed by vernacular tradition, does most of the work in assigning individuals to established social categories.

Racial differences emerged late in human evolution and the vast majority of humans' genetic variation is contained within rather than between races. Africa contains twice the genetic diversity as the rest of the world combined, and we know there are no hard boundaries between races. But this is socially immaterial. Race, like the electromagnetic spectrum, may be a continuum, but, as Dawkins notes, unconscious colour perception interacts with linguistic evolution to produce discrete racial categories. Even if there were a concerted effort to deconstruct the primary colours or our mental images of 'young' and 'old' on the age continuum, these are unlikely to succeed. Likewise, established racial categories will be difficult to recast even as more people occupy the fuzzy boundary between them. For instance, the blurring of races in the Caribbean through intermarriage has not erased the boundary between the small minority of light-skinned mulattoes and the tiny community of whites. A Mexican journalist, Germán Martínez, relates how the white–mestizo boundary in Mexico is similarly binary: a person is white or mestizo, even if observers disagree on which category they belong to.[15] The boundaries may be blurry, but the traditional categories remain.

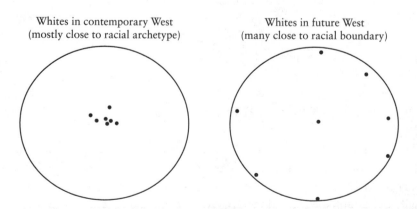

11.4. What races might look like in the West in the future

One way of thinking about what races may look like in the West in the future is to contrast the left and right circles in figure 11.4. The circle on the left shows most whites looking like the racial archetype, as it has developed in our minds due to colour perception and tradition. Most people in the West today cluster towards their racial archetype in the centre, with few in the blurry border zones between categories. The circle on the right paints a picture in which there are fewer who fit the archetype and more who lie near the racial boundary. Whites in this case would be mixed-race individuals who look white enough for most people to classify them as such, i.e. the category I fall under.

WHICH GROUPS ARE FAVOURED BY ASSIMILATION?

Whether mixing will benefit the white *ethnic* majority depends on whether the white group comes to be restricted to those who pass as white, or whether it becomes a transracial ethnic group that unites around common ancestry: i.e. whether it includes those who do not look white but carry other markers that signal their European ancestry. Among the Uighurs of west China, some look more Caucasian, but many are indistinguishable from the Chinese. However, Uighurs are Muslim, which provides an unambiguous differentiating characteristic from the Han. A future English majority population could be similarly multi-hued, with some appearing white and some looking, for instance, Chinese, Indian or black. This group would need a way of distinguishing itself from the unmixed Chinese, Indians and blacks. This would probably involve a combination of naming, culture and religion. Having a European first name (and possibly last name), being secular or Christian, and living a Western lifestyle may be the markers that distinguish whites from other groups. This would be a fuzzier boundary than a religious or racial one – thus native-born members of culturally similar minorities like the native-born Chinese or Afro-Caribbeans might pass as members of the majority. Yet these criteria should still be sufficient to do the job. This kind of blurred boundary exists between many neighbouring ethnic groups in the world today. For instance, the mestizo/ Amerindian line in Mexico, Tatar/Bashkir boundary in Russia or Turkish/Kurdish distinction in Turkey.

The direction of assimilation tends to be towards groups that are closer to the cultural core of a society, or who have high status. Germans assimilated to the Anglo core of the US since the WASPs are both a core group and had a higher status position on what the American writer Samuel Lubell termed the 'ethnic ladder' of opportunity. In Brazil, where German immigrants felt themselves to be of higher status than the Portuguese-origin Brazilian core, assimilation took much longer.[16] In Africa, high-prestige dominant ethnic groups like the Kikuyu of Kenya, Baganda of Uganda, or Wolof of Senegal tend to assimilate members of other groups through intermarriage, mainly in urban areas. Boundaries between dominant and minority groups are often blurred. The assimilation of minorities is leading to a steady reduction in Africa's high level of diversity.[17]

The other obvious factor is group openness. If some groups maintain tight ethnic boundaries, discourage intermarriage and reject those of mixed heritage, they will grow less quickly than more open groups. The groups that are most open to mixing in multiracial societies are African-descended Creoles, mestizo (white–Amerindian) and Indigenous groups. Originally this was because these groups had lower status than Asian and white groups so would accept admixtures with higher-status groups. Yet this manifestation of disadvantage has turned into a significant plus. In Hawaii, for instance, figure 11.5 shows that the Native Hawaiian population has rebounded from under 50,000 in 1900 to some 300,000 today and is projected to reach 700,000 by 2060. There are as few as 7,000 'pure' Native Hawaiians, yet the share of Hawaiians who identify as Native Hawaiian is on track to return to its pre-conquest figure. Though Native Hawaiians make up only 10 per cent of the state's population today, the share could reach 40 per cent by 2060, on its way to majority status towards the end of the century.[18] This is primarily due to a high rate of intermarriage coupled with a strong tendency among those with Native Hawaiian ancestry to identify as Hawaiian – perhaps because of the growing appeal of Native Hawaiian as an 'authentic' indigenous identity.

A similar pattern can be seen among Native American Indians, featuring a large and growing population of mixed-race identifiers. In the US, the Native population increased 18 per cent between 1990 and 2000 and another 26.7 per cent between 2000 and 2010, reaching 1 per cent of the total population. Likewise in Canada, the share reporting

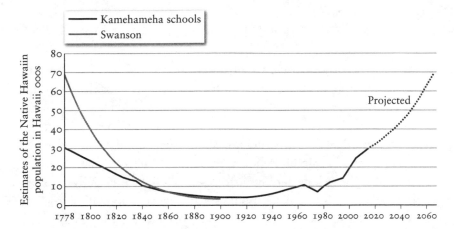

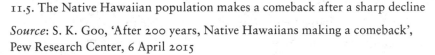

11.5. The Native Hawaiian population makes a comeback after a sharp decline

Source: S. K. Goo, 'After 200 years, Native Hawaiians making a comeback', Pew Research Center, 6 April 2015

aboriginal origins as their single (not partial) ancestry has increased from 2.8 per cent of the population in 1996 to 3.8 per cent in 2006 to 4.9 per cent in 2016.[19] Much of this stems from changing patterns of self-identification, notably among those of part-Native, part-European heritage who once described themselves as white but now call themselves Metis.[20]

Once again, indigenous authenticity forms part of the appeal of identifying as Native. Another is distinctiveness from the average: being American Indian gives people a unique identity. In mixed populations, there is more room for mixed people with 'ethnic options' to choose which of their ancestries to identify with. People can also alter the ancestry they identify with depending on the social situation, or hold dual identities.[21] Something similar can be seen within the white American population, where those who are part Italian and part Scottish are three times more likely to identify with their Italian than their Scottish roots. Among those with English and Italian heritage, Italian is favoured 3:2. This is because Italian is seen as a richer and more distinctive heritage.[22]

WHITES IN THE MELTING POT

White identity is not distinctive in the West because whites define the mainstream. This works against white expansion if exoticism and distinctiveness are prized. Yet only some reach for exotic identities. In the US, for example, whites tend to have multiple European ancestries. Though some identify with Italian, Irish or other singular European origins, a large number simply denote themselves 'white' or 'American'. The latter tend to have long family histories in the US, especially those in rural areas or the south. Their politics leans considerably more towards Trump than those who identify as English or Irish, even though the latter have been in the US for a similar length of time.[23] Liberal New England, for example, contains many English and Irish identifiers, whereas those of similar ancestry in the south tend to call themselves 'American'.

Down the road, the choice among those of mixed-race background may similarly be inflected by politics: conservatives/authoritarians could identify as white, while liberals flag their non-European or aboriginal heritage. Indeed, the Massachusetts senator Elizabeth Warren was dubbed 'Pocahontas' by Donald Trump for identifying with her (disputed) 1/32nd American Indian ancestry.[24] Bill Clinton has talked up his Irish heritage even though this is undocumented. Historically, British liberals and northern US 'Yankees' before the Civil War identified as Anglo-Saxon and British conservatives or southern Americans as Norman-Cavalier; in France, liberals harked back to the Gauls and conservatives to the Franks. In Russia or Hungary, the battle pitted traditionalists who favoured their 'oriental' non-European steppe origins against modernizers who stressed a Western, European heritage.[25] The international context will also be important. Since power, wealth and numbers will increasingly favour non-Western countries, whites in the West may come to feel more embattled and insecure, much like elites in the Muslim world do today. This could further prompt people with partial European ancestry to select it over other ancestries.

In Europe, white majorities in the West will only benefit from assimilation if they can move away from race to name/culture as the defining marker. While a white or part-white appearance will be a sufficient marker, many potential members will not be physically distinct. As a founding group which still has high prestige, the direction of assimilation should flow towards 'whites' the way it favours core ethnic groups like the Wolof of Senegal. On the other hand, this can't work if group boundaries are closed to intermarriage and mixed-race offspring are excluded, the practice of whites in the Caribbean, South Africa or Mauritius. Whites in the West are intermediate in their openness to intermarriage, somewhere between the more open Creole or African groups and more closed Asian groups. Even so, colour perception places a limit on how absorptive whites can be if traditional white appearance remains a *sine qua non* for being a member. On the other hand, if 'white' ethnicity opens up to those of mixed background who identify with their European ancestry – even if they don't look white – then the 'white' share will remain a clear majority.

MELTING POT OR MOSAIC?

If the West moves in a melting-pot direction, will those who assimilate orient around an established ethnic group or form a new hybrid? Mestizos in Mexico, who comprise some 90 per cent of Mexico's population, trace their ancestry to two racial groups, the Aztec Indians and Spanish conquistadors. This myth of origin was developed after the Mexican revolution of 1917 and has become central to both the mestizo majority and the wider Mexican national identity.[26] In other Latin American countries such as Nicaragua or Paraguay, mestizos form the largest ethnic group but their myth of descent doesn't define the nation-state.

Creoles, like mestizos, have a multiracial origin myth. They are prominent in the Caribbean and on the Indian Ocean island of Mauritius. These societies are the most deeply diverse parts of the world in racial terms, with people from several corners of the world coming together from the beginning to form new societies. Though the urban areas of the West are superdiverse, this mixture is recent and geographically concentrated, and has layered on top of a historically white-majority society. In the more diverse Caribbean islands and adjacent coastal areas, ethno-racial diversity came in on the ground floor, creating a polyglot racial matrix early on. Most of the population arrived as slaves or immigrants. There is no large indigenous population that can claim to be the 'true' founding group. Asian, African, European and Amerindian groups all have deep roots.

In these countries, African-origin Creoles maintain looser ethnic boundaries than whites, Indians or Chinese. As a result they have grown by absorbing people of mixed heritage who don't fit other categories.[27] As an open, residual group, Creoles have not only increased in size, but have had a disproportionate influence on the language, culture and national identity of these countries.[28] Figure 11.6 shows their distribution of the population according to three racial categories. The first bar in each country displays the share made up of traditional racial groups, whether Asian, white, black or Amerindian. The second measures the largest 'open' or hybrid racial group, typically Creole or mestizo but including Native Hawaiians. The third bar in each country represents those who tick a 'mixed' box on the census but who in practice may melt back into a traditional group or join a hybrid/open group. The closed and hybrid groups in all societies tend to absorb those of mixed heritage. Where an unclassified 'mixed' group is growing, this is mainly because the Afro-Asians are new and lack a well-developed tradition and myth of descent.[29]

In Hawaii, those of European–Asian mixed origin also lack an established myth to gravitate to, but this could change if an ethnic entrepreneur develops one. Meanwhile, those with some Hawaiian ancestry tend to identify as Hawaiian. Traditional 'unmixed' racial groups such as blacks or Asian Indians are a clear majority only in Suriname and

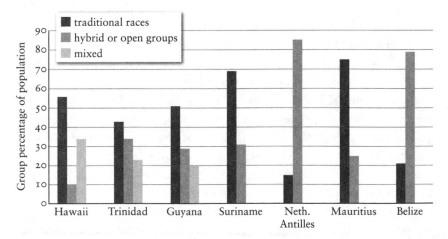

11.6. Diverse societies: salad bowls or melting pots?

Mauritius. In Belize or the Netherlands Antilles, the hybrid Creoles or mestizos dominate, with single-race groups in the minority.

Creole, mestizo or mixed populations are rising in all these cases, with the partial exception of Mauritius, which has a low rate of intermarriage and mixing. Part of this stems from the predominantly Asian makeup of Mauritius, since Asian groups typically maintain stronger proscriptions against intermarriage than African ones. In symbolic terms, mixed groups' myths of ancestry celebrate multiple lines of descent but Gestalt psychology – our need to focus only on a subset of the information hitting our senses to think in terms of unified wholes – makes people select two or three major lineages, screening out smaller influences. Creole myths focus exclusively on African and European heritage, though in Trinidad the new 'mixed' group is Afro-Indian so may develop into a community with an Afro-South Asian myth. At some point this may become the focus of an ethnic revival akin to what occurred in post-1917 Mexico with the myth of 'La Raza', fusing Aztec and Spanish lineages. Something similar took place in Canada with the rise of the Metis – a blend of predominantly French-Canadian settlers and Cree Indians – who developed a set of symbols, including a flag, and mounted a series of political rebellions on the Canadian prairies after 1870.

When the blended white populations of North America, Australia and New Zealand think about their origins in the future, they may morph into Metis/mestizo/Creole groups which focus on a combination of Anglo-European, African and aboriginal lineages as their myth of descent. This process involves a Gestalt-like filtering out of smaller, more recent or less distinctive elements.[30] Prototypes for the potential majorities of the future in settler societies can be found in the Metis population of Canada, the Maori-Anglo mixed group in New Zealand or the Melungeons of the United States who combine European, Native Indian and African ancestry.

Hybridized groups are possible in the New World but unlikely in Europe. While the multi-hued 'white' Europeans of tomorrow may select among European forebears such as Gauls and Gallo-Romans in France, the non-European heritage is too recent to provide the symbolic capital for those seeking a sense of meaning and rootedness. The symbolic cores and ancestry myths of future European 'whites' are more likely to focus exclusively on European origins even as the actual ancestry of the 'white' population becomes more non-European. These white groups will become less physically distinctive but still need some way of distinguishing themselves from others. Looking slightly more Caucasian could be sufficient, but this may provide only an approximate clue to identity – just as having a surname like O'Neill is only an approximate indicator that a person identifies as Irish Catholic. Terence O'Neill is a famous British-Protestant and an Italian-American could also be named O'Neill.[31] Like the Italian O'Neill, some who identify as white may initially be miscategorized as black until people get to know their name, how they speak and more about their outlook. Over time, people get used to the idea that appearance is only a first approximation of identity, not a requirement for membership. Lifestyle or naming practices, as in Brazil, may offer additional clues as to whether someone who appears non-white identifies as white. Having said this, ethnic groups require cultural markers to distinguish themselves from others. When race no longer distinguishes all members of white majorities from other groups, it may be that cultural styles, speech, folkways or naming practices – whether first names or surnames – take over the marking role. A person who exceeds a critical mass of cultural markers is accepted as a member.

COLOUR STRATIFICATION

In the future, many white identifiers will have a more Caucasian appearance than non-whites, but there will be a sliding scale of whiteness based on a person's appearance. This poses two dangers. First, those who are closer to the white archetype may be seen as more authentically white, and, second, they may derive benefits from this. In Latin America, the Indian subcontinent, Africa and the Caribbean, and among African-Americans, advantages accrue to those with lighter skin.[32] Some of this stems from the fact that Europeans were a higher-status civilization during the period of imperial expansion from the 1600s to the mid-1900s, prior to the rise of Asia. In other instances, conquering groups were light-skinned: Aryans in India, Persian-Turkic-Afghan Mughals in India–Pakistan, Arabs in Muslim Africa and Iberians in Latin America. The result is a lamentable system of colour stratification wherein those of lighter complexion are over-represented in higher castes or positions. The mixed-race whites of the future may be at risk of moving towards a colour-coded hierarchy because Caucasian features could be associated with higher status.

Lighter features also reflect feminine beauty ideals in non-Western societies, which often predate European contact. The sociologist Pierre van den Berghe finds that in forty-seven of fifty-one societies where there is anthropological or historical evidence, from Africa to Polynesia to India to East Asia, men prefer lighter features but women usually don't. European beauty ideals may have something to do with this, but in many non-Western societies men prefer lighter hues of their own racial type rather than Europeans, whom they view as similar to albinos, or generally less appealing. One explanation for this is that elite women stayed out of the sun so had lighter complexions than lower-status women. Another is that skin colour is related to youth and to fertile periods of the menstrual cycle.[33] Things can change. Europeans once preferred pale skin for women, but following Coco Chanel's early-twentieth-century innovation of sporting a suntan no longer do. Paleness became associated with having to work indoors and not having leisure time.[34]

Colour stratification need not arise. French-Canadians with British surnames such as the ex-Quebec Premier Pierre-Marc Johnson, or South Tyrolian Germans with Italian surnames, are treated the same as those with ethno-typical surnames. White Americans with Italian names no longer experience an earnings penalty. Among Native Indians, those with a lower share of aboriginal ancestry might not qualify for tribal membership but they are not generally discriminated against by co-ethnics. I recall attending a party as a teenager on the Sechelt reservation in British Columbia with a friend of mine and band member whose father was white. This posed no issues for my friend or his brother, who looked completely Caucasian. Thus it should be possible to have a multi-shaded white group where everyone is treated equally. The rising wealth of the non-European world and peripheral location of many unmixed whites may also flatten the prestige hierarchy which underpins racial stratification. It will be important to exercise vigilance if colourism rears its head, but modern liberal societies are well equipped to monitor bias and adjust for this.

Like unmixed Native Hawaiians or American Indians, or Welsh-speakers in north Wales, unmixed white Swedes, English or Americans in isolated rural areas will be perceived as 'authentic' and archetypal.

They will probably feature more often as film leads, especially in historical productions; but ethnic authenticity and social standing will not be related, thus race would not serve as a basis for discrimination.

PUBLIC OPINION: MAURITIUS OR MEXICO?

Do Westerners prefer their white-majority societies to evolve towards a melting-pot 'white' majority or a multicultural society like Mauritius, where unmixed whites are a small, tight-bounded group? In late 2016, I asked a sample of 572 American respondents from MTurk the following question:

> The year is 2200. Global population growth has stabilized and the gap between rich and poor countries has closed. The US population has largely finished its ethnic transformation. If you had to choose, which of the two possible outcomes would you prefer:
>
> (a) Whites have declined from around 62 per cent of the total in 2016 to 10 per cent in 2200, the smallest major group in a multi-ethnic America which is 30 per cent Asian, 25 per cent black, 25 per cent Hispanic and 10 per cent mixed-race. In order to maintain their group, most whites marry within their own race. They preserve the traditions and memories associated with the Pilgrims, Jamestown, Founding Fathers, Western settlement and the period of European immigration to industrial America.
>
> (b) In 2200 only about 2 per cent of the population is of unmixed white background, mainly living in isolated rural areas. 88 per cent of the American population is mixed-race, with an average European ancestry component of around one-eighth. This mixed population overwhelmingly identifies as 'white'. They preserve the traditions and memories associated with the Pilgrims, Jamestown, Founding Fathers, Western settlement and European immigration to industrial America.

Figure 11.7 shows that most Americans (63 per cent) choose the melting pot over the Mauritian-style salad bowl. There are no clear partisan divides, but non-whites split more evenly, favouring the melting pot over the salad option by a slim 53–47 margin. The one white subgroup which

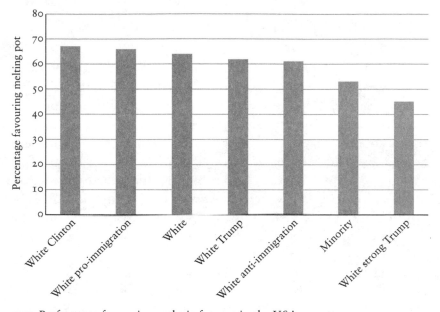

11.7. Preferences for various ethnic futures in the USA

Source: MTurk Survey, 29 November–16 December 2016. N = 499, including 68 non-whites.

favours a tight-bounded white minority over a loose-bounded majority is strong Trump supporters: the sixty-seven whites in the sample who scored Trump a 10 out of 10 preferred the tight-bounded whites-in-salad-bowl option by a modest 55–45.

In Canada, around 85 per cent of a 2017 sample of around 150 people on Prolific chose the melting-pot option over the 'whites as tight-knit group in multicultural society' one. There were few racial or partisan differences. It seems most North American whites prefer a creolized scenario in which the white group absorbs other strains to a mosaic in which whites maintain tight ethnic boundaries.[35] Of course, some may prefer options that were not on offer, such as a multicultural society with no white people or a two-way cosmopolitan melting pot of the kind espoused by Israel Zangwill or John Dewey. Still, these results suggest the idea of an open white majority commands cross-party approval, and certainly more than that of the multicultural salad bowl.

CREOLE NATIONALISTS

In North America, increasing intermarriage has reduced the importance of European 'white ethnic' identities such as Italian. This indicates that people of mixed-race background could become less likely to identify as white as intermarriage proceeds. There are other reasons why the new composite group may move towards the European strand of its heritage. Some argue that the encounter with difference stimulates identity. For example, as the Westernized global culture has spread across the world, non-Western cultures have responded with movements such as Islamism, Arabism and pan-Africanism. A Pakistani youth celebrating the 9/11 attacks in a Chicago Bears T-shirt illustrates how culture can globalize while identity localizes.[36]

Culture is not identity. As we become more culturally similar, the politics of identity becomes more powerful. This in turn may provide the basis for cultural renewal. In the nineteenth century, English steadily replaced Irish and Welsh as the majority language spoken in Ireland and Wales. This anglicization stimulated the Welsh Revival in Wales from the early nineteenth century and the Gaelic Revival in Ireland after 1880. These in turn spawned nationalist political movements which tried to revive the language.[37]

A typical pattern for nationalist movements in empires is that they begin among intellectuals in cosmopolitan cities who are heavily assimilated into the empire's high culture.[38] Think of English-speaking Indian nationalists in the British Empire or German-speaking Czech nationalists in the Habsburg Empire. This encounter with a homogenizing foreign culture – often in multicultural capitals – sharpens the awareness of identity. This can lead to a desire for political independence in the home province. In addition, in provinces where assimilation to the imperial language is also occurring, the encounter with universalism concentrates nationalist minds on how to reverse language loss. Language protection efforts begin and minority nationalist intellectuals try to raise ethnic consciousness in their homelands. They create modern dictionaries for unwritten tongues like Latvian or ancient ones like Irish, and conduct anthropological and historical research to codify their group's history and culture. In the process, myths – such as the legend of King Arthur among the English or William Tell for the Swiss – are invented, revived or reworked.[39]

The diminishing sway of white-Christian majorities in the West involves a loss of cultural traditions of race and religion which can be compared to the fading of the Irish or Welsh languages in the nineteenth century. Indeed, race, religion and language are the three main features which demarcate ethnic groups from each other across the world. The difference is that language can be easily acquired in the second generation, while race and religion are more 'counter-entropic' in Ernest Gellner's parlance and thus more difficult to revive. Yet the loss of religion or race is likely to produce a nostalgia similar to that caused by the loss of language, prompting a desire to slow the process. Populist-right intellectuals such as the 'alt-right' or 'Nouvelle Droite' are therefore mobilizing against the erosion of white-Christian ethnotraditions, attempting to raise consciousness even in parts of their countries that have experienced limited immigration.

Those of hybrid background are prominent in today's cultural nationalist movements, as in the past. A partial list of mixed-ancestry nationalists from the past two centuries would include the Irish president Éamon de Valera (half Spanish), the IRA's Seán Mac Stíofáin (half English), the American pan-Africanist W. E. B. Du Bois (part European) or the Metis leader Louis Riel (seven eighths European). It isn't hard to find examples today, notably the Fijian nationalist George Speight (half English), the leader of the Czech-nationalist Freedom and Democracy party Tomio Okamura (half Japanese), or the part-Indonesian Geert Wilders. In the US, two recent young examples are Joey Gibson, leader of Patriot Prayer (half Japanese) and the paleoconservative Marcus Epstein (half Korean).

Interracial mixing may therefore just as easily increase as reduce the power of white identity. It's certainly true that inter-ethnic mixing among whites reduced the power of individual European identities in America, but the situations are not equivalent. Americans of part-Italian origin could supersede their identity because there was a larger Euro-American category to move to. It's not clear what group mixed-race Americans or Europeans can move to unless a new hybrid myth like the mestizo arises – but the historical resources for this are really only present in New World societies. Instead, global shifts may accentuate the tendency of mixed-race individuals to play up their European origins. As whites decline demographically and economically in the world, their confidence, which incubated both liberalism and left-modernism, is likely to wane. This could make white identity more distinctive and salient while weakening the taboos against it, potentially leading to feelings of pan-European ethnic consciousness that cross the Atlantic.[40] We are already seeing the first stirrings of this.

Returning to the present, we can sketch several alternative paths which ethnic minorities in today's Western societies are moving along, some of which lead to absorption into the ethnic majority. I highlight the main trajectories in figure 11.8. On the left side of the chart is a minority-retention path, in which a minority lives in its ethnic culture, identifies with the homeland, marries within the group and remains distinct from the rest of society. An alternative path is assimilation to the modern mass culture of consumerism and individualism. This is arguably where many native-born minorities are at present. Their national identity is strongly civic, focused on territory, political traditions and the

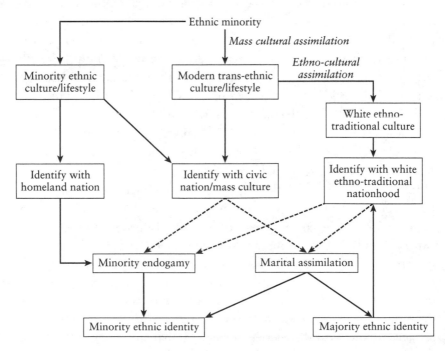

11.8. Minority retention and assimilation paths

mass culture of the nation. Those in this category are more likely to marry out than minority traditionals. They may also identify with 'white' national historical figures such as Christopher Columbus or, in Sweden, the Vikings, rather than the anti-white narrative of the modernist left.

Finally, a portion of these individuals will gravitate to the right-hand side of the diagram, assimilating not just to mass culture but to the ethno-traditions of the majority. This could mean taking part in the national sport, folk dance or traditions of rural origin such as British country shows. It may mean moving to a rural or provincial area. This in turn may be a conduit for ethno-traditional national identity. For instance, in England, the 2011 ONS LS shows that minorities who live in heavily white wards are significantly more likely to identify as English, a more ethnically defined form of national identity than British, compared with minorities in more diverse areas. They are also more inclined to marry outside their group and cease practising a non-Christian religion than their co-ethnics in diverse places. All of which means their offspring have a higher chance of identifying with the ethnic majority.

12

Will 'Unmixed' Whites Go Extinct?

Some argue that white is a relative concept, a category that shifts as demography changes and elites make new economic and political calculations about the minimum coalition they need to stay in power. As mentioned, I'm not convinced by this: critical race theorists' contention that Irish, Italians and other Europeans were not considered white until they became useful for the elite offers no evidence that the term 'white' didn't cover these groups.[1] In fact, the available evidence shows they were viewed as inferior outsiders, but as *white* outsiders in a way blacks or Chinese were not.

If the white category doesn't rest on politics and economics, is it therefore based on natural races defined by demarcated gene pools? No. Whites are not primarily attached to those of their race because they are genetically closer to these people: there are no discrete biological races so our tribal impulses have no obvious boundaries. Furthermore, these instincts can be deflected on to other kinds of group. Recall Dawkins's discussion of racial categories as similar to colours. There are no physical colours or races, but our colour perception and linguistic evolution mean we have a set of racial categories, centred on archetypes, that may prove as difficult to dislodge as the primary colours.

There are two things going on here. First, racial categorization. Like colours, races arise through a blend of unconscious colour-processing and slowly evolved cultural conventions. There is little we can consciously do to alter these categories, except at the fuzzy boundaries. We might be able to think of purple as a shade of red or a kind of blue, but we'll never convince ourselves that what we now think of as red is the same colour as blue. Likewise with race: an Arab or Mexican could be construed as white, but this is difficult to envision in the case of a

478

Chinese person or Nigerian. *Ethnicity* is much more amenable to construction than race, thus ethnic categories can be narrower or wider than racial ones. An Irish or Jewish person with red hair and blue eyes can be othered as inferior and thus not part of the English 'us'. Alternatively, someone who looks black could be included as part of the Native Indian 'us' when we hear they are part Navajo and identify with their Amerindian ancestors. In the future, someone who doesn't look racially white might similarly be accepted as ethnically Norwegian or 'white' American. Even here, however, boundaries typically must emerge from the bottom up. While elite pronouncements can strike a chord, they may also fail to resonate, so the ultimate outcome of the process is not inevitable. The acceptance of those who don't look white as members of the ethnic majority will probably require both intellectual arguments and emergent processes such as intermarriage which make this more compelling.

Whiteness matters because it's a cultural marker, part of a vernacular tradition tied to ethnicity and nationhood. In Western countries, the white racial tradition appears on canvas, engraved on statues and immortalized in family heirlooms and on film. What Michael Lind terms the 'beige' majorities of the future will need to reckon with this inheritance by denying, ignoring or celebrating it.[2] The present impulse on the left is to repress the white racial tradition as racist. On the centre-right, it is sublimated into narratives such as economic nationalism, integration, or law and order. The far right seeks to return to it in idealized form, ironing out the many divisions which existed among whites, and to portray its erosion as primarily due to malevolent forces. In this chapter, I'll examine the future of the white archetype, and, to paraphrase Mark Twain, will suggest that reports of its death are greatly exaggerated.

WHITE GENOCIDE

The theory of white genocide holds that a combination of low white birth rates, non-white immigration and race-mixing will lead to the extinction of the white race in the West. Sometimes this is given a local interpretation, as with the British National Party's Nick Griffin, who speaks of the British government committing 'bloodless genocide' against the 'indigenous people' of Britain.[3] From Charlottesville to Calais, the far-right mantra 'You will not replace us' bespeaks a similar philosophy. This process, argue white nationalists, is being driven by liberals and/or Jews, who have used white guilt over the Holocaust, slavery, Jim Crow and colonialism to open the doors of Western countries to mass non-white immigration and race-mixing. Minorities are permitted to have racial identity but whites are not. Only white countries have liberals who oppose the ethnic majority and welcome large-scale immigration of those from different racial backgrounds.

It's important to address the theory because simply accusing white nationalists of racism or refusing to discuss the fine points of white genocide theory can only give the impression of a cover-up and provide oxygen to these ideas. In addition, the more radical left-modernists get on race, the more people become attracted to theories of white genocide. Consider the relationship between the frequency of searches for the terms 'white privilege' and 'white genocide' on Google I noted earlier. White privilege is searched for more often than white genocide, but when we compare the trends on a 0–100 growth index, mentions of the two terms largely track one another. Both series begin rising in 2012 and are now at unprecedented heights.

WHITE TERRORISM

These ideas may also pose a security risk. On 22 July 2011, a 32-year-old Norwegian extremist, Anders Behring Breivik, set off a car bomb in central Oslo, killing seven people. This was followed by a ninety-minute shooting spree on a small island summer camp for supporters of the governing Labour Party. Breivik hunted down and killed at least eighty-seven children and young people, some under ten years old. In addition to an animus against Islam, the theory of white genocide played a part in Brevik's thinking. In his court statement, he wrote: 'Appreciating diversity does not mean that you support genocide of your own culture and people.'

Breivik is a rarity in Europe thus far. The number of white-nationalist terror incidents is low, both in absolute terms and in proportion to the white majority population. In 2016, Europol reports that Islamists were responsible for 72 per cent of foiled or successful attacks in the EU, compared to 10 per cent for separatists (notably the dissident IRA), 3 per cent for leftists and anarchists and virtually none for the far right.[4] On the other hand, there is evidence that white-nationalist terrorism may be rising in importance. On 16 June 2016, a British Labour MP, Jo Cox, was shot and stabbed to death by a 52-year-old mentally ill man, Thomas Mair, as he yelled: 'This is for Britain.' Mair targeted Cox as a 'passionate defender' of the European Union and immigration, viewing her as a 'traitor' to white people.[5] Britain's PRE-VENT anti-terrorism unit reported that 25 per cent of the 4,000 cases referred to it in 2016 concerned the far right. This is much lower than the 70 per cent for Islamism, but represents a substantial share of the total.[6] Meanwhile, one third of the 400 people referred to CHAN-NEL, the branch of PREVENT focusing on high-priority cases, were linked to the far right.[7] In addition, there are some 55,000 racial and religious hate crimes reported in Britain each year – most involving verbal harassment but with a third involving violence and another 10 per cent concerning arson or criminal damage.[8]

In Germany, attacks on refugee shelters are common. These tripled in frequency between 2013 and 2014, reaching 175 in that year. With the Migration Crisis of 2015, attacks more than quadrupled to 1,031. In 2015, far-right crime rose by a fifth to a total of 23,000 incidents. Clashes between left- and right-wing demonstrators grew dramatically in frequency. 'The sharp increase in politically motivated crime points to a dangerous development in society,' stressed the interior minister, Thomas de Maizière. 'We are witnessing a growing and increasingly pronounced readiness to use violence, both by right and left-wing extremists.'[9] The US also has a history of far-right violence: 106 people were killed by the far right between 12 September 2001 and 31 December 2016, nearly as many as were murdered by jihadis. Much of it is anti-government or anti-abortion, but nearly half is white nationalist or supremacist. Thus far there's a steady drip of casualties rather than any clear rising trend.[10]

IS THE WHITE GENOCIDE
THEORY ENTIRELY FALSE?

White genocide sits at the extreme end of a belief system that has much wider currency. Few believe in the full-throated anti-Semitic conspiracy theory of white genocide. However, a larger number are convinced by some of its claims. Successful ideologies begin with truthful observations which strike a chord, then build a superstructure of mistruths on top of them. The same holds for the theory of white genocide. The simplistic view that every syllable Richard Spencer or Generation Identity utters is a lie is incorrect.

Let's consider where the truth or falsehood lies within white-genocide theory. The argument that minority ethnic groups are encouraged to take pride in their identity while whites are not strikes me as undeniable in the present climate. This isn't to say that whites can't practise aspects of their culture such as rodeo or wearing lederhosen, but rather that they are strongly discouraged from organizing as a community of shared ancestry celebrating a set of traditions, myths and memories. At Georgia State University, Patrick Sharp, aged eighteen, asked: 'If we are already minorities on campus and are soon to be minorities in this country, why wouldn't we have the right to advocate for ourselves and have a club just like every other minority? Why is it when a white person says he is proud to be white he's shunned as a racist?' Mainstream elite opinion is that white clubs are unacceptable. This is justified on the grounds that 'affirmation and uplift are more important to a group that has been oppressed and discriminated against than they are to the dominant majority'.[11] This is flawed in two respects. First, it assumes clubs exist only for political or economic rather than cultural reasons. This materialistic view of the world is hopelessly outdated after the behavioural-economics and evolutionary-psychology revolutions; it is ignorant of the history of ethnic revival in the world, which is often led by romantic intellectuals in search of meaning and authenticity.[12]

It is unclear to me why no members of a dominant group would be interested in their cultural traditions, ethno-history and memories. In common with minorities, some will wish to be part of an ethnic community and celebrate this. No one would protest at the formation of an Italian-American club, but the reality is that Euro-Americans are too blended by now, and are attached to a composite tradition. Minorities are more likely to wish to band together for social purposes, as they differ from the mainstream, but some whites will also have cultural interests. Second, whites are a minority at Georgia State and on many campuses, and are declining year on year, so are growing less secure. This provides further impetus to the desire to form a group. Freezing out legitimate expressions of white identity allows the far right to own it, and acts as a recruiting sergeant for their wilder ideas. The African-American writer Coleman Hughes observes that American society is riven with racial double standards. In a 2018 debate with Jordan Peterson, Hughes observes that the black academic Michael Eric Dyson called Peterson a 'mean, mad, white man' on several occasions, whereas if Peterson labelled Dyson a 'mean, mad, black man' he would be accused of racism. Hughes, a musician who was hired as part of the pop star Rihanna's backup band, recalls a decision to replace his Hispanic friend in the band because she wanted an all-black 'look' for her act. Unlike Dyson's name calling, Rihanna's decision may be justified on artistic grounds. However, if a white performer justified firing a black musician to achieve an 'all-white' image, this would set off a firestorm.[13] Why this white exceptionalism? Should the grandson of a gangster have to endure taunts from the grandchildren of the gangster's victims? Should a gangster's relatives be fair game? Invoking the history of racism to justify harsher treatment of whites reflects a Hatfield–McCoy[14] theory of justice that leans on pre Hobbesian notions of intergenerational culpability, collective punishment, eternal sin and retributive justice.

Moving down the scale of truthfulness, we come to the claim that only white countries have liberals who oppose their own ethnic group and express majority guilt. This is largely but not entirely the case. Most white nationalists wouldn't consider Israel to be part of the West. But in Israel there is a vibrant group of Jewish post-Zionists on the left who oppose the idea of a Jewish state.[15] Some deny their Jewishness, associating it with oppression of Palestinians. In books like *The Invention of the Jewish People* (2009) and *How I Stopped being a Jew* (2014), the Israeli author Shlomo Sand denies the very existence of the Jews as an ethnic group. Instead, he argues, the Jews are either a religion or secular members of their nation-states. Jewish achievements, he adds, are artificially toted up by collecting the works of citizens of many different nations and lumping them together as Jewish. Sand views himself as a secular Israeli citizen, feeling a commonality with Israeli Arabs but not European Jews.[16] Sand is not a crank but a best-selling author and major figure on the Israeli cultural left.

These movements are weaker in Asia, but have a foothold. The island of Taiwan was settled by Chinese beginning in the late 1600s and accelerating after 1760. The chronology is similar to the European settlement of North America. As in North America or Australia, there is an indigenous minority – of Austronesian origin – of around 2 per cent which has lived on the island for over 5,000 years. Aboriginal activists have attacked the Han Chinese majority as exploitative and greedy. Hsieh Shih-chung writes that there is an important group of 'Han humanists, most of them journalists, social critics, writers, or newspaper editors' who support the indigenous resistance and 'have spent considerable energy on self-reflection and confession of Han . . . responsibility for the tragic state of the indigenous people'. The journalist Chia-hsiang Wang 'feels that he himself bears the cross of guilt for [Han Chinese] treatment of indigenous people'. Yu-feng Chen urges something similar to Western multiculturalists: 'accepting and tolerating cultures alien to Han . . . in order to ameliorate the unfortunate situation created by the Han'.[17]

The valorization of indigenes and acceptance of Chinese original sin are similar to the anti-white tropes of the Western modernist left. While these Taiwanese developments may reflect the influence of Western ideas, they also demonstrate how the combination of liberal-democratic modernity and subaltern groups can produce anti-majority politics. They also gain strength from the fact that Taiwanese nationalism is anti-Chinese, which inclines it towards elevating the aboriginal heritage. In that sense, the situation is not precisely analogous to that of the West where there is no nationalist rationale for denigrating the white majority.

But there are other indicators of non-Western cosmopolitanism. Around 8 per cent of people in the World Values Surveys of 1981–2007 say they belong to the world before their country or locality, and another 4 per cent prioritize their continent over the nation. The West reflects this average almost perfectly, with Africa and non-Muslim Asia less cosmopolitan, and the Muslim world and Latin America more cosmopolitan, than average. In addition, in figure 8.13 we saw that fewer Indians, Japanese, Koreans and Mexicans than Westerners want to cut immigration. This could be because few immigrants arrive in these countries, but it's harder to explain why a similar share of folk in these nations consider ethnically motivated immigration restrictions to be racist as Westerners. The difference between the West and the Rest thus lies less in public opinion than in the emergent properties of institutions: people's expectations of what others think the 'correct' view is.

Do liberals intend to transform white societies into non-white ones through immigration and race-mixing? I think this also contains a measure of truth, though it is far from the whole story. For instance, chapter 2 showed that many American business owners, politicians and clerics wanted more Chinese immigration in the period from 1865 until Chinese Exclusion in 1882. This included southern plantation owners. Liberals at this time wanted an open door because they saw this as economically beneficial, part of the country's asylum tradition or reflecting Divine Will. None of this easily fits the left-modernist paradigm. A more explicit cosmopolitanism comes into view with the Liberal Progressives in the 1900s, but even they favoured immigration mainly for reasons of humane liberalism. It is only with the cultural radicalism of the Young Intellectuals after 1912 that an anti-majority ethos took centre stage. Today's left-modernists are motivated by both humanitarianism and multicultural millenarianism. They also look forward to the demise of a white majority because they believe this will pave the way for progressivism despite the fact that this is contradicted by data from figures 7.8 and 7.9. So there is truth to the white nationalists' transformationist charge, but much of the impetus for immigration comes from liberal humanitarianism and economic *laissez-faire* rather than modernist millenarianism.

Are the only countries willing to permit ethnic transformation white ones? The wealthiest countries in the world are Western, Gulf Arab or East Asian. East Asia is relatively closed to migration and the Gulf only admits temporary workers, so here the white genocide story is on solid ground. However, this may have more to do with East Asian and Gulf Arab exceptionalism than white country particularity. Parts of the world where ethnic boundaries have historically been porous – Latin America, Africa and the Caribbean – have been as or more open than the West. Cuba, Mexico or Brazil, for example, were open to East

Asians or Middle Easterners at a time when North America was closed, and consequently have important Asian and Middle Eastern minorities today.[18] Whether they would have remained open in the face of the large-scale flows experienced in North America after 1965 is an open question.

Turkey's openness to 1.8 million Syrian Arab refugees, or Kenya's accommodation of over 500,000 Somalis, South Sudanese, Congolese and Ethiopians shows that countries outside the West often accommodate larger refugee flows of ethnically distinct people. In terms of economic migration, we can spot analogies to the West in Latin America and the Caribbean. In 2017, I visited Costa Rica, one of my ancestral homelands. There the number of Nicaraguans has increased from about 45,000 in 1984 to over 287,000 in 2012. This means those of Nicaraguan origin form 6 per cent of the population. Though both are Hispanic, the Amerindian component of the mestizo population has somewhat different origins in the two countries and is higher in Nicaragua than in Costa Rica. There are also important cultural differences. The share of foreign-born in Costa Rica is 8.6 per cent, but in Belize it is over 15 per cent, consisting mainly of Salvadorians and Guatemalans. English-speaking Creoles and Spanish-speaking mestizos each comprise around 35 per cent of the total, so this new Hispanic migration, if sustained, has the potential to alter the country's ethnic mix.

Nearby, the Caribbean island of Antigua, population 98,000, provides another instance of where Hispanic immigrants are entering an Anglophone Creole-dominated country. The share of Spanish-speakers from the Dominican Republic has increased from virtually zero to 10 per cent of the population since 1981 through a generous programme of work permit allocation.[19] While there is some tension, immigration remains fairly open: 'The Bill to grant amnesty to "thousands" of illegal immigrants received bi-partisan support when it was passed in the Lower House,' reports the local paper.[20] Having said this, a significant portion of the Hispanic population claims to be descended from those who emigrated from Antigua to the Dominican Republic to cut sugar cane in the past. This may affect local perceptions of their right to settle in Antigua.

Whereas ethnic tensions in Antigua, Belize and Costa Rica are modest and haven't led to immigration restriction, the situation in South Africa and Côte d'Ivoire is radically different. In relatively prosperous, demographically mature South Africa, Zimbabweans, Ethiopians, Mozambicans, Nigerians and other groups with little historic presence in the country have grown substantially since the end of apartheid in 1994. Given its proximity to very poor countries at an early stage of their demographic transitions, and with weak border controls across the continent, the potential for large-scale unauthorized immigration is much greater than in Europe or the United States. The share of immigrants has tripled from about 1 million in 1996 to 3 million today, forming 5.5 per cent of the population. In 2015, the number of unresolved refugee claims was second only to Germany. In 2008, pogroms ripped through immigrant neighbourhoods in the country's major cities, resulting in sixty immigrants being killed, with 30,000 homes destroyed and 100,000 people displaced.[21] Mario Khumalo, leader of the new South African First party, is mobilizing this sentiment into a political movement. Khumalo claims the number of illegal immigrants in the country is 13 million, more than four times the actual number.[22]

Likewise, in the West African country of Côte d'Ivoire, civil war broke out in 2002 as northern, mainly Muslim, political actors rebelled against the increasingly discriminatory policies of the southern-Christian-based ruling party of Laurent Gbagbo. In 1922, an estimated 6 per cent of the country was Muslim. The French colonizers, followed by the postcolonial regime of Félix Houphouët-Boigny, recruited Muslim labourers from countries to the north such as Burkina Faso to work the cocoa plantations. Though immigration tailed off in the 1980s and 1990s, Muslim fertility became slightly higher than Christian fertility, perpetuating continued ethnic shifts. By the late 1990s, Muslims formed 38.6 per cent of the population, well in excess of the 29 per cent Christian share. The perception of inexorable Muslim growth combined with the introduction of elections and an economic slump created a dangerous cocktail. Elections in ethnic party systems are often a glorified census which makes ethnic demography a key battleground. Southern politicians claimed that many northerners, including those who were born in the country or had lived there for generations, were not citizens and so should not be allowed to vote. Northerners understandably rebelled, setting off a spiral of conflict.[23] International intervention has helped quell trouble, though another round of violence broke out in 2010–11. Ethnic shifts are not the sole reason for the conflict: divisions along other lines could have emerged and solidified when elections were introduced. Regardless, the main point is that liberal immigration and ethnic change are not unique to the West.

Another claim of the white-genocide theory is that other racial groups are outbreeding whites. But the claim that whites have lower birth rates than non-whites can be dispensed with fairly quickly. Almost all modern populations are in some stage of the demographic transition to low birth and death rates. The transition took place first in the West, between the late eighteenth century and the mid-twentieth century. It happened next in East Asia, and since the mid-twentieth century has more or less spread around the world. Countries like Iran, Brazil, Turkey and Tunisia have total fertility rates (TFR) at or below the replacement level, and the UN predicts that the entire world will be at replacement around 2085. The lowest fertility in the world today is in East Asia, not Europe. France and Northern Europe are emerging as high-fertility regions of the developed world. Fertility remains high in sub-Saharan Africa, but in cities like Addis Ababa the fertility rate is below replacement. Africa is rapidly urbanizing, and I would expect it to follow the wider global trend to lower fertility. The groups most likely to expand in a post-transition world are world-denying fundamentalist sects, all of which, to my knowledge, are exclusively white. But more on this later.

Are Jews or minorities seeking to hasten white decline? I may be biased but I've never seen systematic evidence for this claim. Ethnically conscious members of minority groups wish to boost their numbers and bring in relatives for group-interested reasons, but only a handful of cranks, such as the proponents of the Aztlan reconquest of the American south-west or some European jihadists, dream of political domination. Jews tend to be over-represented among all strands of intellectual thought. They are prominent in left-modernist pro-immigration politics, i.e. the prominent Democratic politician Chuck Schumer or the critical race theorist Noel Ignatiev, but are also in the vanguard of the anti-immigration movement, like Lawrence Auster, Éric Zemmour or Stephen Miller. In the US, Felix Adler had an indirect influence on early pro-immigration thinking, but mainly because his ideas, designed to apply to Jews, were transposed to Anglo-Protestant Americans by John Dewey, a New England Yankee. Similarly, Randolph Bourne, another New Englander, revamped the Jewish Horace Kallen's ideas, which were not anti-WASP, to undercut the identity claims of WASPs and create the asymmetrical multiculturalism of today.

Another white-genocide claim is that whites face imminent extinction through immigration and race-mixing. This is almost certainly false. Straight-line demographic modelling does provide some evidence for this argument, suggesting that on current trends, and assuming no geographic isolation, the last person in Britain will mix with a non-white partner in 980 years.[24] The notion that whites as a race are facing extinction in Europe or America is more of a stretch. As mentioned, there is already non-European ancestry in the white population and even with a good deal more admixture, many will appear Caucasian. Even if non-European ancestry becomes dominant, chance will throw up archetypal white individuals, as periodically occurs when two black parents give birth to a white baby.[25]

More to the point, the modelling most likely underestimates the tenacity of whiteness among committed groups. 'Unmixed' groups of whites already persist as tight-bounded minorities in Africa, the Caribbean, Mauritius and tropical Latin America. Eastern Europe is following the East Asian model of maintaining societies based on closed ethnic boundaries. In the West, whites are likely to endure for millennia in isolated rural communities, just as unmixed Native Indians or Gaelic-speaking Irish do. Immigration to the West is concentrated in urban areas, where the jobs are, with rural hinterlands remaining heavily white. Indeed, cities and suburbs in the West are increasingly diverging from rural areas, portending a widening ethno-geographic divide which could even exceed that of early-twentieth-century America.

FUTURISTIC SCENARIOS

Unmixed whites may persist in rural backwaters, Eastern Europe and a few tight-knit diasporas, but will this be the end of white-majority societies in the West? Sure, I hear you say, the future is unknowable, but the safest prediction in the social sciences is that the West can only become less white. Not necessarily. In order to understand why things are uncertain, let's begin with low-probability scenarios and move to more likely ones.

*

In Ernest Cline's science fiction adventure *Ready Player One* (2011), which takes place in 2044, the protagonist, Wade Watts, lives in 'the stacks', a vertical slum of Oklahoma City made of trailer homes piled on top of each other. Global warming and resource depletion have produced a post-apocalyptic nightmare. In order to escape, people retreat behind visors and gloves into a virtual-reality fantasy world.

Is the world real or a simulation? The problem has vexed metaphysicians for millennia and many techno-optimists point to a future in which the virtual and real have become blurred. The tech magnate Elon Musk, a thought-leader in this area, claims that we may already be living in a simulation. '40 years ago we had Pong – two rectangles and a dot,' Musk told an audience at a tech conference. 'Now 40 years later we have photorealistic, 3D simulations with millions of people playing simultaneously and it's getting better every year. And soon we'll have virtual reality, we'll have augmented reality . . . the games will become indistinguishable from reality.'[26] As the West grows more diverse and white avoidance and hunkering down become impossible, might group-conscious whites 'exit' into a 1950s-style simulation of their countries? Could nationalists set their reality augmentation glasses to reveal an ethnically homogeneous world?

I may be a curmudgeon, but it strikes me there a number of problems here. First, people's need for human interaction, sunlight and fresh air will put the kibosh on the more extreme versions of virtual reality. People are already tiring of screens: for instance, the reading public is moving away from e-readers back to tangible books. Second, individuals have to interact to produce public goods like roads and parks, not to mention the welfare state and democracy. I'm not sure social problems can be solved by putting on a pair of rose-tinted glasses. At some point, people will crave authenticity. There's a reason we find films like *The Matrix* disorienting.

A second techno-futurist line of reasoning is represented by Yuval Noah Harari's *Homo Deus* (2016). Harari claims humans have begun worshipping humanity rather than god and will seek immortality by blending with immortal technologies such as information systems or using biotechnology to renew themselves. Humans have mapped the genome, have cloned animals and are selecting against embryos with genetic errors that produce cystic fibrosis, sickle-cell anaemia, and early-onset Alzheimer's disease. The next stage, which may be no more than a decade or two away, is to use biotechnology to design our offspring. This has implications for ethnic movements because ethnicity concerns ancestry, which has a basis in genetic traits that manifest themselves as phenotypical markers.

The genetic frequencies of ethnic groups have been extensively mapped.[27] Like many, I've done a cheek swab to find out more about my ancestors. While some of the ones I expected – South American Indian, Chinese, Jewish – appeared, many others, such as Swedish, Hungarian and Lowland Scots, surprised me. This was done a decade ago, so I'm not sure the sampling was fine-grained enough! Still, the point is that new technologies can change perceptions of identity. Alondra Nelson's fascinating book *The Social Life of DNA* (2016) chronicles how genetic tests have been used by African-Americans to trace their roots to particular African tribes and even to make claims for reparations for slavery.[28] This can have group-level political implications. The Lemba, a trading minority native to Zimbabwe and South Africa, long believed they were descended from Jews. When genetic tests revealed this to be true, the findings reinforced their myth of descent.[29] In contrast, a study of North African Jews which showed them to be more similar to Arabs than European Jews caused ructions because it challenged existing beliefs.[30]

The active manipulation of genes would be much more consequential, raising a wide range of questions which Francis Fukuyama tackles in *Our Posthuman Future* (2002). The least intrusive form is to use gene therapy to modify our genetic makeup, altering physical traits. A more problematic step is to select which embryo we would like from a range of naturally occurring possibilities so that no one could guess that we engineered our baby's characteristics. Beyond this, biotechnology will permit us to alter genetic characteristics of an embryo which are then passed on to future generations. Fukuyama, like most, urges us to use genetic engineering only to correct defects, not to positively design, but the molecular biologist Lee Silver disagrees. In his controversial *Remaking Eden* (1997), he claims that once some engage in positive design, others will be compelled to follow to keep up. It may even be the case that those who can afford it will have designed themselves into a hyper-intelligent, beautiful *GenRich* species that can't breed with the *GenPoor*.

*

Nothing that is recorded need ever die. George Church, a geneticist at Harvard, claims to be just years away from bringing the extinct Woolly Mammoth to life.[31] Genetic mapping means we can identify the genetic traits which distinguish the Welsh and Cornish from the English. This opens up the possibility that not just religion or language, but race, can be revived.

Though a language dies every 14 days in the world, those that are put to paper or stone can be resurrected by ethnic revivalists and nationalists. Dolly Pentreath passed away in 1777, the last speaker of Cornish, a Celtic dialect from the south-west of England, but today's Cornish nationalists are beginning to revive it to the point where, in 2009, UNESCO altered the language's status from extinct to endangered. One day it may be spoken as widely as Welsh. There are also examples of collective memories that have sprung from the grave. The Assyrian Empire was destroyed and the Assyrian people, like most ancient ethnic groups, subsequently dissolved, their descendants becoming members of surrounding ethnic communities. However, a group of Syriac Christians emerged in the modern period calling themselves Assyrians and claiming descent from the ancients, bringing their collective memories to life. The same is true of the Phoenician and Pharaonic Egyptian civilizations. These vanished, but Lebanese and Egyptian Christians now look to these ancient peoples – not the Arabs – as their ancestors.

The heightened consciousness that arises from ethnic revivals of the kind that surged among minority groups in Europe in the nineteenth century often led to projects of cultural restoration.[32] The newly independent nation-states which emerged out of the Austro-Hungarian, Ottoman or Czarist empires tried to codify their vernaculars as high written languages. Words for modern objects like trains were synthesized from ancient root words. In many cases, the cultural nationalists succeeded. Had they not, languages like Estonian would be on their way to extinction. In some cases, as with Hebrew in Israel, the language hadn't been used since ancient times. Some didn't succeed: Éamon de Valera failed to make Ireland a Gaelic-speaking society in the 1930s and 1940s, and *Provençal* intellectuals in southern France were unable to create a sufficiently large reading public for their language to resist French in the nineteenth century.

As with language, so with religion. The term religious revival is usually reserved for movements which revive religious orthodoxy or, more often, distil religion to a set of imagined fundamentals and attempt to spread this fundamentalist faith as a replacement for the moderate version that actually exists. The Islamic Revival, which emerged after 1970, is an example. Religion can also return to secular soil. Truly non-religious societies are quite new, and shifts from secularism to religion have mainly occurred in ex-Communist societies like the Central Asian 'stans' where Islam has re-emerged.

Nationalism can play a part in religious revival. Sunni Islam is a basis for national identity in Pakistan and Saudi Arabia; Shi'ism for Iranian identity and Orthodox Christianity for the Russians. Nationalists in all these countries have spurred religious revival. In the Sunni cases this boosted fundamentalism in countries that were already religious, but in Iran and Russia some seculars returned to the faith. Religious revival in the West is occurring through religious immigration, but a return to faith among the white majority seems unlikely in today's individualistic climate. Christian *identity* is more likely to revive – indeed, whites in parts of Britain with a higher share of Muslims are significantly more likely to say they are Christian.[33] This might lead some people to reconnect with Christianity through what's known as the 'cultural defence' mechanism whereby ethnic conflicts involving religious markers – as in Northern Ireland – boost religiosity.[34] Yet this requires a cosmological leap which may prove too much for many.

Religious revival is less critical for majority ethnicity as the West becomes less religious. Rather, as the West secularizes and non-Christian minorities remain religious, it is their distinctiveness from a post-Christian secularism which becomes problematic. The agent of assimilation in this case is secularization, which is proceeding slowly among non-Christian groups but may gather pace in the future. What's more central for majority ethnicity in a secular age is race. This discussion becomes important for our story if we imagine the Europe of 2200, in which whites of mixed-race are the dominant group and the white archetype that hangs in museums and is portrayed on movie screens remains a cultural reference point. Would small groups of ultra-nationalists begin whitening themselves, much like tribes tattooed themselves in the past? Even if they didn't, might tomorrow's mixed-race parents – especially of girls – select or engineer embryos for whiter features? Could the cumulative effect of these actions rapidly change the racial composition of society in a few generations? Might whitening threaten the survival of non-whites?

One doesn't have to look far to see that humans will go to great lengths to give themselves or their children an advantage. In a mixed-race nation where light skin carries prestige, such as Mexico, those possessing whiter features tend to marry each other, but darker-skinned people with money, power or fame can whiten their descendants by marrying those with fair skin. One fascinating study of Mexican elite families found that some began as successful mixed-race families who married poor European peasants to whiten their offspring and have since become part of Mexico's white elite. Similarly, poor whites who marry darker-skinned, wealthier Mexicans may produce offspring that cannot pass as white and therefore may pass out of the white racial caste.[35] In South and East Asia today, skin-lightening creams are a $43bn industry, with as many as four in ten East Asian women using them. Hair-straightening is a massive business in African-origin communities. People are even willing to intervene in the process of human reproduction. In Asia, a preference for sons combined with cheap sonograms increased sex-selective abortion to produce a male-skewed sex ratio.[36] If some engage in genetic enhancement in havens where laws were lax, others may feel pressured to follow, creating an unstoppable spiral of the kind Lee Silver describes.

The revival of genetic traits in a population will eventually be technically feasible, but I doubt this will become common. Surveys show that a majority in almost all societies oppose genetic enhancement.[37] Steps are already underway to establish international protocols to protect against this eventuality. The Council of Europe's Convention on Human Rights and Dignity with Regard to Biomedicine, Article 13, states that 'An intervention seeking to modify the human genome may only be undertaken for preventive, diagnostic or therapeutic purposes and only if its aim is not to introduce any modification in the genome of any descendants.' Social norms and legal arrangements can be as durable a barrier as technology, as we see with proscriptions against incest or the spread of nuclear weapons. Even sex-selective abortion tends to die off as societies grow wealthier.

Finally, many believe that engineering offspring would remove some of the enchantment and specialness of life, and thus recoil at the idea of designing their children the way humans designed dog breeds.

Consider the advantages that could be gained from a less radical step like changing one's name. Field experiments show that foreign-sounding names make it harder to get a job. If anything, altering surnames – perhaps by choosing the European surname from among one's parents or finding the nearest one on the family tree – should come first. Yet this doesn't seem to have led to a rash of name-changing. Even among Southern and Eastern European immigrants to the United States, apart from Jews, I calculate that the share who anglicized their surnames may be as low as 3 per cent.[38] Perhaps I'm being naïve, but I think it's unlikely that tomorrow's whites, Native Hawaiians or other highly mixed groups will resurrect their genetics the way ethnic revivalists breathed life into dying languages and extinct origin myths.

WHITE FUNDAMENTALISTS

The mixed-race whites of the West in 2200 are unlikely to embrace virtual reality and genetic engineering. Does this mean unmixed whiteness will survive in only a few pockets or as the odd genetic fluke? Not necessarily. In my *Shall the Religious Inherit the Earth* (2010), I argue that religious fundamentalists who reject the modern world, grow through high birth rates and retain their offspring have hit upon the most consistently successful model for success in liberal societies. So long as they are tolerated, groups like the ultra-Orthodox Jews, Amish, Hutterites, traditionalist Mennonites, Laestadian Lutherans, Orthodox Calvinists, Quiverfull neo-Calvinists and Mormons will expand rapidly. Secular or moderately religious populations make up the vast majority of the world's population but are moving in the direction of below-replacement fertility and population decline. At present, immigration is making up the shortfall in the West, but if this slows down, the fertility advantage of closed fundamentalists will become decisive.

These pro-natalist sects are motivated by religion, but happen to be exclusively white. As such, they are genetic time capsules from particular times and places. Amish, Hutterites and traditionalist Mennonites are German groups whose membership numbered in the hundreds not so long ago. Ultra-Orthodox Jews are mainly Ashkenazi Jews of Eastern European origin. Mormons are mostly English, reflecting the ethnic demography of New England prior to Irish immigration, with an admixture

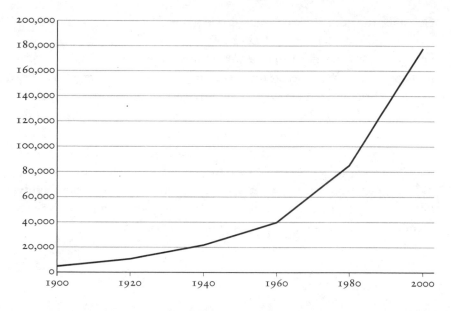

12.1. Old-order Amish in the twentieth century

Source: Michael Blume, 'The reproductive benefits of religious affiliation', in E. Voland and W. Schiefenhövel, *The Biological Evolution of Religious Mind and Behavior*. New York, 2009: Springer-Verlag.

of British and Swedish converts. No wonder Utah, the centre of Mormonism, is the most ethnically English state in the union. The Quiverfull movement, which eschews birth control and aims to reconquer the United States for neo-Calvinism in two centuries through demography, probably reflects the predominantly English, Scotch-Irish or German background of whites in the American Bible Belt.[39]

In most cases these groups are small, but when a group maintains a fertility rate of five to seven children per woman for generations, it multiplies, like compound interest. The American Amish population, for instance, rose 120 per cent between 1992 and 2013, while the US population grew by only 23 per cent. Figure 12.1 shows how 5,000 Amish individuals in 1900 have grown to more than 250,000 today, with a doubling time of twenty-five years.

If the doubling time remains constant, the Amish population growth curve will resemble figure 12.2. In other words, in little more than two centuries they could form half the US population. This presumes they

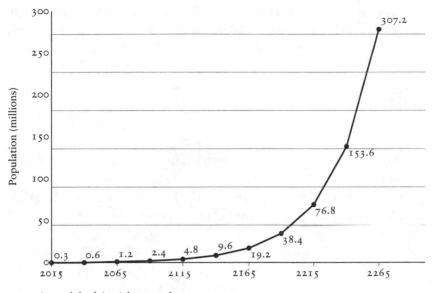

12.2. A model of Amish growth, 2015–2265

are able to keep their fertility and retention at current levels for 200 years. They've done it for a century, but there's no telling whether a Mennonite-style sect-to-church moderating effect might take the edge off their fertility by then. What seems to work against this is the secularism of the modern West, which these groups are reacting to. Whereas a traditionally religious group like Somali Muslim immigrants will reduce their fertility over a generation or two as they become modern, closed religious sects are inoculated against modernity. They've been bathed in it for generations and have learned to resist its charms. As a result, they lose very few members to the wider society.

The US is a big country and the Amish are small, but in some jurisdictions the reverse is true. Take Israel. The ultra-Orthodox model of the segregated scholar-society only developed in the 1950s and 1960s. Ultra-Orthodox, or Haredi, Jews have a fertility rate of around six to seven children per woman. Fewer than 10 per cent leave the fold. Retention is high in closed sects because those who depart are shunned by family and friends and become completely cut off from the world they once knew. Only 2.3 per cent of Israelis over eighty are Haredi, against 16 per cent of those under ten and fully 33 per cent of Jewish first-graders.

Many in Israel are worried because few Haredi men work or serve in the military. 'If the Haredim continue to receive the same [religious] education,' warns Dan Ben David, head of a major think tank, 'I have no doubt Israel will not be able to exist in two decades.' The finance minister, Yuval Steinitz, adds that 'Without a change now, within 10 years the situation will be a catastrophe.' Concerns have reached the highest levels of the country's economic elite. 'This is not sustainable,' urged the Bank of Israel's governor, Stanley Fischer, in July 2010. 'We can't have an ever-increasing proportion of the population continuing to not go to work.'[40]

The Haredim have begun flexing their political muscles. In 2003, Jerusalem elected Uri Lupolianski as the city's first Haredi mayor. Ultra-Orthodox demography and cohesion underpinned his success, with 90 per cent of Jerusalem's Haredi electorate voting compared to 32 per cent of non-Haredim. As Jerusalem has become a centre of Haredi settlement, those who drive on the Sabbath risk getting their cars stoned, ads featuring women's faces have been forced outside the city limits and modest dress is a must in many areas. In the American and British diaspora, the ultra-Orthodox are set to become the majority of observant Jews by 2050 as secular Jews assimilate and average around 1.5 children each. As a deprived, poorly educated community, the ultra-Orthodox will completely up-end stereotypes about Jewish success.[41]

The Haredi birth rate has ethnic implications. Jews now have a higher birth rate than Arabs in Israel. Arab fertility is declining, following global trends, while Jewish fertility continues to rise. The Arab share of Israel, which Jews once feared would grow inexorably due to higher Muslim fertility, will soon peak and begin to fall. Might the same happen elsewhere? The demographic expansion of closed sects can change the ethnic composition of neighbourhoods, cities and regions in the United States and Europe. Centres of ultra-Orthodox population in the United States are growing rapidly. New York City is only one-third non-Hispanic white, but Williamsburg and Borough Park, Brooklyn, the centre of the city's Haredi population, are 77–86 per cent white. Four of the twenty-five fastest increases in white population by ZIP code also occurred in Brooklyn. Population expansion recently led 20,000 Haredim living in Monroe, in upstate New York, to secede from the town to form Palm Tree, the first ultra-Orthodox town in the country.[42]

In the Netherlands, Urk, an Orthodox Calvinist village in the south of the country, is the youngest Dutch community because the Orthodox Calvinist total fertility rate is 3.0, well above the national average of 1.7. In Finland, the Laestadian Lutherans number only 80,000–150,000 but have a fertility rate of around 5.5 in a country where the average is 1.7.[43] Though only 2 per cent of the population, they could begin affecting society in a generation. The one difference from the other sects considered here is that Laestadians have a higher intermarriage rate, which could blunt their growth potential.

The Church of Jesus Christ of Latter-Day Saints, or Mormons, shows how high fertility, concentrated in one jurisdiction, can affect the course of politics. Founded in 1830 by Joseph Smith in upstate New York's 'burned-over district' and carried to the Utah Territory by Brigham Young's band of pilgrims, the cult has turned into a world religion of 12 million communicants. At its core are the Mormons of Utah, who largely descend from the original Yankee, British and Swedish converts and comprise around 61 per cent of the state's population. The high Mormon birth rate has protected the state's Mormon majority in the teeth of large-scale domestic and international migration. Since Mormons are mainly non-Hispanic whites, this means Utah is demographically diverging from the rest of the country. Figure 12.3 shows that among those over eighty-five, Utahans have a similar racial background to those in neighbouring Colorado, and are only 10 points whiter than the country as a whole. But Utah's under-five population is 35 points whiter than the country, and on its way towards stabilizing at 75 per cent of the total. Longer term, the white share of Utah may begin increasing as Latino fertility and immigration decline. Something similar happened in the past, when the share of Mormons in the state's population increased from 60 per cent in 1920 to 75 per cent by 1998.[44]

The state is the most reliably Republican in the country, and it's a pretty safe bet it will vote that way in the future. 'In largely Mormon Utah,' writes Michael Lind, 'there are 90 children for every 1,000 women of child-bearing age, compared to only 49 in the socially liberal Vermont of Howard Dean.' 'In [liberal] Seattle,' adds Philip Longman of the non-partisan New America Foundation, 'there are nearly 45 per cent more dogs than children. In [Mormon] Salt Lake City, there are nearly 19 per cent more kids than dogs.'[45] Utah is just one state and Mormons a small group, but the same can't be said about the rise of

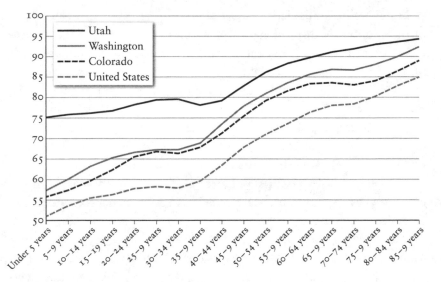

12.3. Non-Hispanic whites, by age group, %

Source: American Community Survey (ACS) 2014.

evangelicals to political prominence in the 1980s. Conservative Protestants increased from around a third of white Protestants born in 1900
to nearly two thirds of those born in 1975. As an important study
shows, three quarters of the change was demographic, to do with
conservative Protestants' one-child fertility advantage over liberal
denominations during the first half of the twentieth century.[46] While
that advantage is now closer to half a child, it will continue to shift the
political composition of the church-attending white population in a
Republican direction. The country's 6.1 million Mormons, who have a
fertility rate of around 3.4 children per woman (close to twice the US
average), are poised to expand significantly.[47] More importantly, with
600,000 ultra-Orthodox Jews, 300,000 Amish, some 50,000 Quiverfull Protestants and tens of thousands of Hutterites and traditionalist
Mennonites, the US is on course to be the second Western country to
experience the demographic rise of world-denying fundamentalism.

The first is Israel. The ultra-Orthodox now control Jerusalem. Without major change, their sway will extend to all of Israel by the end of
this century. The fundamentalist tide is set to sweep America by the
late 2100s. As this occurs, questions of ethnicity and race will fade,

with seculars and moderates of all backgrounds lining up against the fundamentalist sects. This is evident in Israel where anti-Haredi parties such as Shinui and Yisrael Beitenu have notched up impressive results, especially in periods where Arab–Jewish conflict subsides.[48]

THE DURABILITY OF WHITE CORES

If virtual reality and genetic engineering are the stuff of science fiction, and white fundamentalism, if it endures, is two centuries from taking over, where does this leave the white majority in the interim? Arguably the most important way in which unmixed whiteness will endure is through the archetypes around which an ethnic majority orients itself. In the previous chapter, I suggested the mixed group would begin to emerge as the majority in the major immigrant-receiving countries of the West late this century. In what follows, I argue that this mixed population will probably revolve around a white ethnic archetype in Europe and a white or hybrid-white imago in Anglo settler societies. Just as the Greeks absorbed numerically overwhelming Slavic migrations in the Byzantine period, Europeans are likely to absorb non-European admixture. In this sense, unmixed whites will persist in idealized form, even if their share of the population is low.

The key question is how the emerging mixed-race majority will iden- tify. In Europe, I claim, the mixed majority is unlikely to form a separate entity with a distinct tradition and culture from whites because it consists of many different white–other combinations rather than a binary mix like the mestizos (Spanish–Aztec) or Creoles (African– European). In the US and other Anglo settler societies, a hybrid myth is possible, but would most likely be based on established Metis/Melun- geon models which fuse lines of ancestry that have deep native roots.

Either way, I argued in the last chapter that there is a good chance mixed populations will orient around European ancestry. Is there any evidence to sustain this claim? One way of approaching this is to draw an analogy with the way the WASP type continues to serve as a lode- star of all-Americanism within the melting pot that is white America. Milton Gordon and Will Herberg, two Jewish-American writers of the mid-twentieth century, spoke of America as a 'transmuting' pot that converted European immigrants into WASPs. In addition to speaking

English, newcomers' religion, even if Catholic or Jewish, took on the denominational form characteristic of Protestantism. The direction of religious switching also favours Protestantism, though this didn't happen in a significant way until the 1980s. Donald Trump's Vice-President, Mike Pence, an Irish-Catholic-turned-evangelical-Protestant, exemplifies the shift.[49]

Even when newcomers didn't change their surnames or become Protestant, they recognized that what the Jewish-American writer Peter Schrag terms the American 'imago' was WASP.[50] A 1982 survey showed that the English were seen as having made the greatest contribution to America, followed by the Irish, Jews and Germans.[51] In surveys on MTurk during March–April 2017, I asked 467 Americans, 'All surnames are equally American, but if someone from another country asked you what a characteristic American surname was, which of the following would you choose?' Possible choices were (rotated): Browning, Graziano, Hernandez, Schultz and Wong. Eighty-one per cent of those who responded chose Browning, the Anglo surname, including 86 per cent of Clinton voters, 78 per cent of Trump voters, 86 per cent of African-Americans, 85 per cent of Hispanics and 80 per cent of whites. I also asked about the most typical American religion. In this case, 72 per cent of 525 respondents – including 70 per cent of Catholics – selected Protestant as opposed to Catholic or Jewish.

American popular culture, especially film, tends to prefer those who are closer to the WASP archetype. Schrag noticed this in his 1973 comment that:

> Louis B. Mayer took second-generation-Polish calendar models and turned them into WASPs ... The ethnics changed their names – Doris Kappelhoff became Doris Day, Bernie Schwartz turned into Tony Curtis, Margarita Carmen Cansino became Rita Hayworth and Dino Crocetti became Dean Martin ... Those ethnic types who remained sufficiently original for identification were almost invariably second-class citizens: the blundering Irish sidekick, the Filipino valet, the Jewish comic ... The genuine American was John Wayne, Gary Cooper, Clark Gable and Gregory Peck, a mythic man who transcended particular films or plots or situations.[52]

Does this still hold today? Together with Andrea Ballatore, I used data on ancestry from Ethnicelebs.com, a crowdsourced website which lists the ancestry of celebrities from stage, screen, sports, business and politics, past and present. Focusing on Americans, we then ran their surnames through an origins classifier.[53] Twenty-five per cent of American actors were of British descent compared to an estimated 16 per cent in the American population, a significant over-representation. This has declined over time as the pool of actors has shifted to better reflect the US population. The rate of surname anglicization has also declined, suggesting Anglo-conformist pressures in Hollywood have eased since the 1950s.

But figure 12.4 reveals that even among those born after 1980, 40 per cent of Jewish-American actors have Anglo surnames whereas across all professions in the dataset the share of American Jews with Anglo surnames is just 25–30 per cent. A portion of the Anglo over-representation reflects anglicized stage names while some of it may be due to studios' preference for those with Anglo-sounding names. Skylar Astin Lipstein, for instance, takes the stage name Skylar Astin while Halston Schrage is

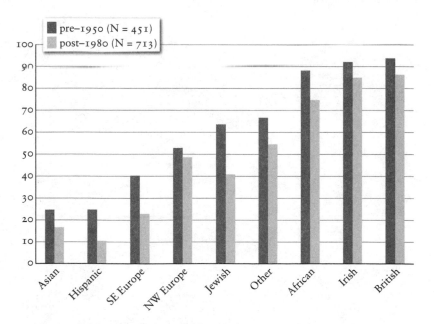

12.4. Share of US actors with British or Irish surnames, pre-1950 vs post-1980 cohorts, by primary ancestry, %

Source: Ethnicelebs.com; Onomap.org surname database.

known as Halston Sage. They are among the approximately forty actors born after 1980 in the database who bear an anglicized surname. Meanwhile, of the five post-1980 generation actors that de-anglicized their surname, three were African-American.

John F. Kennedy was the first non-WASP president, and since then politics has participated in Robert Christopher's elite 'de-WASPing' process.[54] But it is less important for politicians, with the partial exception of the president, to represent national archetypes. This means actors are now WASPier than politicians. Comparing the surnames of prominent American actors and politicians in the Ethnicelebs data in figure 12.5, the Anglo surname share declines from around 85 per cent in the pre-1924 birth cohort to 62 per cent of the 1925–44 cohort. Thereafter, a 10-point gap opens up, with actors significantly more likely to have Anglo surnames than politicians.

Where the divergence is really apparent is among 'serious' American actors in historic and/or Oscar-winning films. These arguably place more of a premium on incarnating an all-American type. Leaving aside the question of racial representation to focus only on white actors,

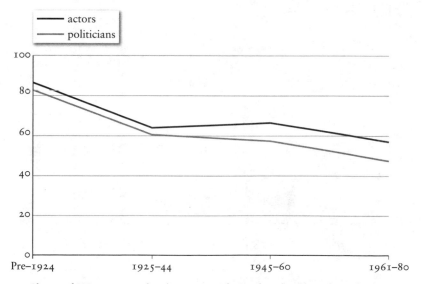

12.5. Share of US actors and politicians with Anglo surnames, by cohort, %

Source: Ethnicelebs.com; Surnames classified by Onomap. N = 85 politicians: 11 (pre-1924), 15 (1925–44), 32 (1945–60), 27 (1961–80); and 1,427 actors.

figure 12.6 shows that there has been no significant shift in the proportion of white actors with British or Irish surnames in these roles over generations. This indicates that while Harry S. Truman is no longer correct about the view that those with 'British or Irish surnames are better Americans', having one of those surnames makes it more likely an actor will star in a film depicting the American national story. Evidently the Anglo-Saxon type which Herberg, Gordon and Schrag – and Teddy Roosevelt before them – remarked upon endures as a focal point of American culture.

If white America orients itself around the WASP type, is there any evidence that non-white Americans orient themselves around whites or blacks as typical Americans? One study finds that respondents of all races tend to associate whites and African-Americans, more than Asians and Hispanics, with American symbols. This also occurs at a subconscious level. In Implicit Association Tests (IATs) researchers find that white and Asian-American subjects identify white faces as American more quickly when paired with American symbols such as the flag than they do Asian faces paired with the same symbols.[55] This intimates that

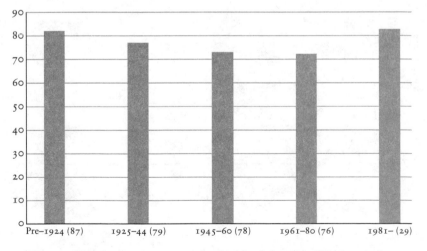

12.6. Share of Anglo surnames among white lead actors in US historical or Academy Award-nominated films, by birth cohort, %

Sources: Ethnicelebs.com; Wikipedia; surnames classified by Onomap.
Note: Number of cases for each cohort in parentheses.

white or Melungeon origin myths could have more resonance among the blended Americans of tomorrow than others.

Politics may play a part in inflecting this: Republicans and conservatives are more likely than liberals to openly say that being white or Christian are important for being a 'true American'.[56] To probe whether respondents have a similar view of blacks and Native Indians, I asked 400 Americans on MTurk the following in September 2017: 'To what extent do you agree with the following: "America includes everyone, but the three most authentically American groups are American Indians, white Anglo-Saxon Protestants and African-Americans because they shaped America from the start."' Respondents could indicate agreement on a 0–100 scale, with 100 as complete agreement. It's a small sample and a very contentious question, but results in figure 12.7 suggest that black and Native Indian Americans, like Trump voters, are more likely to assent to this 'transracial nativism' than Hispanics, Asians or liberals. White Catholics are more likely than white

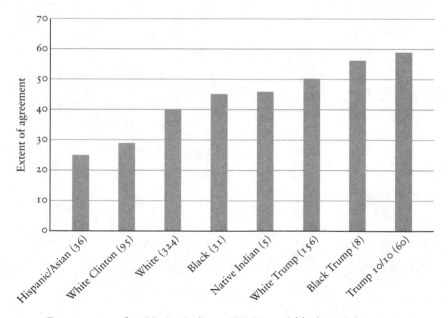

12.7. 'Do you agree that Native Indians, WASPs and blacks are the most "authentically American" groups?', %

Source: MTurk, 20 September 2017. N = 400.
Note: brackets show numbers of cases for each group.

Protestants to agree. Those who rate Trump 10 out of 10 are most likely to concur. One can only speculate how this configuration might translate politically in the future.

Even today, where whites are a majority and we might expect minorities to be on the defensive against them, a significant component of minority Americans express white ethno-traditional nationalism. Part of this is a socioeconomic response to perceived immigrant competition, but also reflects a minority conservatism which values the white narrative of American history and culture. In a survey conducted in August 2017 after the events at Charlottesville and summarized in figures 12.8 and 12.9, around 30 per cent of Hispanics and only slightly fewer Others (mainly Asian) agreed with the view that 'America must protect and preserve its White European heritage.' This was only 3 points lower than the corresponding white answer. Among the 187 Hispanic Trump voters polled, 59 per cent agreed, well above the 47 per cent of

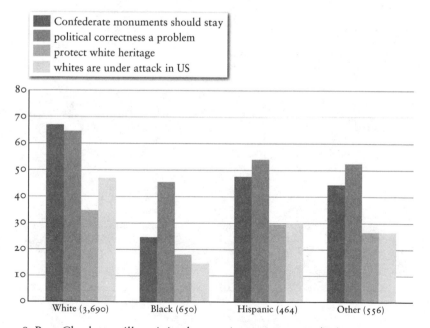

12.8. Post-Charlottesville opinion by race (percentage agreeing)

Source: Reuters/Ipsos/UVA Center for Politics Race Poll. Reuters/Ipsos poll conducted in conjunction with the University of Virginia Center for Politics, 11 September 2017

white Trump voters who did so. In the ANES in 2016, 31 per cent of non-whites wanted lower immigration, rising to 60 per cent among minority Trump voters. With around 30 per cent of Hispanics and Asians voting for Trump, including slightly over half of Hispanic and Asian evangelicals, and between a third and half of minorities backing measures like Proposition 187, this suggests that ideology strongly conditions support for white ethno-traditionalism, regardless of race.[57] African-Americans are only a partial exception.

When the growing mixed-race populations of the West no longer feel on the defensive against a clear white majority, the desire to protect a European or Euro-American legacy may grow more pronounced. Just as German and Scandinavian Americans gravitated towards immigration restriction and support for the Republicans in the early twentieth century and white Catholics moved towards the Republicans in the late twentieth (or towards conservative parties in Protestant Europe),

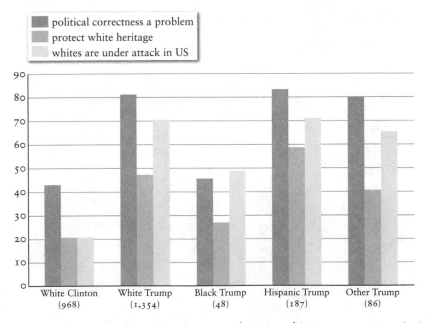

12.9. Post-Charlottesville opinion by race and partisanship (percentage agreeing)

Source: Reuters/Ipsos/UVA Center for Politics Race Poll. Reuters/Ipsos poll conducted in conjunction with the University of Virginia Center for Politics, 11 September 2017

mixed-race voters may follow suit in the middle or late twenty-first. Political outlook should count more than race in determining attitudes to European ancestry and heritage. European ancestry, myths and traditions will form a symbolic archetype around which mixed-race conservatives are likely to cohere. Mixed-race liberals, on the other hand, may prefer a multicultural myth of descent which downplays European ancestry. Figure 12.10 illustrates how ideology acts as a lens which may determine whether an individual identifies with the white or non-white heritage.[58] Like the Slavophile-Westernizer debate in nineteenth-century Russia, ethnic options will carry political freight.[59]

In the interim, of course, the West will become multi-ethnic before it melts, with whites declining. This is likely to pit conservative whites and a subgroup of conservative minorities against a coalition of white liberals and most minorities, as is true today. As whites decline below a critical mass, the pitch of nationalism among white conservatives could rise, as it did in Côte d'Ivoire in the 1990s – albeit without the violence. In the American case, restrictionism surged when Anglo-Protestants' confidence in assimilating Catholics to Protestantism waned in the late nineteenth century. Many American Catholics were unchurched in the nineteenth century and the rapid growth of the American Catholic church at the turn of the century unsettled the confident worldview that the immigrants would become Protestant.[60] When and whether the share of religious and racial minorities reaches a critical mass in the

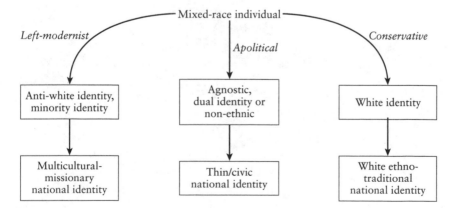

12.10. Ideological lenses and ethnic options for mixed-race majorities

West is unclear. The minority share in Europe is still low, below the quarter of the population Catholics had reached in America by 1900. In America the minority share is approaching 40 per cent, but Latinos are culturally closer to the Euro-Americans than many minorities in Europe are to the ethnic cores of their societies.

In the twenty-first century, whites may come to accept those of mixed-race as part of the same ethnic group, even if racial differences persist for some time. The expansion of ethnic-majority boundaries could reassure despondent whites that their group has a future while simultaneously endowing the mixed group with a new sense of being the inheritors of the European mantle and its racial archetype. This might lead the mixed group to become more politically conservative. Much hinges on whether majority ethnicity can surmount the racial divide in the twenty-first century the way it overcame Protestant–Catholic–Jewish differences in the twentieth. While a white majority depends on this, nothing is certain – whites may be unable to detach themselves from their attachment to race as a boundary marker, opting instead to become a tight-knit minority as in Mauritius. In that event, only those who pass for white will be white while many of those from a mixed background distribute themselves among the more open groups like blacks and Hispanics, producing a multi-polar, multicultural society like the Caribbean ones we encountered in the previous chapter.

13
Navigating *Whiteshift*: Inclusive Majorities in Inclusive Nations

We've looked into the future of white majorities in the West, but what does this mean for the present? As we've seen, large-scale migration is a product of demographic and economic 'push' factors in the developing world and the economic 'pull' of Western companies and governments. But these market forces also operate in Japan and Singapore. Left-modernism is more important, in my estimation, because it provides the moral scaffolding for a globalizing free-market liberalism. The latter has been an impulse among commercial interests and pro-growth politicians for centuries, but has usually been kept in check by popular sentiment. The New Left gave it freer rein. 'In both parties, nationalism and populism are embraced by the rank and file and rejected by the elites,' wrote two American centre-left scholars, John Judis and Michael Lind, in 1995.[1] What Christopher Lasch termed the 'Revolt of the Elites' was well in train by 1989, involving a new bi-partisan spirit of cosmopolitan globalization.[2] Those who wanted slower ethnic change had no party to turn to, which opened space for populist political entrepreneurs like Pat Buchanan in the 1990s and Donald Trump in 2015.

The expansion of the anti-racism taboo from the 1960s and its retreat since the late 1990s is critical because the rise of anti-immigration populism is not simply a matter of what's driving populist voters, but what's no longer restraining them. The rise of the far right led centre-right parties, and sometimes centre-left ones, to breach anti-racist taboos against discussing multiculturalism and immigration.

Many progressives take a 'blank slate' view of the public, believing that anti-immigration messages create anti-immigration sentiment. Their solution is to re-establish broad anti-racism norms in the media and politics to choke off the supply of anti-immigration messaging.

They are partly right: when the media and politicians make anti-immigration noises, this raises the salience of immigration and cues party supporters. But repression is a high-risk strategy: as the Swedish case reveals, migration-led ethnic change leads to latent demand for restriction among conservatives, tinder for the populist match. Once taboos are violated, attempts to reinstate earlier definitions of sacred and deviant actually invigorate populism. When expansive definitions of racism are washed away, it becomes harder to defend the reasonable core of anti-racism. It's difficult to put the genie back in the bottle.

The populist right sets off a positive feedback in which effects become causes. Fence-sitters no longer feel guilty about voting for these parties, which in turn swells the anti-immigration vote, signalling to others that it's okay to vote for them, and so on, creating a self-fulfilling prophesy that only ends when the supply of conservative and order-seeking voters has been exhausted. Such voters are more numerous than liberal voters, but are not necessarily the majority. Much depends on whether right-wing populists can bundle ancillary issues to their core anti-immigration appeal to lure sufficient centrist voters to form a majority.

Once the anti-racist taboo over discussing immigration unravels, the main parties must offer a policy on limiting immigration. I would argue they also need a cultural message for the Somewheres, the roughly 50 per cent of ethnic-majority voters who value continuity and security more than change.[3] If the message is, to quote UN Secretary-General António Guterres, one of demographic inevitability, that: 'societies are becoming multicultural, multiethnic and multi religious', then the populist backlash will only escalate.[4] At a small meeting I participated in at one of the international institutions in Geneva which shall remain nameless, a series of higher-ups in the organization, all white liberals, periodically checked in from meetings in far-flung parts of the world to fire up the troops. One of them, just back from Beirut, said he told the Lebanese that they were way ahead of the curve because they were already diverse and multicultural, and all societies were moving that way.

Only a dyed-in-the-wool utopian could gloss the troublesome history of Lebanon enough to hold it up as a model. This is precisely the kind of cosmopolitan imperialism that needs to be checked if trust is to be restored in liberal and international institutions. Indeed, cosmopolitan overreach by both left and right has fuelled populist-right blowback.[5] An accompanying rhetoric of ever-increasing diversity is equally problematic: already, most voters overestimate the share of immigrants and Muslims by a factor of between two and ten. As noted, a message of change is appropriate only for liberals who prefer novelty to stability.[6] Instead, Somewheres need to hear that minorities are a smaller share than they imagine, and that they will be seamlessly absorbed into 'us' as they have been in the past.[7]

Will they be absorbed? Compared to the melting of Catholics and Jews into the white majorities of the Protestant West, the assimilation process may be more complicated this time. First, the key marker for ethnic-majority groups today is white appearance and religion – be it Christian or secular. Race and religion could prove more resistant to intermarriage than the Protestant–Catholic–Jewish divide. Having said this, the intermarriage rates of groups such as East Asians, Afro-Caribbeans and Franco-Algerians arguably match those of Catholics in Protestant countries during the twentieth century. Indeed, their secularization rate is higher. Nevertheless, where American WASPs and white ethnics could move to an established 'white' category to recover ethno-cultural security, it's harder for many to envisage how the white majority will transition to a mixed-race one. This will entail cultural work to adapt white majority myths of origin and symbol systems to the new mixed population. Naming practices and cultural codes will need to take over the work race did in demarcating ethnic boundaries. The declining unmixed white population would then need to accept the rising mixed group and fuse with it. This vision of *Whiteshift* offers conservative whites a future as an ethnic majority whose group consciousness continues, thereby addressing the cultural and psychological malaise fuelling right-wing populism.

LOCAL AND NATIONAL RESPONSES

Local responses to immigration and diversity are more conditioned by evolutionary psychology than national debates. Locally, most whites, whether liberal or conservative, operate within disproportionately white social networks, tend to avoid settling down in diverse areas and usually marry people from their own group. Local ethnic changes almost inevitably produce higher opposition to immigration. Yet the study of political demography tells us the connection between the local and national can be weak. National ideological actors must plug into local grievances and write them into a wider national script for immigration to become a politically salient issue. In the US, local responses to immigration date from the 1970s and 1980s, but it wasn't until the late 2000s that the issue began to gain traction within the federal Republican Party.

Locally, ethno-tribal impulses count, but when it comes to the nation, ideas determine whether these scale up – i.e. whether people's attitudes to national questions reflect their primordial micro-behaviour. Local behaviour and attitudes to national policy questions are only loosely related because they are mediated by the ideological frames and party identities conveyed by the national press. Liberal cosmopolites tend to live in majority-white neighbourhoods and associate with whites at similar rates to conservatives; but where liberals view the nation as a diverse entity defined by its liberal mission, conservatives imagine it as a larger version of their intimate ethnic community. Those who try to find answers to the populist moment by focusing on local dynamics miss most of the picture.

Whether societies are more conservative on immigration, like Denmark, or more liberal, like Canada, white micro-behaviour – intermarriage, segregation – is similar. In the most liberal societies, like Canada or Sweden, the disjuncture between official liberal cosmopolitanism and local-level tribalism is glaring, bearing out Michael Walzer's dictum that where community boundaries are not maintained nationally, they will reappear locally.[8] The Kurdish-Swedish writer Tino Sanandaji expresses the paradox well: 'From the immigrants' point of view, the Swedish state is warm and generous, while Swedish society is cold and distant . . . The state can share welfare benefits and iPads, but it cannot force Swedes to treat immigrants as equals in daily interactions.'[9] Even where minorities are treated equally, they often find – especially in diverse urban areas – that whites withdraw into their own networks. For my Asian-Latino relatives in suburban Los Angeles, of the many groups in the area the declining white minority is the hardest to get to know.

THE POLITICS OF ETHNO-TRADITIONAL NATIONALISM

The waning of ideological conflict after the Cold War, and the near-absence of interstate war, means there are fewer forces mobilizing state nationalism. Nearly all wars take place within countries, dividing the population along ethnic or sectarian lines. In the West, these conflicts are non-violent or low level, but play an important role in shaping voting patterns. Class and economic ideology are losing importance, to the point the British Tory and Labour parties have the same class composition – an unthinkable development from the vantage point of 1945. Meanwhile, culture wars are increasingly displacing economics as the central axis of politics. Between the 1960s and 1990s, social liberalism – religion, attitudes to homosexuals and women, sexual mores – and the reaction against it, defined a moderate form of cultural politics. Only in the US were religious issues paramount, though the power of the Christian Right peaked in the 1990s and has retreated. As religion declines, most people accept social liberalism. In keeping with Ron Inglehart's value change model, older generations die off and new ones emerge, making society more liberal.[10]

While religion has declined, ethno-traditional nationalism – the desire to limit change to the ethnic composition of the nation – has remained resilient. Attitudes to immigration and the European Union, for instance, have not liberalized in most Western countries. This is because immigration has the potential to transform societies in a way secularization and social liberalism do not. When the share of Hispanics in the US crossed a threshold and began to spread more widely across the country, and when the rate of immigration rose in Europe after 2013, those who oppose immigration began to prioritize this issue, with a rising share of conservative voters ranking it one of their top concerns. This provided the fuel for the populist-right surge. The heightened post-2015 political sensitivity to migration has endured even as migration levels in Europe have subsided to 2013 levels. Whether conservative voters are adopting a 'wait and see' approach before accepting that migration has tapered off or whether this is a new normal is difficult to discern. I suspect that if numbers remain low for long enough, populism will subside.

Right-wing populism has little to do with economics, but arises largely from ethnic change, caused by immigration, which unsettles the existential security of conservative and order-seeking whites. The issue of Muslim immigration is a force multiplier but not the main driver, playing a backup role in the Trump and Brexit votes and only a minor part in Europe prior to 2004. Young people have a more presentist outlook and are used to a higher share of minorities, so right-wing populism is usually weaker among them. But the difference is one of degree: psychological conservatives and authoritarians exist in all age groups. As people age they become more conservative, and Western society is on course to become older than it has ever been in history, with over 40 per cent over sixty in some European countries by 2050. Right-wing populism could become an endemic feature of Western politics for the foreseeable future if immigration remains substantial.

SYMMETRICAL IDENTITY POLITICS

Majority ethnic groups' attachment to their in-group is not racist unless it leads to unequal treatment of outgroups or a quest for racial purity. Social psychologists tell us that attachment to in-group is not correlated with dislike of outgroups. The exception arises when groups are locked in violent zero-sum conflict, such that caring for my in-group entails despising an outgroup. Identifying as white, or with a white tradition of nationhood, is no more racist than identifying as black. Like 75–80 per cent of people across eighteen mainly Western countries, I don't think a white person who wants reduced immigration to help maintain their group's share of the population is being racist, though they are acting in what Shadi Hamid terms their racial self-interest.[11] Whites should feel free to express a group self-interest so long as they accept the need to make compromises with other groups and wider national imperatives. They shouldn't be labelled racists for holding group preferences, and minorities shouldn't be told to stop practising identity politics if they use representative data and scientific methods to highlight discrimination. An enlightened ethnicity, however, is one that balances the desire to maximize group welfare with an equivalent concern for optimizing the common national good of all groups.

One way to move to a positive-sum outlook is for whites to adopt a Hawaiian/Creole strategy, opening up to those of mixed background who identify with their European roots. There is space here for a liberal politics which monitors racial bias and seeks to overcome colour-based stratification through nudge policies and data-driven bias training. If majorities open up even further, minorities should be more likely to identify with the white-inflected national past than the anti-white narrative of the modernist left; and many are potential supporters of European ethno-traditions of nationhood.

Mark Lilla rightfully draws attention to the dangers of identity politics and the need for a conception of the common good. Castigating Hillary Clinton for 'calling out explicitly to African-American, Latino, L.G.B.T. and women voters at every stop,' he argues that 'if you are going to mention groups in America, you had better mention all of them'.[12] It is vital, Lilla argues, that people focus less on their differences and parochial slights, and more on common projects to rectify class inequalities. I agree, in part. However, the civic liberalism and state nationalism Lilla advocates, and his plea to focus on economic issues, is somewhat arid in an age when the state lacks ideological foes or the threat of war to stimulate a sense of shared missionary nationalism. Civic nationalism has not proven sufficient for addressing the anxieties behind right-wing populism.

In ethnically divided regions such as the former Yugoslavia, Serb and Croat nationalists adhered to an unreflexive, biased 'victimhood nationalism' which heightens conflict.[13] Conflict resolution approaches such as truth and reconciliation commissions focus on getting people to move away from the victimhood narratives used by ultra-nationalists. Past crimes are acknowledged, but people come to see that relations were often peaceful, that most members of the other group did not commit atrocities, or that current generations are not guilty for the sins of their ancestors.[14] How odd then that left-modernists, ostensibly progressive, are doing precisely the opposite, stirring up a sense of victimhood among often-reluctant ethnic minorities.

Ethnic identity is not inherently toxic, as some on the right believe, but, like religion or partisanship, needs to be moderate. It's important for all groups to give others the benefit of the doubt and to try to see things in positive-sum terms, accentuating grievances only where there is rigorous evidence. But there is a balance to be struck: a politics of the common good can't succeed unless groups feel they're being treated reasonably fairly. Minorities have experienced discrimination in the past, and some – notably those with Muslim names – continue to experience a penalty. This is a valid identity concern which group representatives can legitimately raise through an evidence-based, sector-specific approach and which begins by advocating unobtrusive 'nudge' remedies. This is not just about material opportunity, but about group status – a wealthy black person may experience no discrimination but will typically wish to raise the status of her ethnic group.

Whites also have concerns. Affirmative action policies, for instance, often discriminate against whites and Asian Americans. When Asians mobilize to defend their interests, this is viewed as a legitimate form of interest group politics. The same should be true for whites, but instead they are stigmatized as racist due to the distortions of the left-modernist belief system. The history of white oppression is real, but moot: grievances need to be examined on their merits against a consistent set of principles using current data. Historic structures of oppression can rapidly dissipate, so their contemporary existence must be demonstrated. There is, for example, a deep history of anti-Catholic oppression in America or Britain, but it no longer exists. If it does, we need to see rigorous proof. Forcing whites to pay cultural reparations for historic misdeeds in the form of denied identity is akin to the French asking the Germans to pay war reparations today. Each ethnic group, regardless of its past, should be able to plead its case with evidence in an atmosphere of toleration, on the understanding that all should support the common good.

Lilla mentions that the left's identity politics ignores whites. There are two conclusions one can take from this. Lilla's is to sublimate identity concerns in favour of the nation. Mine is that there needs to be a moderate and symmetric treatment of group interests before this can happen; not to 'celebrate' difference, but to allow genuine group concerns to be aired and accommodated alongside the wider problem of income inequality. Claims must be backed by modelling, not anecdotes, cherry-picked statistics or sweeping generalizations like 'systemic racism'. The same rules must apply to all groups, regardless of their history as oppressor or oppressed, for one cannot visit the sins of the fathers on the children. As the political theorist Yael Tamir observes with respect to nations:

Liberals often align themselves with national demands raised by 'under-dogs', be they indigenous peoples, discriminated minorities, or occupied nations, whose plight can easily evoke sympathy. But if national claims rest on theoretically sound and morally justified grounds, one cannot restrict their application: They apply equally to all nations, regardless of their power, their wealth, their history of suffering, or even the injustices they have inflicted on others in the past.[15]

And here is where liberalism has an important problem. Where Lilla takes Clinton to task for calling out to minorities like African-Americans, I have no issue with this. I would instead urge that it would be useful to also name-check European and Christian Americans. If that is too much to bear, then mention ethno-cultural reference points dear to whites, but under no circumstances should groups be treated differently. The issue is not so much with recognizing group identity, but consists in the fact subaltern grievances are magnified by left-modernists while majority concerns are stigmatized. This is not what the average non-white American wants. As we've seen, minorities themselves are moderate and much less likely than white liberals to accuse whites who wish to defend their group self-interests of racism. While I reject an identity politics of 'means' which holds that different groups reason differently and therefore can't agree on common stand ards of logic and evidence, a moderate attachment to identity 'ends', i.e. group interests, is perfectly legitimate.

This discussion feeds into the meaning of multiculturalism. If it means identities are important to people and collective interests should form part of public debate, that's fine. The problem arises with what I have termed 'asymmetrical multiculturalism', whereby minority identi-ties are lauded while white majority ones are denigrated.[16] The most rigorous and honest work in multicultural theory is being done by writ-ers like Tariq Modood in Britain. Modood rejects pleas to deconstruct white identity and instead accepts it as one of the components of multi-culturalism.[17] A symmetrical multiculturalism, so long as it is balanced by a concern for the whole rather than narrow group-obsession, can provide a guarantee of fairness which permits people to focus on the national whole. At present, what happens is that minorities set out identity-based concerns which many whites reject as divisive because they have been forced by left-modernism to repress their own ethnicity or because they can't see that their 'national' interests may actually consist of sublimated ethnic desires. If whites set out some explicit identity interests apart from those of the nation, this could allow them to better appreciate minority claims and vice-versa, producing a shared understanding. Rather than serving as a dehumanized whipping boy or hard face of 'the system', whites could be viewed as a group like any other with their own parochial interests. The current dispensation in which white conservatives attack even moderate minority interests as 'identity politics' only leads to polarization.

It's easy to raise fears around the 'dangerous' expression of identities, whether religious, ideological or ethnic, by pointing to rare genocidal events. Those on the left raise the spectre of Nazism whenever white identity or ethno-traditional nationhood is mooted. And, on the other side, while I endorse Jordan Peterson's critique of political correctness, I cannot agree – without systematic comparative modelling – that campus identity politics could land us in the gulag. This is also where I part company with those on the right who believe group sentiments are a problem and we should simply identify as individuals. As communitarian writers note, part of our individuality comes from the multi-generational groups we choose to identify with.[18]

What are white interests? I've mentioned affirmative action, but this doesn't usually apply in Europe. More important is the majority desire to slow immigration to limit cultural dislocation and facilitate assimilation. Critical race theorists dismiss cultural interests, seeing minority identities as political conveniences for resisting oppression. But African-Americans don't form a group only because they were, or are, being oppressed. If the oppression lifted tomorrow, they wouldn't dissolve. People aren't politico-economic automatons. Their ethnicity arises mostly from their attachment to a collective memory and identification with group symbols including physical appearance (encompassing styles) and traditions like the AME Zion Church, the Great Migration, the Harlem Renaissance, the blues and so on.

Whites are no different. Among those for whom majority ethnicity is important, collective memory, along with cultural markers like appearance, religion and cultural traditions, bind them to the group. Like African-Americans, they are not primarily attached to their group as a tool to get more stuff. When Harlem is gentrified by whites and Asians, or Brixton (in London) by hipsters, this is experienced as a loss by blacks. So, too, when a historically ethnic-majority area with strong local traditions like Barking, England, becomes superdiverse, this is experienced as a tragedy. Little can be done within a country since people are welcome to move where they please and must be free to find accommodation. Nevertheless, some measures, even if symbolic, could be taken. In Harlem, attempts could be made to limit gentrification to certain areas, attract potential black residents, protect key historic landmarks and possibly pursue a 'sons and daughters' points policy in public housing to try to slow the rate of change.

Cultural protection is already recognized in the right of Native Indian bands to use cultural criteria to select who is allowed to live on reserves. In the 1990s, the US Congress granted five Pacific Island territories – American Samoa, Micronesia, the Marshall Islands, the Northern Mariana Islands and Palau – the right to control immigration to maintain their ethnic majorities.[19] There is no reason why a similar argument can't be made at the country level in, say, Sweden or the Netherlands. None of which is to say change must be stopped, only that the desire to slow ethnic change is a legitimate expression of the ethnic majority's cultural interest. Indeed, cultural grievances are the main engine behind the right-wing populism we see today and will continue to be important during the coming century of white decline. This in-group attachment is not racist unless it leads to antipathy towards outgroups or racial puritanism.

Ideally, desires for cultural protection should be openly aired, in a respectful way, by members of majority groups who identify strongly with their ethnicity, without drawing the charge of racism. Against this, those who favour more immigration might make the case on economic and humanitarian grounds, or because they are cosmopolitans who would like more cultural diversity. Cosmopolitans, and minorities who want more of their group to enter, should be free to voice their interests without being accused of being unpatriotic the way Scandinavian, German and Irish representatives were during the American congressional immigration discussions of 1929. The normative climate should be neutral and encouraging, with each side trying to see things from the other's point of view. It would then fall to the government to reach an open, transparent accommodation between competing forces, taking *both* cultural and economic considerations on board. The discussion over immigration rates should be no more controversial than the debate over tax rates.

TWO MODELS OF IMMIGRATION

Immigration attitudes are strongly conditioned by cultural anxieties, so these need to be fully and frankly discussed. Let's say white-majority conservatives have a strong desire to slow down the rate of ethnic change and are willing to pay an economic price for this, which British data shows to be the case.[20] When it comes to setting policy, this raises two possibilities. The first is to reduce immigration to the rate the median voter wishes to accept, which in Britain is around 100,000 per year. A second possibility is to introduce cultural elements into the migration-points process, something floated by Paul Collier, thereby allowing a somewhat larger intake.[21] This means selection would focus not only on the economic or humanitarian properties of immigrants, but on how they affect a society's constituent ethnic groups.

Immigration today is not culturally neutral. In favouring relatives, it prioritizes countries with a recent history of sending immigrants. In the US, a diversity lottery was institutionalized in part to encourage migration from European countries whose citizens have few direct family ties and thus don't benefit from family reunification. Since Europe sends few immigrants, this ultimately failed. But the broader point is that cultural considerations must be part of the immigration discussion because they are what matters more to the electorate. Excluding particular people, such as Muslim ethnic groups, is racist, but trying to protect established groups is not. Europeans in the EU already move around freely and in any case the supply of European immigrants is declining for demographic reasons, so their greater assimilability is hardly going to result in racially exclusive immigration policies.

Moreover, it is a left-modernist conceit to think that because countries must treat citizens equally without regard to cultural characteristics they must extend this to non-citizens applying for citizenship. No one would insist that the Knights of Columbus admit non-Catholics: nation-states' relationship to the rest of the world is more akin to that between the Knights and the rest of American society. Countries have a right to regulate membership. All countries discriminate against non-citizens: the latter are not eligible for many social services and employers are under no obligation to treat their job applications the same as those of citizens. Many countries permit members of their diaspora to gain preferential access, as is now being mooted for ethnic Germans in Italy by Austria's Sebastian Kurz. The state must ensure that there is no cultural discrimination against citizens, but, as the US diversity visa lottery shows, countries can introduce cultural selection criteria so long as these are not used to exclude particular groups.

How to do this in a just manner? Excluding particular groups is racist because it denigrates specific ethnic communities, but attempting to insulate established ethnic groups from rapid cultural change isn't. The Oxford economist Paul Collier's argument that immigrants be screened for compatibility with the culture of the nation is problematic because different groups of immigrants will be assessed against a singular definition of national culture.[22] Those further from the ideal will rightly feel they are being viewed as less British or less Norwegian than their co-citizens. Here I buy Michael Blake's argument that if the state says 'group A are more desired than group B' as immigrants, this sends a discriminatory signal to members of group B living in the country.[23]

An alternative approach is to reconcile the interests of society's cultural stakeholders. Points would be granted to prospective immigrants who are more likely to assimilate into the existing ethnic constituencies in a country. To some extent this already happens with language proficiency. But officers could assess further indicators of assimilability such as being in an inter-ethnic marriage or of secular or moderate religiosity. So the cultural points I have in mind will tend to result in the over-representation of groups such as East Asians, Afro-Caribbeans or Franco-Algerians, who have higher intermarriage rates, compared to those like ultra-Orthodox Jews or Salafi Muslims, who do not. This is not because the British state is saying an Afro-Caribbean is a better Briton than an ultra-Orthodox Jew. The state doesn't play favourites, but must carry out its duty to represent the cultural interests of its stakeholder communities in favour of ethnic assimilability.

Again, the reason for cultural points is not because the state prefers immigrants who are more likely to assimilate into some national ideal, but because it must balance the competing interests of its cultural constituencies, weighted by size. If the pool of applicants to Britain was 99 per cent African and European Christian, South Asian Muslims would benefit from a cultural points system. In other words, this is a form of symmetrical multiculturalism designed to slow – but not stop – cultural change. The point is to avoid officially defining Dutchness or Americanness and admitting potential immigrants against that standard – which is what European countries are increasingly doing. This is discriminatory because it suggests ultra-Orthodox Jews or Salafi Muslims are not equally Norwegian or British. The state shouldn't make these judgements but must de-centre itself from the ethnic majority and treat it as just another stakeholder. Majority conservatives would influence selection only by dint of the numbers they command in a democracy. Minority requests will also shape cultural considerations, so the system would act as a cultural brake, moderating the rate of change across all elements of the country's makeup.

In Britain or the Netherlands, for example, the inclusion of cultural assimilation criteria is likely, all else being equal, to favour the immigration of more established Afro-Caribbeans over the more recent Afghans. Again, this is not a quota system, but assigns cultural points alongside economic and humanitarian points, to be weighed in the final decision. The current prohibition on applying cultural considerations to immigration policy (beyond language proficiency) derives from the extension of the racist taboo beyond the legitimate bounds of preventing an obsession with race purity to the illegitimate one of saying all ethno-cultural interests are racist. The religion of anti-racism's expansive stigmatization strategy, not consistent political theory, grounds this approach.[24] Even in the case of the 1924 National Origin quotas in America, the problem was the exclusion of racial minorities and the eugenicist rationale behind the quotas. This clearly stigmatized minorities as second class, established a hierarchy of Americanness and showed animus towards outgroups. However, if the quotas included blacks and Asians in proportion, and were justified on the grounds that immigration should fairly reflect the ethno-cultural attachments of citizens, they would not be racist.

The quotas would, however, be problematic due to the overly rigid ethno-cultural communitarianism they embody. Given demographic realities in today's West, they would result in just a trickle of immigration. Points rather than quotas permit more flexibility. Assimilability to existing groups decelerates cultural change while permitting society to also meet economic and humanitarian objectives. This would have the secondary effect of slowing growth in the share of 'illiberal' groups – a category which doesn't include most Muslims. This is important because many liberal theories are demographically flawed. When ultra-Orthodox Jews are a small share of the population, they can't ban uncovered women's faces from billboards or throw stones at cars caught driving on a Saturday. Now that they control Jerusalem, they do. So the principles which apply when the ultra-Orthodox are a small group, as in Britain, are different from those that hold when they become large. A cultural points system on immigration keeps numbers modest, which means society can be relaxed about conservative minority groups and there is no need for the government to stigmatize them for not integrating. Integrating those who wish to live apart is next to impossible in a free society. Those who reject modern lifestyles cannot, and should not, be coerced into accepting them.

It strikes me that there are two general models for addressing the problem of illiberal minorities. One is to have an open immigration system that doesn't take culture into account but interferes with the rights of illiberal minorities once they are in the country, targeting them through measures such as burqa bans and panicking over their growth. That is the situation we are currently in. A second option is to have a cultural points system of immigration along the lines noted above, but to live and let live once groups are in a country. Growth is contained by the selection process, which removes the imperative for illiberal integration policies and deflates moral panics.

If a Haredi Jew or Salafi Muslim wants to live in a segregated community in Britain, only interacting with their own community, I don't mind. But this is true only because such groups are small. I would rather have a tolerant society, with a small share of illiberal minorities, than a situation like Israel where illiberal minorities are large, growing and beginning to set the tone. If the ethnic majority are aware that immigration policy is being designed to facilitate assimilation, they will become more relaxed about those who don't assimilate, reducing racism. Current Western immigration policy, by pretending culture doesn't exist, can only increase intolerance.

THE TRAGEDY OF SUBLIMATION

Liav Orgad observes that liberal political theories were designed for a time when nation-states were ethnically stable and migration was limited. International law therefore lacks any rights or protections for ethnic majorities, only nation-states and minorities. In order to surmount this, countries tell what he calls 'legal white lies' to try and protect ethnic majorities.[25] Rather than permit white majorities to express their cultural interests, the entrenchment of left-modernist thinking in the institutions of the West since 1965 means these are sublimated into proxy policies that allow for plausible deniability. These harm the very minorities left-modernism claims to defend, giving rise to populist forces which endanger liberal democracy and progressive policies.

For example, when conservative whites' cultural interest in defending their ethnic identity is taboo, they will look for other reasons to reduce immigration. Attacking Muslims as a threat to Jews, homosexuals or free speech offers an acceptable liberal rationale for immigration preferences that are largely motivated by a desire for ethno-cultural protection. Criticizing immigration as a source of crime, terror or economic dependency is a respectably 'civic' argument which appeals to state interests and hence is more acceptable than talking about ethno-traditions or majority-ethnic anxiety. Surely it would be better to plead the case for immigration restriction on the basis of an attachment to an in-group – which is not racist – rather than targeting outgroups, which is. With majority ethno-cultural concerns on the table, other considerations can be introduced and white conservatives can see that they have been listened to rather than stigmatized – and that an accommodation between competing interests has been arrived at democratically.

When liberal institutions such as the press, bureaucracy or courts adopt the positive liberal ethos of left-modernism, this reduces conservatives' trust in liberal democracy. Extending the ambit of anti-racism to apply to discussions of immigration sublimates cultural concerns in unpredictable ways. For instance, Britain leaving the EU to 'control our borders' with (white) Europe is more acceptable than expressing worries about immigration from Asia or the Middle East. One result of displacing immigration anxieties towards Europe is Brexit, which could damage the UK economy. Western left-modernism and immigration policies also undermine efforts to convince East European semi-democracies like Hungary or Poland to shore up the institutions of negative liberalism such as a free press or independent judiciary. In practical terms, the sway of left-modernism within some left-wing parties permits conservatives to win elections more often, making it harder to advance goals such as reducing inequality or mitigating climate change.

FINDING A BALANCE BETWEEN
COSMOPOLITANS AND LOCALS

For all my criticism of the imperialistic cosmopolitanism that exists in Western liberal institutions, I wouldn't want things to flip back to the conformist nationalism of a century ago. We need liberals and the left to keep conservatism in check. Cosmopolitanism must have space to flourish and is a valid form of the good life. Around 8 per cent of the world's people just want to be citizens of the globe, or are attached to trans-ethnic and trans-national identities. It would be wrong to interfere with the right of people to detach themselves from ethnic and national forms of belonging.

At the same time, it's vital not to permit cosmopolitanism to become coercive. Broadening one's tastes and moral horizons is one version of the good life, not an iron moral law. Those who see the world this way have a difficult time accepting that others can be happy pursuing a narrower set of attachments or following comforting routines. Some prefer to holiday in the same place each year, others prefer new vistas. Neither is morally superior. By all means try and persuade, but do not compel. People want different things and negative liberalism permits them to do so. Because cosmopolitanism is de rigueur in the mobile, elite circles where power often resides, its values can crystallize into coercive norms. Those who reject cosmopolitanism, or only seek it in moderation, are accused of racism, nativism, xenophobia, closed-mindedness and parochialism.

The values of large cities, espoused by evangelist mayors like Rahm Emmanuel in Chicago or Sadiq Khan in London, are considered so self-evidently superior that only a bigot could reject them. Large cities are ethnically and socially diverse, are constantly changing, and tend to have low social cohesion and high inequality. Ethnic ties to neighbourhood are always provisional, until the next wave of immigrants moves in. In terms of tradition, 'all that is solid melts into air', to quote Marx. Thus the only approach to life, especially for whites or those of mixed background who lack an ethnic enclave, is modernist: namely, to be an individualist, seek immediate experience, suppress the desire for continuity with previous generations and eschew ethnic ties to the landscape. The goal of left-modernism is a kind of New York-writ-large: to universalize the metropolitan condition. All else is darkness.

The problem is that the metropolitan version of nationhood alienates conservatives who prefer stability and order-seekers who prefer higher cohesion, reducing their trust in society and politics. Instead, a healthy balance must be struck which allows competing preferences space to co-exist in a climate of mutual respect. They also energize each other. 'There can be no cosmopolitans without locals,' writes the Swedish anthropologist Ulf Hannerz.[26] The cultural materials and experiences which cosmopolitans consume derive from rooted ethnic groups. This can't happen if everywhere is diverse Dubai or LA. At the same time, the awareness of cultural distinctiveness which motivates ethnic consciousness arises through travel and encounters with difference in urban areas, so nationals also need cosmopolitans. Cosmopolitan travellers, missionaries and imperial administrators like Tacitus (who first remarked on the characteristics of the English and Germans) codified the names and boundaries of ethnic groups, and their observations sharpen the self-awareness of nations. Nationalists need cosmopolitans and vice-versa.

We might think of the world as a set of parochial locales overlaid by a global network. The network spreads universal ideas and brings people and cultures together across borders. Imagine that the bigger nodes are better connected with each other. Ideas take longer to travel to smaller nodes, even if they are physically proximal. So a fashion trend whisks from London to Los Angeles or Sydney in a heartbeat, but takes days to filter down to Rochdale, in northern England. People are sucked from one end of the network to the other. Economic forces and personal choice determine who moves where. Nations and ethnic groups no longer matter. Over time, the network homogenizes people culturally and ethnically. Every city looks like Brooklyn or Toronto and the network speaks English. Eventually all groups melt into a global, English-speaking whole.

Now imagine a 'flat' world where distance is purely physical. People in London are much closer to those in Rochdale than those in New York. Identity in this segmental world is local and loses force rapidly as it radiates outwards, to region, nation and continent. This is a very inefficient world. It's hard to arrive at common standards to conduct business or solve collective problems. What has actually happened since the late eighteenth century is that the network has penetrated the segmental world that existed in many places before the modern age.

While empires were prominent in the past, the extent and intensity of connections on the network have increased. Nation-states are a hybrid of network integration within the state and segmental differentiation between states. Network integration first produced nation-states but is now pushing towards supranationalism.

Liberals privilege the network and seek the free flow of goods, people and ideas along it, undermining nations. Psychological conservatives prefer a more segmental world – one which protects ethnic groups and nations from global homogenization. Left-modernists want to protect disadvantaged ethnic groups and non-Western nations from the network, but hope the network can undermine majority ethnicity and nationhood in the West. I'd again argue for moderation: let's allow those aspects of the network which are least disruptive to flow, while limiting the more problematic elements. This means regulating people's right to migrate – which voters find most disorienting and which challenges social cohesion most – while encouraging the flow of ideas and allowing free but fair trade.

MULTIVOCALISM: TOWARDS A FLEXIBLE NATIONALISM

English Canada, Australasia and the American Democrats celebrate diversity as the central feature of national identity, but most Western countries emphasize commonality over difference in a bid to build cohesion. Nevertheless, the continued rise of the populist right in Europe suggests civic nationalism is insufficient. If the West faced an existential struggle against an ideological adversary, things might be different, but we left that world behind in 1989. The problem with civic nationalism is that it pursues two diametrically opposing goals: universality and particularity. In order to be inclusive, nationhood is defined in an inoffensive, universal way through liberal values like toleration and fairness embodied in official statements such as 'British values', the American Creed or the French Declaration of the Rights of Man.

However, universalism cannot confer identity in today's world. Western countries are all liberal. This means values-based nationalism can't provide identity except in the guise of missionary nationalism, whereby different countries compete to take the fight to illiberal countries. The problem is that this only fires up a small crew of like-minded people. The muscular missionary nationalism of George W. Bush and Tony Blair is arguably a blind alley. Multiculturalism was wrong to promote diversity as the identity of nations, but it contains an important truth, which is that historic ethnic cultures embody a richness and texture that bland civic nationalism lacks.

What states need is a new synthesis that taps the power of ethnic symbolism while remaining inclusive. Ethnic nationalism has richness, but excludes minorities. Multiculturalism is rich and inclusive, but excludes the majority and can weaken commitment to the nation. My preferred alternative is multivocalism – an idea influenced by the anthropologist Victor Turner, who used 'multivocality' to refer to the many meanings people attach to a symbol like the Union Flag ('Union Jack'), which has functioned as a symbol of the mod subculture, the British far right and the Ulster Unionists of Northern Ireland.[27] Beethoven's 'Ode to Joy' has been an anthem for humanists, Nazis, Soviets and the European Union. If we stop thinking about national identity as a hymn sheet everyone has to sing from and begin to see it as a set of resources people shape in different ways, this opens up new vistas. Instead of a single way of perceiving the nation (i.e. 'British values') that is handed down by the state, national identity today is more of a bottom-up, emergent phenomenon which people take an active part in constructing. The media, sports, everyday routines and peer-to-peer conversations shape the content of popular nationhood.

This means a French woman of Algerian descent living in a Paris suburb sees the nation differently from a farmer from Gascony whose ancestors have been living there for generations. The Gascon identifies through his ancestry and region to France, a more ethno-traditional form of identity with the nation. By contrast, the Franco-Algerian woman might lack the historical-ancestral-rural module of Frenchness. For instance, surveys in Britain show 20–40 point gaps between whites and minorities in their level of identification with the nation's history, ancestry and countryside.[28] Hence our Franco-Algerian may identify with France through her neighbourhood, Franco-Algerian subculture and multicultural Paris. Her French national identity consists of elements which distinguish her from an Algerian in Algeria. The way she imagines the nation will tend to be more multicultural and civic – looking forward more than backward – as compared to the rural villager's. That's fine. There is no single, superior form of national identity: rather it is everywhere and nowhere, with everyone glancing at it from a different angle and belonging to it in their own way. Notice this is not multiculturalism, because the Franco-Algerian woman isn't focused on Algeria, but on France.

Ethnicity, along with region, class and ideology, are lenses through which we interpret the nation.[29] As French people focus on the tricolour flag, they don't see it in precisely the same way. Like mods or Ulster Unionists with the Union Jack, they project their subcultural version of the nation on to it. Where multiculturalism draws people's gaze back to a distant homeland, multivocalism orients them to the nation, albeit viewed through different ethnic lenses. This flexibility maximizes meaning and unity by harnessing the complexity of national identity.

We need to contemplate a world in which the nation can be multicultural, civic and ethnic, all at once. If we censor multicultural or ethno-national imaginings, we alienate both high-identifying minorities and ethno-traditional majorities. The technique of permitting flexible interpretations of tradition in order to maximize loyalty has been used by many organizations. Political parties that give their branches the leeway to adapt to local wishes do better, a technique known as the 'franchise model' of party organization.[30] The Labour Party in Britain, for instance, contains branches dominated by liberal feminists, working-class traditionalists and Muslims. If you permit each to believe the party reflects the full suite of their values without the contradiction between, say, feminism and Islam coming into open conflict, you improve commitment to the cause. This means focusing everyone on one or two universal messages (i.e. opposition to cuts) while allowing the rest of Labour identity in each branch to take a different form. The Muslim Brotherhood in Egypt also succeeded through this form of decentralization, leveraging the bottom-up 'wisdom of crowds', whereas Egyptian communists insisted on a single top-down doctrine, hampering growth and prompting splits and stagnation.[31]

When it comes to social cohesion, Western countries need to rethink state-led, top-down civic nationalism. A weak civic nationalism which celebrates common denominators such as the air we breathe, electricity we use or toleration is very inclusive but totally banal. There have to be non-negotiable values like women's equality and freedom, but these provide little in the way of identity, notwithstanding the Islamic 'threat'.

A stronger civic nationalism which includes a compulsory shared history going back centuries and derides ethnicity is likely to alienate minorities. If it includes left-leaning institutions like the Canadian Broadcasting Corporation (CBC), it puts right-wingers off. Far better to crowd-source national symbols and allow people to read what they want into them, picking and choosing what moves them. This leverages people's unique vantage points, realizing the wisdom of crowds.

Politicians can affirm a multi-vocal understanding of nationhood by tuning into particular audiences. When speaking to liberals or an ethnically diverse crowd, they can talk about diversity and multiculturalism. When addressing conservative whites, it's important to nod to white majority ethno-traditions. This is not hypocrisy, but reflects the reality of complex systems like national identity. Robin Cook's invocation of chicken tikka masala as a symbol of Britain *and* John Major's 'Britain will still be the country of long shadows on county [cricket] grounds' are both valid. The same is true for ethnic change and immigration. When addressing conservatives, leaders should talk about the way immigrants are intermarrying and assimilating, following a time-honoured pattern which leaves 'us' unchanged. They should reference the actual small share of foreigners (since most greatly overestimate the number), connections to the country's long past and timeless countryside. When speaking to liberal groups, today's emphasis on diversity and change is appropriate, but this message is currently aggravating those who don't share this worldview, feeding populism.[32] Some perceive the river to be always changing, others see it as remaining the same. There is truth in both outlooks, and neither should be privileged.

Politicians should maintain what Kissinger called a 'constructive ambiguity' about the content of nationhood, validating many different conceptions instead of attacking multicultural and ethno-traditionalist ones. People hear what they want to hear, read what they want into statements. When pressed on contradictory messages about national identity, leaders should reply that 'there are many ways to be British'. Americans form attachments to different Americas: its politicians should reflect this. There's no single way of being American. All strengthen attachment to the country. Citizens connect to the nation through the particular, not the universal. A top-down approach based on a fixed set of universals flattens and alienates *both* minorities and conservative whites who identify with the nation through their ancestry and traditions. The goal should be to maximize freedom and solidarity. In this way, multivocalism is superior to both civic nationalism and multiculturalism. Instead of focusing on difference, or ironing everyone into commonality, governments should celebrate the different ways we identify in common.

TOWARDS AN OPEN WHITE MAJORITY

I end where I began, with white majorities. Multivocalism helps majorities and minorities pull in the same direction, but social cohesion and public provision are generally better in nations with an ethnic majority, like Botswana, than in those without one, like Tanzania. This is why federations with a clear ethnic majority are more stable than those consisting only of minority units.[33] The ethnic politics of diverse nations can be managed – Mauritius is an example – but it's easier for politics to revolve around class and government competence than ethnicity. I therefore favour *Whiteshift*, a model in which today's white majorities evolve seamlessly and gradually into mixed-race majorities that take on white myths and symbols.

The white majority should be inclusive, though it won't encompass everyone because it's not coterminous with the nation. Only those with some European background can be members, just as only those with some African background can be African-American. White archetypes would form part of the symbol system of the new white group, despite its mixed heritage. For instance, there is a Polynesian racial archetype which Hawaiians view as a symbol of their group even as those who look less Hawaiian aren't treated as second-class members of the community.

Or consider the American accent. Is it part of what makes America distinct? Canadian citizenship officers tell immigrants who have gone through their naturalization ceremony that their accents are all Canadian. At the individual level, this is correct. Once you have citizenship, you are Canadian, so all accents are Canadian. At the level of the whole, however, the statement is absurd. A Canadian accent is clearly distinct from a Jamaican or German accent, and is part of Canadian national identity. Notice what's going on here: you don't have to have an American accent to be an American, but an American accent is a distinguishing feature of the American nation. The first concerns the level of individuals, the second properties of the collective. So too with Protestantism, an Anglo surname like Jackson, and being white, black or Native Indian. These are all ethno-traditions of American nationhood, properties of the Weberian ideal-type which adds to the particularity of the collective: like the American accent, membership in these groups is not a requirement for national belonging, nor are those who lack these archetypal properties second-class citizens. In some cases, few people may possess an archetypal characteristic: most Welsh don't speak Welsh.

What this means, paradoxically, is that someone who is not a member of an ethnic majority might nevertheless be in favour of trying to protect an ethno-tradition of nationhood. A Welshman who speaks English may wish to protect the Welsh language, or a new immigrant to America may love the American accent. This also explains the paradox of British Sikhs being attached to the stereotypical pale skin and blue eyes of many Britons as well as the multicultural mix of people in Britain. Both are distinguishing features, particularities of the national whole which individuals may not personally share, but are attached to and may wish to preserve.

The same needs to hold for the whites of tomorrow: they will come in all shades and most won't look fully Caucasian but they will connect to their ancestors' portraits and statues via the white archetype. Stereotypical racial appearance will be a group symbol – just as distinctively Irish surnames are an Irish group symbol – which many won't possess and which is not an entry barrier. The white group needs to become more open to those who wish to marry in or identify with its culture. But because it is not the nation, the white majority can be symbolically exclusive and celebrate its past. White Swedes are not the Swedish nation-state, so they can cherish exclusive symbols like Lutheranism and the Viking heritage. Just as British Chinese people need not accept Hindu symbols on a par to avoid offending their Hindu neighbours in West London, the new 'white' majority in Western countries doesn't have to change its ethnic archetype, myths or traditions or tear down any statues to accommodate the newcomers who have married into their group. I term this model liberal ethnicity because it is open to outsiders while remaining symbolically exclusive.[34] The nation-state, on the other hand, is compulsory. It must include all citizens, from ethnic majorities to insular religious minorities, so has to be symbolically flexible and multi-vocal rather than promoting the narrative of the majority.

The always sharp centrist commentator Andrew Sullivan nicely elucidates the problem as it appears in America:

> We once had a widely accepted narrative of our origins, shared icons that defined us, and a common pseudo-ethnicity – 'whiteness' – into which new immigrants were encouraged to assimilate. Our much broader ethnic mix and the truths of history make this much harder today – as, of course, they should. But we should be clear-eyed about the consequence. We can no longer think of the Puritans without acknowledging the genocide that followed them; we cannot celebrate our Founding Fathers without seeing that slavery undergirded the society they constructed; we must tear down our Confederate statues and relitigate our oldest rifts. Even the national anthem now divides those who stand from those who kneel. We dismantled many of our myths, but have not yet formed new ones to replace them.[35]

The American nation can't celebrate the divisive American past, but an ethnic majority can because no one is obliged to join it. The solution is to extend Sullivan's 'panethnic' majority to include those of part-white background as white; or perhaps, in the American case, to follow the Mexicans and develop a 'Melungeon' myth which blends the symbols of the oldest founding groups and includes those who have at least some white, black or American Indian background. Those who have no European background can still identify with a national identity that includes the majority ethno-tradition and many will feel warmly towards the majority while maintaining their distinct diaspora ethnicity.

Minorities are free to identify as they choose and are equal members of the nation. There must be a separation of the majority from the nation-state, with the most insular Salafi treated as no less national than a member of the ethnic majority. This separation will also benefit minorities, for, as Mona Chalabi writes, it's important to define whites so they don't simply become the invisible national 'normal' from which minorities deviate.[36]

We need a new 'cultural contract' in which everyone gets to have a secure, culturally rich ethnic identity as well as a thin, culturally neutral and future-oriented national identity. Scrubbing the white ethnic stamp from national identities, as governments are attempting to do, is fine, but to do this while suppressing the expression of white identity is problematic. Majorities like the white British have to stop thinking of themselves as the only true Brits and should appreciate the distinctive Afro-Caribbean or Indian traditions of authentic Britishness that differentiate these communities from their kin abroad. While not as indigenized as African-Americans in the United States, these are now distinctive ethnic groups from their relatives in the homeland. Ideally, British nationhood would celebrate the native-Creole rather than foreign aspects of these groups.

In exchange for de-centring themselves from the nation, white Britons should be given free rein to celebrate their ethnicity and their more historicist, rural, ancestral version of British nationhood. Ideally white Britons would begin to appreciate that minority Britons, especially the native-born, differ greatly from co-ethnics in their ancestral homelands and represent distinct Creole expressions of Britishness which enhance national particularity. With a relaxed and fuzzy line between the majority and minorities, people can focus on their common multi-vocal nationhood.

Despite the de-centring of the ethnic majority and its separation from the nation-state, the majority is likely to serve as a key source of civic glue. Sometimes majorities are more willing to sacrifice parochial ethnic concerns for the benefit of the whole, though this is less the case when they feel insecure. In addition, national cohesion is often a by-product of confident ethnic majorities, who often feel an automatic connection to the state. Britain's cohesion, for example, relies a lot on the taken-for-granted Britishness of the majority English rather than the formal institutions that stretch across the Scots, Northern Irish, Welsh and English such as British values, the BBC or the NHS.

The 'inclusive-majority-within-inclusive nation' model, alongside an immigration system that embodies group cultural interests, is superior to the present mixture of hard-edged civic nationalism and culture-blind immigration. Why? First, majority ethnicity offers a richer set of myths and meanings than civic nationhood. It may do so without fear of offence, because no one is obliged to be a member. Second, it is more liberal because it removes the need for state-driven integration. Those who wish to assimilate to the majority can do so and those who prefer to live as a diaspora are free to. Some may flirt with both.

The immigration system, not coercion and stigmatization, ensures that a balance is struck between diversity and assimilation. If intermarriage slows, the ethnic majority will call for lower numbers or more culturally selective immigration. As assimilation speeds up, immigration can be increased. Clear measures like intermarriage rates can be tracked, as with rates of language proficiency, and used to reassure people and calm panics. An open ethnic majority will be more likely to view outsiders as potential recruits, removing the chance of zero-sum competition leading to the antipathy towards outgroups I define as racism.

Western societies need to reach an accommodation between the freely expressed preferences of cultural conservatives and liberals in which each tries to understand the other. In such a world, the winning formula is to shelve the coercive 'promote diversity' mantra pushed by positive liberals and instead focus on enlarging the circle of freedom. We need to broaden egalitarianism by moving away from a totalizing outlook focused on the white male 'other' towards an evidence-based approach which takes all dimensions of inequality into account and favours 'nudge'-style remedies. Only then can we overcome polarization and work together to solve the pressing material problems we face.

Will right-wing populism continue to surge? Western societies will grow more diverse before *Whiteshift* – melting and cohesion – sets in. Repressing white identity as racist and demonizing the white past adds insult to the injury of this group's demographic decline. This way lies growing populist discontent or even terrorism. Ethnic majorities need a future, and civic nationalism can't offer it. Instead we need writers and politicians to anticipate *Whiteshift*, using it as a vision to open up a conversation about majorities and the European tradition. This will enable conservative whites to find a sense of ethnic continuity in the rising mixed-race population, as well as in the persistence of unmixed whites in rural areas. Majority reassurance, far from leading to oppression, promises to reduce insecurity, opening the way for a return to more relaxed, harmonious and trusting societies.

Acknowledgements

This book benefited greatly from the support of numerous people and institutions. My wife Fran and children Stuart and Alannah deserve credit for putting up with my long sessions at the computer. David Goodhart, first of Demos, then at Policy Exchange, helped me fund and disseminate important new survey research. He also provided useful feedback on the manuscript. Paul Morland, a former doctoral student of mine-turned-successful non-fiction writer, read earlier drafts, pointing out errors of fact and logic while providing encouragement. The Economic and Social Research Council (ESRC) generously awarded me a research grant to use UK datasets to study the white working- class response to ethnic change in Britain during 2012–14. Policy Exchange funded key new survey research which has been important for the book. Credit goes to my employer, Birkbeck, University of London, which has afforded me the time to write. My editors, Casiana Ionita at Penguin and Tracy Carns at Overlook/Abrams Press, have been sources of encouragement and constructive criticism. My agents, Markus Hoffmann in New York and Ed Wilson in London, helped make the project a reality.

Carl Ritter, Sasha Polakow-Suransky, Philippe Lemoine and Will Beaufoy read and commented on earlier drafts, making comments which influenced the final product. Bobby Duffy at Ipsos MORI has done pioneering work on the politics of immigration and generously shared cross-country data on attitudes to immigration and perceptions of racism. Pat Dade of Cultural Dynamics is an influential thinker on public opinion who has shared a great deal of output from his firm's surveys and allowed me to crunch important new data on psychological profiles, immigration attitudes and populist-right support. I've benefited from conversations with Matthew Goodwin, Justin Gest,

Daphne Halikiopoulou, Rob Ford, Ed West, Trevor Phillips, Michael Lind, Sunder Katwala, Shadi Hamid, Reihan Salam, Coleman Hughes, Musa al-Gharbi and Erik Tillman, among others. I've learned a great deal from Ashley Jardina and her work. I would also like to acknowledge the influence of my doctoral supervisor Anthony D. Smith, a giant in the field of nationalism studies, who passed away on 19 July 2016. He will be sadly missed. Needless to say, I alone take responsibility for the thoughts in this book and none of the aforementioned individuals necessarily endorses anything in these pages!

Eric Kaufmann,
London, 1 November 2018

References and Notes

1. The Century of *Whiteshift*

1. 'The New Face of America', *Time*, 18 November 1993.
2. G. Orwell, *The Lion and the Unicorn: Socialism and the English Genius*, London, 1941: Secker & Warburg, p. 48.
3. K. Stenner, *The Authoritarian Dynamic*, Cambridge, 2005: Cambridge University Press.
4. M. Lind, 'The future of whiteness', *Salon*, 29 May 2012.
5. M. Lewis, *Moneyball: The Art of Winning an Unfair Game*, New York, 2003: W. W. Norton.
6. D. Kahneman, *Thinking, Fast and Slow*, New York, 2011: Farrar, Straus and Giroux.
7. Ashley Feinberg, 'What I learned from reading all the media safaris into "Trump country" I could handle before wanting to die', *HuffPost*, 29 December 2017.
8. www.sneps.net/whiteshift.
9. J. B. Judis, *The Populist Explosion: How the Great Recession Transformed American and European Politics*, Columbia Global Reports, 2016; Jan-Werner Müller, *What is Populism?*, London, 2016: Penguin Books.
10. A. Smith, *National Identity*, London, 1991: Penguin Books.
11. E. Kaufmann, 'The lenses of nationhood: An optical model of identity', *Nations and Nationalism* 14:3 (2008), 449–77.
12. E. P. Kaufmann, 'Dominant ethnicity: From background to foreground', Introduction, in E. P. Kaufmann (ed.), *Rethinking Ethnicity: Majority Groups and Dominant Minorities*, London, 2004: Routledge, pp. 1–14.
13. D. Lav, 'Rachid Kaci and Sophia Chikirou: North African roots, French identity, universal ideals', *Middle East Media Research Institute*, 3 June 2007.
14. 'New poll: Some Americans express troubling racial attitudes even as majority oppose white supremacists', *Sabato's Crystal Ball*, 14 September 2017.
15. MTurk sample of 200, including forty-six minorities, 4 January 2017; Prolific Academic sample of fifty-five white Republicans and fifty minority Republicans, 8 January 2017.

16. H. Kohn, 'Western and Eastern nationalisms', in J. Hutchinson and A. D. Smith (eds.), *Nationalism*. Oxford, 1994: Oxford University Press.

17. See the National Geographic's Enduring Voices project website at: http://travel.nationalgeographic.com/travel/enduring-voices/.

18. E. Kaufmann, 'Land, history or modernization? Explaining ethnic fractionalization', *Ethnic and Racial Studies* 38:2 (2015), 193–210; S. Michalopoulos, 'The origins of ethnolinguistic diversity', *The American Economic Review* 102:4 (2012), 1508–39.

19. A. Smith, *The Ethnic Origins of Nations*, Oxford, 1986: Blackwell.

20. V. Skirbekk, 'Human fertility and survival across space and time', World Population Program, IIASA, Working Paper, 2009.

21. E. Kaufmann, 'Demographic change and conflict in Northern Ireland: Reconciling qualitative and quantitative evidence', *Ethnopolitics* 10:3–4 (2011), 369–89.

22. J. A. Goldstone, E. P. Kaufmann and M. Duffy Toft (eds.), *Political Demography: How Population Changes are Reshaping International Security and National Politics*, Boulder, Colo., 2012: Paradigm.

23. United Nations, Department of Economic and Social Affairs, Population Division (2016), *International Migration Report 2015: Highlights* (ST/ESA/SER.A/375), pp. 2–3.

24. M. Duffy Toft, *The Geography of Ethnic Violence: Identity, Interests, and the Indivisibility of Territory*, Princeton, NJ, 2003: Princeton University Press.

25. J. McWhorter, 'Antiracism, our flawed new religion', *Daily Beast*, 27 July 2015; S. Steele, *White Guilt: How Blacks and Whites Together Destroyed the Promise of the Civil Rights Era*, New York and London, 2009: HarperCollins.

26. K. Stenner, *The Authoritarian Dynamic*, Cambridge, 2005: Cambridge University Press.

27. E. Kaufmann and M. J. Goodwin, 'Does diversity produce hostility? A meta-analysis', *Social Science Research*, accepted 15 July 2018.

28. R. A. Billington, *The Protestant Crusade, 1800–1860: A Study of the Origins of American Nativism*, New York, 1938: Macmillan, p. 387.

29. J. Haidt, *The Righteous Mind: Why Good People are Divided by Politics and Religion*, London, 2012: Allen Lane.

30. R. Boyd and P. J. Richerson, 'Culture and the evolution of human cooperation', *Phil. Trans. R. Soc. B* 364:1533 (2009), 3281–8.

31. D. S. Wilson, *Darwin's Cathedral: Evolution, Religion, and the Nature of Society*, Chicago, 2002: University of Chicago Press.

32. D. Bell, *The Cultural Contradictions of Capitalism*, New York, 1996 [1976]: HarperCollins.

33. I. Berlin, *Two Concepts of Liberty*, Oxford, 1958: Clarendon Press.

34. Victor Penney, '"Unprecedented": Ontario Law Society forces members to support "diversity"', *LifeSite*, 26 October 2017.

35. N. Glazer, *We are All Multiculturalists Now*, Cambridge, Mass., 1997: Harvard University Press.
36. McWhorter, 'Antiracism, our flawed new religion'.
37. S. Blinder, R. Ford and E. Ivarsflaten, 'The better angels of our nature: How the antiprejudice norm affects policy and party preferences in Great Britain and Germany', *American Journal of Political Science* 57:4 (2013), 841–57.
38. A. O. Hirschman, *Exit, Voice and Loyalty*, Cambridge, Mass., and London, 1970: Harvard University Press.
39. E. West, *The Diversity Illusion*, London, 2013: Gibson Square.
40. E. Gellner, *Nations and Nationalism*, Oxford, 1983: Blackwell.
41. E. Kaufmann, *Shall the Religious Inherit the Earth? Demography and Politics in the Twenty-First Century*, London, 2010: Profile Books.
42. N. Ignatiev, *How the Irish Became White*, New York and London, 1995: Routledge.
43. P. Kay, B. Berlin and W. Merrifield, 'Biocultural implications of systems of color naming', *Journal of Linguistic Anthropology* 1:1 (1991), 12–25.
44. D. Roberson et al., 'Color categories: Evidence for the cultural relativity hypothesis', *Cognitive Psychology* 50:4 (2005), 378–411.
45. E. Kaufmann, 'Can narratives of white identity reduce opposition to immigration and support for hard Brexit? A survey experiment', *Political Studies*, 5 December 2017 (online).

PART I: FIGHT

2. Prequel to *Whiteshift*

1. J. Higham, 'Cultural responses to immigration', in N. J. Smelser and J. C. Alexander (eds.), *Diversity and Its Discontents: Cultural Conflict and Common Ground in Contemporary American Society*, Princeton, NJ, 1999: Princeton University Press, p. 46.
2. R. Horsman, *Race and Manifest Destiny: The Origins of American Racial Anglo-Saxonism*, Cambridge, Mass., 1981: Harvard University Press, p. 22 (emphasis added).
3. G. VanHoosier-Carey, 'Byrhtnoth in Dixie: The emergence of Anglo-Saxon studies in the postbellum south', in A. J. Frantzen and J. D. Niles (eds.), *Anglo-Saxonism and the Construction of Social Identity*, Gainesville, Fla, 1997: University Press of Florida.
4. T. Roosevelt, *The Winning of the West*, 4 vols., New York, 1889: G. P. Putnam & Sons, vol. 1, p. 27.
5. A. D. Smith, *National Identity*, London, 1991: Penguin Books.

6. M. Gordon, *Assimilation in American Life: The Role of Race, Religion and National Origins*, Oxford, 1964: Oxford University Press, pp. 121–2.

7. E. Gellner, *Nations and Nationalism*, Oxford, 1983: Blackwell.

8. R. A. Billington, *The Protestant Crusade, 1800–1860: A Study of the Origins of American Nativism*, New York, 1938: Macmillan, p. 387.

9. M. A. Jones, *American Immigration*, Chicago and London, 1992 [1960]: University of Chicago Press, pp. 6, 13, 16, 67.

10. H. Kohn, *American Nationalism: An Interpretive Essay*, New York, 1957: Macmillan, p. 138.

11. M. E. Curti, *The Roots of American Loyalty*, New York, 1946: Columbia University Press, pp. 202–3.

12. A. H. Goldman, 'Reconciling Race and Rights: Emerson and the Construction of Nationality', unpublished PhD dissertation, 1992, Harvard University, pp. 242–4.

13. R. W. Emerson, *English Traits*, London and New York, 1902 [1856]: Unit Library, pp. 25–6 (emphasis added).

14. P. Morland, *Demographic Engineering: Population Strategies in Ethnic Conflict*, Farnham, 2014: Ashgate, p. 166.

15. J. Higham, *Strangers in the Land: Patterns of American Nativism, 1860–1925*, New Brunswick, 1955: Rutgers University Press, p. 33.

16. P. Morland, *The Human Tide* (forthcoming).

17. C. Sellers, *The Market Revolution in Jacksonian America*, New York and Oxford, 1991: Oxford University Press, pp. 40, 59–63.

18. E. Foner, *Free Soil, Free Labor, Free Men: The Ideology of the Republican Party before the Civil War*, New York, 1970: Oxford University Press, pp. 236–7.

19. T. F. Gossett, *Race: The History of an Idea in America*, Dallas, 1963: Southern Methodist University Press, p. 294.

20. A. Gyory, *Closing the Gate: Race, Politics, and the Chinese Exclusion Act*, Chapel Hill, NC, 1998: University of North Carolina Press, p. 33; M. Lind, *The Next American Nation: The New Nationalism and the Fourth American Revolution*, New York, 1995: The Free Press, p. 66.

21. L. B. Davis, *Immigrants, Baptists and the Protestant Mind in America*, Urbana, Ill., Chicago and London, 1973: University of Illinois Press, p. 13.

22. B. Gratton, 'Demography and immigration restriction in United States history', in J. A. Goldstone, E. Kaufmann and M. Duffy Toft (eds.), *Political Demography: How Population Changes are Reshaping International Security and National Politics*, Boulder, Colo., 2012: Paradigm, pp. 159–75.

23. J. Hutchinson, *Nations as Zones of Conflict*, London, 2005: Sage.

24. G. F. Seward, *Chinese Immigration in Its Social and Economical Aspects*, New York, 1881: Charles Scribner's Sons, p. 254.

25. E. C. Sandmeyer, *The Anti-Chinese Movement in California*, Urbana, Ill., 1939: University of Illinois Press, p. 30.
26. Gratton, 'Demography and immigration restriction in United States history'.
27. Davis, *Immigrants, Baptists and the Protestant Mind*, pp. 70, 85.
28. J. R. Gusfield, *Symbolic Crusade: Status Politics and the American Temperance Movement*, Urbana, Ill., 1963: University of Illinois Press.
29. C. W. Eagles, *Democracy Delayed: Congressional Reapportionment and Urban–Rural Conflict in the 1920s*, Athens, Ga, and London, 1990: University of Georgia Press, p. 38.
30. Gratton, 'Demography and immigration restriction in United States history', pp. 169–71.
31. E. Kaufmann, *The Rise and Fall of Anglo-America: The Decline of Dominant Ethnicity in the United States*, Cambridge, Mass., 2004: Harvard University Press, p. 33.
32. D. King, *Making Americans: Immigration, Race and the Origins of the Diverse Democracy*, Cambridge, Mass., 2000: Harvard University Press.
33. M. Hyatt, *Franz Boas: Social Activist*, New York and Westport, Conn., 1990: Greenwood Press, p. 100; M. Pittenger, *American Socialists and Evolutionary Thought, 1870–1920*, Madison, Wisc., 1993: University of Wisconsin Press, pp. 183–5.
34. B. Kraut, *From Reform Judaism to Ethical Culture: The Religious Evolution of Felix Adler*, Cincinnati, 1979: Hebrew Union College Press, pp. 122–3.
35. R. B. Westbrook, *John Dewey and American Democracy*, Ithaca, NY, 1991: Cornell University Press, pp. 34–5.
36. R. S. Lissak, *Pluralism and Progressives: Hull House and the New Immigrants, 1890–1919*, Chicago, 1989: University of Chicago Press, p. 156.
37. Kaufmann, *Rise and Fall of Anglo-America*, pp. 92–102.
38. Davis, *Immigrants, Baptists and the Protestant Mind*, pp. 160–61.
39. J. Bodnar, *Remaking America: Public Memory, Commemoration, and Patriotism in the Twentieth Century*, Princeton, NJ, 1992: Princeton University Press, pp. 84–5; K. T. Jackson, *The Ku Klux Klan in the City, 1915–1930*, New York, 1967: Oxford University Press, pp. 99, 150, 247.
40. J. Xing, *Baptized in the Fire of Revolution: The American Social Gospel and the YMCA in China 1919–37*, Cranbury, NJ, and London, 1996: Associated University Presses, p. 72.
41. R. M. Miller, *American Protestantism and Social Issues, 1919–39*, Chapel Hill, NC, 1958: University of North Carolina Press, pp. 291–2.
42. H. M. Kallen, 'Democracy versus the melting pot', *Culture and Democracy in the United States: Studies in the Group Psychology of the American Peoples*, New York, 1924: Boni and Liveright, pp. 67–125.

43. R. S. Bourne, 'Trans-National America', *War and the Intellectuals: Collected Essays, 1915–1919*, ed. C. Resek, New York, 1964 [1916]: Harper & Row, pp. 113–14, 118.

44. W. M. Christie, *1941: The America That Went to War*, New York, 2016: Carrel Books.

45. N. Glazer, *The New Immigration: A Challenge to American Society*, San Diego, 1988: San Diego State University Press, pp. 2–3.

46. J. F. Perea, *Immigrants Out! The New Nativism and the Anti-Immigrant Impulse in the United States*, New York and London, 1997: New York University Press, pp. 48–51.

47. F. FitzGerald, *America Revised: History Schoolbooks in the Twentieth Century*, Boston, Mass., and Toronto, 1979: Little, Brown and Company, p. 80. Despite this, in his speech on the subject, JFK mainly talks with reverence about the founders, soft-pedalling arguments about post-1890 immigrants.

48. Ibid., pp. 80–81.

49. B. M. Ziegler, *Immigration: An American Dilemma*, Boston, Mass., 1953: D. C. Heath & Co., pp. 97–9.

50. C. C. O'Brien, *God-Land: Reflections on Religion and Nationalism*, Cambridge, Mass., 1988: Harvard University Press.

51. Eagles, *Democracy Delayed*, p. 118.

52. W. G. Mayer, *The Changing American Mind: How and Why American Public Opinion Changed between 1960 and 1988*, Ann Arbor, Mich., 1992: University of Michigan Press.

53. R. Inglehart, *Culture Shift in Advanced Industrial Society*, Princeton, NJ, 1990: Princeton University Press, p. 96.

54. Paul Krugman, 'Unacceptable prejudices', *The New York Times*, 9 August 2013.

55. R. J. Simon, *Public Opinion and the Immigrant: Print Media Coverage, 1880–1980*, Lexington, Mass., 1985: Lexington Books, pp. 36–40; R. J. Simon and S. H. Alexander, *The Ambivalent Welcome: Print Media, Public Opinion and Immigration*, Westport, Conn., 1993: Praeger Publishers, p. 41.

56. C. H. Anderson, *White Protestant Americans: From National Origins to Religious Group*, Englewood Cliffs, NJ, 1970: Prentice-Hall, p. 131; Mayer, *The Changing American Mind*, p. 382.

57. C. W. Mills, *The Power Elite*, London, 1956: Oxford University Press, p. 60.

58. R. C. Christopher, *Crashing the Gates: The De-WASPing of America's Power Elite*, New York and London, 1989: Simon & Schuster, p. 41.

59. R. D. Alba, *Ethnic Identity: The Transformation of White America*, New Haven and London, 1990: Yale University Press; S. Lieberson, 'Unhyphenated whites in the United States', in R. D. Alba (ed.), *Ethnicity and Race in*

the U.S.A.: Toward the Twenty-First Century, Boston, Mass., and London, 1985: Routledge & Kegan Paul, pp. 159–80.

60. D. R. Roediger, *The Wages of Whiteness: Race and the Making of the American Working Class*, New York and London, 1991: Verso.

61. T. Devos and M. R. Banaji, 'American = white?', *Journal of Personality and Social Psychology* 88:3 (2005), 447.

62. R. J. Simon and M. A. Abdel-Moneim, *Public Opinion in the United States: Studies of Race, Religion, Gender, and Issues That Matter*, New Brunswick, NJ, 2010: Transaction.

63. S. Huntington, *Who are We? The Cultural Core of American National Identity*, New York and London, 2004: Simon & Schuster; D. E. Sherkat, 'Tracking the restructuring of American religion: Religious affiliation and patterns of religious mobility, 1973–1998', *Social Forces* 79:4 (2001), 1459–93.

64. A. E. Jardina, 'Demise of dominance: Group threat and the new relevance of white identity for American politics', PhD dissertation, University of Michigan, 2014, pp. 90–93.

3. The Rise of Trump

1. P. Martin, 'Trends in migration to the U.S' Population Reference Bureau, 19 May 2014.

2. 'Modern immigration wave brings 59 million to U.S., driving population growth and change through 2065', Pew Research Center, 28 September 2015, p. 31.

3. W. H. Frey, *Diversity Explosion: How New Racial Demographics are Remaking America*, Washington, DC, 2014: Brookings Institution Press, p. 4.

4. Miami–Dade County Facts, 2009: http://www.miamidade.gov/planning/library/reports/2009-miami-dade-county-facts.pdf.

5. V. Skirbekk, E. Kaufmann and A. Goujon, 'Secularism, fundamentalism or Catholicism? The religious composition of the United States to 2043', *Journal for the Scientific Study of Religion* 49:2 (2010), 293–310.

6. J. M. Krogstad, J. S. Passel and D. Cohn, '5 facts about illegal immigration in the U.S.', Pew Research Center, 27 April 2017.

7. C. Rose, *What Makes People Tick: The Three Hidden Worlds of Settlers, Prospectors and Pioneers*, Kibworth Beauchamp, 2011: Matador.

8. http://www.sneps.net/whiteshift.

9. P. Schrag, *The Decline of the WASP*, New York, 1973: Simon & Schuster, pp. 71–2.

10. B. Altemeyer, *Right-Wing Authoritarianism*, Winnipeg, 1981: University of Manitoba Press.

11. K. Stenner, *The Authoritarian Dynamic*, Cambridge, 2005: Cambridge University Press.

12. E. Kaufmann, 'Levels or changes? Ethnic context, immigration and the UK Independence Party vote', *Electoral Studies* 48 (2017), 57–69.

13. E. Kaufmann and M. J. Goodwin, 'Does diversity produce hostility? A meta-analysis', *Social Science Research*, accepted 15 July 2018.

14. D. Stockemer, 'The success of radical right-wing parties in Western European regions – new challenging findings', *Journal of Contemporary European Studies* 25:1 (2017), 41–56; R. Kappe, Media attention, party positioning and public support for right-wing populist parties: The emergence of the "Alternative für Deutschland" (AfD) party in Germany', paper presented at the ePop conference, University of Kent, UK, 2016.

15. J. Hutchinson, *The Dynamics of Cultural Nationalism: The Gaelic Revival and the Creation of the Irish Nation-State*, London, 1987: Allen & Unwin; L. Morowitz and E. Emery, *Consuming the Past: The Medieval Revival in Fin-de-Siècle France*, Aldershot, 2003: Ashgate.

16. L. Greenfeld, *Nationalism: Five Roads to Modernity*, Cambridge Mass., 1992: Harvard University Press.

17. R. L. Dorman, *Revolt of the Provinces: The Regionalist Movement in America, 1920–1945*, Chapel Hill, 1993: University of North Carolina Press.

18. R. Brubaker, 'The return of assimilation? Changing perspectives on immigration and its sequels in France, Germany and the United States', *Ethnic and Racial Studies* 24:4 (2001), 531–48.

19. M. Kenny, 'The political theory of recognition: The case of the white working class', *British Journal of Politics & International Relations* 14:1 (2012), 19–38; J. Gest, *The New Minority: White Working Class Politics in an Age of Immigration and Inequality*, New York, 2016: Oxford University Press.

20. T. Gallagher, *Edinburgh Divided: John Cormack and No Popery in the 1930s*, Edinburgh, 1987: Polygon.

21. N. Marzouki, D. McDonnell and O. Roy (eds.), *Saving the People: How Populists Hijack Religion*, New York, 2016: Oxford University Press.

22. http://www.gallup.com/poll/1660/immigration.aspx, accessed 20 July 2017.

23. J. Dunaway, R. Branton and M. A. Abrajano, 'Agenda setting, public opinion, and the issue of immigration reform', *Social Science Quarterly* 91:2 (2010), 359–78.

24. D. Bell, *The Cultural Contradictions of Capitalism*, New York, 1996 [1976], HarperCollins, p. 54.

25. E. Kaufmann, *The Rise and Fall of Anglo-America: The Decline of Dominant Ethnicity in the United States*, Cambridge, Mass., 2004: Harvard University Press, p. 225.

26. R. N. Bellah, *Habits of the Heart*, 2nd edn, London and Berkeley, Calif., 1996 [1985]: University of California Press, p. 71

27. D. Bell, *The Cultural Contradictions of Capitalism*, New York, 1976: HarperCollins.

28. S. Zukin, 'Art in the arms of power', *Theory and Society* 11 (1982), 423–51.

29. S. Bruce, *God is Dead: Secularization in the West*, Malden, Mass., 2002: Blackwell Pub.

30. C. D. Kam, 'Who toes the party line? Cues, values, and individual differences', *Political Behavior* 27:2, 163–82.

31. P. L. Martin, 'The United States', in W. A. Cornelius, P. L. Martin and P. M. Orrenius (eds.), *Controlling Immigration: A Global Perspective*, 3rd edn, Stanford, Calif., 2014: Stanford University Press, pp. 57–8.

32. https://www.wola.org/wp-content/uploads/2017/01/border.png, accessed 1 February 2018.

33. Jason DeParle, 'The anti-immigration crusader', *The New York Times*, 17 April 2011.

34. Kaufmann, *Rise and Fall of Anglo-America*, p. 269.

35. Ibid.

36. Ibid., p. 263.

37. D. J. Schildkraut, *Press One for English: Language Policy, Public Opinion, and American Identity*, Princeton, NJ, 2005: Princeton University Press; '84% still support English as official U.S. language', *Rasmussen Reports*, 14 May 2013.

38. R. and J. S. Delgado (eds), *Critical White Studies: Looking behind the Mirror*, Philadelphia, 1997: Temple University Press, p. 91.

39. Kaufmann, *Rise and Fall of Anglo-America*, pp. 264, 281.

40. F. Fukuyama, *The End of History and the Last Man*, London, 1992: Hamish Hamilton.

41. M. Hout, A. Greeley and M. J. Wilde, 'The demographic imperative in religious change in the United States', *American Journal of Sociology* 107:2 (2001), 468–500.

42. E. Kaufmann, *Shall the Religious Inherit the Earth? Demography and Politics in the Twenty-First Century*, London, 2010: Profile Books.

43. Ibid., pp. 85–9

44. J. Hunter, *Culture Wars: The Struggle to Define America*, New York, 1991: Basic Books.

45. J. Guth et al., 'Religious influences in the 2004 presidential election', *Presidential Studies Quarterly* 36:2 (2006), 223–42.

46. F. FitzGerald, *The Evangelicals: The Struggle to Shape America*, New York, 2017: Simon & Schuster.

47. Kaufmann, *Shall the Religious Inherit the Earth?*, pp. 109–11.

48. Ibid., p. 105.
49. R. D. Putnam and D. Campbell, *American Grace: How Religion Unites and Divides Us*, New York, 2010: Simon & Schuster, p. 121.
50. M. Lipka, 'Millennials increasingly are driving growth of "nones"', Pew Research Center, 12 May 2015.
51. http://www.gallup.com/poll/117328/marriage.aspx.
52. American Jewish Historical Society, 'Jews and the conservative rift', *The Free Library*, 1999, accessed 24 July 2017: https://www.thefreelibrary.com/Jews+and+the+Conservative+Rift.-a063090928.
53. S. M. Lipset, *American Exceptionalism: A Double-Edged Sword*, New York, 1996: W. W. Norton & Co.
54. P. Brimelow, *Alien Nation: Common Sense about America's Immigration Disaster*, New York, 1995: Random House, p. 264.
55. G. Hawley, *Making Sense of the Alt-Right*, New York, 2017: Columbia University Press, p. 27.
56. Kaufmann, *Rise and Fall of Anglo-America*, pp. 278–9.
57. John Judis and Michael Lind, 'For a new nationalism', *New Republic*, 27 March 1995.
58. M. Lind, *The Next American Nation*, New York, 1995: Free Press; S. Huntington, *Who are We? The Cultural Core of American National Identity*, New York and London, 2004: Simon & Schuster; E. Kaufmann, 'The Meaning of Huntington', *Prospect*, no. 155 (February 2009).
59. Patrick J. Buchanan, 'West's doors closing', Patrick J. Buchanan Official Website, 7 June 1993.
60. M. J. Rozell and C. Wilcox, *God at the Grass Roots, 1996: The Christian Right in the American Elections*, Lanham, Md, 1997: Rowman & Littlefield, p. 121.
61. Sam Tannenhaus, 'When Pat Buchanan tried to make America great again', *Esquire*, 5 April 2017; Tim Alberta, 'The ideas made it, but I didn't', *Politico*, May/June 2017.
62. Private correspondence with Pat Buchanan, 22 November 2017.
63. Ibid.
64. R. and J. S. Delgado (eds.), *Critical White Studies*, p. 187.
65. Kaufmann, *Rise and Fall of Anglo-America*, pp. 267–9.
66. R. M. Alvarez and T. L. Butterfield, 'The resurgence of nativism in California? The case of Proposition 187 and illegal immigration', *Social Science Quarterly* 81:1 (2000), 167–79; R. Branton et al., 'Anglo voting on nativist ballot initiatives: The partisan impact of spatial proximity to the US–Mexico border', *Social Science Quarterly* 88:3 (2007), 882–97.
67. M. V. Hood and I. L. Morris, 'Brother, can you spare a dime? Racial/ethnic context and the Anglo vote on Proposition 187', *Social Science Quarterly* 81:1 (2000), 194–206.

68. L. Y. Newton, 'Why some Latinos supported Proposition 187: Testing economic threat and cultural identity hypotheses', *Social Science Quarterly* 81:1 (2000), 180–93.
69. C. Joppke, 'Why liberal states accept unwanted immigration', *World Politics* 50:2 (1998), 266–93.
70. M. Abrajano and Z. L. Hajnal, *White Backlash*, Princeton, NJ, 2015: Princeton University Press, pp. 165–6.
71. M. Wright and J. Citrin, 'Saved by the stars and stripes? Images of protest, salience of threat, and immigration attitudes', *American Politics Research* 39:2 (2010), 323–53 (at p. 330).
72. R. P. Branton and J. Dunaway, 'Spatial proximity to the US–Mexico border and newspaper coverage of immigration issues', *Political Research Quarterly* 62:2 (2009), 289–302.
73. D. J. Hopkins, 'Politicized places: Explaining where and when immigrants provoke local opposition', *American Political Science Review* 104:1 (2010), 40–60.
74. A. E. Jardina, 'Demise of dominance: Group threat and the new relevance of white identity for American politics', PhD dissertation, University of Michigan, 2014, pp. 51–3.
75. N. A. Valentino, E. Brader and A. E. Jardina, 'Immigration opposition among US whites: General ethnocentrism or media priming of attitudes about Latinos?', *Political Psychology* 34:2 (2013), 149–66.
76. Frey, *Diversity Explosion*, p. 72; 'Arcadia embraces Hispanic population amid immigration talks', *Telegraph-Herald*, 24 April 2017.
77. M. Spicuzzi, 'Politics of immigration take root in Walker's hometown', *Wisconsin News*, 5 July 2015.
78. Kaufmann and Goodwin, 'Does diversity produce hostility?'
79. B. J. Newman, 'Acculturating contexts and Anglo opposition to immigration in the United States', *American Journal of Political Science* 57:2 (2013), 374–90.
80. Michael S. Teitelbaum, 'Migration and conflict in OECD countries', in Isabelle Cote, Matthew Mitchell and Monica Duffy Toft (eds.), *People Changing Places: New Perspectives on Demography, Migration, Conflict, and the State*, London, 2018: Routledge, p. 187.
81. K. E. Walker and H. Leitner, 'The variegated landscape of local immigration policies in the United States', *Urban Geography* 32:2 (2011), 156–78.
82. T. J. Vicino, *Suburban Crossroads: The Fight for Local Control of Immigration Policy*, Lanham, Md, 2012: Lexington Books, pp. 76, 88–90, 120.
83. Ibid., pp. 128–9.
84. Ibid., pp. 132–4.
85. Frey, *Diversity Explosion*, p. 37.
86. https://en.wikipedia.org/wiki/Arizona_SB_1070#Opinion_polls.

87. Ibid.
88. '2015 Immigration Report', National Conference of State Legislatures, 3 August 2015:http://www.ncsl.org/research/immigration/2015-immigration-report.aspx.
89. 'Senate immigration bill suffers crushing defeat', CNN, 28 June 2007.
90. DeParle, 'The anti-immigration crusader'.
91. Molly Ball, 'The unsung architect of Trumpism', *The Atlantic*, 20 March 2017.
92. C. Parker, 'The (real) reason why the house won't pass comprehensive immigration reform', Brookings, 4 August 2014; C. Parker, '2011 multi-state survey of race and politics': http://depts.washington.edu/uwiser/racepolitics_research2011.html.
93. V. Williamson, T. Skocpol and J. Coggin, 'The Tea Party and the remaking of Republican conservatism', *Perspectives on Politics* 9:1 (2011), pp. 32–3.
94. Parker, 'The (real) reason'.
95. Teitelbaum, 'Migration and conflict in OECD countries', pp. 187–8.
96. J. M. Box-Steffensmeier and S. De Boef, 'Macropartisanship and macroideology in the sophisticated electorate', *The Journal of Politics* 63:1 (2001), 232–48; A. I. Abramowitz and K. L. Saunders, 'Exploring the bases of partisanship in the American electorate: Social identity vs. ideology', *Political Research Quarterly* 59:2 (2006), 175–87; M. J. Hetherington and J. D. Weiler, *Authoritarianism and Polarization in American Politics*, Cambridge, 2009: Cambridge University Press.
97. D. J. Ahler and G. Sood, 'The parties in our heads: Misperceptions about party composition and their consequences', Working Paper (2016), University of California, Berkeley.
98. S. R. Lichter, Stanley Rothman and L. S. Lichter, *The Media Elite*, Bethesda, Md, 1986: Adler & Adler.
99. D. B. Hindman and K. Wiegand, 'The big three's prime-time decline: A technological and social context', *Journal of Broadcasting & Electronic Media* 52:1 (2008), 119–35.
100. S. DellaVigna and E. Kaplan, 'The Fox News effect: Media bias and voting', *Quarterly Journal of Economics* 122:3 (2007), 1187–234.
101. H. Gil de Zúñiga, T. Correa and S. Valenzuela, 'Selective exposure to cable news and immigration in the US: The relationship between FOX News, CNN, and attitudes toward Mexican immigrants', *Journal of Broadcasting & Electronic Media* 56:4 (2012), 597–615.
102. Ball, 'The unsung architect of Trumpism'.
103. 'Trump told Christie he didn't think he'd last past October 2015', CNN, 15 November 2016.
104. Ball, 'The unsung Architect of Trumpism'; Steve Bannon's *Wikipedia* page, accessed 25 July 2017.

105. Steve Benen, 'Both sides blame Trump in case about campaign-season violence', MSNBC, 17 April 2017.

106. Moira Weigel, 'Political correctness: How the right invented a phantom enemy', *Guardian*, 30 November 2016.

107. A. Case and A. Deaton, 'Mortality and morbidity in the 21st century', Brookings, 1 May 2017.

108. D. Kahneman, *Thinking, Fast and Slow*, New York, 2011: Farrar, Straus and Giroux.

109. N. Silver, 'Education, not income, predicted who would vote for Trump', *Five Thirty-Eight*, 22 November 2016; 'Brexit: voter turnout by age', *Financial Times*, 24 June 2016.

110. P. Surridge, 'Education and liberalism: Pursuing the link', *Oxford Review of Education* 42:2 (2016), 146–64; B. Lancee and O. Sarrasin, 'Educated preferences or selection effects? A longitudinal analysis of the impact of educational attainment on attitudes towards immigrants', *European Sociological Review* 31:4 (2015), 490–501.

111. 'Election 2016: Exit polls', *The New York Times*: https://www.nytimes.com/interactive/2016/11/08/us/politics/election-exit-polls.html.

112. D. Goodhart, *The Road to Somewhere: The Populist Revolt and the Future of Politics*, London, 2017: Hurst.

113. http://edition.cnn.com/election/results/exit-polls.

114. J. Hainmueller and D. J. Hopkins, 'Public attitudes toward immigration', *Annual Review of Political Science* 17 (2014), 225–49. While the authors accept that concern over economic effects on others could be driving opinion, my own experimental work suggests this is a minor factor compared to values.

115. C. Young, 'It's nativism: Explaining the drivers of Trump's popular support', Ipsos (2016).

116. Newton, 'Why some Latinos supported Proposition 187'.

117. 'New poll: Some Americans express troubling racial attitudes even as majority oppose white supremacists', *Sabato's Crystal Ball*, 14 September 2017.

118. D. J. Schildkraut, 'Defining American identity in the twenty-first century: How much "there" is there?', *Journal of Politics* 69:3 (2007), 605–7.

119. D. J. Hopkins, 'Politicized places: Explaining where and when immigrants provoke local opposition', *American Political Science Review* 104:1 (2010), 55.

120. E. D. Knowles and L. R. Tropp, 'Donald Trump and the rise of white identity in politics', *The Conversation*, 21 October 2016.

121. Kaufmann and Goodwin, 'Does diversity produce hostility?'

122. R. Alba, R. G. Rumbaut and K. Marotz, 'A distorted nation: Perceptions of racial/ethnic group sizes and attitudes toward immigrants and other minorities', *Social Forces* 84:2 (2005): 901–9.

123. Jardina, 'Demise of dominance', pp. 50–53, 70, 82.
124. M. A. Craig and J. A. Richeson, 'More diverse yet less tolerant? How the increasingly diverse racial landscape affects white Americans' racial attitudes', *Personality and Social Psychology Bulletin* 40:6 (2014), 691–9.
125. R. Willer, M. Feinberg and R. Wetts, 'Threats to racial status promote Tea Party support among white Americans', SSRN Working Paper, 4 May 2016: https://ssrn.com/abstract=2770186 or http://dx.doi.org/10.2139/ssrn.2770186.
126. Jardina, 'Demise of dominance', pp. 158–60.
127. 'Trump's Muslim ban comes into effect', *Al Jazeera*, 30 June 2017.
128. 'Donald Trump's travel ban heads back to the Supreme Court', *Economist*, 23 January 2018.
129. Alan Gomez, 'Immigration arrests up 38% nationwide under Trump', *USA Today*, 17 May 2017.
130. Kevin Drum, 'Southwest border apprehensions continue their big decline', *Mother Jones*, 19 August 2017.
131. Dara Lind, 'What Obama did with migrant families vs. what Trump is doing', Vox, 21 June 2018.
132. Ariel Edwards-Levy, 'More Americans blame undocumented parents than Trump for family separations', *Huffpost*, 22 June 2018.
133. Brendan O'Neill, 'This photo isn't what it seems – and that really matters', *Spiked*, 25 June 2018.
134. Rich Lowry, 'The truth about separating kids', *National Review*, 28 May 2018.
135. G. Hawley, *Making Sense of the Alt-Right*, New York, 2017: Columbia University Press; Cecile Alduy, 'What a 1973 French novel tells us about Marine Le Pen, Steve Bannon and the rise of the populist right', *Politico*, 23 April 2017.
136. Tom Newton Dunn, 'Migrants "harm UK": Donald Trump says Britain is "losing its culture" because of immigration', *Sun*, 12 July 2018.

4. Britain

1. A majority of Scots voted Remain, many for nationalist reasons. They view Europe as a club which can reduce Scotland's dependence on the United Kingdom. But 90 per cent of the UK's population resides in England and Wales.
2. Chris Hanretty, 'The EU referendum: How did Westminster constituencies vote?', *Medium*, 29 June 2016.
3. ONS LS 2011: http://webarchive.nationalarchives.gov.uk/20160105160709/http://www.ons.gov.uk/ons/dcp171776_369571.pdf.
4. P. Morland, *The Human Tide* (forthcoming).

5. M. J. Mitchell, *New Perspectives on the Irish in Scotland*, Edinburgh, 2008: John Donald.

6. B. Gratton, 'Demography and immigration restriction in United States history', in J. A. Goldstone, E. Kaufmann and M. Duffy Toft, *Political Demography: How Population Changes are Reshaping International Security and National Politics*, Boulder, Colo., 2012: Paradigm, pp. 159–75.

7. Figures from Migration Watch UK.

8. D. Goodhart, *The British Dream: Successes and Failures of post-War Immigration*, London, 2013: Atlantic, p. 140.

9. E. Bleich, *Race Politics in Britain and France: Ideas and Policymaking since the 1960s*, Cambridge and New York, 2003: Cambridge University Press, pp. 44–7.

10. 'Charles de Gaulle on Algerian independence': https://berkleycenter.georgetown.edu/quotes/charles-de-gaulle-on-algerian-independence.

11. R. Hansen, *Citizenship and Immigration in Post-War Britain*, Oxford and New York, 2000: Oxford University Press, pp. 83, 191.

12. L. McLaren and M. Johnson, 'Resources, group conflict and symbols: Explaining anti-immigration hostility in Britain', *Political Studies* 55:4 (2007), 709–32.

13. Hansen, *Citizenship and Immigration in Post-War Britain*.

14. E. West, *The Diversity Illusion: What We Got Wrong about Immigration and How to Set It Right*, London, 2013: Gibson Square, p. 14.

15. 'Hague fuels asylum row', BBC News, 30 April 2000.

16. K. Kumar, *The Making of English National Identity*, Cambridge, 2003: Cambridge University Press; A. Roshwald, *The Endurance of Nationalism*, Cambridge, 2006: Cambridge University Press.

17. D. Leal, J. Hagan and N. Rodriguez, 'Religion, migration and nationalism', paper presented at the Association for the Study of Ethnicity and Nationalism (ASEN) conference, London, 2016.

18. YouGov survey, 5–6 February 2018.

19. G. H. Mead, *Mind, Self and Society*, Chicago, 1934: University of Chicago Press.

20. 'Cracking up: Immigration and the polarization of nations', plenary talk at the ASEN conference, London, 2016.

21. D. Goodhart, *The Road to Somewhere: The Populist Revolt and the Future of Politics*, London, 2017: Hurst.

22. BBC/YouGov Englishness survey, 9–26 March 2018. See https://www.bbc.co.uk/news/uk-england-44142843.

23. Sophie Gaston and Sacha Hilhorst, 'At home in one's past: Nostalgia as a cultural and political force in Britain, France and Germany', Demos, May 2018.

24. T. Modood, 'Multicultural nationalism', at the *Symposium on National Identity and Diversity*, King's College, London, 17 March 2017.

25. T. Modood, *Multiculturalism*, Cambridge, 2013: Polity Press.
26. Tom Baldwin and Gabriel Rozenberg, 'Britain "must scrap multicultural-ism"', *The Times*, 3 April 2004.
27. P. Jenkins, *God's Continent: Christianity, Islam, and Europe's Religious Crisis*, Oxford and New York, 2007: Oxford University Press, p. 221.
28. J. Kawalerowicz and M. Biggs, 'Anarchy in the UK: Economic deprivation, social disorganization, and political grievances in the London riot of 2011', *Social Forces* 94:2 (2015), 673–98.
29. R. Brubaker, 'The return of assimilation? Changing perspectives on immigration and its sequels in France, Germany and the United States', *Ethnic and Racial Studies* 24:4 (2001), 531–48.
30. 'Britain Rediscovered: Roundtable on Britishness with Gordon Brown', *Prospect*, no. 109 (April 2005).
31. Gordon Brown, 'The future of Britishness', speech to Fabian Society, 14 January 2006.
32. Ibid.
33. http://www.bbc.co.uk/news/world-europe-11559451.
34. 'Nicolas Sarkozy declares multiculturalism had failed', *Telegraph*, 11 February 2011.
35. Modood, *Multiculturalism*.
36. David Willetts, quoted in 'Diversity versus solidarity', RSA/*Prospect* round-table debate, 28 January 2003, p. 1.
37. M. Lind, *The Next American Nation*, New York, 1995: Free Press.
38. Trevor Phillips, 'Genteel xenophobia is as bad as any other kind', *Guardian*, 16 February 2004.
39. Nicholas Watt and Patrick Wintour, 'How immigration came to haunt Labour: The inside story', *Guardian*, 24 March 2015.
40. S. Jivraj, 'How has ethnic diversity grown 1991–2001–2011?' Centre on Dynamics of Ethnicity (CoDE), University of Manchester, December 2012.
41. S. Hix, E. Kaufmann and T. J. Leeper, 'UK voters, including Leavers, care more about reducing non-EU than EU migration', LSE EUROPP [European Politics and Policy] blog, 30 May 2017.
42. 'What do Europeans think about Muslim immigration?', Chatham House, 7 February 2017.
43. E. Kaufmann and M. J. Goodwin, 'Does diversity produce hostility? A meta-analysis', *Social Science Research*, accepted 15 July 2018.
44. E. Kaufmann, 'Levels or changes? Ethnic context, immigration and the UK Independence Party vote', *Electoral Studies* 48 (August 2017), 57–69.
45. Seumas Milne and David Gow, 'Ford president signs pact to end Dagenham racism', *Guardian*, 26 October 1999.
46. T. C. Schelling, *Models of Segregation*, Santa Monica, Calif., 1969: Rand Corp.

47. E. Havekes, M. Bader and M. Krysan, 'Realizing racial and ethnic neighborhood preferences? Exploring the mismatches between what people want, where they search, and where they live', *Population Research and Policy Review* 35:1 (2016), 101–26.

48. J. Gest, *The New Minority: White Working Class Politics in an Age of Immigration and Inequality*, New York, 2016: Oxford University Press.

49. Meeting with Margaret Hodge, London, 26 July 2017.

50. Gest, *The New Minority*.

51. R. Ford and M. J. Goodwin, 'Angry white men: Individual and contextual predictors of support for the British National Party', *Political Studies* 58:1 (2010), 11.

52. J. Rydgren and P. Ruth, 'Contextual explanations of radical right-wing support in Sweden: Socioeconomic marginalisation , group threat, and the halo effect', *Ethnic and Racial Studies* 36:4 (2013), 711–28.

53. G. Harris, 'The rise and fall of the British National Party: The demand for extreme right politics in the UK', unpublished PhD dissertation, Department of Politics, Birkbeck College, University of London, 2012.

54. D. Kahneman, *Thinking, Fast and Slow*, New York, 2011: Farrar, Straus and Giroux.

55. E. Ivarsflaten, *Reputational Shields: Why Most Anti-Immigrant Parties Failed in Western Europe, 1980–2005*, Annual Meeting of the American Political Science Association, Philadelphia, 2006.

56. S. Blinder, R. Ford and E. Ivarsflaten, 'The better angels of our nature: How the antiprejudice norm affects policy and party preferences in Great Britain and Germany', *American Journal of Political Science* 57:4 (2013), 841–57.

57. R. Ford and M. Goodwin, *Revolt on the Right: Explaining Support for the Radical Right in Britain*, London, Routledge, p. 199.

58. Blinder et al., 'The better angels of our nature'.

59. T. Bale, *The Conservative Party: From Thatcher to Cameron*, Cambridge and Malden, Mass., 2016: Polity Press.

60. G. Evans, 'European integration, party politics and voting in the 2001 election', *Journal of Elections, Public Opinion and Parties* 12 (2002), 95–110.

61. Ford and Goodwin, *Revolt on the Right*, p. 73.

62. Gaby Hinsliff, 'It feels like the BNP, only in blazers', *Observer*, 30 May 2004.

63. G. Evans and K. Chzhen, 'Explaining voters' defection from Labour over the 2005–10 electoral cycle: Leadership, economics and the rising importance of immigration', *Political Studies* 61:S1 (2013), 138–57.

64. Ford and Goodwin, *Revolt on the Right*, p. 174.

65. G. Evans and J. Tilley, *The New Politics of Class: The Political Exclusion of the British Working Class*, Oxford, 2017: Oxford University Press, pp. 150, 195.

66. Ibid., pp. 174–4, 186.
67. Rosa Prince, 'David Cameron: net immigration will be capped at tens of thousands', *Telegraph*, 10 January 2010.
68. Ford and Goodwin, *Revolt on the Right*, p. 279.
69. Hix, Kaufmann and Leeper, 'UK voters, including Leavers, care more about reducing non-EU than EU migration'.
70. Ibid.
71. West, *The Diversity Illusion*, p. 230.
72. Hix, Kaufmann and Leeper, 'UK voters, including Leavers, care more about reducing non-EU than EU migration'.
73. Kaufmann, 'Levels or changes?'.
74. G. Evans and J. Mellon, 'How immigration became a Eurosceptic issue', LSE Brexit blog, 5 January 2016.
75. Ford and Goodwin, *Revolt on the Right*, p. 198; H. D. Clarke, M. Goodwin and P. Whiteley, *Brexit: Why Britain Voted to Leave the European Union*, Cambridge, 2017: Cambridge University Press, pp. 88–9.
76. Ibid., p. 88.
77. P. Kellner, 'Labour's lost votes', *Prospect*, no. 200 (November 2012).
78. M. J. Goodwin and C. Milazzo, *UKIP: Inside the Campaign to Redraw the Map of British Politics*, Oxford, 2017: Oxford University Press.
79. Matthew Holehouse, 'Nigel Farage puts ethnic minority Ukip candidates centre stage in bid to kill racism row', *Telegraph*, 8 May 2014.
80. Clarke, Goodwin and Whiteley, *Brexit*, p. 89.
81. Ipsos MORI Political Monitor, 'Attitudes to immigration', based on survey of 1,000 British adults, 8–12 March 2014.
82. Timothy Kennett, 'Why we should be worried about Ukip becoming more politically correct', *Independent*, 15 October 2014.
83. Lord Ashcroft, 'They're thinking what we're thinking: understanding the UKIP temptation', Lord Ashcroft Polls, 2012.
84. R. Mann and S. Fenton, *Nation, Class and Resentment: The Politics of National Identity in England, Scotland and Wales*, London, 2017: Palgrave Macmillan, pp. 86, 91.
85. M. Skey, *National Belonging and Everyday Life*, Basingstoke, 2011: Palgrave Macmillan, pp. 86, 107.
86. Rowena Mason, 'Emily Thornberry resigns from shadow cabinet over Rochester tweet', *Guardian*, 20 November 2014.
87. E. Kaufmann, 'The shy English nationalists who won it for the Tories and flummoxed the pollsters', LSE British Politics and Policy blog, 12 May 2005.
88. 'David Cameron promises in/out referendum on EU', BBC News, 23 January 2013.
89. M. J. Goodwin and O. Heath, 'The 2016 referendum, Brexit and the left behind: An aggregate-level analysis of the result', *Political Quarterly* 87:3 (2016), 323–32.

90. L. Hooghe and G. Marks, 'Calculation, community and cues: Public opinion on European integration', *European Union Politics* 6:4 (2005), 419–43.

91. Clarke, Goodwin and Whiteley, *Brexit*, p. 65. Surveys may have oversampled pro-EU voters somewhat, but the trend still stands.

92. 'Nigel Farage's anti-migrant poster reported to police', *Guardian*, 16 June 2016.

93. Clarke, Goodwin and Whiteley, *Brexit*, pp. 28–9.

94. Ibid., pp. 162–3.

95. E. Kaufmann, 'Trump and Brexit: Why it's again NOT the economy, stupid', LSE British Politics and Policy blog, 9 November 2016.

96. N. Silver, 'Education, not income, predicted who would vote for Trump', *Five Thirty-Eight*, 22 November (2016); John Burn-Murdoch, 'Brexit: Voter turnout by age', *Financial Times*, 24 June 2016.

97. B. Lancee and O. Sarrasin, 'Educated preferences or selection effects? A longitudinal analysis of the impact of educational attainment on attitudes towards immigrants', *European Sociological Review* 31:4 (2015), 490–501.

98. D. Goodhart, *The Road to Somewhere: The Populist Revolt and the Future of Politics*, London, 2017: Hurst.

99. S. Feldman and K. Stenner, 'Perceived threat and authoritarianism', *Political Psychology* 18:4 (1997), 741–70.

100. J. R. Alford, C. L. Funk and J. R. Hibbing, 'Are political orientations genetically transmitted?' *American Political Science Review* 99:2 (2005), 153–67.

101. K. Swales, presentation at the conference on 'Understanding Society's EU Referendum Project', University of Essex, 28 June 2017.

102. Clarke, Goodwin and Whiteley, *Brexit*, p. 32.

103. Ibid., p. 164.

104. Eric Kaufmann, 'Can narratives of white identity reduce opposition to immigration and support for Hard Brexit? A survey experiment', *Political Studies*, published online 18 November 2017.

105. Goodhart, *The Road to Somewhere*.

106. Kaufmann, 'Can narratives of white identity reduce opposition?'

107. S. Katwala, J. Rutter and S. Ballinger, 'Time to get it right: Finding consensus on Britain's future immigration policy', London, 2017: British Future . . .

108. J. Hainmueller and D. J. Hopkins, 'The hidden American immigration consensus: A conjoint analysis of attitudes toward immigrants', *American Journal of Political Science* 59:3 (2015), 529–48; N. A. Valentino et al., 'Economic and cultural drivers of immigrant support worldwide', *British Journal of Political Science*, published online 1 November 2017, 1–26.

109. E. Kaufmann, 'Why culture is more important than skills: Understanding British public opinion on immigration', LSE British Politics and Policy blog, 30 January 2018.

110. Lord Ashcroft, 'How the United Kingdom voted on Thursday . . . and why', Lord Ashcroft Polls, 4 June 2016; Lord Ashcroft, 'How did this result happen? My post-vote survey', Lord Ashcroft Polls, 9 June 2017.

111. R. Duffy and T. Frere-Smith, 'Perception and reality: 10 things we should know about attitudes to immigration in the UK', January 2014, Ipsos MORI, p. 17.

112. M. T. Grasso et al., 'Thatcher's children, Blair's babies, political socialization and trickle-down value change: An age, period and cohort analysis', *British Journal of Political Science*, published online 26 January 2017, pp. 1–20.

113. A. Gallego, F. Buscha, P. Sturgis and D. Oberski, 'Places and preferences: A longitudinal analysis of self-selection and contextual effects', *British Journal of Political Science* 46:3 (2016), 529–50.

114. Duffy and Frere-Smith, 'Perception and reality', p. 18.

115. Roger Daltrey, 'I will never forgive Labour for their immigration policies', *Telegraph*, 17 November 2013.

116. I am indebted to Nick Wright of Luntz Polling for sharing these results.

117. Ashcroft, 'How did this result happen?'

118. Glen Owen, 'Nigel Farage could return to frontline politics with "Ukip 2.0" if scandal-hit party leader is ousted', *Mail Online*, 20 January 2018.

5. The Rise and Rise of the Populist Right in Europe

1. 'Austria elects Green candidate as president in narrow defeat for far right', *Guardian*, 23 May 2016.

2. Tracy McNicoll, 'French election history: Jean-Marie Le Pen's "thunderclap" shocker 15 years on', *France 24*, 21 April 2017.

3. T. Bale, 'Cinderella and her ugly sisters: The mainstream and extreme right in Europe's bipolarising party systems', *West European Politics* 26:3 (2003), 67–90.

4. S. Blinder, R. Ford and E. Ivarsflaten, 'The better angels of our nature: How the antiprejudice norm affects policy and party preferences in Great Britain and Germany', *American Journal of Political Science* 57:4 (2013), 841–57.

5. C. Mudde, *Populist Radical Right Parties in Europe*, Cambridge and New York, 2007: Cambridge University Press, pp. 132–3.

6. J. Veugelers, 'Ex-colonials, voluntary associations, and electoral support for the contemporary far right', *Comparative European Politics* 3:4 (2005), 408–31.

7. D. Horowitz, *Ethnic Groups in Conflict*, Berkeley, Calif., 1985: University of California Press.

8. E. Kaufmann, 'Ethnic nationalism or relaxed assimilation? The response of English "Sons of the Soil" to immigration', in I. Cote and M. Mitchell, *Sons of the Soil* (Routledge, forthcoming).

9. M. and T. B. Hewitson (eds.), *Nationalism in Europe 1789–1914: Civic and Ethnic Traditions*, Oxford, 2004: Oxford University Press, p. 328.

10. Ibid., pp. 71–4, 115–16.

11. O. Zimmer, *Remaking the Rhythms of Life: German Communities in the Age of the Nation State*, Oxford, 2013: Oxford University Press.

12. D. McDonnell, 'The Lega Nord: The new saviour of Northern Italy', in N. Marzouki, D. McDonnell and O. Roy (eds.), *Saving the People*, London, 2016: Hurst and Co., pp. 13–28.

13. P. Morland, *The Human Tide* (forthcoming).

14. A. Wimmer, *Nationalist Exclusion and Ethnic Conflict: Shadows of Modernity*, Cambridge, 2002: Cambridge University Press, pp. 258–9.

15. R. Inglehart, *Culture Shift in Advanced Industrial Society*, Princeton, NJ, 1990: Princeton University Press.

16. R. D. Putnam, *Bowling Alone: The Collapse and Revival of American Community*, New York, 2000: Simon & Schuster.

17. J. Haidt, *The Happiness Hypothesis: Finding Modern Truth in Ancient Wisdom*, New York, 2006: Basic Books.

18. K. Arzheimer, '15 electoral sociology – who votes for the Extreme Right and why – and when?', in C. Mudde (ed.), *The Populist Radical Right: A Reader*, London and New York, 2016: Routledge, Taylor and Francis.

19. M. Lubbers, M. Gijsberts and P. Scheepers, 'Extreme right-wing voting in Western Europe', *European Journal of Political Research* 41:3 (2002), 345–78.

20. G. Lucassen and M. Lubbers, 'Who fears what? Explaining far-right-wing preference in Europe by distinguishing perceived cultural and economic ethnic threats', *Comparative Political Studies* 45:5 (2012), 547–74.

21. E. Kaufmann and M. J. Goodwin, 'Does diversity produce hostility? A meta-analysis', *Social Science Research*, accepted 15 July 2018.

22. P. M. Sniderman, L. Hagendoorn and M. Prior, 'Predisposing factors and situational triggers: Exclusionary reactions to immigrant minorities', *American Political Science Review* 98:1 (2004), 44

23. H. Kohn, 'Western and Eastern nationalisms', in J. Hutchinson and A. D. Smith (eds.), *Nationalism*, Oxford, 1994: Oxford University Press, p. 165; R. Brubaker, *Citizenship and Nationhood in France and Germany*, Cambridge, Mass., and London, 1992: Harvard University Press.

24. Inglehart, *Culture Shift*.

25. L. S. Davis and S. S. Deole, 'Immigration, attitudes and the rise of the political right: The role of cultural and economic concerns over immigration', CESifo Working Paper no. 5680, Center for Economic Studies and Ifo

Institute, Munich, December 2015; T. J. Hatton, 'Immigration, public opinion and the recession in Europe', *Economic Policy* 31:86 (2016), 205–46.

26. Private correspondence with Simon Hix of the London School of
Economics.

27. A. E. Kessler and G. P. Freeman, 'Public opinion in the EU on immigration
from outside the Community', *Journal of Common Market Studies* 43:4
(2005), 825–50.

28. E. Kaufmann, *Shall the Religious Inherit the Earth? Demography and Politics in the Twenty-First Century*, London, 2010: Profile Books, p. 172

29. M. Fertig and M. Kahanec, 'Projections of potential flows to the enlarging
EU from Ukraine, Croatia and other eastern neighbors', published online
December 2015, p. 6.

30. Gilles Kepel, *The War for Muslim Minds: Islam and the West*, Cambridge,
Mass., 2004: Belknap Press of Harvard University Press, p. 255.

31. P. Jenkins, *God's Continent: Christianity, Islam, and Europe's Religious
Crisis*, Oxford and New York, 2007: Oxford University Press, pp. 240–45.

32. 'Ministers lose religious bill bid', *BBC*, 1 February 2006.

33. Leila Hadj-Abdou, 'The "religious conversion" of the Austrian Freedom
Party', in Marzouki et al. (eds.), *Saving the People*, pp. 36–7.

34. Sniderman et al., 'Predisposing factors and situational triggers', p. 45.

35. Sasha Polakow-Suransky, *Go Back to Where You Came From: The Backlash against Immigration and the Fate of Western Democracy*, London,
2017: Hurst and Co., pp. 31–2.

36. Gregory Crouch, 'Dutch immigration kit offers a revealing view', *The New
York Times*, 16 March 2006.

37. J. K. Puar, *Terrorist Assemblages: Homonationalism in Queer Times*, Dur-
ham, NC, 2007: Duke University Press.

38. J. Lester Feder and Pierre Buet, 'How France's Nationalist Party is winning
gay support', *Buzzfeed*, 2 February 2017.

39. O. Roy, 'The French National Front: From Christian identity to *laïcité*', in
Marzouki et al. (eds.), *Saving the People*, p. 90.

40. Gianluca Mezzofiore, 'France's National Front: Rise in Jews voting for
Marine Le Pen – survey', *International Business Times*, 15 September 2014.

41. 'France's Le Pen to propose new name for National Front', *Reuters*, 11 February 2018.

42. E. Ivarsflaten, S. Blinder and R. Ford, 'The anti-racism norm in Western
European immigration politics: Why we need to consider it and how to
measure it', *Journal of Elections, Public Opinion and Parties* 20:4 (2010),
421–45.

43. E. Ivarsflaten, 'Reputational shields: Why most anti-immigrant parties
failed in Western Europe, 1980–2005', paper presented at the annual meeting of the American Political Science Association, Philadelphia, 2006.

44. E. Harteveld and E. Ivarsflaten, 'Why women avoid the radical right: Internalized norms and party reputations', *British Journal of Political Science* 48:2 (2018), 369–84.

45. D. Murray, *The Strange Death of Europe: Immigration, Identity, Islam*, Bloomsbury: 2017, pp. 80–81.

46. Polakow-Suransky, *Go Back to Where You Came From*, p. 109.

47. P. Collier, *Exodus: How Migration is Changing Our World*, New York, 2013: Oxford University Press.

48. 'Number of potential migrants worldwide tops 700 million', *Gallup News*, 8 June 2017.

49. M. A. Clemens, 'Does development reduce migration?', in R. E. B. Lucas (ed.), *International Handbook on Migration and Economic Development*, Cheltenham and Northampton, Mass., 2014: Edward Elgar, pp. 152–85.

50. L. M. Mbaye, '"Barcelona or die": understanding illegal migration from Senegal', *IZA Journal of Migration* 3:1 (2014), 1–21.

51. Ben Quinn, 'Migrant death toll passes 5,000 after two boats capsize off Italy', *Guardian*, 23 December 2016.

52. Fertig and Kahanec, 'Projections of potential flows to the enlarging EU', p. 6.

53. D. S. Massey and K. A. Pren, 'Unintended consequences of US immigration policy: Explaining the post-1965 surge from Latin America', *Population and Development Review* 38:1 (2012), 1–29.

54. B. Gratton and E. K. Merchant, 'An immigrant's tale: The Mexican American southwest 1850 to 1950', *Social Science History* 39:4 (2015), 521–50.

55. Murray, *Strange Death of Europe*, p. 81.

56. 'European leaders in talks on creating asylum centre outside EU', *Reuters*, 5 June 2018.

57. 'EU leaders clinch migration deal in marathon summit', *Politico*, 28 June 2018.

58. P. Collier and A. Betts, *Refuge: Rethinking Refugee Policy in a Changing World*, New York, 2017: Oxford University Press.

59. 'European governments return nearly 10,000 Afghans to risk of death and torture', Amnesty International, 5 October 2017.

60. J. Hollifield, P. L. Martin and P. M. Orrenius, 'The dilemmas of immigration control', in W. A. Cornelius, P. L. Martin and P. M. Orrenius (eds.), *Controlling Immigration: A Global Perspective*, 3rd edn, Stanford, Calif., 2014: Stanford University Press, pp. 8–9.

61. C. Joppke, 'Why liberal states accept unwanted immigration', *World Politics* 50:2 (1998), 266–93.

62. Alexander Betts, 'How to fix the refugee crisis', *Prospect*, no. 254 (May 2017).

63. Tweet can be found @MarianaSeMendes.

64. R. Duffy and T. Frere-Smith, 'Perception and reality: 10 things we should know about attitudes to immigration in the UK', January 2014, Ipsos MORI, p. 17; H. G. Boomgaarden and R. Vliegenthart, 'How news content influences anti-immigration attitudes: Germany, 1993–2005', *European Journal of Political Research* 48:4 (2009), 516–42; L. Morales, J.-B. Pilet and D. Ruedin, 'The gap between public preferences and policies on immigration: A comparative examination of the effect of politicisation on policy congruence', *Journal of Ethnic and Migration Studies* 41:9 (2015), 1495–516; J. Dennison, A. Geddes and T. Talò, 'The Dutch aren't turning against immigration – the salience of the immigration issue is what drives Wilders' support', LSE EUROPP [European Politics and Policy] blog, 3 March 2017.

65. 'Perils of Perception 2015' survey, Ipsos MORI, published online 2 December 2015.

66. Dennison et al., 'The Dutch aren't turning against immigration'.

67. J. Dennison et al., 'Explaining the rise of anti-immigration parties in Western Europe', Working Paper, shared privately by author, 1 January 2018.

68. Nick Gutteridge, 'The Great Wall of Europe: Hungary splits continent in two with huge fence to stop migrants', *Express*, 29 February 2016.

69. 'Migrant crisis: More EU states impose border checks', *BBC*, 14 September 2015.

70. Murray, *Strange Death of Europe*, p. 230.

71. R. Brubaker, 'Between nationalism and civilizationism: The European populist moment in comparative perspective', *Ethnic and Racial Studies* 40:8 (2017), 1191–226.

72. Janosh Delcker, 'Viktor Orbán, Bavaria's hardline hero', *Politico*, 23 September 2015.

73. J. Hoerner and S. Hobolt, 'The AfD succeeded in the German election by mobilising non-voters on the right', LSE EUROPP [European Politics and Policy] blog, 29 September 2017.

74. Stefan Wagstyl, 'Refugee crisis helps put Germany's FDP back in the political game', *Financial Times*, 7 June 2016.

75. Philip Oltermann, 'German coalition talks collapse after deadlock on migration and energy', *Guardian*, 20 November 2017.

76. L. M. McLaren, 'The cultural divide in Europe: Migration, multiculturalism, and political trust', *World Politics* 64:2 (2012), 199–241.

77. K. Stenner, *The Authoritarian Dynamic*, Cambridge, 2005: Cambridge University Press.

78. Rick Noack, '2,000 men "sexually assaulted 1,200 women" at Cologne New Year's Eve party', *Independent*, 11 July 2016.

79. Polakow-Suransky, *Go Back to Where You Came From*, p. 121.

80. Ibid., pp. 2–3

81. M. Sobolewska, R. Ford and P. Sniderman, 'Democratic resilience: How some individuals resist the threat of terrorism and maintain their core values of tolerance', paper presented at the 'Elections, Public Opinion and Parties' (ePop) conference, University of Kent, UK, 10 September 2016.

82. P. English, M. Cinalli and S. Van Hauwaert, 'The limits of desire: Policy making and public opinion toward the Integration of Muslims in the United Kingdom and France', paper presented at the ePoP conference, University of Kent, UK, 10 September 2016.

83. W. de Koster, P. Achterberg and J. van der Waal, 'The new right and the welfare state: The electoral relevance of welfare chauvinism and welfare populism in the Netherlands', *International Political Science Review* 34:1 (2013), 3–20.

84. V. Skirbekk et al., 'The future of the global muslim population: Europe', Pew Research Center, 27 January 2011.

85. Morales et al., 'The gap between public preferences and policies on immigration'.

86. Y. R. Velez and H. Lavine, 'Racial diversity and the dynamics of authoritarianism', *The Journal of Politics* 79:2 (2017), 519–33.

87. K. Manevska and P. Achterberg, 'Immigration and perceived ethnic threat: Cultural capital and economic explanations', *European Sociological Review* 29:3 (2011), 437–49; J. Karreth, S. P. Singh and S. M. Stojek, 'Explaining attitudes toward immigration: The role of regional context and individual predispositions', *West European Politics* 38:6 (2015), 1174–202.

88. R. Inglehart and P. Norris, 'Trump, Brexit, and the rise of populism: Economic have-nots and cultural backlash', HKS Working Paper No. RWP16-026, 2016.

89. Almost all non-blacks vote for the Democratic Alliance (DA), though black South Africans largely divide their votes between the African National Congress (ANC), Inkatha Freedom Party (IFP) and Economic Freedom Fighters (EFF).

90. J. Downes, 'The 2008–2013 economic crisis in Europe: Extreme right-wing and center right party competition on the salience of immigration', PhD dissertation, University of Kent, 2016.

91. T. Bale et al., 'If you can't beat them, join them? Explaining social democratic responses to the challenge from the populist radical right in Western Europe', *Political Studies* 58:3 (2010), 410–26.

92. Jamey Keaten, 'Sarkozy: Burqas are "not welcome" in France', *Huffington Post*, 22 June 2009.

93. Bale et al., 'If you can't beat them, join them?'

94. S. B. Hobolt, and R. Klemmensen, 'The dynamics of issue diversity in party rhetoric', Working Paper: http://citeseerx.ist.psu.edu/viewdoc/download?doi=10.1.1.542.6668&rep=rep1&type=pdf (2008).

95. Pauline Bock, 'On immigration, Macron's words draw borders', *New Statesman*, 11 August 2017.

96. Shellie Karabell, 'French elections part II: Macron victory trumps far right in Europe', *Forbes*, 7 May 2017.

97. Will Kirby, 'Macron's Europe ULTIMATUM: French president ORDERS EU to support his reforms ... or CRUMBLE', *Express*, 25 August 2017.

98. Kaufmann, *Shall the Religious Inherit the Earth?*, p. 169.

99. C. Caldwell, *Reflections on the Revolution in Europe: Immigration, Islam, and the West*, New York, 2009: Doubleday, pp. 24–5.

100. '18 prozent der Deutschen würden Sarrazin wählen', *Berliner Morgenpost*, 6 September 2010.

101. Polakow-Suransky, *Go Back to Where You Came From*, pp. 289–91.

102. P. Bruckner, *The Tyranny of Guilt: An Essay on Western Masochism*, Princeton, NJ, 2012: Princeton University Press.

103. David Frum, 'The roots of a counterproductive immigration policy', *The Atlantic*, 28 January 2017.

104. R. Jackson et al., *The Graying of the Great Powers: Demography and Geopolitics in the 21st Century*, Washington, DC, 2008: Center for Strategic and International Studies.

6. Canadian Exceptionalism

1. R. Gibson, I. McAllister and T. Swenson, 'The politics of race and immigration in Australia: One Nation voting in the 1998 election', *Ethnic and Racial Studies* 25:5 (2002), 823–44.

2. Ben Raue, 'Rise of One Nation thickens the plot in Queensland election', *Guardian*, 11 November 2017.

3. 'Top 10 countries for Australian migration in April 2017', *Registered Migration Australia*, 14 June 2017.

4. 'Cultural diversity in Australia', Australian Bureau of Statistics, 2016.

5. 'The newcomers: how many and from where', *ENZ.org*, accessed 1 December 2017.

6. Aboriginal groups can also be added to the white share to give a sense of the size of the established majority because they are indigenous and many have mixed with the white population. The aboriginal population is largest in New Zealand, with 18 per cent claiming some Maori ancestry, and forms about 4 per cent of the total in Canada and 1 per cent in Australia and the United States.

7. US Census Bureau, with Canadian figures approximated from P. Dion et al., 'Long-term contribution of immigration to population renewal in

Canada: A simulation', *Population and Development Review* 41:1 (2015), 109–26. No projections available for Australia.

8. Alexis de Tocqueville, *Democracy in America*, London, 1994: David Campbell. First published in French in 1835.

9. A. M. Ceobanu and X. Escandell, 'Comparative analyses of public attitudes toward immigrants and immigration using multinational survey data: A review of theories and research', *Annual Review of Sociology* 36 (2010), 309–28.

10. J. Citrin and J. Sides, 'Immigration and the imagined community in Europe and the United States', *Political Studies* 56 (2008), 33–56.

11. MTurk/Prolific data, November 2017. Limited to white respondents. N = 243 (152 USA, 72 Canada, 49 UK).

12. Reuters Polling Explorer, accessed 12 December 2017.

13. W. Zelinsky, *The Cultural Geography of the United States*, Englewood Cliffs, NJ, 1973: Prentice-Hall, p. 10.

14. Citrin and Sides, 'Immigration and the imagined community'.

15. Simon Romero and Daniel Politi, 'Argentina's Trump-like immigration order rattles South America', *The New York Times*, 4 February 2017.

16. E. Kaufmann, 'The decline of the WASP in the United States and Canada', in E. Kaufmann (ed.) *Rethinking Ethnicity: Majority Groups and Dominant Minorities*, London, 2004: Routledge, p. 76.

17. A. B. Anderson and J. S. Frideres, *Ethnicity in Canada: Theoretical Perspectives*, Toronto, 1981: Butterworth and Co., p. 277.

18. Kaufmann, 'The decline of the WASP in the United States and Canada', pp. 72–3.

19. H. E. Palmer, *Immigration and the Rise of Multiculturalism*, Toronto, 1975: Copp Clark, p. 119.

20. M. A. Schwartz, *Public Opinion and Canadian Identity*, Berkeley, Calif., 1967: University of California Press, p. 119.

21. *Report of the Grand Lodge of British America*, 22 June 1955, p. 14.

22. J. Errington, *The Lion, the Eagle and Upper Canada: A Developing Colonial Ideology*, Kingston, Ont., and Montreal, 1987: McGill–Queen's University.

23. D. J. Cheal, 'Ontario loyalism: A socio-religious ideology in decline', *Canadian Ethnic Studies* 13:2 (1981), 40–51.

24. D. Duffy, *Gardens, Covenants, Exiles: Loyalism in the Literature of Upper Canada/Ontario*, Toronto, 1982: University of Toronto Press, p. 119.

25. N. Tienhaara, *Canadian Views on Immigration and Population: An Analysis of Post-War Gallup Polls*, Ottawa, 1974: Manpower and Immigration Canada.

26. F. Underhill, in Peter Russell (ed.), *Nationalism in Canada*, Toronto and New York, 1966: McGraw-Hill, p. xvii.

27. K. McRoberts, *Misconceiving Canada: The Struggle for National Unity*, Toronto, 1997: Oxford University Press.

28. Jessica Smith Cross, 'Forty-one per cent say "too many" minorities immigrating to Canada: survey', *Toronto Metro*, 13 March 2015.

29. *Canadian Election Study 2011*: https://ces-eec.arts.ubc.ca/english-section/surveys/; Reuters Polling Explorer (US): http://polling.reuters.com; *Mapping Social Cohesion: The Scanlon Foundation Surveys 2017* (Monash University): https://www.monash.edu/__data/assets/pdf_file/0009/1189188/mapping-social-cohesion-national-report-2017.pdf; 'Most important problems facing New Zealand in 2017', Roy Morgan, published online 27 February 2017.

30. J. Gordon and S. Jeram, 'Friendly Canada? Explaining the absence of a Canadian anti-immigration party', paper presented at American Political Science Association, San Francisco, 1 September 2017.

31. Martin Collacott, 'Opinion: Canada replacing its population a case of wilful ignorance, greed, excess political correctness', *Vancouver Sun*, 22 June 2017; on the right of the political spectrum, see Faith Goldy, 'Canada: identity vs values', *YouTube*, 25 November 2017.

32. Mike Medeiros, 'The populism risk in English Canada', Policy Options, 8 January 2018.

33. Ishmael Daro, 'David Suzuki says Canada is "full" and calls country's immigration policy "crazy"', Canada.com, 11 July 2013.

34. Doug Todd, 'There's nothing racist about Metro Vancouver housing study', *Vancouver Sun*, 15 November 2015; 'Justin Fung: An open letter to those who play the race card in the Vancouver housing affordability debate', *Georgia Straight*, 11 July 2016.

35. Matty Meuse, '9 in 10 Vancouverites support foreign home-buyers' tax, poll finds', CBC, 29 July 2016.

36. Ujjal Dosanjh, 'The silencing of the white men of the West!', Ujjaldosanjh. org, 2 January 2016.

37. D. M. Rayside, *On the Fringe: Gays and Lesbians in Politics*, Ithaca, NY, 1998: Cornell University Press, p. 129.

38. E. Ambrose and C. Mudde, 'Canadian multiculturalism and the absence of the far right', *Nationalism and Ethnic Politics* 21:2 (2015), 229.

39. C. Berger, *The Writing of Canadian History: Aspects of English-Canadian Historical Writing, 1900–1970*, Toronto, 1976: Oxford University Press, pp. 130–36.

40. Personal correspondence and C. Breton, 'Making national identity salient: Impact on attitudes toward immigration and multiculturalism', *Canadian Journal of Political Science/Revue canadienne de science politique* 48:2 (2015), 357–81.

41. E. C. Malenfant, A. Lebel and L. Martel, *Projections of the Diversity of the Canadian Population: 2006 to 2031*, Statistics Canada, catalogue no. 91-551-X.

42. 'ADQ immigration cap motion rebuffed at Quebec legislature', CBC News, 12 March 2008; 'ADQ leader gets boost, pushes immigration policy', CBC News, 17 March 2017.

43. 'CAQ wants to let fewer immigrants into Quebec', CBC News, 30 August 2016.

44. Jillian Kestler-Lamours, 'Explained: "Increased legitimacy" of Quebec's far-right', Al Jazeera, 15 November 2017; Anna Maria Tremonti, 'Are actions of police legitimizing far-right groups in Quebec?', CBC Radio, 28 November 2017.

45. Medeiros, 'The populism risk in English Canada'.

46. E. Kaufmann, 'Condemned to rootlessness: The Loyalist origins of Canada's identity crisis', *Nationalism and Ethnic Politics* 3:1 (1997), 110–35; D. H. Akenson, *The Irish in Ontario: A Study in Rural History*, Kingston, Ont., and Montreal, 1984: McGill–Queen's University Press.

47. R. N. Rosecrance, 'The radical culture of Australia', in L. Hartz (ed.), *The Founding of New Societies*, New York, 1964: Harcourt, Brace & World, pp. 275–318.

48. 'Quebec politics: Major support for Bill 62, far less approval for government's handling of border issues', Angus Reid Institute, 4 October 2017.

49. Philip Authier, 'CAQ at historic high in Quebec poll, Trudeau still top choice for PM', *Montreal Gazette*, 26 June 2018.

50. Michael Lind, 'The rubes and the elites', *Salon*, 15 April 2008.

51. D. H. Fischer, *Albion's Seed: Four British Folkways in America*, New York, 1989: Oxford University Press.

52. A. E. Jardina, 'Demise of dominance: Group threat and the new relevance of white identity for American politics', PhD dissertation, University of Michigan, 2014.

53. Ambrose and Mudde, 'Canadian multiculturalism', p. 226.

PART II: REPRESS

7. Left-Modernism

1. N. Elias, *The Civilizing Process*, Oxford, 1994: Blackwell.

2. M. Douglas, *Purity and Danger: An Analysis of Concepts of Pollution and Taboo*, in M. Douglas, *Collected Works*, London, 2003: Routledge.

3. K. T. Erikson, 'Notes on the sociology of deviance', *Social Problems* 9:4 (1962), p. 322.

4. E. Durkheim, *The Elementary Forms of Religious Life*, New York and London, 1995: Free Press; K. T. Erikson, 'On the sociology of deviance', in P. A. and P. Adler, *Constructions of Deviance: Social Power, Context, and Interaction*, Belmont, Calif., and London, 2003: Wadsworth, pp. 11–18.

5. J. Haidt, *The Righteous Mind: Why Good People are Divided by Politics and Religion*, London, 2012: Allen Lane.

6. A. Fog, *Cultural Selection*, Dordrecht and Boston, Mass., 1999: Kluwer Academic Publishers, ch. 8.

7. Ibid.

8. A. Hartocollis, 'A campus argument goes viral. Now the college is under siege', *The New York Times*, 16 June 2017; Scott Jaschik, 'Who defines what is racist?', *Inside Higher Ed*, 30 May 2017; Lisa Pemberton, '80 Evergreen protesters sanctioned for breaking student-conduct code', *Seattle Times*, 1 October 2017.

9. Bret Weinstein, 'The campus mob came for me – and you, professor, could be next', *Wall Street Journal*, 30 May 2017.

10. Jaschik, 'Who defines what is racist?'

11. Fog, *Cultural Selection*, ch. 8.

12. Emma Rosen, 'More than 90 per cent of universities are restricting free speech, study finds', 14 February 2017; Arj Singh, 'Universities "could face fines or de-registration" if they fail to uphold freedom of speech', *Independent*, 19 October 2017.

13. Julia Carre Wong, 'UC Berkeley cancels "alt-right" speaker Milo Yiannopoulos as thousands protest', *Guardian*, 2 February 2017.

14. April Kelly-Woessner, 'How Marcuse made today's students less tolerant than their parents', *Heterodox Academy*, 23 September 2015.

15. 'April Kelly-Woessner on declining political tolerance', *Half Hour of Heterodoxy* (YouTube), 5 June 2017.

16. Eugene Volokh, 'Freedom of expression on campus: An overview of some recent surveys', *Washington Post*, 23 October 2017.

17. Emily Elkins, 'The state of free speech and tolerance in America', Cato Institute, 31 October 2017.

18. A. Harell, 'Political tolerance, racist speech, and the influence of social networks', *Social Science Quarterly* 91:3 (2010), 724–40; Kelly-Woessner, 'How Marcuse made today's students less tolerant'.

19. S. Atran and R. Axelrod, 'Reframing sacred values', *Negotiation Journal* 24:3 (2008), 221–46.

20. Doug Todd, 'David Suzuki shifts immigration debate into new territory', *Vancouver Sun*, 12 July 2013.

21. J. Gray, *Black Mass: Apocalyptic Religion and the Death of Utopia*, London, 2007: Penguin Books.

22. D. Bell, *The Winding Passage: Essays and Sociological Journeys, 1960–1980*, Cambridge, Mass., 1980: ABT Books, pp. 275–6.

23. A. Giddens, *Modernity and Self-Identity*, Cambridge, 1991: Polity Press.

24. E. Doss, *Benton, Pollock and the Politics of Modernism: From Regionalism to Abstract Expressionism*, Chicago and London, 1991: University of Chicago Press.

25. D. Brooks, *Bobos in Paradise: The New Upper Class and How They Got There*, New York, 2001: Simon & Schuster.

26. D. Bell, *The Cultural Contradictions of Capitalism*, New York, 1976: HarperCollins, p. 111.

27. Marie-Danielle Smith, 'Governor general apologizes for calling indigenous people "immigrant" after interview backlash', *National Post*, 19 June 2017.

28. Rachel Mendelson, 'Jonathan Kay resigns as editor of The Walrus amid "appropriation prize" backlash', *Toronto Star*, 14 May 2017.

29. M. Racco, 'Trudeau family criticized for overdoing it on their traditional Indian outfits', Global News (Canada), 21 February 2018.

30. R. Brubaker, 'The Dolezal affair: race, gender, and the micropolitics of identity', *Ethnic and Racial Studies* 39:3 (2016), 414–48.

31. N. Marzouki, D. McDonnell and O. Roy (eds.), *Saving the People: How Populists Hijack Religion*, New York, 2016: Oxford University Press.

32. A. D. Smith, *Nations and Nationalism in a Global Era*, Cambridge, 1995: Polity Press.

33. F. Meinecke, *Cosmopolitanism and the National State*, Princeton, NJ, 1970: Princeton University Press.

34. E. Kaufmann, 'The rise of cosmopolitanism in the 20th-century West: A comparative-historical perspective on the United States and European Union', *Global Society* 17:4 (2004), 359–83.

35. P. M. Kennedy, 'The decline of nationalistic history in the West, 1900–1970', *Journal of Contemporary History*, no. 8 (1977), pp. 91–2.

36. P. Nora, 'Between memory and history', Introduction in P. Nora and L. Kritzman (eds.), *Realms of Memory: Rethinking the French Past*, vol. 1: *Conflicts and Divisions*, New York, 1996: Columbia University Press; J. H. Plumb, *The Death of the Past*, London, 1969: Macmillan.

37. F. FitzGerald, *America Revised: History Schoolbooks in the Twentieth Century*, Boston, Mass., and Toronto, 1979: Little, Brown and Company.

38. R. D. Hutchins, *Nationalism and History Education: Curricula and Textbooks in the United States and France*, New York, 2016: Routledge.

39. Kaufmann, 'Rise of cosmopolitanism in the twentieth-century West'; D. Gorman, *The Emergence of International Society in the 1920s*, Cambridge, 2012: Cambridge University Press.

40. Kaufmann, 'Rise of cosmopolitanism in the twentieth-century West'.

41. E. Kaufmann, *The Rise and Fall of Anglo-America: The Decline of Dominant Ethnicity in the United States*, Cambridge, Mass., 2004: Harvard University Press, pp. 187–8.

42. R. Inglehart, *Culture Shift in Advanced Industrial Society*, Princeton, NJ, 1990: Princeton University Press.

43. Kaufmann, *Rise and Fall of Anglo-America*, p. 192.

44. John McWhorter, 'Educated liberals overuse the term "racist"', CNN, 21 October 2017.

45. J. Toby, 'The charge of racism against James S. Coleman', *Academic Questions* 29(4) (2016), 404–9.

46. F. Rojas, *From Black Power to Black Studies: How a Radical Social Movement Became an Academic Discipline*, Baltimore, 2007: Johns Hopkins University Press.

47. Bell, *Cultural Contradictions*, pp. 130, 132.

48. J. Dorman, *Arguing the World: The New York Intellectuals in Their Own Words*, Chicago, 2001: University of Chicago Press.

49. J. L. Duarte et al., 'Political diversity will improve social psychological science', *Behavioral and Brain Sciences* 38 (2015).

50. Jonathan Haidt, 'New study indicates existence of eight conservative social psychologists', *Heterodox Academy*, 2 January 2016.

51. N. Carl, 'The political attitudes of British academics', *Open Quantitative Sociology and Political Science*, published online January 2018; Chris Hanretty, 'Is the left over-represented within academia?', *Medium*, published online 9 March 2016.

52. Duarte et al., 'Political diversity will improve social psychological science'.

53. Atran and Axelrod, 'Reframing sacred values'.

54. John McWhorter, 'Antiracism, our flawed new religion', *Daily Beast*, 27 July 2015; S. Steele, *White Guilt: How Blacks and Whites Together Destroyed the Promise of the Civil Rights Era*, New York, 2006: HarperCollins.

55. 'Is it okay for restaurants to racially profile their employees?', *Freakonomics Radio*, 24 June 2015.

56. A. L. Stinchcombe, *Constructing Social Theories*, New York, 1968: Harcourt, Brace & World, pp. 117–18.

57. N. Haslam, 'Concept creep: Psychology's expanding concepts of harm and pathology', *Psychological Inquiry* 27:1 (2016), 1–17; Jason Manning, 'Victimhood culture and concept creep', The Victimhood Report, 2 February 2018.

58. R. K. Carney and R. D. Enos, 'Conservatism and fairness in contemporary politics: Unpacking the psychological underpinnings of modern racism', Harvard University Working Paper, 2018.

59. M. Lavergne and S. Mullainathan, 'Are Emily and Greg more employable than Lakisha and Jamal? A field experiment on labor market discrimination', *The American Economic Review* 94:4 (2004): 991–1013.

60. Ibid.; R. Darolia et al., 'Race and gender effects on employer interest in job applicants: new evidence from a resume field experiment', *Applied Economics Letters* 23:12 (2016), 853–6.

61. J. Rich, 'What do field experiments of discrimination in markets tell us? A meta-analysis of studies conducted since 2000', October 2014: http://ftp.iza.org/dp8584.pdf.

62. C. L. Adida, D. D. Laitin and M.-A. Valfort, 'Identifying barriers to Muslim integration in France', *Proceedings of the National Academy of Sciences* 107:52 (2010), 22384–90.
63. Rich, 'What do field experiments of discrimination in markets tell us?'
64. Marco Della Cava, 'Blacks face longer wait times on Uber, Lyft than other races – worse for taxis, study says', *USA Today*, 28 June 2018.
65. J. J. Fyfe, 'Who shoots? A look at officer race and police shooting', *Journal of Police Science & Administration* 9:4 (1981), 367–82; R. A. Brown and J. Frank, 'Race and officer decision making: Examining differences in arrest outcomes between black and white officers', *Justice Quarterly* 23:1 (2006), 96–126.
66. Tess Townsend, 'Google is still mostly white and male', *Recode*, 29 June 2017.
67. Ironically the firm is being simultaneously sued by women who claim it systematically underpays and under-promotes women, and by James Damore and David Gudeman, who argue the company has created a hostile environment which openly discriminates against whites, conservatives and men. It is possible that both are true.
68. R. S. Bourne, 'Trans-National America', in C. Resek (ed.), *War and the Intellectuals: Collected Essays, 1915–1919*, New York, 1964 [1916]: Harper & Row, pp. 107–23.
69. E. Kaufmann, 'The Orange Order in Ontario, Newfoundland, Scotland and Northern Ireland: A macro-social analysis', in D. A. Wilson (ed.), *The Orange Order in Canada*, Dublin, 2007: Four Courts Press; E. Kaufmann, 'Condemned to Rootlessness: The Loyalist Origins of Canada's Identity Crisis', *Nationalism and Ethnic Politics* 3:1 (1997), 110–35.
70. R. Brubaker, 'The return of assimilation? Changing perspectives on immigration and its sequels in France, Germany and the United States', *Ethnic and Racial Studies* 24:4 (2001), 531–48.
71. D. Murray, *The Strange Death of Europe: Immigration, Identity, Islam*, London, 2017: Bloomsbury.
72. S. Pinker, *The Better Angels of Our Nature: Why Violence Has Declined*, New York, 2011: Viking, p. 49.
73. G. Lukianoff and J. Haidt, 'The coddling of the American mind,' *The Atlantic*, September 2015.
74. P. Bruckner, *Shall the Religious Inherit the Earth? An Essay on Western Masochism*, Princeton, NJ, 2012: Princeton University Press.
75. L. L. Cavalli-Sforza and W. F. Bodmer, *The Genetics of Human Populations*, Mineola, NY, 1999: Dover.

8. Left-Modernism versus the Populist Right

1. 'Unite the Right rally', *Wikipedia*, accessed 6 November 2017.
2. William Saletan, 'What Trump supporters really believe', *Slate*, 29 August 2017.
3. 'Polls [*sic*] shows majority of Americans think Confederate statues should remain', *Guardian*, 22 August 2017.
4. N. Haslam, 'Concept creep: Psychology's expanding concepts of harm and pathology', *Psychological Inquiry* 27:1 (2016), 1–17; Jason Manning, 'Victimhood culture and concept creep', *The Victimhood Report*, 2 February 2018.
5. T. Kuran, *Private Truths, Public Lies: The Social Consequences of Preference Falsification*, Cambridge, Mass., 1995: Harvard University Press.
6. Pamela Wood, 'Christopher Columbus monument vandalized in Baltimore', *Baltimore Sun*, 21 August 2017.
7. Pat Buchanan, 'Trump embraces the culture war', Patrick J. Buchanan Official Website, 10 October 2017.
8. 'Polls [*sic*] shows majority of Americans'.
9. B. Campbell and J. Manning, *The Rise of Victimhood Culture: Microaggressions, Safe Spaces, and the New Culture Wars*, Cham, Switz., 2018: Palgrave Macmillan.
10. Zach Goldberg, Twitter posts @ZachG932, 31 May–28 June 2018.
11. A. Nagle, *Kill All Normies: Online Culture Wars from 4chan and Tumblr to Trump and the Alt-Right*, Winchester and Washington, DC, 2017: Zero Books.
12. Marion Mourge, 'Laurent Wauquiez s'insurge contre "les élites"', *Le Figaro*, 25 October 2017.
13. J. Duckitt and C. G. Sibley, 'A dual-process motivational model of ideology, politics, and prejudice', *Psychological Inquiry* 20:2–3 (2009), 98–109.
14. Lee Roden, 'Why Sweden is talking about immigration more than before', *The Local* (Sweden), 6 July 2016.
15. Yascha Mounck, 'Germany has been a beacon of stability at a time of unrest. That's about to end', *Slate*, 20 November 2017.
16. Charlotte Greenfield and Ana Nicolaci da Costa, 'Hard Labour: NZ's Ardern takes tougher line on immigration', *Reuters*, 22 August 2017.
17. 'The Overton Window: a model of policy change': https://www.mackinac.org/OvertonWindow.
18. D. Murray, *The Strange Death of Europe: Immigration, Identity, Islam*, London, 2017: Bloomsbury, p. 230.
19. Nick Robins-Early, 'Hungary's Prime Minister calls For "ethnic homogeneity"', *HuffPost*, 1 March 2017.

20. Peter Zimonjic, 'Tory leadership candidate Kellie Leitch wants immigrants to be asked: "Are men and women equal?"', CBC News, 7 March 2017; Craig Smith, 'Candidate's call to save "Canadian values"? Un-Canadian, critics say', *The New York Times*, 26 May 2017.

21. Campbell Clark, 'Justin Trudeau rolls the dice on immigration', *Globe and Mail*, 1 November 2017.

22. Irvin Studin, 'Review: Doug Saunders's Maximum Canada argues the more the merrier', *Globe and Mail*, 6 October 2017.

23. Ciaran D'Arcy, 'Merrion Hotel cancels launch of anti-immigration political party', *Irish Times*, 16 November 2016.

24. Douglas Todd, 'The dangers of Trudeau's "postnational" Canada', *Vancouver Sun*, 13 March 2016.

25. Katharine Murphy, 'Australians growing more concerned over immigration – Guardian Essential poll', *Guardian*, 23 April 2018.

26. B. Prins, 'The nerve to break taboos: New realism in the Dutch discourse on multiculturalism', *Journal of International Migration and Integration/Revue de l'integration et de la migration internationale* 3:3–4 (2002), 363–79.

27. Matthew Weaver, 'Angela Merkel: German multiculturalism has "utterly failed"', *Guardian*, 17 October 2010.

28. R. Brubaker, 'The return of assimilation? Changing perspectives on immigration and its sequels in France, Germany and the United States', *Ethnic and Racial Studies* 24:4 (2001), 531–48; 'The Mayor's vision for a diverse and inclusive city', London, 2017: Greater London Authority.

29. T. Bale, 'Cinderella and her ugly sisters: The mainstream and extreme right in Europe's bipolarising party systems', *West European Politics* 26:3 (2003), 67–90.

30. S. Polakow-Suransky, *Go Back to Where You Came From: The Backlash against Immigration and the Fate of Western Democracy*, London, 2017: Hurst and Co., p. 213.

31. David Blunkett, 'Race relations not helped by pseudo-cultural political correctness', *Guardian*, 23 March 2015.

32. A. L. Janus, 'The influence of social desirability pressures on expressed immigration attitudes', *Social Science Quarterly* 91:4 (2010), 928–46.

33. J. Gordon and S. Jeram, 'Friendly Canada? Explaining the absence of a Canadian anti-immigration party', paper presented at American Political Science Association, San Francisco, 1 September 2017.

34. L. Bursztyn, G. Egorov and S. Fiorin, 'From extreme to mainstream: How social norms unravel', National Bureau of Economic Research Working Paper no. 23415, May 2017; C. R. Sunstein, 'Yes, Trump is making xenophobia more acceptable', Bloomberg Opinion, 26 May 2017.

35. T. R. Gurr and A. Pitsch, 'Ethnopolitical conflict and separatist violence', in W. Heitmeyer and J. Hagan (eds.), *International Handbook of*

Violence Research, Dordrecht and London, 2003: Kluwer Academic Publishers.

36. T. R. Gurr, and B. Harff, *Ethnic Conflict in World Politics* (2nd edn), Boulder, Colo., and Oxford, 2004: Westview Press.

37. M. G. Marshall and T. R. Gurr, *Peace and Conflict 2003: A Global Survey of Armed Conflicts, Self-Determination Movements, and Democracy*, College Park, Md, 2003: Integrated Network for Societal Conflict Research.

38. Ana Knauf, '"Go Back to the Zoo": How Evergreen State College became a target for right-wing trolls', *The Stranger*, 14 June 2017.

39. Greg Scorzo, 'Politics and the new counter-culture part 1: The outraged Establishment': http://www.cultureontheoffensive.com, accessed 16 November 2017.

40. K. Joyce, *Quiverfull: Inside the Christian Patriarchy Movement*, Boston, Mass., 2009: Beacon Press.

41. Kate Shellnutt, 'Evangelicals to Trump: Don't deport our next generation of church leaders', *Christianity Today*, 1 September 2017.

42. D. Sacks and P. Thiel, *The Diversity Myth: 'Multiculturalism' and the Politics of Intolerance at Stanford*, Oakland, Calif., 1995: The Independent Institute; N. Glazer, *We are All Multiculturalists Now*, Cambridge, Mass., 1997: Harvard University Press.

43. Aaron Colton, 'The problem with political correctness is not the content – it's the delivery', *Paste Magazine*, 30 November 2016; Brandon Morse, 'Bernie Sanders explains why anti-political correctness helped win Trump the election', *The Blaze*, 13 December 2017.

44. Ryan Maloney, 'Most Canadians say political correctness has gone "too far": Angus Reid Institute Poll', *HuffPost (Canada)*, 29 August 2016.

45. Tom Clark, 'Free speech? New polling suggests Britain is "less PC" than Trump's America', *Prospect*, no. 264 (February 2018).

46. H. Fingerhut, 'Republicans much "colder" than Democrats in views of professors', Pew Research Center, 13 September 2017.

47. Michell Hemmer, 'Eternally frustrated by "liberal" universities, conservatives now want to tear them down', Vox, 8 March 2017.

48. Measured as perceived discrimination against whites divided by discrimination against blacks.

49. Ashley Jardina, 'The white backlash to "crying racism": How whites respond to calling racial preferences racist', paper presented at American Political Science Association meeting, San Francisco, 2 September 2017.

50. N. A. Valentino, F. G. Neuner and L. M. Vandenbroek, 'The changing norms of racial political rhetoric and the end of racial priming', *Journal of Politics*, published online November 2016.

51. Frank Bruni, 'Crying wolf, then confronting Trump', *The New York Times*, 1 September 2016.

52. Shadi Hamid, 'There's no "good" or "bad" America', *Washington Post*, 18 November 2017.
53. M. Z. Bookman, *The Demographic Struggle for Power: The Political Economy of Demographic Engineering in the Modern World*, London and Portland, Ore., 1997: Frank Cass; D. Horowitz, *Ethnic Groups in Conflict*, Berkeley, Calif., 1985: University of California Press, pp. 175–81.
54. M. B. Brewer, 'The psychology of prejudice: Ingroup love and outgroup hate?', *Journal of Social Issues* 55:3 (1999), 429–44.
55. Ibid.
56. E. Kaufmann, 'Land, history or modernization? Explaining ethnic fractionalization', *Ethnic and Racial Studies* 38:2 (2015), 203.
57. M. Abrajano and Z. L. Hajnal, *White Backlash*, Princeton, NJ, 2015: Princeton University Press, pp. 133–7.
58. M. Sobolewska, R. Ford and P. Sniderman, 'Democratic resilience: How some individuals resist the threat of terrorism and maintain their core values of tolerance', paper presented at the 'Elections, Public Opinion and Parties' (ePop) conference, University of Kent, 2016.
59. 2016 ANES pilot survey; YouGov–Birkbeck–Policy Exchange survey, 7–8 December 2016.
60. No underlining is visible to respondents.
61. E. L. Uhlmann, D. A. Pizarro, D. Tannenbaum and P. H. Ditto, 'The motivated use of moral principles', *Judgment and Decision Making* 4:6 (2009), 476–91. When it comes to civilian casualties in war, the reverse is true, with conservatives more willing to endorse military action if casualties are foreign than American, with liberals being the even-handed ones.
62. 'Political typology reveals deep fissures on the right and left', Pew Research Center, 24 October 2017, p. 5.
63. J. Haidt, *The Righteous Mind: Why Good People are Divided by Politics and Religion*, London, 2012: Allen Lane.
64. I am indebted to Bobby Duffy of Ipsos MORI for doing this.
65. For further details, see E. Kaufmann, 'Racial self-interest is not racism: ethno-demographic interests and the immigration debate', *Policy Exchange*, 3 March 2017.

PART III: FLEE

9. Hunkering Down

1. M. van Ham and D. Manley, 'Social housing allocation, choice and neighbourhood ethnic mix in England', *Journal of Housing and the Built Environment* 24:4 (2009), 407–22.

2. G. Knies, A. Nandi and L. Platt, 'Life satisfaction, ethnicity and neighbourhoods: Is there an effect of neighbourhood ethnic composition on life satisfaction?', *Social Science Research* 60 (2016), 110–24.

3. S. L. S. Arbaci, 'The residential insertion of immigrants in Europe: Patterns and mechanisms in southern European cities', PhD dissertation, University of London, 2007.

4. C. Peach, 'Social geography: New religions and ethnoburbs – contrasts with cultural geography', *Progress in Human Geography* 26:2 (2002), 252–60.

5. J. Rich, 'What do field experiments of discrimination in markets tell us? A meta-analysis of studies conducted since 2000', October 2014: http://ftp.iza.org/dp8584.pdf.

6. Computed from the Longitudinal Tract Database: https://s4.ad.brown.edu/projects/diversity/Researcher/LTDB1.htm, accessed 25 September 2017.

7. W. H. Frey, 'White neighborhoods get modestly more diverse, new census data show', Brookings, 13 December 2016.

8. R. Johnston, M. Poulsen and J. Forrest, 'Multiethnic residential areas in a multiethnic country? A decade of major change in England and Wales', *Environment and Planning A* 45:4 (2013), 753–9.

9. G. Catney, 'Has neighbourhood ethnic segregation decreased?', Centre on Dynamics of Ethnicity (CoDE) Bulletin, University of Manchester, February 2013, pp. 1–4.

10. R. D. Alba and S. Romalewski, 'The end of segregation? Hardly. A more nuanced view from the New York metropolitan region', Center for Urban Research, New York, City University of New York, 2013.

11. J. Logan and W. Zhang, 'Global neighborhoods: New evidence from Census 2010', US2010 Project, February 2011.

12. *Housing in London 2014*, London, 2014: Greater London Authority, p. 8.

13. I. Gordon, 'Implications for residential displacement', in *How is London being Transformed by Migration?*, London, 2014: London School of Economics.

14. Ben Judah, 'Undercover as an Eastern European migrant in London, I discovered the pain of Brexit Britain', *New Statesman*, 1 December 2016.

15. S. Bell and J. Paskins (eds.), *Imagining the Future City: London 2062*, London, 2013: Ubiquity Press.

16. Å. Bråmå, '"White flight"? The production and reproduction of immigrant concentration areas in Swedish cities, 1990–2000', *Urban Studies* 43:7 (2006), 1127–46.

17. R. Andersson, 'Ethnic residential segregation and integration processes in Sweden', in K. Schonwalder (ed.), *Residential Segregation and the Integration of Immigrants: Britain, the Netherlands and Sweden*, Berlin, 2009: WZB, p. 89.

18. G. Bolt, R. van Kempen and M. van Ham, 'Minority ethnic groups in the Dutch housing market: Spatial segregation, relocation dynamics and housing policy', *Urban Studies* 45:7 (2008), 1359–84.

19. C. B. Ong, 'Tipping points? Ethnic composition change in Dutch big city neighbourhoods', *Urban Studies* 54:4 (2017), 1016–37.

20. ONS LS, London, 2011: Office of National Statistics. The permission of the Office of National Statistics to use the Longitudinal Study is gratefully acknowledged, as is the help provided by staff of the Centre for Longitudinal Study Information & User Support (CeLSIUS). CeLSIUS is supported by the ESRC Census of Population Programme (Award Ref: RES-348-25-0004). The author alone is responsible for the interpretation of the data. Census output is Crown copyright and is reproduced with the permission of the Controller of HMSO and the Queen's Printer for Scotland.

21. M. Hall and K. Crowder, 'Native out-migration and neighborhood immigration in new destinations', *Demography* 51:6 (2014), 2179–202.

22. E. Kaufmann and G. Harris, *Changing Places: Mapping the White British Response to Ethnic Change*, London, 2014: Demos.

23. E. Kaufmann, 'The religious demography of London since 1980', in D. Goodhew and A.-P. Cooper (eds.), *No Secular City: Church Growth and Decline in London, 1980 to the Present* (forthcoming).

24. W. H. Frey, *Diversity Explosion: How New Racial Demographics are Remaking America*, Washington, DC, 2015: Brookings Institution Press, p. 72.

25. 'U.S. Latino population growth and dispersion has slowed since onset of the Great Recession', Pew Research Center, 8 September 2016.

26. http://www.sneps.net/whiteshift.

27. Frey, *Diversity Explosion*, p. 143.

28. Hawaii is omitted to improve granularity of focus.

29. W. H. Frey and K.-L. Liaw, 'Migration within the United States: Role of race-ethnicity', Brookings–Wharton Papers on Urban Affairs, Washington, DC, 2005: Brookings Institution Press, pp. 207–62.

30. J. R. Logan, B. Stults and Z. Xu, 'Validating population estimates for harmonized census tract data, 2000–2010', *Annals of the American Association of Geographers* 106:5 (2016), 1013–29.

31. L. Aldén, M. Hammarstedt and E. Neuman, 'Ethnic segregation, tipping behavior, and native residential mobility', *International Migration Review* 49:1 (2015), 36–69; D. Card, A. Mas and J. Rothstein, 'Tipping and the dynamics of segregation', Cambridge, Mass., 2008: National Bureau of Economic Research.

32. UKHLS, US (2017), Waves 1–9, 2009–16. Institute for Social and Economic Research and National Centre for Social Research, Colchester, Essex, UK Data Archive, SN#6614.

33. E. Havekes, M. Bader and M. Krysan, 'Realizing racial and ethnic neighborhood preferences? Exploring the mismatches between what people want, where they search, and where they live', *Population Research and Policy Review* 35:1 (2016), 101–26.

34. W. A. V. Clark, 'Residential preferences and residential choices in a multi-ethnic context', *Demography* 29:3 (1992), 451–66; C. Z. Charles, 'Can we live together? Racial preferences and neighborhood outcomes', in X. Briggs (ed.), *The Geography of Opportunity*, Washington, DC, 2005: Brookings Institution Press, pp. 46–80; M. Krysan, 'Whites who say they'd flee: who are they, and why would they leave?' *Demography* 39:4 (2002), 675–96; M. van Londen, 'Exclusion of ethnic minorities in the Netherlands: The effects of individual and situational characteristics on opposition to ethnic policy and ethnically mixed neighbourhoods', PhD dissertation, Nijmegen, Netherlands, Radboud University, 2012.

35. M. Permentier, M. van Ham and G. Bolt, 'Neighbourhood reputation and the intention to leave the neighbourhood', *Environment and Planning A* 41:9 (2009), 2162–80.

36. Van Londen, 'Exclusion of ethnic minorities in the Netherlands', p. 93.

37. Card et al., 'Tipping and the dynamics of segregation'.

38. E. Kaufmann and G. Harris, '"White Flight" or positive contact? Local diversity and attitudes to immigration in Britain', *Comparative Political Studies* 48:12 (2015), 1563–90.

39. P. Watt, G. Millington and R. Huq, 'East London mobilities: The "Cockney Diaspora" and the remaking of the Essex ethnoscape', in P. Watt and P. Smets (eds.), *Mobilities and Neighbourhood Belonging in Cities and Suburbs*, Basingstoke, 2014: Palgrave MacMillan, pp. 16–17.

40. Ibid., p. 18.

41. L. Hedman and E. Hoplmqvist, 'Producing and reproducing ethnic residential segregation. Is "white flight" enough to capture the mobility motives of natives?', Uppsala, 2012: Institute for Housing and Urban Research, Uppsala University.

42. B. Bishop and R. G. Cushing, *The Big Sort: Why the Clustering of Like-Minded America is Tearing Us Apart*, Boston, Mass., 2008: Houghton Mifflin.

43. A. Gallego et al., 'Places and preferences: A longitudinal analysis of self-selection and contextual effects', *British Journal of Political Science* 46:3 (2016), 529–50.

44. 'Political Polarization in the American Public', Pew Research Center, 12 June 2014.

45. J. G. Gimpel and I. Hui, 'Inadvertent and intentional partisan residential sorting', *Annals of Regional Science* 58:3 (2017), 441–68.

46. E. Kaufmann, 'Is there "white flight" in England and Wales?', paper prepared for the 'Understanding Society' conference, University of Essex, June 2017.

47. Office for National Statistics and Home Office, 'Communities Group, Home Office Citizenship Survey, 2010–2011, UK Data Archive Study

#7111', London, 2011; Office for National Statistics and Home Office, 'Communities Group, Home Office Citizenship Survey, 2009–2010, UK Data Archive Study #6733', London, 2011.

48. A. Enjeti, 'Ghosts of white people past: Witnessing white flight from an Asian ethnoburb', *Pacific Standard*, 25 August 2016.

49. 'Where are all the white people in San Francisco schools?', Priceonomics, 24 March 2015; P. Lorgerie and J. A. Smith, 'San Francisco schools' changing demographics', *San Francisco Public Press*, 2 February 2015.

50. C. Hamnett, T. Butler and M. Ramsden, '"I wanted my child to go to a more mixed school": schooling and ethnic mix in East London', *Environment and Planning A* 45:6 (2013), 553.

51. Michael Lind, 'The open-borders "Liberaltarianism" of the new urban elite', *National Review*, 15 September 2016.

52. R. C. Christopher, *Crashing the Gates: The De-WASPing of America's Power Elite*, New York and London, 1989: Simon & Schuster.

53. Kaufmann, 'Is there 'white flight' in England and Wales?'

54. M. J. Hetherington and J. D. Weiler, *Authoritarianism and Polarization in American Politics*, Cambridge, 2009: Cambridge University Press.; 'Political polarization in the American public', Pew Research Center; Ross Butters and Christopher Hare, 'Three-fourths of Americans regularly talk politics only with members of their own political tribe', *Washington Post* (Monkey Cage), 1 May 2017.

55. Social Integration Commission, 'How integrated is modern Britain', London, 2014. Report at: http://socialintegrationcommission.org.uk/SIC_Report_WEB.pdf.

56. K. Lewis et al., 'Tastes, ties, and time: A new social network dataset using Facebook.com', *Social Networks* 30:4 (2008), 330–42.

57. D. Stolle, S. N. Soroka and R. Johnston, 'When does diversity erode trust? Neighborhood diversity, interpersonal trust and the mediating effect of social interactions', *Political Studies* 56:1 (2008), 65.

58. K. G. Banting, 'The multicultural Welfare State: International experience and North American narratives', *Social Policy & Administration* 39:2 (2006), 15.

59. J. Tolsma and T. W. G. van der Meer, 'Losing wallets, retaining trust? The relationship between ethnic heterogeneity and trusting coethnic and noncoethnic neighbours and non-neighbours to return a lost wallet', *Social Indicators Research* 131:2 (2017), 631–58.

60. P. T. Dinesen and K. M. Sønderskov, 'Ethnic diversity and social trust: Evidence from the micro-context', *American Sociological Review* 80:3 (2015), 550–73.

61. J. Laurence and L. Bentley, 'Does ethnic diversity have a negative effect on attitudes towards the community? A longitudinal analysis of the causal

claims within the ethnic diversity and social cohesion debate', *European Sociological Review* 32:1 (2016), 54–67.

62. David Willetts, quoted in 'Diversity versus Solidarity', RSA/*Prospect* round-table debate, 28 January 2003, p. 1.

63. E. Kaufmann, 'Land, history or modernization? Explaining ethnic fractionalization', *Ethnic and Racial Studies* 38:2 (2015), 203.

64. Ibid.; J. G. Montalvo and M. Reynal-Querol, 'Ethnic polarization, potential conflict, and civil wars', *American Sociological Review* 95:3 (2005), 796–816.

65. W. Easterly and R. Levine, 'Africa's growth tragedy: Policies and ethnic divisions', *Quarterly Journal of Economics* 111:4 (1997), 1203–50.

66. Elliott D. Green, 'Endogenous ethnicity', paper presented at the APSA Annual Meeting, 2011. Available at SSRN: https://ssrn.com/abstract=1899822.

67. J. Habyarimana et al., 'Why does ethnic diversity undermine public goods provision?', *American Political Science Review* 101:4 (2007), 709–25.

68. A. Alesina, R. Bakir and W. Easterly, 'Public goods and ethnic divisions', *Quarterly Journal of Economics* 114:4 (1999), 1243–84; M. Abrajano and Z. L. Hajnal, *White Backlash*, Princeton, NJ, 2015: Princeton University Press, p. 139.

69. A. Alesina et al., 'Immigration and redistribution', National Bureau of Economic Research, Working Paper 24733, 2018.

70. A. Chua, *World on Fire: How Exporting Free Market Democracy Breeds Ethnic Hatred and Global Instability*, New York, 2002: Doubleday.

71. Stolle et al., 'When does diversity erode trust?'

72. Abrajano and Hajnal, *White Backlash*, p. 139.

73. J. Laurence, 'The effect of ethnic diversity and community disadvantage on social cohesion: A multi-level analysis of social capital and interethnic relations in UK communities', *European Sociological Review* 27:1 (2011), 70–89.

74. J. Laurence, 'Reconciling the contact and threat hypotheses: does ethnic diversity strengthen or weaken community inter-ethnic relations?', *Ethnic and Racial Studies* 37:8 (2014), 1328–49.

75. W. Kymlicka and K. G. Banting, *Multiculturalism and the Welfare State: Recognition and Redistribution in Contemporary Democracies*, Oxford and New York, 2006: Oxford University Press, p. 50.

76. S. Beugelsdijk and M. J. Klasing, 'Diversity and trust: The role of shared values', *Journal of Comparative Economics* 44:3 (2016), 522–40.

77. J. Rydgren, 'Is extreme right-wing populism contagious? Explaining the emergence of a new party family', *European Journal of Political Research* 44:3 (2005), 413–37.

78. J. Laurence, K. Schmid and M. Hewstone, 'Ethnic diversity, inter-group attitudes and countervailing pathways of positive and negative inter-group

contact: An analysis across workplaces and neighbourhoods', *Social Indicators Research* 136:2 (2018), 719–49.

79. 'Perils of Perception 2016' survey, Ipsos MORI, published online 14 December 2016.

80. C. J. Wong, '"Little" and "big" pictures in our heads: Race, local context, and innumeracy about racial groups in the United States', *Public Opinion Quarterly* 71:3 (2007), 392–412.

81. YouGov survey data courtesy of David Goodhart.

82. J. A. Goldstone, E. Kaufmann and M. Duffy Toft (eds.), *Political Demography: How Population Changes are Reshaping International Security and National Politics*, Boulder, Colo., 2012: Paradigm; J. D. Fearon and D. D. Laitin, 'Sons of the soil, migrants, and civil war', *World Development* 39:2 (2011), 199–211.

83. R. Nordas, 'The devil in the demography? Religion, identity and war in Côte d'Ivoire', in Goldstone, Kaufmann and Duffy Toft, *Political Demography*, pp. 252–67.

84. P. L. van den Berghe, *The Ethnic Phenomenon*, New York, 1979: Elsevier.

PART IV: JOIN

10. Mixing or Moulding?

1. E. Kaufmann and G. Harris, '"White flight" or positive contact? Local diversity and attitudes to immigration in Britain', *Comparative Political Studies* 48:12 (2015), 1563–90.

2. E. Kaufmann, 'Levels or changes? Ethnic context, immigration and the UK Independence Party vote', *Electoral Studies* 48 (2017), 57–69.

3. J. Rydgren and P. Ruth, 'Contextual explanations of radical right-wing support in Sweden: Socioeconomic marginalization, group threat, and the halo effect', *Ethnic and Racial Studies* 36:4 (2013), 711–28.

4. L. McLaren and M. Johnson, 'Resources, group conflict and symbols: Explaining anti-immigration hostility in Britain', *Political Studies* 55:4 (2007), 709–32.

5. J. Dennison et al., 'Explaining the rise of anti-immigration parties in Western Europe', Working Paper, shared privately by author, 1 January 2018.

6. E. Kaufmann and M. J. Goodwin, 'Does diversity produce hostility? A meta-analysis', *Social Science Research*, accepted 15 July 2018.

7. R. Inglehart and P. Norris, 'Trump and the populist authoritarian parties: The silent revolution in reverse', *Perspectives on Politics* 15:2 (2017), 443–54.

8. J. Tilley and G. Evans, 'Ageing and generational effects on vote choice: Combining cross-sectional and panel data to estimate APC effects', *Electoral Studies* 33 (2014), 19–27.

9. James Tilley, 'Do we really become more conservative with age?', *Guardian*, 3 November 2015.

10. Eurobarometer data.

11. A. Rigney, 'Remembrance as remaking: Memories of the nation revisited', *Nations and Nationalism*, 24:2 (2018), 240–57.

12. Menachem Wecker, 'Dating to save your tiny religion from extinction', *The Atlantic*, 27 March 2016.

13. A. Wimmer, *The Making and Unmaking of Ethnic Boundaries: Toward a Comparative Theory*, New Haven, Conn., 2007: Yale Center for Comparative Research.

14. E. Kaufmann, *The Rise and Fall of Anglo-America: The Decline of Dominant Ethnicity in the United States*, Cambridge, Mass., 2004: Harvard University Press, p. 192; G. Livingston and A. Brown, 'Intermarriage in the U.S. 50 years after Loving v. Virginia', Pew Research Center, 18 May 2017.

15. 'Cheerios commercial featuring mixed race family gets racist backlash (VIDEO)', *Huffpost*, 31 May 2013.

16. Livingston and Brown, 'Intermarriage in the U.S.'.

17. Ibid.

18. F. Hou et al., 'Cross-country variation in interracial marriage: A USA–Canada comparison of metropolitan areas', *Ethnic and Racial Studies* 38:9 (2015), 1591–609.

19. Zosia Bielski, 'Where is the love: How tolerant is Canada of its interracial couples?', *Globe and Mail*, 3 October 2016.

20. L. Lucassen and C. Laarman, 'Immigration, intermarriage and the changing face of Europe in the post war period', *The History of the Family* 14:1 (2009), 52–68; R. Alba and N. Foner, 'Mixed unions and immigrant-group integration in North America and Western Europe', *Annals of the American Academy of Political and Social Science* 662:1 (2015), 38–56.

21. 'Muslim Life in Germany', Nuremberg, 2009: Federal Office for Migration and Refugees, pp. 273, 280.

22. Lucassen and Laarman, 'Immigration, intermarriage and the changing face of Europe'; Alba and Foner, 'Mixed unions', pp. 42–7.

23. E. Kaufmann, *Shall the Religious Inherit the Earth? Demography and Politics in the Twenty-First Century*, London, 2010: Profile Books, p. 178.

24. E. Gellner, *Nations and Nationalism*, Oxford, 1983: Blackwell.

25. D. Martin, *A General Theory of Secularization*, Aldershot, 1993 [1978]: Gregg Revivals.

26. My own calculations from ONS LS data.

27. Kaufmann, *Shall the Religious Inherit the Earth?*, p. 175.

28. Scott London, 'The face of tomorrow: Reflections on diversity in America': http://scottlondon.com/articles/newface.html, accessed 4 December 2017.

29. Richard Dawkins, 'Race and creation', *Prospect*, no. 103 (October 2004).

30. J. Goldstein, J. B. Davidoff and D. Roberson, 'Knowing color terms enhances recognition: Further evidence from English and Himba', *Journal of Experimental Child Psychology* 102:2 (2009), 219–38.

31. 'The surprising pattern behind color names around the world', Vox/You-Tube, 16 May 2017.

32. M. A. Webster et al., 'Adaptation to natural facial categories', *Nature* 428:6982 (2004), 557–61.

33. Ethnicelebs.com, accessed 5 December 2017.

34. D. T. Levin, 'Classifying faces by race: The structure of face categories', *Journal of Experimental Psychology: Learning, Memory, and Cognition* 22:6 (1996), 1364.

35. 'Slaves, sinners and saints', BBC, 27 February 2009.

36. 'Video of white supremacist learning he is 14 percent black may be the best thing ever', *Huffpost*, 12 November 2013.

37. A. S. A. Guimarães, 'The Brazilian system of racial classification', *Ethnic and Racial Studies* 35:7 (2012), 1157–62; A. Saperstein and A. M. Penner, 'Racial fluidity and inequality in the United States', *American Journal of Sociology* 118:3 (2012), 676–727.

38. Saperstein and Penner, 'Racial fluidity'.

39. Michael Lind, 'The future of whiteness', *Salon*, 29 May 2012; Richard Alba, 'The likely persistence of a white majority', *American Prospect*, 11 January 2016.

40. R. Alba and T. Islam, 'The case of the disappearing Mexican Americans: An ethnic-identity mystery', *Population Research and Policy Review* 28:2 (2009), 109–21.

41. William Darity, 'The Latino flight to whiteness', *American Prospect*, 11 February 2016.

42. R. Salam, *Melting Pot or Civil War? A Son of Immigrants Makes the Case against Open Borders*, New York, 2018: Sentinel, pp. 86–7.

43. Darity, 'The Latino flight to whiteness'; B. Duncan and S. J. Trejo, 'The complexity of immigrant generations: Implications for assessing the socio-economic integration of Hispanics and Asians', *ILR Review* 70:5 (2017), 1146–75.

44. Spencer Piston, 'Lighter-skinned minorities are more likely to support Republicans', *Washington Post* (Monkey Cage), 1 September 2014; J. Iceland, *Where We Live Now: Immigration and Race in the United States*, Berkeley, Calif., 2009: University of California Press.

45. John Judis, 'Redoing the electoral math', *New Republic*, 14 September 2017.

46. Jamelle Bouie, 'Demography is not destiny', *Democracy: A Journal of Ideas* 31 (Winter 2014).

47. Lind, 'The future of whiteness'.

48. Kirk Semple, 'A Somali influx unsettles Latino meatpackers', *The New York Times*, 15 October 2008.

49. Alba, 'The likely persistence of a white majority'; R. Alba and G. Yrizar Barbosa, 'Room at the top? Minority mobility and the transition to demographic diversity in the USA', *Ethnic and Racial Studies* 39:6 (2016), 917–38.

50. Hou et al., 'Cross-country variation in interracial marriage'.

51. S. Jivraj, 'How has ethnic diversity grown 1991–2001–2011?', Centre on Dynamics of Ethnicity (CoDE), University of Manchester, December 2012; 'Into the melting pot', *Economist*, 10 February 2014.

52. 'Europe's growing Muslim population', Pew Research Center, 29 November 2017.

53. R. Alba, 'Bright vs. blurred boundaries: Second-generation assimilation and exclusion in France, Germany, and the United States', *Ethnic and Racial Studies* 28:1 (2005), 20–49.

54. Iceland, *Where We Live Now*, pp. 124–40; W. A. V. Clark and R. Maas, 'The geography of a mixed-race society', *Growth and Change* 40:4 (2009), 565–93.

55. M. Ellis et al., 'The effects of mixed-race households on residential segregation', *Urban Geography* 28:6 (2007), 554–77.

56. D. T. Lichter, D. Parisi and M. C. Taquino, 'Together but apart: Do US whites live in racially diverse cities and neighborhoods?', *Population and Development Review* 43:2 (2017), 239.

11. The Future of White Majorities

1. S. Huntington, *Who are We? The Cultural Core of American National Identity*, New York and London, 2004: Simon & Schuster, pp. 307–11.

2. R. Brubaker, 'Migrations of ethnic unmixing in the "New Europe"', *International Migration Review* 32:4 (1998), 1047–65.

3. A. Wimmer, *Waves of War: Nationalism, State Formation, and Ethnic Exclusion in the Modern World*, Cambridge, 2013: Cambridge University Press.

4. S. Pinker, *The Better Angels of Our Nature: Why Violence Has Declined*, New York, 2011: Viking.

5. S. Jivraj, 'Who feels British? The relationship between ethnicity, religion and national identity in England', Centre on Dynamics of Ethnicity (CoDE), University of Manchester, 2013.

6. P. Morland, *Demographic Engineering: Population Strategies in Ethnic Conflict*, London and New York, 2016: Routledge.

7. J. Laponce, 'National self-determination and referendums: The case for territorial revisionism', *Nationalism & Ethnic Politics* 7:2 (2001), 33–56.

8. A. Smith, *The Ethnic Origins of Nations*, Oxford, 1986: Blackwell, ch. 8.

9. 'Multiracial in America', Pew Research Center, 11 June 2015.

10. P. Dion et al., 'Long-term contribution of immigration to population renewal in Canada: A simulation', *Population and Development Review* 41:1 (2015), 109–26.

11. G. Lanzieri, 'Two projections by foreign/national background', in Scientific Series: 'International Migration of Population: Russia and the Contemporary World' (ed. V. Iontsev), Moscow, 2014, pp. 50–77.

12. D. Coleman, 'The changing face of Europe', in J. Goldstone, E. Kaufmann and M. Duffy Toft, *Political Demography: How Population Changes are Reshaping International Security and National Politics*, Boulder, Colo., 2012: Paradigm, p. 182.

13. D. Coleman, 'Immigration and ethnic change in low-fertility countries – towards a new demographic transition?', paper presented to the Population Association of America annual meeting, Philadelphia, 31 March–2 April 2005.

14. 'World Population to 2300', New York, 2004: United Nations (Economic and Social Affairs).

15. Conversation with the Mexican writer Germán Martínez, London, 28 December 2015.

16. K. W. Deutsch, *Nationalism and Social Communication: An Inquiry into the Foundations of Nationality*, 2nd edn, New York, 1966: MIT Press.

17. E. Green, 'Industrialization and ethnic change in the modern world', *Ethnic and Racial Studies*, published online 2017, 1–20.

18. S. K. Goo, 'After 200 years, Native Hawaiians make a comeback', Pew Research Center, 6 April 2015.

19. 'Aboriginal peoples in Canada: Key results from the 2016 Census', Statistics Canada, 25 October 2017.

20. Kristy Kirkup, 'Canada's indigenous population growing 4 times faster than rest of country', Global News (Canada), 25 October 2017.

21. M. C. Waters, *Ethnic Options: Choosing Identities in America*, Berkeley, Calif., 1990: University of California Press.

22. Ibid., pp. 32–5, 142–3.

23. S. Lieberson, 'Unhyphenated whites in the United States', in R. D. Alba, *Ethnicity and Race in the U.S.A.: Toward the Twenty-First Century*, Boston, Mass., and London, 1985: Routledge & Kegan Paul, pp. 159–80; 'Which white people support Trump?', *Buzzfeed*, 9 October 2016.

24. Gregory Krieg, 'Here's the deal with Elizabeth Warren's Native American heritage', CNN, 28 November 2017.

25. J. Hutchinson, *Nations as Zones of Conflict*, London, 2005: Sage; G. Van-Hoosier-Carey, 'Byrhtnoth in Dixie: The emergence of Anglo-Saxon studies in the postbellum south', in J. D. Niles and A. J. Frantzen (eds.), *Anglo-Saxonism*

and the Construction of Social Identity, Tallahassee, 1997: University Press of Florida; T. Hofer, 'The "Hungarian Soul" and the "Historic Layers of National Heritage": Conceptualizations of the Hungarian folk culture, 1880–1944', in I. Banac and K. Verdery (eds.), *National Character and National Ideology in Interwar Eastern Europe*, New Haven, Conn., 1995: Yale Center For International and Area Studies, pp. 65–81.

26. A. Knight, 'Racism, revolution, and indigenismo: Mexico, 1910–1940', in R. Graham (ed.), *The Idea of Race in Latin America, 1870–1940*, Austin, Tex., 1990: UT Press, pp. 71–113.

27. T. H. Eriksen, *Common Denominators: Ethnicity, Nation-Building and Compromise in Mauritius*, Oxford and New York, 1998: Berg.

28. A. St Hilaire, 'Ethnicity, assimilation and nation in plural Suriname', *Ethnic and Racial Studies* 24:6 (2001), 998–1019.

29. 'Census: Mixed population on the rise', *Trinidad Daily Express*, 19 February 2013.

30. E. Kaufmann, *The Rise and Fall of Anglo-America: The Decline of Dominant Ethnicity in the United States*, Cambridge, Mass., 2004: Harvard University Press, p. 301.

31. W. L. Yancey, E. P. Ericksen and G. H. Leon, 'The structure of pluralism: "We're all Italian around here, aren't we, Mrs. O'Brien?"', in R. D. Alba (ed.), *Ethnicity and Race in the U.S.A.: Toward the Twenty-First Century*, Boston, Mass., and London, 1985: Routledge & Kegan Paul, pp. 94–116.

32. See, for instance, D. Gabriel, *Layers of Blackness: Colourism in the African Diaspora*, London, 2007: Imani Media.

33. P. L. van den Berghe and P. Frost, 'Skin color preference, sexual dimorphism and sexual selection: A case of gene culture co-evolution?' *Ethnic and Racial Studies* 9:1 (1986), 87–113.

34. 'Human skin color', *Wikipedia*, accessed 15 December 2017.

35. Question wording asked people to choose between: (a) ' "White" Canadians – those with at least some European ancestry – form over 90 percent of what has become a very homogeneous country. Though the average white Canadian has only about 1/8 European ancestry they identify with their European forebears. "Unmixed" whites are a dwindling group forming half a percent of the population'; or (b) 'White Canadians have become a close-knit community that, to preserve themselves, rarely marries out, forming 5 percent of the population in a multicultural country.'

36. B. R. Barber, *Jihad vs. McWorld*, New York, 1996: Ballantine Books; T. H. Eriksen 'Nationalism and the Internet', *Nations and Nationalism* 13:1 (2007), 1–17.

37. W. Connor, *Ethnonationalism: The Quest for Understanding*, Princeton, NJ, 1994: Princeton University Press; J. Hutchinson, *The Dynamics of Cultural Nationalism: The Gaelic Revival and the Creation of the Irish*

Nation-State, London, 1987: Allen & Unwin; P. Morgan, 'From a death to a view: The hunt for the Welsh past in the Romantic period', in Eric Hobsbawm and T. Ranger, *The Invention of Tradition*, Cambridge, 1983: Cambridge University Press, pp. 43–100.

38. M. Hroch, *Social Preconditions of National Revival in Europe: A Comparative Study of the Social Composition of Patriotic Groups among the Smaller European Nations*, New York, 2000 [1985]: Columbia University Press.

39. A. D. Smith, *The Ethnic Revival*, Cambridge, 1981: Cambridge University Press; J. Leerssen, 'Nationalism and the cultivation of culture', *Nations and Nationalism* 12:4 (2006), 559–78.

40. A. E. Jardina, 'Demise of dominance: Group threat and the new relevance of white identity for American politics', PhD dissertation, University of Michigan, 2014.

12. Will 'Unmixed' Whites Go Extinct?

1. E. Kaufmann, 'The dominant ethnic moment: Towards the abolition of "whiteness"?', *Ethnicities* 6:1 (2006), 231–53.

2. Michael Lind, 'The future of whiteness', *Salon*, 29 May 2012.

3. Matthew Taylor, 'Archbishop condemns BNP leader's "bloodless genocide" claim', *Guardian*, 23 April 2009.

4. '2017 EU Terrorism Report: 142 failed, foiled and completed attacks, 1002 arrests and 142 victims died', *Europol*, 15 June 2017.

5. 'Jo Cox murder', *Wikipedia*, accessed 14 December 2017.

6. Harry Yorke, 'One in four "extremists" reported to Government's deradicalisation programme are far-Right sympathisers, figures show', *Telegraph*, 15 February 2017.

7. Richard Ford and Fiona Hamilton, 'Tommy Robinson accused of exploiting Finsbury Park assault as far-right fans flames of hate', *The Times*, 20 June 2017.

8. Figures for 2015–16. Courtesy of Richard Norrie, formerly of Policy Exchange, originally obtained from the Crown Prosecution Service (CPS) and Home Office.

9. Katie Connolly, 'Germans greet influx of refugees with free food and fire-bombings', *Guardian*, 30 July 2015; Lizzie Dearden, 'Refugee crisis sparks record year for political violence in Germany as right and left wing clash', *Independent*, 24 May 2016.

10. Miriam Valverde, 'A look at the data on domestic terrorism and who's behind it', *Politifact*, 16 August 2017; 'A dark and constant rage: 25 years of right-wing terrorism in the United States', Anti-Defamation League, 2017.

11. Michael McGough, 'Could there be a benign "European American" group? No', *Los Angeles Times*, 1 January 2015.

12. Smith, *Ethnic Revival*.

13. Coleman Hughes, 'The high price of stale grievances', *Quillette*, 5 June 2018.

14. Referring to the infamous multi-generational feud between the west Virginia Hatfield family and the Kentucky McCoys.

15. E. Nimni, *The Challenge of Post-Zionism: Alternatives to Fundamentalist Politics in Israel*, London, 2003: Zed Books.

16. Anshel Pfeffer, 'Shlomo Sand to secular Jews: I'm not Jewish and neither are you', *Haaretz*, 15 November 2014.

17. H. Shih-Chung, 'Images of the majority people in Taiwan', in Dru C. Gladney (ed.), *Making Majorities*, Stanford, Calif., 1998: Stanford University Press, pp. 100–103.

18. D. S. FitzGerald, *Culling the Masses: The Democratic Origins of Racist Immigration Policy in the Americas*, Cambridge, Mass., 2014: Harvard University Press.

19. B. Farquhar, 'The Spanish language in Antigua and Barbuda: Implications for language planning and language research', paper presented at the University of the West Indies conference, 2004.

20. Martina Johnson, 'Parliament "legitimises" status of illegal immigrants', *Daily Observer*, 20 February 2015.

21. S. Polakow-Suransky, *Go Back to Where You Came From: The Backlash against Immigration and the Fate of Western Democracy*, London, 2017: Hurst and Co., pp. 246–7.

22. Sinthia Chiumia, 'How many international migrants are there in SA?', Africa Check, 14 August 2016; Kate Wilkinson, 'Claim that 13 million international migrants live in SA wildly incorrect', Africa Check, 21 February 2017.

23. R. Nordas, 'The devil in the demography? Religion, identity and war in Côte d'Ivoire', in J. A. Goldstone, E. Kaufmann and M. Duffy Toft, *Political Demography: How Population Changes are Reshaping International Security and National Politics*, Boulder, Colo., 2012: Paradigm, pp. 252–67.

24. Coleman, 'The changing face of Europe', pp. 188–90.

25. Sophie Warnes and Anna Leach, 'How a white baby can be born to a black mother – the statistics of skin colour', *Mirror*, 1 September 2014.

26. Andrew Griffin, 'Elon Musk: The chance we are not living in a computer simulation is "one in billions"', *Independent*, 2 June 2016.

27. L. L. Cavalli-Sforza, *Genes, Peoples and Languages*, Stanford, Calif., 2001: University of California Press.

28. A. Nelson, *The Social Life of DNA: Race, Reparations, and Reconciliation after the Genome*, 2016: Boston, Mass.: Beacon Press.

29. 'Lemba tribe in southern Africa has Jewish roots, genetic tests reveal', World Jewish Congress, 8 March 2010.

30. G. Lucotte and G. Mercier, 'Y-chromosome DNA haplotypes in Jews: Comparisons with Lebanese and Palestinians', *Genetic Testing*, 7:1 (2003), 67–71.

31. 'Can we grow woolly mammoths in the lab? George Church hopes so', *New Scientist*, 16 February 2017.

32. Smith, *Ethnic Revival*.

33. E. Kaufmann, 'The religious demography of London since 1980', in D. Goodhew and A.-P. Cooper (eds.), *No Secular City: Church Growth and Decline in London, 1980 to the Present* (forthcoming).

34. D. Martin, *A General Theory of Secularization*, Aldershot, 1993 [1978]: Gregg Revivals.

35. Conversation with the Mexican writer Germán Martínez, London, 28 December 2015.

36. V. M. Hudson and A. Den Boer, *Bare Branches: The Security Implications of Asia's Surplus Male Population*, 2004: MIT Press.

37. 'CGS summary of public opinion polls – Opinions about inheritable genetic modification (IGM)', Center for Genetics and Society, 4 February 2014.

38. E. Kaufmann and A. Ballatore, 'New York Yankees and Hollywood Anglos: The persistence of Anglo-conformity in the American motion picture industry', Working Paper, 2017.

39. E. Kaufmann, *Shall the Religious Inherit the Earth? Demography and Politics in the Twenty-First Century*, London, 2010: Profile Books, ch. 3; K. Joyce, *Quiverfull: Inside the Christian Patriarchy Movement*, Boston, Mass., 2009: Beacon Press.

40. Amir Shoan, Ynetnews.com, 7 December 2010; Jason Koutsoukis, 'Haredi way of life poses an "existential threat"', *Sydney Morning Herald*, 14 August 2010.

41. Kaufmann, *Shall the Religious Inherit the Earth?*, ch. 6.

42. 'Hasidic Jews in upstate New York: Monroe's referendum and a peculiar population boom', *Economist*, 2 November 2017.

43. Kaufmann, *Shall the Religious Inherit the Earth?*, ch. 5.

44. A. L. Mauss, *The Angel and the Beehive: The Mormon Struggle with Assimilation*, Urbana, Ill., 1994: University of Illinois Press, p. 49.

45. Michael Lind, 'Red-state sneer', *Prospect*, no. 106 (January 2005); Philip Longman, 'The liberal baby bust', *USA Today*, 13 March 2006.

46. M. Hout, A. Greeley and M. J. Wilde, 'The demographic imperative in religious change in the United States', *American Journal of Sociology* 107:2 (2001), 468–500.

47. M. Lipka, 'Mormons more likely to marry, have more children than other U.S. religious groups', Pew Research Center, 22 May 2015.

48. Kaufmann, *Shall the Religious Inherit the Earth?*, pp. 235–8.
49. Huntington, *Who are We?*; D. E. Sherkat, 'Tracking the restructuring of American religion: Religious affiliation and patterns of religious mobility, 1973–1998', *Social Forces* 79:4 (2001), 1459–93.
50. P. Schrag, *The Decline of the WASP*, New York, 1973: Simon & Schuster, pp. 71–2.
51. R. J. Simon and M. A. Abdel-Moneim, *Public Opinion in the United States: Studies of Race, Religion, Gender, and Issues That Matter*, New Brunswick, NJ, 2010: Transaction, pp. 61–2.
52. Schrag, *Decline of the WASP*, p. 37.
53. Thanks to Paul Longley of University College London, co-creator of Onomap's onomastics software.
54. R. C. Christopher, *Crashing the Gates: The De-WASPing of America's Power Elite*, New York and London, 1989: Simon & Schuster.
55. T. Devos and M. R. Banaji, 'American = white?', *Journal of Personality and Social Psychology* 88:3 (2005), 447; S. Cheryan, and B. Monin, 'Where are you *really* from? Asian Americans and identity denial', *Journal of Personality and Social Psychology* 89:5 (2005), 717.
56. D. J. Schildkraut, 'National identity in the United States', *Handbook of Identity Theory and Research*, New York, 2011: Springer, pp. 845–65.
57. Ryan Burge, 'How does being white shape evangelicals' voting habits?', Religion in Public blog, 6 November 2017.
58. E. Kaufmann, 'The lenses of nationhood: an optical model of identity', *Nations and Nationalism* 14:3 (2008), 449–77.
59. J. Hutchinson, *Nations as Zones of Conflict*, London, 2005: Sage.
60. E. S. Gaustad, 'The pulpit and the pews', in W. R. Hutchison, *Between the Times: The Travail of the Protestant Establishment in America, 1900–1960*, Cambridge and New York, Cambridge University Press, p. 37.

13. Navigating *Whiteshift*

1. John Judis and Michael Lind, 'For a new nationalism', *New Republic*, 27 March 1995.
2. C. Lasch, *The Revolt of the Elites and the Betrayal of Democracy*, New York and London, 1995: W. W. Norton.
3. D. Goodhart, *The Road to Somewhere: The Populist Revolt and the Future of Politics*, London, 2017: Hurst.
4. 'Secretary-General's address to the General Assembly': www.un.org, 19 September 2017.
5. C. Ritter, 'The poverty of cosmopolitan historicism', *Quillette*, 17 November 2017.

6. K. Stenner, *The Authoritarian Dynamic*, Cambridge, 2005: Cambridge University Press.

7. Eric Kaufmann, 'Can narratives of white identity reduce opposition to immigration and support for hard Brexit? A survey experiment', *Political Studies*, published online 5 December 2017.

8. M. Walzer, *Spheres of Justice: A Defence of Pluralism and Equality*, Oxford, 1983: Blackwell, p. 39.

9. T. Sanandaji, *Mass Challenge: Economic Policy against Social Exclusion and Antisocial Behaviour*, forthcoming.

10. R. Inglehart and P. Norris, 'Trump, Brexit, and the rise of populism: Economic have-nots and cultural backlash', HKS Working Paper No. RWP16-026, 2016.

11. Shadi Hamid, 'There's no "good" or "bad" America', *Washington Post*, 18 November 2017.

12. Mark Lilla, 'The end of identity liberalism', *The New York Times*, 18 November 2016.

13. J.-H. Lim, 'Victimhood nationalism in contested memories: National mourning and global accountability', in A. Assmann and S. Conrad (eds.), *Memory in a Global Age: Discourses, Practices and Trajectories*, London, 2010: Palgrave Macmillan, pp. 138–62.

14. D. Bar-Tal, 'From intractable conflict through conflict resolution to reconciliation: Psychological analysis', *Political Psychology* 21:2 (2000), 351–65.

15. Y. Tamir, *Liberal Nationalism*, Princeton, NJ, and Chichester, 1993: Princeton University Press, p. 11.

16. E. Kaufmann, 'Liberal ethnicity: Beyond liberal nationalism and minority rights', *Ethnic and Racial Studies* 23:6 (2000), 1086–119.

17. T. Modood, 'Multicultural nationalism', at the symposium on 'National Identity and Diversity', King's College, London, 17 March 2017; T. Modood, *Multiculturalism*, Cambridge, 2013: Polity Press.

18. C. Taylor and A. Gutmann, *Multiculturalism and 'The Politics of Recognition': An Essay*, Princeton, NJ, 1992: Princeton University Press.

19. E. West, *The Diversity Illusion: What We Got Wrong about Immigration and How to Set It Right*, London, 2013: Gibson Square, p. 69.

20. S. Hix, E. Kaufmann and T. J. Leeper, 'UK voters, including Leavers, care more about reducing non-EU than EU migration', LSE EUROPP [European Politics and Policy] blog, 30 May 2017.

21. P. Collier, *Exodus: How Migration is Changing Our World*, New York, 2013: Oxford University Press.

22. Ibid.

23. M. Blake, 'Discretionary immigration', *Philosophical Topics* 30:2 (2002), 273–89.

24. D. Miller, *Strangers in Our Midst*, Cambridge, Mass., 2016: Harvard University Press, pp. 103–5.
25. L. Orgad, *The Cultural Defense of Nations: A Liberal Theory of Majority Rights*, Oxford, 2015: Oxford University Press, pp. 232–3.
26. U. Hannerz, 'Cosmopolitans and locals in world culture', *Theory, Culture and Society*, 7 (1990), 237–51.
27. V. W. Turner, *The Forest of Symbols: Aspects of Ndembu Ritual*, Ithaca, NY: Cornell University Press.
28. BBC/YouGov Englishness survey, 9–26 March 2018: https://www.bbc.co.uk/news/uk-england-44142843.
29. E. Kaufmann, 'The lenses of nationhood: an optical model of identity', *Nations and Nationalism* 14:3 (2008), 449–77.
30. R. K. Carty, 'The politics of Tecumseh Corners: Canadian political parties as franchise organizations', *Canadian Journal of Political Science* 35:4 (2002), 723–46.
31. Z. Munson, 'Islamic mobilization: Social movement theory and the Egyptian Muslim brotherhood', *Sociological Quarterly* 42:4 (2001), 487–510.
32. E. Kaufmann, 'From multiculturalism to multivocalism: Complexity, national identity and political theory', in M. Antonsich, E. Mavroudi and S. Mihelj, 'Building inclusive nations in the age of migration', *Identities*, 24:2 (2017), 156–76.
33. B. O'Leary, 'An iron law of nationalism and federation? A (neo-Diceyian) theory of the necessity of a federal Staatsvolk, and of consociational rescue', *Nations and Nationalism* 7:3 (2001), 273–96.
34. Kaufmann, 'Liberal ethnicity'.
35. Andrew Sullivan, 'America wasn't built for humans', *New York*, 19 September 2017.
36. Mona Chalabi, 'What is white culture, exactly? Here's what the stats say', *Guardian*, 26 February 2018.

Index

INDEX